THE HARMONY ILLUSTRATED ENCYCLOPEDIA OF

COUNTRY MUSIC

HARMONY BOOKS

NEW YORK

THE HARMONY ILLUSTRATED ENCYCLOPEDIA OF

COUNTRY MUSIC

A Salamander Book

Credits

Acknowledgements

Published in the United States in 1987 by Harmony Books, a division of Crown Publishers, Inc., 225 Park Avenue South, New York, New York 10003 and represented in Canada by the Canadian MANDA Group.

Originally published in Great Britain as THE ILLUSTRATED ENCYCLOPEDIA OF COUNTRY MUSIC by Salamander Books Limited, 52 Bedford Row, London WC1R 4LR.

HARMONY and colophon are trademarks of Crown Publishers, Inc.

Manufactured in Belgium

Library of Congress Cataloging-in-Publication Data

Deller, Fred.
  The Harmony illustrated encyclopedia of country music.

  Red. ed. of: The illustrated encyclopedia of country music. 1977.
  Includes index.
  1. Country music—Dictionaries.   2. Country musicians—Biography.   3. Country music—Discography.
  1. Cackett, Alan.   II. Thompson, Roy.   III. Green, Douglas B.   IV. Deller, Fred.   Illustrated encyclopedia of country music.   V. Title.
ML102.C7D4   1987   784.5′2′00321   86-18423
ISBN 0-517-56502-1
ISBN 0-517-56503-X (pbk.)

10 9 8 7 6 5 4 3 2 1

First revised Edition

Managing Editor: Ray Bonds
Editors: Ros Bacon, Jocelyn Finnis
Designer: Angela King
Picture Research: Kay Rowley, Richard Wootton
Indexer: Isobel McLean
Filmset by Flair plan Photo-typesetting Ltd
Colour Reproduction by Rodney Howe Ltd
Printed in Belgium by Proost International Book Production, Turnhout, Belgium.

Picture Credits

Many of the photographs in this book were provided by the record companies mentioned in the Acknowledgements, and we are very grateful for their help. Additionally we would like to again thank Douglas B. Green and Grease Brothers for pictures supplied for original edition and re-used here, and also the following individuals and companies:

National Film Archive: 117.
Photo Guild, Nashville: 9, 37, 108.
David Redfern: front cover, 1.
Jim Shea: 21.
Ian Tilbury: 5, 6, 29.

The authors acknowledge the debt they owe to Malone and McCulloch's Stars Of Country Music, Melvin Shestack's Country Music Encyclopedia, Stambler and Landon's Encyclopedia Of Folk, Country And Western Music, Kenn Kingsbury's Who's Who In Country And Western Music, Jerry Osborne's 55 Years Of Recorded Country/Western Music, Bill C. Malone's Country Music USA, Rick Marshall's Encyclopedia Of Country And Western Music, John Morthland's The Best Of Country Music, Country Music People, Country Rhythms, Country Music Round-Up, Leslie Halliwell's Filmgoer's Companion, Billboard, Music City News, Country Song Roundup, NME, Melody Maker and Joel Witburn's essential series of chart books.

We would also like to thank all the record companies who supplied many of the record sleeves and illustrations used in this book, while special thanks are also due to Byworth-Wootton (Europe's country publicists par excellence), Cynthia Leu of RCA, New York, Lee Simmonds, Anne Barraclough, Kathy Gangswitsch, Mervyn Conn, Jim Halsey, all the music maniacs at Making Waves, Ricky Skaggs, Warren Davies, Kay Rowley and, of course, Roy Thompson, Dave Redshaw and Douglas B. Green, without whose special work this volume would not exist.

THIS BOOK IS DEDICATED TO EDWIN LEWIS ROSE JR.

The Authors

FRED DELLAR is one of the busiest journalists of the British music scene. He began his career providing rock and country articles for Audio Record Review (now Hi-Fi News) in 1968 and has since contributed to a huge number of publications though he is probably best known for his weekly Fred Fact column in the New Musical Express. His books include The Book Of Country Music Lists, The NME Guide To Rock Cinema, The Hip, Where Did You Go To My Lovely plus, more surprisingly, The Book Of Rock And Pop Crosswords.

ALAN CACKETT, a freelance journalist and printing works manager, is best known for his contributions to Country Music People. In the late Sixties he edited and published Britain's first monthly country music magazines – Country Record Exchange and Country Music Monthly.
   Since 1969 he has contributed a regular country music column for the Kent Evening Post and has also written for Record Mirror and Sounds, as well as providing pop music and country music columns for the Kent Messenger Group of publications.

ROY THOMPSON is a country music fanatic who met Fred Dellar several years ago while working for a publishing company. Roy, who owns one of the largest collections of country records in England, has during the past few years worked with Fred on a number of musical projects.

DOUGLAS B. GREEN is one of America's leading country music historians. Once head of the Oral History Project at the Country Music Foundation in Nashville, he has written several well-received books and has contributed to some two score music publications including liner notes for several country albums, one of which was nominated for a Grammy Award. Currently he is heading a band of his own, Riders In The Sky, and is a member of the Grand Ole Opry.

Foreword

Country music is many things to many different folk.
To some, it is songs of the prairie sung by the likes of Roy Rogers and The Sons of the Pioneers – the sort of music that enlivened a thousand Western movies and kept us entertained even when the six-gun action had ended.

To others, it is the blues of Jimmie Rodgers, the western swing of Bob Wills, the bluegrass breakdowns of Bill Monroe and the trucking anthems of Dave Dudley, the soulful ballads of Tammy Wynette or the contemporary sounds of Alabama.

That's what I love about country music. It knows no boundaries, applies no shackles. Country can be one guy playing fiddle on an Appalachian front porch or a millionaire leading a big band in Hollywood. It is the true musical backdrop to the American Dream. It is the stuff legends are made of and has, in turn, provided more than a few legends of its own.

Roy Acuff, a one-time conductor on the L&N Railroad, made his way through country music to become nominated as Governor of Tennessee. Jimmy Davis who, if his sole contribution to the history of America had been the writing of 'You Are My Sunshine,' would still have been elected to the Country Music Hall Of Fame. But, he fought off the legendary Huey Long to become Governor of Louisiana for a second term.

Not that they were all winners. Some were pushed aside along the way, some got a grasp on the top of the pole only to slide back down and out of the limelight. Others, tragically, found that their time on earth was up before they had barely gotten started.

All these people – and more – are featured in the pages of this marvellous work of reference. Not only Americans, but Canadians, Mexicans, New Zealanders, Australians – *and* a British rocker (hi, Elvis!) who has worked with me and George Jones. In fact, just about anyone who has ever contributed anything of importance to the world of country music has a place in these pages.

So, because I, in common with the authors of this book, care about the many shapes and sounds that help form country music, and because I believe that this affection has been carefully translated into the written word within these pages, I'm honored to have been asked to provide this introductory note.

I trust librarians will file this one under 'E' – for essential!

Ricky Skaggs

Introduction

When I got together with Roy Thompson and Douglas B. Green to produce the first edition of this encyclopedia nearly 10 years ago, we little realised just how essential a publication we were fashioning. The resulting book, which also included input from the then Country Music People journalist, David Redshaw, became the definitive textbook, even used by such organisations as Nashville's Country Music Foundation library. Since that time, much has changed. Many of the singers and musicians whose lives we documented have sadly gone, while others have taken their places. Accordingly, the work which had taken us all so many, many months to research became out-of-date. But, though some attempts were made to fill the gap by others, nobody succeeded in providing a replacement of equal appeal.

At the close of 1985, it was decided that we would provide a completely revised encyclopedia – 'we' being myself and Alan Cackett, whose writing for Country Music People I had always admired. Roy Thompson was, unfortunately, too busy to fully participate in the new undertaking while Doug Green had moved on to become a country star in his own right, leading Nashville's Riders In The Sky. Alan Cackett was as aware of country music history as most pundits. He was also usually one step ahead when it came to new names and thoughts for the future. Furthermore, he provides accurate, clean and well-written copy. Which is why he was an apt candidate for the enormous task ahead.

We agreed that we would stick to the original format, listing artists in alphabetical order, classifying them under their surnames, while groups would be listed under their full title – The Binkley Brothers Clodhoppers, for instance, being logged under 'B'. But so many new artists were to be included that something had to make way. It was to this end that we opted to include an all-embracing appendix, listing not only performers who failed to get into the main body of the book, but also information on such items as the Country Music Association, Nashville, Austin etc. – subjects which had initially formed part of the main text. The emphasis was to be placed on musicians and singers. Rightly or wrongly, this was the decision we took.

Equally, there had to be changes in the way we approached the discographies. In the 1977 edition of this book we merely listed everything that was available at the time of publication. This proved space-consuming and not entirely satisfactory. Scores of the albums we listed were mere duplications – revamps of 'Greatest Hit' collections and suchlike. Also, because of record company policies, many of them were deleted even before we had got around to reading the first proofs. So this time, we have gone for the easy option and merely listed selected discographies, providing first the American label and then the British one, including the reissue Bear Family series (actually of German origin) among the latter. Not every entry in the book is new. Rewriting merely for the sake of rewriting was considered a pointless exercise. After all, if a subject was adequately covered in the original book and nothing else has happened since – as is the case with such artists as say, Cowboy Copas, Robert Lunn and Henry Whitter – then the original text might just as well be left intact.

We are extremely proud of the results. We have not achieved perfection because I do not think that any such thing is possible on such an all-embracing project. For instance, it is difficult to even pin down definite dates of birth because some people just will not reveal such details, while others just downright lie about their time of arrival. Some choose to claim a huge array of hits in their press releases, a 'nationwide No. 1' in one singer's handout probably relating to a record that merely went Top 20! A word here about our chart references which, unless otherwise stated, all relate to Billboard magazine's country music Top 75, which we feel is the most authentic and accurate of its type.

But, I repeat, despite providing the most comprehensive country encyclopedia we could possibly devise, perfection is not claimed. In fact, we look to you to supply us with any details that you feel should be revised, any artist you feel we have neglected.

Fred Dellar

Tennessee in 1944 and 1946, Acuff failed to get past the primaries. But in 1948 he won the Republican primary, failing to win the ensuing election but nevertheless gaining tremendous support, earning a larger slice of the vote than any previous Republican candidate had ever earned in that particular political confrontation. Also in '48, Acuff opened his Dunbar Cave resort, a popular folk music park which he owned for several years.

Four years later, after being requested to change his style by Columbia, Acuff left the label, switching in turn to MGM, Decca and Capitol. And though his live performances still continued to go well and his publishing empire seemed ever-expanding, Acuff's record sales failed to maintain their previous high – **So Many Times** (1959), **Come and Knock** (1959) and **Freight Train Blues** (1965), all on his own Hickory label, being the only releases to create any real interest during the '50s and '60s.

However, his tremendous contribution to country music was recognized in November 1962, when Acuff became the first living musician to be honoured as a member of the Country Music Hall Of Fame.

Severely injured in a road accident during 1965, Acuff was back and touring within a few months, at one stage making several visits to the Vietnam War front. On May 24, 1973, he entertained returned POWs at the White House and, on March 16, 1974, was chosen to provide the President with yoyo lessons at the opening of the new Nashville Opryhouse, an incident which Acuff considers as one of the high points in his career. Acuff guested on the Nitty Gritty Dirt Band's triple album set **Will The Circle Be Unbroken?** in 1972 lending credence to contemporary and country-rock music.

Country Music Hall Of Fame, Roy Acuff, Courtesy Hickory Records.

Known as the 'King of Country Music', Roy Acuff has sold more than 30 million records throughout the years – his most successful disc being his Columbia version of Wabash Cannonball, which went gold in 1942. His film appearances include 'Grand Ole Opry' (1940), 'Hi Neighbor' (1942), 'My Darling Clementine' (1943), 'Sing, Neighbor, Sing' (1944), 'Cowboy Canteen' (1944) and 'Night Train To Memphis (1946)'.

Roy Acuff

Son of a baptist minister, Roy Claxton Acuff was born September 15, 1903, in a three-room shack in Maynardsville, Tennessee. As a child, Roy, who had two brothers (Briscoe and Claude) and two sisters (Juanita and Sue) learnt jews harp and harmonica. However, it seemed that he was destined to become an athlete for, following a move to Fountain City, near Knoxville, Acuff (at that time nicknamed 'Rabbit' because he weighed only 130 pounds) gained 13 letters at high school, eventually playing minor league ball and being considered for the New York Yankees. Severe sunstroke put an end to

Time, Roy Acuff, Courtesy Hickory Records.

this career, confining Acuff to bed for much of 1929 and 1930.

Following this illness Acuff, whose jobs had included that of callboy on the L&N Railroad, hung around the house, learning fiddle and listening to records by old-time players – also becoming adept with a yoyo.

In Spring, 1932, he joined a travelling medicine show, led by a Dr Haver, playing small towns in Virginia and Tennessee, by 1933 forming a group the Tennessee Crackerjacks, in which Clell Summey played dobro, thus providing the distinctive sound that came to be associated with Acuff (Pete 'Bashful Brother Oswald' Kirby providing the dobro chores in later Acuff aggregations). Soon he obtained a programme on Knoxville radio station WROL, moving on to the rival KNOX for the Mid-day Merry-Go-Round show, starting point for Kitty Wells, Bill Carlisle and many others. On being refused a raise (each musician received fifty cents per show) the band returned to WROL once more, adopting the name of the Crazy Tennesseans.

Acuff married Mildred Douglas in 1936, that same year recording two sessions for ARC (a company controlling a host of labels, later merged with Columbia), the temperature on one date being so high that the band recorded in their underwear. Tracks from these sessions included **Great Speckled Bird** and **Wabash Cannonball**, two classic items, the latter having a vocal by Dynamite Hatcher.

Above: Roy Acuff, first living member of the Country Music Hall of Fame.

Though Acuff's contract was with Columbia, the band's discs appeared on ARC's subsidiary labels Melotone, Conqueror and Perfect, and Columbia's subsidiary labels Okeh and Vocalion, and were not available on the main, red label until the mid '40s.

Making his first appearance on the Grand Ole Opry in 1938, Acuff soon became a regular on the show, changing the name of the band once more to the Smoky Mountain Boys, winning many friends with his sincere, mountain-boy, vocal style and his dobro-flavoured band sound, eventually becoming as popular as Uncle Dave Macon, who was until that time undisputed Opry main attraction.

In 1942, together with songwriter Fred Rose, Acuff organised Acuff-Rose, a music publishing company destined to become one of the most important in country music. During that same period Acuff's recordings became so popular that he headed Frank Sinatra in some major music polls and reportedly caused Japanese troops to yell 'To hell with Roosevelt, to hell with Babe Ruth, to hell with Roy Acuff' as they banzai-charged at Okinawa. The war years also saw some of his biggest hits, including **Wreck on the Highway** (1942), **Fireball Mail** (1942), **Night Train to Memphis** (1943), **Pins And Needles**, **Low And Lonely** (1943).

Nominated to run as governor of

Alabama

Jeff Cook, lead guitar; Teddy Gentry, bass; Mark Herndon, drums; Randy Owen, guitar.

This American country-rock group has been the most successful country act of recent years, with all their singles since signing with RCA in 1980 having made No. 1 on the country charts and each album reaching gold or platinum status. Initially formed in 1969 at Fort Wayne, Alabama, as Wild Country, the group was a semi-professional outfit with the nucleus of cousins Jeff Cook and Randy Owen, plus Teddy Gentry. They turned fully professional in 1973 when they landed a club residency in Myrtle Beach, South Carolina.

By this time they had started writing songs and Teddy Gentry's **I May Never Be Your Love, But I'll Always Be Your Friend** was recorded by Bobby G. Rice and made the country charts in 1975. The band had recorded for small labels as Wild Country in the mid '70s and made the name change to Alabama when they signed to GRT Records at the beginning of 1977, making their first mark on the country charts with **I Want To Be With You**.

Alabama were now undertaking tours all across the Southern States, but without a major record deal or hit singles they were struggling. Larry McBride, a Dallas businessman, took an interest in them and signed them to a management deal. He set up MDJ Records and the group's first record, **I Wanna Come Over**, made the country charts in the autumn of 1979. Under the production of Harold Shedd they came up with another hit, **My Home's In Alabama**. At the same time their drummer decided to quit and the group spent several months as a three-piece until they found Mark Herndon, the fourth member of Alabama.

Below: Alabama, the hottest new group in country music. Multi-award winners, all their singles go automatically to the top of the charts; their albums go gold or platinum.

40 Hour Week, Alabama, Courtesy RCA Records.

The group signed with RCA Records at the beginning of 1980 and hit the top of the country charts with **Tennessee River**, following up with **Why Lady Why**, **Feels So Right**, **Love In The First Degree**, **Mountain Music**, **The Closer You Get** and **40 Hour Week**. Each album has gone gold and some, like **40 Hour Week**, **Mountain Music** and **Alabama's Greatest Hits**, have gone platinum. They have been named CMA Group Of Year consistently since 1981 and have also won Entertainer Of The Year in 1982 and 1983.

Alabama's commercial success changed the thinking in Nashville away from the solo performer. They have created the group sound rather than a singer accompanied by a group of musicians and set things in motion for other outfits like Atlanta, Exile and Bandana. Though they could have turned their back on country music, Alabama are keen to retain their country connection. However, at the beginning of 1986 they were busy recording with pop-soul-singer Lionel Richie.

Albums:
The Closer You Get (RCA/–)
Feels So Right (RCA/–)
Mountain Music (RCA/–)
40 Hour Week (RCA/RCA)

Susie Allanson

A young lady who made her initial impression in showbusiness in the musicals 'Hair' and 'Jesus Christ Superstar' in the early '70s, Susie Allanson was born in Minneapolis, Minnesota, March 17, 1952. She started out in country music as a background vocalist, and was picked out by record producer Ray Ruff who groomed her for stardom. Signed to Ruff's Oak Records, she subsequently made the country charts with **Baby Don't Keep Me Hangin' On** in September 1977.

Ray and Susie were married, and later divorced; he guided her through such hits as **Maybe Baby** (1978), **Words** (1979) and **Two Steps Forward And Three Steps Back** (1980) as she recorded for Warner/Curb, Elektra and Liberty Records. In her spare time Susie, an experienced horserider, takes part in show jumping competitions.

Albums:
Susie Allanson (ABC/–)
We Belong Together (Warner/Warner)
Heart To Heart (Elektra/–)

Deborah Allen

One of Nashville's leading songwriters and, more recently, crossover recording artists, Deborah Allen was born in Memphis Tennessee in 1955 and always dreamt of being a country singer. The black-haired beauty first made the move to Nashville in 1972 and worked as a waitress at the International House of Pancakes. Legend has it that she served Roy Orbison, told him she could sing, and was booked as a back-up singer on Roy's next session.

For a time she sang and danced in the chorus line of Opryland, working a show with Jim Stafford who offered her a job in Los Angeles on his TV Variety Show. Accepting the offer, she worked with Stafford both on TV and show dates for the next three years, making a move back to Nashville in 1977. She then signed a writer's contract with MCA Music and soon had songs recorded by Zella Lehr, Brenda Lee and Janie Fricke, who scored her first No. 1 country hit with Deborah's **Don't Worry 'Bout Me** in 1980. After teaming up with fellow writer Rafe Van Hoy, the pair came up with hits for John Conlee, Janie Fricke, Brenda Lee and Sheena Easton.

Deborah's first chance to record came in 1979 when she was asked to do vocal overdubs on some Jim Reeves recordings. These were so successful that Deborah received label credit and the next year was signed to Capitol Records for whom she recorded the album **Trouble In Mind**, a highly acclaimed mix of country, folk and gospel. She failed to gain a major hit single and though she recorded a second album for Capitol it was never released.

In 1983 she joined RCA and immediately came up with the crossover hit **Baby I Lied**, which she co-wrote with Raf Van Hoy, whom she married in 1982. Van Hoy was also Deborah's producer and her first RCA album, **Cheat The Night**, contained further country hits, **I Hurt For You** and **I've Been Wrong Before**.

Her next album, **Let Me Be The First**, took her closer to pop music and was the first totally digitally recorded, mixed and mastered album to come out of Nashville.

Albums:
Trouble In Mind (Capitol/–)
Cheat The Night (RCA/–)

Rex Allen

Known as the 'Arizona Cowboy', Allen was born Willcox, Arizona, December 31, 1924. A rodeo rider in his teens, he learnt to play guitar and fiddle at an early age. He took an electronics course at University College of Los Angeles but opted instead for a singing career, finding his first job with radio station WTTM, Trenton, New Jersey, during the mid '40s. Like Gene Autry before him, he was a popular singer on the NBD before entering films. In 1951 he was awarded his own Hollywood radio show by CBS, subsequently getting high ratings.

He has since recorded for Decca, Mercury, Buena Vista, and others, and has made films for Fox, Republic and Universal, having the distinction of being the last of the singing cowboys on screen; but he is perhaps best known nowadays for his singing and narration chores in various Disney productions.

He had a Top 20 hit with **Don't Go Near The Indians**, a Mercury single, in September 1962, having previously won a gold disc for his version of **Crying In The Chapel** in 1953.

Albums:
Golden Songs of the West (Vocalion/–)
Under Western Skies (–/Stetson)
Boney-Kneed, Hairy-Legged Cowboy Songs (–/Bear Family)

Rex Allen Jr

The son of singing cowboy Rex Allen, this young singer with a rich baritone has made quite an impression on the country scene in the last ten years with hit singles like **Two Less Lonely People**, **Lonely Street** and **Me And My Broken Heart**. He started while still a youngster, playing rodeos and state fairs with his father.

A move to Nashville in the early '70s set him up for a promising career in country music, signing with Shelby Singleton's SSS International label. A change to Warner Brothers records in 1973 started a long run of hit singles and distinctive albums like the concept **Oklahoma Rose** and **The Singing Cowboys**, featuring guest appearances by his father and Roy Rogers. He moved to the smaller Moonshine Records in 1984 and produced the excellent album **On The Move** which, like many of his previous recordings, he co-produced.

Albums:
Ridin' High (Warner/–)
Brand New (Warner/Warner)
Oklahoma Rose (Warner/–)
Cats In The Cradle (Warner/–)
On The Move (Moonshine/–)

Rosalie Allen

Known as 'The Prairie Star' in her heyday, Rosalie Allen was a great cowgirl yodeller in an era full of them. Actually, she was born Julie Marlene Bedra, the daughter of a Polish-born chiropractor, in Old Forge, Pennsylvania, on June 6, 1924.

Entranced by the cowboy image and music, she gained a radio spot with long-time New York City favourite Denver Darling in the late '30s, and through the '40s and '50s she was a fixture of the northeast states. She signed with RCA, her biggest solo efforts being yodelling spectaculars **I Want To Be A Cowboy's Sweetheart** and **He Taught Me How To Yodel**. She was frequently paired with Elton Britt, another legendary yodeller, for a number of records. The best sellers from these records were **Quick-Silver**, **The Yodel Blues** and **Beyond the Sunset**.

She turned to a career as a disc jockey over WOV in the '50s, preferring not to travel, and gradually left her performing and recording career behind.

For several years she owned a record shop in New Jersey specializing in country music. She currently lives in rural Alabama.

Amazing Rhythm Aces

Barry 'Byrd' Burton, guitar, dobro; Jeff Davis, bass; Billy Earheart III, keyboards; Butch McDade, drums; Russell Smith, lead vocals, guitar.

A Memphis-based rock band, Amazing Rhythm Aces were formed during the early '70s. The group's **Third Rate Romance** single, penned by Smith, became a Top 20 hit in September 1975. Members Davis and McDade previously toured and recorded with singer-songwriter Jesse Winchester.

They enjoyed further hits with **Amazing**

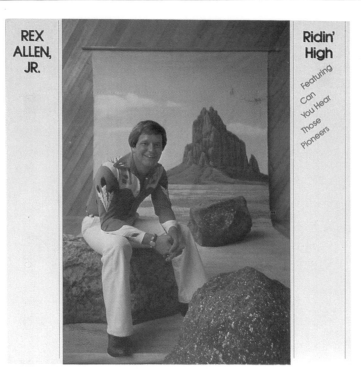

Riding High, Rex Allen Jr, Courtesy Warner Bros Records.

Grace (Used To Be Her Favourite Song) and **The End Is Not In Sight** and released several critically acclaimed albums before finally splitting up in 1981.

Russell Smith has since embarked upon a promising solo career, recording for Capitol. He has also written a number of hit songs for a range of country stars including Mel McDaniel, Conway Twitty and George Jones.

Albums:
Stacked Deck (ABC/ABC)
Too Stuffed To Jump (ABC/ABC)
Toucan Do It Too (ABC/–)
Burning The Ballroom Down (ABC/ABC)
The Amazing Rhythm Aces (ABC/ABC)
Russel Smith (solo album) The Boy Next Door (Capitol/–)

Stacked Deck, Courtesy ABC Records – a well-received first album.

Bill Anderson

Nicknamed 'Whispering Bill' because of his lack of any real voice, Anderson was born Columbia, South Carolina, November 1, 1937. Training initially to be a journalist, he obtained a BA degree at the University of Georgia, singing and acting as a disc jockey in his spare time. Along the way, he worked as a sports writer for the weekly 'DeKalb New Era' and as correspondent for the 'Atlanta Journal', opting for a full time musical career in 1958 after Ray Price heard him singing his self-penned **City Lights** on a car radio and promptly covered it, thus earning a gold disc.

Many other Anderson songs were then recorded by Hank Locklin, Jim Reeves, Porter Wagoner, Faron Young, Jean Shepherd, and others, while his own discs

(for Decca) also sold well. However, his real breakthrough as a recording artist came in 1962, with a crossover hit **Mama Sang A Song**, this being followed by **Still** and **8 × 10**, both covered in Britain by singing comedian Ken Dodd. Since that time, Anderson has waxed a stream of hits including **I Get The Fever** (1966), **For Loving You** with Jan Howard (1967), **Wild Weekend** (1968), **Happy State Of Life** (1968), **My Life** (1969), **But You Know I Love You** (1969), **Quits** (1971), **The Corner Of My Life** (1973), and many others.

Anderson discovered Mary Lou Turner, who became another successful duet

The Bill Anderson Story, Courtesy MCA Records.

partner in the '70s (**Sometimes** and **I Can't Sleep With You**). When his records failed to make an impression, he turned to disco songs and came up with disco-country numbers such as **I Can't Wait Any Longer** and **Three Times A Lady**.

Winner of countless awards, Anderson and his band the Po' Boys (named after his early hit **Po' Folks**) have played concerts throughout the world. In recent years he has become a TV personality, starting with his own syndicated Bill Anderson Show in the '60s and leading up to game shows like 'Mister and Mrs'. He now records for the small Atlanta-based Southern Tracks label without too much success on the country charts.

Live From London, Courtesy MCA Records.

As well as being among the first country artists to move into the realms of country disco, Anderson was the first country musician to appear on a satellite broadcast.

Albums:
The Bill Anderson Story (MCA/MCA)
Don't She Look Good? (MCA/–)
Always Remember (MCA/–)
Whispering Bill (MCA/–)
Live From London (–/MCA)
Ladies Choice (MCA/Bulldog)
Bright Lights and Country Music (Decca/Stetson)
Golden Greats (–/MCA)

John Anderson

This honky tonk country singer with a rich bluesy vocal style was born December 12, 1955 in Apopka, Florida. He played in a rock 'n' roll band called Living End whilst still in high school in Florida. One week after graduation he moved to Nashville and for two years he was singing in lounge bars with his older sister Donna. Anderson signed a recording contract with the small Ace Of Hearts label, releasing his first single **Swoop Down Sweet Jesus** in 1974 and landed a writer's contract with Al Gallico Publishing. For the next three years he tried his hand at various jobs during the day whilst working the Nashville clubs and bars. A move to Warner Bros. Records in 1977 started a consistent run of chart successes with hard country songs like **The Girl At The End Of The Bar** at the end of 1978, **Your Lying Blue Eyes**, a Top 20 hit in 1979 and reflective **1959** in 1980. Since then Anderson hasn't looked back, being hailed as the new George Jones and Lefty Frizzell with Top 5 country hits including **I'm Just An Old Chunk Of Coal, Swingin'** – a hard-core country blues number which crossed over into the American pop charts in 1983 – and the cleverly constructed **Tokyo, Oklahoma**. These hits plus his excellent albums have consolidated his position as one of the finest young country vocalists and writers on the contemporary scene.

Albums:
Wild And Blue (Warner/Warner)
I Just Came Home To Count The Memories (Warner/–)
Best Of John Anderson (Warner/Warner)
Eye Of A Hurricane (Warner/–)
Tokyo, Oklahoma (Warner/–)

Below: John Anderson's Swingin' was CMA Single Of The Year in 1983, the same year that he won the Horizon award.

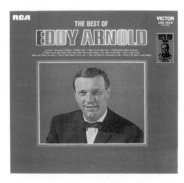

Liz Anderson

Born Elizabeth Jane Haaby, at Rosean, Minnesota, March 13, 1930, Liz married Casey Anderson, May 26, 1946 and gave birth to daughter Lynn Anderson in September 1947.

After business college, she worked as a secretary but became a singer-songwriter, signing a recording contract with RCA in 1964. An Anderson-penned song **(My Friends Are Gonna Be) Strangers** provided Merle Haggard with a disc success in 1965, the same singer having a No.1 country hit with **I'm A Lonesome Fugitive**, another Anderson song, in December 1966. Liz herself logged over a dozen country chart-fillers while with RCA, the biggest of these being **Wife Of The Party** (1966), **The Game Of Triangles**–with Bobby Bare and Norma Jean (1966), **Mama Spank** (1967), **Tiny Tears** (1967) and **Husband Hunting** (1970). Nowadays she lives in virtual retirement. Her past albums include **Favourites, Cookin' Up Hits, Like a Merry Go Round** and **Liz Anderson Sings** (all on RCA).

Lynn Anderson

Singer Lynn Rene Anderson, daughter of Casey and Liz Anderson, was born in Grand Forks, North Dakota, September 26, 1947. Later, the family moved to Sacramento, where Lynn became an equestrian success, winning the title of California Horse Show Queen at the 1966 State Fair.

Also during 1966 she joined Chart Records, recording around 100 songs for the label and producing 17 hits during the late '60s, the biggest of these being a cover version of Ben Peters' **That's A No No** (1969). After marrying producer-songwriter Glen Sutton, Lynn signed for Columbia Records, her first single for the label being **Stay There Till I Get There**, a

Above: Lynn Anderson has spent a lot of time collecting funds for charity.

hit written by her husband. In the same year (1970), Lynn's recording of **Rose Garden** became a monster hit winning her a Grammy and the CMA Female Vocalist Of The Year awards. Other hits include **You're My Man, Keep Me In Mind, Top Of The World, I've Never Loved Anyone More** and **Isn't It Always Love**. She and Sutton were divorced in the mid '70s and Lynn is now married to her second husband, Harold Stream and concentrates on her horse riding skills, though she still does the occasional session as a background vocalist.

Albums:
Rose Garden (Columbia/CBS)
What A Man My Man Is (Columbia/CBS)
I've Never Loved Anyone More (Columbia/CBS)
Outlaw Is Just A State of Mind (Columbia/CBS)
All The King's Horses (Columbia/–)
Rose Garden/How Can I Unlove You? (Columbia/–)
Country Girl (–/Embassy)
Lynn Anderson Is Back (Permain/–)

Area Code 615

David Briggs, keyboards; Ken Buttrey, drums, vocals; Mac Gayden, guitar, french horn; Wayne Moss, guitar; Weldon Myrick, steel guitar; Norbert Putnam, bass, cello; Buddy Spicher, fiddle, viola, cello; Bobby Thompson, banjo, guitar.

Supergroup comprising Nashville and Muscle Shoals sessionmen, Area Code 615 was originally formed by Mike Nesmith, who still owns unreleased tapes of Code's initial sessions. They later made two albums for Polydor then split, three members forming Barefoot Jerry.

Albums:
Area Code 615 (Polydor/Polydor)
Trip In The Country (Polydor/Polydor)

Eddy Arnold

A country crooner with a smooth, very commercial voice, Arnold has probably sold more records than any other C&W artist. Born on a farm near Henderson, Tennessee, May 15, 1918, Richard Edward Arnold first became interested in music while at elementary school, his father – an old-timer fiddler – teaching him guitar at the age of ten. Arnold left high school during the early '30s to help his family run their farm. During this period he played at local barn dances, sometimes travelling to such dates on the back of a mule. He made his radio debut in Jackson, Tennessee during 1936, six years later gaining a regular spot on Jackson station WTJS. His big break came as singer/guitarist with Pee Wee King's Golden West Cowboys providing exposure on Grand Ole Opry.

As a solo act he signed for RCA in 1944, sparking off an amazing tally of hit records with **It's A Sin** and **I'll Hold You In My Heart** in 1947, the latter becoming a million-seller. This achievement was matched by later Arnold recordings: **Bouquet Of Roses, Anytime, Just A Little**

The Best Of Eddy Arnold, Courtesy RCA Records.

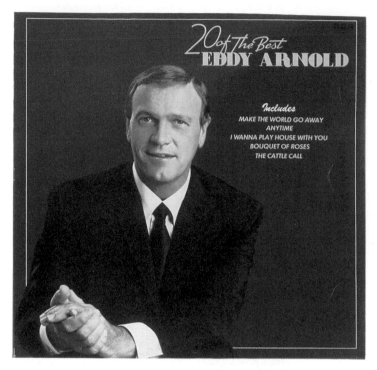

20 Of The Best, Eddy Arnold, Courtesy RCA Records.

Lovin' Will Go A Long Long Way (1948); **I Wanna Play House With You** (1951) and **Cattle Call** (1955), while many others sold nearly as many.

Arnold's records sold to people who normally bought straight pop, so his TV appearances were not confined to just Grand Ole Opry and country shows; he guested on programmes hosted by Perry Como, Milton Berle, Arthur Godfrey, Dinah Shore, Bob Hope, Spike Jones and other showbiz personalities. Arnold also had his own syndicated TV series, Eddy Arnold Time, plus other shows on NBC and ABC networks.

Though his record sales dropped slightly by the end of the '50s, **What's He Doing In My World?**, **Make The World Go Away**, **I Want To Go With You**, **Somebody Like Me**, **Lonely Again**, **Turn The World Around** and **Then You Can Tell Me Goodbye**, all topped the country charts during the '60s. By the beginning of the '70s Arnold, nicknamed 'The Tennessee Plowboy', had sold well in excess of 60 million discs.

In 1966, Arnold was elected to the Country Music Hall of Fame. A hit single **Cowboy** marked Arnold's return to the RCA fold in 1976 after a brief period with MGM and he has continued recording for RCA, cutting a sprinkling of hits including **Let's Get It While The Gettin's Good** and **That's What I Get For Loving You**. Both of these records reached the Top 10 in 1980.

Eddy, Courtesy RCA Records. A fine, Owen Bradley-produced, album.

Albums:
Best Of Vol. 1 (RCA/RCA)
Best Of Vol. 2 (RCA/–)
Cattle Call (RCA/–)
So Many Ways/If The World Stopped Turnin' (MGM/–)
Country Gold (RCA/–)
Pure Gold (RCA/–)
Eddy (RCA/RCA)
A Legend And His Lady (RCA/–)
Famous Country Music Makers (–/RCA)

Ernie Ashworth

Born in Huntsville, Alabama on December 15, 1928, Ernie Ashworth in his teens played guitar and sang on local radio stations, later moving to Nashville and working for stations WSIX. Carl Smith and Little Jimmy Dickens were among those to record Ashworth's songs, prompting MGM to sign him to a recording contract in 1955, a number of the discs being cut for the label under the name of Billy Worth. Wesley Rose, who had initiated the MGM contract, won Ashworth another deal, this time with Decca, his first release **Each Moment (Spent With You)** becoming a major hit in May 1960. After further successes with **You Can't Pick A Rose In December** and **Forever Gone** came a move to Hickory Records, the hits continuing via **Everybody But Me** (1962), his first Hickory single, and **Talk Back Trembling Lips**, a No. 1 in the 1963 country charts.

Wins in the Most Promising C&W Artist sections of the Cashbox and Billboard polls came in 1963 and 1964. Ashworth was rewarded with appearances and membership on Nashville's Grand Ole Opry and other leading shows. A consistent hit-maker throughout the '60s, Ashworth's **A Week In The Country**, **I Love To Dance With Annie** and **The DJ Cried**, all figured in the charts. In 1965 he appeared in a movie, 'The Farmer's Other Daughter' and made two Hickory albums as **Talk Back Trembling Lips** and **Ernie Ashworth**. Nowadays he entertains tourists in Pigeon Forge, Tennessee.

Asleep At The Wheel

Wheel, a western swing unit, began life on vocalist-guitarist Ray Benson's rent-free 1,500 farm, near Paw Paw, West Virginia, where he, Leroy Preston (vocals, guitar) and Reuben Gosfield often called 'Lucky Oceans' (pedal steel guitar) formed a small country band. With various personnel changes, the band gained further shape when female vocalist Chris

Pasture Prime, Asleep At The Wheel, Courtesy Capitol Records.

O'Connell, just out of high school, became the fourth permanent member. Following a move to San Francisco, pianist Floyd Domino joined, bringing jazz influence to the band.

The first UA album by the Wheel was near country in character but subsequent albums for Epic, Capitol, MCA have seen the band employing more diverse material, linking country, R&B and jazz in best western swing tradition, often employing contributions by guesting ex-Texas Playboy Johnny Gimble. Once merely back-up band for singer Stoney Edwards in their early days, the Wheel have been working out of Austin since February 1974, gaining an enviable reputation and getting voted Top Touring Band by the ACM in 1977. They also won a Grammy for their

Collision Course, Asleep At The Wheel, Courtesy Capitol Records.

version of Count Basie's **One O'Clock Jump** in 1978, and in 1980 appeared on the soundtrack of the film 'Roadie'.

They do what they do and it's often full of surprises. In fact the only thing about the band that can be guaranteed is that the Wheel will feature a changed personnel next time you hear them – at the last count some 60 musicians claim to have worked with the band at one point or another!

Albums:
Comin' Right At Ya (UA/–)
Texas Gold (Capitol/Capitol)
Wheelin' and Dealin' (Capitol/Capitol)
Wheel (Capitol/Capitol)
Collision Course (Capitol/Capitol)
Pasture Prime (MCA Dot/Demon)

Bob Atcher

Robert Owen Atcher, born in Hardin County, Kentucky on May 11, 1914, grew up in North Dakota in a family of folk singers and championship fiddlers, and the duality of these locations gave him a broad knowledge of both traditional folk songs and cowboy songs as well, although he proved to be a very commercial country singer during his long association with Columbia Records (1937–1958).

Bob's clear tenor voice was a fixture and a cornerstone of the once-thriving country music scene in Chicago; he appeared there on WJJD and WBBM and on a host of network programmes from 1931–34 and 1937–48, then joined the National Barn Dance as its top star from 1948 right through to its demise in 1970.

Appearing on and off with a series of girl singers known as 'Bonnie Blue Eyes', Bob Atcher achieved his greatest popularity on radio. He recorded for Kapp and Capitol as well as Columbia Records (his biggest hit for them was a comedy version of **Thinking Tonight Of My Blue Eyes**), wrote songs, pioneered television in Chicago, and appeared as a singing cowboy in several Columbia pictures.

Although he continued to perform, Atcher's interest gradually turned to the financial and civic, and he spent nearly two decades as mayor of the Chicago

suburb of Schaumburg.

His past albums have included **Early American Folk Songs**, **Songs Of The Saddle**, **Dean Of The Cowboy Singers** (all Columbia); **Bob Atcher's Best** (Harmony) and **Saturday Night At The Old Barn Dance** (Kapp).

Chet Atkins

Chester Burton Atkins was born June 20, 1924, on a 50-acre farm near Luttrell, Tennessee. His elder half-brother, Jim, was a proficient guitarist who later went on to play with Les Paul. At 18, Chet became fiddler on station WNOX in Knoxville, Tennessee, then toured with Archie Campbell and Bill Carlisle, playing fiddle and guitar. After marrying Leona Johnson in 1945, Atkins joined Red Foley

20 Of The Best, Chet Atkins, Courtesy RCA Records.

in 1946, then moved to Nashville in 1950 with The Carter Sisters and Mother Maybelle, signing a record contract with RCA and initially cutting more vocals than instrumentals – the latter got the airplay.

He became top session guitarist for RCA's Nashville sessions at the end of the '40s, moving up to the post of A&R assistant under Steve Sholes in 1952. His first solo album, **Gallopin' Guitar** was released in 1953. After assisting Sholes on Presley's **Heartbreak Hotel** sessions in 1955, Atkins was placed in charge of the new RCA studio, becoming Nashville A&R manager in 1960 and vice-president of RCA Records just eight years later, holding the post until he retired in 1979.

A guitarist able to tackle many styles, Atkins has appeared at the Newport Jazz Festival, and was featured soloist with the Atlanta Symphony Orchestra. He has produced hit records for Hank Snow, Waylon Jennings, Perry Como, Al Hirt and many, many others, and also had his own major hits with **Poor People Of Paris** (1956), **Boo Boo Stick Beat Beat** (1959), **One Mint Julep** (1960), **Teensville** (1960), **Yakety Axe** (1965) etc. Along with Floyd Cramer, Hank Garland and others, he is credited with creating the highly commercial 'Nashville Sound' that brought pop acts scurrying to record in the area. For 14 consecutive years he won 'Best Instrumentalist' award in the 'Cashbox' poll. He signed with Columbia Records in 1983 and made a big impact with his album **Stay Tuned**, with fellow guitarists Larry Carlton, George Benson, Mark Knopfler and Earl Klugh. With more than 100 albums to his credit covering all styles of music, and having guided the careers of Jerry Reed, Jim Reeves, Hank Locklin etc, he is one of Nashville's leading country figures. He was elected to the Country Music Hall of Fame in 1973.

Above: A track-suited Chet Atkins. In the '80s he did Stay Tuned, an album for the jogging generation.

Albums:
Country Pickin' (Camden/)
Finger Pickin' Good (Camden/–)
For The Good Times (RCA/–)
Me And Jerry Reed (RCA/–)
Superpickers (RCA/RCA)
Picks On The Hits (RCA/RCA)
Picks The Beat (RCA/–)
Chester And Lester (RCA/RCA)
Me And Chet Atkins with Jerry Reed (RCA/RCA)
Famous Country Music Makers (–/RCA)
Atkins-Travis Travelling Show (RCA/RCA)
Stay Tuned (Columbia/CBS)

Below: Gene Autry in the movie, 'The Last Roundup'. He once appeared in a sci-fi serial entitled 'The Phantom Empire', the plot of which concerned a lost empire located under Gene's own ranch!

Gene Autry

Orvon Gene Autry, the most successful of all singing cowboys to break into movies, was born in Tioga, Texas, September 29, 1907. Taught to play guitar by mother Elnora Ozment Autry, Gene joined the Fields Brothers Marvelous Medicine Show while still at high school, but after graduation in 1925 became a railroad telegrapher with the Frisco Railway at Sapulpar, Oklahoma. Encouraged by Will Rogers following a chance meeting, Autry took a job on radio KVOO, Tulsa, in 1930, billing himself as 'Oklahoma's Singing Cowboy', and singing much in the style of Jimmie Rodgers.

In 1929 he had visited New York and began recording with such labels as Victor, Okeh, Columbia, Grey Gull and Gennett (often under a pseudonym), sometimes working with Jimmy Long, a singer-songwriter-guitarist, once Autry's boss on the Frisco line. On many he was

assisted by Frank and Johnny Marvin. Shortly after, Autry began broadcasting regularly on the WLS Barn Dance programme for Chicago, his popularity gaining further momentum with the 1931 release of **Silver Haired Daddy of Mine** (penned by Autry and Long), a recording that eventually sold over five million copies.

Next came a move to Hollywood where, following a performance in a Ken Maynard western 'In Old Santa Fe', he was asked to star in a serial 'The Phantom Empire'. Thereafter, Autry appeared in innumerable B Movies, usually with the horse, Champion. His list of hit records during the '30s and '40s – he was easily the most popular singer of the time – is awesome, including **Yellow Rose of Texas** (1933), The Last Roundup (1934), **Tumbling Tumbleweeds** (1935), **Mexicali Rose** (1936), **Back In The Saddle Again** (1939), **South Of The Border** (1940), **You Are My Sunshine** (1941), **It Makes No Difference Now** (1941), **Be Honest With Me** (1941), **Tweedle-O-Twill** (1942) and **At Mail Call Today** (1945).

Autry enlisted in the Army Air Corps in July 1942 and became a pilot, flying in the Far East and North Africa with Air Transport Command. Discharged on June 17 1945, he formed a film company, continuing to star in such movies as 'Sioux City Sue' (1947), 'Guns And Saddles' (1949) and 'Last Of The Pony Riders' (1953). He also appeared in the long-running 'Melody Ranch' radio programme from 1939 until 1956.

His other activities included opening a chain of radio and TV stations and running a record company, a hotel chain and a music publishing firm, plus a major league baseball club, the California Angels. Since **Silver Haired Daddy**, Autry has had three other million-selling discs in **Here Comes Santa Claus** (1947), **Peter Cottontail** (1949) and the other nine million-seller **Rudolph The Red Nosed Reindeer** (1948).

Writer of scores of hit songs, Gene Autry has also starred in a series of annual rodeos held in Madison Square Garden and even had an Oklahoma town named after him. In 1969 he was elected to the Country Music Hall Of Fame.

Albums:
Country Music Hall Of Fame (Columbia/–)
All American Cowboy (Republic/–)
Cowboy Hall of Fame (Republic/–)
Favourites (Republic/Ember)
South Of The Border (Republic/Ember)
Live From Madison Square Garden (Republic/Ember)

Hoyt Axton

Born in Oklahoma, son of two teachers, John Thomas Axton and his wife Mae – a lady who worked for Grand Ole Opry and wrote many fine songs including **Heartbreak Hotel**, the Elvis Presley classic – Axton began playing guitar and singing in West Coast clubs during 1958. After a brief spell in the Navy, he cut his first record **Follow The Drinking Gourd** in Nashville, along with sessionmen Jimmy Riddle (harmonica) and Grady Martin (guitar). Axton's **Greenback Dollar** became a hit when recorded by The Kingston Trio in 1963, while **The Pusher**, another Axton song, was heard by John Kay in 1964 and subsequently became an enormous success for Kay's rock group, Steppenwolf. Other Axton compositions, **Joy To The World** and **Never Been To Spain**, proved winners for Three Dog Night and **No No Song** scored for Ringo Starr.

While Axton was once thought of primarily as a folk singer, he is now considered as one of the finest writers in country music, his songs being recorded by Waylon Jennings, Tanya Tucker, John Denver, Glenn Yarborough, Lynn Anderson, Glen Campbell, Commander Cody and many others. He featured in the country charts during the late '70s with **Flash Of Fire**, **A Rusty Old Halo** and **Della And The Dealer**, the latter making an impression in Britain. Axton has also made

Below: Hoyt Axton. One of country's odd men out, he has written hits for such rock stars as Steppenwolf, Three Dog Night and Ringo Starr. He also once recorded an album of Bessie Smith songs, while his mother wrote Heartbreak Hotel, the Elvis hit.

Free Sailin', Hoyt Axton, Courtesy MCA Records.

his mark in films appearing in 'The Black Stallion', 'Gremlins' and many more. He also has his own record company, Jeremiah, named after the bullfrog in the song **Joy To The World**.

Albums:
Less Than The Song (A&M/A&M)
Life Machine (A&M/A&M)
Southbound (A&M/A&M)
Fearless (A&M/A&M)
Snowblind Friend (MCA/MCA)
A Rusty Old Halo (Jeremiah/Youngblood)

The Bailes Brothers

Homer Bailes, fiddle, vocals; Johnny Bailes, guitar, vocals; Kyle Bailes, string bass, vocals; Walter Bailes, guitar, vocals.

Despite the number of Bailes Brothers members, the act of that name rarely consisted of all four brothers, but instead any combination of two or three was likely. The heart of the act, however, comprised Johnny and Walter, whose song-writing and singing made them one of the most popular groups of the 1940s.

Johnny was actually the first to work professionally, teaming up with Red Sovine in 1937. By the time he had gone to Beckley, West Virginia (1939), he had not only acquired the services of Skeets Williamson but also those of his sister Laverne, who became known as Molly O'Day. Yet another bandmember was Little Jimmy Dickens. During the same period, Kyle and Walter were billing themselves as the Bailes Brothers; before long it was Walter and Johnny.

In 1942, Roy Acuff heard them and arranged for an audition – which was successful – for the Grand Ole Opry, a tenure which lasted through to 1948 when they joined the Louisiana Hayride. It was during the Opry years that they recorded many of the songs that made them famous: **Dust On The Bible**, **I Want To Be Loved**, **Remember Me**, **As Long As I Live** and others, mainly for Columbia.

The act eventually broke up in 1949, Homer and Walter entering the ministry, although both Johnny and Walter, and Home and Kyle worked as gospel duets intermittently in the '50s. By the late '70s, Kyle was in the air-conditioning business, Homer had become a minister and Johnny was managing one of Webb Pierce's radio stations, leaving Walter, though actively involved in church work, as the other brother still performing on a semi-regular basis, doing gospel numbers (largely self-written) like his classic **Whiskey Is The Devil In liquid Form**.

Albums:
The Bailes Brothers: Johnny And Homer (Old Homestead/–)
I've Got My One Way Ticket (Old Homestead/–)

DeFord Bailey

Though black musicians are a rarity in country music, it was Bailey, a black harmonica player, who opened the WSM Barn Dance programme – playing **Pan American Blues** – on the night George D. Hay named the show, 'Grand Ole Opry'. Born Carthage, Tennessee, in 1899, Bailey was afflicted by infantile paralysis at the age of three. Although he recovered, his growth was stunted and he suffered from a deformed back. Apart from being the first performer on the Opry, the 4ft 10in tall Bailey was amongst the first musicians to record in Nashville, cutting several sides for Victor on September 28, 1928.

He remained a member of the Opry for many years but later drifted into obscurity, turning down offers of records, films and personal appearances in favour of operating a shoeshine stand in the Nashville area. When Bailey died in July, 1982, several Opry members were present at the funeral, Bill Monroe acting as a pall bearer.

Razzy Bailey

A rough-voiced singer with a penchant for country blues, Rasie (later Razzy) Bailey spent his boyhood on a Five Points Alabama farm which had no running water or electricity. A back porch picker, he learnt guitar and joined a string band sponsored by the Future Farmers Of America Organisation before going solo and working at a Georgia nightclub, which closed down four months later. He then became, in turn, a truck driver, an insurance salesman, a furniture company representative and a meat cutter for a butcher, trying to keep both a band and a family together, the former wanting to quit and his wife first seeking a divorce and then psychiatric help. In 1972, he recorded just one release for MGM and in 1975 he cut **Peanut Butter** for Capicorn, but nothing really jelled, though his marriage miraculously held together.

But in 1976, amid a contract hassle, he was told by a psychic that not only his contractual problems would be cleared up but another artist would record a Bailey song and that it would change his whole way of life. Soon after, Dickey Lee recorded Razzy's **9,999,999 Tears** and had a Top 5 hit. Another of the psychic's predictions came true when RCA signed Bailey in 1978 and his first single, **What Time Do You Have To Be Back In Heaven** went Top 20, followed by **Tonight She's Gonna Love Me (Like There Was No Tomorrow)** (1978), **If Love Had A Face, I**

Makin' Friends, Razzy Bailey, Courtesy RCA Records.

Ain't Got No Business Doin' Business Today, I Can't Get Enough Of That (all 1979), and **Too Old To Play Cowboys** (1980), his first chart-toppers coming with **Loving Up A Storm** and **I Keep Coming Back**, in 1980.

By 1981 he was 'Billboard' magazine's Country Singles Artist Of The Year, he played Lake Tahoe, Disneyland, the New York Savoy, the Palomino and many other major venues.

Many artists wait until their record sales plummet before they jump labels but Razzy switched from RCA to MCA while still a happy hit-maker in 1984. And at last his feel for things raunchy and bluesy seemed to be paying off. His last Top 20 hit for RCA was a version of Wilson Pickett's **In The Midnight Hour**, while his first album with his new label, **Cut From A Different Stone**, saw Bailey linking with soul guitar ace Steve Cropper to write several songs, also reprising Eddie Floyd's R&B classic **Knock On Wood**.

Albums:
Makin' Friends (RCA/RCA)
Razzy Bailey's Greatest Hits (RCA/–)
The Midnight Hour (RCA/–)

Below: People used to ask Razzy if he was a pop singer or an R&B artist. But he is really into country blues.

Moe Bandy

A provider of undiluted honky-tonk, Bandy was born in Meridan, Mississippi, February 12, 1944, one of six children born to a piano-playing mother and a guitar-picking father. The family settled near San Antonio, Texas, when Moe was six, his father there organizing a band called the Mission City Playboys. A guitar player from an early age, Bandy initially preferred bronco-busting and opted for a rodeo career until a surfeit of broken bones convinced him to return to a less hazardous occupation. At the age of 19, he formed a group Moe Bandy and The Mavericks, eventually gaining his first record contract with Satin, a local label. Then came stints with Shannon (during which Bandy first met producer Ray Baker) and GRC, the latter releasing **I Just Started Hating Cheatin' Songs Today** (1974), Bandy's first hit. the label released three more Top 20 hits – **It Was Always So Easy** (1974), **Don't Anybody Make Love At Home Anymore?**, and **Bandy the Rodeo Clown** (1975), after which GRC folded and Moe moved on to Columbia and renewed success with **Hank Williams You Wrote My Life** (1975).

With Baker masterminding his career

(acting as producer and also as song-finder, sometimes finding well over a thousand songs which were whittled down to a final 20), Bandy became a hit-making machine, logging two Top 20 songs in 1976, three in 1977, and three in 1978, peaking in 1979 when he provided five major records including two chart-toppers, **Just Good Ol' Boys** (a duet with Joe Stampley) and **I Cheated Me Right Out Of You**.

Since that time, little has changed, except for Moe's acquisition of a beard! He still sings songs about seeing life through a bottle or of love gone sour; he still refuses to cross over in search of pop success; and he still maintains that steady stream of country hits, some of the more recent being **I Still Love You In The Same Ol' Way**, **You're Gonna Lose Her Like That**, **Let's Get Over Them Together** (1983), **It Took A Lot Of Drinking' To Get That Woman Over Me**, **Woman Your Love** (1984) and **Daddy's Honky Tonk** (1985). The latter was another duet with Joe Stampley, Bandy's partner on the 1984 Top 10 **Where's The Dress?**, a hilarious send-up of the pop transvestite scene.

A frequent award winner, Moe Bandy was also linked with Stampley at the 1980 CMA Awards ceremony; on this occasion, the twosome won the Vocal Duo Of The Year category.

Above: Moe Bandy, a one-time rodeo clown, handles drinking songs in a way even teetotallers would approve of.

Albums:
Bandy The Rodeo Clown (GRC/–)
Hank Williams You Wrote My Life
  (Columbia/–)
Soft Lights And Hard Country Music
  (Columbia/CBS)
It's A Cheatin' Situation (Columbia/CBS)
Just Good Ol' Boys – with Joe Stampley
  (Columbia/CBS)

R. C. Bannon

From Dallas, Texas, Bannon initially moved into Nashville as a DJ, holding down a five year residency at the city's Smuggler's Inn. Prior to this, he had spent many years on the road, performing at clubs throughout the southwest, at one point acting as warm-up act for the Marty Robbins roadshow.

In Nashville he was introduced to songwriter Harlan Sanders who nudged Warner Brothers Music into signing Bannon as a writer. By 1977 he had gained a recording contract with Columbia, logging a trio of minor hits that year and a couple in 1978. But the big breakthrough came in 1979 when he married Louise Mandrell, the two of them also getting together on record for Epic and recording a number of chart duets, one of which, **Reunited**, went Top 20. However, his own solo career refused to move up a gear and 1980 brough only three further mid-chart singles, leaving Bannon searching for the right song to really establish himself as a headline act.

Albums:
R. C. Bannon Arrives (Columbia/–)
Inseparable – with Louise Mandrell (Epic/–)

Bobby Bare

The provider of such million selling singles as **Detroit City** and **500 Miles Away From Home** and one of country's ranconteurs supreme, Bare was born in Ironton, Ohio, April 7, 1935. Motherless at the age of five, his sister being sent for adoption because

of the father's inability to feed the whole family, Bare became a farm worker at 15, later obtaining a job in a clothing factory. He built his own guitar and learnt to play, eventually winning a job with a country band in the Springfield-Portsmouth area, for which he received no pay. He recorded his own song **All American Boy** in 1958, then joined the army, the tapes of his song being offered to various record companies and taken up by Fraternity, who released the disc as by 'Bill Parsons'. But although the single became the second biggest selling record in the USA in December, Bare hardly benefitted financially, having sold the song rights for $50.

Upon service discharge, Bare began performing and writing once more, contributing three songs for the Jimmy Clanton-Chubby Checker movie 'Teenage Millionaire', a year later having his own hit record with an RCA release, **Shame On Me**. Richard Anthony then recorded a French version of **500 Miles Away From Home** (a folk song adapted and arranged by Bare, Hedy West and Charles Williams) and obtained a gold disc, Bare also achieving hit status with the same song. A year later, Bare appeared in an acting role in the cavalry western 'A Distant Trumpet' and also provided RCA with further hits via his versions of Hank Snow's **Miller's Cave** and Ian and Sylvia's **Four Strong Winds**.

After numerous other hit singles including **The Streets Of Baltimore** (1966) and **(Margie's At) The Lincoln Park Inn** (1966), Bare left RCA to join Mercury in 1970 supplying his new label with such Top 10 country hits as **How I Got To Memphis** (1970), **Come Sundown** (1970) and actually charting with every release. But he rejoined RCA (1972) and began working on a series of fine albums, commencing with one of his most successful, **Lullabys, Legends and Lies** (1973), an album penned almost entirely by Shel Silverstein and one that spawned such Top 10 hits as **Daddy What If** (1973) and **Marie Laveau**, a 1974 No. 1. After an album with his whole family **Singing In The Kitchen** (1974), he moved on to produce **Hard Time Hungries** (1975),

Below: Bare – "Tom T. Halls talks me into drinking brandy. He says 'It's only fruit juice, Bobby Joe.' But, man, that fruit juice wipes me out quick!"

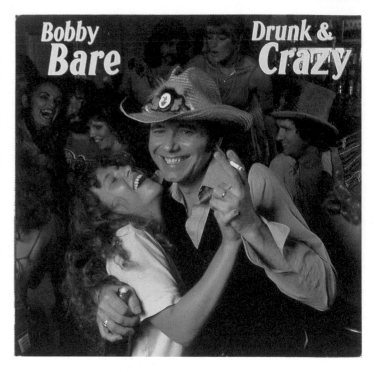

Drunk And Crazy, Bobby Bare, Courtesy CBS Records.

another critically acclaimed LP. Other hit singles followed but, unhappy with RCA, Bare signed for Columbia in 1978, first cutting **Bare** (1979), a well received, self-produced album. He then moved on to make **Sleeper Wherever I Fall**, reputed to have cost nearly $100,000, making it one of the most expensive albums ever to have been made in Nashville at that time.

Managed by rock mogul Bill Graham at this period, it seemed that Bare would once more cross over into the pop market. But, despite a number of other exemplary albums and a potentially chartbusting single in **Numbers** (1980), a Shel Silverstein-written parody of the movie '10', Bare's recording career gradually lost impetus and, despite the kudos gained by hosting the highly acclaimed 'Bobby Bare And Friends' TV show on the Nashville Network, by the mid '80s, Bare – still without any well-deserved CMA award – eventually signed to EMI-America.

Albums:
Famous Country Music Makers (RCA/RCA)
Lullabys, Legends And Lies (RCA/RCA)
Hard Time Hungries (RCA/RCA)
Bare (Columbia/CBS)
Sleeper Wherever I Fall (Columbia/CBS)
Drinkin' From The Bottle, Singin' From The
  Heart (Columbia/CBS)

Barefoot Jerry

Formed from the remnants of Area Code 615, Barefoot Jerry were headed by Wayne Moss from Charleston, West Virginia, a guitar player at 12 who later worked with several rock and R&B bands before becoming a member of Brenda Lee's back-up unit for two and a half years. After becoming a Nashville sessionman, also forming a band called The Escorts along with steelie Russ Hicks, Wayne Moss fashioned Barefoot Jerry, an often inventive country-rock outfit that recorded variously for Capitol, Warner

You Can't Get Off . . . Barefoot Jerry, Courtesy Monument Records.

Bros and Monument, 1971–76, Hicks being present on most of the albums.

Albums:
Barefoot Jerry (Warner Bros/Warner
  Bros)
Watchin' TV (Monument/Criminal)
You Can't Get Off With Your Shoes On
  (Monument/Monument)
    Barefootin' (Monument/Monument)

Randy Barlow

A Detroit-born singer, Barlow was a student at West Kentucky University, majoring in clinical psychology, and was about to graduate when Dick Clark's travelling Caravan of Stars arrived in Bowling Green without an MC and offered Barlow the position, which he accepted. Eventually he arrived in California, becoming a solo singer on the lounge circuit and also formulating a recording career with Capitol, his first chart record coming with **Throw Away The Pages** in 1974. Together with producer, manager and co-writer Fred Kelly he formed his own label, Gazelle, and immediately notched seven hits in a row, the biggest of these being **Twenty Four Hours From Tulsa** (1976) and **Kentucky Woman** (1977).

By 1978 Barlow had signed to Gene Autry's Republic label, coming up with three Top 10 records in **Slow And Easy**, **No Sleep Tonight** and **Fall In Love With Me Tonight**, other major singles arriving with **Sweet Melinda** and **Lay Back In The Arms Of Someone** (1979). A one-time heavy drinker "I wasn't a stumblin'-around, falling down drunk – I just crawled", he quit the bottle shortly before this successful period.

Switching to Paid Records in 1980, Barlow has since had one further Top 20 single with **Love Dies Hard** (1981).

Albums:
Arrival (Gazelle/–)
Fall In Love With Me (Republic/London)

Bashful Brother Oswald – See Pete Kirby

Dr Humphrey Bate (And The Possum Hunters)

Oscar Albright, bass; Alcyone Bate, vocals, ukelele, piano; Buster Bate, guitar, tipple, harmonica, jews harp; Dr Humphrey Bate, harmonica; Burt Hutcherson, guitar; Walter Leggett, banjo; Oscar Stone, fiddle; Staley Walton, guitar.

The harmonica-playing leader of the most popular string band on the Grand Ole Opry, Dr Bate – a graduate of the Vanderbilt Medical School who earned his living as a physician – was born in Summer County, Tennessee, in 1875. He had fronted a great many popular local string bands before he began to play on Nashville radio in 1925, joining the forerunner of the Opry late in that year. Not long after, they recorded a number of tunes and songs for Brunswick Records. After Dr Bate's death in 1936, Oscar Stone headed the band until 1949, when Staley Walton and Alcyone Bate took over the leadership of the Possum Hunters, whose remaining members were absorbed when four old time Opry bands were amalgamated into two during the '60s. Bate's daughter, Alcyone (now Alcyone Beasley), joined her father's band at the age of 13 as a vocalist, eventually becoming pianist with the Crook Brothers Band and logging well over half a century as an Opry member.

Above: Dr Humphrey Bate And The Possum Hunters, the first string band to be featured on the Grand Ole Opry. A real doctor from Sumner County, Tennessee, he led a group that featured his 13 year-old daughter.

Molly Bee

Only ten years old when she made her debut on the Rex Allen Tuscon radio show, Molly Bee (real name Molly Beachwood) was born in Oklahoma City, Oklahoma, August 18, 1939. When 11, she became a regular on Cliffie Stone's Los Angeles-based Hometown Jamboree TV show, following this with stays on the nationally networked Pinky Lee and Tennessee Ernie Ford TV programmes.

A successful actress and vocalist, Molly was booked into several Las Vagas nightspots and other major venues, breaking house records with some of her appearances. During the '60s, she also began starring in West Coast productions of such stage musicals as 'The Boy Friend', 'Paint Your Wagon' and 'Finian's Rainbow', in 1967 making a well-received tour of Japan. Additionally, she recorded for Capitol and MGM, and made films that included 'The Chartroose Caboose' (1960) and 'The Young Swingers' (1963), vying for the teen-queen crown worn by Sandra Dee. Fading somewhat from the country and pop scene during the '70s, she still turned up on TV from time to time, singing and dancing in variety shows, and even got together with one-time mentor Cliffie Stone to record for his Granite label, gaining mini-hits with **She Kept On Talkin'** (1974) and **Right Or Left At Oak Street** (1975).

Albums:
Swingin' Country (MGM/–)
Good Golly Miss Molly (Granite/Pye)

Carl Belew

Singer-songwriter and guitarist Carl Robert Belew was born in Salina, Oklahoma, April 21, 1931. For many years he played minor venues and country fairs, eventually gaining a spot on Shreveport KWKH's Lousiana Hayride and obtaining a recording contract with Decca. His first major hit for the label was **Am I That Easy To Forget?**, a self-penned song that became a Top 10 country hit in 1959, the success of this disc being matched by **Hello Out There**, an RCA release waxed by Belew in 1962. Other hits followed throughout the mid '60s, namely **In The Middle Of A Memory**, **Crystal Chandelier**, **Boston Jail**, **Walking Shadow**, **Talking Memory**, **Girl Crazy** and **Mary's Little Lamb**.

After 1968 Belew's name was absent from the charts for a long period, returning in 1971 when **All I Need Is You**, a duet recorded with Betty Jean Robinson, became a mini-hit. A further success with **Welcome Back To My World**, an MCA release in 1974, augured well for the furtherance of Belew's chart career. But it was not to be.

The Bellamy Brothers Best, Courtesy MCA/Curb Records.

Albums:
Carl Belew (Vocalion/–)
12 Shades (Victor/–)
Songs (Vocalion/–)

The Bellamy Brothers

David and Howard Bellamy hail from Derby, Florida, the sons of a farmer who played dobro and fiddle in a bluegrass band. Keyboardist David worked as organist with a soul band The Accidents in 1965, backing Percy Sledge, Little Anthony and The Imperials plus others, while Howard learnt guitar, the family playing together for the first time at an annual Tampa event, Rattlesnake Round Up.

During 1968 the brothers formed a pop band Jerico, playing the club circuit in Georgia, Mississippi and South Carolina, but disbanded in 1971 and returned to the family farm. There the duo began songwriting, also providing jingles for the local radio and TV stations.

After one of David's songs, **Spiders And Snakes**, proved a two million seller for Jim Stafford in 1973, they headed for California, and there embarked on a recording career of their own making an initial impact with **Nothin' Heavy**, a regional hit (1975). They moved on to gain an international reputation with their version of **Let Your Love Flow**, a song written by Neil Diamond and roadie Larry Williams, thus providing the brothers with a US pop No.1 in 1976. Fashioning a rock-styled yet often acoustic-based kind of country music, the Bellamys achieved their second major success with **If I Said You Had A Beautiful Body Would You Hold It Against Me** (1979), a song which was voted Single Of The Year by the CMA of Great Britain.

Since that time, there have been no further pop hits for the Bellamys, but they

have proved a popular touring act at the same time as regaling the country charts with such No. 1s as **Sugar Daddy**, **Dancin' Cowboys** (1980), and **When I'm Away From You** (1983) plus many other major hits. In the meantime **Let Your Love Flow** has become something of a standard and has been employed as the music to a TV jeans commercial plus the closing theme to the Tatum O'Neal film 'Little Darlings' (1980).

Albums:
The Bellamy Brothers Best (MCA/MCA)

Beverly Hillbillies

An early, California-based outfit, the Hillbillies had a radio show on KEJK (later KMPC) Beverly Hills, in 1928, the group – then comprising Zeke and Tom Manners, Hank Skillet and Ezra Paulette – having a hit single, **When The Bloom Is On The Sage/Red River Valley**, released during the following year. Elton Britt, Stuart Hamblen, Wesley Tuttle and Glen Rice were all members of the Hillbillies at some point in the group's career, Rice forming his own version of the band in later years after Zeke Manners and Elton Britt moved to New York in 1935.

The Binkley Brothers' Dixie Clodhoppers

Tom Andrews, guitar; Amos Binkley, banjo; Gale Binkley, fiddle; Jack Jackson, guitar, vocals.

An early Grand Ole Opry string band whose fine music, like most of the Opry's early acts, was severely under-recorded. Both watch repairman by trade, the

Binkley Brothers kept their band going on Nashville radio – with and without Jackson, a fine singer and yodeller – well into the mid '30s, but only recorded during Victor's 1928 field trip to Nashville, with **Hungry Hash House** and **I'll Rise When The Rooster Crows** outstanding.

Bill Black Combo

Winners of the No 1 Country Band award in both Cashbox and Record World, the Combo was first formed by bassist Bill Black (born in Memphis, Tennessee, on September 17, 1926), a one-time session-man for Sun Records, who became a regular sideman with Elvis Presley. When Presley joined the army in 1958, Black formed his own rock-inclined instrumental combo and signed for Hi Records, the band's first release, **Smokie** (1959), selling over two million copies. Throughout the early '60s, the Combo, which included Reggie Young (guitar) and Buddy Emmons on piano, notched hit after hit in the pop charts and after Bob Tucker took over the leadership in 1962.

Just prior to Black's death in October, 1965, the flow of pop hits began to peter out, but the band worked on, Tucker signing an agreement with Black's widow to keep the Combo active as a recording and touring concern. Gradually, the band swung from being predominantly rock with a little bit of country to one that provided things more on a 50/50 basis, and by 1975 they came up with their first real country album **Solid And Country**; one track, **Boilin' Cabbage**, a sax-assisted fiddle breakdown, became the biggest country instrumental of the year.

Since that time, 75 per cent of the band's gigs have been at country venues, while they have occasionally managed to edge into the country chart with **Back Up And Push** 1975, **Fire On The Bayou**, **Redneck Rock** (1976) and **Cashin' In** (1978).

Above: The Bellamy Brothers, who provided the world of music with If I Said You Had A Beautiful Body Would You Hold It Against Me.

Albums:
The World's Greatest Honky Tonk Band (Hi/–)
Solid And Country (Hi/–)

Jack Blanchard and Misty Morgan

Both were born in the same Buffalo, New York, hospital, both in May (Jack on May 8, 1942 and Misty on May 23, 1945), both have brown hair and blue eyes, both have parents John and Mary, plus sisters also named Mary, and both moved to Ohio while young.

Jack Blanchard spent many years as a sax player in a small combo, while Misty Morgan, who had been involved in music since the age of nine, played piano and organ on the Cincinatti club circuit for a time before moving to Florida where she met and eventually married Blanchard.

Five years passed, however, before they began working as a duo. Blanchard became a solo pianist, working for big bands as a director-arranger, later producing records in Nashville. It was at this time that he decided to cut **Big Black Bird** as a duet with his wife, thus coming up with a mild country hit. Next came **Tennessee Birdwalk**, one of the '70s biggest sellers, establishing Blanchard and Morgan as a top-ranking act.

Since then they have played many high-rated TV shows and obtained an equal number of prestige-filled dates, their other hits (on Mega Wayside and Epic) including **You've Got Your Troubles**, **Humphrey The Camel** (1970), **There Must Be more To Life**, **Somewhere in Virginia**

In The Rain (1970), **Just One More Song**, **Something On Your Mind**, **Down The End Of The Wine** (1974), **Because We Love**, **I'm High On You** (1975).

Albums:
Birds Of A Feather (Wayside/–)
Two Sides Of . . . (Mega/–)

The Blue Sky Boys

Bill Bolick, vocals, mandolin; Earl Bolick, vocals, guitar.

Both born in Hickory, North Carolina: Bill on October 28, 1917, Earl on December 16, 1919, they were sons of Garland Bolick, who grew tobacco and worked in a textile mill. The Bolicks began playing traditional material, working in and around the Hickory area. In 1935, Bill sang for The East Hickory String Band – a name later changed to The Crazy Hickory Nuts, after J. W. Fincher of the Crazy Water Crystal Company who had offered them a job in Nashville – and the same year, the brothers began singing duets on the local radio station. In 1936, they recorded for Victor, whose A&R man believed them to be copies of the Monroe Brothers.

Their first release – on Bluebird – was **The Sunnyside Of Life**, written by Bill. During the late '30s and early '40s, the Bolicks' mixture of old-timey and religious music became very popular but, following World War II, country fans began seeking something more commercial and RCA asked the Boys to employ an electric guitarist in their lineup – a request they refused.

The Blue Sky Boys (Bill And Earl Bolick), Courtesy RCA Records.

In 1951, the Blue Sky Boys broke up, Bill entering college but leaving to work for the Post Office before he had gained his degree in business, Earl working as a machinist for Lockheed. Persuaded by Starday Records to come out of retirement in 1963 and cut an album titled **Together Again**, they also decided to play the odd date or two at folk festivals and colleges, providing a youth audience with an opportunity to hear their fine harmony vocals. They also recorded an album for Capitol in 1965 and another for Rounder as late as 1976.

But these albums and the occasional live dates were but gestures. After 1951 the Boys – soured by their experiences in the music business – never returned to full-time music careers.

Albums:
The Blue Sky Boys (Rounder/–)
The Sunny Side Of Life (Rounder/–)
Presenting The Blue Sky Boys (JEMF/–)

Legendary Singer And Banjo Player, Dock Boggs, Courtesy Folkways.

Dock Boggs

Possessor of a unique banjo style, Moran Lee 'Dock' Boggs was born Norton, Virginia, February 7, 1898. A miner for 41 years, Boggs played five string banjo merely as a hobby – his religious wife frowning upon any deep involvement in 'sinful' music. Acquiring his unusual playing style (using two fingers and a thumb instead of the normal one finger and thumb claw hammer method) from a black musician he met in Norton, Boggs gradually developed his technique and recorded a number of sides for Brunswick in 1927, thoroughly displeasing his wife. But upon his retirement from mining, Boggs turned more of his attention to music and found himself to be an in-demand performer at various folk festivals where his playing, his eerie, haunting songs like **Oh Death** and his nasal vocal delivery, attracted much attention, encouraging Mike Seeger to record Boggs for the Folkways label. He died in 1971.

Albums:
Dock Boggs Vols 1 & 2 (Folkways/–)
Dock Boggs Vols 3 & 4 (Folkways/–)

Johnny Bond

Singing cowboy film star, Johnny Bond, was born Cyrus Whitfield Bond, at Enville, Oklahoma, on June 1, 1915.

After his family moved to a Marietta, Oklahoma farm in the '20s, he bought a 98 cent ukelele through a Montgomery Ward catalogue and began playing it, moving on to guitar and becoming proficient on that instrument by the time he'd entered high school. In 1934, Bond made his debut on an Oklahoma City radio station. Three years later, after performing at many local venues, he joined the Jimmy Wakely Trio (then known as The Bell Boys) – a group heard by Gene Autry – and signed for Autry's Melody Ranch CBS show in 1940.

Cooley and Jimmy Wakely, becoming co-host of Compton's Town Hall Party Show and partner with Tex Ritter in music publishing.

A fine songwriter, Bond is responsible for such standards as **Cimarron** and **I Wonder Where You Are Tonight**, **Gone And Left Me Blues**, **Your Old Love Letters**, **Tomorrow Never Comes** plus around 500 other compositions. His contract with Autry's Republic Records provided that label with **Hot Rod Lincoln**, a Top 30 pop hit in 1960; a 1965 recording of **Ten Little Bottles** giving another company, Starday, a top selling single. In the late '60s he signed for Capitol, cutting an album with Merle Travis, and then, after seeing one of his Starday tracks **Here Come The Elephants** become a mild hit (1971), moved on to Lamb and Lion who released one album, **How I Love Them Old Songs** (1975).

Bond toured the UK in 1976, the same year that his book 'The Tex Ritter Story' was published by Chappell. A writer of some talent he also wrote a book on Gene Autry plus 'Reflections', an autobiography which was published by the John Edwards Memorial Foundation.

His death occurred in Burbank, California, on June 12, 1978, after an illness which lasted for almost a year and forced him to cancel a proposed 1978 Spring tour of Britain.

Albums:
The Best Of Johnny Bond (Starday-Gusto/–)

The Best Of Debbie Boone, Courtesy Warner Bros.

That same year, Bond began recording for Columbia Records, with whom he recorded **Cimarron**, **Divorce Me, C.O.D.**, **Smoke, Smoke, Smoke**, **Tennessee Saturday Night**, **Cherokee Waltz**, **A Petal From A Faded Rose**, **'Til The End Of The World** and many others. His strong association with Autry also led to minor parts and sidekick roles in scores of films, while during the '50s and '60s he guested on TV shows hosted by Autry, Spade

Debby Boone

Daughter of singer Pat Boone and granddaughter of Red Foley, Debby was born Hackensak, New Jersey, September 22, 1956. The third of four sisters, she had a religious upbringing and attended Bible college after finishing high school.

An onstage performer at an early age, Debbie, her sisters and her mother (singer-actress Shirley Jones) provided the backing for Pat's act as The Boone Girls. Debby and her sisters later formed a gospel quartet, The Boones, before she opted to go solo, gaining a massive hit with **You Light Up My Life** (1977), claimed to be the biggest selling single in over 20 years, the record providing her with a Grammy as Best New Artist. It also gave Debby her first major country hit and won her the Top New Vocalist category at the Academy Of Country Music presentations in 1978. That same year Debby achieved another country chart hit **God Knows**, following this with such climbers as **My Heart Has A Mind Of Its Own** and **Breakin' In A Brand New Broken Heart** in 1979, the year that she was nominated in the Top Female Vocalist category at the CMA Awards. By 1980 she had her first country No. 1 in **Are You On The Road To Lovin' Me Again**, her other big hits being **Free To Be Lonely Again** (1980) and **Perfect Fool** (1981).

A non-smoker and non-drinker, she once claimed on a TV show that, prior to her 1979 marriage to Gabriel Ferrer, she had no trouble warding off the advances of would-be seducers. "I just tell them

who my Dad is, and that sort of takes care of it!"

An autobiography 'Debby Boone – So Far' was published in 1981.

Albums:
Debby Boone (Warner Bros/–)
Love Has No Reason (Warner Bros/–)

Don Bowman

Top country comedian of the '60s, Bowman was born in Lubbock, Texas, August 26, 1937. While a child he sang in church, later learning to play guitar – though part of his stock in trade is that he professes to play it badly! During Bowman's school years he became a DJ choosing this as his profession, though he was forced to sell hub caps and pick cotton along with several other menial jobs in order to survive.

Becoming more established as a DJ, at one time working with Waylon Jennings, he began working more and more of his own routines into shows, eventually opting to become a full-time fun maker, appearing at clubs in the south and southwest. In the mid-'60s, Chet Atkins signed Bowman to RCA, the result being **Chet Atkins Made Me A Star**. In 1966 came smaller successes with **Giddy Up Do-Nut** and **Surely Not**, which helped Bowman win the Billboard award as favourite C&W Comedian of the Year.

His other hits have included **Folson Prison Blues No. 2** (1968) and **Poor Old Ugly Gladys Jones** (1970).

Albums:
Support Your Local Prison (RCA/–)
All New (Mega/–)

Boxcar Willie

A singer, whose train whistle impressions helped him become a UK favourite before he had established any real reputation in his homeland, Boxcar was born Lecil Martin, Sterret, Texas, September 1, 1931. The son of a railroad worker, he worked in many jobs while pursuing a part-time

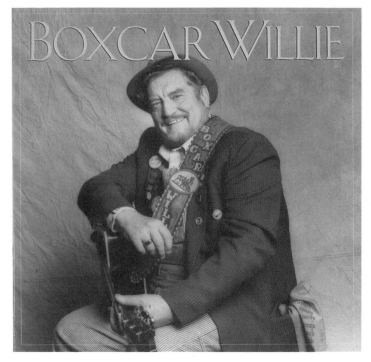

Boxcar Willie: his debut album for MCA Records.

profession as an entertainer for 37 years. During this period he was a DJ, a garage owner and a refrigeration engineer, also becoming a certified flight engineer. Determined to become a top-line country artist, he assumed a hobo-like persona during the mid-'70s and moved to Nashville, giving himself three years in which to make the grade. Seen by Scottish agent Drew Taylor at Nashville's Possum Hollow Club in 1977, he was signed to play his first British tour the following year, playing to small clubs. Gradually, after further tours, he built something of a reputation and gained a spot on the 1979 Wembley Festival Bill where he proved a sensation. Also in 1979 he made his first appearance on the Grand Ole Opry winning a standing ovation.

Boxcar Willie: a 1979 release by the sage of the train (Big R Records).

He returned to Wembley for a further triumph in 1980, reaching the Top 5 in the UK album charts that year with a TV-advertised album, **King Of The Road**. In the US he logged his first single in the Country charts, his **Train Medley** nudging into the Top 100.

A fine entertainer who deals mainly in material of a traditional nature, Boxcar remains a major crowd-puller in Europe, and one who has slowly been building on his success in the USA, achieving a respectable number of hits on the Main Street label during the '80s.

He and his family live in Arlington, Texas, though Boxcar spends much of his time in Nashville, where he owns a railway museum.

Albums:
King Of The Road (–/K.Tel)
Daddy Was A Railway Man (–/Big R)
Live In Concert (–/Pickwick)

Bill Boyd

Singer, guitarist, bandleader and film actor, William Boyd was born in Fannin County, Texas, on September 29, 1910.

A true cowboy raised on a ranch, Boyd, together with his brother Jim (born on September 28, 1914), formed Alexander's Daybreakers in the late '20s, this group metamorphosing into the Cowboy Ramblers, a Greenville, Texas, band. They began recording for Bluebird in 1934 initially cutting versions of traditional numbers plus cowboy songs like **Strawberry Roan** – of these, **Under The Double Eagle** (1935), a fiddle and guitar version of the popular march, proving most successful. Boyd, whose band grew from a four-man string band in 1934 to a ten-man western swing outfit in 1938, recorded over 300 sides for RCA, including such best-sellers as **New Spanish Two Step** and **Spanish Fandango** (1939) plus **Lone Star Rag** (1949), and had his own radio show on station WRR, Dallas for many years. His last recording session was February 7, 1950 and he retired soon after. He died in 1977.

After his brother's death, Jim Boyd, who had worked with the Light Crust

Bill Boyd's Cowboy Ramblers, Courtesy RCA Records.

Doughboys in 1938–9 and the Men Of The West in 1949–51, continued the family tradition, performing with the Light Crust Doughboys before modern day audiences in the Dallas-Forth Worth area.

Albums:
Bill Boyd's Cowboy Ramblers (Bluebird/–)
Bill Boyd And His Cowboy Ramblers 1934–47 (Texas Rose/–)

Owen Bradley

A Nashville producer, musician and executive, Owen Bradley had as much, if not more, to do with the creation of the Nashville Sound and the growth of Nashville studios than any other single individual.

Born on October 10, 1915, in Westmoreland, Tennessee, Bradley was a band-leading pianist who had one of the most popular dance bands in the Nashville area for some time and served as director of WSM radio from 1940–1958, leading their staff orchestra from 1947. That same year, Decca's Paul Cohen asked Bradley to do some producing for him in Nashville, as Decca had already cut Ernest Tubb, Red Foley and a few others there. Bradley accepted and by 1952 he and his younger brother Harold (later a leading Nashville session musician) had built their first studio.

By 1956 they had built their legendary Quonset hut on 16th Avenue South (which is now Columbia Studio B) which was the beginning of large scale Nashville studio activity and of the area which has come to be known as Music Row. In the Studio, which became known as Bradley's Barn, Bradley became instrumental in pioneering the so-called Nashville Sound during the '50s, smoothing out country music and providing it with a more pop, uptown treatment, often featuring lush strings and background voices.

Bradley, whose own recording career had started with the Bullet label, made many successful records of his own during the '50s, frequently appearing with a rockin' band as featured pianist. But as MCA's chief staff producer he achieved more fame, producing just about every one of their major artists: Loretta Lynn, Conway Twitty, Brenda Lee, Bill Anderson and so on.

He was quite open about dispensing with steel guitars, fiddles etc, and pursuing a sophisticated recording sound which many felt was castrating country as an individual form. There is much truth in this accusation, although at the same time Bradley, with the Nashville Sound, formulated a safe, broadly appealing

Big Guitar, Owen Bradley, Courtesy Charly Records.

sound (making much money in the process) and can justifiably be said to have brought country music in from the cold when it needed help most. Had the music not gone through this stage of its development, it might well not enjoy its huge current acceptability.

In 1958 he moved up the corporate ladder to become country A&R director, a position he held for over a decade until his promotion to vice president of MCA's Nashville operation. In 1974 he was elected to the Country Music Hall Of Fame and, after retirement from MCA, continued to produce independently.

Albums:
Big Guitar (–/Charly)

Elton Britt

Born in Marshall, Arkansas, June 27, 1917, Elton Britt's real name was James Britt Baker. He was the son of a champion fiddle player. While still at school he learnt guitar on a model purchased from Sears Roebuck for $5.

Below: Elton Britt, one of the greatest yodellers who, in 1944, won the first official gold disc for a country hit.

Britt worked in the fields as a boy, picking cotton, digging potatoes etc. While only 14, he was discovered by talent scouts who signed him to a year's contract with station KMPC, Los Angeles, where he appeared with the Beverly Hillbillies, recording for ARC, Decca and Varsity, both with the group and as a solo act. In 1937 he signed for RCA Records, staying with the label for over 20 years, during which time he recorded 672 singles and over 50 albums. Following this, he moved on to record for Decca, Ampar and ABC-Paramount.

Britt, who was considered to be one of the world's greatest yodellers, obtained the first gold disc awarded to any country star when, in 1944, his version of **There's A Star Spangled Banner Waving Somewhere**, originally released in May 1942 as a B-side, reached the million sales mark. His other successful singles include **Chime Bells** (1948), **Jimmie Rodgers Blues** (1968) and **Quicksilver** (1949), the latter being one of the many duets he recorded with Rosalie Allen.

Britt, who died June 23, 1972, appeared in several films, including 'Laramie' and 'The Prodigal Son'. He also made many TV appearances during the '50s and '60s, although he was a semi-retired gentleman farmer from around 1954 to 1968.

Albums:
16 Great Country Performances (ABC/–)
Elton Britt Yodel Songs (RCA/–)

Karen Brooks

A singer who first established a reputation as the writer of such songs as **Couldn't Do Nothing' Right** (for Rosanne Cash) and **Tennessee Rose** (for Emmylou Harris), Karen was born in Dallas and raised by her mother, a film makeup artist. A commercial artist who claims she always had a yen to be a cowgirl, Karen became a country singer on the Austin, Texas scene, working with Jerry Jeff Walker, Townes van Zandt, Steve Fromholz and then-husband, Gary P Nunn, the latter recording her **Fool For A Tender Touch** on an album. In Austin she was heard by Rodney Crowell who suggested she move to California, where she sang backup with Crowell's band. Her debut solo album, **Walk On**, received substantial critical acclaim, while such singles as **If That's What You're Thinking**, **Walk On** (both 1983), **Born To Love You**, **Tonight I'm Here With Someone Else** (both 1984) provided her with chart placings. In 1983 she was named Best New Female Vocalist by the Academy of Country Music. A one-time roomer with Carlene Carter when she first arrived in Nashville, Karen now owns her own ranch in Tennessee, where she rears quarter horses and cattle.

Albums:
Walk On (Warner Bros/–)
Heats On Fire (Warner Bros/–)

Below: Karen Brooks. She and Carlene Carter were the terrible twins of Nashville when the duo roomed together.

The Browns

The Browns – Ella Maxine Brown, born in Sampti, Louisiana, April 27, 1932; her brother Jim Edwards, born in Sparkman, Arkansas, March 1, 1934; and younger sister Bonnie, born in Sparkman, Arkansas, July 31, 1937 – began as a duo in the early '50s when Jim and Maxine won a talent contest on Little Rock's KLRA radio station, eventually matriculating to a featured spot on Little Rock's KWKH's Louisiana Hayride. In 1955, following an extensive concert tour, Bonnie came in to form a trio, the threesome becoming a headline act on the Ozark Jubilee show. Initially signed to Abbott Records, The Browns moved to RCA after being brought to the label's attention by Jim Reeves. They scored an initial hit with a version of the Louvin Brothers' **I Take A Chance** in 1956 and after Jim Ed had completed his army service (his place during the interim period being taken by yet another sister, Norma), they recorded **The Three Bells**, an adaptation of Edith Piaf's Euro-hit **Les Trois Cloches** which proved to be a 1959 million-seller.

Hits such as **Scarlet Ribbons** (1959), **The Old Lamplighter**, **Teen-Ex**, **Send Me The Pillow You Dream On**, **Blue Christmas** (all 1960) and **Ground Hog** (1961) followed, plus a number of well received overseas tours.

In 1963 The Browns became Opry members but Bonnie and Maxine, both married, wanted to spend more and more time with their families. As a result, the group disbanded in 1967, despite having

Above: The Browns biggest record was a cover of an Edith Piaf song.

country chart success that same year with **I Hear It Now** and **Big Daddy**. However, Maxine later returned to record as a solo artist for Chart, scoring with **Sugar Cane Country** (1968), while Jim Ed Brown began a solo career on RCA.

Albums:
The Best Of The Browns (RCA/–)
20 Of The Best Of The Browns (–/RCA)

Jim Ed Brown

In 1965, Bonnie and Maxine of The Browns persuaded Chet Atkins to record Jim Ed as a soloist, his first single, **I Heard From A Memory Last Night**, being a chart entry. Following this, Jim Ed began to record more frequently as a soloist, enjoying hits with **I'm Just A Country Boy**, **A Taste Of Heaven** (1966), **Pop A Top**, **Bottle, Bottle** (1967), and others. When the Browns eventually disbanded in 1967, Jim Ed was easily able to reshape his stage act and continue as a star attraction, making his debut as a fully-fledged solo performer at Atlanta, Georgia, early in 1968, immediately gaining a lucrative booking at a leading Lake Tahoe niterie.

Throughout the '70s and early '80s, Jim Ed's Midas touch continued to function. In 1970 he charted with **Morning**, a song successfully covered by singer Val Doonican in Britain, while Top 10 entries also came with **Southern Loving**, **Sometime Sunshine** (1973), and **It's That Time Of Night** (1974). During 1976 he teamed with Helen Cornelius and grabbed a country No. 1 with **I Don't Want To Marry You**, followed this with another

I Don't Want To Have To Marry You, Courtesy RCA Records.

duet, **Saying Hello, Saying I Love You, Saying Goodbye**, which only just missed the top spot. Since that time, Brown and Cornelius have also had major records with **If The World Ran Out Of Love Tonight, You Don't Bring Me Flowers** (1978), **Lying In Love With You, Fools** (1979), and **Morning Comes Too Early** (1980), the twosome's final chart record for RCA being **Don't Bother To Knock** (1981). An award winner way back in 1967, when The Browns won the Cash Box poll as the best country vocal group, Jim Ed also shared the CMA vocal duo award with Helen Cornelius ten years later.

Angel's Sunday, Jim Ed Brown, Courtesy RCA Records.

Albums:
Morning (RCA/RCA)
Barrooms and Pop A Tops (RCA/–)
I Don't Want to Have To Marry You – with Helen Cornelius (RCA/RCA)
I'll Never Be Free – with Helen Cornelius (RCA/–)

Milton Brown

One of the founders of western swing, Brown was born in Stephenville, Texas, September 8, 1903. In 1918 his family moved to Fort Worth, Brown attending Arlington Heights High School until graduation in 1925. After a spell in the police, with whom he broadcast as part of the Fort Worth Policeman's Quartet, Brown moved on to become a salesman. But, following a meeting with Bob Willis in 1931, he began singing professionally as part of Wills' Fiddle Band, actually just a duo comprised of Wills (fiddle) and Herman Arnspiger (guitar). Then followed a number of sponsored radio shows, the band name-changing to The Aladdin Laddies when promoting Aladdin Mantle Lamps, and The Light Crust Doughboys as pluggers of Light Crust Flour.

Following some personnel changes – which included the enrolment of Milton's brother Durwood Brown (guitar) – the band cut some sides for Victor in the guise of The Fort Worth Doughboys. But soon after, Brown formed his own unit, The Musical Brownies, to play on radio KTAT, Fort Worth, the lineup eventually stabilizing at Milton Brown (vocals), Durwood Brown (guitar and vocals), Jesse Ashlock and Cecil Brower (fiddles), Wanna Coffman (bass) and Fred 'Papa' Calhoun (piano). This line-up – minus Ashlock – recorded a number of sides for Bluebird in April 1934, the fiddler returning for the band's second Bluebird session in August of that year.

With the addition of jazz-playing guitarist Bob Dunn – the first in country to electrify his instrument – some three months later, a complete western swing sound was achieved, the band offering little allegiance to conventional country music. At the same time, Brown concluded a contract with the new Decca Record Company and with this label the Brownies began cutting a miscellany of titles ranging from jazz items like **St Louis Blues**, **Memphis Blues** and **Mama Don't Allow** through to such western songs as **Carry Me Back To The Lone Prairie** and **The Wheel Of The Wagon Is Broken**, enjoying several best-sellers. But, just when the band began moving into top gear, Brown died following a car accident. He had been returning home from a Crystal Springs Dance Pavilion date when his car tyre burst while Brown was travelling at over 90 mph, the vehicle eventually hitting a telegraph pole, seriously injuring Brown but instantly killing his passenger, vocalist Katherine Prehoditch. Though rushed to hospital, complications set in and Brown died on April 13, 1935.

For a while the Brownies continued to fulfil contractual obligations but the band finally folded in early 1938. Brown is considered, along with Wills, as the co-founder of western swing but, unfortunately, did not live to fulfil his early promise, nor to reap the financial rewards the music enjoyed in the '40s.

Albums:
Taking Off (String/)
Dance-O-Rama (Rambler/–)

Ed Bruce

Recording for Phillips under the name Edwin Bruce, this singer had a brief career as a '50s rocker – but he soon returned to selling semi-shabby Chevvys at his father's used car lot in Memphis. By the mid '60s he'd moved to Nashville, there recording over a dozen singles for RCA with the aid of producer Bob Ferguson, having mild chart reaction with **Walker's Woods** (1967), **Last Train To Clarksville** (1967), and **Painted Girls And Wine** (1968), his rich voice also being heard on an album, **If I Could Just Go Home**.

In 1968, Bruce joined Monument Records cutting a fine album, **Shades Of Ed Bruce**, also having minor singles success with **Song For Jenny** and **Everybody Wants To Go Home** (1969). However, despite his strong commercial appeal, it wasn't until the '70s and an association with UA Records that Bruce finally established himself as a record seller of any consequence, his **Mamas Don't Let Your Babies Grow Up To Be Cowboys** moving high into the charts

I Write It Down, Ed Bruce, Courtesy MCA Records.

Above: Mainstream country singer Ed Bruce was a Memphis based rockabilly who sold used cars.

during early 1976. The song, written by Bruce and his wife Patsy, was later covered by Waylon Jennings and Willie Nelson whose joint version climbed to No. 1 in 1978, gaining Bruce a nomination both for a Grammy and for the CMA's Song Of The Year. Later, Tony Joe White was to chart with an 'answer' song, **Mamas Don't Let Your Cowboys Grow Up to Be Babies**!

In the interim, Bruce provided UA with a bunch of further mini-hits plus some excellent albums, including **Ed Bruce** which saw him moving from a pop stance to a more basic country sound. In the wake of his last single for UA, a version of Alex Harvey's **Sleep All Mornin'**, Bruce

signed for Epic (1977), only mustering mid-chart singles in 1977–9.

Throughout 1979 Bruce spent his time writing and recording, fashioning new material for his new label, MCA, for whom he signed in 1980. That year he logged three major singles, **Diane**, **The Last Cowboy Song** and **Girls, Women And Ladies** plus an album, again titled **Ed Bruce**, which re-established him as a major country music name. Well-known on TV ads where he had dressed in Daniel Boone manner to advertise Tennessee – gaining Bruce the title of The Tennessean – his acting career flourished initially when he was signed to appear in 'The Chisholms' mini-series and then gained a further fillip in 1981 when James Garner asked him to play Tom Guthrie in the 'Bret Maverick' TV series.

Since that time there have been such

other excellent albums as **One To One** (1981) and **I Write It Down** (1982), along with hit singles that include **Everything's A Waltz, You're The Best Break This Heart Ever Had** (1981), **Love's Found You And Me, Ever Never Lovin' You** (1982), **My First Taste Of Texas** and **After All** (1984), 1984 also seeing the man who has written hits for such artists as Kitty Wells, Tanya Tucker, Crystal Gayle, Tommy Roe, Kenny Price and Charlie Louvin, once more back on RCA, gaining a Top 5 single with **You Turn Me On (Like A Radio)**.

Albums:
Shades Of Ed Bruce (Monument/Monument)
Ed Bruce (UA/–)
The Tennessean (Epic/–)
Ed Bruce (MCA/–)
I Write It Down (MCA/–)
The Best Of Ed Bruce (–/MCA)

Cliff Bruner

The leader of an early swing/honky tonk band, Cliff Bruner was born April 25, 1915, at Houston, Texas, and got his start as a fiddler in Milton Brown's Musical Brownies, cutting 48 sides with Brown before the bandleader's tragic death in 1936.

At that point Bruner formed his own band, The Texas Wanderers (sometimes known just as Cliff Bruner's Boys) and began a long recording association with Decca in 1937. His biggest hit on the label was the first version released of Floyd Tillman's **It Makes No Difference Now** (1938), although one of the band's most historic milestones was cutting the first truck driving song on record: Ted Daffan's **Truck Driver's Blues** (1939).

Bruner – who also recorded for the Ayo label in the '40s – became increasingly inactive as the years passed and by the early '50s had become an insurance salesman and executive, performing only occasionally. By the late '70s he was living in the Houston suburb, League City.

Boudleaux and Felice Bryant

Boudleaux Bryant, born Shellman, Georgia, February 13, 1920, originally aimed at a career in classical music, studying to become a concert violinist and, in 1938, playing a season with the Atlanta Philharmonic. Then came a switch to more popular music forms, Bryant joining a jazz group for a period. It was during this time he met his wife-to-be Felice (born Milwaukee, Wisconsin, August 7, 1925), then an elevator attendant at Milwaukee's Shrader Hotel. After marriage, the duo began writing songs together, in 1949 sending one composition, **Country Boy**, to Fred Rose who published it, thus providing Little Jimmy Dickens with material to fashion into a Top 10 hit.

In 1950 the Bryants moved to Nashville and began writing hit after hit, supplying Carl Smith with a constant supply of chartbusters, one of these songs, **Hey Joe** (1953), becoming a million seller when covered by Frankie Laine. During 1955, Eddy Arnold charted with the Bryants' **I've Been Thinking** and **The Richest Man**, but it was the duo's association with the Everly Brothers that brought the song-writing team their biggest string of successes, **Bye Bye Love, Wake Up Little Susie, Problems, Bird Dog, All I Have To Do Is Dream, Poor Jenny, Take A Message To Mary**, all Bryant-penned songs, ending up on million-selling discs.

Other Bryant hits have included **Raining In My Heart** (Buddy Holly 1959), **Let's Think About Living** (Bob Luman 1960), **Mexico** (Bob Moore, 1960), **Baltimore** (Sonny James 1964), **Come Live With Me** (Roy Clark 1973) and the oft-recorded **Rocky Top**, which Felice and Boudleaux wrote in just ten minutes. In 1974 Billboard was able to publish a list of well over 400 artists who had recorded songs by the Bryants, and in 1986 the duo were honoured by being elected to the Songwriters' Hall Of Fame.

Left: Fiddler Cliff Bruner played jazz for honky tonks but also recorded one of the first trucking songs.

Wilma Burgess

A consistent maker of country hits during the '60s and early '70s, vocalist Wilma Burgess was born Orlando, Florida, June 11, 1939. A city girl who acquired a love of country music during high school days, it wasn't until she attended Stetson University, Florida, to major in physical education that she began singing in public. In 1960, Wilma travelled to Nashville to demo songs for publishers, and was heard by Charlie Lamb of Sound Format publications, who brought her to the attention of Decca's Owen Bradley. Signed by Decca, and also gaining regular appearances on various Nashville radio and TV shows, Wilma built a reputation that soared following major hits with **Baby** (1965), **Don't Touch Me**, **Misty Blue** (1966) and **Tear Time** (1967). Later her popularity waned but she continued supplying lesser hits for the Shannon label, these including **I'll Be Your Bridge** (1973), **Love Is Here** (1974) and **Sweet Lovin' Baby** (1975).

Album:
Wilma Burgess Sings Misty Blue (Decca/–)

Johnny Bush

Born Houston, Texas, February 17, 1935, Bush – voted Most Promising Male Vocalist of The Year by Record World in 1968, an accolade duplicated by Music City News 12 months later – moved to San Antonio, Texas in 1962, obtaining his first

musical job at the Texas Star Inn, where he played rhythm guitar and sang.

At a later stage, he opted to become a drummer, eventually joining a band organized by his friend Willie Nelson during the early '60s. After a year's stay with this outfit, he then became a member of Ray Price's Cherokee Cowboys, with whom he played for three years before returning to Nelson's side once more. With Nelson he became front man for the band, The Record Men, also branching out as a solo artist on Stop Records, his first release for the label, a Nelson original titled **You Ought To Hear Me Cry**, being a mild hit in 1967. His next release, **What A Way To Live**, yet another Nelson song, climbed even further up the charts.

Primarily a honky tonk singer in the Ray Price tradition, Bush switched from Stop – with whom he had major hits with **Undo The Right** (1968) and **You Gave Me A Mountain** (1969) – to RCA in 1972, enjoying his greatest-ever disc success with Willie Nelson's **Whiskey River** that year.

Throughout 1973 the hits kept on coming but began to peter out during the following year, Bush's name then being absent from the chart until 1977 when he had low-level success with **You'll Never Leave Me Completely**, a Gusto-Starday release. There were other chart-nudgers in 1978 and 1979 while in 1981, the man known as the Country Caruso got his name into the listings again with **Whiskey River**. All of which is quite remarkable considering that Bush lost his speaking voice in the early 1970s and in recent

Here's Johnny Bush, Courtesy Starday Records.

Carl Butler & Pearl's Greatest Hits, Courtesy CBS Records.

years has only been able to sing up to half an hour at a time!

Albums:
You Gave Me A Mountain (Stop/Stop)
Undo The Right (Gusto/)
Whiskey River (RCA/RCA)

Carl and Pearl Butler

A highly popular duo during the '60s, honky tonk vocalist Carl Roberts Butler (born Knoxville, Tennessee, June 2, 1927) and his wife Pearl (born Pearl Dee Jones, Nashville, Tennessee, September 20, 1900?) first performed as a team in 1962. Prior to this, Carl had been a highly successful recording artist with Capitol and Columbia, having hits for Columbia with **Honky Tonkitis** (1961) and **Don't Let Me Cross Over** (1962), the later being released as a Carl Butler solo item but featuring Pearl on harmony vocals.

When **Cross Over** became a country No. 1 the Butlers realized they had hit on a winning formula and began recording as a duo, logging a fair number of chart entries during the '60s including **Loving Arms** (1963), **Too Late To Try Again** (1964), **I'm Hanging Up The Phone** (1964), **Just Thought I'd Let You Know** (1965), **Little Pedro** (1966) and **I Never Got Over You** (1969). Granted Opry status in 1962, the Butlers appeared in the movie 'Second Fiddle To A Steel Guitar' during 1967.

Albums:
Greatest Hits (Columbia/–)

Jerry Byrd

Born in Lima, Ohio, March 9, 1920, Jerry Byrd went on to become one of the genuine giants of the electric steel guitar. Unequalled for purity of tone and taste, he was in demand for record sessions for years, although he was never comfortable with the increasingly popular pedal steel style, preferring Hawaiian stylings. Finally, growing weary of Nashville and the music business, he chucked it all and caught a plane to Honolulu where he became revered as practically a national monument for his advancement of the Hawaiian guitar.

Album:
Master Of Touch And Tone (Midland/–)

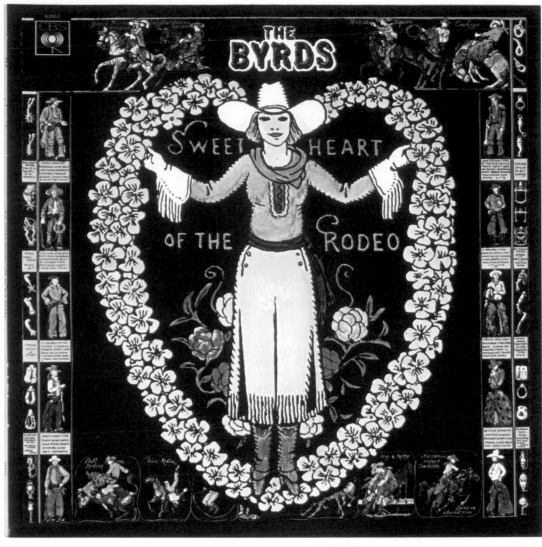

Sweetheart Of The Rodeo, The Byrds, Courtesy CBS Records. This was one of the first and finest of all country rock albums. The sleeve design was taken from a catalogue of Western clothes.

The Byrds

Initially an LA folk-rock group formed in 1964, The Byrds recorded a country-influenced album **The Notorious Byrd Brothers** in 1968, using such guest musicians as Lloyd Green, John Hartford, Earl Ball and Byrd-to-be, Clarence White. That same year, the group, heavily influenced by newcomer Gram Parsons, produced **Sweetheart Of The Rodeo**, arguably the first real country-rock album, containing songs penned by the Louvin Brothers, Woody Guthrie, Merle Haggard and others. Thereafter, most Byrds albums featured some country-style tracks, though leader Roger McGuinn is said to have fought against the trend.

The group, which folded in 1972 (McGuinn attempting a musically unsuccessful reunion album on Asylum the following year), featured several musicians who have made some contribution to the furtherance of country music. Since that time, McGuinn has continued on his own solo way, sometimes re-uniting with such ex-Byrds as Gene Clark and Chris Hillman, but little of real musical consequence, country or otherwise, has resulted.

Album:
Sweetheart Of The Rodeo (Columbia/CBS)

The Callahan Brothers

Homer C. ('Bill') Callahan, guitar, mandolin, bass and vocals; Walter T. ('Joe') Callahan, guitar and vocals.

Natives of Laurel, North Carolina (Walter born on January 27, 1910 and Homer born on March 27, 1912), the Callahan Brothers became a popular duet team of the south eastern style in the 1930s, and by 1933 were already busy on radio and were recording for the ARC complex of labels. They spent some time at WHAS in Louisville and WWVA in Wheeling before serving other stretches at WLW (1937–1939) and KVOO in Tulsa, before settling down in the North Texas area, basing their operations from either Dallas or Wichita Falls for over ten years.

It was here, for reasons best known to themselves, that they changed their names from Walter and Homer to Bill and Joe, and changed their music as well, performing more and more western and swing material, the highlight probably being their double-yodel version of **St Louis Blues**. Except for a single session with Decca (1941) and one Bill Callahan session with Cowboy Records, their 91 recorded sides were with ARC or Columbia, over a period stretching from 1934 to 1951. They became increasingly inactive in the '50s and '60s.

Homer/Bill died on September 10, 1971.

Album:
The Callahan Brothers (Old Homestead/–)

Archie Campbell

Honoured as Comedian Of The Year in 1969 by the CMA, Campbell has been writer and star of the Hee Haw TV show.

Born in Bulls Gap, Tennessee, on November 17, 1914, his career really rocketed through stints on WNOX, Knoxville in 1949, an eventual TV show on WATE, Knoxville (1952–1958), coming his way. He joined the Prince Albert portion of the Grand Ole Opry in 1958, also signing a recording contract with RCA, for whom he cut a number of comedy routines including **Beeping Sleauty** and **Rindercella**.

On the serious side he scored with the narration, **The Men In My Little Girl's Life** (1965), as well as duets with Lorene Mann, the most popular being **At The Dark End Of The Street** (1968). Away from show business he is a talented sculptor, poet and painter and is also a keen golfer of almost professional standard.

Albums:
Live At Tupelo (Elektra/–)
Bedtime Stories For Adults (RCA/–)

Glen Campbell

The seventh son of a seventh son, singer-songwriter-guitarist-banjoist Glen Campbell was born in Delight, Arkansas, on April 22, 1936. A reasonable guitarist at the age of six, he joined Dick Bills' (his uncle) western band while a teenager, later forming his own outfit in New Mexico,

Below: Archie Campbell – not only a humourist but also a humanist.

Glen Campbell, a 1962 album, Courtesy Capitol Records.

where he met Billie Nunley and married her.

Armed with his 12-string, in 1960 he opted to become one of Hollywood's busiest session musicians but found time to cut sides as a solo performer, one, **Turn Around, Look At Me**, becoming a 1961 pop hit on the local Crest label. Signed immediately to Capitol, Campbell graced the 1962 charts with Al Dexter's **Too Late To Worry, Too Blue To Cry** and Merle Travis' **Kentucky Means Paradise**, and in the mid '60s supplied a couple of other minor hits while continuing his work as a sideman with the Beach Boys, Jan and Dean, Association, Rick Nelson, Elvis Presley and many others. Then in 1967 he recorded John Hartford's **Gentle On My Mind**, following this monster hit with an even bigger one in **By The Time I Get To Phoenix**, a song written by Jimmy Webb. From then on came a succession of high selling albums and singles, the most successful of the latter being **Wichita Lineman** (1968), **Galveston, Where's The Playground, Susie?, Try A Little Kindness** (1969), **Honey Come Back, It's Only Make Believe, All I Have To Do Is Dream** – with Bobbie Gentry – (1970), **Dream Baby** (1971), **Country Boy** and **Rhinestone**

Above: Glen Campbell and a friend of Colonel Sanders on the Louisiana Hayride. A scene from the movie 'Norwood'.

Left: The seventh son of a seventh son, Glen Travis Campbell was guitarman on Tequila, a 1958 million seller for The Champs, a rock band that also included Seals and Crofts.

Cowboy (1975), and **Southern Nights** (1977).

Campbell made the headlines over his on-off affair with singer Tanya Tucker while they toured and recorded together and, in a barrage of publicity, they finally split up in 1981. He left Capitol Records and has since recorded with Atlantic-America, though he has never regained the commercial success he enjoyed in the late '60s and early '70s.

Possessor of 12 gold records; featured artist on countless TV shows, including his own Glen Campbell Show; co-star with John Wayne in the film 'True Grit' (1969) and star of 'Norwood' (1969); Campbell is also a golf fanatic, hosting the Glen Campbell Los Angeles Open, a major event on the PGA circuit.

Albums:
Glen Travis Campbell (Capitol/Capitol)
I Remember Hank Williams (Capitol/ Capitol)
Reunion (Capitol/Capitol)
Rhinestone Cowboy (Capitol/Capitol)
Ernie Sings And Glen Picks (Capitol/ Capitol)
Words (–/Ember)
More Words (–/Ember)
20 Golden Greats (–/Capitol)
Old Home Town (Atlantic-America/ Atlantic-America)
It's Just A Matter Of Time (Atlantic-America/Atlantic-America)

Judy Canova

A sort of slicked up Minnie Pearl of the 1940s, Judy Canova was a country comedienne who was successful on Broadway in some two dozen movies, and on record, as well as having a long running radio show (1943–1953).

Born on November 20, 1916 in Jacksonville, Florida, she and her sister Annie and brother Zeke moved to New York in 1934 to crack the big time, and were successful on the stage and on radio. The act broke up in the late '30s, with Judy going solo, eventually moving to Hollywood in the early '40s as film roles and her network radio show beckoned, a dual career which lasted into the late '50s.

She recorded for the ARC complex of labels with her siblings, and for Okeh, Varsity, Mercury, Sterling and RCA in her long career, with her theme song **Go To Sleep, Little Baby** probably the most popular, along with the haunting wartime ballad **Goodnight Soldier**.

Henson Cargill

From a family of political and legal background, Cargill was brought up on a ranch, where he spent considerable efforts in fighting off all intentions to turn him into a budding attorney. But though his initial aim was to become a successful rancher, he suddenly switched ambitions and headed for Nashville to cut a record session and seek a deal with a record

Welcome To My World, Henson Cargill, Courtesy CBS Records.

label. There, with the aid of guitar-playing producer Fred Carter Jr he made a disc called **Skip A Rope**, which earned him a contract with Monument Records and a 1967 million-seller.

After other major hits with **Row, Row, Row** (1968), **None Of My Business** (1969) and **The Most Uncomplicated Goodbye** (1970), Cargill signed for the Mega label, there having minor chart entries with **Pencil Marks On The Wall** and **Naked And Crying** (both 1971). He joined Atlantic Records in 1974, his only notable success being **Some Old California Memory**.

In the mid '70s, Cargill moved to Oklahoma, living there with his wife and three children, and recorded briefly for Copper Mountain Records making the country charts with **Silence On The Line** in the early months of 1980.

Below: **Cliff (left) and Bill Carlisle with Shannon Grayson on banjo.**

Albums:
Coming On Strong (Monument/ Monument)
None Of My Business (Monument/–)
Henson Cargill Country (Atlantic/–)

Bill and Cliff Carlisle

Cliff Carlisle, born in Taylorsville, Kentucky, on May 6, 1904, was among the first top-line dobro players. As a boy he toured as a vaudeville act, first recording for Gennett in 1930 with guitarist Wilbert Ball. An excellent yodeller, Cliff – who backed Jimmie Rodgers on some of his recordings – eventually formed a duo, the Carlisle Brothers, with his younger brother, Bill (born in Wakefield, Kentucky, December 19, 1908), playing dates in the Louisville-Cincinnati area. The brothers, who spiced their vocal and instrumental act with a fair degree of comedy, obtained

regular radio exposure on station WLAP, Lexington, Kentucky during 1931, and six years later had their own show, The Carlisle Family Barn Dance, on radio station WLAP, Louisville.

In 1947 Cliff retired (he now lives near Lexington, Kentucky) and Bill eventually formed a new group, the Carlisles. In 1954, following hits with **Rainbow At Midnight**, **No Help Wanted** and **Too Old To Cut The Mustard**, the Carlisles joined Grand Ole Opry, remaining cast members to this day, scoring a further hit with **What Kinda Deal Is This?** (1966).

During his career, Bill Carlisle has won over 60 various country awards, his past albums including **Fresh From the Country** (King) and **The Best Of Bill Carlisle** (Hickory).

Fiddling John Carson

An old-time fiddler, he became (on June 14, 1923, in Atlanta, Georgia) the first country musician to be recorded by field recordist Ralph Peer. The tracks cut, **Little Old Log Cabin In The Lane** and **That Old Hen Cackled And The Rooster's Goin' To Crow**, were initially released on 500 unlabelled discs, all immediately sold at a local old-time fiddler's convention. Following a re-release on Okeh, Carson was awarded a contract with the label.

Born on March 23, 1868, in Fannin County, Georgia, Carson was, at various times, a teenage jockey, a foreman in a cotton mill, a house painter and a moonshiner. Seven times fiddler champion of Georgia, he made his radio debut on September 9, 1922. Often working with a string band, the Virginia Reelers (which included his daughter Rosa Lee Carson, also known as Moonshine Kate), he cut around 150 discs for Okeh between 1923 and 1931. Following the Depression, Carson moved to RCA, mainly re-cutting earlier successes.

In later life an elevator operator, Carson died December 11, 1949.

Album:
That Old Hen Cackled (Rounder/–)

Martha Carson

A country gospel singer whose repertoire appealed not only to Opry fans but also the audiences at such ritzy venues as New York's Waldorf Astoria, Martha Carson was one of the most popular vocalists in her genre during the 50s.

Born Irene Ambergay, in Neon, Kentucky, on March 19, 1921, her first broadcasts were relayed over station WHIS, Bluefield, West Virginia in 1939. During the '40s she toured as one half of Martha and James Carson, the other half of the duo being her husband, the singing and mandolin-playing son of Fiddlin' Doc Roberts. They were longtime fixtures of the WSB Barn Dance in Atlanta becoming known as the Barn Dance Sweethearts. Together they recorded many magnificent sides, including **The Sweetest Gift**, **Man of Galilee** and **Budded on Earth**.

Divorced in 1951, Martha began gracing the Opry with her fervent style during the following year.

The writer of well over 100 songs, including **I'm Gonna Walk And Talk With My Lord**, **I Can't Stand Up Alone** and **Satisfied**, Martha has recorded for such labels as RCA, Capitol, Cadence and Decca.

Carter Family

One of the most influential groups in country music, the original line-up was headed by Alvin Pleasant (A.P.) Delaney Carter, born in Maces Spring, Virginia, on April 15, 1891. One of nine children, A.P. initially sang in a church quartet alongside two uncles and an elder sister. Later he met Sara Dougherty (born in Wise County, Virginia, on July 21, 1898), a singer, guitarist, autoharp and banjo player, and they married on June 18, 1915. The third member of the group, Maybelle Addington (born in Nickelsville, Virginia, on May 10, 1909), joined after marrying A.P.'s brother, Ezra Carter, in 1926. She too played guitar, autoharp and banjo.

The Carter Family were first recorded by Ralph Peer for Victor on August 1, 1927 (at the same session that Jimmie Rodgers cut his first sides) completing six titles, including **Single Girl, Married Girl**, at a makeshift studio in Bristol, Tenessee. After some success the family began a whole series of sessions for Victor, often recording A.P.'s own songs, though **Wildwood Flower**, a traditional item cut at Camden, New Jersey, on May 9, 1928, proved to be the group's biggest seller, registering over a million sales for 78 rpm discs alone. Another important recording

20 Best Of The Carter Family, Courtesy RCA Records.

Above: The Carter Family today – Anita, June, Helen and Carlene, the show-stopping line-up that appeared at the 1986 Wembley Festival.

date occurred during June 1931, when Peer cut sides featuring the collective talents of the Carters and Jimmie Rodgers.

After recording around 20 songs at one Victor session on December 11, 1934, the family moved on to ARC, waxing some 40 titles for that label during May 5–10, 1935.

Sara and A.P. obtained a divorce during the following year but continued working together in the group, next recording for Decca before moving to Texas to appear on various radio stations in the San Antonio and Del Rio areas. During this three-year period, other members of the Carter Family joined the group – Anita, June and Helen (Maybelle and Ezra's three daughters) and Janette and Joe (Sara and A.P.'s children). Sara then remarried, to Coy Bayes, and though the Family cut further sides for Columbia and Victor (the last session by the original Carter Family taking place on October 14, 1941) they disbanded in 1943, having waxed over 250 of their songs including such standards as **Wabash Cannonball**, **Lonesome Valley** and **I'm Thinking Tonight Of My Blue Eyes**. Maybelle then formed a group with her three daughters and began a five-year stint on station WRVA, Richmond, Virginia, after which came a switch to Nashville, where the quartet became regulars on Grand Ole Opry as a group and as individuals. A.P. began his career again too, working on some sides for the Acme label during 1952–6. But this version of the Carter

Family – employing Sara, Joe and Janette – made little impact. A.P. died on November 7, 1960, ten years before the Carter Family's election to the Country Music Hall Of Fame. Sara Carter died on January 8, 1979, in Lodi, California following a long illness.

Following A.P.'s death, Maybelle and her daughters began working as the Carter Family (previously they'd been the Carter Sisters and Mother Maybelle), June Carter eventually going solo and becoming part of the Johnny Cash road show. In 1961, Maybelle Carter, plus Helen and Anita, also joined Cash, becoming regulars on his TV show in 1966. Anita's daughter Lori and Helen's son David have since appeared as part of the Carter Family road show.

The Carter Family have carried on into the '80s through Carlene Carter (born in Tennessee, on September 26, 1955), the daughter of June Carter and her husband Carl Smith. Following tours with the Carter Family in the '60s and early '70s, Carlene has launched a solo career in rock music with a strong country influence. British-based during the early 1980s (she was married to Nick Lowe for a while), she appeared in the London production of the show 'Pump Boys and Dinettes'.

Albums:
Best Of The Carter Family (Columbia/–)
Famous Country Music Makers (–/RCA)
Carter Sisters – Maybelle, Anita, June & Helen (–/Bear Family)
Musical Shapes – Carlene Carter (–/F-Beat)
Favourite Family Songs (Liberty/–)
Travelling Minstrel Band (Columbia/–)

Maybelle Carter

During the '60s Maybelle became a mother figure to the New Generation folkies (it was at a time when singers like Joan Baez had begun to discover and re-record Carter Family songs) and appeared on many folk bills throughout the country, winning much acclaim at the Newport Folk Festival of 1963. At a later Newport Festival, in 1967, she reunited with Sara Carter to record the live album **An Historic Reunion**, their first recording together for 25 years. In 1971, she also appeared on Nitty Gritty Dirt Band's **Will The Circle Be Unbroken** album, leading the singing on the title track. She died on October 23, 1978 in Nashville.

Album:
Mother Maybelle Carter (Columbia/–)

Mother Maybelle Carter, Courtesy CBS Records.

Wilf Carter

Born in Guysboro, Nova Scotia, on December 18, 1904, singer-songwriter-guitarist Carter is a one-time Canadian cowboy, who branched out from rodeo to radio in the early '30s when he began broadcasting on Calgary station CFCN, at the same time commencing a recording career with RCA Victor. Later, on a New York CBS radio show he adopted the guise of 'Montana Slim' under which name he became known in the United States. One of the many yodelling singers influenced by Jimmie Rodgers, Carter has written over 500 songs and recorded for such labels as Bluebird, Decca and Starday, his singles including **The Hindenberg Disaster**, **The Life And Death Of John Dillinger**, and **I'm Only A Dude In Cowboy Clothes**.

Album:
Montana Slim's Greatest Hits (Camden/–)

Johnny Carver

Raised and schooled in Jackson, Mississippi, where he was born on November 24, 1940, Carver is a modern-styled country singer who started out in a gospel group with two aunts and an uncle. Whilst at high school he lead a band and following graduation took to the road, appearing all over America. He finally based himself in Milwaukee with a club residency. A move to the West Coast in 1965 led to his being hired as the featured singer in the house band at the famed Palomino Club. He signed with Imperial Records and scored minor country hits with **Your Lily White Hands** and **Hold Me Tight** in the late '60s.

As a writer he has provided fellow artists like Roy Drusky, Ferlin Husky and Connie Smith with material, but failed to make an impression himself as he moved through recording associations with United Artists and Epic. However, an affiliation with ABC-Dot Records in 1973 took the warm-voiced Carver to the top of the ladder. His covers of pop hits such as **Tie A Yellow Ribbon**, **Afternoon Delight** and **Living Next Door To Alice** were all big country hits in the mid '70s. He has since recorded for Equity, Tanglewood and Monument during the '80s without too much success.

Albums:
Don't Tell That Sweet Old Lady Of Mine (ABC-Dot/–)
Afternoon Delight (ABC-Dot/–)
Best Of Johnny Carver (ABC-Dot/–)

Afternoon Delight, Johnny Carver, Courtesy MCA/Dot Records.

Johnny Cash

Winner of six CMA awards in 1969 (best male vocalist, entertainer of the year, best single, best album, outstanding service award and even one with June Carter for best vocal group), John R. Cash was born in Kingsland, Arkansas, on February 26, 1932, son of a poverty stricken cotton farmer, Ray Cash and his wife Carrie. In 1935 the Cash family moved to the government resettlement Dyess Colony, surviving the Mississippi river flood of 1937, an event documented in a 1959 Cash song **Five Feet High And Rising**. One son, Roy, put together a country band, The Delta Rhythm Ramblers, which broadcast on KCLN, Blytheville. However, tragedy struck the Cashes in 1944 when son Jack died after an accident with a circular saw, which had a lasting effect on the young John.

After high school graduation in 1950, J.R. took a job in a Detroit body plant, then worked for an Evadale margarine firm, sweeping floors and cleaning vats. But by July of that year he had enlisted in the Air Force for a four-year term. It was while serving in Germany that Cash learnt guitar and wrote his first songs.

Upon discharge in July 1954, having achieved the rank of staff sergeant, Cash married Vivian Liberto and then headed for Memphis where he became an electrical appliance salesman.

In Memphis he met electric guitar player Luther Perkins and bassist Marshall Grant and began performing with them – for no pay – on station KWEM. Eventually they gained an audition with Sam Phillips of Sun Records, from which came a recording session and a single **Hey Porter/ Cry, Cry, Cry**, both songs being Cash originals. Upon release, the disc – listed as by Johnny Cash and the Tennessee Two – became a hit, selling in the region of 100,000 copies. Following a success with his follow-up disc **Folsom Prison Blues** in December 1955, Cash joined KWKH's Louisiana Hayride, Shreveport. He also began touring, the dates becoming even more plentiful after the release of **I Walk The Line**, a crossover hit that sold a million ,and **There You Go**, another 1956 winner. In 1957, Cash joined the Opry then trekked

Heroes – an album that teamed Johnny Cash and Waylon Jennings, Courtesy CBS Records.

Below: Elected to the Country Music Hall of Fame in 1980, Johnny Cash has cut albums in San Quentin and Folsom prisons and shot a documentary film in the Holy Land. But his album with Bob Dylan still remains unissued.

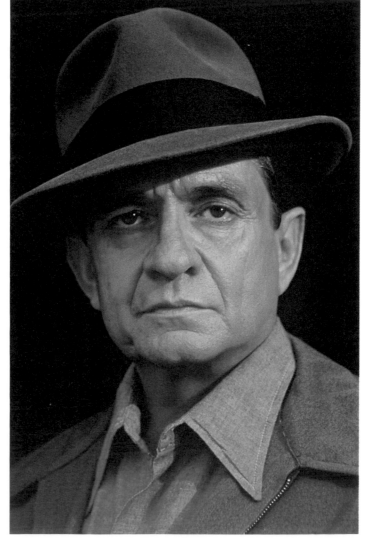

to Hollywood to play a maniacal killer in a 'B' movie entitled 'Five Minutes To Live' (1958). Next came tours in Canada and Australia, grossing a quarter of a million dollars, and Cash signed for Columbia Records. Drummer W. S. Holland joined the Tennessee Two in 1960 (at which point they became the Tennessee Three), Cash and his enlarged band playing the nightclub circuit for the first time. Much in demand, he was playing nearly 300 gigs a year; he was pill-popping to provide enough energy.

Cash first began working with June Carter in December '61, June trying to steer him through 1962, a heavy schedule year that included a 30-hour tour of Korea and a disastrous Carnegie Hall date. At the Newport Folk Festival of 1964 he sang with Bob Dylan, and that same year he recorded **Bitter Tears**, a classic album of songs regarding the mistreatment of the American Indian, much of the material being written by Peter LaFarge. But the pill-popping worsened and in October, 1965, Cash was arrested by the narcotics squad in El Paso and received a 30-day suspended sentence and a $1,000 fine. In 1966 he was jailed once more – for embarking on a 2am flower-picking spree! Also in 1966, Carl Perkins became a regular part of the Cash touring show.

Though in poor health and with his weight down to 140 pounds, he produced **Carrying On**, an album with June Carter – but while his recorded work maintained a high standard, his personal life headed ever downwards, with Vivian Cash sueing him for divorce in mid 1966. The pill addiction continued, but he undertook

treatment, gradually fighting back until by the close of the '60s he was restored to complete health once more.

Since signing for Columbia in 1958, Cash had cut a tremendous quota of hit singles – the biggest of these being **All Over Again** (1958), **Don't Take Your Guns To Town** (1959), **I Got Stripes** (1959), **Ring Of Fire** (1963), **Understand Your Man** (1964), **It Ain't Me, Babe** (1964), **Orange Blossom Special** (1965), **The One On Your Right Is On Your Left** (1966), **Folsom Prison Blues** (1968), **Daddy Sang Bass** (1968) and **A Boy Named Sue** (1969). More importantly, he had also cut some of the most striking albums to emerge from country music – including **Ride This Train** (1960), a kind of musical hobo-ride through America; **Blood, Sweat And Tears** (1964), a tribute to the working man; the already-mentioned **Bitter Tears** (1964); **Ballads Of The True West** (1965), a double album glance at western folklore; and **At Folsom Prison** (1968), an award winning affair recorded in front of perhaps the world's toughest, but most appreciative audience.

Look At Them Beans, Johnny Cash, Courtesy CBS Records.

His partnership with June Carter, whom he married in March 1968 (Merle Kilgore was best man), proved successful both on and off stage, the duo gaining a Grammy award for **Jackson**, adjudged the best country performance by a group during 1967. And as the '60s rolled away, the CMA showered a whole flood of awards on the craggy-faced man in black, while the film critics applauded his portrayal of an ageing gun-fighter in 'The Gunfight', a 1970 release in which he pitted his acting ability against that of Kirk Douglas. During the '70s, Johnny Cash turned increasingly towards religion, visiting Israel to make a film about life in the Holy Land, and appeared on shows headed by evangelist Billy Graham.

He was elected to the CMA Hall of Fame in 1980, but in 1983 Cash nearly died before undergoing abdominal treatment at Nashville's Baptist Hospital. "It was abuse," he claimed, admitting that he had

Bitter Tears, Johnny Cash, Courtesy CBS Records.

once more begun dabbling with pills, "Many, many long years of abuse."

But he has since pulled back, resuming his touring career and playing European dates in 1986. He has also carried on making records, tackling songs of various dimensions. But thanks to his obvious sincerity and his crumbling rock of a voice (often placed out front over the most meager of rhythm patterns) everything he sings about, no matter how twee, always comes out sounding completely believable.

Albums:
At Folsom Prison (Columbia/CBS)
At San Quentin (Columbia/CBS)
Blood, Sweat And Tears (Columbia/–)
Holy Land (Columbia/–)
Man In Black (Columbia/CBS)
Ride This Train (Columbia/–)
Ballads Of The True West (–/Embassy)
The Gospel Road (–/CBS)
America (Columbia/CBS)
Silver (Columbia/CBS)
Rockabilly Blues (Columbia/CBS)
The Adventures Of Johnny Cash
  (Columbia/CBS)

Rosanne Cash

The eldest daughter of Johnny Cash and his first wife, Vivian Liberto, Rosanne was born on May 24, 1955 in Memphis, Tennessee at a time when her father's career was just starting to take off. Her parents were divorced when she was eleven and Rosanne and her three sisters were raised in California, though she did retain a close friendship with her father. She moved to Nashville following graduation and along with her stepsister, Rosey, she joined the Johnny Cash roadshow, working initially in the wardrobe department but after a few months singing back-up vocals to her famous father. After three years with the Cash Show, Rosanne left to pursue her interest in acting, moving to London with the intention of enrolling in drama school. Instead she landed a job at CBS Records, helping to co-ordinate the Wembley International Country Music Festival. Returning to America, she spent a year studying drama at Nashville's Vanderbilt University then moved back to California to study at Lee Strasberg's Theatre Institute. A vacation in Germany during the Christmas break led to a change in career direction. She was offered the opportunity to record for Ariola Records and made her first album in Munich during the summer of 1978. On her return to America she decided to make music her career and, having teamed up with singer-songwriter Rodney Crowell whom she married in 1979, signed with Columbia Records and recorded the acclaimed **Right Or Wrong** album.

Rosanne soon found herself on the country charts, firstly with **No Memories Hangin' 'Round**, a duet with Bobby Bare, then with **Couldn't Do Nothing' Right** and **Take Me, Take Me**. With her first daughter on the way, Rosanne was unable to fully promote her recordings. Her next album, **Seven Year Ache**, gave Rosanne a major breakthrough with the self-penned title song hitting No. 1 on the country charts and also making the American pop Top 20. She had further country number ones with **My Baby Thinks He's A Train** and **Blue Moon With A Heartache**, the album gaining gold

Seven Year Ache, Rosanne Cash,
Courtesy CBS Records.

status. Sadly her next album, **Somewhere In The Stars**, released towards the end of 1982, failed to match the commercial success of its predecessor. Rosanne spent the next two years raising her two daughters, Caitlin and Chelsea, also going through a self-described 'depressing period' of marital discord, drug treatment and introspection. But the period of inactivity also gave her the time to write material for her critically acclaimed **Rhythm And Romance** album (1985) which

contained the hit singles **Hold On** and **I Don't Know Why You Don't Want Me**, and led to her winning a Grammy for Best Female Vocalist Performance in February, 1986.

Albums:
Right Or Wrong (CBS/–)
Seven Year Ache (CBS/–)
Somewhere In The Stars (CBS/CBS)
Rhythm And Romance (CBS/CBS)

Below: Rosanne Cash once worked in CBS' London office. Now she is one of the label's biggest stars.

Tommy Cash

Younger brother of superstar Johnny Cash, Tommy was born in Mississippi County, Arkansas, on April 5, 1940.

He learnt the guitar at 16 after watching his brother play chords and listening to other guitarists. His first public appearance was as a performer at Treadwell High School in 1957; he then joined the army at 18, becoming a disc jockey for AFN, Frankfurt, Germany and having his own show 'Stickbuddy Jamboree'. He met his wife Barbara during this period.

Six White Horses, Tommy Cash, Courtesy Epic Records.

Cash began appearing with a band at various service clubs and eventually launched his professional career by performing alongside Hank Williams Jr at Montreal in January, 1965. He recorded for Musicor and United Artists, but it was not until he signed to Epic in 1969 that he made a commercial breakthrough with **Six White Horses**, a hit in 1969 and **Rise And Shine** and **One Song Away**, hits in 1970. During the '70s, Cash continued to tour with his band, the Tom Cats, and recorded for Elektra, United Artists and Monument without gaining any further chart hits.

Albums:
Best of Tommy Cash Vol 1 (Epic/–)
Six Horses/Lovin' Takes Leavin' (Epic/–)
Only A Stone (Elektra/–)

Pete Cassell

A long-popular blind singer with a fine smooth voice which anticipated the likes of Jim Reeves. Most popular in the '40s and early 50's, Pete recorded for Decca, Majestic and Mercury, but died all too young in 1953, a few years too early to cash in on the smooth Nashville Sound for which his voice was so well suited.

Ray Charles

Although best known as a Rhythm & Blues performer, Ray Charles has made a telling contribution to the cause of country music. Born Ray Charles Robinson, in Albany, Georgia, on September 23, 1930, he could play piano before he was five. At six he contracted glaucoma, which eventually left him blind. Later he learnt composition and became proficient on several instruments, leaving school to work with dance bands around Florida.

In 1947 Ray moved to Seattle and

began working with a Nat Cole R&B styled group but in 1953 he switched style and utilized a more fervent, gospel-styled approach, signing for Atlantic Records and piling up an imposing array of hits. Among the material he covered were some country songs but it was not until 1962, when he made the remarkable **Modern Sounds In Country Music** album for ABC Records, that he really edged into country, the album selling a million and spawning some massive hit singles. Although black artists had earlier welded soul and country – predominantly Ivory Joe Hunter in the late '40s and early '50s – Charles' success paved the way for many other black artists to cut Nashville-oriented albums, these including Esther Phillips, Dobie Gray, Joe Tex, Bobby Womack and Millie Jackson.

After fashioning a sequel to **Modern Sounds**, he moved on yet again, touching all bases but settling for none, seemingly losing direction. However, in 1982 he returned to country music once more, cutting a fine album for Columbia, **Wish You Were Here Tonight**, replete with a set of pickers who included Buddy Emmons, Terry McMillan, Phil Baugh, Hoot Hester, Buddy Spicer etc, and following this with the equally impressive **Do I Ever Cross Your Mind** (1984) and **Friendship** (1984), a collection of duets that found Ray swopping vocal licks with Johnny Cash, Mickey Gilley, Ricky Skaggs, Hank Williams Jr and others, the partnerships with George Jones (**We Didn't See A Thing**), B. J. Thomas (**Rock And Roll Shoes**) and Willie Nelson (**Seven Spanish Angels**) furnishing hit singles, the last named reaching No. 1 in the charts.

Below: The rugged looking Guy Clark, who has been called 'the best poet in Texas' has been known to wear false silver fingernails in order to keep his digits in full picking order.

Do I Ever Cross Your Mind, Ray Charles, Courtesy CBS Records.

Albums:
Modern Sounds In Country & Western Music (ABC/HMV)
Modern Sounds In Country & Western Music (ABC/HMV)
Country And Western Meets Rhythm & Blues (ABC/HMV)
Love Country Style (ABC/Probe)
Wish You Were Here Tonight (Columbia/CBS)
Do I Ever Cross Your Mind (Columbia/CBS)
Friendship (Columbia/CBS)

Lew Childre

A native of Opp, Alabama (born on November 1, 1901), 'Doctor Lew' was a Hawaiian guitar player and sophisticated rural comedian of long tenure (1945–1961) on the Grand Ole Opry.

A veteran of vaudeville – as were many early country comedians – he specialized in routines involving letters to a rural physician – 'Doctor Lew' – who gave outrageous advice. He was also an adept singer and musician who featured old standards like **I'm Looking Over A Four Leaf Clover**. He and Stringbean formed a comedy team for a period (1945–8), before each carved out a solo Opry career.

He recorded little material; so much so that a recently reissued album on Starday has long been regarded as a collector's item.

Guy Clark

Writer of such fine contemporary songs as **Desperados Waiting For A Train, L.A. Freeway, Texas 1947** and **The Last Gunfighter Ballad**, Clark is a Texan (born on November 6, 1941), who spent most of his early years in the town of Monihans, living with his grandmother in a run-down hotel, which provided the inspiration for many of his later songs.

During the '60s he moved to Houston, there working as an art director on a local TV station, also meeting Jerry Jeff Walker and Townes Van Zandt. After a stint on the coffee house circuits of Houston, Dallas and Austin he headed for Los Angeles where he eventually signed as a writer with Sunbury Music.

He moved to Nashville in 1971, cutting an album but scrapping it due to personal dissatisfaction. Then in 1975 came **Old No. 1**, which critics hailed as the finest album for many years. Clark writes almost poetically about losers and low-life ladies. He joined Warner Bros Records in 1978 and recorded three more superb albums as well as penning Ricky Skaggs' chart-topper **Heartbreak** and hit songs for Emmylou Harris, Steve Wariner, Gary

Stewart and others.

Albums:
Old No. 1 (RCA/RCA)
Texas Cooking (RCA/RCA)
The South Coast Of Texas (Warner/–)
Better Days (Warner/–)

Roy Clark

Multi-talented star of the Hee Haw TV series, Roy Linwood Clark was born in Meherrin, Virginia, on April 15, 1933. Son of a guitar-playing tobacco farmer, Clark soon picked up the rudiments of guitar technique but at an early age became even more proficient on banjo, winning the National Country Music Banjo championship two years in succession in the late '40s. Following a move to Washington DC, Roy played as part of the Clark family group, performing at local square dances and eventually winning a solo spot on the Jimmy Dean TV Show – but getting fired due to perpetual lateness. A subsequent job found him getting fired by Marvin Rainwater – this time for earning more applause than the star himself. Better luck followed when, as a cast member of a George Hamilton IV TV series, he gained wide recognition.

Recording initially for Four Star as Roy Clark and the Wranglers, he later moved on to Debbie, Coral and – following a tour with Wanda Jackson – Capitol, enjoying his first sizeable hit with a Capitol single, **Tips Of My Fingers**, in 1963. Following a contract with Dot, the hits really began to proliferate, via titles like **Yesterday When I Was Young** (1969), **I Never Picked Cotton, Thank God And Greyhound** (both 1970), **A Simple Thing Called Love** (1971), **Come Live With Me** (1973), **Honeymoon Feeling** (1974) and **If I Had To Do It All Over Again** (1976). He has since failed to make the Top

Roy Clark Sings Gospel, Courtesy Word Records.

10, though he has remained one of country music's top in-concert attractions. A jovial international ambassador for country music, Clark was presented with the CMA Entertainer Of The Year award in 1973. Since 1982 he has been with Churchill Records, a label formed by his long-time manager, Jim Halsey.

Albums:
My Music And Me (Dot/–)
Roy Clark Sings Gospel (Word/Word)
A Pair Of Fives – with Buck Trent (Dot/ABC)
Back To The Country (MCA/MCA)
Live From Austin City Limits (Churchill/–)
The Entertainer (Dot/Ember)
I'll Paint You A Song (–/Ember)
20 Golden Pieces (–/Bulldog)
Makin' Music (MCA/MCA)

Yodelling Slim Clark

Born Raymond LeRoy Clark, on November 12, 1917, in Springfield, Massachusetts, Yodelling Slim worked for a long period as a woodman. Winner of the World Yodelling Championship in 1947, be hegan recording for such labels as Continental, Remington, Wheeling and Palomino, his albums including **Yodel Songs** (Remington 1950), **Jimmie Rodgers Songs** and **Wilf Carter Songs** (Palomino 1965 and 1967).

Jack Clement

Few people have mastered more phases of the music business than Jack 'Cowboy' Clement, who was born on April 5, 1931, in Memphis, Tennessee. As a youth he mastered a variety of instruments and played all kinds of music from big band to bluegrass as he worked his way into the production end of the business, where he fell in with Sam Phillips at Sun Records as a session musician, engineer and producer. During that era, Clement also wrote a great many songs including **Guess Things Happen That Way** and **Ballad Of A Teenage Queen** for Johnny Cash.

Since the mid '60s he has concentrated his energies in Nashville, where he built an extremely successful publishing firm – Jack Music – ran Jack Clement Studio, assisted in the careers of Charley Pride, Tompall & The Glasers and continued to write as well. He even found time to produce a horror film, 'Dear Dead Delilah'. In 1971 he formed JMI Records, working with Allen Reynolds, Bob McDill and Don Williams, but the company folded in 1974.

All I Want To Do In Life, Jack Clement, Courtesy Elektra Records.

Clement made a comeback in the late '70s as a producer with Johnny Cash and Waylon Jennings and started recording for the first time in almost 20 years for Elektra. Amongst his most notable songs are **Miller's Cave**, **I Know One**, **A Girl I Used To Know** and **The One On The Right Is On The Left**.

Album:
All I Want To Do In Life (Elektra/Elektra)

Vassar Clements

A much respected fiddle player who worked for some time as a sessioneer in Nashville before finding a degree of solo fame. Born on April 25, 1928, at Kinard,

Nashville Jam, Vassar Clements, Courtesy Flying Fish Records.

South Carolina, Vassar has heen in the bands of Bill Monroe, Jim and Jesse, Faron Young and the contemporary-slanted Earls Scruggs Revue.

He appeared on the Nitty Gritty Dirt Band's **Will The Circle Be Unbroken** and his consequent familiarity to the general public after years of being a name among recording sessions credits has meant that he has been able to get his own show together and travel the road.

Albums:
Superbow (Mercury/–)
Hillbilly Jazz (Flying Fish/Sonet)
Bluegrass Session (Flying Fish/Sonet)

Zeke Clements

'The Alabama Cowboy' was born near Empire, Alabama, on September 9, 1911, and has had one of the longest careers in country music, having appeared on radio shows in all sections of the country, as well as having the unusual distinction of having been a member of all three of the major barn dances in the course of his career.

Zeke began on the National Barn Dance in 1928, toured for some years with Otto Gray's Oklahoma Cowboys, then joined the Grand Ole Opry in 1933 as a member of their first cowboy group, the Bronco Busters. After spending some time on the west coast on radio and in films (where he was, among many other screen parts, the voice of the yodelling dwarf Bashful in Walt Disney's 'Snow White and the Seven Dwarfs'), he returned to the Opry in 1939, where he became one of the Opry's major stars throughout the '40s. He also became known as a songwriter during this era, especially for **Blue Mexico Skies**, **There's Poison In Your Heart**, and as co-writer of **Smoke On The Water**, the top country record of 1945.

Clements later appeared on the Louisiana Hayride and on many other Deep South stations. He pursued a business career in Nashville in the late

'50s and '60s, then moved to Miami, Florida, where he spent nearly a decade playing tenor banjo in a dixieland band before returning to the Nashville area.

Bill Clifton

Perennial globetrotter Clifton was born at Riderwood, Maryland, in 1931. A vocalist, guitarist and autoharp player, he became

Below: Opry and Hayride star Zeke Clements supplied the voice of Dopey in Walt Disney's 'Snow White'.

interested in the music of the Carter Family during the 1940s, later forming his own group, the Dixie Mountain Boys, which established a considerable reputation among bluegrass aficionados, and also cut sides for Starday and other labels. In 1961, he recorded 22 Carter Family songs for a Starday album but some months later turned up in Britain where, using contracts made as a founder member of the Newport Folk Festival, he became instrumental in setting up tours by Bill Monroe, the Stanley Brothers, the New Lost City Ramblers and others during the '60s. He also enhanced his own

Blue Ridge Mountain Bluegrass, Bill Clifton, Courtesy County Records.

reputation as a bluegrass musician, embarking on tours of Europe and recording a programme of old-time music for transmission on Radio Moscow in 1966.

By 1967, Clifton was on the move once more, he, his wife and seven children sailing for the Philippines, where he became an active member of the Peace Corps. Still in the Pacific area at the commencement of the '70s, he arrived in New Zealand, playing at a banjo players' convention and cutting an album with

A Bluegrass Jam Session 1952, Bill Clifton, Courtesy Bear Family.

Hamilton County Bluegrass Band, a local outfit. Since that time, Clifton has been active in Europe, the States, and Japan.

Albums:
Happy Days (–/Golden Guinea)
Blue Ridge Mountain Blues (County/Westwood)
Going Down To Dixie (–/Bear Family)
Mountain Folk Songs (Starday/–)

Patsy Cline

Patsy Cline (real name Virginia Patterson Hensley) was born in Winchester, Virginia, on September 8, 1932. Winner of an amateur tap dancing contest at the age of four, she began learning piano at eight, and in her early teens became a singer at local clubs. In 1948, an audition won her a trip to Nashville, where she appeared in a few clubs before returning home – but her big break came in 1957 when she won an Arthur Godfrey Talent Scout show, singing **Walking After Midnight**. Her Decca single of the contest-winning song then entered the charts, both pop and country, enjoying a lengthy stay in both. In 1961 came **I Fall To Pieces**, one of Patsy's biggest hits, followed in quick succession by **Crazy, Who Can I Count On?, She's Got You, Strange** and **When I Get Through With You**, most of them being massive sellers.

Sweet Dreams – the soundtrack to the Patsy Cline biopic – Courtesy MCA.

During the same period she became a featured singer on the Opry, soon attaining the rank of top female country singer and challenging Kitty Wells as 'Queen Of Country Music'. Such hits as **Imagine That, So Wrong** and **Leavin' On Your Mind** continued to proliferate until, on March 5, 1963, Patsy died in an air disaster at Camden, Tennessee. She had been returning home from a Kansas City benefit concert with Hawkshaw Hawkins and Cowboy Copas, both of whom were also killed in the crash.

But even after her death, Patsy's records continued to sell, **Sweet Dreams (Of You)** and **Faded Love** being top hits during '63, **When You Need A Laugh** and **He Called Me Baby** entering the country charts in 1964, and **Anytime** appearing in the latter as late as 1969.

Patsy has continued to be a major influence on singers like Loretta Lynn, who recorded a tribute album in 1977, Reba McEntire and Sylvia. In 1973 she was elected to the Country Music Hall of Fame and her recordings and those of Jim Reeves were spliced together to produce a duet effect resulting in hits with **Have You Ever Been Lonely** and **I Fall To Pieces** during 1981 and a best selling album. A film tracing her career, 'Sweet Dreams', based on the biography written by Ellis Nassour, was made in 1985 and led to Patsy's recording making yet another comeback on the country charts.

Albums:
The Legendary (–/Music For Pleasure)
Country Hall Of Fame (–/MCA)
The Patsy Cline Story (MCA/–)
Always (MCA/MCA)
Sweet Dreams (MCA/MCA)

Jerry Clower

Country comedian Jerry Clower was born at Liberty, Mississippi, on September 28, 1926, and grew up in Amite County amid the folks he now brings to life as part of his hilarious routines. After graduation in 1944 he joined the navy, following in the path of elder brother Sonny, who joined soon after Pearl Harbour. Upon discharge came a football scholarship at Southwest

The Heart of Hank Cochran, Courtesy Monument.

Junior College, Summit, where he won a further scholarship to Mississippi State University, playing for the State football team and majoring in agriculture.

After becoming a field representative with the Mississippi Chemical Company, Clower rose to become Director of Field Services with the company, in charge of a large sales force. Sales talks became part of his stock in trade and so his **Coon Hunt Story** and other routines were introduced to make such speeches more acceptable. A friend then suggested that Clower should record an album of his routines and, after further prompting, it was agreed that an album be cut on the Lemon label. Named **Jerry Clower From Yazoo City Talkin'** and advertised only by word of mouth, the album sold over 8,000 copies in a short period, gaining Clower a contract with MCA in 1971. His album later went into the Billboard charts for a lengthy stay

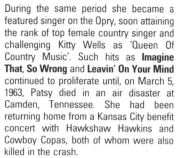

Ambassador Of Goodwill, Jerry Clower, Courtesy MCA Records.

and, following the release of other high-selling LPs, he became accepted as country music's funniest man, winning many spots on TV shows including frequent appearances on Grand Ole Opry. The father of four children, Clower, deeply religious like many country stars, is a Yazoo City Baptist deacon, an active member of the Gideon Bible Society and author of the best selling book, 'Ain't God Good'. For several years he was co-host

of the syndicated TV show 'Nashville On The Road'.

Albums:
Clower Power (MCA/–)
Country Ham (MCA/–)
Live In Picayune (MCA/–)
The Ambassador Of Goodwill (MCA/–)

Hank Cochran

Singer-songwriter Henry 'Hank' Cochran was born in Greenville, Mississippi, on August 2, 1935. After completing school he moved to New Mexico, working in the oil-fields during the mid '50s, and eventually made his way to California, where he began entertaining in small clubs, occasionally obtaining radio and TV work. In 1954, he and Eddie Cochran (no relation) formed a duo, the Cochran Brothers, initially recording country material for the Ekko label but later switching to rock after watching Elvis Presley perform in Dallas.

After two years, the Cochrans went their separate ways, Hank going on to join the California Hayride TV show in Stockton, then in 1960 moving to Nashville in order to sell his songs. One such composition, entitled **I Fall To Pieces**, written with the aid of Harlan Howard, became a 1961 winner for Patsy Cline, after which came **Make The World Go Away** (a hit for both Ray Price and Eddy Arnold), **A Little Bitty Tear** and **Funny Way Of Laughing** (Burl Ives), **I Want To Go With You** (Eddy Arnold), and others. Signed by Liberty as a recording artist in 1961, Cochran's name appeared in the charts during '62 with **Sally Was A Good Old Girl** and **I'd Fight The World**, the singer later scoring with **A Good Country Song** on Gaylord in 1963, and **All Of Me Belongs To You** on Monument in 1967.

Married for many years to Jeannie Seely, Hank re-emerged in the mid '70s writing hit songs for Willie Nelson (**Angel Flying Too Close To The Ground**) and Mel Tillis (**Uphill All The Way**). He once again took up performing and recording, signing to Capitol Records in 1978 and making the album **With A Little Help From His**

Friends, featuring Merle Haggard, Willie Nelson, Jack Greene and Jeannie Seely. Two years later he recorded an album for Elektra, **Make The World Go Away**, featuring mainly his classic songs from the '60s.

Albums:
Make The World Go Away (Elektra/–)
With A Little Help From His Friends (Capitol/–)
Going In Training (RCA/–)
Heart (Monument/–)

Commander Cody And His Lost Planet Airmen

This zany, modern western-swing outfit was named after space movie characters. Formed in 1967 by leader George 'Commander Cody' Frayne (born Boise, Idaho), previously Farfisa organ player with various small-time rock bands and a one-time lifeguard, it acquired a sizeable reputation in California. The Airmen signed to ABC-Paramount in 1969, recording the fine **Lost In The Ozone** album and subsequently gaining a Top 20 hit with a version of Johnny Bond's **Hot Rod Lincoln** (1972). In 1974 they moved to Warner Bros releasing two studio albums and a live double, **We've Got A Live One Here**, recorded during the band's 1976 British tour, after which the band split.

Line-up changes have always affected Cody's unwieldy aggregation – amongst those who have worked with the band are Bobby Black (pedal steel), Lance Dickerson (drums), Bruce Barlow (bass), Norton Buffalo (harmonica, trombone) and vocalist Nicolette Larson – but somehow he has always managed to put something together and in the early '80s logged a hit in Europe with **Two Triple Cheeseburgers (Side Order Of Fries)**, an MCA release.

Album:
Lost In The Ozone (Paramount/ABC)

We've Got A Live One Here, Commander Cody, Courtesy Warner Bros.

Hot Licks, Cold Steel (Paramount/ABC)
Live – Deep In The Heart Of Texas (Paramount/ABC)
Tales From The Ozone (Warner Bros/Warner Bros)
We've Got A Live One Here (Warner Bros/Warner Bros)

David Allan Coe

This flamboyant and outrageous country star, born in Akron, Ohio, on September 6, 1939, made his initial impression in country music writing the hit songs, **Would You Lay With Me In A Field Of Stone** (Tanya Tucker) and **Take This Job And Shove It** (Johnny Paycheck). He spent most of his youth in various reform schools and prisons, once escaping the death penalty only by the timely abolition of capital punishment in his home state. Released from jail in 1967, Coe attempted a career as a singer and eventually went south to Nashville. At that time, however, Coe was primarily a blues artist. He signed a recording contract with Shelby Singleton in Nashville and came up with **Penitentiary Blues**, an autobiographical album reflecting Coe's 20 years of prison life. He followed this with **Requiem For A Harlequin**, another blues-filled, but poetic LP.

Next came a switch to country music and following a few unsuccessful singles on SSS International, he signed with Columbia Records in 1972 and with the album **The Mysterious Rhinestone Cowboy** he launched a successful career that saw him turning out top-selling albums such as **Once Upon A Rhyme**, **Longhaired Redneck**, **David Allan Coe Rides Again**, **Human Emotions** and **Family Album**. Very much a fan of black music, Coe has a rich and raunchy voice which takes easily to soul, blues and country. He finally made a big impression on the country singles chart with **The Ride**, the tale of a ghostly meeting with Hank Williams, which topped the charts in 1983. He had further success with the reflective **Mona Lisa's Lost Her Smile** in 1984, but has remained very much as album artist, something which is rather unusual in country music, where a star's stature is

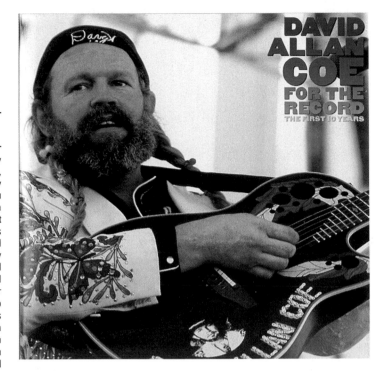

For The Record, David Allan Coe, Courtesy CBS Records.

measured by the number of Top 10 singles.

Albums:
Once Upon A Rhyme (Columbia/CBS)
Family Album (Columbia/–)
Human Emotions (Columbia/–)
Rough Rider (Columbia/–)
Tennessee Whiskey (Columbia/–)
Castles In The Sand (Columbia/CBS)

Tommy Collins

One of the musicians who helped to put Bakersfield on the country music map – Buck Owens was once a member of his band – Tommy Collins (real name Leonard Raymond Sipes) was born in Oklahoma City, Oklahoma, on September 28, 1930. A boyhood guitarist, he began performing at

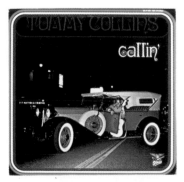

Callin', Tommy Collins, Courtesy Gusto–Starday Records.

local clubs while at Oklahoma State College, making appearances on such radio stations as KLPR, KOCY, KBYE and WKY. During the early '50s, he became both a resident of Bakersfield and a Capitol recording artist, his halcyon days being in 1954–5 when Collins followed **You Better Not Do That**, a half-million seller, with a quartet of other Top 20 discs. In 1966 he presented Columbia with a Top 10 item in **If You Can't Bite, Don't Growl**, but

his later discs, such as **Birmingham** (1967) and **I Made The Prison Band** (1968) only achieved moderate chart placings.

As a songwriter, he provided Merle Haggard with some of his best numbers including the chart-topping **Roots Of My Raising** in 1976. Hag repaid Collins by writing a song about him called **Leonard**, which was a successful country single in 1981.

Collins' past albums include **This Is Tommy Collins** (Capitol), **Dynamic** (Columbia), **On Tour** Columbia) and two albums recorded in Britain during 1980, **Country Souvenir** and **Cowboys Get Lucky Some Of The Time** for the small G&W label.

Jessi Colter

Writer and singer of the 1975 No. 1, **I'm Not Lisa**, Jessi Colter (real name Miriam Johnson) was born in Phoenix, Arizona, on May 25, 1947, the sixth of seven children whose father was a racing car builder. A church pianist at the age of 11, Jessi married guitarist Duane Eddy just five years later, touring England, Germany, South Africa and other countries as part of the Eddy show. A singer-songwriter, she was recorded by Eddy and Lee Hazelwood for the Jamie and RCA labels, meeting Waylon Jennings during some Phoenix-based sessions.

She split from Eddy in 1965 and,

Jessi, Jessi Colter, Courtesy Capitol Records.

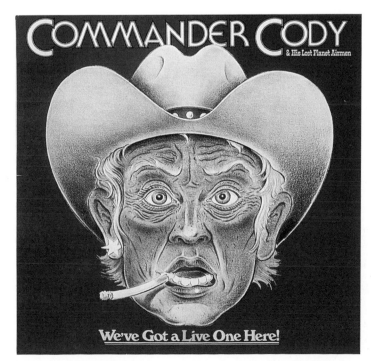

We've Got a Live One Here!

Above: Jessi Colter – she participated in the massive Democratic fund-raising telethon of 1983. A one-time church pianist, her self-penned I'm Not Lisa, produced by her husband Waylon Jennings and Ken Mansfield, topped the charts in 1975.

changing her name to Jessi Colter because her great, great uncle was a member of the Jesse James Gang, she moved to Nashville, signed a new contract with RCA and recorded the critically-acclaimed album, **A Country Star Is Born**, in 1966.

By this time she had made an impression writing songs recorded by Eddy Arnold, Dottie West, Anita Carter, Patsy Sledd and Don Gibson. She teamed up with Waylon Jennings, and following her divorce from Eddy, the pair married in 1969 and recorded a series of duets including **Suspicious Minds** and **Under Your Spell Again**, which made the charts in 1970 and 1971 respectively.

Jessi signed a solo contract with Capitol Records in 1974 and scored hits with **I'm Not Lisa**, which she wrote in five minutes, **What Happened To Blue Eyes** (1975), **It's Morning** (1976) and **Maybe You Should've Been Listening** (1978). She appeared on the best-selling RCA album titled **Outlaws** (1976) and has continued touring and recording with Waylon, but devotes much of her time to their children, Buddy and Jennifer.

Albums:
I'm Jessi Colter (Capitol/–)
Jessi (Capitol/Capitol)
Diamond In The Rough (Capitol/–)
That's The Way A Cowboy Rocks 'n' Rolls (Capitol/–)
Ridin' Shotgun (Capitol/–)
Leather & Lace – with Waylon Jennings (RCA/RCA)

Compton Brothers

Voted Most Promising Vocal Group of 1968–9 by Cashbox magazine, the Comptons, Harry and Bill, from St Louis, Missouri, won a 1965 talent contest that resulted in a Columbia recording contract. However, they later became associated with the Dot label, supplying a number of minor hits during the late '60s and early '70s. Only two of these, namely **Haunted House** (1969) and **Charlie Brown** (1970), ever attained Top 20 status. The brothers are owners of the Wepedol Publishing Co.

John Conlee

The singer with the saddest voice in modern country music, Conlee was born on August 11, 1946 in Versailles, Kentucky and raised on a tobacco farm. Music played an important role throughout his childhood and by his early teens he was a member of a folk trio and later joined a rock group.

Following graduation he worked for six years as a mortician but still had a hankering for a job in music and finally landed himself a DJ stint on a Fort Knox Station. A move to Nashville in 1971, playing rock music, enabled him to make important music contacts, which led to him playing local clubs in the evenings and the signing of a recording contract with ABC Records.

His initial releases failed to make much impression but his fourth release, **Rose Coloured Glasses**, a song he co-wrote

Songs For The Working Man, John Conlee, Courtesy MCA Records.

with a newsreader at the radio station, made the country Top 5 in May 1978. That same year ABC Records were absorbed by MCA, for whom John scored more than 30 Top 10 hits, including **Lady Lay Down**, a chart-topper in 1978, **Backside Of Thirty** (1979), **Friday Night Blues** (1980), **Miss Emily's Picture** (1981), **Common Man** (1983) and **As Long As I'm Rockin' With**

Below: John Conlee – he worked for six years as a mortician.

You (1984). At the beginning of 1986 John signed with Columbia Records. When he joined the Grand Ole Opry in 1979, John was the first new member in five years.

Albums:
Rose Coloured Glasses (MCA/MCA)
Forever (MCA/–)
Friday Night Blues (MCA/–)
Busted (MCA/–)
In My Eyes (MCA/–)
Blue Highway (MCA/–)
Harmony (Columbia/–)

Earl Thomas Conley

Country music singer, songwriter and philosopher, Conley, who was born in Portsmouth, Ohio, made a major breakthrough in the early '80s with a string of number ones including **Fire And Smoke**, **Tell Me Why**, **Heavenly Bodies** and **Your Love's On The Line**. His father was a railroad man but with the advent of diesel locos was put out of work in the early '50s, which led to the large Conley family being on the breadline for many years. The young Earl took to carving, painting and drawing and when he left home in his teens he drifted around living off money earnt from his artistic skills. During army service in Germany he became interested in country music and, following demob, started singing in clubs in Alabama.

A move to Nashville led to him making an impression as a songwriter, providing Mel Street with **Smokey Mountain Memories**, a Top 10 hit in 1975, and Conway Twitty with the chart-topping **This Time I've Hurt Her More Than She Loves Me** the following year. Earl was signed to GRT Records and had a few minor hits including **I Have Loved You Girl** (1975) and **High And Wild** (1976).

He added the Thomas to the middle of his name in 1978 to save confusion with John Conlee and Con Hunley and signed with Warner Brothers, scoring his biggest hit with **Dreamin's All I Do** in 1979. A move to the small Sunbird label the following year and the release of his debut album, **Blue Pearl**, led to a Top 10 hit with **Silent Treatment** (1980) and a No. 1 with **Fire And Smoke** the following August.

Conley's contract with Sunbird was acquired by RCA and the next few years saw him emerge as the most successful country singer of recent times. Using mainly self-written tunes, he's been hailed for his sensitive, introspective writing talents, blending traditional strains with elements of modern country and soul and bringing a fresh spirit to the country forms he celebrates.

Albums:
Blue Pearl (Sunbird/–)
Fire And Smoke (RCA/–)
Don't Make It Easy For Me (RCA/–)
Treadin' Water (RCA/–)
Somewhere Between Right And Wrong (RCA/–)
Greatest Hits (RCA/–)

Ry Cooder

One-time Los Angeles session man, Cooder is of interest to country fans in that his music is soaked generally in southern folk styles. Born in Los Angeles, California,

Above: Earl Conley added a middle name to avoid confusion with John Conlee.

on March 15, 1947, he first came to public notice with his tasteful and well-timed mandolin excursions on bluesman Taj Mahal's first CBS album and he played with Taj's band, the Rising Sons. Later, he was to impress again with his mandolin work on the Rolling Stones' **Let It Bleed** album.

His solo career began in 1970 with the first in a series of highly acclaimed albums for Warner Brothers which featured long forgotten or little known gospel, old-timey country, Cajun and blues tunes given a very distinctive treatment. He also became proficient on slide guitar and is now a rated exponent of that style. One of his finest albums is **Chicken Skin Music**, which introduced Tex-Mex music to a wide audience and featured accordionist

Alamo Bay – Soundtrack, Ry Cooder, Courtesy Slash/London Records.

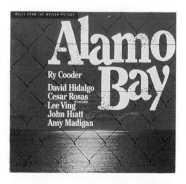

Flaco Jiminez and his Conjunto musicians from San Antonio.

Ry has also been in demand for writing and playing on film soundtracks such as 'The Long Riders', for which he created western music of a style played in saloons during the gunfighter era of Jesse James and Cole Younger, and the country blues used as the backcloth for the 1984 movie, 'Paris, Texas'. During 1985 he produced yet another soundtrack score – this time for the Louis Malle film 'Alamo Bay'.

Albums:
Chicken Skin Music (Reprise/Reprise)
The Long Riders (Reprise/Reprise)
Into The Purple Valley (Reprise/Reprise)
Paradise And Lunch (Reprise/Reprise)

Spade Cooley

One-time King Of Western Swing, Donell C. Cooley had literally one of the biggest bands in country music, sometimes numbering around two dozen musicians.

Born in Grand, Oklahoma, on February 22, 1910, Cooley, of Scottish-Irish descent plus a dash of Cherokee Indian, acquired the nickname of Spade from an exceptional run of spades he once held during a poker game.

Both his father and his grandfather were fine fiddle players and Cooley, who was first taught cello, also became adept on fiddle, playing at square dances while still a boy, earning his first fee as a musician at the age of eight.

During the late '30s he became a

Swinging The Devil's Dream, Spade Cooley, Courtesy Charly Records.

Hollywood extra, eventually obtaining roles in movies produced by RKO, Universal, Republic, Warner, Lippert and Columbia.

By 1942 Cooley was leading his own very successful band, in '46 leasing the Santa Monica ballroom for long term use as the band's headquarters. A radio performer during the early '40s, he was signed for a Hollywood country TV show in 1948, shortly after returning from a

C&W Dance-O-Rama, Spade Cooley, Courtesy MCA Records.

lengthy tour with his band. Playing a mixture of jazz, country and pure dance music, the Cooley outfit gained further fame, but the fiddle-playing leader's

The Lady's Not For Sale, Rita Coolidge, Courtesy A&M Records.

career came to a dramatic end when he was jailed for wife-slaying. His death occurred shortly after his release from prison: Cooley suffered a heart attack on November 23, 1969 while playing at a sheriff's benefit concert in Oakland, California.

During his career, his records were released on such labels as Okeh, Columbia, RCA Victor and Decca, Cooley's biggest hit being with the self-penned **Shame On You** in 1945.

Albums:
Spade Cooley (Columbia/–)
The King Of Western Swing (Club Of Spade/–)
Swinging The Devil's Dream (–/Charly)

Rita Coolidge

Nashville born, on May 1, 1944, Rita Coolidge and her two sisters first began singing in a church choir (their father was a Baptist minister). Rita later worked with a rock band, the Moonpies, playing at fraternity parties at the University of Florida and at Florida State. In college, she also sang with a folk rock unit, then, after leaving, went to Memphis and began working for Pepper Records, cutting some sides with the label. Her sister Priscilla began working with and then married the popular R&B organist-bandleader Booker T. Jones, which brought Rita into further contact with the rock scene – and engagements with such artists as Delaney and Bonnie Bramlett, Leon Russell, Eric Clapton and Joe Cocker.

Following a tour with Cocker's Mad Dogs And Englishmen in 1970, on which she was featured as a vocalist and pianist, Rita was signed to A&M as a solo artist, her first album, **Rita Coolidge**, being released in 1971. Forming a band known as the Dixie Flyers, she then began touring, playing engagements in Britain and Canada during 1971. Some time later she met Kris Kristofferson, whom she married in 1973.

The duo appeared on several tours and many TV shows, also recording together and scoring such hits as **A Song I'd Like To Sing** (1973) and **Loving Arms** (1974).

Known as the Delta Lady (Leon Russell named the song in her honour), Rita is considered to be one of the leading performers in country rock with such solo hits as **Higher And Higher** and **We're All Alone** (1977), **The Way You Do The Things You Do** (1978) and **One Fine Day** (1980). Kris and Rita went their separate ways in the late seventies and were divorced in 1980.

Albums:
Rita Coolidge (A&M/–)
Fall Into Spring (A&M/–)
The Lady's Not For Sale (A&M/A&M)
Breakaway – with Kris Kristofferson
    (Monument/Monument)
Natural Act – with Kris Kristofferson
    (A&M/A&M)
Very Best (A&M/A&M)

The Coon Creek Girls

Violet Koehler, vocals, guitar, mandolin; Daisy Lange, vocals, bass; Black Eyed Susan Ledford, bass; Lily Mae Ledford, vocals, banjo, fiddle; Rosie Ledford, vocals, guitar.

The Coon Creek Girls were an extremely popular all girl string band of the '30s and '40s (although their career actually proceeded in fits and stars right up until Lily Mae Ledford's death in 1976), led by the singer and multi-instrumentalist Lily Mae Ledford of Pinch-em-tight Holler, Kentucky.

Lily Mae began her career as a fiddler on the National Barn Dance in 1936, but it was John Lair who conceived the idea of an all-girl band built around Lily Mae. It first consisted of Daisy Lange and Violet Koehler as well as younger sister Rosie Ledford, but in later years the band consisted of the three Ledford sisters only. They spent their entire career on the Renfro Valley Barn Dance (1938–1958), first over WLW and then over WHAS, and regrouped sporadically for events like the Newport Folk Festival.

Their most popular record was their theme song, **You're A Flower That Is Blooming There For Me** (Vocalion).

Wilma Lee and Stoney Cooper

Born at Harman, West Virginia, on October 16, 1918, singer-songwriter-fiddler Dale T. 'Stoney' Cooper came from a farming family of some considerable musical ability. By the time he was 12, he had become an accomplished musician and upon leaving school joined the Leary Family, a religious singing group, who were in need of a fiddle player. One member of the group was Wilma Lee Leary (born at Valley Head, West Virginia, on February 7, 1921), a singer-songwriter, guitarist and organist, whom Stoney courted and eventually married in 1939.

For several years the duo remained members of the Leary Family, appearing on radio shows and performing in churches and other venues. Then, in the mid '40s, the Coopers decided to go their own way and began playing dates on many radio stations throughout the country, in 1947 joining the WWVA Jamboree at Wheeling, West Virginia, on

Wilma Lee and Stoney Cooper, Courtesy Rounder Records.

a regular basis.

After a ten-year stay with WWVA, during which time they switched record labels from Columbia to Hickory (1955), the Coopers headed for Nashville, becoming members of the Opry in 1957. Soon after they scored hits with **Come Walk With Me**, **Big Midnight Special** and **There's A Big Wheel**, all three discs being Top 5 country hits during 1959. Further successes followed, including **Johnny My Love** (1960), **This Old House** (1960), and

Below: Wilma Lee and Stoney Cooper. The duo met and married while members of a religious singing group.

Wreck On The Highway (1961), then, though the duo left Hickory for Decca, the hit supply seemed to dry up. However, the Coopers continued to be a tremendous onstage attraction and in the mid '70s were still rated as one of the Opry's most popular acts. Stoney Cooper's death, caused by a heart attack, on March 22, 1977 put the future of the act in doubt, although Wilma Lee continued with daughter Carol Lee Snow (married to Hank Snow's son, Jimmie Rodgers Snow) and the Clinch Mountain Clan, performing old time mountain and bluegrass songs.

Albums:
Satisfied (–/DJM)
Wilma Lee and Stoney Cooper (Rounder/–)
A Daisy A Day (Leather/–)
Early Recordings (County/–)
Wilma Lee Cooper (Rounder/–)

Cowboy Copas

A victim of the 1963 plane crash that also claimed the lives of Patsy Cline and Hawkshaw Hawkins, Copas' 1960 recording of **Alabam** had just placed him back on top of the heap again, following his virtual disappearance from the country charts during the late '50s. Born in Muskogee, Oklahoma, on July 15, 1913, Lloyd 'Cowboy' Copas was brought up on

The Best Of Cowboy Copas, Courtesy Gusto Records.

a ranch, where his grandfather taught him western folklore and songs. Learning guitar at the age of 16, Copas then formed a duo with an Indian fiddler, Natchee. After winning a talent contest, the twosome then played a series of dates throughout the country, Copas himself performing on 204 radio stations in North America between 1939 and 1950. When Natchee went his own way in 1940, Copas then obtained a regular spot on a Knoxville station, eventually being featured on WLM's Boone County Jamboree and signing for King Records, for whom he made a number of hits including **Filipino Baby**, **Tragic Romance**, **Gone And Left Me**

Blues and **Signed, Sealed And Delivered**.

Becoming a featured vocalist with Pee Wee King's Golden West Cowboys on the Opry in 1946, he furthered his reputation with **Kentucky Waltz** and **Tennessee Waltz**. For a while he became a performer with an SRO reputation but after the advent of **Strange Little Girl**, a 1951 chart-climber, Copas dropped from sight. Signed to Starday in 1959, his hit recording of **Alabam** seemed set to launch him on a new career. Then came the plane disaster.

Album:
The Best of Cowboy Copas (Starday/ Starday-Midland)

Helen Cornelius

Finding fame in 1976 as Jim Ed Brown's singing partner and as a member of the Nashville On The Road TV Show, Helen Cornelius has also made a considerable impression as a songwriter, her compositions being recorded by Dottsy, LaCosta, Liz Anderson, Bonnie Guitar, Barbara Fairchild and many other artists.

Brought up on a farm in Hannibal, Missouri, where she was born on December 6, 1950, Helen was one of an eight-strong musical family, with her sisters Judy and Sharon combining with Helen to form a vocal trio, their father chauffeuring them from town to town in order to provide the threesome with opportunities to perform. As a solo act, Helen began obtaining work at various local gigs, playing some radio and TV dates, won the Ted Mack Amateur Hour and eventually employed a backup group known as the Crossroads. At 17 she graduated from high school in Monroe City, Missouri, marrying just a year later and working for a short period as a secretary. But by 1970 she was songwriting as a profession, signing a contract with Columbia-Screen Gems and cutting some discs with Columbia Records some time later, these meeting with little response.

Signing for RCA Records in September, 1975, her first release was **We Still Love Songs In Missouri**, a well received single. However, being cast as the ideal vocal foil for Jim Ed Brown proved to be the real breakthrough, the duo's version of **I Don't Want To Have To Marry You** becoming both a controversial release – many radio stations banning the disc – and a country No. 1. In early 1977, **Saying Hello, Saying I Love You, Saying Goodbye** found the Cornelius-Brown partnership chart-topping yet again. Further hits followed with **Born Believer** (1977), **If The World Ran Out Of Love Tonight** (1978) and **Lying In Love With You** (1979). Helen has been concentrating on a solo career since 1982, but has so far failed to score a major hit.

Albums:
I Don't Want To Have To Marry You – with Jim Ed Brown (RCA/RCA)
Born Believer – with Jim Ed Brown (RCA/–)
Helen Cornelius (MCA-Dot/–)

Elvis Costello

The Irish-born pop star fulfilled a life-long ambition when he appeared on Nashville's Grand Ole Opry on January 3, 1982 during

Above: Country Gazette, 1974 – Alan Munde, Bryon Berline, Rodger Bush and Kenny Wertz.

an American tour. An ardent admirer of George Jones, Elvis took his band, the Attractions, to Nashville to record **Almost Blue**, an album of country standards produced by Billy Sherrill in 1980.

Although snubbed by the American country establishment, he scored a British chart-topper with an update of the old George Jones' hit, **A Good Year for The Roses**, and recorded a duet with Jones of **A Stranger In The House**, a sad country ballad that Costello had written.

Album:
Almost Blue (Columbia/F-Beat)

Country Gazette

With the famous Flying Burrito Brothers now in abeyance, it was left to Country Gazette, the remains of the Burrito

Don't Give Up Your Day Job, Country Gazette, Courtesy UA Records.

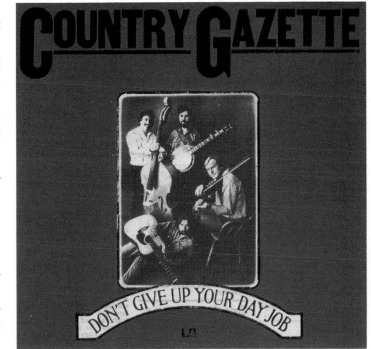

aggregation, to perpetuate the line. Byron Berline had originally been a championship-winning fiddle player and in-demand session man and he teamed up with Roger Bush (string bass), Kenny Wertz (guitar, vocals), Roland White (guitar, mandolin, vocals) and Alan Munde (banjo, vocals), to bring a souped-up, '70s-style bluegrass sound to the nation.

Since bluegrass was commonplace in America their appeal there was rather limited, but in Britain and Europe they found themselves preaching to a new audience. A first British tour of clubs and colleges was hailed warmly. Gazette drew on a mixture of self-penned originals and revered standards and rounded it off with some cornpone humour in which the puckish figure of Roger Bush, with upturned moustache, featured prominently.

They have perhaps never bettered their first album for UA, **Traitor In Our Midst**, but in spite of personnel changes they have always maintained a standard of instrumental slickness and attractive vocal harmonies and have proved to the outside world that top-class country bands do not necessarily have to operate out of Nashville. On more than one ocasion they have been voted Top Country Group in

British award polls. Berline eventually left the band to form Sundance and was replaced for a time by Dave Ferguson. Far more popular abroad than at home, the band has continued regardless of numerous line-up changes.

Albums:
All This And Money Too (Ridge Runner/–)
American And Clean (Flying Fish/–)
Traitor In Our Midst (UA/)
Don't Give Up Your Day Job (UA/–)
From The Beginning (–/Sunset)

Country Gentlemen

One of the first progressive bluegrass groups, the Country Gentlemen played their first date on July 4, 1957.

During the group's embryonic days the personnel consisted of Charlie Waller, John Duffy, Bill Emerson and Eddy Adcock, though by the mid '70s, lead singer and flat top guitarist Waller (born in Jointerville, Texas, on January 19, 1935) was the only remaining member of the original line-up.

Initially from the Washington DC area, the group played two nights a week for ten years at a Georgetown niterie known as the Shamrock Club – but during the '60s the Gentlemen gained a nationwide reputation, being featured on many networked TV shows, the group's popularity gaining ground along with the bluegrass explosion. Voted Best Band by 'Muleskinner News' in 1972 and 1973, they became the first Washington bluegrass band to play in Japan.

Eclectic in their choice of material – drawing equally from Bob Dylan, Charlie Poole, Lefty Frizzell and even Hollywood film composers – the Country Gentlemen have recorded for such labels as Folkways, Rebel, Mercury, Starday and Vanguard.

Albums:
Country Songs Old And New (Folkways/–)
Folksongs and Bluegrass (Folkways/–)
Bringing Mary Home (Rebel/–)
Play It Like It Is (Rebel/–)
New Look, New Sound (Rebel/–)
The Award Winning Gentlemen (Rebel/–)
Live At Roanoke (Zap/–)
Sit Down Young Stranger (Sugar Hill/–)

Cousin Jody

James Clell Summey began his career as a straight musician and was one of the fine early practitioners of the dobro. In fact, it was as a member of Roy Acuff's Smoky Mountain Boys that he recorded several of the early Acuff hits, including **Wabash Cannonball** and **The Great Speckled Bird**, and it was he, as well, who first joined the Opry with Acuff in 1938.

He branched out as a musician, playing electric steel (one of the first do do so on the Opry stage) with Pee Wee King's Golden West Cowboys before delving into comedy with Oral Rhodes as Odie and Jody, then joining Lonzo and Oscar for a number of years prior to gaining his own solo Opry spot for over a decade.

Summey was born near Sevierville, Tenessee, on December 14, 1914. Plagued by ill health in his late years, he died of cancer in 1976.

Billy 'Crash' Craddock

Known as 'Mr Country Rock', Craddock was born on June 16, 1939 in Greensboro, North Carolina. Initially part of a group called the Four Rebels, along with his brother Clarence, Billy later signed to Columbia as a solo artist, scoring heavily with a 1959 single, **Don't Destroy Me**, which made a big impression in Australia. He claims he then quit the business because Columbia insisted on casting him in a pop role, while he saw his future in country music.

After taking many menial jobs – for a while working in a cigarette factory – he eventually signed for Ron Chancey's Cartwheel label coming up with a whole string of rock-oriented country hits including **Ain't Nothin' Shakin'**, **Dream Love** and **Knock Three Times**, a revamped version of Dawn's pop hit. Cartwheel was

The Country Sounds Of Billy 'Crash' Craddock, Courtesy MFP Records.

Above: Billy 'Crash' Craddock – he won his nickname because of his football prowess at school.

then absorbed into ABC-Dot and Craddock enjoyed further hits with **Rub It In** (1974), **Easy As Pie** (1976) and **Broken Down In Tiny Pieces** (1977). Since joining Capitol Records in 1978 he has continued with such hits as **I Cheated On A Good Woman's Love** (1978) and **I Just Had You**

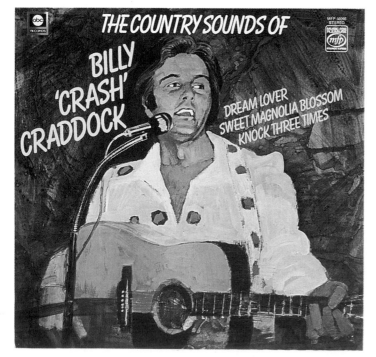

On My Mind (1980). Highly respected for his stunning in-concert antics, which recall the early days of Elvis Presley, he is regarded as one of the most exciting performers in country music.

Albums:
Two Sides Of Crash (ABC/–)
The Country Side Of (–/MFP)
Gratest Hits Vol. 1 (ABC/–)
The New Will Never Wear Off Of You (Capitol/–)
Laughing And Crying (Capitol/–)
Greatest Hits (Capitol/–)

Floyd Cramer

Pianist on a large proportion of Nashville hits during the late '50s – including Elvis Presley's **Heartbreak Hotel** – Cramer was born at Shreveport, Louisiana, on October 27, 1933, and grew up in Huttig, Arkansas, playing his first dates at local dances.

On completing high school in 1951 he returned to Shreveport where he appeared on KWKH's Louisiana Hayride show, played on sessions at the Abbott Record company and fitted in tours with Presley and other major acts.

Following various Nashville session dates, Chet Atkins advised Cramer to become a regular Music City sideman. This he did in 1955, quickly establishing himself as one of the city's most active musicians, helping to create the new Nashville Sound with his distinctive 'slipnote' piano style. He also toured and performed on many radio and TV shows including Grand Old Oprv.

20 Of The Best, Floyd Cramer, Courtesy RCA Records.

Signed to RCA, his first hit record was **Flip, Flop And Bop** in 1958, following this with two self-penned million sellers, **Last Date** (1960) and **On The Rebound** (1961).

Winner of countless polls and awards, Cramer has enjoyed many other high selling discs including **San Antonio Rose** (1961), **Chattanooga Choo Choo**, **Hot Pepper** (1962) and **Stood Up** (1967).

In 1977 Floyd emerged with **Keyboard Kick Band**, an album on which he played no less than eight keyboard instruments including various ARP synthesizers.

Albums:
Super Hits (RCA/–)
Best Of Class Of (RCA/–)
Last Date (RCA/–)
Plays The Big Hits (Camden/–)
In Concert (RCA/–)
Piano Masterpieces (RCA/–)
This Is Floyd (RCA/–)
Keyboard Kick Band (RCA/–)

Hugh Cross

One of country music's earliest professional entertainers was Hugh Cross, born in east Tennessee in 1904. At the age of 16 he joined a medicine show, and by the mid '20s was a popular singer on radio and record. A guitarist, banjoist and songwriter (**Don't Make Me Go To Bed And I'll Bed Good**), he joined the Cumberland Ridge Runners on the National Barn Dance from 1930-3, then struck out on his own again, playing stations in the west, north west and east, including WWVA in Wheeling.

He spent a long tenure on the WLW Boone County Jamboree, teaming there with Shug Fisher for a number of years beginning in 1938, and eventually drifted into announcing and executive capacities.

Rodney Crowell

One of Nashville's most successful contemporary songwriters and producers, Rodney was born on August 7, 1950 in Houston, Texas and moved to Nashville in the early '70s, detmined to become a songwriter. He was signed to Jerry Reed's publishing firm but struggled to make a living. All set to move back to Texas, his luck changed when a chance meeting with Brian Ahern, husband of Emmylou Harris, led to a move to California where he joined Emmylou's Hot Band in 1975.

Rodney worked with Emmylou for just over two years, during which time he wrote several songs like **Bluebird Wine**, **Til I Gain Control Again** and **Leaving**

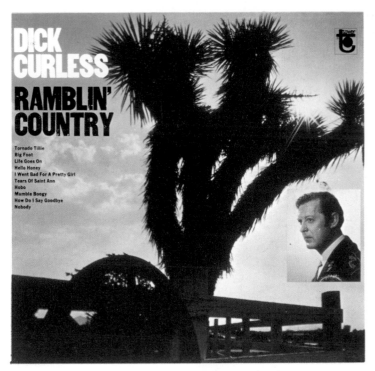

Ramblin' Country, Dick Curless, Courtesy Capitol Records.

Louisiana In The Broad Daylight, which she recorded. He embarked on a solo career towards the end of 1977 coming up with the critically acclaimed **Ain't Living Long Like This** album. In 1979 he married Rosanne Cash (daughter of Johnny) and produced her successsful albums, **Right Or Wrong**, **Seven Year Ache** and **Somewhere In The Stars**.

As a songwriter Crowell has penned hits for Waylon Jennings, Crystal Gayle, The Oak Ridge Boys, Johnny Cash and many others. He has also recorded solo albums for Warner Brothers, which have proved a gold mine for other singers looking for material, but have failed to make Rodney a star in his own right.

Albums:
Ain't Living Long Like This (Warner/ Warner)
Rodney Crowell (Warner/–)
But What Will The Neighbours Think (Warner/–)

The Cumberland Ridge Runners

Hugh Cross, banjo; Karl Davis, mandolin; Red Foley, bass; Doc Hopkins, guitar, vocals; John Lair, leader, announcer, harmonica; Slim Miller, fiddle; Linda Parker, vocals, guitar, banjo, dulcimer; Harty Taylor, guitar.

The Cumberland Ridge Runners were a popular string band brought to the National Barn Dance by John Lair in 1930, and which more or less dissolved in 1935, mainly because Karl and Harty, Doc Hopkins, and especially Red Foley had gone on to stardom in their own right, Hugh Cross had left WLS, and Linda Parker, 'The Sunbonnet Girl', who was the real star of the act, had met an unfortunate early death.

As popular as they were for a time, their place in history is assured far more by their individual members than by the entire band itself.

Dick Curless

Born at Fort Fairfield, Maine, on March 17, 1932, Richard Curless joined a local group, Trail Blazers, soon after leaving high school. In 1948 he gained his own radio show in Ware, Massachusetts, but shortly after his marriage to wife Pauline in 1951 he was drafted into the army and sent to Korea as a performer. There he had his own programme on the Armed Forces Network and achieved great popularity using the guise 'The Rice Paddy Ranger'. Discharged in 1954, Curless returned to his home in Bangor and worked as a vocalist in a local club, but left a year later after a bout of ill health. By 1957, however, he was playing Las Vegas and Hollywood clubs, having won first place on Arthur Godfrey's TV talent show.

Then, once more, he faded from sight, first involving himself in a logging business, later playing small clubs in the Maine area. His luck changed for the better when, in 1965, he recorded **A Tombstone Every Mile** for Allagesh Records. As soon as it began chart climbing, Tower Records a subsidiary of Capitol, bought the master and signed Curless to a contract. Following **Tombstone**, one of 1965's major country hits, Curless then proceeded to provide Tower with ten more high-selling singles before moving on to the parent Capitol label in 1970, scoring once more with songs like **Hard Time Travellin' Man** and **Drag 'Em Off The Interstate Sock It To 'Em J. P. Blues**. During 1966 Curless joined Buck Owens' All-American Music Show, touring for two years, and in 1969 he recorded soundtrack items for the film, 'Killers Three'.

Although he has always been – and still is – a true country singer, Curless, who wears a pirate-like patch over his right eye, has never been a Nashvillite, remaining a resident of the New England area to this very day.

Albums:
Hard Travelling Man (Capitol/–)
Last Blues Song (Capitol/–)
Keep On Truckin' (Capitol/–)
The Great Race (Rocade/–)

Ted Daffan

Born in Beauregard County, Louisiana, on September 21, 1912, singer-songwriter-guitarist Theron Eugene Daffan spent his childhood in Texas, graduating from Houston's Jeff Davis High School in 1930. During the early '30s he led the Blue Islanders, a Hawaiian band, in 1934 moving on to become steel guitarist with the Blue Ridge Playboys, a unit featuring Floyd Tillman on lead guitar. He later worked with the Bar X Cowboys, a Houston band, and after a long stay, formed band of his own. In 1939 he wrote **Truck Driver's Blues**, reputed to be the first trucking song, this being recorded for Decca by Cliff Bruner with Moon Mullican. This became such a high-selling disc that Daffan and his band, The Texans, were signed by Columbia, providing that label with a 1940 hit in **Worried Mind**, which sold 350,000 copies.

The future seemed assured for Daffan but, after cutting some two dozen of his own songs for Columbia (sometimes using the song-writing nom-de-plume of Frankie Brown), World War II intervened and The Texans were forced to disband. Within two years Daffan was recording once more, cutting **No Letter Today** and **Born To Lose**, a double-sided hit that won him a gold disc for a million sale. He also formed a new band to play at the Venice Ballroom, Los Angeles, California, during the mid '40s heading back to Texas to once more organize bands in the Fort Worth-Dallas area. Throughout the '50s many singers recorded Daffan's songs – including Faron Young and Hank Snow, the latter becoming a partner in a Daffan music publishing enterprise in 1958.

By 1961, Daffan was once more a resident of Houston, this time as general manager of a publishing house. And that same year yet another of his compositions ended up on a million selling disc, Joe

Below: Ted Daffan, writer of the first truck-driving hit.

Barry winning an award for his recording of Daffan's **I'm A Fool To Care**, which had been a hit nearly a decade earlier for Les Paul and Mary Ford. Other hits from the prolific Daffan pen include **Blue Steel Blues**, **Heading Down The Wrong Highway**, **I've Got Five Dollars And It's Saturday Night**, and **A Tangled Mind**.

Vernon Dalhart

A seminal figure in country music development, Vernon Dalhart (real name Marion Try Slaughter) was born in Jefferson, Texas, on April 6, 1883, the son of a ranch owner. While a teenager, he and his mother moved to Dallas, where Dalhart obtained a job in a hardware store, later becoming a piano salesman. He also began attending Dallas Conservatory of Music.

Next came a series of jobs in New York, during which time Dalhart sang in churches and vaudeville, auditioning for light opera. In 1912, he obtained a part in Puccini's 'Girl Of The Golden West' and later worked in other similar productions, though his first traceable recording, Edison cylinder **Can't Yo' Heah Me Callin' Caroline**, released June 1917, featured a 'coon' song. Following this came a deluge of Dalhart recordings on various labels, the singer tackling operatic arias, popular songs, patriotic World War I ditties, etc. He recorded mountain musician Henry Whitter's **The Wreck Of The Old '97** for Edison in May 1924, then cut the same song, backed with **The Prisoner's Song**, an adaptation of a traditional folk tune, for Victor, the disc having a November 1924 release. It promptly became a massive hit, encouraging Dalhart to record more hillbilly material, though more often than not he was content to re-record his hits. **The Wreck Of The Old '97**, sung by Dalhart in various guises, appears on more than 50 labels. Meanwhile, Victor sold over six million copies of the original version, making the disc their biggest seller of the pre-electric period.

Above: Lacey J Dalton. She and her Dalton Gang sometimes play tough.

Many of Dalhart's follow-ups, mainly written by Carson J. Robinson, dealt with the subject of disasters or news events – **The Death of Floyd Collins**, **The John T Scopes Trial** – and his records sold well until 1930. But between 1933 and 1938 Dalhart was absent from the recording studio and in 1942, following some unsuccessful 1939 sessions for Bluebird, he took a job as a nightwatchman with a Bridgeport, Connecticut firm, finally becoming a night checkout clerk in a local hotel, shortly before his death.

After a heart attack early in 1948, he suffered yet another and died on September 14, 1948, at Bridgeport Hospital. During his lifetime Dalhart recorded under more than a 100 pseudonyms, made an estimated 5,000 releases and sold around 75 million discs, most of which were country songs, this notable contribution to the history of country music gaining due recognition in 1981 when Dalhart was elected to the Country Music Hall of Fame.

Albums:
Old-Time Songs 1925–39 (Davis Unlimited/–)

Lacy J. Dalton

'A voice so unique it rises above the rest. Lacy J. Dalton possesses that exciting style and quality that makes her special.' So said Billy Sherrill about Lacy J. Dalton shortly before the release of her CBS debut album.

Born in 1948 and raised near Bloomsburg, Pennsylvania, Lacy (real name Jill Byrem) hails from a musical family, her father being a guitarist and mandolinist. At 18 she moved to Los Angeles and, soon after, settled in Santa Cruz where she played the local club circuit for 12 years, at one point becoming lead singer of a psychedelic rock group,

Office, also accruing a hefty catalogue of self-penned songs. After a series of demo discs was recorded, one, **Crazy Blue Eyes**, found its way to CBS who signed Lacy to a contract in May, 1979, and immediately released a Sherrill-embellished version of **Crazy Blue Eyes** which went to the Top 20. Lacy, with her band the Dalton Gang, began a heavy schedule of gigs, sometimes headlining, sometimes opening for such artists as Willie Nelson, Emmylou Harris, Christopher Cross, and the Oak Ridge Boys, her first two albums, **Lacy J. Dalton** and **Hard Times** becoming Top 20 chart items in 1980, that same year providing a haul of hit singles that included **Tennessee Waltz**, **Losing Kind Of Love**, **Hard Times** and **Hillbilly Girl With The Blues**.

A constant Top 20 hit maker since – with **Whisper**, **Takin' It Easy**, **Everybody**

Hard Times, Lacey J Dalton, Courtesy CBS Records.

Makes Mistakes (1981), **Slow Down, 16th Avenue** (1982), **Dream Baby** (1983), **If That Ain't Love** (1984), **You Can't Run Away From Your Heart** (1985) – Lacy J. retains a solid country feel yet still appeals to a rock audience, a fact that should ensure her a long-lasting career.

Albums:
Hard Times (Columbia/CBS)
Takin' It Easy (Columbia/CBS)

Charlie Daniels

Once categorized as a southern boogie band, the Charlie Daniels Band has, over the years, moved further and further into the pure country fold. This was hardly surprising, considering Daniels' history as a bluegrass player and regular Nashville sessionman.

Born in Wilmington, North Carolina, in 1937, the son of a lumberjack, the guitar- and fiddle-playing Daniels spent the years 1958–67 (except for a short period during which he found employment in a Denver junkyard) playing with a band known as The Jaguars. He claims that the band played every honky-tonk, dive and low-life

High Lonesome, Charlie Daniels, Courtesy Epic Records.

joint from Raleigh to Texas – and it was in Texas that Daniels met producer Bob Johnson, who headed him in the direction of Nashville where he became a sessioneer with Flatt and Scruggs, Marty Robbins, Claude King and Peter Seeger, also playing on Ringo Starr's country album and Dylan's **Nashville Skyline**. A classy songwriter – Daniels' songs have been recorded by Elvis Presley, Gary Stewart, Tammy Wynette, etc – he began involving himself more in this area during the early '70s and in 1971 was offered a recording contract. At which point the Charlie Daniels Band came into being.

Full Moon, Charlie Daniels, Courtesy Epic Records.

For four years the band recorded for Kama Sutra, gaining a gold album with **Fire On The Mountain** and hit singles in **Uneasy Rider** (1973) and **The South's Gonna Do It** (1975). During 1974, Daniels began his series of annual Volunteer Jam concerts, featuring some of the biggest names in country and rock, and during the following year did a deal with Epic Records, who signed the CDB to a contract worth a reported three million dollars. The band worked 250 days that year and kept up the rate when Epic put out **Saddle Tramp**, the first album for their new label in 1976 – their chores that year including benefits for presidential candidate Jimmy Carter. By 1986, Daniels was lined-up to appear in a TV movie 'Lone Star Kid', also becoming author of his first book, a series of short stories.

The quality of the albums kept moving up and up – and so did their public acceptance. The high came in 1979 when a multimillion selling **Million Mile Reflections** provided a huge spin-off single in **Devil Went Down To Georgia**, a Top 5 pop chart single that was full of country fiddling, won Daniels a Grammy for Best Country Vocal and also gained him Opry bookings. When the 1979 CMA Awards came around, the CDB won the Single Of The Year and Best Band categories, also retaining the latter title in 1980, the year that the band appeared in the John Travolta movie 'Urban Cowboy'.

Since then Daniels has kept up a heavy road schedule, published a collection of original short stories (entitled 'The Devil Went Down To Georgia' after the 1979 hit), managed to maintain the array of stars at his Volunteer Jams – the 1984 Jam included The Jordanaires, Carl Perkins, Emmylou Harris, Roy Acuff, Boxcar Willie, Crystal Gayle, Exile, Tammy Wynette and many others.

In 1985, **Me And The Boys** was released, the first CDB studio album in over three years.

Albums:
Nightrider (Kama Sutra/Kama Sutra)
Volunteer Jam (Capricorn/Capricorn)
Saddle Tramp (Epic/Epic)
Fire On The Mountain (Epic/Epic)
High And Lonesome (Epic/Epic)
Full Moon (Epic/Epic)

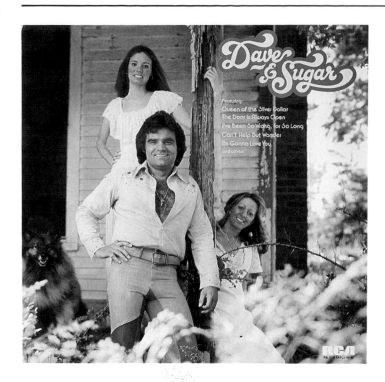

Dave and Sugar

A one man, two girl vocal group, that, in the late '70s, was momentarily hailed as Nashville's answer to Abba. Original members were Dave Rowland, a beefy, soulful singer from LA, Vicki Hackman, from Louisville, Kentucky and Jackie Franc (born in Sidney, Ohio).

Rowland started out as a dance band vocalist, becoming a trumpeter with the 75th Army Band after being drafted. During his tour of duty he became the only serviceman to receive a theatrical scholarship from the Entertainment Division of the Army. Graduating from the Stamps School of Music in Texas he became a member of the Stamps Quartet, toured with Elvis Presley and eventually became a member of The Four Guys. While still a member of the Guys he backed Charley Pride and heard that Pride required a new backup group for vocal harmony work. So Rowland held auditions, signed ex-trumpeter Franc and Hackman (who later married Pride's guitarist) and had the group signed to Chardon, the company that so astutely masterminded Pride's own meteoric rise. The trio had an immediate No. 1 single with **The Door Is Always Open**, in mid-1976, following this with a second chart-topper **I'm Gonna Love You**, just a few months later. Rowland then experienced some changes in partners but the hits — all Top 10s — continued to flow profusely, 1977 bringing **Don't Throw It All Away, That's The Way Love Should Be** and **I'm Knee Deep In Loving You**; 1978 providing **Gotta Quit Lookin' At You Baby** and **Tear Time** (a No. 1); and 1979 supplying **Golden Tears** (yet another No. 1), **Stay With Me** and **My World Begins And Ends With You**, all RCA releases.

By 1980, the group, now labelled Dave Rowland And Sugar, began to slide in terms of record sales with only one single, **New York Wine And Tennessee Shine**, going Top 20. Then followed a label switch, to Elektra, where **Fool By Your Side** (1981) saw the group momentarily back in the Top 10 again, after which they moved on once more, joining MCA Records in 1985.

Dave And Sugar, the group's debut album. Courtesy RCA Records.

Albums:
Dave And Sugar (RCA/RCA)
New York Wine And Tennessee Shine (RCA/RCA)
Stay With Me (RCA/RCA)
Greatest Hits (RCA/–)

Gail Davies

A talented singer-songwriter, Davies was born in Broken Bow, Oklahoma (1948), the daughter of a country musician who kept a home juke-box stacked with classic country singles. When her parents split up, Gail, her mother and her brother Ron relocated in Seattle. A one-time keypunch operator for Westinghouse, quitting after only two weeks, she opted for a singing career, she and her brother forming a Californian-based folk-rock duo and recording an unreleased album for A&M. Ron moved further into the world of rock during the early '70s, recording initially for A&M and writing **Long Hard Climb** (Helen Reddy) and **It Aint Easy** (Three Dog Knight).

Meanwhile, Gail, who had lost her voice and been advised to stop singing for a while, also turned to songwriting and then headed for Nashville, scoring immediately as the writer of **Bucket To The South**, a 1978 Top 20 hit for Ava Barber. That same year Gail herself began logging country hits, signing for the Lifesong label and notching two Top 20 singles in **No Love Have I** and **Poison Love**. In the wake of one further Lifesong hit, **Someone Is Looking For Someone Like You** (1979), came a Warner contract and Top 10 success with **Blue Heartache** (1979) and **I'll Be There If You Ever Want Me** (1980).

After further winners, Gail switched

Below: Gail Davies. In 1986 she became lead singer with a band, Wild Choir.

Where Is A Woman To Go?, Gail Davies, Courtesy RCA Records.

labels once more, signing with RCA and immediately charting high with **Jagged Edge Of A Broken Heart** (1984), a single that had all the hallmarks of a high-grade pop crossover, though one that ultimately did not gain the attention it deserved. Nevertheless, her country chart career continued to prosper and in 1985, the year in which Gail made her debut appearance at Britain's Wembley Festival, she had major hit singles with **Break Away**.

Albums:
What Can I Say? (Warner/–)
Where Is A Woman To Go? (RCA/RCA)

Danny Davis

Davis, real name George Nowlan, was born in Randolph, Massachusetts, on April 29, 1925. He first played trumpet with high school bands during the '30s, paying for his instrument by acting as delivery boy for a Boston fruiterer. At 17 he became a sideman with some of the best bands of the swing era, including those of Gene Krupa, Hal McIntyre and Bob Crosby, also developing a singing style that brought him work with Vincent Lopez, Blue Barron, Sammy Kaye and others. Later, he recorded under his own name, having a hit with **Trumpet Cha Cha Cha**, and in 1958 became a record producer, first with Joy Records, then with MGM, where he helped Connie Francis on her way to several No. 1 singles.

During a trip to Nashville, Davis — who terms himself 'a Yankee Irishman' — met publisher Fred Rose and Chet Atkins and became the latter's production assistant at RCA in 1965. He then conceived the idea of adding a brass sound to a pop-oriented country rhythm section, recording the results under the name The Nashville Brass. The band proved a success right from the first single, **I Saw The Light**, the Nashville-cum-Alpert sound of the Davis outfit appealing to such a cross-section of the public that the band's first 14 albums all sold in excess of 100,000 copies, while such singles as **Wabash Cannonball** and **Columbus Stockade Blues** also made their way into the charts.

By the early '70s, Davis was living in a fabulous ranch house near Nashville, had a stake in several oil wells and a seaside motel and was also the proud owner of a private airliner. For six straight years, from 1969 through to 1974, Davis and The Nashville Brass were voted Instrumental Band of the Year at the CMA Awards Ceremony, Davis also picking up a Grammy in 1969 for his **More Nashville Sounds** album. And although the trumpeter logged few hit singles during the '70s,

record company work. He lived much of his early life in Atlanta, Georgia and after attending high school he worked for the Georgia State Board of Probation. In his spare time he formed a band and toured in the south, playing mainly rock'n'roll. Later he took a job as a Regional Manager (in Atlanta) for Vee-Jay Records, then going to Liberty Records.

In 1968 Lou Rawls recorded one of Davis's songs, **You're Good For Me**, and Elvis Presley recorded his **In The Ghetto**. The latter was a funky departure for Presley at the time and it really brought Davis to prominence. At this point he was writing under non-de-plumes to avoid confusion with lyricist Mack David, although he finally switched back to using his own name.

He wrote some material for Presley's first TV spectacular and also provided some material for such films as 'Norwood', starring Glen Campbell. Additionally, he wrote hits for Kenny Rogers And The First Edition (**Something's Burning**) and Bobby Goldsboro (**Watching Scotty Grow**).

In 1970 he guested on TV shows with Johnny Cash and Glen Campbell and the following year cut a debut album for CBS called **I Believe In Music**, the title track being covered by over 50 artists, the most successful version being that released by Gallery in 1972. That same year Davis came up with the big one, **Baby Don't Get Hooked On Me**, his first US pop chart-topper, following this with such hits as **One Hell Of A Woman, Stop And Smell The Roses** and **Rock'n'Roll (I Gave You The Best Years Of My Life)**, all in 1974. In 1974, too, he began hosting his own TV show.

After this period, the flood of pop chart hits began to ebb but Davis's country audience stayed faithful and he logged four country chart singles in 1975, two in 1976, one in both 1977 and 1978 and, after signing a new deal with Casablanca in 1979, three Top 10 singles, **It's Hard To Be Humble, Let's Keep It That Way** and **Texas In My Rear View Mirror** (all 1980). A brilliant live performer, ever being able to ring the changes – which is why he has been able to command high fees at all the best Las Vegas niteries – Davis has also developed a career as an actor, appearing

Above: Danny Davis, the self-dubbed Yankee Irishman who has become Nashville's answer to Herb Alpert.

by 1980 he was back in the Top 20 once again thanks to **Night Life**, a release culled from the hit album **Danny Davis & Willie Nelson with The Nashville Brass**.

Albums:
Bluegrass (RCA/–)
The Best Of Danny Davis (RCA/RCA)
Moving On (RCA/–)
Danny Davis & Willie Nelson with The
  Nashville Brass (RCA/–)

Jimmie Davis

Elected Governor of Louisiana in both 1944 and 1960, James Houston Davis (born in Quitman, Louisiana, on September 11, 1902) is also an eminently successful recording artist and songwriter, his writing credits including such standards as **You Are My Sunshine, It Makes No Difference Now, Sweethearts Or Strangers** and **Nobody's Darlin' But Mine**.

Gaining a BA at Louisiana College and an MA at Louisiana State University, Davis became a professor of history at Dodd College in the late '20s. During the next decade he forwarded his musical career – recording for RCA, Victor and Decca – at the same time still managing to hold down various positions of public office. A popular performer by the end of the '30s, in 1944 he appeared in the movie 'Louisiana'. When his first term of office as State Governor came to an end in 1948, Davis returned to the entertainment industry once more, concentrating much of his activity within the sphere of gospel music where he won an award as Best Male Sacred Singer in 1957.

In 1960, Davis was asked to run in the primary, proving successful again. He also won against the might of the Huey Long machine in the ensuing election. During this second stint as Governor he had a hit in 1962 **Where The Old Red River Flows**.

Returning to active duty on the recording front in 1964, he provided Decca with an album, **Jimmie Davis Sings**, his other late '60s and early '70s releases including **At The Crossing, Still I Believe, Amazing Grace** and **Christ Is Sunshine**.

In 1972, Davis was elected to the Country Music Hall Of Fame.

Memories Coming Home, Jimmie Davies, Courtesy MCA Records.

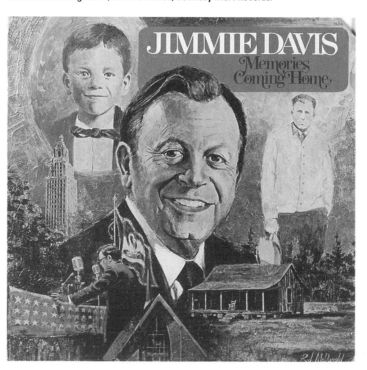

Albums:
Greatest Hits (MCA/–)
You Are My Sunshine (MCA/–)
Christ Is Sunshine (Canaan/Canaan)
Country Side Of Jimmie Davis (MCA/–)
Rockin' Blues (–/Bear Family)

Mac Davis

Born at Lubbock, Texas, on January 21, 1941, Mac Davis's career has taken in rock'n'roll, songwriting, performing and

Song Painter, Mac Davis, Courtesy Columbia Records.

in movies such as 'North Dallas Forty', 'Cheaper To Keep Her' and 'The Sting II'. Glen Campbell once said of him: 'Mac Davis don't write songs, he paints them.' Hence the album title, **Song Painter**.

Albums:
Song Painter (Columbia/CBS)
Its Hard To Be Humble (Casablanca/
  Casablanca)

Skeeter Davis

Suspended by the Opry in December 1973 for criticizing the Nashville Police Department on a WSM broadcast – following a week in which two Opry performers had been murdered and Tom T. Hall's house burned down – Skeeter Davis has always had an eventful career.

She began life (in Dry Ridge, Kentucky, on December 30, 1931) as Mary Frances Penick, the eldest of seven Penick children. At high school, she and her friend Betty Jack Davis (born in Corbin, Kentucky, on March 3, 1932) formed a harmony vocal team, the Davis Sisters, providing local performances that led to a regular programme on radio station WLEX, Lexington, Kentucky. This, in turn, led to other radio shows in Detroit and Cincinnati and, eventually, to a recording contract first with Fortune, then with RCA Victor. In 1953, their first RCA effort, **I Forget More Than You'll Ever Know**, became a No. 1 record, claiming a chart position for 26 weeks – and it appeared that the Davis Sisters were set for a long career. But while travelling to Cincinnati on August 2, 1953, the girls became involved in a car accident which killed Betty Jack and critically injured Skeeter.

It was some considerable time before she resumed work once more but, after a brief spell working as a duo with Betty Jack's sister Georgia, Skeeter began a solo career, her first real breakthrough occurring in 1959 when her recording of **Set Him Free** established her as a chart name. A 1962 release, **The End Of The World**, proved the real clincher, the disc earning Skeeter a gold record and worldwide reputation – and though she asked her agency not to book her into clubs where liquor was being served (Skeeter claimed that she did not want her non-drinking fans drawn into a situation where they might be tempted to imbibe) her bookings became more and more prestigious, a date at New York's Carnegie Hall figuring among them. And her records continued to sell, **I'm Saving My Love** (1963), **Gonna Get Along Without You Now** (1964), **What Does It Take?** (1967) and **I'm A Lover, Not A Fighter** (1969)

She Sings They Play, Skeeter Davis with NRBQ, Courtesy Rounder Records.

proving to be her biggest sellers. Along the way she also recorded two best selling duets with Bobby Bare – **A Dear John Letter** (1965) and **Your Husband, Your Wife** (1971) – and appeared on disc with such artists as Porter Wagoner and George Hamilton IV.

Ever pop-connected – during the 1960s she toured with the Rolling Stones and even in 1985 she did an album with nutty rock outfit NRBQ, one cut proving to be a version of **Someday My Prince Will Come** done in 4/4 time! – Skeeter has often been accused of betraying her country heritage. But she claims: "I've been with the Opry since joining in 1959 – which proves that my heart's in country."

Albums:
The Hillbilly Singer (RCA/RCA)
Bring It On Home (RCA/RCA)
She Sings They Play – with NRBQ (Rounder)
20 Of The Best (–/RCA)
Tunes For Two – with Bobby Bare (RCA/RCA)

Eddie Dean

Born Edgar Dean Glossup in Posey, Texas, July 9, 1907, Eddie began his professional career as a gospel singer with both the James D. Vaughan Quartet and with the V.O. Stamps Quartet. He and his older brother Jimmy appeared both on the WLS National Barn Dance in Chicago and on WNAX, in Yankton, South Dakota, before returning to Chicago, where Jimmy appeared for a year and a half on the CBS radio soap, Modern Cinderella.

Eddie and Jimmy headed west in 1937 to try their luck in films, and both landed jobs with Gene Autry which Eddie left to join Judy Canova's radio show. He appeared in scores of films before finally gaining his own series of 20 films with PRC from 1946 to 1948, in which, incidentally, Lash LaRue got his start.

Eddie's big booming, magnificent voice somehow never seemed to find the right

vehicle for a hit record, though he recorded for a great many labels, including Decca, Majestic, Mercury, Crystal, Sage And Sand, Capitol and Shasta, his biggest singles being **On The Banks Of The Sunny San Juan** (Decca), **No Vacancy** (Majestic), **One Has My Name, The Other Has My Heart** (Crystal) and **I Dreamed Of A Hillbilly Heaven** (Sage And Sand) – the last two being genuine country music classics which he co-wrote.

Resident in California for many years, he has continued playing at various nightspots and festivals from time to time, also cutting a few records.

Albums:
Sincerely Eddie Dean (Shasta/–)
The Great American Singing Cowboys (Republic/London)

Jimmy Dean

The writer and performer of **Big Bad John**, a five million selling disc of semi-recitative nature, Jimmy Dean was born on a farm near Plainview, Texas, on August 10, 1928. He began his musical career at the age of ten, first learning piano and then mastering accordion, guitar and mouth harp. Whilst in the Air Force during the '40s, he joined the Tennessee Haymakers, a country band comprised of service personnel who played off-duty gigs around Washington DC, Dean continuing to play in that area after discharge in 1948.

Impresario Connie B. Gay hired him to perform for US Forces in the Caribbean during 1952 and, following this tour, Dean and his band, the Texas Wildcats, began playing on radio station WARL, Arlington, Virginia, obtaining a hit record on the Four Star label with **Bummin' Around** (1953). By 1957 he had his own CBS-TV network show, a programme which proved popular with everyone except the sponsors, Dean gaining a CBS recording contract that same year. Initially he found hits hard to come by, but in 1961 he wrote **Big Bad John**, a somewhat dramatic tale of

Everybody's Favourite, Jimmy Dean, Courtesy CBS Records.

mineshaft heroism, and then began to supply CBS with a run of Top 20 discs that included **Dear Ivan, Cajun Queen, PT109** (all 1962) and **The First Thing Every Morning**, the latter becoming a country No. 1 in 1965.

A star of ABC-TV during the mid-1960s, Dean switched his record allegiance to RCA in 1966. But though this relationship began encouragingly with **Stand Beside Me**, a Top 10 record, Dean's country pop approach seemed to lose much of its appeal as the '70s drew near – though such releases as **I'm A Swinger** (1967), **A Thing Called Love** (1968), **A Hammer And Nails** (1968) and **Slowly**, a duet with Dottie West (1971), all fared well.

After something of a lull, Dean was back in the Top 10 once more in 1976, with **I.O.U.**, a single which was re-released with some success by the Churchill label in 1983. And though such records proved all too few at the start of the 1980s, Dean, a sausage entrepreneur, was hardly forgotten. On TV he had a syndicated music show, Jimmy Dean's Country Beat, while honours-wise he was still gaining nominations, becoming the 11th inductee into the Texas Hall Of Fame, his presentation being made by Roy Orbison and Buddy Holly's widow.

Albums:
Greatest Hits (Columbia/–)
I.O.U. (GRT/–)

Penny De Haven

From Winchester, Virginia (born on May 17, 1948), Penny De Haven was the first female country star to entertain the armed forces in Vietnam. A frequent Opry guest in the '60s and early '70s, she appeared in three films, 'Valley Of Blood', 'Travelling Light' and 'The Country Music Story' and had a number of minor hits on the Imperial and UA labels, her highest chart placing being gained with **Land Mark Tavern**, a 1970 duet with Del Reeves.

Since that time her name has continued to pop up in the lower reaches of the country charts, De Haven achieving some success with **(The Great American) Classic Cowboy** on the Starcrest label in

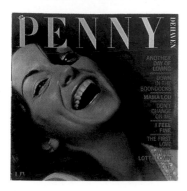

Penny De Haven. An excellent 1972 offering, Courtesy UA Records.

1976, and, more recently, with such Main St releases as **Only The Names Have Been Changed** (1983) and **Friendly Game Of Hearts** (1984).

Album:
Penny De Haven (UA/–)

Delmore Brothers

Longtime Opry favourites and writers of a huge number of songs, including the oft-recorded **Blues Stay Away From Me**, the Delmore Brothers – Alton (born on December 25, 1908) and Rabon (born on December 3, 1910) – both hailed from Elkmont, Alabama. Farm raised, they were taught fiddle by their mother, Aunt Mollie Delmore, in 1930 winning an old-time fiddle contest in Athens, Alabama. Equally adept on guitar, the brothers soon won a contract with Columbia Records, for whom they recorded in 1931. Prior to that date, the duo had never faced a microphone of any kind, the Delmores' first experience of radio coming with a WSM Grand Ole Opry date during 1932. Proving extremely popular, the Delmores enjoyed a tenure of some six years on the show, leaving in 1938.

During the '40s came appearances on scores of radio stations, plus record dates for King, the duo's single of **Blues Stay Away From Me** becoming a Top 5 hit in 1949 and enjoying a chart stay of no less than 23 weeks. While with King, they also recorded with Grandpa Jones and Merle Travis as the Brown's Ferry Four. Soon after, the Delmores became based in Houston, where Alton began drinking heavily due to the death of his daughter Sharon. And Rabon also became seriously ill with lung cancer, returning to Athens, where he died on December 4, 1952.

Alton later moved to Huntsville, where he became a door-to-door salesman and part-time guitar teacher. His death occurred on June 9, 1964, the cause being diagnosed as a haemorrhage brought on by a liver disorder.

The Delmores were posthumously honoured in October 1971, when they became elected to the Songwriters Hall Of Fame. Proficient musicians and precise harmonizers, they brought a new degree of professionalism to the Opry when they joined. Their other hits include: **Brown's Ferry Blues**, **Freight Train Boogie**, **Nashville Blues**, **When It's Time For The Whipoorwill To Sing** and **Gonna Lay Down My Old Guitar**.

Album:
When They Let The Hammer Fall (–/Bear Family)

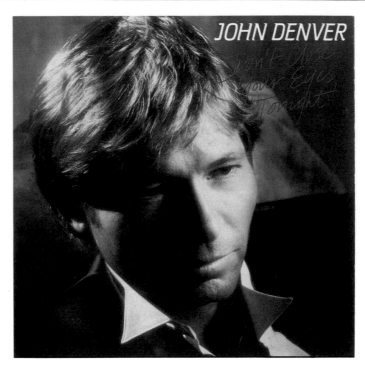

John Denver

The cheerful straw-haired product of the hippie generation, Denver is now one of the biggest draws in showbiz.

Born John Henry Deutschendorf on December 31, 1943, he grew up in an Air Force family and was educated in schools around the USA. His father was a pilot with three world records in military aviation and John also had flying ambitions until the music bug caught him, first via Elvis and rock'n'roll and then through the campus folk music explosion of the '60s. He took guitar lessons early as a boy on an old 1910 Gibson but it was during his time at Texas Tech, where he was majoring in architecture, that he felt he should try for a showbiz career, subsequently playing in west coast clubs and eventually replacing Chad Mitchell in

Rocky Mountain High, John Denver, Courtesy RCA Records.

Don't Close Your Eyes Tonight, a 1985 John Denver single from RCA.

the trio of that name. Four years later, his own solo talents were sufficiently developed for RCA to sign him.

He has never been purely country, although he confesses to country music having been a major influence in his career. His albums tend to contain elements of country, folk, rock and ballads. However, he has written one all-time country standard, **Country Roads**, a lyrical, uplifting song now recorded by countless artists, and he has logged many country chart hits including such No. 1s as **Home Again** (1974), **Thank God I'm A Country Boy** (1975), and **I'm Sorry** (1975).

John Denver's appeal is that of a clean-cut all-American country boy but one who has always been able to appeal to two generations, perhaps enhancing his credit rating with the youth when he spoke against censorship in pop at the 1985 Washington Wives investigation.

Back Home Again, John Denver, Courtesy RCA Records.

Albums:
Back Home Again (RCA/RCA)
Rocky Mountain High (RCA/RCA)

Al Dexter

Born in Jacksonville, Texas, on May 4, 1902, Dexter was the leader of a country outfit known as the Texas Troopers. The singer (real name Albert Poindexter) is best remembered for his self-penned **Pistol Packin' Mama**, a song that provided both he and Bing Crosby with million-selling discs. Based on the story of Mollie Jackson whose family ran an illicit whisky still in Kentucky, the resulting disc brought Dexter a fortune in royalties and made him an overnight star – though he spent much of his later career performing at his own club in Dallas, Texas.

One of the first artists to use the term 'honky tonk' in a song (**Honky Tonk Blues**), Dexter died in Lewisville, Texas, on January 28, 1984. He was a prolific hitmaker in the '40s – apart from **Pistol Packin' Mama**, he will also be remembered for **Too Late To Worry, Too Blue To Cry**, **Rosalita**, **Guitar Polka** and **So Long Pal**, all No. 1 songs in that era.

Album:
Pistol Packin' Mama (Harmony/–)

Below: Al Dexter who, it was claimed, went around in a shirt emblazoned with the words "Al Dexter, Star Of Brunswick Records". Dexter was nominated top artist by the Juke Box Operators back in 1946.

acceptance speech after being elected to the CMA Country Music Hall Of Fame.

Albums:
May The Bird Of Paradise (Columbia/–)
Little Jimmy Dickens Sings (Decca/–)

The Dillards

Initially an ethnically-rated bluegrass band who scored on crossover appeal to a rock audience, Rodney (born on May 18, 1942) and Doug Dillard (born on March 6, 1937) from Salem, Missouri, were the nucleus. They joined up with Mitch Jayne, a local radio announcer, and Dean Webb (from Independence, Missouri) and travelled to California where they were signed by Elektra Records – in the period before Elektra became known as a connoisseur's rock label.

The Dillards came from a strong bluegrass tradition but their novel, lighthearted approach, coupled with the fact that they themselves were a younger group, won them the plaudits of a wide public. They cut their **Back Porch Bluegrass** and **Live! Almost!** albums before meeting fiddler Byron Berline, with whom they made

DeZurich Sisters

Mary and Caroline DeZurich were a popular yodelling team on the WLS National Barn Dance for years, specializing in sky-high Alpine yodels. During their long career they were also known as the Cackle Sisters. Their career lasted from the mid '30s to the early '50s.

Below: Little Jimmy Dickens, with the big stetson, was elected to the Country Music Hall of Fame in 1982.

Above: The yodelling DeZurich Sisters, once stars of WLS.

Little Jimmy Dickens

The provider of **May The Bird Of Paradise Fly Up Your Nose**, a monster crossover hit in 1965, the four foot eleven inch Dickens had, at that time, already been hitmaking for some 16 years.

Born in Bolt, West Virginia, on December 19, 1925, Dickens, the youngest of 13 children, was raised on a ranch, went to a local school and later attended the University of West Virginia. At 17, he won a spot on a Beckley, West Virginia, early morning radio show, moving on to appear on WIBC Indianapolis, WLW Cincinnati and WKNX Saginaw, Michigan, there meeting Roy Acuff, who invited him to appear on a guest spot on the Grand Ole Opry. Two weeks after the date, the Opry management invited Dickens back as a regular.

Signed to Columbia Records in the late '40s, Dickens' first Top 10 disc was **Take An Old Cold Tater And Wait** (1949). This the diminutive showman followed with hits such as **Country Boy**, **Pennies For Papa** (1949), **A-Sleeping At The Foot Of The Bed**, **Hillbilly Fever** (1950), **The Violet And The Rose** (1962) and **May The Bird Of Paradise Fly Up Your Nose** (1965) before label-hopping from Columbia to Decca, UA, Starday, Little Gem and then back to Columbia and UA again, enjoying a number of minor hits along the way, the last being **Try It, You'll Like It** on UA in 1972.

Known affectionately as 'Tater', though he originally worked as Jimmy The Kid, Dickens claims to be the first country artist to circle the globe on a world tour. His TV credits are impressive and include dates on Hullabaloo, The Jimmy Dean Show, Johnny Carson's Tonight programme and Hee Haw. But the biggest night of his life came in 1982, when the little man with the big stetson climbed on stage at the Opry and, with tears in his eyes, made a short

Roots And Branches, The Dillards. Courtesy UA Records.

Pickin' And Fiddlin', an album now much rated and sought after by fans of old-time music. Doug Dillard left to be replaced by Herb Pederson and the Dillards then pursued a more commercial, rock direction. **Wheatstraw Suite** and **Copperfields** are albums from this period and the material took in Tim Hardin's **Reason To Believe** and Lennon-McCartney songs.

After recording albums for the Anthem and Poppy labels, the Dillards – then Rodney (vocals, guitar), Dean Webb (mandolin), Jeff Gilkinson (vocals, bass, cello), Paul York (drums) and Billy Ray Latham (banjo, guitar) – moved on to Flying Fish in 1977 releasing an album titled **The Dillards Vs The Incredible L.A. Time Machine**, which included an LA to Nashville board game ('audition for The Earl Scruggs Revue but your notes are all flat – go back three squares') at centre sleeve.

Since that time Rodney has continued to head the band, cutting such albums as **Decade Waltz** (1979), **Mountain Rock** (on Crystal Clear, 1980) and **Homecoming And Family Reunion** (1980), while Doug, who recorded solo albums in the early '70s, now seems to have opted for a career as a studio musician.

Albums:
Back Porch Bluegrass (Elektra/Elektra)
Pickin' and Fiddlin' (Elektra/Elektra)
Wheatstraw Suite (Elektra/Elektra)

Dottsy

For a while, Dottsy Brodt (born at Seguin, Texas, on April 6, 1953) swept all before her. A talent show winner at 12, by 14 she was a regular on a weekly TV series on a San Antone station. After quitting college in 1972, she was signed by Happy Shahan to play five shows a day at the impresario's Alamo Village, Brackettville, Texas. Later came tours with Johnny Rodriguez, whom Shahan also managed. By 1974 she was in Nashville and signed to RCA. Cute and country, petite and sweet, Dottsy seemed set to become a superstar.

Her first single, **Storms Never Last**, went Top 20 in 1975. Her next, **I'll Be Your San Antone Rose**, climbed even higher. Further major records came with **(After Sweet Memories) Play Born To Lose Again** (1977), **Here In Love** (1978), and **Trying To Satisfy You** (1978), a Waylon Jennings song that had Waylon helping out on the chorus. Then things fell apart. She and RCA parted company. Her name vanished from the charts. During 1981 she turned up on Tanglewood Records and made a bid to get her record career on course again with **Somebody's Darling, Somebody's Wife** and **Let The Little Bird Fly**, both moderately successful singles. But, sadly, the effort was not enough. Dottsy's fans are still waiting for her to come up with another big one.

Albums:
The Sweetest Thing (RCA/RCA)
Tryin' To Satisfy You (RCA/RCA)

Below: Pete Drake in his studio. One of the most outstanding pedal steel men in country music, he was also among the first to play the instrument on rock sessions.

Pete Drake

Session man supreme, producer, owner of a studio and part-owner of a record company and music publishing firm, Pete Drake has played with everyone, from Jim Reeves to Bob Dylan, George Harrison, and Ringo Starr. Born in Atlanta, Georgia, on October 8, 1932, Drake did not take up guitar until 1951 but rapidly became so proficient on the instrument that, within a year, he was leading his own band, The Sons of the South.

After playing on radio station WLWA, Atlanta and WTJH, East Point, Georgia, he worked with Wilma Lee and Stoney Cooper, moving to Nashville with the duo in 1959.

He claims that he "starved for a year and a half" before catching the ears of Roy Drusky and George Hamilton IV, who both asked him to play on their sessions the following week – after which he did 24 sessions in the next month and quickly became one of the most sought after sessioneers in Nashville, at one point appearing on 59 of the 75 records listed in the Billboard country singles charts. Drake also began cutting solo discs, his 1964 **Forever**, on the Smash label, becoming a Top 30 pop hit.

Recordings bearing Drake's name as an artist have also appeared on such labels as Starday, Stop, Hillside, Cumberland and Canaan, while he can be heard playing on the soundtracks of several Elvis Presley movies.

As a producer, he is particularly proud of his **Amazing Grace** album for B. J. Thomas, a Grammy and Dove Award winner in 1982; as a music publisher he is equally proud of backing Linda Hargrove, a no-hoper in the eyes of some Nashville publishers, but one who was named Writer Of The Year for providing Olivia Newton-John with **Let It Shine**.

Steel Away, Pete Drake. Courtesy Canaan Records.

Albums:
Forever (Smash/–)
Talking Steel Guitar (Smash/–)

Jimmie Driftwood

Singer-guitarist-fiddler-banjoist Driftwood (real name James Morris) was born in Mountain View, Arkansas, on June 20, 1917, and grew up in the Ozark Mountains, where he learnt the songs and traditions of the early settlers. During high school he played at local dances continuing his role as a part-time musician and collector of folklore even after qualifying to become a teacher.

During the '50s he began performing at various festivals and concerts and in 1958 signed for RCA producing an album entitled **Newly Discovered Early Folk Songs**.

One song from the album, a revamped version of an old fiddle tune, **The 8th Of January**, recorded under the title of **The Battle Of New Orleans**, became a hit

Songs Of Billy Yank and Johnny Reb, Jimmie Driftwood. Courtesy RCA Records.

single for Johnny Horton during 1959, and was covered in Britain by skiffle star Lonnie Donegan. Other Driftwood songs, including **Sal's Got A Sugar Lip** and **Soldier's Joy**, also came into popular use. Another song, entitled **Tennessee Stud**, provided Eddy Arnold with a big hit which stayed for 20-weeks in the 1959 charts.

Driftwood ceased recording in 1966 but still managed to devote much of his time to the cause of folk music, helping to run the Rackensack Folklore Society and assisting with some folk festivals. His **The Battle Of New Orleans** continues to be a much recorded number, Harpers Bizarre charting with the song yet again in 1968. The song proved popular again in 1975 with The Nitty Gritty Dirt Band and Buck Owens both cutting versions.

As well as being heavily involved in American folklore since he was brought up amongst a wealth of old American traditions in The Ozark Mountains, Driftwood has gained a great deal of inspiration from the American Civil War.

Album:
Famous Country Music Makers (–/RCA)

Roy Drusky

Born in Atlanta, Georgia, on June 22, 1930, Roy Frank Drusky did not acquire an interest in country music until the late '40s, when he signed for a two-year term in the navy. While on ship, he met some C&W fans who had organized their own band – at which point Drusky bought a guitar and taught himself to play. Upon return to civilian life, he initially tried for a degree in veterinary medicine at Emory University. Then in 1951 he formed a band, the Southern Ranch Boys, who played a daily show on a Decatur radio station where Drusky subsequently became a DJ. Next came a three-year residency as a vocalist at a local venue, during which time Drusky, a one-time star athlete, made his TV debut and signed for Starday Records.

Following a later DJ stint on KEVE, Minneapolis, he took over another residency, this time at the city's Flame Club, where he began writing more of his own songs. These he began recording with Decca, one – **Alone With You** – being covered by Faron Young providing the Shreveport singer with a hit. However, after a move to Nashville, the Drusky hitmaking machine really went into action, his first solo successes coming with **Another** and **Anymore** in 1960, followed by five more winners before the singer opted for a switch to the Mercury label in 1963. With Mercury he maintained his supply of

Above: Roy Drusky, the Perry Como of country music.

chart records right through to the early '70s, **Peel Me A Nanner** (1963), **From Now On All My Friends Are Going To Be Strangers** (1965), **Yes, Mr Peters** (a duet with Priscilla Mitchell that went to No. 1 in 1965), **The World Is Round**, **If The Whole World Stopped Lovin'** (both 1966) **Where The Blue And The Lonely Go**, **Such A Fool** (both 1969), and **I'll Make Amends**, **Long Texas Road** and **All The Hard Times** (all 1970), being Top 10 entries.

Also during this period, Drusky appeared in two country movies – 'The Golden Guitar' and 'Forty Acres Feud' – enjoying disc success with **White Lightning Express** the title song of another.

In 1974, Drusky, still a consistent, if lower level hitmaker, changed labels yet again – this time joining Capitol. But after a brace of minor successes, he decided to label-hop to Scorpion, supplying two more mini-hits in **Night Flying** and **Betty's Song** (both 1977). Since that time, however, Drusky's name has been sadly absent from the charts, though, as the Como-like, smooth-voiced singer proved during his Wembley Festival visits to the UK of the early 1980s, he remains very much a crowd-pleaser.

Albums:
All My Hard Times (Mercury/–)
Country Special (Mercury/–)

Dave Dudley

One of the several country stars who could have made the grade in baseball, Dudley (born in Spencer, Wisconsin, on May 3, 1928) gained his first radio date after receiving an arm injury playing for the Gainsville Owls, Texas. While recuperating, he stopped by radio station WTWT and began playing along with the DJ's choice of discs. It was then suggested that he should sing live, which he did, obtaining a positive reaction from listeners. Following stints on stations in the Idaho region during 1951–52, Dudley moved on to lead a couple of small groups, his career taking a setback in the early '60s when he was hit by a car while packing away his guitar after a late night gig – after which he spent several months in hospital. However, record-wise this period proved kind to the near-rockabilly performer, hits coming on such labels as Vee, Jubilee and Golden Wing, the most important of these being **Six Days On The Road**, a release reputed to have commenced the whole modern truck song cycle.

In 1964 came a contract with Mercury Records and four Top 10 discs in **Last Day in The Mines** (1963), **Mad** (1964), **What**

Dave Dudley Sings, Courtesy Mercury Records.

We're Fighting For and **Truck Drivin' Son-Of-A-Gun** (both 1965), the Nashville local branch of the truckers' union providing Dudley with a solid gold security card in appreciation of his musical efforts on behalf of their chosen profession. With his band, The Roadrunners, he has since

continued on his truckstop way, switching labels and moving from Mercury to Rice, UA and Sun, providing each of them with hits of various sizes, including **The Pool Shark** (a No. 1 in 1970 and just one of the 25 major successes he had with Mercury until quitting the label in 1973), **Fireball Rolled A Seven** and **Me And Ole CB** (both 1975), **One A.M. Alone** (1978) and **Rolaids, Doan's Pills And Preparation H** (1980).

Album:
Truck Songs (–/Mercury)

Duke of Paducah

A homespun comedian, always ready to close his routine with a rousing banjo solo, Benjamin Francis 'Whitey' Ford was born in DeSoto, Missouri, on May 12, 1901.

Brought up by his grandmother in Littlerock, Arkansas, he joined the navy in 1918, learning banjo while at sea. During the '20s he toured with his own Dixieland band then, after some time in vaudeville and a stay with Otto Gray's Oklahoma Cowboys, he became MC on Gene Autry's WLS Chicago show, acquiring the title the Duke of Paducah during this period. Next came an opportunity to host and script NBC's Plantation Party on WLW Cincinnati. In 1937 he, John Lair, Red Foley and Red's brother Cotton Foley, founded the Renfro Valley Barn Dance. In 1942 the comedian began a tour of various service installations, playing to the forces.

Following this tour, Ford gained his first date on the Grand Ole Opry, creating such an impression that he remained a member until 1959, thereafter becoming a constant visitor to the show. A former regular member of the Hank Williams Jr Road Show and a performer on countless TV shows originating out of Nashville, Ford, with his famous wind-up line – "I'm going to the wagon, these shoes are killin' me" – toured for many years, often providing a serious lecture, 'You Can Lead A Happy Life', at colleges, sales functions and various conventions. His films include 'Country Farm' and 'Country Music On Broadway'.

Below: Whitey Ford, The Duke of Paducah also known as 'Mr Talent', who, after a fight against cancer, died in Nashville on June 20, 1986.

Johnny Duncan

Born on a farm near Dublin, Texas, on October 5, 1938, Johnny Duncan came from a music-loving family, his mother Minnie being able to both play and teach guitar. At first, Duncan thought of himself as an instrumentalist and Chet Atkins, Les Paul and Merle Travis were his idols. Then during his mid-teens, he realized that his singing ability was an equal asset. After attending high school in Dublin, he went on for a stay at Texas Christian University, meeting and marrying his wife Betty during this period. Shortly after their marriage, in 1959, the Duncans moved to Clovis, New Mexico, where John joined forces with Buddy Holly and producer Norman Petty with whom he worked for the next three years. Then in 1964, following a spell as a DJ in the south west, he headed for Nashville, where he applied his talents to a number of menial jobs – including a stint at bricklaying – while waiting to break into the music industry. After an appearance on WSM-TV Nashville, Don Law of Columbia Records signed Duncan, lining him up first with producer Frank Jones then, after 1970, with Bobby Goldsboro and Bob Montgomery.

His first hit came in 1967 with the release of **Hard Luck Joe**, after which Duncan, who for a while became a regular part of the Charley Pride, began slotting two or three records into the country charts, going Top 10 with **Sweet Country Woman** (1973) and achieving

Australia, in June, 1927, has sold more locally made records in his own land than any other artist. A champion of frontier ballads and music of the bush country, he has fought for survival since the beginning of his career.

A songwriter at the age of 12, he first recorded for EMI in late 1946, two songs from those sessions, **When The Rain Tumbles Down In July** and **My Faded World**, becoming the biggest-selling Australian records made up to that time. He rose to worldwide prominence, however, with **A Pub With No Beer** (1958) and its sequel **Answer To The Pub With No Beer** (1958), both of which were awarded with the first gold records ever presented in Australia.

Made an MBE in 1970 he continued winning both fans and polls, claiming the Most Popular Australian Country Artist award in 1976, 1977 and 1978. And as the '80s moved in, Dusty continued his hitmaking ways, fashioning a No. 1 single, **Duncan**, to begin the new decade.

Album:
No. 50 – The Golden Anniversary Album (EMI Australia/–)

Tommy Duncan

Although best known – and deservedly so – as Bob Wills' longtime lead singer, Tommy Duncan also had a long and significant solo career. Born January 11, 1911, in Hillsboro, Texas, he was steeped in the music of Jimmie Rodgers and loved

both 'hillbilly' and the blues when he joined the Light Crust Doughboys in 1932. When their fiddler, Wills, split from the Doughboys, Duncan joined him in the newly formed Playboys, soon known as the Texas Playboys.

Duncan's years with Wills were great for both, his mellow, bluesy, high baritone appearing on hundreds of records, including **New San Antonio Rose**, the biggest of them all. He struck out on a career of his own in 1948 (taking a number of Texas Playboys with him) and though many of his Capitol recordings were worthy enough, it was generally considered that neither Wills nor Duncan were as great apart as they had been together. He spent many years touring with his new band, the Western All Stars, but it was to everyone's delight when he and Bob Wills joined forces once more for a series of albums for Liberty in the '60s.

Although not to the inspired greatness of the '30s and '40s, these albums are tributes to the genius of two of country music's greats and now form part of the legacy of Duncan, who died from a heart attack on July 25, 1967.

Album:
Hall Of Fame – Bob Wills And Tommy Duncan (UA/–)

Eagles

The Eagles is a now defunct west coast country and soft rock band which featured lucid, flowing instrumental work and

exquisite rough harmonies. They followed on from the Byrds and the Flying Burrito Brothers in helping bring a dash of country to acid heads and rock fans.

Founded by Randy Meisner (ex-Poco and Rick Nelson's Stone Canyon Band), Bernie Leadon (ex-Linda Ronstadt, Dillard & Clark and Flying Burrito Brothers), Glenn Frey (ex-Linda Ronstadt and John David Souther) and Don Henley (ex-Shiloh), they emanated from the ethnically loose musical scene in Los Angeles but cut their first album in England under Rolling Stones' producer Glyn Johns. Later personnel changes saw guitarist and slide guitarist Don Felder boosting the line-up and Joe Walsh joining in place of Bernie Leadon.

The Eagles scored a No. 1 single in the US with the memorable **The Best Of My Love**, and subsequent singles, **Lyin' Eyes** and **One Of These Nights**, notched up hit status in Britain.

In 1980 they disbanded to pursue solo careers, but many of their best known songs have since been recorded by a number of established country acts. These include Conway Twitty, Tanya Tucker and Nat Stuckey.

Albums:
Eagles (Asylum/Asylum)
Desperado (Asylum/Asylum)
On The Border (Asylum/Asylum)
One Of These Nights (Asylum/Asylum)
Hotel California (Asylum/Asylum)
Their Greatest Hits (Asylum/Asylum)

One Of These Nights, The Eagles, Courtesy WEA Records.

Greatest Hits, Johnny Duncan. Courtesy CBS Records.

No. 1s with **Thinking Of A Rendezvous** (1976), **It Couldn't Have Been Any Better** (1978), several of his most successful records featuring vocal assistance from Janie Fricke. It seemed that Duncan would have no difficulty extending his run of hits well into the '80s, but in the wake of an ill-titled and ill-received album, **The Best Is Yet To Come**, the Texan's luck ran out and the hits inexplicably began to dry up. In 1986 he turned up on the Indie Pharoah label.

Albums:
Johnny One Time (Columbia/–)
There's Something About A Lady (Columbia/–)
The Best Of Johnny Duncan (Columbia/–)
Johnny Duncan (–/CBS)

Slim Dusty

Australia's top-ranking country singer for four decades, Slim Dusty, born David Gordon Kirkpatrick in Kempsey, NSW,

Above: This is the Leadon, Frey, Henley, Meisner, Felder, Eagles line-up of 1974.

Steve Earle

A young country-rockabilly singer from San Antonio, Texas, Steve has built up a cult following since his first single, **Nothin' But You**, on Epic Records hit the country charts in October, 1983.

He moved to Nashville from Texas in 1974 and almost immediately landed a job as an 'extra' in the Robert Altman film 'Nashville'. For the next few years he performed in local Nashville bars, linking up with other singer-writers like Guy and Susanna Clark, Rodney Crowell and Townes Van Zandt.

In 1980, Steve relocated to Mexico for a while, then returned to San Antonio where he picked up a couple of musicians and took to the road as Steve Earle & The Dukes. A move back to Nashville in 1981 led to him being signed as a writer by Pat Carter and Roy Dea, and also being asked to run their music publishing company in Music Row. This enabled him to cut demos of his songs and, using his two-piece back-up group, he recorded a four-song EP which perfectly captured all the excitement of 1950s rockabilly with a definite contemporary feel.

Consequently, Steve was offered a recording contract by Epic Records in early 1983, and came up with a few minor hits. At this time he also wrote songs which were subsequently recorded by Johnny Cash, Waylon Jennings and several other country stars.

A move to MCA Records at the beginning of 1986 resulted in the acclaimed **Guitar Town** album, one of the most exciting records by a new Nashville-based artist in years.

Album:
Guitar Town (MCA/–)

Below: Connie Eaton was suspended from a Nashville college for leaving her dorm after hours.

Connie Eaton

A recording artist with Chart, GRC, Stax and ABC, Connie is the daughter of Bob Eaton, a one time Opry artist best known for his 1950 hit **Second Hand Heart**, and was born that same year on March 1, in Nashville, Tennessee. Following an acting award in 1968, she met Chart Records' A&R man Cliff Williamson (whom she later married) and began appearing on TV talent shows, winning £1,000 and a trophy on one major programme and beating The Carpenters in the process. In 1970 Connie was voted Most Promising Female Artist by both Cashbox and Record World magazines, also having a fair-sized record hit that year with her version of **Angel Of The Morning**. After providing several other minor hits (including two duets with Dave Peel) for Chart, Connie moved on briefly to GRC and Stax before signing to ABC in 1974 and having her most successful release in **Lonely Men, Lonely Women**, a Top 20 single in the spring of '75. An album, **Connie Eaton**, was released later that year but has since been deleted.

Stoney Edwards

Stoney, a soulful black country singer of Afro-Indian parents, was born on December 24, 1937 in Oklahoma, and grew up listening to the country sounds of Hank Williams and Lefty Frizzell, as depicted in his 1973 hit, **Hank And Lefty Raised My Country Soul**.

Life was hard for Stoney who worked as a farm hand, truck driver, janitor, crane operator and dock worker before becoming a singer in small Texas clubs and finally in Oakland, California, where he made a minor breakthrough in 1970 when he signed with Capitol Records.

For the next decade or so, Stoney built up a cult following with his traditionally styled honky tonk sound that was firmly rooted in the 1950s. He scored minor country hits with **Poor Folks Stick Together** (1971), **She's My Rock** (1972),

Mississippi You're On My Mind (1975) and Blackbird (Hold Your Head High) (1976). In his own modest way, he paved the way for the acceptance in the 1980s of similarly styled singers like Con Hunley, John Anderson and John Conlee, but sadly Stoney has never really achieved the success he deserved. He was dropped by Capitol in 1977 and has since recorded for JMI Records and Music America and tours regularly, mainly in the southern states, especially Texas, where he is something of a country hero.

Albums:
Mississippi You're On My Mind (Capitol/–)
Down Home In The Country (Capitol/–)

Rambling Jack Elliott

Born in Brooklyn, New York, on August 1, 1931, Rambling Jack became known as an individualistic, bohemian, folk singer – a travelling troubadour of the great outdoors and particularly the western states. Although born in New York he is widely believed to be from a rural background. He has in fact frequently wisecracked about being 'born on a 40,000 acre ranch in Brooklyn'.

Elliott flunked out of college to live in Greenwich Village and it was there that he met Woody Guthrie, a friendship that was to prove fruitful in getting him accepted as a performer. He was well received in Europe and enjoyed TV exposure and successful club bookings. In New York he also began to find popular success in Greenwich Village. He played the Newport Folk Festival in 1963, and continues to play colleges, coffee houses and folk festivals.

Albums:
Country Style (Prestige/–)
Ramblin' (Prestige/–)
Talkin' Woody Guthrie (Delmark/Topic)
Essential Ramblin' Jack Elliott (Vanguard/–)
Muleskinner (–/Topic)

Young Brigham, Ramblin' Jack Elliott. Courtesy WEA Records.

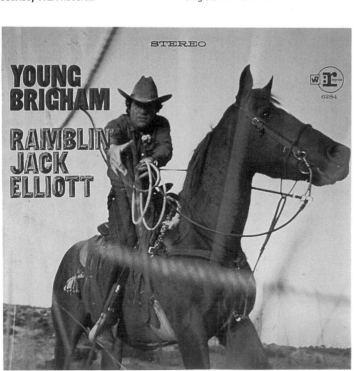

Joe Ely

One of the most promising new singers to emerge from Texas in the late 1970s, Ely, born February 9, 1947, has never matched his cult following and rave reviews with commercial success.

Raised in Lubbock, a stone's throw away from where Buddy Holly lived, Joe never finished school, but instead hit the road playing bars and cafes, jamming with the likes of Johnny Winter. For a time he joined a theatre company and ended up on a European tour playing the arts circuit including shows in London and Edinburgh.

On his return to Texas in the early '70s, Joe teamed up with Butch Hancock and Jimmy Dale Gilmore to form The Flatlanders, an acoustic country group. They played throughout the South, and in 1972 the trio recorded an album for Shelby Singleton in Nashville. The record was not

Live Shots, Joe Ely. Recorded live in Britain. Courtesy MCA Records.

released at the time, though it did surface in the late '70s when Joe was beginning to make a name for himself with his rockin' honky tonk music.

A move back to Lubbock in 1974 led to Joe forming a new band, an electric country-rock outfit designed to play up-tempo honky tonk music for dancing audiences. A regular gig at The Cotton Club, a large honky tonk on the outskirts of Lubbock, led to the Joe Ely Band gaining record company interest. An album cut at Chip Young's studio in Murfreesboro, Tennessee was released by MCA in 1977, and **Joe Ely** gained widespread critical acclaim but minimal sales.

Further albums like **Honky Tonk Masquerade** and **Down On The Drag** showed that the first album was no fluke. Each one was a mind-blowing celebration of Texas honky tonk music, mixing rock sounds with the traditional to bring it slap-bang up-to-date. Ely and band proved to be a very popular live act in Texas and also Europe, where they toured several times in the late '70s and early '80s.

Songs like the reflective **She Never Spoke Spanish To Me**, the rocking **Fingernails** and the wry **Tennessee Is Not The State I'm In**, were just three numbers that should have become big hits for Ely, but his high-energy presentation fell in the no-man's land between country and rock radio formats, which meant his records did not get the American radio exposure they both needed and deserved.

Albums:
Joe Ely (MCA/MCA)
Honky Tonk Masquerade (MCA/MCA)
Hi-Res (MCA/MCA)
Flatlanders – One Road More (–/Charly)

Buddy Emmons

A multi-instrumentalist of exceptional ability – he is a first class pianist, an able bass player and not a bad singer, either – Emmons is generally considered in terms of his brilliantly inventive steel guitar work.

Born in Mishawaka, Indiana, on January 27, 1937, he was given a six-string 'lap' guitar at the age of 11 and subsequently studied at the Hawaiian Conservatory of Music, South Bend, Indiana. At 16 he appeared in Calumet City, Illinois, playing around the local clubs for most nights of the week and jamming in Chicago at weekends. By 1955 he had moved on to Detroit where, after deputizing for steelman Walter Haynes at a Little Jimmy Dickens gig, Emmons was awarded a permanent position with Dickens' band, which, in turn, led to dates on the Opry.

Steel Guitar, Buddy Emmons. Courtesy Flying Fish Records.

During the years that followed came lengthy stints with Ernest Tubb and Ray Price, also the founding of the Sho-Bud company, he and his then partner Shot Jackson marketing the first steel guitar with push-rod pedals. In 1969 Emmons left Nashville, joined Roger Miller as a bassist and became based in LA, playing west coast sessions with Ray Charles, Linda Ronstadt, Henry Mancini and many others between tours with Miller.

When he and the King Of The Road parted company in December '73, Emmons returned to Nashville once more and since that time has involved himself in an incredible amount of session work, also spending some time in promoting his own Emmons Guitar Company, his association with Sho-Bud having terminated some years before.

Albums:
Sings Bob Wills (Flying Fish/Sonet)
Steel Guitar (Flying Fish/Sonet)
Buddies – with Buddy Spicher (Flying Fish/Sonet)
Minors Aloud – with Lenny Breau (Flying Fish/Sonet)

Dale Evans

Wife of singing cowboy superstar Roy Rogers, Dale was born Frances Smith, at Ulvalda, Texas, on October 31, 1912.

Brought up in Texas and Arkansas, attending high school in the latter state, Dale married Thomas Fox in 1928, she and her husband parting two years later – at which time she began concentrating upon a career as a popular vocalist.

During the '30s she became a band singer with the Anson Weeks Orchestra, then became resident vocalist on the CBS News And Rhythm Show. Following many appearances on major radio shows, including a stay on the Edgar Bergen/Charlie McCarthy Show, Dale moved into films, appearing in such productions as 'Orchestra Wives' (1942), 'Swing Your Partner' (1943), 'Casanova In Burlesque'

In The Sweet By And By, Roy Rogers and Dale Evans. Courtesy Word.

(1944), 'Utah' (1945), 'Bells Of Rosarita' (1945), 'My Pal Trigger' (1946), 'Apache Pass' (1947), 'Slippy McGee' (1948), 'Susanna Pass' (1949), 'Twilight In The Sierras' (1950), 'Pals Of The Golden West' (1951), etc, many of these movies starring Roy Rogers, whom she married in 1947.

With Rogers, she has recorded a number of albums for such labels as RCA, Capitol and Word, some of these being in gospel vein, and is also the author of an armful of small books of an inspirational/ religious nature.

Albums: (with Roy Rogers)
In The Sweet Bye And Bye (Word/Word)
The Good Life (Word/Word)
The Bible Tells Me So (Capitol/–)

Leon Everette

In the space of a few short years, Leon Everette, born in South Carolina but raised in the Queens district of New York, has emerged as one of the most exciting and successful new names on the country scene. However, the transition from obscurity to overnight fame was not easy for the rugged, good-looking performer.

Rejection by the major labels in Nashville led to some frustrating years with small independent labels like Doral Records and True Records, and finally the formation of Orlando Records, a company organized with the sole intention of establishing Leon as a major name in country music.

Carroll Fulmer, a Florida businessman, financed Orlando Records in the spring of 1978 and subsequent extensive recording sessions in Nashville were produced jointly by Jerry Foster, Bill Rice (the famed songwriting team), Ronnie Dean and Leon himself. The first two singles, **We Let Love Fade Away** and **Giving Up Easy**, failed to make much impression, but the third release, **Don't Feel Like The Lone Ranger**, made the country Top 40 in the summer of 1979.

Further hits on Orlando including **I Love**

That Woman (Like The Devil Loves Sin), I Don't Want To Lose and Over You, the latter his first entry into the Top 10, led to interest from major labels and in October 1980 Everette signed with RCA Records and was given the creative freedom and control of his own recordings.

He soon proved that RCA's faith in him was justified with such Top 5 country hits as **Giving Up Easy**, **If I Keep On Going Crazy**, **Hurricane** and **Don't Be Angry**. With his own five-piece band, initially called Tender Loving Care but changed to Hurricane in 1981, Leon has also made an impact as a dynamic stage performer with a fast moving act that has gained rave reviews and praise from fellow performers like Hank Williams Jr and Waylon Jennings.

Though he continued to chalk up Top 10 hits for RCA with **Soul Searchin'**, **Give Me What You Think Is Fair** and **Midnight Rodeo**, Leon was not entirely happy with the promotion he was receiving from the label and at the end of 1984 he changed

This Is Leon Everette. A British compilation. Courtesy RCA Records.

labels and signed with Mercury Records.

Bill Rice (now parted from Jerry Foster) was engaged as producer and gave Everette a contemporary country styling that resulted in such hit singles as **Feels Like Forever**, **Too Good To Say No To** and **'Til A Tear Becomes A Rose**.

Albums:
This Is Leon Everette (–/RCA)
Where's The Fire? (Mercury/–)

Everly Brothers

A mid-'50s teen heart-throb duo, the Everly Brothers came from a solid country music background, made rock 'n' roll history and then returned to country.

Born in Brownie, Kentucky, Don in 1937 and Phil in 1939, they were the sons of Ike and Margaret Everly, well known local country stars (Ike was an influential guitar player). Early on the boys were joining their parents on tour and their first radio appearance with the show was on KMA, Shenendoah, Iowa.

After high school, Don and Phil branched out on their own and in 1957 they procured a record contract with Cadence. They had previously made one unsuccessful Columbia single. At Acuff-Rose music publishers they were introduced to Felice and Boudleaux Bryant, the result of this liaison being their first hit, **Bye Bye Love**. The Everlys' sound was characterized by harmony singing which contrived to be velvety and whining at the same time, and which was matched with pounding, open-chord guitars and songs which perfectly caught the era's mood of teenage frustration. In no time at all they were causing riots at theatres, yet they were also acceptable to adults because of their evidently modest demeanor and clean-cut looks.

Bye Bye Love was a huge international hit for them, topping pop and country charts in America and becoming the most hummed international hit that year. With rock 'n' roll losing some of its early steam the time was exactly right for this distinctive and poignant teen sound. Subsequent hits included **Wake Up Little Susie**, **Bird Dog**, **Claudette** and **All I Have To Do Is Dream**, all huge sellers and the last-named making No. 1 in the American and British pop charts.

In 1960 they left Cadence for Warner Bros, thus losing the Nashville production team (which had included Chet Atkins) and the Bryant songwriting team. However, the self-composed **Cathy's Clown** was an immediate hit for them and

The Everly Brothers Sing Great Country Hits. Courtesy WEA Records.

they followed up with **Ebony Eyes** and **Walk Right Back**. After a spell in the Marines they managed an excellent 1965 hit with **Price Of Love** but it was to be their last really big pop winner. Don had suffered a nervous breakdown on their 1963 tour of England and gradually the brothers began to go their separate ways.

They returned to their country roots with the albums **Great Country Hits**, **Roots** and **Pass The Chicken And Listen**, the latter album, recorded in Nashville in 1972, reuniting them with producer Chet Atkins. Shortly after this Don and Phil split to pursue solo careers, Don based in

Pass The Chicken, The Everly Brothers. Courtesy RCA Records.

Nashville and Phil in Los Angeles. Apart from a few spasmodic successes, they never really made a big impression as solo artists. In 1983 they reunited for what was to be a one-off concert appearance at London's Royal Albert Hall. It was such a huge success that the following year they undertook a world-wide tour, signed a new recording contract with Phonogram and had a hit with the Paul McCartney-penned **On The Wings Of A Nightingale**.

Albums:
Born Yesterday (Mercury/Mercury)
1984 (Mercury/Mercury)
In The Studio (–/Ace)
Very Best Of The Everly Brothers (Warner/ Warner)
Pure Harmony (–/Ace)
Great Country Hits (Warner/Warner)
Stories We Could Tell (RCA/RCA)
Pass The Chicken And Listen (RCA/RCA)

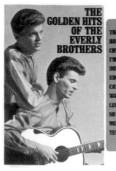

Golden Hits, The Everly Brothers. Courtesy WEA Records.

Don Everly solo:
Brother Jukebox (Hickory/DJM)
Sunset Towers (Ode/A&M)

Phil Everly solo:
Phil's Diner (Pye/Pye)
Star Spangled Springer (RCA/RCA)
Phil Everly (–/Capitol)

Exile

Steve Goetzman, drums; Marlon Hargis, keyboards; Sonny Le Mairne, bass, vocals; J. P. Pennington guitar, vocals; Les Taylor, guitar, vocals.

This spirited five-piece band silenced any arguments about its rock 'n' roll origins with a string of No. 1 country singles throughout 1985 and 1986 and rivalled Alabama as the top country band of the mid '80s.

Originally a pop group who scored with the chart-topping **Kiss You All Over** in 1978, Exile made their initial impact as a country group with **High Cost Of Leaving**, a country Top 10 entry in August 1983. Previously J. P. Pennington and Sonny Le Maire had made an impression as songwriters when Alabama, Kenny Rogers, Dave & Sugar, Janie Fricke and Bill Anderson all recorded their songs in a country setting.

Hang On To Your Heart, Exile. Courtesy Epic Records.

After their demise from the pop charts, they moved naturally towards country, as the group who were at that time based in Lexington, Kentucky had often played on country sessions long before they made it as a pop attraction. J. P. Pennington had a further connection with country music in his aunt, Lila May Ledford, who was one of the Coon Creek Girls.

Signed to Epic Records in Nashville, where the new band now have their headquarters, Exile have enjoyed No. 1 hits with **I Don't Want To Be A Memory**, **Give Me One More Chance**, **Crazy For Your Love**, **She's A Miracle**, **Hang On To Your Heart** and **I Could Get Used To You**, all up-mood numbers with infectious country arrangements that have given them a new lease of life.

Albums:
Kentucky Hearts (Epic/Epic)
Hang On To Your Heart (Epic/Epic)

Barbara Fairchild

A husky-voiced blonde, Barbara Fairchild was born in Knobel, Arkansas (population around 350) on November 12, 1950. Spending her high school years in St Louis, Missouri, at 15 she had recorded for a local station and had a regular spot on a weekly TV show. Later came the inevitable move to Nashville and a meeting with MCA staffman Jerry Crutchfield, who signed her to the company as a songwriter, Barbara's own recorded efforts appearing on Kapp.

Still working primarily as a songwriter she made some demos that came to the attention of Columbia's Billy Sherrill, the result being a new recording contract and a subsequent flow of minor hits with **Love Is A Gentle Thing** (1969), **A Girl Who'll Satisfy Her Man** (1970), **(Loving You Is) Sunshine** (1971), **Love's Old Song** (1971), **Thanks For The Memories** (1972) and others, her real breakthrough coming with **Teddy Bear Song** (1973), **Kid Stuff** (1973) and **Baby Doll** (1974), all three becoming Top 5 singles.

For a couple of years Barbara faltered on the charts, but made a minor comeback with the Top 20 hit **Cheatin' Is**

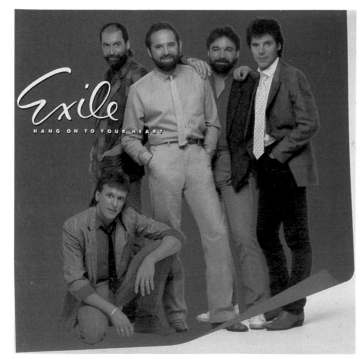

Above: Barbara Fairchild, who signed to Capitol Records in 1986.

towards the end of 1976 and **Let Me Love You Once Before You Go** the following year. Though she has faded from the scene in recent years, Barbara made an impression with British country fans following tours in 1978 and 1979 and recorded a successful duet with Billy Walker of **The Answer Game** in 1982.

Love's Old Song, Barbara Fairchild. Courtesy CBS.

Albums:
Free And Easy (Columbia/CBS)
This Is (Columbia/CBS)
Mississippi (Columbia/CBS)
Greatest Hits (Columbia/CBS)

Donna Fargo

Born Yvonne Vaughn on November 10, 1949, the daughter of a Mount Airey, North Carolina tobacco farmer, Donna attended High Point, North Carolina, Teachers' College and also spent some time at the University of Southern California, her musical education consisting of just four piano lessons taken at the age of ten. Nevertheless, she found herself torn between two careers, teaching, in the Corvin, California, area, and singing, which she did under a stage name, in LA clubs.

After meeting record producer Stan Silver, whom she married in 1969, Donna set out for Phoenix where she cut some sides for Ramco Records. Her initial

On The Move, Donna Fargo. Courtesy WEA Records.

releases flopped so Donna continued with her teaching chores, later switching her recording activities to the Challenge label, also with little success.

Taught guitar by Silver, who also encouraged her to songwrite, Donna finally won a contract with a major company, ABC-Dot, repaying their belief in her talent via a self-penned No. 1 in **Happiest Girl In The Whole USA**, the CMA Single Of The Year for 1972. All possibilities of her being a one-hit wonder were soon dispelled when **Funny Face**, another 1972 Fargo original, climbed the charts, to be followed by **Super Man**, **You Were Always There**, **Little Girl Gone** (all

1973), **You Can't Be A Beacon** (1974), **It Do Feel Good** (1975) and **Don't Be Angry** (1976), all Top 10 entries that benefitted from the distinctive, dry-throated, Fargo vocal style. In 1977 she became part of the growing roster of Warner Bros Records' country artists scoring such hits as **That Was Yesterday** (1977), **Do I Love You (Yes In Every Way)** (1978) and **Somebody Special** (1979). In 1979 she was stricken with Multiple Sclerosis, but has fought against the crippling disease and continued with her career, though on a lesser scale than previously, recording for RCA, Cleveland, International and MCA-Songbird.

Albums:
The Happiest Girl In The Whole World (Dot/–)
All About A Feeling (Dot/–)
Country Sounds Of (–/MFP)
On The Move (Warner/Warner)
Dark Eyed Lady (Warner/–)
Brotherly Love (MCA-Songbird/–)
Just For You (Warner/–)

Charlie Feathers

An early Sun rockabilly artist, still active (in a family group) in the Memphis area. Born on June 12, 1932 in Hollow Springs, Mississippi, he recorded for Flip, Sun, King, Kay, Memphis and Holiday Inn records, and is thought of as an artistic influence who somehow never found the right rockabilly record.

Album:
Rockabilly's Main Man (–/Charly)

Below: Narvel Felts, who started out as a rocker in the 1950s.

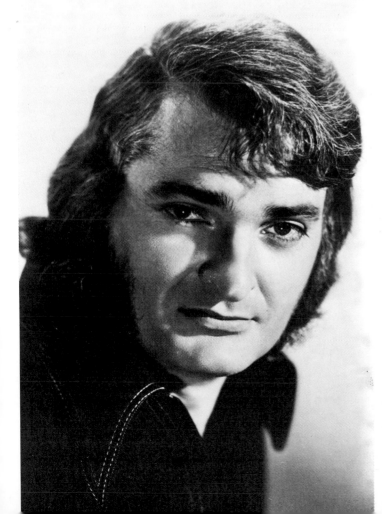

Narvel Felts

A native of Missouri, born on November 11, 1938, Felts grew up with country music, became known as a rock 'n' roller in the mid-'50s and returned to country later in his career. As a boy, the first singer he remembers hearing was Ernest Tubb: 'I used to wonder what his girlfriend was doing on the floor and him walking over her.'

In 1956 he won a high school talent contest by singing **Blue Suede Shoes** and in an effort to trace him and have him sing on the station, KDEX in Bernie, Missouri, put out a message for him. Narvel and his father drove the eight miles into Bernie in their pickup truck to find a telephone.

Performing on the station's Saturday show led to Narvel landing the bass guitar spot in Jerry Mercer's band. When Mercer left, Narvel became band leader. Felts worked with both Conway Twitty (then plain Harold Jenkins) and Charlie Rich at Sun Records in 1957.

He then signed first with Mercury and then with Pink Records where **Honey Love** and **3000 Miles** made the charts. In 1970, while contracted to Hi Records, he came to Nashville hoping to find a solid country label with good distribution. Then, discussing his problems with friend and DJ Johnny Morris, they decided to evolve a new label, Cinnamon Records. In 1973, **Drift Away** (written by Mentor Williams and a pop hit for Dobie Gray) was an impressive country hit for Narvel. Later that year he scored again with **All In The Name Of Love** and in 1974 with **When**

Narvel The Marvel, Narvel Felts. Courtesy MCA/Dot Records.

Your Good Love Was Mine.

When Cinnamon folded in 1975, Narvel joined ABC-Dot Records, coming up with **Reconsider Baby**, which was a No. 1 hit and was chosen by Billboard as No. 1 Song of the Year and Cashbox as No. 1 Country Song of the Year. It also crossed over to the pop charts. **Somebody Hold Me (Until She Passes By)** (1975), **Lonely Teardrops** (1976) and **The Feeling's Right** (1977) have all been Top 20 country hits for Narvel. Since 1979 he has recorded for a variety of small labels, including College, GMC, Lobo, Compleat and Evergreen. He has a strong, nasal voice, distinctive enough to handle country or rock, as his career has demonstrated.

Albums:
Drift Away (Cinnamon/–)
Reconsider Me (ABC-Dot/–)
Greatest Hits (ABC-Dot/–)
A Touch of Felts (ABC-Dot/–)
Inside Love (ABC-Dot/–)

Freddy Fender

A maverick country artist, Fender (real name Baldermar Huerta) waited 20 years for record success. Born on June 4, 1937 in San Benito, a South Texas border town, early in life Fender found himself part of the migratory worker life pattern. His family worked as casual farm labourers throughout the year but made it back to

Rock'n'Country, Freddie Fender. Courtesy MCA/Dot Records.

the San Benito valley each Christmas. Fender remembers that music helped to make a hard life happy and that he always managed to persuade his mother to buy him a new guitar when the old one wore out.

He dropped out of high school at 16 and joined the Marines for three years but found that he preferred playing guitar in the barracks to professional soldiering. In the late '50s he was back in San Benito playing bars and Chicano dances. By 1958 his records, in which he utilized all-Spanish lyrics, were doing well in both Texas and Mexico.

In 1959 he had turned to the more commercial fields of rhythm and blues and country for inspiration. To give Fender exposure, local club owner Wayne Duncan founded his own Duncan label. The nationally established Imperial Records took an interest and Fender and Duncan leased them material. The second such release, **Wasted Days And Wasted Nights**, written by Fender and Duncan, was a big hit in 1960.

In May of 1960 Fender was arrested for possession of drugs, betrayed by a paroled informer. Fender served three years of his five-year sentence in the Angola State Penitentiary, Louisiana, cutting several titles for the Goldband and Powerpack labels while inside. The Governor of Louisiana, Jimmie Davis, himself something of a country singer, helped secure Fender's release but a condition of his parole was that he should leave the entertainment business.

Fender managed to pick up his career again though, foregoing record hits but gigging steadily. He also worked as a mechanic and even went to college for two years. In 1974 though, he was introduced to noted Louisiana R&B producer Huey Meaux who set about putting Fender's distinctive voice in a country setting. In Houston, Texas, they put down many tracks, among them a re-recording of **Wasted Days And Wasted Nights** and an update of **Before The Next Teardrop Falls**, performed partly in English and partly in Spanish. The latter was

picked up by ABC-Dot and became a big pop and country hit, which led to the record being named CMA Single Of The Year (1975) and Fender being named Top Male Vocalist by the ACM.

Further country and pop successes followed with **Secret Love** (1975), **You'll Lose A Good Thing** and **Vaya Con Dios** (both 1976), **The Rains Came** (1977) and **Talk To Me** (1978). He joined Starflite Records in 1979, then signed with Warner Brothers in 1982, but has been unable to regain the enormous success he enjoyed in the late '70s.

Albums:
Before The Next Teardrop Falls (Dot/ABC)
Are You Ready For Freddy? (Dot/ABC)
If You're Ever In Texas (Dot/ABC)
Rock 'n' Country (Dot/ABC)
Swamp Gold (ABC-Dot/–)
The Texas Balladeer (Starflite/–)
Best Of (–/MCA)

Lester Flatt Live! Courtesy RCA Records.

Flatt & Scruggs

Lester Raymond Flatt, born on June 19, 1914, in Overton County, Tennessee and Earl Eugene Scruggs, born on January 6, 1924, in Cleveland County, North Carolina, pioneered a particular type of bluegrass under Bill Monroe's leadership – especially Scruggs' 'three-finger banjo' technique – and thus helped popularize bluegrass immensely.

Both came from highly musical families. Lester's parents both played the banjo (in

Flatt And Scruggs. A fine budget release by UK Hallmark.

the old 'frailing' style) and Lester practised on both guitar and banjo. He also sang in the church choir. Earl came from an area east of the Appalachians which was already using a three-finger style on the five-string banjo. The style was not new anyway (although the strict universal style then involved either two-finger picking or simply brushing or frailing the strings): a three-finger style had been used by Uncle Dave Macon and Charlie Poole, and Earl himself had heard such banjoists as Snuffy Jenkins locally. But then Scruggs evolved a newer style, syncopated and rhythmic, blending in his three-finger banjo eventually to make the bluegrass style sound fresh and alive, and often as fast as an express train.

Lester became a textile worker but still listened to a lot of 'hillbilly' music, while also continuing to play instruments. His wife could also play guitar and sing. He

was particularly a fan of Bill and Charlie Monroe who were heard a great deal on Carolina radio stations in the years before World War Two. Lester was living in Covington, Virginia, and he got together with some old friends from Tennessee to play. By 1939 they had become pretty proficient and were to be heard on Radio WDBJ, Roanoke, as the Harmonizers. Then followed a period in which Lester played with the Happy-Go-Lucky Boys, one of whose members was Clyde Moody who had played and recorded with Bill Monroe. In 1943 Lester and his wife Gladys were hired by Charlie Monroe. Lester sang tenor harmony and played mandolin. He tired of the travelling and quit, tried his hand at trucking and then procured a position with a North Carolina radio station. It was there that he received a telegram from Bill Monroe asking Lester to come and play with him on the Grand Ole Opry.

Earl had played in public with his brothers from the age of six and by 15 he was playing on a North Carolina radio station with the Carolina Wildcats. At this time (1939) he also played with the Morris Brothers on Radio WSPA, Spartanburg, South Carolina. He became a textile worker too (during the war years) but the end of the war saw him playing with 'Lost' John Miller in Knoxville. Shortly after, he began to be heard widely when Miller started broadcasting on Radio WSM from Nashville. Miller then stopped touring and Earl, out of work, was hired by Bill Monroe.

At this time Monroe was known mainly around the south east but the Opry was becoming more and more popular, and Bill's show (which had featured artists and was a 'show' in the genuine sense) rapidly gained a broader appeal. Monroe switched musical duties around and Lester Flatt's high tenor voice easily adapted to singing lead when necessary. Less easy was the pace Lester was required to keep on guitar. He shortcut his guitar part sometimes by developing a characteristic run with which to catch up and finish the lines. This became known as the 'Lester Flatt G Run' since it was usually played in that chord position. Lester had also become compere and link man to the Monroe package.

Dueling Banjos, Earl Scruggs. Courtesy CBS Records.

Scruggs was given full rein by Monroe to develop his fluid banjo technique and helped popularize songs such as **Blue Grass Breakdown**, numbers which would remain associated with him after his departure from Monroe. Monroe even put the names of Flatt and Scruggs on some of his records. This precision and teamwork which characterized Monroe's sound was attracting many new listeners to the music and, by association, to the

Above: The Foggy Mountain Boys on the Opry during the mid-1950s.

Opry itself.

In 1948, within weeks of each other, Earl and Lester resigned from Monroe to escape the constant travelling (Monroe has always been a dedicated touring man). Almost inevitably the two then decided to team up and do some radio work. They recruited ex-Monroe men Jim Shumate, on fiddle, and Howard Watts (stage name Cedric Rainwater), on bass, and then moved to Hickory, North Carolina, where they were joined by Mac Wiseman. That year, 1948, they made their first recordings for Mercury Records.

The band took its name from an old Carter Family tune, **Foggy Mountain Top**, calling themselves the Foggy Mountain Boys. Wiseman left and was replaced by mandolin player Curly Seckler. Many of the fiddle players they used had previously worked with Bill Monroe. Earl's banjo was now more to the fore and the mandolin was used less. Both Lester and Earl were prone to using guitars, Earl developing a more aggressive, Merle Travis-influenced sound on lead. The only mellow thing was Lester's vocal – in most other respects they promoted a harder, more driving music than that of Monroe.

In 1948 they moved to Bristol on the Tennessee-Virginia border and while broadcasting on radio WCYB there met the Stanley Brothers and Don Reno, both of whom developed this new sound into what we now know as 'bluegrass' and

'Scruggs-style banjo'. They broadcast for many radio stations in the south east and also booked their own outdoor concerts, complete package shows that also featured local performers and at which the artists sold records and souvenirs.

In 1949 they recorded **Foggy Mountain Breakdown** and it was released the following year. It has remained one of their most consistently popular numbers and was included in the film 'Bonnie And Clyde' as background to the famous car chase. In 1950 they were offered a lucrative contact by Columbia Records. However, before moving, they fulfilled some contractual obligations to Mercury by recording a series of older folk numbers and giving them the new, bluegrass treatment. Songs such as **Roll In My Sweet Baby's Arms** and **Old Salty Dog Blues** were heard in a new setting, one which many people now associate with them.

Earl also introduced the 'Scruggs peg', a device which allowed him to change easily the tuning of his banjo strings for the number **Earl's Breakdown** (1951). That year a boost was given to their career when they appeared on a show headlined by the then fashionable Ernest Tubb and Lefty Frizzell. In 1953 the band began broadcasting 'Martha White Biscuit Time' on Nashville's WSM Radio, a show which not only ran for years but which saw them coming well and truly into country music prominence. In 1955 their position was consolidated with an equivalent syndicated TV show and at this time they

also became Grand Ole Opry members. They were travelling more than they had ever done with Bill Monroe and they were also winning magazine fan polls and industry awards. The '60s folk revival also helped them, since by this time 'Scruggs picking' was already in instrument tutor terminology, Folkways released an album, compiled by Mike Seeger, titled **American Banjo Scruggs Style** and both Mercury and Columbia released similar albums with the artist himself featured.

Further recognition came in the shape of the CBS-TV series 'The Beverly Hillbillies'. The theme tune, played by Lester and Earl, **The Ballad Of Jed Clampett**, was No. 1 on the country charts for three months from December 1962. They became a household name and a symbol of this exciting, syncopated musical style. During the '60s they consolidated their position and sold a vast amount of records. Towards the end (mainly pushed by Earl) they began experimenting with new folk songs, with drums and with gospel-style harmonies. Some of their older fans were unhappy about these changes and in 1969 they split up, Lester returning to more traditional sounds and making reunion albums with his old buddy Mac Wiseman. Lester formed the Nashville Grass, composed mainly of the Foggy Mountain Boys, but Earl defiantly went off in new directions with his Earl Scruggs Revue, utilizing his own sons and later dobro player Josh Graves in a unit which could also appeal to young, rock audiences. Earl also played

a big part in getting together the old stars for the 1971 Nitty Gritty Dirt Band album **Will The Circle Be Unbroken**.

Lester Flatt died on May 11, 1979, and in recent years Earl Scruggs has cut back his activities, whilst his sons have made their mark as songwriters, producers and multi-instrumentalists in contemporary country music.

Albums:
Foggy Mountain Breakdown (Hillside/–)
Carnegie Hall (Columbia/–)
Changin' Times (Columbia/–)

Earl Scruggs Albums:
Nashville's Rock (Columbia/–)
Duelling Banjos (Columbia/–)
Kansas State (Columbia/–)
I Saw The Light (Columbia/–)
Earl Scruggs Revue (Columbia/CBS)
Scruggs Revue Vol. 2 (Columbia/–)
Rockin' Cross (Columbia/–)
Family Portrait (Columbia/–)
Live From Austin City Limits (Columbia/–)

Lester Flatt Albums:
Before You Go (RCA/–)
Foggy Mountain Breakdown (RCA/RCA)
Over The Hills to the Poorhouse – with
　　Mac Wiseman (RCA/–)
Best Of . . . (RCA/RCA)
Flatt Gospel (Canaan/–)
Lester Raymond Flatt (Flying Fish/–)
Live Bluegrass Festival – with Bill Monroe
　　(RCA/–)
Living Legend (CMH/–)
The One And Only (Nugget/–)

Flying Burrito Brothers

The band was formed in 1968 by ex Byrds, Gram Parsons and Chris Hillman, to bring country music to the rock fans of California. A&M Records felt that the charismatic Parsons might help generate some big sales with this new concept and they subsequently put much promotional money behind the first album, **Gilded Palace Of Sin**. Bizarre photo sessions in the desert resulted in an album sleeve depicting the Burritos in extravagant Nudie suits. The marijuana leaves embroidered on the suits emphasised a new approach. **Gilded Palace** featured some of Parsons' best-ever songs and beefed up his sensitive but none too strong voice with a rock production and Chris Hillman prominent on vocals. The line-up for this album was: Parsons (guitar, vocals), Chris Hillman (guitar, mandolin, vocals), Chris Ethridge (bass), Sneaky Pete Kleinow (pedal steel guitar) and Jon Corneal (drums). There was little country-styled music being played in Los Angeles at this time, and this band served to provide a real opportunity for pickers such as Sneaky Pete to make it on a national level.

In 1969, Corneal and Ethridge dropped out and Bernie Leadon (guitar, vocals) and Mike Clarke (drums) joined, Hillman switching to bass. The next two albums, **Burrito De Luxe** and **The Flying Burrito Brothers** were straighter productions but still with a good dash of country included. Parsons left between the two albums (in 1970) and in 1971 Bernie Leadon also left, feeling that he was not being fully stretched, and subsequently formed the highly successful band, The Eagles. Sneaky Pete also left to undertake production and session work.

1971 saw a vastly expanded line-up in which Byron Berline, a top fiddle player who had recorded with The Rolling Stones, Al Perkins (pedal steel guitar), Kenny Wertz (guitar, banjo, vocals) and Roger Bush (string bass) all joined. This line-up saw the release of a good live

Flying Again, Flying Burrito Brothers. Courtesy Columbia/CBS Records.

album, **Last Of The Red Hot Burritos**, which featured much in the way of favourite material.

The addition of Alun Munde (banjo) in 1971 completed a floating aggregation which rejoiced under the title, Hot Burrito Revue. The band was already perpetuating a legend on the strength of Parsons and the whole LA country rock syndrome, and had built up quite a following particularly in Holland. Those bluegrass-oriented members of this loose set-up who finally decided to stay became known as Country Gazette.

However, the Burritos were to re-form again in 1974. With a line-up of Sneaky Pete, Gib Guilbeau (a Cajun fiddle player), Gene Parsons (drums), Chris Ethridge and a new singer Joel Scott-Hill, they toured America and Europe cutting albums for CBS.

By 1979, the Burritos were down to a two-piece consisting of Guilbeau and John Beland. Known as The Burrito Brothers, they moved from the west coast to Nashville in 1981 determined to make an impression as a country act. They signed a recording contract with Curb Records who were licensed through Columbia and scored Top 20 country hits with **She's A Friend of Mine** (1982), **Does She Wish She Was Single Again** and **She Belongs To Everyone But Me** (both 1983). By 1985, the pair had split, Beland concentrating on his songwriting skills and Guilbeau teaming up with Sneaky Pete Kleinow for yet another re-formed Flying Burrito Brothers line-up which undertook a world tour and recorded a live album in Japan.

Albums:
Gilded Palace Of Sin (A&M/Demon)
Last Of The Red Hot Burritos (A&M/–)
Flying Burrito Brothers (A&M/A&M)
Close Up The Honky Tonks (A&M/A&M)
Flying Again (Columbia/CBS)
Sleepless Nights – with Gram Parsons (A&M/A&M)
The Flying Burrito Brothers – Live From Tokyo (–/Sundown)
Cabin Fever (Relix Records/–)

Dan Fogelberg

Fogelberg grew up in the little town of Preoria, Illinois (where he was born on August 13, 1951), and attended the University of Illinois as an art student before settling on a musical career. He established himself in the mid '70s as a pop-country singer-songwriter with a series of albums on Full Moon Records.

Although he has lived in Colorado for a number of years, most of his songs have a mid-western setting. His writings on freedom, lost love and women have proved to be decidedly effective and timely pieces. Dan showcased his country roots on the highly acclaimed 1985 album, **High Country Snows**.

Utilising the talents of Ricky Skaggs, Herb Pedersen, Chris Hillman, Doc Watson, Al Perkins and Vince Gill, Dan produced a first-rate bluegrass-flavoured album, blending his own self-penned songs with those of Carter Stanley and Flatt & Scruggs. He made inroads on the country charts with **Go Down Easy** and **Down The Road (Mountain Pass)** during 1985.

Album:
High Country Snows (Full Moon/Full Moon)

Red Foley

Elected to the CMA Hall Of Fame in 1967, Clyde Julian 'Red' Foley was born in Bluelick, Kentucky, on June 17, 1910.

A star athlete at high school and college, at the age of 17 he won the Atwater-Kent talent contest in Louisville, in 1930 moving to Chicago to become a member of John Lair's Cumberland Ridge Runners on the WLS National Barn Dance Show. Seven years later he helped to originate the Renfro Valley Show with Lair, by 1939 appearing on Avalon Time, a programme in which he co-starred with Red Skelton, thus becoming the first country star to have a network radio show.

His Decca records soon proved eminently popular, Foley's versions of **Tennessee Saturday Night, Candy Kisses, Tennessee Polka**, and **Sunday Down In Tennessee** all becoming Top 10 discs during 1949. In 1950 sales escalated even further, with no less than three Foley titles – **Chattanoogie Shoe Shine Boy** and the spirituals **Steal Away** and **Just A Closer Walk With Thee** – becoming million sellers.

Below: Red Foley on the Opry in the early '50s. The bassist is Ernie Newton.

The Red Foley Story. Courtesy MCA Records.

The following year, his success with religious material continued, Foley's recording of Thomas A. Dorsey's **Peace In The Valley** selling well enough to become an eventual gold disc winner. Meanwhile, his more commercial songs also accrued huge sales, **Birmingham Bounce** becoming a 1950 No. 1, and **Mississippi** (1950), **Cincinatti Dancing Pig** (1950), **Hot Rod Race** (1951), **Alabama Jubilee** (1951), **Midnight** (1952), **Don't Let The Stars Get In Your Eyes** (1953), **Hot Toddy** (1953), **Shake A Hand** (1953), **Jilted** (1954), **Hearts Of Stone** (1954) and **A Satisfied Mind** (with Betty Foley, 1955), all providing him with Top 10 placings.

An Opry star during the '40s, in 1954 he moved to Springfield, Missouri, where he hosted the Ozark Jubilee – one of the first successful country TV series. During the early '60s, Foley co-starred with Fess Parker on an ABC-TV series 'Mr. Smith Goes To Washington' and he continued appearing on radio and TV and making many personal appearances right up to the time of his death on September 19, 1968, in Fort Wayne, Indiana.

Albums:
Beyond The Sunset (MCA/–)
Red Foley Story (MCA/–)
Red & Ernie – with Ernest Tubb (–/Stetson)

Dick Foran

Although Herbert J. Yates and Nat Levene are generally given credit for creating the singing cowboy genre and casting Gene Autry in what was to become one of the most popular film genres of all time, it appears that Warner Brothers had come up with pretty much the same idea at the same time, for not long after the release of Autry's first major film in 1934 came a Warner Brothers western starring Dick Foran (real name Nicholas Foran) as a singing cowboy.

Possessed of a fine voice – which sounded more at home on the Broadway stage than on the range – Foran was born in New Jersey on June 18, 1910, the son of a US Senator. Educated at Princeton he aspired to a career on the stage and later on film, but despite his singing cowboy westerns for Warner and Universal, he aspired to, and was quite successful in, roles in high budget westerns and in other types of films.

Foran retired around the start of the '70s and lived in Southern California up to the time of his death in 1979.

Tennessee Ernie Ford

The singer who recorded **Sixteen Tons**, a mining song which sold over four million copies during the mid-'50s, Ernie Jennings Ford was born in Bristol, Tennessee, on

Ernie Sings & Glen Picks. Courtesy Capitol Records.

February 13, 1919. At school he sang in the choir and played trombone in the school band – but he also spent much time at the local radio station, WOAI, where in 1937 he began working as an announcer.

Four years later, following a period of study at the Cincinnati Conservatory of Music and further announcing stints with various radio stations, Ford enlisted in the Air Force, becoming first a bombadier on heavy bombers, then an instructor. After discharge, he returned to announcing, working on C&W station KXLA, Pasadena, where he met Cliffie Stone and appeared as a singer with Stone's quartet on the 'Hometown Jamboree' show.

In 1948, Ford signed with Capitol Records, for whom his warm bass voice provided immediate hits in **Mule Train** and **Smokey Mountain Boogie** (1949), subsequently scoring with **Anticipation Blues** (1949), **I'll Never Be Free** (with Kay Starr – 1950), **The Cry Of The Wild Goose** (1950) and **Shotgun Boogie**, a Ford original that became a 1950 million seller.

His own radio shows over the CBS and ABC networks gained Ford further popularity, then in 1955, following another handful of hits, he recorded **Sixteen Tons**, a superb Merle Travis song that came decked out in a fine Jack Marshall arrangement. This quickly became a massive hit, winning Ford his own NBC-TV show – a series which the singer hosted until 1961, when he took a break to spend more time with his family in California.

Since the early '60s, Ford has tended to cut down on his work, though he has appeared before capacity audiences, been on many TV shows and enjoyed some chart success with **Hicktown** (1965), **Honey-Eyed Girl** (1969) and **Happy Songs Of Love** (1971). During his career he has also recorded many religious albums, the biggest seller being **Hymns**, reputed to be the first million-selling album in country music and one which won Ford a platinum-plated master in 1963.

Albums:
Favourite Hymns (Capitol/–)
Hymns (Capitol/–)
America The Beautiful (Capitol/–)
Civil War Songs Of The North (Capitol/–)
Civil War Songs Of The South (Capitol/–)
Country Hits Feelin' Blue (Capitol/–)

The Very Best Of Tennessee Ernie Ford (–/Capitol)
Ernie Sings And Glen Picks – with Glen Campbell (Capitol/–)
Swing Wide Your Gate Of Love (Word/Word)

The Forester Sisters

Kathy, June, Kim and Christy, four sisters from Georgia, burst upon the country scene at the beginning of 1985 when their very first single, **(That's What You Do) When You're In Love**, gave them a country Top 10 entry.

The girls, who count Bonnie Raitt, Linda Ronstadt and Emmylou Harris as being their main influence and inspiration, began by singing at weddings, funerals and community events around their Lookout Mountain home. Specializing in sweet harmonies, with Kim and eldest sister Kathy handling most of the lead vocals, they cut a demo tape in Muscle Shoals, Alabama, which eventually found its way to Warner Brothers Records in Nashville.

Jim Ed Norman signed the girls to the label at the end of 1984 and, under the guidance of Jerry Wallace and Terry Skinner, they recorded their debut album in Muscle Shoals, resulting in not only a country hit with their first single, but subsequent No. 1s with **I Fell In Love Again Last Night** and **Just In Case**.

In addition to Kathy's keyboards and Kim's guitar, the girls make use of a four-piece band, including Kathy's husband on bass, who also acts as The Forester's road manager.

Album:
The Forester Sisters (Warner/–)

Wally Fowler

Cheerful, gladhanding Wally Fowler was born in February, 1917, in Bartow County, Georgia. He first achieved success as a singer and songwriter, leading an Opry band called the Georgia Clodhoppers, and writing such hits of the late 1940s as **I'm Sending You Red Roses** and **That's How Much I Love You, Baby**.

His interest turned to gospel music a little later on and he was a member of the John Daniel Quartet before forming and leading the Oak Ridge Quartet, forerunner of the Oak Ridge Boys. In later years he turned his hand to gospel promoting, sponsoring the first all-night sing (in Nashville in 1948) among numerous other promotions. In his prime Wally recorded for both the Decca and King labels.

Curly Fox And Texas Ruby

Curly Fox, the fiddling son of a fiddler, was born Arnum LeRoy Fox in Graysville, Tennessee, on November 9, 1910. He joined a medicine show at the age of 13, and recorded as early as 1929, with the Roane County Ramblers. He also played with the Carolina Tarheels and headed his own band, the Tennessee Firecrackers, over WSB in Atlanta in 1932.

Texas Ruby was Tex Owens' sister,

born on June 4, 1910 in Wise Country, Texas, who had come to the Grand Ole Opry as early as 1934 with Zeke Clements and his Bronco Buster. She and Celements worked for a while on WHO in Des Moines, before she and Curly Fox teamed up on WSM in 1937. Not long after this they became one of the most popular acts on the Opry and in country music, with their winning combination of Ruby's deep, strong, sultry voice and Curly's masterful trick fiddling.

After marrying in 1939, their biggest years were on the Grand Ole Opry in the '40s, where they were stars of the Purina portion, and they recorded for Columbia (1945–6) and King (1947). In 1948 they journeyed to New York and then Houston, where they were to spend seven years over KPRC-TV before returning to the Grand Ole Opry.

They recorded an album for Starday during this second Nashville period, just prior to Texas Ruby's death in March of 1963, when a fire raged through their house trailer. Curly went into virtual retirement afterwards, living in rural Illinois, but in the mid-'70s he began to appear at occasional bluegrass festivals and other gatherings.

Dallas Frazier

A respected singer-songwriter, Frazier is capable of penning country songs that 'cross-over' without losing too much individuality in the process (although it must be said that one big success in this area, **Alley Oop**, moulded into a novelty hit by Kim Fowley for the Hollywood Argyles, was pure gimmickry).

Born in Spiro, Oklahoma, in 1939, Frazier was a featured stage performer before he reached his teens and a best-selling songwriter by 21. Early on, his family moved to the up-and-coming country centre of Bakersfield, California. In a talent contest sponsored by Ferlin Husky he won first prize and Husky offered him a place on his show.

He was signed by Capitol Records and

My Baby Packed Up My Mind And Left Me, Dallas Frazier. Courtesy RCA.

moved to Nashville to pitch his songs, and also starred on radio and TV there. Ferlin Husky had one of his most famous hits with Frazier's **Timber, I'm Falling** and there were other cross-overs with **There Goes My Everything** (Engelbert Humperdinck) and **Son Of Hickory Holler's Tramp** (O. C. Smith). But he could also pen a convincing dues-paying country song as he showed with **California Cotton Fields**, a title recorded by Merle Haggard.

Frazier made a comeback as a writer in the last ten years with the Oak Ridge Boys' updated version of **Elvira**, a million seller in 1981, and several other singers raiding his vast catalogue of songs. He has been helped in his writing career by having a stronger voice than many composers and this has enabled him to succeed as a performer also. His albums have included **My Baby Packed Up My Mind And Left Me** and **Singin' My Song** (RCA).

Janie Fricke

Regarded as the most versatile female vocalist in country music, Janie, who was born on Deecmber 19, 1952 near South Whitney, Indiana, came from a musical family. Her father was a guitarist and her mother taught piano and played organ at the local church.

Between study lessons at Indiana University, Janie was earning extra cash by singing jingles for an advertising agency in Memphis. After completing her studies, she tried her luck in Los Angeles as a background vocalist but failed to make any impression. Consequently, she returned to Memphis in the summer of 1972 and during the next few years she was busy building a first-rate reputation as a jingle singer.

In 1975 she moved to Nashville where she joined The Lea Jane Singers, one of Music City's busiest vocal groups. Janie's natural vocal ability allowed her to stand out in the cut-throat Nashville session business where talented background vocalists are two-a-penny. On a Johnny Duncan session she was asked to sing some solo lines on **Jo And The Cowboy**, which became the Texas balladeer's first

Above: The versatile Janie Fricke, top CMA female vocalist in 1982 and 1983.

Top 10 hit at the end of 1975.

Janie was used on subsequent Johnny Duncan recordings of **Stranger** and **Thinkin' Of A Rendezvous** (both 1976) and **It Couldn't Have Been Any Better** (1977). During this period she contributed to more than 20 Top 10 country singles by Ronnie Milsap, Crystal Gayle, Mel Tillis and Vern Gosdin.

After being coaxed into a solo

Singer Of Songs, Janie Fricke. Courtesy CBS Records.

recording contract in 1977 with Columbia Records, where she was initially produced by Billy Sherrill, Janie enjoyed Top 20 hits with **What're You Doing Tonight, Baby It's You** and **Please Help Me I'm Falling** from her first album. Due to her reluctance to give up her session work to form a band and do show dates, she was dubbed 'the reluctant superstar'. But Janie was building her solo career slowly and carefully.

Further hits with **I'll Love Away Your Troubles For Awhile** (1979) and **Pass Me By** (1980) were followed by a change of producer with Jim Ed Norman being responsible for **Down To My Last Broken**

Heart (1980), I'll Need Someone To Hold Me (When I Cry) (1981) and Janie's first No. 1, Don't Worry 'Bout Me Baby (1982).

By this time, Janie had made the transition from secure anonymity as one of Nashville's most successful jingle and session singers to the forefront as a country star. She was named CMA Female Vocalist in both 1982 and 1983 and enjoyed further chart toppers with He's A Heartache (Looking For A Place To Happen) (1983), Let's Stop Talking About It (1984) and She's Single Again (1985). Her recordings were now being produced by Bob Montgomery and her career was managed by her husband, Randy Jackson. With her own Heart City Band, which she used on the acclaimed It Ain't Easy LP, Janie gained a reputation as one of country music's most dynamic female entertainers.

She has recorded duets with George Jones, Ray Charles and Merle Haggard, making the top of the charts in company with the latter on the sensitive Natural High (1985), but is now fully established as a successful solo star in her own right.

Albums:
Sleeping With Your Memory (Columbia/CBS)
Love Notes (Columbia/CBS)
The First Word In Memory (Columbia/CBS)

Kinky Friedman

Leader of outlandish country rock band, The Texas Jewboys, Richard Friedman was born in Palestine, Texas, October 31, 1944, the son of a of a Texas University

Below: Richard Friedman, provider of such titles as Get Your Biscuits In The Oven And Your Buns In The Bed.

Sold American, Kinky Friedman. Courtesy Vanguard Records.

professor.

Brought up on a ranch, he later attended the University in nearby Austin, in which town he formed his first band, King Arthur And The Carrots. Then came some time spent in Borneo, where he was a member of the Peace Corps.

In 1971 he headed for LA with his band, The Texas Jewboys, establishing a reputation as the Frank Zappa of country music in Sold American, for Vanguard.

He was signed to ABC Records during 1974 but by 1976 Friedman had moved on once more, to Epic, cutting Lasso From El Paso, an all-star album featuring such dignitaries as Bob Dylan and Eric Clapton.

Although he has appeared on the Opry, Friedman's country is generally far-out and not really meant for mainstream fans. These days he is resident in New York where he often headlines at the Lone Star Cafe, entertaining both city cowpokes and rock fans alike.

Albums:
Sold American (Vanguard/Vanguard)
Kinky Friedman (ABC/ABC)
Lasso From El Paso (Epic/Epic)

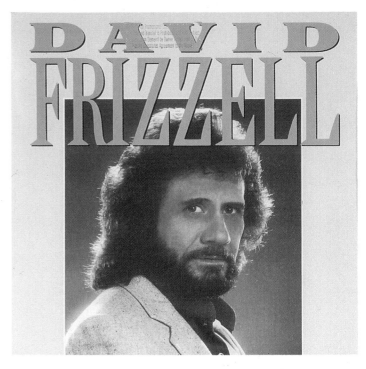

David Frizzell

A younger brother of legendary Lefty Frizzell, David, born on September 26, 1941, Texas, spent 23 years recording for seven different labels under eight separate contracts before he made a major breakthrough in 1981, when he teamed up with Shelly West (daughter of singer Dottie West) on the chart-topping duet of You're The Reason God Made Oklahoma.

He was not quite a teenager when his famous brother was enjoying the peak of his success, and by the time David was

Solo, David Frizzell. Courtesy WEA/Viva Records.

old enough to embark upon a music career, Lefty had almost become a 'has-been'. He hitch-hiked from his Texas home to California to be with Lefty in the late '50s and his first recordings were made under the guidance of Don Law for Columbia Records in 1958.

A handful of country-rockabilly singles were released, but all sank without trace. Following a stint in the US Army, he re-signed with Columbia in the late '60s, scoring a modest hit with I Just Can't Help Believing in 1970. David spent a few years working with Buck Owens, making regular appearances on Owens' Ranch Show syndicated TV programme. A few recordings for Capitol were released, David scoring minor hits with Words Don't Come Easy (1973) and She Loved Me Away From You (1974).

Further recording stints followed with RSO and MCA without too much success, and David was quite happy to remain a little known cabaret act appearing in clubs in Reno and California. David invested in his own club at Concord, California in 1977, and it was the following year that Shelly West, along with David's younger brother Allen Frizzell, joined him at the club.

Shelly and David toyed with a few duets and did a demo tape of We're Lovin' On Borrowed Time. Producer Snuffy Garrett heard the tape and recorded an album, setting up a deal with Casablanca West, the country division of the disco-orientated Casablanca Records. The pair's first single was set for release when Casablanca decided to close down their country division and dropped David and Shelly from their books.

However, Garrett had great faith in the completed album and began shopping around for a new deal. He found no takers in Nashville and played the tape to actor Clint Eastwood, his partner in Viva Records, who immediately liked one song, You're The Reason God Made Oklahoma, and decided to use it in the soundtrack of his upcoming film, 'Any Which Way You Can'.

The rest was like a dream for David and

David Frizzell

Shelly. The song was put out as a single at the beginning of 1981, made it to the top of the country charts and the pair walked off with a CMA Award for the top country duo for 1981, a feat they repeated the following year. More duet hits followed with **A Texas State Of Mind** (1981), **Another Honky Tonk Night On Broadway** (1982) and **Cajun Invitation** (1983).

Both were keen to pursue solo careers, and David was first to record a solo album, **The Family's Fine, But This One's All Mine**, which resulted in the No. 1 country hit, **I'm Gonna Hire A Wino To Decorate Our Home**. He has continued to score solo hits with **A Million Light Beers Ago** (1983), **When We Get Back To The Farm** (1984) and **Country Music Love Affair** (1985), whilst the pair have also chalked up duet successes with **Another Dawn Breaking Over Georgia** (1984) and **Do Me Right** (1985).

Albums:
On My Own Again (Warner-Viva/–)
The David Frizzell & Shelly West Album (Warner-Viva/–)
Our Best To You – with Shelly West (Warner-Viva/–)

Lefty Frizzell

Acquiring the nickname 'Lefty' after disposing of several opponents with his left hand during an unsuccessful

Treasures Untold, Lefty Frizzell. Courtesy Bear Family Records.

The Legendary Lefty Frizzell. Courtesy MCA Records.

attempt to become a Golden Gloves boxing champion, the Texas-born (Corsicana, March 31, 1928) singer-songwriter-guitarist began life as William Orville Frizzell, the son of an itinerant oil driller.

A childhood performer, at 17 he could be found playing the honky tonks and dives of Dallas and Waco, moulding his early, Jimmie Rodgers stylings to the requirements of his environment, thus formulating a sound that was very much his own.

In 1950, Frizzell's Columbia recording of **If You've Got The Money, I've Got The Time** became a massive hit, claiming a chart position for some 20 weeks, the ex-pugilist following this with two 1951 No. 1s in **I Want To Be With You Always** and **Always Late**.

Becoming an Opry star, throughout the rest of the decade he continued to supply a series of chart high-flyers, many of these in honky tonk tradition. The '60s too found Frizzell obtaining more than a dozen hits, though only **Saginaw, Michigan** – a 1964 No. 1 – and **She's Gone, Gone, Gone** (1965) proved of any real consequence. His last hit for Columbia was with **Watermelon Time In Georgia** (1970).

He joined ABC Records in 1973 and was beginning to make a comeback with **I Never Go Around Mirrors** and **Lucky Arms** (both 1974) and **Falling** (1975) when he died on July 19, 1975 after suffering a stroke. Elected to the Country Music Hall Of Fame in 1982, Frizzell's influence can still be heard in the work of Merle Haggard, George Strait and many others.

Albums:
Lefty Frizzell Boxed Set (–/Bear Family)
The Classic Style (ABC/–)
The Legend Lives On (Columbia/–)
Songs Of Jimmie Rodgers (Columbia/–)
Lefty Goes To Nashville (Rounder/–)

Steve Fromholz

Purveyor of what he terms "free from country folk science fiction gospel cum existential bluegrass-opera music", the hirsute Fromholz (born June 8, 1945, Temple, Texas) once looked likely to become the most talented has-been in Austin, a situation later reflected in the title of his first solo album – **A Rumour In My Own Time**.

At 18, he attended North Texas State University, meeting singer-songwriter Michael Murphey, the duo becoming part

A Rumor In My Own Time, Steve Fromholz. Courtesy Capitol Records.

of the Dallas County Jug Band. After an abbreviated stay in the navy, Fromholz befriended another singer-songwriter, Dan McCrimmon, the twosome forming Frummox and recording an album **From Here To There** for Probe (1969), the disc featuring Fromholz's ambitious **Texas Trilogy**.

By 1971 the Texan had become part of Steve Stills' band, but later went solo cutting **How Long Is The Road To Kentucky**, an LP for Mike Nesmith's Countryside label, the completed record never being released.

Fromholz moved to Austin (1974), there becoming an accepted part of the outlaw community, providing material and singing on Willie Nelson's **Sound In Your Mind**. The first real Fromholz solo album, **A Rumour In My Own Time**, an all-star soiree featuring Red Rhodes, Willie Nelson, Doug Dillard, John Sebastian, B. W. Stevenson and the Lost Gonzo Band, found a Capitol release in 1976 and fulfilled all the hopes of Fromholz's cult following. However, a later album, **Frolicking In The Myth**, proved him to be moving on in search of new frontiers to breach.

In 1979, Fromholz signed to Nelson's Lone Star label, releasing one album, **Jus' Playin' Along**, had three songs on the film soundtrack of 'Outlaw Blues', and is now working on the Texas country-rock circuit.

Albums:
A Rumour In My Own Time (Capitol/–)
Frolicking In The Myth (Capitol/–)
Jus' Playin' Along (Lone Star/–)

Larry Gatlin

Born in Seminole, Texas, on 28 May, 1948, but raised in nearby Odessa, clear-voiced Larry Wayne Gatlin is a singer-songwriter whose roots are in gospel music. When only five he could be found watching the Blackwood Brothers. At the same age he appeared in a talent contest as part of The Gatlins (along with his two brothers and one of his sisters), a gospel group that toured throughout the southern states. But his breakthrough came while he was working with The Imperials, in Vegas, as part of The Jimmy Dean Show.

There Gatlin met Dottie West, one of Dean's guests, who offered to help him. In May, 1971, he sent her eight songs – from which she selected and recorded two, **Once You Were Mine** and **You're The Other Half Of Me**. A few months later, when Dottie formed her own First Generation Music Company, Gatlin was the first writer to gain a contract. Following further songs for Dottie, including **My Mind's Gone Away**, Gatlin

Treasures Untold:
The Early Recordings of
Lefty Frizzell

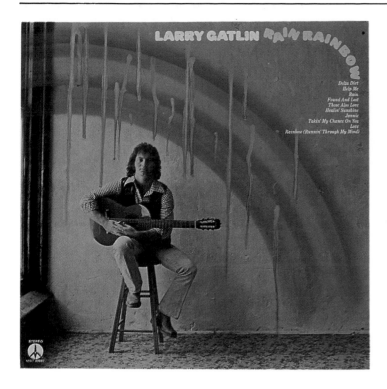

Rain Rainbow, Larry Gatlin. Courtesy Monument Records.

sang the verse plus harmony vocals on Kristofferson's **Why Me?** hit, Johnny Cash employing several Gatlin compositions for his 'Gospel Road' movie. Due to Kristofferson's insistence, Monument signed Gatlin in 1972, releasing singles by both he and The Gatlins that year, Larry's first album, **The Pilgrim**, appearing in 1974. Also in 1974 he made his Top 20 debut

Below: The Gatlin Brothers. Larry (centre) is one of country's most controversial characters. An engrossing performer, his behaviour has often been erratic.

with **Delta Dirt**, going Top 5 with a late 1975 release, **Broken Lady**, a song that won a Grammy as the best country song of 1976.

During 1975 too, Gatlin produced some sides for fellow Texan Johnny Duncan, one of which, **Jo And The Cowboy**, provided Janie Fricke with her debut as a backup singer.

He also reunited with his brothers Rudy and Steve, forming a band and reshaping his whole musical approach once more, the next major hit, **Statues Without Hearts** (1976), being released as by Larry Gatlin, With Family And Friends, culled from an album of the latter title. During 1977, in the wake of a flood of hits, he scored his first

No. 1 with **I Wish You Were Someone I Love**. There were three more Top 10 singles in 1978 along with two hit albums, **Oh Brother** and **Greatest Hits Vol 1**, but the Monument label was slowly folding and in early 1979 Gatlin switched to Columbia, his act now being billed as Larry Gatlin And The Gatlin Brothers Band. The result was another No. 1, **All The Gold In California** (1979) and such Top 10 singles as **Take Me To Your Lovin' Place** (1980), **What Are We Doin' Lonesome** (1981), **Sure Feels Like Love** (1982), **Houston** (a No. 1 in 1983), **Denver** and **The Lady Takes The Cowboy Everytime** (both 1984). But the strain of constant writing, recording and touring took its toll. On December 10, 1984 he voluntarily checked himself into a California drug and alcohol abuse centre, Gatlin making a public statement that 'My disease is fatal unless it is changed'. Happily, he was soon back to full health once more, he and his brothers cutting **Smile**, an album produced by jazz-funk guitarist Larry Carlton, in 1985.

Albums:
The Pilgrim (Monument/–)
Rain, Rainbow (Monument/Monument)
Larry Gatlin With Family And Friends
  (Monument/Monument)
Greatest Hits Vol 1 (Monument/
  Monument)
Houston to Denver (Columbia/–)
Straight Ahead (Columbia/CBS)

Crystal Gayle

Loretta Lynn's younger sister (real name Brenda Gail Webb), Crystal was the last of eight children born to the Webbs and the only one who arrived in a hospital. Born in Paintsville, Kentucky, in 1951, at 16 she toured with Conway Twitty and Loretta, her name change being inspired by the

Crystal, Crystal Gayle. Courtesy UA Records.

Krystal hamburger chain. In 1970, she placed her first Decca release, **I Cried (The Blue Right Out Of My Eyes)** on the country charts, but there was little other chart action during this period.

After the Decca deal ended, Crystal moved to UA Records, refusing to record any material associated with Loretta, and there began an association with producer Allen Reynolds, the man who had galvanized Don Williams' career. Reynolds' own composition, **Wrong Road Again**, brought Crystal back into the country charts, this being followed by two other singles that followed the same pattern, all of them from her successful debut album **Crystal Gayle**. This 1975 comeback was the start of a consistent run of hitmaking, Crystal's **Somebody Loves You** single going Top 10 that year. The following year saw the singer having two country chart-toppers, **I'll Get Over You** and **You Never Miss A Real Good Thing**, plus a best-selling third album, **Crystal**, all bearing the Reynolds hallmark of quality. 1977 saw the advent of two further monster hits in **I'd Do It All Over Again** and the bluesy **Don't It Make My Brown Eyes Blue**, Crystal's first major crossover single, while 1978 saw her

These Days, Crystal Gayle, Courtesy CBS Records.

logging three No. 1s in a row with **Ready For The Times To Get Better**, **Talking In Your Sleep** and **Why Have You Left The One You Left Me For**.

The flood of hits continued in 1979, though Crystal switched labels to Columbia, providing her new record company with further No. 1s, **It's Like We Never Said Goodbye** and **If You Ever Change Your Mind**, in 1980. Incredibly consistent – there was another No. 1, **Too Many Lovers**, for Columbia in 1981 before she signed for Elektra and carried on where she left off – logging yet another chart-topper with **Till I Gain Control Of You** (1982) Crystal Gayle has become the type of artist who can play country shows, rock concerts, MOR family affairs and plain pop shindigs, all with equal aplomb.

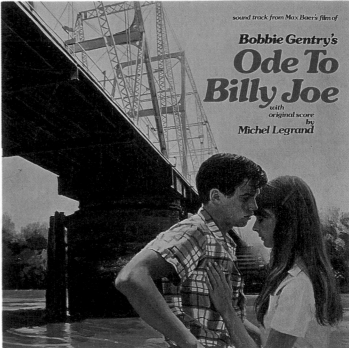

Ode To Billy Joe. The film soundtrack album. (Courtesy WEA Records).

Above: Crystal Gayle. Only her hair is longer than her list of best-selling records.

In recent years she has had a hit duet with Eddie Rabbit (**You And I**), further No. 1s with such Warner releases as **Our Love Is On The Faultline**, **Baby What About You**, **The Sound Of Goodbye** (1983) and **Turning Away** (1984), while in early 1986, she and Gary Morris had a Top 5 duet in **Making Up For Lost Time**, a song penned by Morris and Jim Ed Norman. Only her hair is longer than her list of best-selling records.

Albums:
Crystal Gayle (UA/UA)
Somebody Loves You (UA/UA)
Crystal (UA/UA)
When I Dream (UA/UA)
The Crystal Gayle Collection (-/CBS)

Bobbie Gentry

In July 1967, **Ode to Billy Joe**, a song about the suicide of a certain Billy Joe Macallister, was released. Bedecked in an imaginative, swamp-flavoured, Jimmy Haskell arrangement, it was one of the year's finest singles and subsequently sold a million. Thus was the public introduced to the singing and songwriting talent of Bobbie Gentry.

Of Portugese descent, she was born Roberta Streets, in Chickasaw County, Mississippi, on July 27, 1944, later changing her name to Gentry after seeing 'Ruby Gentry', a movie about swampland passion involving Jennifer Jones and Charlton Heston. A childhood singer and guitarist, Bobbie spent her early years in Greenwood, Mississippi, and then moved with her family to California, there attending high school in Palm Springs and, later, UCLA, where she majored in philosophy. Already proficient on several instruments (she plays guitar, banjo, bass, piano and vibes) Bobbie attended the LA Conservatory of Music, studying theory.

Signed to Capitol Records in 1967, she cut **Ode To Billy Joe** at one half-hour session and became a star virtually overnight. Then followed a number of other crossover hits including **Okolona River Bottom Band** (1967), **Fancy** (1969), **Let It Be Me** (1969) and **All I Have To Do Is Dream** (1970), the last two being duets with Glen Campbell.

Extremely popular in Britain where she had her own BBC-TV series and gained a No. 1 with **I'll Never Fall In Love Again** (1970), Bobbie's sales waned as the '70s moved on. But in 1976 a film, 'Ode To Billie Joe', based on the events documented in the Gentry song, reactivated some interest in her Delta ditties once more, boosting her appeal on the Vegas-Reno circuit and at the Hughes hotel chain, her contract with the latter touted to be in the multimillion dollar bracket.

Albums:
Ode to Billy Joe (Capitol/Capitol)
Bobbie Gentry's Greatest (Capitol/Capitol)

Don Gibson

A rich-voiced singer-songwriter whose wares enabled him to move into the pop market of the 1960s, Don Gibson was born in Shelby, North Carolina, on April 3, 1928. A competent guitarist before he left

20 Of The Best, Don Gibson. Courtesy RCA Records.

school, Gibson built up a regional following via live gigs and radio broadcasts. After finishing his education, he moved to Knoxville, where he was heard on the WNOX Tennessee Barn Dance. His first big writing success came from **Sweet Dreams**, a song which was a hit for Faron Young, while in 1958 **I Can't Stop Loving You**, his best known compositon, became a hit for Kitty Wells. Later, Ray Charles was to have international success with the same song and virtually make it his own property. Gibson himself recorded the number as the B-side of **Oh Lonesome Me**, but the former broke through for him and gave him a name-making pop hit in the process. Total sales of **I Can't Stop Loving You** were not long in reaching the one million mark, other songs that provided hit records for Don himself including **Give Myself a Party**, **Blue Blue Day**, **Sea Of Heartbreak** and **Lonesome Number One**, the last three, and particularly **Sea Of Heartbreak**, showing that Gibson's deep

I Wrote A Song, Don Gibson. Courtesy RCA Records.

voice and neatly novel songs could cross over into the pop charts sometimes.

But, consistently successful in the country charts, Gibson has always kept his country image and has often been critical of the inroads rock has made into his chosen style of music. Though regarded mainly as a 1960s singer because of his crossover hits during that period, he was a fairly prolific hitmaker in the 1970s when, signed to Hickory and

Don't Stop Loving Me, Don Gibson. Courtesy Hickory Records.

ABC-Hickory, he logged nearly 40 chart records, including a number of duets with Sue Thompson, one of his solo cuts, **Woman (Sensuous Woman)**, going to No. 1 in 1972. More recently, he has recorded for MCA (1979) and Warner (1980) providing both with some chart action. A purveyor of classic songs dealing with heartbreak and loneliness, Gibson once wrote: 'If loneliness meant world acclaim, then everyone would know my name – I'd be a legend in my time.' And he is, he really is.

Above: Mickey Gilley achieved international fame when 'Urban Cowboy' was shot at his Houston club.

Albums:
20 Of The Best (–/RCA)
Don't Stop Loving Me (Hickory/DJM)
Rockin' Rollin' Gibson (–/Bear Family)
The Best Of Don Gibson (RCA/RCA)

Mickey Gilley

The piano-playing cousin of Jerry Lee Lewis and a performer in similar vein, Mickey Gilley was born in Ferriday, Louisiana. He moved to Houston at the age of 17 to do construction work and began playing at local clubs, cutting the rock'n'roll songs **Tell Me Why** and **Oo-ee-baby** for the Houston-based Minor label. This brought no rewards so Gilley travelled on, recording for Dot in Memphis, Rex in New Orleans and Khoury in Lake Charles, Louisiana. In 1960 he recorded a Warner Mack song, **Is It Wrong**, for Potomac, and gained a regional best seller – but the label folded and Gilley continued label-hopping, cutting sides with Lynn, Sabra and Princess.

In 1964, he formed his own record company Astro, his second release **Lonely Wine** proving another regional hit, an album of the same name (later retitled **Down The Line**, when reissued by Paula) also being released. However, 1965 found Gilley on 20th Century Fox, from there moving to Paula, where he enjoyed a mild 1968 hit in **Now I Can Live Again** – but it was not until 1974 and some reaction to his Astro version of George Morgan's old **Roomful Of Roses** winner, that things slotted together for Gilley. The single was picked up by Hugh Hefner's Playboy label and immediately went to No. 1 in the

charts, to be followed by further chart-toppers in **I Overlooked An Orchid**, **City Lights** (both 1974) and **Window Up Above** (1975). Two more No. 1s came in 1976 – **Don't The Girls All Get Prettier At Closing Time** and **Bring It One Home To Me** – at which point he garnered the Entertainer Of The Year, Top Male Vocalist, Song Of The Year, Single Of The Year and Album Of The Year awards from the ACM.

After further hits for Playboy, including **She's Pulling Me Back Again**, a 1977 No. 1, Gilley signed with Epic, his career gaining an added fillip in 1980 when the

Welcome To Gilley's, Mickey Gilley. Courtesy PRT Records.

movie 'Urban Cowboy', shot at Gilley's – the Houston club the singer bought in the early '70s – provided him with international exposure and a pop hit in **Stand By Me**, one of Gilley's three country No. 1s that year, the others being **True Love Ways** and **That's All That Matters**. Since then the flow of hits has continued along with an additional array of league leaders in **A Headache Tomorrow (Or A Heartache Tonight)**, **You Don't Know Me**, **Lonely Nights** (1981), **Put Your Dreams Away**, **Talk To Me** (1982), **Fool For Your Love** (1983), and **You've Really Got A Hold On Me** (1984). Also in recent years Gilley has recorded a number of hit duets with Charly McClain.

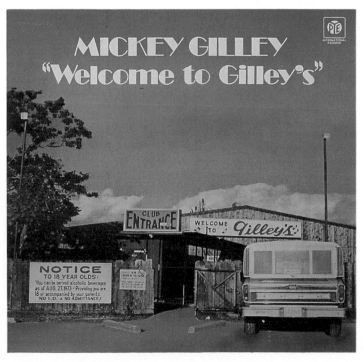

Albums:
At His Best (Paula/–)
Welcome To Gilley's (Playboy/Pye)
Greatest Hits Vol. 1 (Playboy/Pye)
Down The Line (–/Charly)
That's All That Matters To Me (Epic/Epic)
Gilley's Smokin' (Epic/–)
It Takes Believers – with Charly McClain
  (Epic/–)

Johnny Gimble

A brilliant session fiddle player and mandolinist, also the writer of **Fiddlin' Around**, a tune nominated for a 1974 Grammy Award, Johnny Gimble was born in 1926 and grew up on a farm in Texas.

With his brothers Gene, Jerry, Jack and

Texas Dance Party, Johnny Gimble. Courtesy CBS Records.

Bill, the 12-year-old Johnny began playing at local gigs, Gene, Jerry and Johnny combining with James Ivie during their high school days to form the Rose City Swingsters, a group that played on radio station KGKB. Leaving home in 1943, Gimble played fiddle and banjo with Bob and Joe Shelton at KWKH, Shreveport, Louisiana, also working as part of the Jimmie Davis band.

Gimble spent two or three stints with Bob Wills and his Texas Playboys, playing an essential part in creating the best of Bob's post war bands, although when western swing's popularity sagged he left the music business and settled down in barbering and working in a hospital.

A resident of Dallas for a while, he began working as a studio musician with Lefty Frizzell, Ray Price, Marty Robbins and others, eventually moving to Nashville,

Below: The incredible Johnny Gimble, one of the world's finest fiddle-players and an excellent mandolinist.

where he gained even more work, both in the studio and as a touring back-up man with such stars as Merle Haggard, Loretta Lynn and Johnny Rodriguez. He has also played many dates as a headliner and has appeared on such TV shows as 'Hee Haw' and 'Austin City Limits' with some frequency, his accomplishments winning him the CMA Instrumentalist Of The Year award in 1975, while the Academy Of Country Music adjudged him Top Fiddle Player in 1978 and 1979.

In the late '70s Johnny moved from Nashville to Austin but he still turns up on countless Nashville sessions and tours with Merle Haggard, Asleep At The Wheel, Willie Nelson, and various all star bands, playing both jazz and pure country with equal fluency.

Albums:
Texas Dance Party (Columbia/–)
Still Swingin' – with The Texas Swing
  Pioneers (CMH/–)

Girls Of The Golden West

Authentic westerners, both from Muleshoe, Texas, Dorothy Laverne 'Dolly' Good (born December 11, 1915) and Mildred Fern 'Millie' Good (born April 11, 1913) were one of the most popular acts in early country music, and helped pave the way for the other women singers who followed, as well as being among the earliest to exploit the cowboy image in dress and in song.

They began their career on WIL and KMOX in St Louis in 1930, then spent three years in Milford, Kansas, and on XER in Mexico, before coming to nationwide renown on the National Barn Dance from 1933–7. The Goods, both of whom sang and played guitar, were even more popular on the Boone County Jamboree and the Midwestern Hayride (both over WLW) in Cincinnati, where they were voted the most popular act on WLW in 1945. Their appearances and performance tailed off in the '50s and they did not perform after about 1963, Dolly dying on November 12, 1967, while Millie was still living in Cincinnati, Ohio at the start of the 1980s.

In their prime they recorded for RCA, Columbia and Conqueror, also recording for such labels as FJC, Manco and Bluebonnet (which put out a full six volumes of their material) late in their career. They never had any great success on record, but were among the most

Still Swingin', Johnny Gimble. Courtesy CMH Country Classics.

popular groups of their era – and one of the most influential.

Album:
The Girls Of The Golden West (Old
  Homestead/–)

Vern Gosdin

A singer whose success was a long time in coming, Vern Gosdin spent many years as a West Coast sessionman, providing back-up vocals for The Byrds, The Burritos, Leon Russell and otherrs.

Born in Woodland, Alabama, he lived on a farm where there was no TV set, only an old monster-sized Philco radio that ran on batteries. Each Saturday night was spent tuning in to the Opry, Gosdin assimilating the sounds of the Louvin Brothers, their harmonies becoming a major influence upon his own vocal style. He sang six days a week on a gospel show over WVOK, Birmingham, Alabama during the late '50s, then moved out to California, where he and his brother Rex recorded as The Gosdin Brothers and had a fair-sized hit with **Hangin' On** on the Bakersfield International label in 1967, this being followed by another mini-winner in **Till The End** (1968) for Capitol. But things fell apart and during 1972 Vern moved to Atlanta with his wife and two sons, taking a job selling and delivering glassware.

During the mid '70s he was encouraged, by record producer Gary S. Paxton, to make a fresh start in Nashville, cutting new versions of **Hangin' On** (1976), with Emmylou Harris singing harmony, and **Till The End** (1977), both these Elektra releases going Top 10, along with **Yesterday's Gone**, another Gosdin Top 10 entry in 1977. In the wake of chart entries with **Till The End** and an album of the same title, Vern eventually was asked to make an entry on his revered Opry, following this with such other major hits as **Never My Love, Break My Mind** (1978), **You've Got Somebody, I've Got Somebody** (1979). He switched to the Ovation label in

1981 and had a couple of hits including **Dream Of Me**, while by 1982 Gosdin was on AMI and still going Top 10 with **Today My World Slipped Away**. A consistent label-hopper – in 1983 he signed for Compleat – he has remained an equally consistent provider of major singles, providing his new employers with Top 10 records in **If You're Gonna Do Me Wrong (Do It Right), Way Down Deep,** and **I Wonder Where We'd Be Tonight** (1983), **I Can Tell By The Way You Dance (You're Gonna Love Me Tonight)** (his first No. 1), **What Would Your Memories Do,** and **Slow Burning Memory** (1984).

Albums:
Till The End (Elektra/Elektra)
The Best Of Vern Gosdin (Elektra/–)
There Is A Season (Compleat/PRT
  Compleat)

Billy Grammer

Originator of the Grammer guitar, a fine flat-top instrument, Billy Grammer's first guitar was installed in the Country Music Hall Of Fame in March, 1969, along with the first pick-up for amplifying a bass electronically, the latter designed by Everett Hull.

One of 13 children fathered by an Illinois coalminer, Grammer (born Benton, Illinois, August 28, 1925) became a major star during the late '50s and early '60s. He performed on WRAL, Arlington in 1947 and by 1955 had earned a regular spot on the Washington-based Jimmy Dean TV Show, moving with Dean on to a CBS network programme later.

A popular bandleader, Grammer signed with Monument Records in 1958, having his first hit – a million seller – with **Gotta Travel On**, a song adapted by The Weavers from a traditional melody. Becoming an Opry regular in 1959 and obtaining a double-sided hit that year with **Bonaparte's Retreat/The Kissing Tree**, Grammer recorded for numerous labels throughout the '60s, with minor hits on most of them, via such titles as **I Wanna Go Home** (Decca, 1963), **The Real Thing** (Epic 1966), **Mabel** (Rice, 1967), **Ballad Of**

Above: Billy Grammer. Once lead guitarist with Clyde Moody and Jimmy Dean, he hit paydirt with Gotta Travel On.

John Dillinger (Mercury, 1968) and Jesus Is A Soul Man (Stop, 1969).

Albums:
Country Guitar (Decca/–)
Favorites (Vocalion/–)

Claude Gray

A popular singer, guitarist and bandleader, Gray enjoyed a spate of best-selling singles at the commencement of the '60s when, after recording Willie Nelson's **Family Bible** and gaining a Top 10 hit, he signed for Mercury and immediately scored two 1961 Top 5 entries with **I'll Just Have Another Cup Of Coffee** and **My Ears Should Burn**, the latter being a Roger Miller composition. Several minor hits later, in 1965, the six feet five inch tall Gray switched to Columbia, stopping to provide one healthy seller in **Mean Old Woman** (1966), then moved on to join Decca, with whom he enjoyed a healthy stay that extended into the '70s, this relationship commencing with two best sellers, **I Never Had The One I Wanted** (1966) and **How Fast Them Trucks Can Go** (1967).

Gray, who once again popped into the charts during 1973 with **Woman Ease My Mind**, on the Million label, has since logged a number of mini-hits for the Granny White label – the most recent being **Let's Go All The Way**, a duet with Norma Jean (1982). He was born in Henderson, Texas, on January 26, 1932.

Mark Gray

A one-time gospel singer, a composer of jingles for 17 years and a writer of pop hits for Englebert Humperdinck and Melissa

Manchester, Mark Gray was born at Vicksbury, Mississippi, in 1952. The youngest of seven children, his mother died when he was just two and he was raised by his aunt and uncle who lived near Chattanooga, Tennessee. His aunt was part of a gospel group and Gray toured with them for several years, at 19 moving on to work with the Oak Ridge Boys publishing company and appearing with them onstage whenever they needed a pianist to deputize for Tony Brown, then their regular keyboardist. After seven years he returned to Mississippi and began concentrating on his songwriting career.

Eventually he made his way back to

That Feeling Inside, Mark Gray. Courtesy CBS Records.

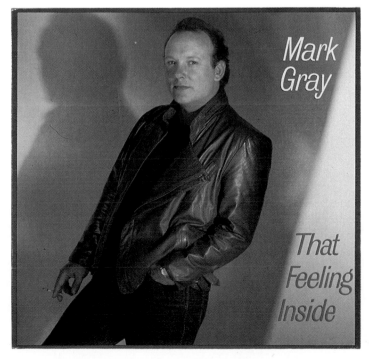

Nashville, becoming lead singer with Exile but continuing to write songs, his credits including **Take Me Down** and **The Closer You Get** (both No. 1s for Alabama) and **It Ain't Easy (Bein' Easy)**, a chart-topper for Janie Fricke. One of his demo-tapes for the latter was heard by a Columbia Records executive and led to Gray gaining a contract as a solo act with the label in 1983. Proffering a crossover image – country songs provided by a city guy in a trilby hat – Gray made an immediate impact, notching a Top 20 single that year with **Wounded Hearts**. By 1984 he was up among the frontrunners, logging three Top 10 records (**Left Side Of The Bed**, **If All The Magic Is Gone**, and **Diamond In The Dust**) and in 1985 Gray teamed with Tammy Wynette in a Top 10 duet, **Sometimes When We Touch**, returning to

solo mode for **Please Be Love** (1986).

Able to touch many bases, Gray once said: 'I love all kinds of music but country is where I want to be because it isn't fake music for me. I feel it. For me, country music is that line betwen gospel and R&B. And that's where I am.'

Albums:
Magic (Columbia/CBS)
This Ol' Piano (Columbia/CBS)
That Feeling Inside (Columbia/CBS)

Otto Gray

One of the most popular and influential of the very early country professional bands was Otto Gray and his Oklahoma Cowboys, who toured in custom-made limousines, helped popularize country music in the north east, and presented a very slick, very rehearsed, very effective stage show.

Gray himself was from Oklahoma, but achieved his greatest success in the north east, particularly over WGY in Schenectady, New York. Not much of a musician himself, he was host and MC for the Oklahoma Cowboys, whose more prominent members included his wife 'Mommie', his son Owen, and at one time also both Zeke Clements and Whitey 'The Duke Of Paducah' Ford.

Gray had organized the Oklahoma Cowboys as early as 1924, and the band actually lasted through the mid-'40s. They recorded for Gennett, Vocalion and Okeh.

Lloyd Green

One of Nashville's top sessionmen, Mensa member Green was born in Mississippi, on October 4, 1937, and grew up in Mobile, Alabama. He began taking lessons on steel guitar at the age of seven, playing professionally three years later. During his high school days he played weekends at clubs and bars where 'real rough fights, shootings and stabbings were common', using material drawn mainly from the Eddy Arnold and Hank Williams songbooks. He attended the University of Southern

Lloyd Green And His Steel Guitar. Courtesy M&M Records.

Mississippi as a psychology major but left after two years to play in Nashville. He initially worked there with Hawkshaw Hawkins and Jean Shepard, then toured with Faron Young and George Jones, his first recording session in Music City being on Jones' **Too Much Water Runs Under The Bridge** single in 1957. Though he has had hard times since – at one period being forced to take a job in a shoe shop – Green is now an in-demand steelie and plays on some 500 sessions a year. A recording artist in his own right, he has also had a few hit singles, the biggest of these being **I Can See Clearly Now**, on Monument in 1973.

Albums:
Steel Rides (Monument/Monument)
Cool Steel Man (Chart/Chart)
Green Velvet (Little Darlin'/President)

Greenbriar Boys

A New York-based bluegrass group, Greenbriar Boys was formed in 1958 by Bob Yellin, John Herald and Eric Weissberg. Extremely popular at various folk festivals in the 1960s, they recorded for Elektra and Vanguard and produced several well-regarded albums. Changing much through the years, their personnel can claim to have included legendary mandolinist Frank Wakefield, fiddler Buddy Spicher and Ralph Rinzler, one-time manager of Bill Monroe, organizer of numerous festivals, and a leading authority on old time country music. Original member Weissberg teamed with Steve Mandell in 1972 to provide **Dueling Banjos** – an instrumental from the film 'Deliverance' – which turned a million-selling single the following year.

Albums:
Best Of The Greenbriar Boys (Vanguard/–)
Ragged But Right (Vanguard/–)
Better Late Than Never (Vanguard/–)

Below: Jack Greene, In 1966 he logged eight Top 5 singles in a row and won four CMA Awards in 1967.

Jack Greene

Yet another of the long list of country entertainers who could play guitar at an early age, Jack Henry Green (born Maryville, Tennessee, January 7, 1930), also a fine drummer, first became a full-time musician with the Cherokee Trio, an Atlanta GA group, moving on to become sticksman with the Rhythm Ranch Boys in 1950. Then came two years of army service, followed by a stint with another Atlanta band, the Peachtree Cowboys.

Joining Ernest Tubb's Texas Troubadours in 1962, the amiable six-footer, dubbed 'the Jolly Giant', soon became a favourite. And while still a member of Tubb's band, he began having solo discs released by Decca, one single, **Ever Since My Baby Went Away**, charting in mild fashion during 1965, this being followed by two No.1s in **There Goes My Everything** (1966) and **All The Time** (1967). During 1967, Greene gained four CMA awards – Best Male Vocalist, Best Album, Best Song and Single Of The Year (for **There Goes My Everything**, a Dallas Frazier composition). Thereafter he continued on his hit-making way, providing Decca with five more top singles during the late '60s.

In 1969, Greene and Jeannie Seely, his co-vocalist on the Ernest Tubb TV show, put together a roadshow and began touring with a band called the Green Giants, the twosome enjoying immediate success on record with **Wish I Didn't Have To Miss You**. The first country act to play the Rooftop Lounge, King Of The Road, Nashville, in 1972, Greene and Seely received considerable acclaim for their 1974 Madison Square Garden concert.

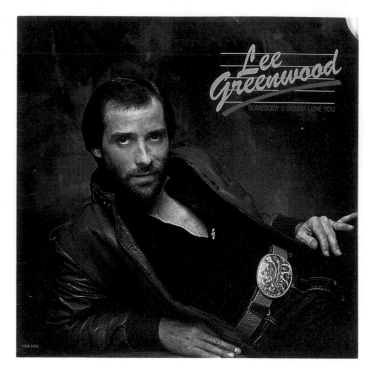

Somebody's Gonna Love You, Lee Greenwood. Courtesy MCA Records.

The duo played host and hostess at the Wembley Country Festival two years later. But at the beginning of 1981, after many thousands of miles on the road together, they went their separate ways, Greene claiming that the split gave him the opportunity to provide a less Vegas-styled presentation and a back-to-basics approach. Also, during the start of the '80s he began having hits again, for the first time since 1975. But his deal with the Frontline label fell through and Greene was out in the cold once more, his happy relationship with the country charts being resumed yet again in 1983 when he signed with EMH Records.

Albums:
Greatest Hits (MCA/–)
The Best Of (–/MCA)
Greene Country (MCA/–)
Two For The Show – with Jeannie Seely (MCA/–)
Jack Greene And Jeannie Seely (MCA/–)

Lee Greenwood

The son of half-Cherokee parents who split when he was just a year old, Lee Greenwood was left in the care of his grandparents who had a chicken farm near Sacremento. A sax-player and a pianist, he became a schoolboy member of a local band known as My Moonbeams. Later reunited with his mother in Los Angeles, he played for various jazz and rock bands in the LA area but, after returning to Sacremento in 1958, he moved into country music, joining a band headed by Capitol recording artist Chester Smith and appearing on TV at the age of 15. Hired by Del Reeves for his sax expertise (he can also play guitar, bass and banjo), he learnt the art of showmanship from Reeves, then formed his own band, Apollo, which became based in Las Vegas in 1962. By 1965 Apollo had evolved into The Lee Greenwood Affair, a pop band signed to Paramount

Records.

For a while, Greenwood took the band back to the west coast in an attempt to break into the pop market. But the Paramount label folded and so did the Affair shortly afterwards, Greenwood returning to Vegas where he took up jobs as a bandleader, back-up singer, musical arranger, bar-room pianist and card dealer in the casinos. Heard singing in a bar by Mel Tillis' bandleader Larry McFaden in 1979, he was asked to fly to Nashville to record some demo discs but afterwards returned to jobs in Vegas and Reno. He also began concentrating on his songwriting, switching from showbiz material to more country-oriented fare at McFaden's insistence. The latter took Greenwood's demos to various Nashville-based labels and eventually got MCA to sign a deal in June, 1981, McFaden becoming the singing musician's manager some months later.

A distinctive singer with a voice loaded with finely sifted gravel, Greenwood went Top 20 with his first MCA single, **It Turns Me Inside Out**, in mid-1981 and followed this with three Top 10 hits during the following year – **Ring On Her Finger, Time On Her Hands, She's Lying, Ain't No Trick (It Takes Magic)** – all of which appeared on his debut album **Inside And Out**. But 1983 was really Greenwood's year, not only providing him with three hit singles – **IOU, Somebody's Gonna Love You**, and **Going, Going, Gone**, the last two being country No.1s and all three crossing over into the pop charts – but also with the Male Vocalist Of The Year title at the CMA Awards.

Since that time, he has had further winners with **God Bless The USA, Fool's Gold, You've Got A Good Love Comin', To Me**, a duet with Barbara Mandrell, (all 1984), **Dixie Road, I Don't Mind The Thorns (If You're The Rose)**, and **Don't Underestimate My Love For You** (1985). A superior songwriter who has had his material recorded by Kenny Rogers, Mel Tillis, Brenda Lee and others, he is also the voice on many commercials, singing the praises of McDonald's and Nestles Crunch, to name but a mouthful. In Britain, however, Lee is known for **The Wind Beneath My Wings**, a single which

Above: The multi-talented Lee Greenwood, once a Las Vegas croupier, now raking in the loot from disc buyers.

entered the UK pop charts in 1984.

Albums:
Inside And Out (MCA/MCA)
Somebody's Gonna Love You (MCA/MCA)
Meant For Each Other – with Barbara Mandrell (MCA/–)

Ray Griff

The writer of many hundreds of songs, Ray Griff was born in Vancouver, British Columbia, Canada, on April 22, 1940, moving with his family to Calgary, Alberta, shortly before reaching his teens. A drummer in a band at the age of eight, Griff also mastered guitar and piano, becoming a bandleader on the nightclub circuit at 18. His reputation as a songwriter was enhanced when Johnny Horton recorded **Mr Moonlight**, a Griff composition, during the late '50s, Jim Reeves cutting **Where Do I Go?**, another Griff original, in 1962.

Encouraged by Reeves, he became Nashville-based in 1964, initially involving himself in songwriting and music publishing, but later recording some sides for RCA's Groove label. An MGM release,

Above: The Gully Jumpers, an early WSM string band.

Sugar From My Candy, on Dot, a few months later. Label-switching again, he recorded Clarence Carter's **Patches** for Royal American, gaining a 1970 success, climbing even higher with **The Morning After Baby Let Me Down**, in 1971, also enjoying Top 10 discs with **You Ring My Bell** (1975) and **If I Let Her Come In** (1976), both on Capitol.

Since that time, Griff has supplied a few mini-hits during the '80s for Vision and RCA but it is as a songwriter that the one-time inveterate stutterer (for years he hardly gave an interview) has really staked a claim to fame, his compositions including **Canadian Pacific** (recorded by George Hamilton IV), **Baby** (Wilma Burgess), **Better Move It On Home** (Porter Wagoner and Dolly Parton), **Step Aside** (Faron Young), **Who's Gonna Play This Old Piano** (Jerry Lee Lewis) and many others, the majority of these being published by Griff's own Blue Echo company.

Your Lily White Hands, provided him with his first hit (1967), Griff following this with

Below: Ray Griff, one of several Canadians who have enhanced country music.

Albums:
Ray Griff (Capitol/–)
The Last Of The Winfield Amateurs (Capitol/–)
Canada (Boot/–)

Rex Griffin

A popular singer, guitarist and songwriter, Rex Griffin is best known for his composition **The Last Letter**, although he has several other hits to his credit, including **Just Call me Lonesome**.

Born on August 22, 1912, he became popular over WSB in Atlanta and as host of the KRLD Texas Roundup. Probably the most fascinating aspect of his career was that he recorded **Lovesick Blues** for Decca, a record which went nowhere; nearly a decade later Hank Williams learnt and recorded Griffin's version identically, with tremendous success. Plagued with ill-health in latter years due to a lifelong drinking problem, Griffin died on October 11, 1959.

The Gully Jumpers

Charlie Arrington, fiddle; Roy Hardison, banjo; Burt Hutcherson, guitar; Paul Warmack, mandolin and guitar.

The Gully Jumpers were one of the early popular Opry string bands and participated in that early Nashville recording session for Victor in October 1928. Led by Paul Warmack, an auto mechanic by trade, they remained with basically the same personnel for well over two decades (they had joined the Opry about 1927) and in fact were one of the most popular and most used bands of the Opry's early years. The group was dissolved in the mid-'60s when four of the old-time Opry bands were accordioned into two.

Though few recordings of The Gully Jumpers are available on vinyl, the band can be heard on Nashville – **The Early String Bands Vol. 1** (County) playing **Robertson County** and **Stone Rag**.

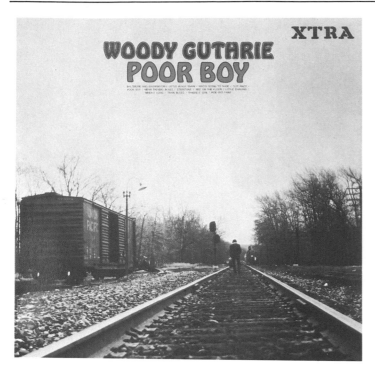

Poor Boy, Woody Guthrie. Courtesy Xtra Records.

Woody Guthrie

An influential country folk singer, Guthrie's visual attitude and thin, fragmented vocal style have been copied by many, most notably Bob Dylan.

Born Woodrow Wilson Guthrie, in Okema, Oklahoma, in 1912, a hard rural upbringing amid a background of natural disasters set the tone for many of his songs. He championed the rural poor and the loser (as on **Dustbowl Ballads**) yet he was also capable of joyous hymns to the country itself and the idea of man as owner of it (**This Land Is Your Land**).

He roamed the land extensively, incorporating what he found into songs. He later wrote that he saw things happen to oil people, cattle people and wheat folks, and detailed these happenings in songs which he broadcast over the LA station KFVD. He gave rise to what is sometimes called 'The Dustbowl Tradition', other exponents of which include Cisco Houston, Rambling Jack Elliott, and Ry Cooder. The slogan on his guitar read 'This machine kills fascists' and as he roamed America during the depression, singing in union halls and for picket lines, it was hardly surprising when the authorities, already scared by the crisis, tried to tag the 'red' label on him. In a parallel with the '60s decade, those who pointed the need for social change could find themselves ostracized or even in danger.

Guthrie's mother had died of Huntingdon's Chorea (a hereditary nerve disease) and Woody himself succumbed to it in 1967, having been in hospital since 1954 (where Bob Dylan visited him). He was a country singer in the very widest sense, a drifting son of the earth, crafting his simple songs out of experience and his own perception. During 1976, the singer's autobiography 'Bound For Glory' became the subject of a film directed by Hal Ashby with David Carradine in the role of Guthrie.

Albums:
Dust Bowl Ballads (Folkways/–)
Bound For Glory (Folkways/–)
This Land Is Your Land (Folkways/–)

The Hackberry Ramblers

Luderin Darbone, fiddle and leader; Edwin Duhon, mandolin; Floyd Rainwater, bass; Lonnie Rainwater, guitar; Lennis Sonnier, guitar and vocals; Joe Werner, guitar.

An early and influential Cajun band whose records both in English and Cajun French helped win the music a wider audience in the 1930s. In their prime – the '30s – they recorded mainly for Bluebird.

They disbanded in 1939, but in the '60s Luderin Darbone reformed the Hackberry Ramblers for appearances at folk festivals and at week-end dances in various local taverns.

Albums:
Hackberry Ramblers (Arhoolie/–)
Country Music: Songs Of The South And West (New World/–)

Merle Haggard

Country's most charismatic living legend, Merle Haggard is the proof that you do not have to forsake your musical roots to achieve fame.

The Haggard family had been driven from their farm in dustbowl East Oklahoma and were living in a converted boxcar in Bakersfield, California, when Merle was born, on April 6, 1937. Merle's father was a competent fiddle player although after their marriage Mrs Haggard, a strict Church of Christ member, insisted that he at least stopped playing in honky tonks.

Merle was nine when his father died, and without his father's influence and music he began to run wild. His mother put him in a juvenile home for a spell to try and scare him into straightening out. He embarked on a series of petty thefts and frauds and was in and out of local prisons, and in 1957 he was charged with attempted burglary and sentenced to six months to fifteen years in San Quentin.

Whilst in prison Merle did some picking and songwriting and was in San Quentin when Johnny Cash came to perform. A spell in solitary confinement talking with the men on death row convinced him to get himself straight, and when he left jail in 1960 he was determined to try and make a go of performing, since Bakersfield was by then growing into a respectable little country music centre.

He was helped initially by Bakersfield *eminence gris*, Buck Owens, and by Bonnie Owens, Buck's former wife whom Merle himself eventually married. At this time Merle ran into Fuzzy Owen, an Arkansas musician who was playing the Bakersfield clubs (the town's country music venues included a share of 'apprentice serving clubs' frequented by whooping cowboys and oil hands). Fuzzy, who is Merle's manager to this day, helped Merle get work locally and encouraged him, and when Merle returned from a stint with a band at Las Vegas in 1962 Fuzzy had him recording some sides for Tally, a label Owen had purchased from his cousin Lewis Tally.

Recording in a converted 'garage' studio, they produced a single which sold 200 copies. However, the next year saw them reach No. 19 in the country charts with **Sing A Sad Song** and in 1964 **Sam Hill** reached No. 45. In 1965 they put out **All My Friends Are Gonna Be Strangers**, and although it languished for some time on Tally, Capitol Records later took over the Tally Catalogue and recycled the single, getting a Top 10 country hit with it.

The song was a Liz and Casey Anderson composition and in 1966 Merle had his first country No. 1 with **I'm A Lonesome Fugitive**, also written by them. It was the first in a long line of country hits. Merle had been trying to suppress the news of his prison record, but as the story came out the hard core country public were fascinated by this man who so obviously had lived the songs he wrote.

In 1966 Merle released **The Bottle Let Me Down** (Emmylou Harris would later include the song on an album), in 1967 **Branded Man**, 1968 **Mama Tried** (which referred to his wild childhood and prison

Kern River, Merle Haggard, Courtesy Epic Records.

record), 1969 **Hungry Eyes** and **Workin' Man Blues** and in 1970 the well-covered standard **Today I Started Loving You Again** (co-written with Bonnie Owens).

Two other apparently innocent songs were committed to record in 1970: **Okie From Muskogee** and **The Fightin' Side Of Me**. Okie re-stated redneck values in the face of then current campus disturbances and Vietnam marches, yet Merle had written it as a joke, picking up a remark one of his band members had made about the conservative living habits of Oklahoma natives as the coach rolled through Muskogee one day. **Fightin' Side Of Me** was another apparent putdown of those who were so bold as to disparage America's image. When Haggard premiered **Okie** for a crowd of NCOs at the Fort Bragg, North Carolina, camp, they went wilder than he had expected and from then on the song became a silent majority legend.

Haggard had been gaining a reputation as the new Woody Guthrie before **Okie**, and his hippy following was stunned yet intrigued by this new turn of events. Even President Nixon was said to have written to congratulate Haggard on the song.

Merle himself has admitted to feeling scared at the reaction the song provoked and he then backed away from further right wing involvement, refusing a proposal that he had been offered to endorse George Wallace politically. Indeed, for his next single he wanted to record a song about an inter-racial love affair (**Norma Jackson**) but Capitol advised against it.

After the **Okie** controversy had died down Merle was able to settle into the straightforward country career he felt most comfortable with. He has not appeared over much on television. For one thing he lacks the easy, flip manner which TV companies seem to want from a host, and secondly he has not bothered to cultivate the medium. He once walked out on an Ed Sullivan show when they tried to tell him which songs to sing and how to sing them. However, this principled, non-conforming attitude, which probably lost him lucrative work, only strengthened the bond between Merle and country fans.

Since **Okie**, hits have come consistently: **I Wonder What She'll Think**

Merle Haggard
KERN RIVER

pair were married on October 7, 1978 and recorded several duets which failed to make much of an impression. Five years later they were separated with Merle concentrating fully on his musical career.

A move to Epic Records towards the end of 1981 led to duet recordings with George Jones (**A Taste Of Yesterday's Wine** album in 1982) and Willie Nelson (**Poncho & Lefty**, which was named CMA Album Of The Year in 1983). His solo hits continued with **Big City** (1982), **That's The Way Love Goes** (1983), **Natural High** (1984), **Kern River** (1985) and **I Had A Beautiful Time** (1986).

Usually, legendary figures are larger than life, but somehow Merle Haggard has managed to become a legend in his own time without losing the reality of being a down-to-earth human being. Perhaps this is because his songs deal so closely with the reality of being human. A classic uncompromising country artist, his voice is hurting, yet subtle, with no showbiz nuances and he gives the impression, with his sparsely instrumented band The Strangers, of being more comfortable before audiences of working men than in Las Vegas hotel lounges.

Albums:
Same Train, A Different Time (Capitol/Capitol)
Okie From Muskogee (Capitol/–)
The Fightin' Side Of Me (Capitol/Capitol)
A Tribute To The Best Damn Fiddle Player In The World (Capitol/–)
Hag (Capitol/Capitol)
I Love Dixie Bues (Capitol/Capitol)
Keep Moving On (Capitol/Capitol)
It's All In The Movies (Capitol/Capitol)
My Love Affair With Trains (Capitol/Capitol)
Very Best Of Merle Haggard (–/Capitol)
A Portrait Of Merle Haggard (–/Capitol)
The Roots Of My Raising (Capitol/Capitol)
Songs For The Mama That Tried (MCA-Songbird/–)
Rambling Fever (MCA/MCA)
My Farewell To Elvis (MCA/MCA)
Back To The Barrooms (MCA/MCA)
Going Where The Lonely Go (Epic/Epic)
That's The Way Love Goes (Epic/Epic)
The Epic Collection (Recorded Live) (Epic/Epic)
Amber Waves (Epic/Epic)

Monte Hale

Just as Republic Pictures brought in young Roy Rogers to keep their recalcitrant star, Gene Autry in line, so they brought in Monte Hale when Roy became a star just in case he decided to become balky at contract time.

Hale – who was born on June 8, 1921 in San Angelo, Texas – went on to star in some 19 Republic Westerns from 1945 to 1951, making him one of the last of the singing cowboys in chronological terms. Although possessed of a strong, smooth voice, his records – mainly for MGM – were not particularly successful; his singing highlights tended to come in his films, where he was backed mostly by Foy Willing and the Riders Of The Purple Sage.

After his film-making days were over (other than for a few non-singing television roles), Monte toured for a time as a singer with rodeos before bowing out of musical and acting careers while still a young man. He currently lives in Nevada, and makes occasional appearances at Western film festivals.

Above: Merle Haggard. In 1985 he planned to send a train across America, carrying a message of hope to farmers. But the sponsors then pulled out.

About Me Leaving and **It's Not Love But It's Not Bad** (written by Hank Cochran and Glenn Martin) in 1972, and **If We Make It Through December** in 1975. Albums have provided an area for experimentation including one with a dixieland jazz band, **I Love The Blues (So I Recorded Live In New Orleans)** and, one of Haggard's most auspicious projects, **A Tribute To The Best Damn Fiddle Player In The World** in which he recruited original members of

Bob Wills' band and teamed them with his own.

Haggard had grown up with western swing, and Wills returned the compliment by inviting him to appear on Wills' own album **For The Last Time**. This was a fateful occasion since Wills suffered a stroke during these sessions from which he never recovered. Haggard has also recorded other concept albums, notably on trains (he is fascinated by the old American railroads) and religion.

In 1977, he joined MCA Records and although he enjoyed major hits with **If We're Not Back In Love By Monday** (1977), **I'm Always On A Mountain When I**

Fall (1978) and **The Way I Am** (1980), it was not altogether a successful association. His tribute album, **My Farewell To Elvis** (1977), was slated by the critics, though it came across in typical Haggard fashion. In no way did he try to mimmick the Elvis style, but his identifiable delivery captured the soul of Presley's music, creating an enjoyable encounter with past Presley hits.

By this time Merle and Bonnie Owens had divorced, though she did continue to run his business affairs. Leona Williams, a country singer in her own right, joined the Haggard group as backing vocalist and soon a stormy relationship developed. The

Theron Hale And Daughters

Theron Hale, fiddle; Elizabeth Hale, fiddle; Mamie Ruth Hale, piano.

Theron Hale (1883–1954) led one of the most interesting and popular of the early Opry bands from 1926 until the early 1930s. Unlike most of the raucous hoedown bands, their music was gentle and reminiscent of parlour music of the preceding century, highlighted by lovely twin fiddling.

Like many other early Opry bands, they recorded only during Victor's 1928 field trip to Nashville. They were best known for poularizing **Listen To The Mocking Bird** as a trick-fiddling tune.

Bill Haley

Born William John Clifton Haley, in Highland Park, Michigan, on July 6, 1925, the leader of a series of good local country bands in the late '40s and '50s, he was undoubtedly more surprised than anyone when his creative mixture of R&B, boogie and country music took off like a rocket in 1955, with the success of **Rock Around The Clock** and later **Shake, Rattle And Roll** turning him into an international superstar overnight.

Haley had led bands which pretty much describe their musical approach – Bill Haley and The Four Aces Of Western Swing, Bill Haley and the Saddle Pals – before attempting to fuse the then all black sound of R&B with that of swing, western and country music. The result met such a phenomenal reaction that it vaulted him out of the ranks of country into the ranks of rock, never to return.

It is more than significant, however, that until that turning point his roots and approach had been firmly – if experimentally – country, a trait he shared with many of rock's originators. Having become the first real star of rock 'n' roll, Bill died in his sleep on February 9, 1981 at home in Harlingen, Texas.

Albums:
Greatest Hits (MCA/MCA)
Rock The Joint (–/Roller Coaster)
Golden Country Origins (–/Australian Grass Roots)

Tom T. Hall

The Mark Twain of country music – even his band is called The Storytellers – Tom T. Hall's songs are full of colourful characters and intriguing or humourous situations. Born in Olive Hill, Kentucky, on May 25, 1936, the son of a preacher, he first learned to play on a broken Martin guitar, which his father, the Reverend Virgil L. Hall, restored to working order.

At the age of 14, Tom T. quit school and went to work in a clothing factory, two years later forming his first band, the Kentucky Travellers, playing local dates and appearing on radio station WMOR, Morehead, Kentucky. After the band broke up, Hall continued with WMOR as a DJ for a period of five years.

After enlistment in the army in 1957, Hall was posted to Germany, where he worked on the AFN radio network, taking

Above: Tom T. Hall: "People who write songs are often as equally amazed by them as those who listen to them."

the opportunity to try out a number of his own compositions – with some success. Discharged in 1961, he returned to WMOR, also working with The Technicians, another local band that enjoyed but a brief existence.

More stints as a DJ followed, during which time Hall penned **DJ For A Day**, a major hit for Jimmy Newman in 1963. Next, Dave Dudley scored with **Mad** (1964), another Hall composition, and Hall promptly moved to Nashville to begin supplying songs to such acts as Roy Drusky, Stonewall Jackson and Flatt & Scruggs, eventually having his own hit disc with **I Washed My Face In The Morning Dew**, a release on the Mercury label in 1967.

A year later, Jeannie C. Riley recorded

Harper Valley PTA – a brilliant and highly commercial song about a fast-living woman and a band of small-town hypocrites – and Hall became the writer of a million seller.

During the early '70s he became something of a star performer, sending the audience and press into raptures at his 1973 Carnegie Hall concert, while record buyers readily snapped up such Hall releases as **A Week In A County Jail** (1969), **The Year That Clayton Delaney Died** (1971), **Old Dogs, Children And Watermelon Wine, Ravishing Ruby** (both 1973), **I Love, That Song Is Driving Me Crazy, Country Is** (all 1974) and **Faster Horses** (1976), all chart toppers from Nashville's prime yarn spinner.

His albums include **Songs Of Fox Hollow**, which Hall described as 'an LP of songs for children of all ages', and **The Magnificent Music Machine**, a bluegrass collection that spawned a popular single

in **Fox On The Run**, a Tony Hazzard song which was a 1969 pop chartbuster for Manfred Mann. It is a song that has long been a favourite with a variety of bluegrass bands.

In 1977, Hall signed with RCA Records, and though he recorded some fine singles like **What Have You Got To Lose** (1978), **The Old Side Of Town** (1979) and **Soldier Of Fortune** (1980), his record sales slumped quite dramatically. At this point he took time off from performing to write books, resulting in the best-seller, 'The Storyteller's Nashville', and became host of the syndicated TV show, 'Pop Goes The Country'.

On returning to the recording studio, a link-up with bluegrass musician Earl Scruggs led to the acclaimed album, **The Storyteller and The Banjoman** (1982), a stunning set that mixed traditional country songs with contemporary tunes, Hall's laconic vocal style working perfectly with

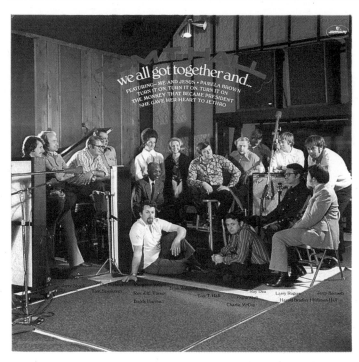

We All Got Together And . . ., Tom T. Hall. Courtesy Mercury Records.

Scruggs' fluid banjo work. The success of the album led to Hall rejoining Mercury Records, and his career took off again with the top selling single, **Everything From Jesus To Jack Daniels** (1983). This teamed him once more with producer Jerry Kennedy, who had worked with Hall on his earlier hits, and he has enjoyed further hits with **Famous In Missouri** (1984) and **P.S. I Love You** (1985).

Albums:
Homecoming (Mercury/Mercury)
I Witness Life (Mercury/–)
The Storyteller (Mercury/Mercury)
Songs Of Fox Hollow (Mercury/–)
Country Classics (–/Phillips)
The Magnificent Music Machine (Mercury/–)
Ol' T's In Town (RCA/RCA)
Places I've Done Time (RCA/RCA)
Everything From Jesus To Jack Daniels (Mercury/Mercury)

Wendell Hall

Although he was by no means a true country entertainer, it was Hall's hillbilly-like recording of **It Ain't Gonna Rain No Mo'**, a 1923 million-seller, that encouraged Victor to embark on a search for possible country hitmakers.

Born in St George, Kansas, on August 23, 1896, Hall attended the University of Chicago and, after military service during World War 1, began touring in vaudeville, singing and playing ukelele. Known as the Red-Headed Music Maker, Hall was a friend of Carson Robinson. It was with Robinson that he went to New York, where the pair recorded for Victor during the early '20s.

Director of many shows during the '30s, Hall was still active in the music business up to the time of his death in Alabama, on April 2, 1969.

The writer of such songs as **My Carolina Rose** and **My Dream Sweetheart**, he frequently guested on the WLS National Barn Dance show.

Stuart Hamblen

Born in Kellyville, Texas, on October 20, 1908, singer and bandleader Stuart Hamblen achieved considerable fame during the '50s as a songwriter. He attended the McMurray State Teachers College, Abilene, Texas in the '20s but later switched to a musical career, working and broadcasting in the California area, sometimes appearing in minor roles in Western films.

In 1949, Hamblen had a Top 10 hit with a Columbia release, **But I'll Go Chasin' Women**, following this with **(Remember Me) I'm The One Who Loves You**, a few months later.

An attempt to run for the Presidency of the United States, on a Prohibition Party ticket, proved a predictable failure in 1952, but in '54 he had more luck when his self-penned **This Ole House** (a song written after Hamblen had discovered a man laying dead inside a dilapidated hut many miles from the nearest habitation) became a country hit, prompting a million-selling cover version by Rosemary Clooney. This same song was later successfully revived by Shakin' Stevens, who topped the British charts with his updated rendition during the summer of 1981.

Hamblen, who was responsible for many other popular songs of the '50s, later turned increasingly to religious material, including the gospel standard **It Is No Secret (What God Can Do)**. Other Hamblen-penned classics include **My Mary** and **Texas Plains**, both of which first became popular in the early '30s.

Albums:
Cowboy Church (Word/Word)
A Man And His Music (Lamb & Lion/–)

George Hamilton IV

A pleasant-voiced vocalist who has gained tremendous popularity in Canada and England as well as his native country, George Hamilton was born on July 19, 1937 and raised in Winston Salem, North Carolina. Becoming a country music fan after watching Gene Autry and Tex Ritter films at Saturday matinees, he bought his first guitar at the age of 12, earning the necessary cash on a paper round.

He then began buying Hank Williams discs, frequently catching the Greyhound bus out to Nashville, where he saw the Grand Ole Opry and met people like Chet Atkins, Eddy Arnold, Hank Snow and others.

Later he began a High School band at Reynolds High, Winston Salem, in his senior year making a demo recording of Little Jimmy Dickens' **Out Behind The Barn**, sending the results to talent scout Orville Campbell. Through Campbell, Hamilton met John D. Loudermilk and recorded his **A Rose And Baby Ruth**, which sold over a million in 1956–7. **Baby Ruth** was considered a pop hit rather than a country item and Hamilton found himself booked on the Alan Freed Show during

20 Of The Best, George Hamilton IV. Courtesy RCA Records.

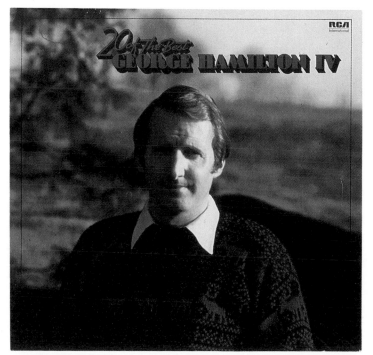

Bluegrass Gospel, George Hamilton IV. Courtesy Lamb And Lion Records.

the autumn of 1956, also gaining a place on various package shows featuring Buddy Holly, Gene Vincent and the Everly Brothers.

Frustrated with his teenage-bopper image, Hamilton moved to Nashville in 1959, joined the Grand Ole Opry and signed with RCA Records. He commenced singing primarily C&W fare, then in the early sixties, became influenced by the folk revival headed by such as Bob Dylan, Peter, Paul and Mary and Gordon Lightfoot. Becoming friendly with Lightfoot in 1965, Hamilton began recording a series of the Canadian's songs, eventually recording more Lightfoot compositions than any other artist. Through this Canuck connection, he began to work more and more with Canadian writers and later signed with RCA's Canadian division.

After a dozen years in Nashville, Hamilton moved to North Carolina once more because he felt such a move would prove beneficial to his family – by this time he had acquired a wife, two teenage boys and a daughter.

First visiting England in 1967 en route to Nashville following a tour of US bases in Germany, he subsequently did a guest spot on the BBC's 'Country Meets Folk' programme, later becoming a regular on many British programmes and being booked several times for Mervyn Conn's Country Music Festival at Wembley. In Canada, Hamilton hosted his own TV show 'North Country' for five years, while in 1977 he became signed to Anchor, a British record label, rejoining ABC-Dot for

Canadian Pacific, George Hamilton IV. Courtesy RCA Records.

American releases only.

For several years he has been managed by Mervyn Conn in Britain, where George spends most of his time, though he has remained a member of the Grand Ole Opry in Nashville, and his recordings have been geared very much to the British market. Known as the International Ambassador of Country Music he was the first American country singer to perform in Russia and

Above: Probably the best ambassador that country music has ever known, the likeable George Hamilton IV is a welcome visitor in many lands.

Czechoslovakia, where he recorded an album with Czech country group, Jiri Brabeck and Country Beat, and has also hosted successful country music festivals in Sweden, Finland, Norway, Holland and Germany.

Albums:
Bluegrass Gospel (Lamb & Lion/Lamb & Lion)
Canadian Pacific (RCA/RCA)
Country Music In My Soul (–/RCA)
Famous Country Music Makers (–/RCA)
Travellin' Light (–/RCA)
Fine Lace And Homespun Cloth (Dot/Anchor)
Feel Like A Million (Dot/Anchor)
Songs For A Winter's Night (–/Ronco)
Music Man's Dream (–/Range)
George Hamilton IV (MCA-Dot/MCA)

Arleen Harden

One-time secretary for an insurance company, Arleen Harden (born England, Arkansas, March 1, 1945) was part of the Harden Trio, a family group, whose **Tippy Toeing** charted for 21 weeks in 1966, gaining the trio Opry membership from 1966–8. During this time they supplied Columbia with other hits in **Seven Days Of Crying** (1966), **Sneakin' Across The Border** (1967) and **Everybody Wants To Be Somebody Else** (1968).

Arleen also became signed to the label as a solo artist, having a first hit with **Fairweather Lover** in 1967, and following the break up of the Harden Trio in '68 she enjoyed a string of minor successes, **Lovin' Man** (1970) proving the most potent.

Following a stay with UA, Arleen later signed for Capitol, cutting a warm, easy-listening, Cam Mullins-arranged album, **I Could Almost Say Goodbye**, in 1975. She has since recorded for Elektra without too much success and spends much of her time working as a background vocalist on Nashville recording sessions.

Albums:
Sings Roy Orbison (Columbia/–)
I Could Almost Say Goodbye (Capitol/–)

Great Country Hits, The Harden Trio. Courtesy Harmony.

Linda Hargrove

A superior singer-songwriter and an outstanding guitarist (at least, Pete Drake and Mike Nesmith have said so), Linda was born on February 3, 1950 and was raised in Tallahasee, Florida, where she took piano lessons at the age of five and moved on to become a French horn player in a high school band before getting bitten by the rock bug.

Influenced by Dylan's **Nashville Skyline**, she packed her bags and headed for Nashville in 1970, there hitting hard times until Sandy Posey recorded one of her songs. Pete Drake, who sat in on the Posey session, then offered Linda a songwriting contract plus some session chores as a guitarist. Some time later, he taught her to handle the console at Drake's own studio.

An album featuring Linda was cut by Mike Nesmith for his ill-fated Countryside label but was never released. However, her songs met a better fate, Leon Russell employing two on his **Hank Wilson's Back** LP, Jan Howard, Billie Jo Spears, Melba Montgomery, David Rogers and many others also utilizing Linda's compositions on various recordings.

Since the abortive Nesmith dates, Linda has recorded for Elektra, cutting such albums as **Music Is Your Mistress** and **Blue Jean Country Queen**. After joining Capitol Records in 1975, she made a breakthrough to the singles chart with **Love Was (Once Around The Dance Floor)** (1975), and came up with the acclaimed album, **Love You're The Teacher**. Following a change of labels to RCA in 1978 and the release of two singles, Linda became a born-again Christian and no longer sings her secular material, devoting her life instead to her religious teachings.

Albums:
Music Is Your Mistress (Elektra/–)
Impressions (Capitol/–)
Love You're The Teacher (Capitol/–)

Kelly Harrell

A country music pioneer who recorded as early as 1924 for Ralph Peer, then with Okeh Records, Crockett Kelly Harrell was born in Drapers Valley, Virginia, on September 13, 1899. A one-time rambler, he became a loom fixer in a mill around 1927, but also continued with a musical career, making a number of important early records for Victor, including **Cuckoo**, **She's A Pretty Bird**, **New River Train**, **Rovin' Gambler**, **I Wish I Was Single Again**, **Charles Guiteau** and **The Butcher Boy**. Often accompanied by banjo, fiddle and guitar, Harrell himself did not play an instrument.

Despite the success of his early records, and his songwriting efforts in two popular early songs, **Away Out On The Mountain** (as recorded by Jimmie Rodgers) and **The Story Of The Mighty Mississippi** (as recorded by Ernest Stoneman), his musical career was a brief one, and he ended his short life working in a rural Virginia towel factory. He died of a heart attack on July 9, 1942.

Album:
Kelly Harrell And The Virginia String Band (County/–)

Emmylou Harris, Gliding Bird. A pirate version of Emmylou's debut album.

Blue Kentucky Girl, Emmylou Harris. Courtesy WEA Records.

Emmylou Harris

The First Lady of contemporary country music, Emmylou, with the help of Gram Parsons' songs, has been as responsible as anyone for making country acceptable to a wider audience. Born in Birmingham, Alabama, on April 2, 1949, she developed an early interest in country music and when her family moved to Washington DC she performed in the folk clubs there and in New York. An early album release on the Jubilee label in 1969 came to nothing. After this she made the ritual pilgrimage to Nashville, a fruitless journey, and also suffered a broken marriage.

Living in Virginia in the late '60s, Emmylou had become sufficiently known locally to be invited to Los Angeles by Gram Parsons to work on his first album for Warner Bros, GP. Warner Bros were making a big effort to relaunch Parsons' career (by this time he was in a wasted state due to drugs and drink) and they had hired musicians from Elvis Presley's backing band to play on the album.

With Emmylou helping out and a new set of Parsons' songs, it looked as if the country rock star might be on the verge of a new career. In 1973 Gram, Emmylou and the Fallen Angel Band embarked on a small tour. A tape of this tour and the evidence of those around them seemed to indicate that perhaps Gram might be finding a way back. Already, they had formulated the sound with which Emmylou would later ride to success. Gram's death occurred shortly after the recording of **Grievous Angel** in 1973 and this record is real evidence of what might have been.

Emmylou had been close to Gram and was stunned by his death, and when she picked up the threads of her own career, it was to Gram's material that she turned. In 1975 she recorded **Pieces Of The Sky** for Reprise Records, an album which mixed country songs with some light rock 'n' roll, and although none of Gram's songs were included on this album she was using his material in her act.

Right: Emmylou Harris. Her Hot Band has featured such musicians as Ricky Skaggs, Albert Lee and Rodney Crowell.

Pieces Of The Sky had not made a great impact on its release although her version of The Louvin Brothers' **If I Could Only Win Your Love** from the album did achieve No.1 status. But as Emmylou toured America and Europe her pure voice and impeccable backing band were to enchant listeners. She also has a fragile, Californian sort of beauty and those who had admired her recorded work found that her stage act was everything they had hoped for. The erstwhile Elvis Presley musicians, James Burton (guitar) and Glen D. Hardin (piano), were proving a big draw, Hardin having previously played with Buddy Holly's Crickets.

Her huge success in Europe particularly focused attention on Emmylou. Her voice had a pure, innocent, classic quality and it also lacked the nasal sound which so many non-country fans find hard to take. The second album, **Elite Hotel**, was released in 1976 and it featured three of Gram Parsons' better compositions: **Wheels**, **Sin City** and **Ooh Las Vagas**. As usual, it was a well-balanced mix of country, ballads and rock. Emmylou's band at this time was Glen D. Hardin (piano), James Burton (guitar), Hank De Vito (pedal steel guitar), Emory Gordy (bass), Rodney Crowell (rhythm guitar) and John Ware (drums). Crowell has proved himself a capable songwriter, having had a hand in three of Emmylou's best loved numbers: **Amarillo**, **Till I Gain Control Again** and **Leaving Louisiana In The Broad Daylight**.

Emmylou's famed Hot Band has featured such musicians as Albert Lee, a British rock musician who replaced James Burton on lead guitar in 1977, and Ricky Skaggs, a fiddle player and mandolinist who brought a bluegrass influence to Emmylou's music and was largely responsible for the more traditional arrangements used on **Roses On The Snow**. This 1980 release finally brought recognition from a country audience and was to lead Skaggs to becoming a major country artist in his own right, and was also notable for being the first introduction many had to the family group The Whites, who like Skaggs became a top country act during the early 1980s.

Always striving to vary her music, Emmylou certainly caught a lot of her fans out with her inventive re-workings of the old pop songs **Mister Sandman** and **How High The Moon** in 1981, and in the same year she teamed up with Don Williams for the chart-topping duet of **If I Needed You**. Throughout Emmylou's recordings, the greater the challenge the song provides, the more inspired her performance

becomes. In recent years she has recorded such diverse material as Donna Summer's **On The Radio**, Jule Styne's **Diamonds Are A Girl's Best Friend**, Bruce Springsteen's **Racing In The Streets** and the early Presley classic **Mystery Train**.

Possibly her most ambitious project has been the concept album, **The Ballad Of Sally Rose**, which Emmylou wrote and produced with British-born songwriter Paul Kennerley during 1985, which tells the story of a young girl who rises from rags to riches as a singer and entertainer, but finds life empty without the one she loves beside her. Featuring the talents of Waylon Jennings, Dolly Parton, Linda Ronstadt, Vince Gill, Gail Davies, Albert Lee and Hank De Vito, it was both an artistic and commercial success.

Emmylou and Kennerley were married on November 8, 1985 in Maryland, and as well as writing songs with Emmylou, Kennerley has assumed control of her recordings, being responsible for the overall production.

Albums:
Pieces Of The Sky (Reprise/Reprise)
Elite Hotel (Reprise/Reprise)
Luxury Liner (Reprise/Reprise)
Quarter Moon In A Ten Cent Town (Warner/Warner)
Roses In The Snow (Warner/Warner)
Cimarron (Warner/Warner)
Profile: Best Of Emmylou Harris (–/Warner)
White Shoes (Warner/Warner)
The Ballad Of Sally Rose (Warner/Warner)
Thirteen (Warner/–)

Freddie Hart

Born in Lockapoka, Alabama, on December 21, 1933, Hart is said to have run away from home at seven, becoming – amongst other things – a cotton picker, a sawmill worker, a pipeline layer in Texas and a dishwasher in New York.

By the age of 14, he had become a marine, three years later helping to take Guam, having already been to Iwo Jima and Okinawa. A physical fitness expert and currently the possessor of a black belt in karate, he taught this form of self defence at the LA Police Academy in the '50s, eventually moving into the music business with the aid of Lefty Frizzell with whom he worked until 1953 when Hart signed a recording contract with Capitol.

He subsequently recorded for Columbia (having his first hit in 1959 with **The Wall**), Monument and Kapp throughout the mid '60s, logging around a dozen chart entries, becoming a major artist after re-signing for Capitol in 1969 and having a million-selling single, **Easy Loving** (1971), which won him the CMA Song Of The Year award in both 1971 and '72.

For the next few years Hart enjoyed a run of success, most of his singles claiming Top 5 status, **My Hang Up Is You**, **Bless Your Heart**, **Got The All Overs For You** (all 1972), **Super Kind Of Woman**, **Trip To Heaven** (1973), **If You Can't Feel It**, **Hang On In There Girl**, **The Want To's** (1974), **The First Time** (1975) and **Why Lovers Turn To Strangers** (1977) being just a few of his major hits.

In 1980 he joined the small Sunbird label and scored minor hits with **Roses Are Red** (1980) and **You Were There** (1981), however, in recent years he has slipped in popularity. Now extremely

Please Don't Tell Her, Freddie Hart. Courtesy Pickwick Records.

wealthy, Hart owns many acres of plum trees, a trucking company and over 200 breeding bulls, and runs a school for handicapped chlidren.

Albums:
Easy Loving (Capitol/–)
That Look In Her Eyes (Capitol/–)
The Pleasure's Been All Mine (Capitol/Capitol)
Only You (Capitol/–)
The First Time (Capitol/–)
Greatest Hits (Capitol/–)

John Hartford

This banjoist, fiddler, guitarist, singer-songwriter is one of the most exciting solo entertainers in country music today. Born in New York, on December 30, 1937, but raised in St Louis by his doctor father and painter mother, he first learnt to play on a banjo which he claims was beat up and had no head. By the time he was 13 he had also mastered fiddle and played at local square dances; next he graduated to the dobro then on to guitar.

Upon leaving school, he worked as a sign painter, a commercial artist, a deck-hand on a Mississippi riverboat and as a disc jockey. After marriage and the birth of a son, Hartford headed for Nashville, becoming a session musician. His work on these sessions gained him a recording contract with RCA, for whom he cut eight albums and several singles, the first of which was **Tall Tall Grass**, a single released in 1966.

Soon many acts began recording Hartford's songs, and one, **Gentle On My Mind**, from his 1967 **Earthwords And Music** album, became a million seller when covered by Glen Campbell. It entered the charts in both July 1967 and September 1969, winning three Grammies in the process and becoming the most recorded song of the period.

After appearances on the 'Smothers Brothers Comedy Hour' and a regular spot on the 'Glen Campbell Goodtime Hour',

Hartford toured with his own band for a while but eventually opted to become a solo performer. His 1976 **Mark Twang** album presents him in this role, unaccompanied by any rhythm section, Hartford providing all the percussive sounds with his mouth and feet! It went on to win a Grammy of its own, in the best ethnic/traditional category.

An entertaining performer who utilizes his own songs and those drawn from the traditions of country music, he often performs at bluegrass festivals and plays and records with bluegrass musicians. Due to his keen sense of humour and natural entertaining skills he has been a regular guest on such TV shows as 'Hee-Haw', 'Today Show', 'Dinah Shore' and 'Merv Griffin'.

Albums:
The Love Album (RCA/–)

Mark Twang, John Hartford. Courtesy Sonet Records.

Aero Plain (Warner/Warner)
Mark Twang (Flying Fish/Sonet)
Nobody Knows What You Do (Flying Fish/Sonet)
All In The Name Of Love (Flying Fish/Sonet)
Slumbering On The Cumberland (Flying Fish/–)

Iron Mountain Depot, John Hartford. Courtesy RCA Records.

Alex Harvey

The writer of **Delta Dawn**, **Reuben James**, **Tulsa Turnaround** and many other hits, Harvey was born in Brownsville, Tennessee, in 1945.

He attended Murray State University, Kentucky, where he obtained a degree in music and became conductor of the University Symphony Orchestra. Later he became involved in various bands and during the mid '60s moved to Nashville where he transcribed songs from tape for such aspiring writers as Kris Kristofferson, who proved unable to either read or write music.

Establishing himself as a quality singer-songwriter through such songs as **Molly** (a hit for Jim Glaser), **Love Of A Gentle Woman** (John Gray) and **Reuben James** (Kenny Rogers), Harvey was awarded his own TV show, 'Fun Farm', and also gained a Capitol recording contract.

He became a resident of Hollywood in 1970 but continued to provide an equal flow of pop and country material, Tompall and The Glaser Brothers having a hit with

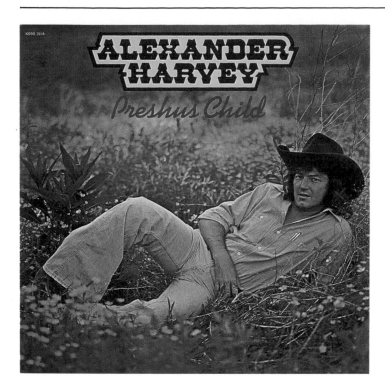

Preshus Child, Alex Harvey. Courtesy Karma Sutra Records.

Rings in 1971, Tanya Tucker achieving a crossover success via **Delta Dawn** in '72 and Kenny Rogers recording **Ballad Of Calico**, a whole album of Harvey songs, that year.

Songs that Alex has written have sold in excess of 50 million copies when recorded by such stars as Helen Reddy, Jimmy Buffett, Waylon Jennings, Three Dog Night, Conway Twitty and Jerry Lee Lewis. He has also made his mark in film music, contributing a score to the film 'Fools'.

Below: John Hartford who recorded Don't Leave Your Records In The Sun in suitably warped-disc fashion!

Albums:
Preshus Child (Karma Sutra/–)
Souvenirs (Capitol/Capitol)
Alex Harvey (Capitol/Capitol)

Hawkshaw Hawkins

Another victim of the plane crash that killed Patsy Cline and Cowboy Copas, Harold Hawkins was born in Huntingdon, West Virginia, on December 22, 1921. A guitarist at the age of 15, he then won a local amateur talent show, the prize being a $15 a week spot on radio station WSAZ.

By the time of Pearl Harbour, Hawkins had established himself as a radio

The All New Hawkshaw Hawkins. Courtesy London Records.

personality, but he then enlisted and was sent for service in the Pacific area. By 1946 he was home again and singing on WWVA, Wheeling, West Virginia. Then came a recording contract with King and hit records in **I Wasted A Nickel** (1949) and **Slow Poke** (1951), plus a country classic in **Sunny Side Of The Mountain**.

Despite some recordings for RCA and a 1955 contract with the Grand Ole Opry, Hawkins enjoyed no further chart success until 1959, when a Columbia single **Soldier's Joy** climbed high in the country list. Four years later – he was at this time married to Jean Shepard – his first country No. 1 came with the release of **Lonesome 7-7203**, a song penned by Justin Tubb. But on March 5, 1963, just two days after the disc had entered the charts, Hawkins was lying dead among the aircraft wreckage near Kansas.

Album:
16 Greatest Hits (Gusto/–)

Ronnie Hawkins

Country rock 'n' roller Ronnie was born on January 10, 1935 in Huntsville, Madison County, Arkansas and came from a country music background. He formed his first band whilst still in his teens, playing 'hopped-up hillbilly' music.

During the '50s he developed into a fully fledged rockabilly performer with his group The Hawks, who later went on to play with Bob Dylan and became The Band, the highly successful rock band of the late '60s.

Ronnie landed a contract with Roulette Records in 1958 and the following year enjoyed success on the American pop charts with **Mary Lou**, **40 Days** and **Who Do You Love?**. Unlike most of the '50s rock 'n' rollers, Ronnie has never changed his style to easy-listening pop or country music but has continued to perform genuine rock 'n' roll, mainly in Canada, where he has lived since the early '60s.

Album:
Sings Songs Of Hank Williams (–/PRT)

George D. Hay

Founder of the Grand Ole Opry, George Dewey Hay (born Attica, Indiana, November 9, 1895) was once a reporter for the Memphis Commercial Appeal. Shortly after World War 1, while on an assignment in the Ozarks, he attended a mountain cabin hoedown, and conceived the idea which later resulted in country music obtaining its most famous showcase.

When the Appeal moved into radio, setting up station WMC, Hay became radio editor, later, in 1924, taking up an appointment as an announcer on Chicago station WLS. With WLS he helped begin the National Barn Dance programme, gaining high ratings, this success leading to the position of director with the newly established WSM, Nashville, in 1925.

Again he instigated a similar Barn-dance programme, the first broadcast taking place on November 28, 1925, although it did not become a regularly scheduled programme until December of that year. The show rapidly grew in quality

The Solemn Ol' Judge, George D. Hay, the man who named the Opry.

and popularity.

It was on December 10, 1927, that the WSM Barn Dance became officially retitled Grand Ole Opry. The show had been preceded by a programme featuring the NBC Symphony Orchestra and, after an introductory number by De-Ford Bailey, Hay, who announced the show, declared: 'For the past hour we have been listening to music taken from Grand Opera – but from now on we will present the Grand Ole Opry.' And so the Opry it became.

Hay, known as the Solemn Old Judge, continued to expand and develop the Opry throughout the rest of his career, extending the range of WSM's broadcasts, encouraging the best country entertainers in the country to appear in Nashville, and recruiting new talent to keep the show both vital and fresh. However, he began to show some signs of mental instability, and in 1951 he retired to live with his daughter in Virginia and died at Virginia Beach, Virginia, on May 9, 1968, having been elected to the Country Music Hall of Fame in 1966.

Roy Head

A rock 'n' roll based country singer, Roy was born on January 9, 1943, in Three Rivers, Texas. He started out in the early '60s with his own band The Traits reworking old rock 'n' roll songs in clubs and bars across Texas.

A recording contract with New York's Scepter Records in 1964 proved to be a failure, so Roy returned to Texas and joined the small Back Beat label, making a breakthrough with the R&B-styled **Treat Her Right**, which reached the Top 3 on the American pop charts towards the end of 1965.

Further pop success followed with **Apple Of My Eye** and **To Make A Big Man Cry** (both 1966), which led to Scepter re-releasing his singles from 1964 resulting in **Just A Little Bit** making the Top 40.

By the end of the '60s Roy was very much a pop has-been and was finding his music becoming more closely aligned with country. He signed to Mega Records in Nashville and scored a minor hit with Mickey Newbury's **Baby's Not Home**

(1974). A move to Shannon Records led to his biggest country hit, **The Most Wanted Woman In Town** (1975).

This resulted in a move to the major labels, beginning with ABC-Dot, for whom he had further hits with **The Door I Used To Close** (1976) and **Come To Me** (1977). Next came Elektra and success with **In Our Room** (1979) and **The Fire Of Two Old Flames** (1980). Since then Roy has recorded with a number of smaller labels including Churchill, NSD and Avion without exactly setting the charts on fire.

Albums:
Ahead Of His Time (ABC-Dot/–)
The Many Sides Of Roy Head (Elektra/–)

Bobby Helms

A crossover performer, Helms had a Top 10 pop hit with **Jingle Bell Rock** in 1957, the same year that he was adjudged the nation's leading country singer by Cashbox magazine.

Born in Bloomington, Indiana, on August 15, 1933, guitarist, singer-song-writer Helms appeared on radio at the age of 13, making his debut on the Grand Ole Opry four years later. In 1957, he achieved a No. 1 country hit with **Fraulein**, the disc remaining in the charts for a whole year, while his version of Jimmy Duncan's **My Special Angel** became both a C&W and pop hit, selling over a million copies.

The impetus was maintained through-out 1958, with **Jacqueline** (from the film 'A Case Against Brooklyn') and **Just A Little Lonesome** providing him with best sellers – but despite constant seasonal reappearances by **Jingle Bell Rock** (which took five years to become a million seller), Helms' recording career faded rapidly. Between 1960 and '67 his name was absent from the charts, but later he achieved a series of mini hits on such labels as Little Darlin' and Certon, as he drifted in and out of the business.

Albums:
My Special Angel (–/President)
Sings His Greatest Hits (Power Pak/–)
My Special Angel (Vocalion/–)
Fraulein (Harmony/–)

Goldie Hill

Though she went into semi-retirement shortly after her marriage to Carl Smith, Goldie Hill is still remembered as one of the most popular female country singers of the 1950s, her version of **Don't Let The Stars Get In Your Eyes** becoming a Top 5 hit in 1953.

Born in Karnes County, Texas, on January 11, 1933, Goldie began her professional singing career during the early '50s, signing for Decca and appearing on Shreveport's Louisiana Hayride Show in 1952, joining the Opry the following year after the success of **Don't Let The Stars**.

During the mid '50s she toured on several major shows, working on some with Carl Smith, whom she married in 1957. Though she had a best-selling disc with **Yankee Go Home** in 1959, Goldie restricted her number of personal appearances during the '60s, occasionally visiting the recording studios to cut such sides as **Loveable Fool**, a 1969 success. There are currently no Goldie Hill albums in the catalogue.

Chris Hillman

For most of his musical career, Chris Hillman, who was born December 4, 1944 in Los Angeles, California, has chosen to take a back seat leaving the spotlight on others. But he has been recognised as the musical backbone of each band he has been with.

He played mandolin in his first group, the bluegrass-orientated Scottsville Squirrell Barkers, which by the early '60s had become The Hillmen. Later he had careers with several well known bands where he was usually unnoticed or underrated.

During a stint with The Byrds, Hillman, with Gram Parsons' support, urged the folk-rock group to make a country LP, **Sweetheart Of The Rodeo**, the pioneering

All New Just For you, Bobby Helms.
Courtesy Little Darlin' Records.

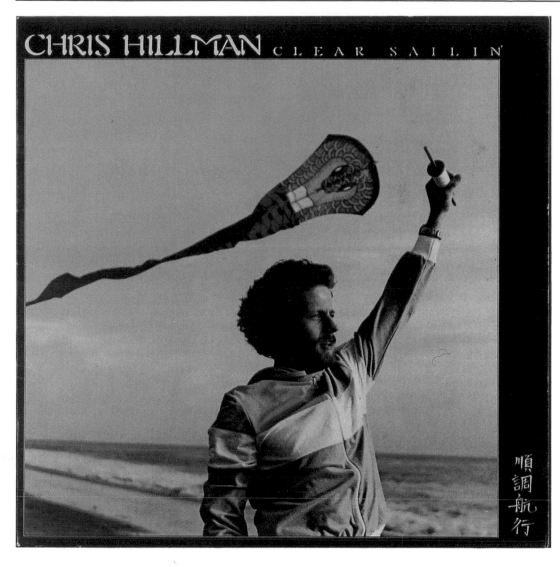

Clear Sailin', Chris Hillman. Courtesy WEA Records.

country-rock album of 1968. Chris and Gram left the band soon afterwards, developing their country-rock ideas into The Flying Burrito Brothers.

Throughout the '70s, Chris worked with various country-rock outfits such as Manassas (with Steve Stills), The Souther-Hillman-Furay Band (with J. D. Souther and Richie Furay), Firefall (with Rick Roberts) and McGuinn, Clark & Hillman (with Roger McGuinn and Gene Clark).

Since 1980, Chris has made his mark as a solo performer with a series of albums that have neatly blended his country and bluegrass roots with rock. He has also worked regularly as a background vocalist and instrumentalist on recordings by Linda Ronstadt, Dan Fogelberg, John Denver and many other contemporary country acts, and penned **Step On Out**, the title tune of The Oak Ridge Boys' 1984 album.

Albums:
Desert Rose (Sugar Hill/Spindrift)
Morning Star (Sugar Hill/–)
Clear Sailin' (Asylum/Asylum)

Adolph Hofner

A native Texan of German-Slavic descent, Adolph Hofner has had a long and fascinating career playing both western swing and ethnic dance music for Texas' large German-American community. He began his career in San Antonio in the

'30s, and continues to this day, travelling five days a week within the Texas state line, sponsored by Pearl Beer.

Hofner recorded for Bluebird and Okeh before World War II, and during the war hit the west coast dance circuit – where his billing was changed to Dub Hofner due to the similarity of his name to that of Germany's Fuhrer. He later returned to Texas, where he recorded for Columbia, Decca and Sarge, his biggest hits, **Alamo Steel Serenade** and **Cotton Eyed Joe**, being with Columbia.

Album:
South Texas Swing (Arhoolie/–)

Buddy Holly

One of rock's prime movers in its early years, Buddy Holly actually began his career as a country singer, and the sound was never to leave him during his short but brilliant life; nor has the power of his songwriting seemed to diminish, as **That'll Be The Day**, **Everyday** and **It's So Easy** have all been pop and country hits in recent years.

Charles Hardin Holley (the 'e' in his last name was dropped only after he signed his first record contract) was born on September 7, 1936, in Lubbock, Texas, and grew up listening to the blues and Tex-Mex music as well as to Hank Williams and Bill Monroe. His first band, with longtime friend Bob Montgomery, tells the story of their musical approach; they were called Buddy and Bob: Western and Bop.

Holly's first professional session was, in fact, a country session for Decca, produced in Nashville by Owen Bradley early in 1956, and featured not Holly's own band, The Crickets, but a group of Nashville sidemen. However, the combination of slick Nashville sound and

Nashville, Tennessee. Buddy Holly. Part of MCA's wonderful boxed-set.

raw Texas rockabilly did not mix well and the records were not successful. It is ironic that Holly's great success came on Coral Records, a Decca subsidiary, after the parent label had dropped him.

His career as a rock star – although many country stations continued to play his records and many country fans continued to buy them – was brief and hectic, filled with hit records like **Oh Boy!**, **Peggy Sue**, **Rave On**, **Fool's Paradise** and **Raining In My Heart**. It was on one of his hectic tours that he died in a plane crash on February 3, 1959.

His songs, his style, and his sidemen – Waylon Jennings, Tommy Allsup, Bob Montgomery and Sonny Curtis – have all left great marks on country music, and Holly was a genuine influence on it at this pivotal point in its history.

Album:
The Complete Buddy Holly (6 LP Box Set) (–/MCA)

Doyle Holly

Born on June 30, 1936, in Perkins, Oklahoma, Holly learnt bass guitar at an early age, forming a band with his older brothers and playing at rodeos and other venues.

A Kansas oilfield worker at 13, he remained in this occupation until 1953 when he joined the army, performing tours of duty in Okinawa and Korea.

In 1957, Holly was discharged and returned to oilfield work, this time in the Bakersfield area of California. As a part-timer he played in Johnny Burnette's band along with Fuzzy Owen and Merle Haggard, then, following a number of ups and downs that sometimes found him on the breadline, he joined Buck Owens, becoming a regular member of the Buckaroos from August 1963 until late 1970, often being cast in the role of resident funnyman.

With his own band, The Vanishing Breed, he became signed to Barnaby Records during the early '70s, registering low level hits with **Lila**, **Queen Of The Silver Dollar** (1973), **Lord, How Long Has This Been Going On**, **A Rainbow In My**

Hand, Just Another Cowboy Song, and
Richard And The Cadillac Kings (1974).

Album:
Doyle Holly (Barnaby/–)

Homer & Jethro

From Knoxville, Tennessee, Henry D.
Haynes (Homer), (born July 29, 1917), and
Kenneth C. Burns (Jethro), (born March
10, 1923), formed a duo in 1932, the two
boys winning a regular stop on station
WNOX, Knoxville.

Discovering that their parodies gained
more attention than their 'straight'
material, they opted to become country
comics, holding down a residency at the
Renfro Valley, Kentucky, until war service
caused a temporary halt to their career.
With Japan defeated, the duo re-formed,
for a decade appearing as cast members
of the National Barn Dance on Chicago
WLS, also guesting on the Opry and many
networked radio and TV shows.

Signed to RCA Records in the late '40s,
they cut **Baby It's Cold Outside** with June
Carter in 1948, obtaining later hits with
That Hound Dog In The Window (1953),
Hernando's Hideaway (1954), **The Battle
Of Kookamonga** (1959) and **I Want To Hold
Your Hand** (1964). The duo also recorded a
number of instrumental albums (Haynes
on guitar, Burns on mandolin), at one time
teaming with Chet Atkins to form a
recording group known as The Nashville
String Band.

The 39-year-old partnership terminated
on August 7, 1971, with the death of Henry
Haynes, but Burns continued with his
musical career. A brilliant mandolinist, he
has often been involved with country-jazz,
playing almost in Django Reinhardt
fashion.

Albums:
Country Comedy (–/RCA)
The Far Out World Of Homer & Jethro
(RCA/–)

Jethro Burns Albums:
Jethro Burns (Flying Fish/–)
Back To Back – with Tiny Moore
(Kaleidescope/–)

The Hoosier Hot Shots

Frank Kettering, banjo, guitar, flute,
piccolo, bass, piano; Hezzie Triesch, song
whistle, washboard, drums, alto horn;
Kenny Triesch, banjo, tenor guitar, bass
horn; Gabe Ward, clarinet.

'Are you ready, Hezzie?' always signalled
the arrival of the Hoosier Hot Shots on the
National Barn Dance, a first-rate group of
comedians and musicians who had one of
the most popular novelty acts in the
country before Spike Jones came along.

They started out as a small dance band
but their flair for comedy and unusual
instruments got the better of them, and
when they joined WLS in 1935 it was as a
novelty group, and their success was
immediate. They appeared in many films
both with and without other Barn Dance
cast members, and eventually retired to
California.

Their records (for the ARC complex of
labels and Vocalion) did well, but they
were primarily a visual comedy act.

Doc Hopkins

Doctor Howard Hopkins – yes, that is his
real name – was born on January 26, 1899
in Harlan County, Kentucky. He was
associated for a long time (1930–49) with
station WLS and the National Barn Dance,
and during that period became well
known as one of the best and most
authentic of American folk singers.

Although he spent a great deal of time
on WLS and has recorded for many labels
(including Paramount, Decca and others),
he has somehow never received the
recognition as a country music pioneer
that he richly deserves.

Johnny Horton

With **Battle Of New Orleans**, a Jimmie
Driftwood song said to be based on an old
fiddle tune known as **The 8th Of January**,
Horton achieved one of the biggest selling
discs of 1959, a cover version by skiffle
king Lonnie Donegan becoming a Top 5
record in Britain.

Born in Tyler, Texas, on April 3, 1929,
Horton went to college in Jacksonville and
Kilgore, Texas, later attending the
University of Seattle, Washington.
Spending some time in the fishing industry
in Alaska and California, he then became
a performer under the title of The Singing
Fisherman, when he began starring on
Shreveport's Louisiana Hayride during the
mid-'50s.

Completing recording stints with both
Mercury and Dot, he moved on to
Columbia, his first hit being with **Honky
Tonk Man** (1956) and his first country
No. 1 with **When It's Springtime In Alaska**
(1959).

Following the runaway success of the
million-selling **Battle Of New Orleans**,
Horton became a nationwide star, having
hits with **Johnny Reb/Sal's Got A Sugar
Lip** (1959) and **Sink The Bismarck** (1960),
also being asked to sing Mike Phillips'
North To Alaska in the John Wayne film

**The Spectacular Johnny Horton. Courtesy
Columbia Records.**

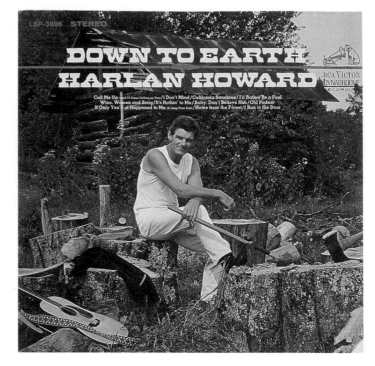

Down To Earth, Harlan Howard. Courtesy
RCA Records.

of that title, the resulting record providing
the Texan with yet another million seller in
1960.

On November 5, 1960, Horton was killed
in a car accident while travelling to
Nashville, but his records continued to sell
throughout the '60s and his songs have
been recorded by Claude King, Dwight
Yoakam and many other country stars
over the years. In fact, Claude King
recorded a tribute album to Johnny in the
late '60s, and in 1983 a biography entitled
'Your Singing Fisherman' was published.

Albums:
Honky Tonk Man (Columbia/–)
Makes History (Columbia/–)
On Stage (Columbia/–)
Spectacular (Columbia/–)
Greatest Hits (–/CBS)
Rockin' Rollin' (–/Bear Family)
America Remembers (CSP-Gusto/–)

David Houston

A direct descendant of Sam Houston and
Robert E. Lee, Houston was born in
Shreveport, Louisiana, on December 9,
1938.

Brought up in Bossier City, where he
was taught guitar by his aunt, Houston
was aided in his career by his godfather
Gene Austin (a pop singer who had 1920s
million sellers with **My Blue Heaven** and
Ramona).

By the age of 12, Houston had won a
guest spot on Shreveport's famed
Louisiana Hayride radio show, later joining
the cast as a regular member. During his
teen years he completed his college
education, then, in the late '50s, began
touring avidly, appearing also on many TV
and radio shows.

Signed to Epic Records in 1963, he
gained an instant hit with **Mountain Of
Love** which stayed in the charts for 18
weeks, winning Houston 'Most Promising
Country Newcomer' plaudits from music
magazines.

An accomplished yodeller and a
talented guitarist-pianist, Houston went
from strength to strength throughout the
'60s, having No. 1 hits with **Almost
Persuaded** (1966), **With One Exception**
(1967), **You Mean The World To Me** (1967),
My Elusive Dreams (1968) and **Baby, Baby
(I Know You're A Lady)** (1969), winning
two Grammy awards for **Almost
Persuaded** and earning a part in a 1967
film, 'Cottonpickin' Chickenpickers'.

During the early '70s, Houston's discs
continued to chart regularly, **I Do My
Swinging At Home** (1970), **After Closing
Time** (with Barbara Mandrell – 1970),
Wonders Of The Wine (1970), **A Woman
Always Knows** (1971), **Soft Sweet And
Warm** (1972), **Good Things** (1973) and
She's All Woman (1973) all being Top 10
contenders.

Since the mid '70s David's decline has
been rapid, as he has moved through a
succession of labels including Colonial,
Elektra, Derrick, Country International and
Excelsior looking for the one song that
might take him back into the Top 10.
However, he has continued to work
steadily, usually touring with his manager

Tillman Franks, who also doubles as David's guitarist when he appears with a pick-up band.

Albums:
Greatest Hits (Epic/Epic)
Best Of Houston And Mandrell (Epic/–)
Day Love Walked In (Epic/–)
A Perfect Match – with Barbara Mandrell (Epic/–)
A Man Needs Love (Epic/–)
From The Heart Of Houston (Derrick/–)
From Houston To You (Excelsior/–)

Harlan Howard

An outstanding performer, Howard (born Lexington, Kentucky, September 8, 1929) has generally preferred to remain a songwriter, picking up numerous awards, and running his Wilderness Music Publishing Company. Raised in Detroit, he began songwriting at the age of 12. Spending four years in the paratroops following high school graduation, he became based in Fort Benning, Georgia, spending his weekends in Nashville.

Later, in Los Angeles, he met Tex Ritter and Johnny Bond who began publishing his songs, hits emerging with **Pick Me Up On Your Way Down** (Charlie Walker, 1958), **Mommy For A Day** (Kitty Wells, 1959) and **Heartaches By The Number** (Ray Price and Guy Mitchell, 1959). In 1960, Howard along with his wife, singer Jan Howard, moved to Nashville where, proving to be a veritable hit machine, he became known as the 'king' of country songwriters, a title only challenged perhaps by Dallas Frazier and Bill Anderson.

His many songs have included **I've Got A Tiger By The Tail**, **Under The Influence Of Love**, **A Guy Named Joe**, **Streets Of Baltimore**, **Heartbreak USA**, **Busted**, **No Charge**, **I Fall To Pieces** and **Three Steps To The Phone**, Howard winning no less than ten citations – a record number – for the BMI in 1961.

As a recording artist, he has cut albums for Monument, RCA and Nugget.

Rock Me Back To Little Rock, Jan Howard, Courtesy MCA Records.

Above: Paul Howard and his Arkansas Cotton Pickers, one of the '40s best western swing bands. Note the drum kit – banned by the Opry for many years.

Jan Howard

The daughter of a Cherokee maid and an Irish immigrant, Jan was born at West Plains, Missouri, March 13, 1932, acquiring her present surname after marriage to songwriter Harlan Howard.

An avid country music record collector early on, her first public performance came as a result of a meeting with Johnny Cash, a tour with Johnny Horton and Archie Campbell ensuing.

At the close of the 1950s, she began recording for the Challenge label, her first release being **Yankee Go Home**, a duet with Wynn Stewart. This Jan followed with **The One You Slip Around With**, a 1960 hit that won her several awards in the Most Promising Newcomer category.

In the wake of recordings for such labels as Capitol and Wrangler, she moved to Nashville during the mid '60s, there signing for Decca Records, also teaming with Bill Anderson as a featured part of his road and TV shows. With Anderson she cut a number of hit duets that included **I Know You're Married** (1966), **For Loving You** (a 1967 No. 1), **If It's All The Same To You** (1969), **Someday We'll Be Together** (1970) and **Dissatisfied** (1971).

Proving similarly successful as a solo act, a score or so of her releases attained chart status, the most prominent of these being **Evil On Your Mind** (1966), **Bad Seeds** (1966), **Count Your Blessings, Woman** (1968) and **My Son** (1968), the last named being a self-penned tribute to her son Jim, who died in Vietnam just two weeks after the song had been recorded.

Following the tragic death of the second of her three sons, Jan, once contender for the Queen of Country Music crown, opted for retirement during the early '70s. However, she later joined the Carter Family appearing on Johnny Cash's road show, and in 1985 she recorded her first album in many years when she signed with the reactivated MCA-Dot.

Albums:
Rock Me Back To Little Rock (Decca/–)
Sincerely (GRT/–)
Jan Howard (MCA-Dot/–)

Paul Howard

Although hot western swing on the stage of the staid Grand Ole Opry sounds a little far fetched, that was exactly Paul Howard's role in the 1940s, the height of western swing's popularity. Born July 10, 1908 in Midland, Arkansas, Howard drifted in and out of music until 1940 when he joined the Opry as a solo singer.

Always entranced by western swing, he began to build a bigger and bigger band, which grew to some nine or ten pieces, sometimes with multiple basses to make up for the lack of drums which were then still taboo on the Opry stage. His band, the Arkansas Cotton Pickers, was one of the hottest of the era, and he recorded for Columbia and King.

Frustrated by the lack of attention western swing got in the south east, Howard left the Opry in 1949 for a circuit of radio programmes and dances in Louisiana, Arkansas and Texas.

For many years, Paul lived in Shreveport where he led a band playing dances. He died on June 18, 1984 in Little Rock, Arkansas.

Con Hunley

Conrad Logan Hunley, born on April 9, 1946, Knoxville, Tennessee, the eldest of six children, found success in country music towards the end of the '70s with a run of Top 20 successes that started with **Week-end Friend**.

Country music's blue-eyed soul man grew up listening to the country music of Lefty Frizzell and George Jones, but he switched to a soul-country sound modelled on Ray Charles' country-pop successes of the early '60s. He played with various local bands for a dozen years and in 1976 put together his own group and landed a regular gig at The Village Barn in Knoxville.

Businessman Sam Kirkpatrick took an interest in Hunley's career, setting up a new record label, Prairie Dust, and paying for the singer to travel to Nashville and record. During 1976 and '77, Con enjoyed several minor hits on Prairie Dust including **Breaking Up Is Hard To Do** and **I'll Always Remember That Song**.

This led to the major record companies showing an interest in Con Hunley and in 1978 he signed to Warner Brothers with **Week-end Friend** (1978), beginning a run of Top 20 successes which included **You've Still Got A Place In My Heart** (1978), **I've Been Waiting For You All My Life** (1979), **They Never Lost You** (1980), **She's Stepping Out** (1981) and **Oh Girl** (1982).

A short stint recording for MCA Records (1983–84) was followed by a contract with Capitol which resulted in minor hits with **I'd Rather Be Crazy**, **All American Country Boy** (both 1985) and **What Am I Gonna Do About You** (1986).

Albums:
Ask Any Woman (Warner Bros/–)
Oh Girl (Warner Bros/–)

Ferlin Husky

Born in Flat River, Missouri, on December 3, 1927, comedian-singer-songwriter-guitarist Husky grew up on a farm. It is claimed that his first attempt to own a guitar was foiled when the hen that he swopped it for failed to lay eggs, causing neighbours to cancel the deal.

He did, however, obtain a guitar at a later date and, following stints in the

Above: Ferlin Husky's alter ego, Simon Crum, hick philospher supreme, in typical pose.

merchant marines and as a DJ, began performing in the Bakersfield, California, area using the name Terry Preston and eventually being discovered by Tennessee Ernie Ford's manager, Cliffie Stone, who asked Husky to deputize for Ford during a vacation period. About this time, Husky also created a character called Simon Crum, a kind of hick philosopher who became so popular that Capitol signed the singer to cut several sides as his alter ego.

Later, recording as Terry Preston, Husky had his first hit with **A Dear John Letter**, a duet recorded with Jean Shepard in 1953, eventually obtaining a minor hit under his own name with **I Feel Better All Over**, two years on. During 1957, he appeared on a Kraft TV Theatre show playing a dramatic role. Also, in the same year, he recorded **Gone**, a remake of a Smokey Rogers' song originally cut by Husky in his Terry Preston era, this new version becoming a million seller. By 1958 it was Crum's turn to become a chartbuster, a comedy song **Country Music Is Here To Stay** hitting the No. 2 spot in the country listings. 1958 also saw Husky obtain a film role in 'Country Music Holiday', alongside Zsa Zsa Gabor and Rocky Graziano.

Since 1957 his long list of record hits has included **A Fallen Star**, **Wings Of A Dove** and **The Waltz You Saved For Me**,

all crossover successes, and **Once** and **Just For You**, both country Top 10 items. Father of seven children – the youngest being named Terry Preston in memory of Husky's earlier identity – the singer has made many radio, TV and film appearances in recent years and recorded for ABC during the early and mid '70s. He tours with his group The Hush Puppies.

The Country Sounds of Ferlin Husky. Courtesy MFP Records.

Albums:
The Best Of Ferlin Husky (Capitol/–)
True True Lovin' (ABC/–)
Sings The Foster-Rice Songbook (ABC/–)
Country Sounds Of Ferlin Husky (–/Music For Pleasure)
Freckles And Polliwog Days (ABC/–)
Audiograph Live (Audiograph/–)

Carl Jackson

A fast-pickin' banjo and guitarist player who was for several years an integral part of the Glen Campbell Show, Jackson was born in Louisville, Kentucky, in 1953. He learnt banjo at the age of five and at 13 began playing with a family bluegrass outfit. During his schooldays he toured as part of Jim and Jesse's band, cutting an album, **Bluegrass Festival**, for Prize Records during this period. In 1972, he

Banjo Player, Carl Jackson. Courtesy Capitol Records.

visited the Ohio State Fair, Columbus, and learnt that Larry McNeely, Campbell's banjoist was leaving the group. McNeely then set up a meeting between Jackson and Campbell, the latter being so

impressed by the 19 year old's playing that he immediately signed him as part of his touring show, later playing and producing Jackson's first solo album for Capitol, **Banjo Player** (1973).

Jackson stayed 12 years with Campbell, during this time cutting another album for Capitol and three for Sugar Hill. Then he split, opted for a true solo career, signed for Columbia and in 1984 gained his first ever hit single with **She's Gone, Gone, Gone**, a Lefty Frizzell standard, following this with another mid-chart entry, **Dixie Train**, in 1985. Recently, Jackson has also been providing vocal back-ups on Emmylou Harris sessions.

Albums:
Banjo Player (Capitol/Capitol)
Banjo Man – A Tribute To Earl Scruggs (Sugar Hill/–)
Banjo Hits (Sugar Hill/–)

Aunt Mollie Jackson

An early protest singer, Aunt Mollie was born Mary Magdalene Garland, in Clay County, Kentucky, in 1880. The daughter of a miner, her mother died of starvation in 1886, her brother, husband and son all died in pit accidents, and her father and another brother were blinded by further mining misadventures. Jailed at the age of ten for her union activities, she became a union organizer, singing at meetings and on picket lines, and moved back to New York in 1936 after being blacklisted throughout Kentucky because of her beliefs.

In New York, Aunt Mollie, along with her sister, Sarah Ogan Gunning, continued her combined singing and union activities and recorded a great wealth of material for the Library of Congress – though her only commercial disc was **Kentucky Miner's Wife**, a Columbia single. She died on September 1, 1960.

Album:
Library Of Congress Recordings (Rounder/–)

Stonewall Jackson

This is his real name; he was named after the Confederate general. Born in Tabor City, North Carolina, on November 6, 1932, he had an impoverished childhood and obtained his first guitar at the age of ten by trading an old, tyre-less bike. He figured out the chords by watching other youngsters on their guitars and would sit listening to the radio, using what he heard as the basis for constructing his own songs.

After submarine service in the navy, during which time he sometimes

Stonewall Jackson's Greatest Hits.
Courtesy CBS Records.

entertained the crews, he worked on farms and within two years, by 1956, had saved enough money to go to Nashville. Wesley Rose, head of Acuff Rose publishing, heard him and signed him to a long-term contract. He had outstanding appeal as a performer and was immediately successful across the country via TV.

In 1958 he had a big country hit with **Life To Go** and 1959 saw his monster crossover smash **Waterloo**, an international pop hit in which a neat country backing was combined with novelty lyrics drawing military analogies to a love affair. As a result of the hit, he starred on Dick Clark's American Bandstand. Other Jackson-composed standards are **Don't Be Angry**, **Mary Don't You Weep** and **I Washed My Hands In Muddy Water**. In 1967 he came back strongly with **Stamp Out Loneliness** and

Capitol Country Classics, Wanda Jackson. Courtesy Capitol Records.

also had a very successful album based around the title.

Albums:
At The Opry (Columbia/–)
Greatest Hits (Columbia/–)

Wanda Jackson

Child prodigy Wanda Jackson was born Maud, in Oklahoma, on October 20, 1937, the daughter of a piano-playing barber. By the age of ten she could play both guitar and piano, three years later obtaining her own radio show. By 1954 she was cutting discs for Decca – charting with a Billy Gray-aided duet **You Can't Have My Love** – and she began touring with Hank Thompson's band. In 1955–6, Wanda toured with Elvis Presley, then became Capitol Records' leading female rocker, scoring heavily in the 1960 pop charts with **Let's Have A Party**. However, 1961 saw her return to more country-oriented fare – and her hits such as **Right Or Wrong** and **In The Middle Of A Heartache** went into both pop and country charts.

Through the '60s, Wanda racked up over a score of hits – even having a major success in Japan with the rocking **Fujiyama Mama** – and though her chartbusting continued into the '70s, in 1971 she asked for her release from Capitol and switched instead to pure gospel music, cutting sides for the religious Word and Myrrh labels. Even so, Wanda can still easily be persuaded to revive her old rockabilly and country hits onstage.

Albums:
The Best Of Wanda Jackson (Capitol/Capitol)
Capitol Country Classics (–/Capitol)

Make Me Like A Child Again, Wanda Jackson. Courtesy Myrrh Records.

Up Against The Wall, Stonewall Jackson.
Courtesy PRT Records.

Sonny James

Sonny James is still thought of by many in terms of his pace-setting 1950s teen hit **Young Love** and there is no denying that his music has often been easily accessible to the MOR market, for he has a deep rich voice with much commercial appeal.

Born in Hackleburg, Alabama, on May 1, 1929 (real name Jimmy Loden), into a showbiz family, he made his stage debut at the age of four, touring with his sisters

200 Years Of Country Music, Sonny James. Courtesy CBS Records.

after making his radio debut. At seven he had learned to play violin, later becoming signed to a full-time contract with a Birmingham, Alabama, radio station. Following 15 months in Korea – there performing before his fellow servicemen – he returned home and pacted with Capitol Records, obtaining his first hit with **For Rent** in 1956, that same year recording **Young Love**, an eventual million seller. After one more Top 10 entry, with the pop-slanted **First Date, First Kiss, First Love** (1957), he saw little chart action until 1963 when he scored with **The Minute You're Gone**. That the song was successfully covered in Britain by Cliff Richard proves again just how suited James was to pop-oriented material.

During 1964, **Baltimore, Ask Marie** and **You're The Only World I Know** all charted for James, the last commencing an incredible run of Top 5 singles (most of them reaching the No. 1 spot!) that extended well into the mid '70s. After supplying one final No. 1 hit, **That's Why I Love You Like I Do**, for Capitol in mid-1972, James switched to the rival Columbia label, claiming an immediate chart-topper with **When The Snow Is On The Roses**. He turned producer to fashion a hit record, **Paper Roses**, for Marie Osmond in 1973, and continued with his own flow of vinyl winners for a while, going to No. 1 yet again with **Is It Wrong (For Loving You)**

In Prison, In Person. Sonny James. Courtesy CBS Records.

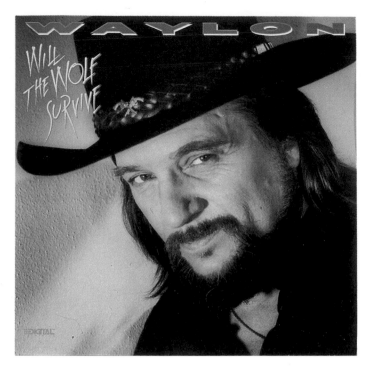

Will The Wolf Survive? Waylon Jennings. Courtesy MCA Records.

in 1974 and adding to his tally of Top 10 entries with **A Mi Esposa Con Amor** (1974), **A Little Bit South Of Saskatoon**, **Little Band Of Gold**, **What In The World's Come Over You** (1975), **When Something's Wrong With My Baby, Come On In** (1976), and **You're Free To Go** (1977). During this period he also made a couple of out-of-the-rut albums in **200 Years Of Country Music** (1976) and **In Prison, In Person** (1977), the latter produced by Tammy Wynette's husband George Richey inside Tennessee State Prison.

Since then, the career of the man known as the Southern Gentlemen has slowed down a mite, his more recent hits on Monument and Dimension gaining low placings in the charts. But he has been a remarkably consistent performer, is an able musician, capable of producing great licks on a number of instruments, and has even nudged his way into a number of minor films along the way, once appearing in 'Hillbilly In A Haunted House', a movie that also featured Lon Chaney and Basil Rathbone. In fact, the only thing he has missed out on is a CMA Award – which seems something of an oversight.

Albums:
The Best Of Sonny James (Capitol/Capitol)
Country Artist Of The Decade (Columbia/–)
200 Years Of Country Music (Columbia/CBS)
In Prison, In Person (Columbia/–)

Waylon Jennings

A strong voice and a strong personality have enabled this charismatic man to aspire to country music's heights. From a modestly successful career as a mainstream country and folk-country artist, he became the definitive 'outlaw' figure, a man who, with Willie Nelson, spearheaded the movement away from orchestral blandness in country towards exciting, gritty, more personalized music.

Born in Littlefield, Texas, on June 15, 1937, the son of a truck-driver, Waylon could play guitar by his teens. He gained a DJ job on a Littlefield radio station at 12 and, although interested in pop in his teens, he had developed an interest in country by 21.

In 1958 he moved to Lubbock, working as a DJ there, also meeting Buddy Holly. In 1958–9 he toured as Holly's bassist. When Holly's plane crashed in 1959, killing the singer and two others, it was Waylon who, at the last moment, had given up his seat to J. P. Richardson, the 'Big Bopper' of **Chantilly Lace** fame.

In the early '60s, Waylon settled in Phoenix, Arizona, forming The Waylors to back him and becoming locally known at Phoenix's famous JD's club. Chet Atkins signed him to RCA in 1965 and the

Below: Waylon Jennings – taken during the mid '70s, when he, Jessi, Tompall and Willie became an outlaw gang.

following year Waylon moved to Nashville. He was featured on the Grand Ole Opry TV show, on ABC-TV's 'Anatomy Of Pop' Special and on TV generally. He also appeared in the film 'Nashville Rebel'.

But Waylon was to become more than just a celluloid rebel. Nashville, and particularly its major labels such as RCA, was often tightly business-minded. Certain staff producers were insisted upon, the label's own Nashville studios were used and so were an elite band of session musicians. Artists were not encouraged to record with their own bands and, consequently, much of the Nashville product sounded similar. Waylon wanted to break out sufficiently to be able to have his say on material, musicians and production. He upset the RCA Nashville hierarchy by going direct to the New York bosses with his ideas about what his contract should contain. He was guaranteed an independent production package in which he would provide RCA with a number of sides each year for them to promote and sell. The big musical change for Waylon had already become apparent on the **Ladies Love Outlaws** album, where he at last succeeded in folding his own band, The Waylors, in with the sessionmen and picking some distinctive and evocative current song material; Hoyt Axton's **Never Been To Spain** and Alex Harvey and Larry Collins' **Delta Dawn**.

But **Honky Tonk Heroes**, released the following year, in 1973, proved an even bigger watershed. Waylon extensively plundered the repertoire of Billy Joe Shaver to come up with an album variously produced by himself, Tompall Glaser, Ronnie Light and Ken Mansfield, and featuring music sounding as hard and 'outlaw' as the reputation Waylon himself was already being given. The themes, instead of lightly hymning marriage situations, love nests and the occasional bit of drinking or slipping around, were of self-doubt, questing wanderers and good ol' boys alienated by the twentieth century – mostly couched in the imagery of the old west. The music was often as sparse as the poetry but it had a sting in the tail.

Leaving Town, Waylon Jennings. Courtesy RCA Records.

Waylon was well and truly 'outlaw' country. The 1973 Nashville DJ Convention saw him ignoring the major label roster shows and setting up a bill of his own at the Sheraton Hotel with Willie Nelson, Troy Seals and Sammi Smith. There were mutterings in high places about the new music. But others felt that Waylon was giving country a shot in the arm. Jennings was still patently country (a fact he always emphasised in interviews) but his use of a heavier instrumentation and his rock star approach tended to mislead people. True, he played on a San Francisco bill with the Grateful Dead, but the Dead's splinter group, New Riders Of The Purple Sage, were themselves of a trucking, rock-country nature and the alliance undoubtedly weaned new fans on to country.

In 1974 Waylon made the US pop charts with a double-sided single, **Bob Wills Is Still The King/Are You Sure Hank Done It This Way?** In 1976 he scored again with **Suspicious Minds**, an evocative duet with his wife Jessi Colter. The previous year had seen him making an inroad into the CMA Awards by winning the Male Vocalist Of The Year category. But in 1976 **Suspicious Minds** involved Waylon in two awards, Duo Of The Year and Single Of The Year. He was also involved in Album Of The Year (**The Outlaws**), and it was evident that the new contemporary strain of country had finally gained official acceptance.

It was a period during which Jennings could do little wrong. In 1977, he had two No. 1 singles in **Luckenbach, Texas (Back To The Basics Of Love)** and **The Wurlitzer Prize**, while in 1978 he came up with another chart-topping solo single, **I've Always Been Crazy** gaining another by teaming with Willie Nelson for **Mammas Don't Let Your Babies Grow Up To Be Cowboys**. Additionally the albums of identical titles also went to No. 1 in their division, while a duet single with Johnny Cash, **There Ain't No Good Chain Gang**, only just missed out on the top spot.

By 1979, grabbing No. 1 singles had become almost routine. **Amanda** and

Come With Me raised the total further, as did **I Ain't Living Long Like This** and **Good Ol' Boys**, Waylon's self-penned theme to the TV series 'The Dukes Of Hazzard' in 1980. A **Greatest Hits** compilation also did the Jennings reputation no harm at all. When the sales were totted up they amounted to three million. But it seemed that Waylon had peaked. There were no No. 1s in 1981, though **Shine** climbed into the Top 5 and a couple of duets with Jessi Colter also sold well. Nevertheless, with the help of duet partner Willie Nelson, he returned to his chart-topping ways with **Just To Satisfy You** during 1982, following this with a solo effort, **Lucille (You Won't Do Your Daddy's Will)** in 1983. A liaison with Willie Nelson, Johnny Cash and Kris Kristofferson resulted in the best-selling album **Highwayman** in 1985, plus a No. 1 single of that same title. That year he also made an album called **Turn The Page** for RCA and claimed it was the first one he had ever recorded without the help of drugs. The album also saw him quitting the label he had been with for 20 years. His next album, **Will The Wolf Survive?** came out on MCA.

Albums:
Ladies Love Outlaws (RCA/RCA)
Honky Tonk Heroes (RCA/RCA)
Leather And Lace – with Jessi Colter (RCA/RCA)
Waylon Live (RCA/RCA)
Waylon And Willie (RCA/RCA)
I've Always Been Crazy (RCA/RCA)
Wanted! The Outlaws – with Jessi Colter, Willie Nelson And Tompall Glaser (RCA/RCA)
Waylon And Company (RCA/RCA)

Jim And Jesse

Bluegrass-playing brothers Jim and Jesse McReynolds were both born in Coeburn, Virginia, Jim on February 13, 1927, Jesse on July 9, 1929. From a musical family – their grandfather was an old-time fiddler who recorded with Victor – the duo began playing at local get-togethers.

With Jim on guitar and Jesse on mandolin, they made their radio debut in

1947 and cut some records for the Kentucky label during the early '50s, later signing for Capitol. However, the duo's progress was terminated for a while during the Korean war when Jesse was called up for service in the armed forces, reforming to play on Knoxville's WNOX Tennessee Barn Dance in 1954.

During the '60s, Jim and Jesse with their band The Virginia Boys – which at that period included such musicians as Bobby Thompson and Vassar Clements – signed for Epic Records and began notching up a number of fair-sized chart entries with **Cotton Mill Man** (1964),

We Like Trains/Diesel On My Trail, Jim & Jesse. Courtesy Epic Records.

Diesel On My Trail, **Ballad Of Thunder Road** (both 1967), **The Golden Rocket** (1968) and other titles before switching to Capitol once more for a 1971 success in **Freight Train**.

Regulars on the Opry since 1964, Jim and Jesse are a fine, no-frills, bluegrass outfit, specialising in smooth, haunting, sky-high harmony vocals. They have played the Newport Folk Festival, have appeared at Britain's Wembley Festival many times and, in addition to their own 'Jim And Jesse' TV show have played on scores of TV shows throughout Europe and America. They have recorded well over 40 albums and in 1982 even made a return to the singles charts, having a mild hit with **North Wind**, a single that saw them teaming with Charlie Louvin.

The Jim And Jesse Show. Courtesy Old Dominion/DJM Records.

Albums:
We Like Trains/Diesel On My Trail (Epic/–)
The Jim And Jesse Show (Old Dominion/DJM)
All-Time Greatest Country Instrumentals (Columbia/–)

George Jones

Known as the 'Rolls Royce Of Country Singers', George Glenn Jones' nasal, blues-filled, vocal styling has influenced a host of country performers.

Born in Saratoga, Texas, on September 12, 1931, Jones grew up against a musical background. His mother played piano at the local church and his father was an amateur guitarist. He got his first guitar at the age of nine and was soon performing at local events. In his late teens he served with the Marines in Korea, and upon discharge began working as a house painter while also playing evening gigs. By 1954 he had gained a sufficiently good reputation to attract the interest of industry executive H. W. 'Pappy' Dailey at Starday Records in Houston.

Jones saw his first big country hit, **Why Baby Why**, in 1955. He stayed with Starday till 1957, cutting both country and rockabilly sides, before moving on to Mercury, his first No. 1 for his new label coming with **White Lightning**, an up tempo song with a novelty chorus, in 1959.

After 18 hits including another No. 1 (**Tender Years** – 1961) he changed labels again and landed at UA Records, where he hit a fertile period, turning out songs that have become country standards but have also remained identified with Jones' name. He proved particularly strong with the anguished, two-timing women type of song, delivering them in a manner that suggested he had lived the lyric out and that his only aim in life was to impart the agony of broken love to his fellow men.

So he hit big with **Window Up Above** (1961), **She Thinks I Still Care**, an archetypal Jones song and one covered by countless other artists (1962), **We Must Have Been Out Of Our Minds**, performed with his travelling co-star Melba Montgomery (1963), and the classic **Race Is On** (1964).

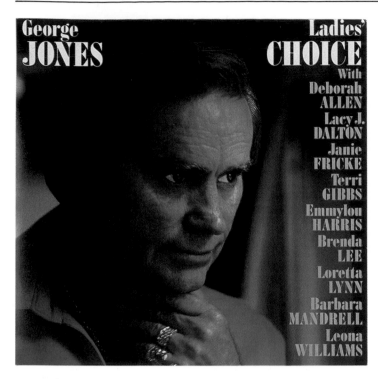

Ladies Choice, George Jones. Courtesy Epic Records.

In 1965 he renewed acquaintance with Pappy Dailey. Dailey had left Starday to form his own company, Musicor, and Jones was an obvious target for him. Although this proved a successful liaison and Jones' tally of hits continued to grow via such singles as **Things Have Gone To Pieces, Love Bug, Take Me** (1965), **I'm A People, 4033** (1966), **Walk Through This World With Me, I Can't Get There From Here, If My Heart Had Windows,** and **Say It's Not You** (1967). But the singer became increasingly unhappy with the way he was being recorded and began a fight to shake off the Musicor contract. At this period of his life he went through a rough patch, having become divorced from his wife. He began drinking heavily as he undertook endless overseas tours. He

Below: George Jones shows up for a photo call.

seemed to be increasingly living out his honky-tonk songs and became associated with stories of wild and destructive living, sometimes having to be helped onstage. During 1967 he met Tammy Wynette, when the two played the same package tour. Tammy was having problems with her marriage and she and George became romantically entwined. When, in the wake of his 1968 hits, **Say It's Not You, As Long As I Live** and **When The Grass Grows Over Me,** he released **I'll Share My World With You** (1969), the fans knew it was Tammy he was singing about. They bought it and the record went to No. 2 – kept out of the No. 1 spot by Tammy's **Stand By Your Man.** That year, both George and Tammy joined the Opry. They also got married, being hailed as 'Mr And Mrs Country Music'.

Though Jones continued having hits with Musicor – **If Not For You, She's Mine**

We Love To Sing About Jesus. George Jones & Tammy Wynette. Courtesy Epic.

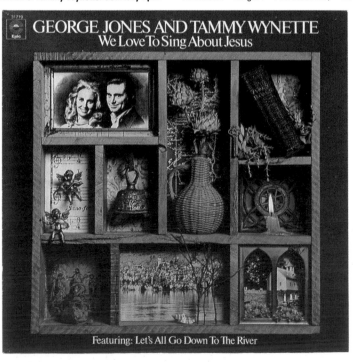

(1969), **A Good Year For The Roses** (1970), **Sometimes You Can't Win, Right Won't Touch A Hand** (1971), – he still wished to quit the label and eventually did so in 1971, joining Tammy and producer Billy Sherrill on Epic. Tammy was massive during this period (she had five chart-toppers during 1972–3) and though George had his share of hits, it was only when the twosome (now the subjects of a soap-opera romance set to music) worked together that he really hit the heights, the duo's **We're Gonna Hold On** (1973), providing him with a half-share in his first No. 1 since 1967. In 1974, things began to swing around. Tammy had only one hit, while George had two No. 1s with **The Grand Tour** and **The Door.** Also that year, the two stars swung apart, Tammy filing for a legal separation. And in 1976 she remarried – in the same year that her and George's duets, **Golden Ring** and **Near You,** went top of the charts.

Though Jones was named Country Singer Of The Year by rock magazine 'Rolling Stone' in 1976, the hits stopped flowing as regularly as they once did. He had one solo Top 10 record in 1978 with **Bartender's Blues** and duetted to good effect with Johnny Paycheck on **Mabellene.** Although in bad health, George began to put together what he hoped would be a show-stopping album in **My Very Special Guests,** a 1979 release that saw him working with Elvis Costello, Pop And Mavis Staples, Linda Ronstadt, Dr Hook, Emmylou Harris, Willie Nelson and others. But the results were not all they might have been.

Nevertheless, Jones was on his way back. During 1980, he released three chart albums (one with Tammy, another with Johnny Paycheck) and five Top 20s, one, **He Stopped Loving Her Today,** reaching No. 1 and helping George win a Grammy Award for the Best Male Country Vocal Performance. Also in 1980 he was adjudged Male Vocalist Of The Year by the CMA, a title he claimed again in 1981.

Jones continues to create his own problems. He frequently fails to turn up at events and sometimes appears to be living through a permanent nightmare, as documented in Bob Allen's biography 'George Jones – The Saga Of An American Singer'. Nevertheless, he

continues supplying such hits as **If Drinkin' Don't Kill Me (Her Memory Will), Still Doin' Time** (1981), **Same Ole Me** (1982), **Yesterday's Wine** and **C. C. Waterback** – both with Merle Haggard (1982), **Shine On, I Always Get Lucky With You, Tennessee Whiskey** (1983), **We Didn't See A Thing** – with Ray Charles (1983), **You've Still Got A Place In My Heart, She's My Rock** (1984), **Who's Gonna Fill Her Shoes** (1985), and **The One I Loved Back Then** (1986). And, as Janie Fricke once proclaimed: 'With respect to all that have come before him ... Jones will always be recognized as the greatest vocal interpreter of country music.'

Albums:
White Lightning (–/Ace)
Anniversary – Ten Years Of Hits (Epic/Epic)
The King Of Country Music (–/Liberty)
My Very Special Guests – with various guests (Epic/Epic)
The Best Of The Best (–/RCA)
Burn The Honky Tonk Down (Rounder/–)
Alone Again (Epic/Epic)
I Am What I Am (Epic/Epic)
George Jones And Tammy Wynette – Greatest Hits (Epic/Epic)
What's In Our Hearts – with Melba Montgomery (Liberty/UA)
George Jones Meets Hank Williams and Bob Wills (–/EMI)
Ladies Choice – with various guests (Epic/Epic)

Grandpa Jones

A long-time regular on both the Opry and 'Hee-Haw', high-kicking, joke-cracking, story-telling, foot-stomping vaudevillian Grandpa Jones is one of the most colourful figures in country music.

Born Louis Marshall Jones, in Niagra, Kentucky, on October 20, 1913, he began playing guitar on an instrument costing only 75 cents. At 16 he had become so proficient a musician that he won a talent contest promoted by Wendell Hall, while the year 1935 found him working with Bradley Kincaid's band, playing regularly in the north east.

Though only in his twenties, it was during this period that Jones began disguising himself as an old-timer, at the same time becoming a banjo picker in the exuberant Uncle Dave Macon style. By 1937 he was leading an outfit known as Grandpa Jones And His Grandchildren, this unit becoming regulars, first on WWVA's Wheeling Jamboree, and then Cincinnati WLW, during the late '30s and early '40s. It was here that he began recording for King Records, by himself, with Merle Travis, and with the Delmore Brothers as Brown's Ferry Four. In 1944 Jones joined the army and was posted to Germany, where he played on AFN Radio until his discharge in 1946. Almost immediately he became a member of the Opry, remaining so for many years (although he defected to pioneer television in the Washington DC area for several years), along the way having a brace of hit records in **All American Boy** (1959) and a version of Jimmie Rodgers' **T For Texas** (1962). Other numbers associated with Jones include **Old Rattler, Old Rattler's Pup, Mountain Dew, Tragic Romance** and **Eight More Miles to Louisville.** Elected to the Country Music Hall Of Fame in 1978, in 1984 he published an autobiography 'Grandpa: 50 Years Behind The Mike', written in co-operation with Charles Wolfe.

The Man From Kentucky, Grandpa Jones. Courtesy Bulldog Records.

Below: The Jordanaires, Nashville's most overworked vocal group, team up with their most famous client. They were Grammy award winners in 1968.

Albums:
16 Greatest Hits (King-Gusto/–)
The Grandpa Jones Story (CMH/–)
Everybody's Grandpa – Hits From Hee Haw (Monument/–)
20 Of The Best (–/RCA)

Jordanaires

A vocal group that has appeared on hundreds of Nashville recordings, The Jordanaires were formed in Springfield, Missouri during 1948. Initially a male barbershop quartet, performing mainly gospel material, they worked in Tennessee and nearby states, sometimes including female singers on their dates, gaining their first Opry appearance in 1949.

A year later they were featured on Red Foley's million-selling version of **Just A Closer Walk With Thee** and in 1956 sprang to even wider fame by commencing a long and extremely successful association with Elvis Presley. Grammy award winners in 1965 (for best religious album), the Jordanaires, who have undergone myriad personnel changes since their inception (Gordon Stoker, lead tenor, is the only constant member), have appeared on many TV and radio shows, also lending their talents to an impressive number of movie scores. But just how they find the time to indulge in their multifarious activities is beyond comprehension. Stoker himself admits that he has no way of knowing how many sessions the group has sung on, though he says even Led Zeppelin once gave him a call.

Album:
The Jordanaires (Columbia/–)

The Judds

A mother (Naomi) and daughter (Wynonna) vocal duo who have managed to go 'New Country' while retaining links with traditional roots, the twosome emigrated from Ashland's, Kentucky, to Hollywood in 1968. During the next seven years Wynonna attended public school while Naomi worked at various jobs, becoming, among other things, a model, a secretary for the pop group The Fifth Dimension and Girl Friday to an oriental millionaire.

In 1976, when Wynonna was 12 years old, they moved back to Morrill, Kentucky, close to their hometown, where Naomi pursued a career in nursing for a while. Because they had no TV, they began singing duets at home and realized they were good enough to embark on a musical career. They began singing at local functions, bought a 30 dollar tape deck and began making demo tapes, all the time honing their harmonies to perfection. Following a move back to California, Naomi completed her nursing training in San Francisco, and then decided to really push for a career in music, she and her daughters (Naomi, a child bride who missed high school graduation giving birth to Wynonna, also has a younger daughter, Ashley) headed for Nashville in 1979, where Wynonna finished High School, winning a talent

Why Not Me?, The Judds. Courtesy RCA Records.

contest while in the 10th grade.

As a duo they worked on WSM's Ralph Emery Show but their big break came when Naomi met producer Brent Mahler while nursing his daughter, taking the opportunity to pass on one of her demo tapes. Eventually, with the help of Mahler, Woody Bowles (a veteran Nashville manager and publicist) and manager Ken Stilts, they landed an RCA recording contract after an unprecedented live audition before the company's executives.

Immediate Top 20 chart jumpers with **Had A Dream (For The Heart)** a late 1983 release, the twosome's new career really took off in 1984 when they gained two No. 1s with **Mama He's Crazy** and **Why Not Me**, also netting a Grammy for Best Country Performance for the former title and Single Of The Year for the latter at the CMA Awards, a ceremony that also saw them being adjudged Best Vocal Group. Since that time, the girls have logged further massive hits with **Love Is Alive**, **Girls Night Out**, **Have Mercy** (1985), **Grandpa (Tell Me About The Good Old Days)** and **Rockin' With The Rhythm Of The Rain** (1986), though many still rate **John Deere Tractor**, on **The Judds**, as the best thing they have ever done.

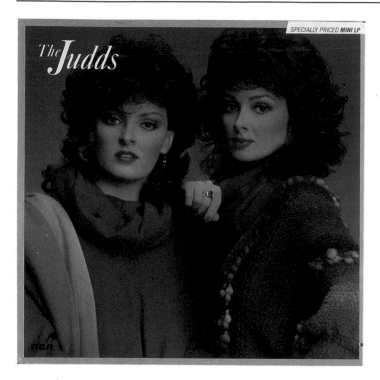

The Judds, the duo's debut mini-album. Courtesy RCA Records.

Albums:
The Judds (RCA mini-LP/–)
Why Not Me? (RCA/RCA)
Rockin' With The Rhythm (RCA/RCA)

Karl and Harty

Karl Victor Davis (born December 17, 1905) and Hartford Connecticut Taylor (born April 11, 1905, died October, 1963), both of Mt Vernon, Kentucky, composed one of the earliest and most influential of the mandolin-guitar duets. They were brought to WLS' National Barn Dance by John Lair in 1930 as members of the Cumberland Ridge Runners and remained on the show for some 20 years.

Their records for the ARC complex of labels (and later, Capitol) were popular in their era, especially **I'm Just Here To Get My Baby Out Of Jail** (1934), **The Prisoner's Dream** (1936) and **Kentucky** (1938), all written by Karl, the mandolin player. They both left the recording and performing field in the '50s, Karl continuing to work at WLS as a record turner for many years.

Best known as a songwriter (all the above have been recorded and been hits by several groups at different times, from Mainer's Mountaineers and The Blue Sky Boys, to Linda Rondstadt and Emmylou Harris), Davis was also able to write a hit song as late as the '60s, Hank Locklin's **Country Music Hall Of Fame** (1967) being one of Karl's compositions.

Buell Kazee

Born in Burton Fork, Kentucky, on August 29, 1900, Kazee was a college-educated, fully ordained minister of the church, who had an avid interest in a wide range of traditional material. During 1927–9 he recorded 58 titles for Brunswick, 46 of which were released – Kazee singing and playing five-string banjo on such songs as **Hobo's Last Ride** and **Rock Island Line**, also cutting some two-part sketches that included **A Mountain Boy Makes His First Record** and **Election Day, Kentucky**.

Author of a book, 'Faith In The Victory', Kazee performed at many folk concerts throughout his life and recorded some material for the Library of Congress. He died on August 31, 1976.

Album:
Buell Kazee Plays And Sings (Folkways/–)

Wayne Kemp

Born in Muldrow, Oklahoma, in 1941, honky tonk style vocalist Kemp, the son of a motor mechanic, naturally enough became interested in automobile racing during his early teens – though music rapidly became his main occupation.

After forming his own band and touring throughout the south-west, he met Buddy Killen, who in 1963 signed him to a songwriting contract with Free Music and a recording deal with the Dial label. It was as a songwriter that he first made the grade, George Jones recording Kemp's **Love Bug** in 1965 and gaining a major hit. From Dial, Kemp switched to Jeb, a newly formed label, his first release, **The Image Of Me**, gaining little public attention but proving strong enough to encourage a cover version by Conway Twitty which went into the Top 10. Twitty then recorded several other Kemp songs including **Next In Line**, **Darling You I Know**, **I Wouldn't Lie** and **That's When She Started Loving You** – all these going high in the charts.

This association with Twitty enabled Kemp to win a recording contract with Decca, for whom he began supplying such minor hits as **Won't You Come Home**, **Bar Room Habits** (1969), **Who'll Turn Out The Lights?**, **Award To An Angel** and **Did We Have To Come This Far?** (1971), this gradual acceptance leading to a debut Decca album, **Wayne Kemp**, in 1971. During 1973 he went Top 20 with **Honky Tonk Wine** and since that time has been remarkably consistent – albeit at the lower end of the charts – recording hits variously for MCA, UA, Mercury and Door Knob, his more recent winners including **Don't Send Me No Angels** (1983) and **I've Always Wanted To** (1984).

Albums:
Wayne Kemp (MCA/–)
Kentucky Sunshine (MCA/–)

Kendalls

A father and daughter team, Royce Kendall was born in St Louis, Missouri, on 25 September, 1934, while Jeannie hails from the same town, born on 30 November, 1954. Royce began guitar-picking at five and by the age of eight was on radio with his brother Floyce, the twosome forming an act called The Austin Brothers and touring. After serving in the army, Royce worked in various jobs, eventually settling in St Louis where he and his wife Melba started a barbershop and beauty salon.

When the Kendall's only child, Jeannie, began singing duets with her father for fun, Royce realized that he and his daughter had an outstanding harmony sound. In 1969 Royce and Jeannie took a trip to Nashville, cutting a demo that caught the ear of Peter Drake, who signed the couple to his Stop label, The Kendalls' debut single **Leavin' On A Jet Plane**, climbing to 52 in the country charts in 1970. Encouraged, Royce packed his clippers away and moved the family to Nashville, where The Kendalls began recording for Dot, with limited success. During this three-year period they made numerous appearances on TV shows and played the Opry, while Jeannie notched a Beatle connection, singing harmony on Ringo Starr's **Beaucoup Of Blues** album.

After Dot, they signed to UA for a year, but still could not make the desired breakthrough, at which point the duo took a six month hiatus from recording to reassess their way of doing things. In 1977 they returned to the studio once more, this time working for the Ovation label, their first release, a version of an old country standard **Making Believe**, nudging into the lower regions of the charts. The follow-up **Live And Let Live** was well received but looked no chartbuster until some country stations reported interest in the single's 'B' side and Ovation flipped the release and began plugging **Heaven's Just A Sin Away**, which soared to No. 1. At the next CMA Awards ceremony in 1978 The Kendalls romped away with the Single Of The Year plaudit after being nominated in three categories. Additionally, they were adjudged Best Country Group at the Grammy Awards.

The Kendalls stuck with Ovation through to 1981, continually having major hits with such songs as **It Don't Feel Like Sinnin' To Me**, **Pittsburgh Steelers** and

Below: The Kendalls, the father and daughter twosome who spend much of their lives singing cheatin' songs.

their second No. 1 **Sweet Desire** (all 1978), **I Had A Lovely Time, Just Like Real People, I Don't Do Like That No More, You'd Made An Angel Wanna Cheat** (1979), **I'm Already Blue, Put If Off Until Tomorrow** (1980) and **Heart Of The Matter** (1981). When their first Mercury releases came out in 1981 the duo continued their charting ways with **Teach Me How To Cheat** and **If You're Waiting On Me (You're Backing Up)**, while 1983 saw them twice going Top 20 via **Precious Love** and **Movin' Train**, since which time they have had several monster hits, one of which, **Thank God For The Radio** (1984), gave The Kendalls their hat-trick of chart-toppers.

An unlikely pair in some ways – the idea of father and daughter swopping choruses on cheatin' songs has often led to the twosome being asked if they are married to each other – they have stayed country and paid the price by seeing their records never really cross over into the more lucrative pop market.

Albums:
Heaven's Just A Sin Away (Ovation/ Polydor)
Just Like Real People (Ovation/Ovation)
Heart Of The Matter (Ovation/Ovation)
Movin' Train (Mercury/–)

Below: A National Barn dance regular 1926–1931 after making an impact on a one-off WLS Chicago show, Bradley Kincaid was usually billed as 'The Kentucky Mountain Boy with his Hound-Dog Guitar'.

Doug Kershaw

Cajun fiddler Douglas James Kershaw, born at Tiel Ridge, Louisiana, on January 24, 1936, first appeared onstage as a child, accompanying his mother (singer-guitarist-fiddler Mama Rita) at the Bucket Of Blood, Lake Arthur. In 1948, together with his brothers, Russell Lee ('Rusty') and Nelson ('Pee Wee') Kershaw, he formed the Continental Playboys, gaining a spot on Lake Charles KPLC-TV in 1953. Rusty and Doug then began recording as a duo for the Feature label, later obtaining a contract with Hickory. At this time they also appeared on Shreveport's Louisiana Hayride show.

With an Everly-like treatment of a Boudleaux Bryant song, **Hey Sheriff**, the Kershaws made an indent on the country charts in October 1958 and even briefly joined the Opry. After Doug completed his military service, the duo resumed their joint career, scoring with country classics **Louisiana Man** and **Diggy Diggy Lo**, the former being penned by Doug.

After cutting sides for Victor and Princess, the twosome parted in 1964, Doug moving on to record for Mercury, MGM, Warner Bros, Starflyte and Scotti Bros. He has also guested on scores of sessions, appearing on albums with the legendary Longbranch Pennywhistle (J. D. Souther, Gelnn Frey, Ry Cooder, etc), Bob Dylan, Johnny Cash, John Stewart and even Grand Funk Railroad. After playing a cameo role in the film 'Zachariah' (1971), he also appeared in 'Medicine Ball Caravan' (1971) and 'Days Of Heaven' (1978).

Albums:
The Cajun Country Rockers – Rusty And Doug (–/Bear Family)
The Cajun Way (Warner Bros/–)
Devil's Elbow (Warner Bros/Warner Bros)
Douglas James Kershaw (Warner Bros/ Warner Bros)
Louisiana Man (Warner Bros/–)

Merle Kilgore

Born Wyatt Merle Kilgore, in Chickasha, Oklahoma, on September 8, 1934, his family moved to Shreveport, Louisiana, when he was still young. He learnt guitar as a boy and got a job as a DJ on Shreveport's KENT when he was just 16. At this time he was already attracting attention as a performer and writer and by the age of 18 Kilgore had his first hit composition, **More, More, More**. Invited to join the Louisiana Hayride, he became the principal guitarist on the show. In 1952 he appeared on the Opry and in that same year attended Louisiana Tech. The following year saw him working at the American Optical Company but performing at night. He appeared on the Hayride throughout the '50s, initially recording for the Imperial and D labels, but his first big hit came in 1959 with **Dear Mama**, a Starday release, Johnny Horton scoring with **Johnny Reb**, a Kilgore composition, around the same time.

Another of Kilgore's Starday releases, **Love Has Made You Beautiful**, charted in 1960, as did **Gettin' Old Before My Time**, while in 1962 he co-wrote **Wolverton Mountain** with Claude King (the song becoming a worldwide pop hit for King) and **Ring Of Fire** with June Carter, the later composition providing Johnny Cash with a million-selling single in 1963.

Though his record sales fared less successfully as the '60s wore on, the six foot four inch Kilgore became established as an impressive western actor, appearing in such movies as 'Nevada Smith' (1966), 'Five Card Stud' (1968) and a number of others.

Album:
Merle Kilgore (Mercury/–)

Bradley Kincaid

A pioneer broadcaster of traditional Kentucky mountain music, Kincaid (born Point Leavell, Kentucky, July 13, 1895) began singing folk songs on WLS, Chicago, in August, 1925, while still attending that city's George Willams College. By 1926 he had become a regular on the WLS Chicago Barn Dance,

remaining with the show (later to be known as the National Barn Dance) until 1930. Following graduation in June, 1928, Kincaid began touring, at the same time collecting folk songs from a variety of sources, publishing these in a series of songbooks.

His recording career also began in 1928, when he made a number of sides for Gennett, these discs appearing on myriad labels, sometimes under a pseudonym. Later sessions for Brunswick, in 1930, produced a similar crop of multi-labelled releases, while during the later '30s and '40s, Kincaid's name appeared on discs marketed by Decca, RCA, Majestic, Varsity, Mercury and Bullet.

A banjo picker at the age of five, Kincaid, who became known as 'The Kentucky Mountain Boy', purveyed such material as **I Gave My Love A Cherry**, **The Letter Edged In Black** and **Barbara Allen**, singing the latter over WLS every Saturday night for four successive years. An ever-active radio performer, he bought his own station (WWSO, Springfield, Ohio) in 1949 but sold it again in 1953. His more recent recordings include albums for Bluebonnet (for whom he cut 162 titles in 1963) and McMonigle, the latter sessions stemming from 1973.

Besides appearing on nearly every major barn dance, Kincaid played for years in the north-east, introducing folk and country music to a whole new area before retiring in Springfield.

Albums:
Mountain Ballads And Old Time Songs
(Old Homestead/–)

Claude King

Wolverton Mountain – a distinctive and menacing country-styled 'Jack And The Beanstalk' saga – was a 1962 million seller for King and co-writer Merle Kilgore.

Born in Shreveport, Louisiana, on February 5, 1933, King attended the University of Idaho and then returned to Shreveport, to business college. He had been interested in music, having bought his first guitar from a farmer for 50 cents when he was 12.

During the '50s he began writing and performing, playing clubs, radio and TV. He was signed to a record contract by Columbia in 1961, gaining country hits as follows; **Big River, Big Man** (1961), **The Comancheros** (1961), **Burning Of Atlanta** (1962), **I've Got The World By The Tail** (1962), **Sheepskin Valley** (1963), **Building A Bridge** (1963), **Hey Lucille** (1963), **Sam Hill** (1963), **Tiger Woman** (1965), **All For The Love Of A Girl** (1969), **Friend, Lover, Woman, Wife** (1969), **Mary's Vineyard** (1970). **Big River**, **The Comancheros**, **Wolverton Mountain** and **Burning Of Atlanta** also crossed over into the pop charts.

During the early '60s, Nashville expected King to become a superstar whose flow of massive hits would extend well into the next decade. But it was not to be. Public taste seemed to move away from butch sagas of the great outdoors and, as a result, the '70s failed to prove kind to the singer, though he did see some chart action with **Montgomery Mabel** (Warner Bros, 1974) and **Cotton Dan** (True, 1977).

Albums:
Claude King's Best (Gusto/Gusto)
Meet Claude King (Columbia/–)

Pee Wee King

The leader of what was claimed to be the first band to use an electric guitar and drums on the Opry, King is also a noted songwriter, being writer or co-writer of such hits as **Slow Poke**, **Bonaparte's Retreat**, **You Belong To Me** and **Tennessee Waltz**, the last named being declared the state song of Tennessee in February 1965.

Born in Abrams, Wisconsin, on February 18, 1914, of Polish descent, Frank 'Pee Wee' King originally trained as a draftsman, though he had learnt harmonica, accordion and fiddle while still a boy, broadcasting over radio stations in Racine and Green Bay at the age of 14, his father having been the leader of a locally popular polka band.

After stints with the WLS (Chicago) Barn Dance during the early '30s, he joined the Gene Autry Show, taking over the band in 1934 when Autry headed for Hollywood. Renamed The Golden West Cowboys, the band – which featured such stars as Eddy Arnold, Redd Stewart, Cowboy Copas, Ernest Tubb and guitarist Clem Sumney at various points in its history – first graced the Opry in the mid-'30s, in 1938 following Autry to Hollywood to make 'Gold Mine In The Sky' for Republic Pictures, the first in a series of cowboy movies (usually with Johnny Mack Brown as the Durango Kid) featuring King and The Golden West Cowboys. By 1941, the band could be found touring as part of the 'Camel Caravan', a show organized by the Opry to entertain at army camps and other military posts, Billboard later estimating that, by late 1942, the Caravan had played 175 shows at 68 venues, spread over a total of 19 states.

From 1947 to 1957 King hosted his own radio and TV show on Louisville WAVE, also in 1947 signing a record deal with RCA-Victor. Additionally, he did a weekly television circuit, taking in Cincinnati, Chicago and Cleveland.

Above: Pee Wee King, co-writer of Slowpoke and You Belong To Me.

Success as a composer came when **Tennessee Waltz**, penned by King and Stewart, became a hit record for Cowboy Copas in 1948. Around the same time, King himself began logging a tally of hits: **Tennessee Tears** (1949), **Slow Poke** (a 1951 million seller), **Silver And Gold** (1952) and **Bimbo** (1954) all becoming Top 10 entries.

Voted top country band during 1951-5, The Golden West Cowboys were hit by the rise of rock and roll during the late '50s, King adding horns in an effort to compete with the all-conquering rockers. However, by 1959 the financial struggle

Brother Oswald, Pete Kirby. Courtesy Rounder Records.

had become uneven and King disbanded the Cowboys, forming another unit several months later when Minnie Pearl asked him to accompany her on a roadshow. When Minnie ceased touring in 1963, King kept the unit – which included Redd Stewart and the Collins Sisters – together for a while, playing on package shows until 1968. Then he disbanded once again, relying on local musicians to support him at any of his flow of dates.

Though King's records have failed to sell in any tremendous quantities since he terminated his contract with RCA in 1959, he remains a popular and highly respected member of the country music profession, worthily being elected to the Country Music Hall Of Fame in 1974. His 1986 dates included an appearance on the Grand Ole Opry's 60th Anniversary show, lining up alongside Kitty Wells, Bill Carlisle, the Crook Brothers, Charlie Louvin and many others.

Albums:
Ballroom King (–/Detour)
The Legendary Pee Wee King (Longhorn/–)
The Best Of Pee Wee King And Redd Stewart (Starday/–)
Rompin, Stompin', Singin', Swingin' (–/Bear Family)

Pete Kirby (Bashful Brother Oswald)

Real name Beecher Kirby, born in Sevier County, Tennessee, this guitarist, banjoist and dobro player was one of eight brothers and two sisters, all of whom played instruments, their father being proficient on fiddle, banjo and guitar. As a young man, Kirby worked in a sawmill, a cotton mill and on a farm before becoming a guitarist in an Illinois club. Over the road at a rival establishment was a musician playing dobro and drawing large crowds – so Kirby too bought a dobro in order to compete.

During the World's Fair in Chicago, he played in local beer joints, passing the hat around, also working part-time in a

restaurant in order to survive. Then came a move to Knoxville, Tennessee, where he joined Ray Acuff's Crazy Tennesseans on radio station WRL, becoming one of the band's stars when, as the Smoky Mountain Boys, Acuff's unit became a regular part of the Opry at the beginning of 1939. As Bashful Brother Oswald, the bib-overall-clad Kirby sang and duetted with Acuff, playing the banjo for most solo work, and reverting to dobro whenever Acuff's distinctive band sound was required. A member of the Smoky Mountain Boys for many years, Kirby could be found looking after Acuff's Nashville museum in the '70s, often indulging in good-time pickin' in order to attract extra customers.

One of the stars to appear on the Nitty Gritty Dirt Band's **Will The Circle Be Unbroken** (1971), Kirby cut a fine series of albums for the Rounder label during the '70s, some of the sessions lining him up alongside fellow Smoky Mountain Boy Charlie Collins.

Albums:
Brother Oswald (Rounder/–)
That's Country – with Charlie Collins
(Rounder/–)

Eddie Kirk

A one-time singer and guitarist with the Beverly Hillbillies, Kirk was an amateur flyweight boxer whose yodelling ability won him the National Yodelling Championship in 1935 and 1936. A singer much in the smooth style of Eddy Arnold, he performed on the Gene Autry Show and on Compton's Town Hall Party shows during the late '40s, also appearing in several films. Signed to Capitol Records in 1947, he recorded **Blues Stay Away From Me** with Ernie Ford and Merle Travis, obtaining two solo hits in 1949 with **Candy Kisses** and **The Gods Were Angry With Me**.

Born in Greeley, Colorado, on March 21, 1919, Kirk was one of the musicians who fought during the '40s to have the description 'hillbilly' replaced by the more acceptable term 'country music'.

Kris Kristofferson

Born in Brownsville, Texas, on June 22, 1936, the son of a retired Air Force Major-General, Kristofferson's family moved to California during his high school days. Living in San Mateo, he went to Pomona College, having success in football and taking part in the Golden Gloves boxing championship. In 1958, he won a Rhodes Scholarship to Oxford University, England, where he began writing his second novel, becoming a songwriter as a sideline, using the name of Kris Carson.

His novels rejected by publishers, he became disenchanted with a literary career and left Oxford after a year, first getting married, then joining the army and becoming a helicopter pilot in Germany. While in the army he began singing at service clubs in Germany, also sending some of his songs to a Nashville publisher. Upon discharge in 1965, Kristofferson headed for Nashville, initially becoming a janitor in Columbia Records' studio, then spending time flying men and equipment to oil rigs in the Gulf Of Mexico. Broke and with his marriage in tatters, he was about

Above: Kris Kristofferson as Billy The Kid in Sam Pekinpah's 1973 western 'Pat Garrett And Billy The Kid'.

to take a construction job when Roger Miller recorded one of his songs, **Me And Bobby McGee**, the composition also being covered by Janis Joplin, whose version became a million seller in 1971. During 1970, Johnny Cash waxed **Sunday Morning Coming Down**, another Kristofferson original and the Texan cut his first album for Monument, Cash writing a poem documenting the singer-songwriter's lean years, for use as a sleeve note.

Appearances on Cash's TV show and other triumphs followed, including a debut engagement at a name club (The Troubadour, L.A.) and another hit via Sammi Smith's version of his **Help Me Make It Through The Night** – a million seller in 1971. During the following year, Kristofferson's **Silver Tongued Devil And I** single went gold, while in November, 1973, another single, **Why Me?** also qualified as a gold disc. Additionally in 1973, the year that he married singer Rita Coolidge, two albums, **The Silver Tongued Devil And I** and **Jesus Was A Carpenter**, provided the Texan with further gold awards.

He and Rita merged bands and began recording together, though still continuing with their solo careers. But Kris's recording career was burning out and sales started to dip. However, he had made his debut as an actor in 'Cisco Pike' (1972) and from there on gained role after role, he and Rita appearing in 'Pat Garrett And Billy The Kid' (1973), the real breakthrough coming with 'Alice Doesn't Live Here Anymore' (1974), after which came major roles in movies such as 'The Sailor Who Fell From Grave With The Sea' (1976), 'A Star Is Born' (1976), 'Convoy' (1978), 'Heaven's Gate' (1980), 'Rollover'

(1981), etc.

Meanwhile, Kirstofferson has continued recording and playing live dates. He kicked a 20 year drinking problem at the end of the '70s (too late to save his marriage to Rita Coolidge, which ended in 1979) and in recent years has been singing better than at any time in his life, even getting his name on a No. 1 album in 1985 when he joined with Willie Nelson, Johnny Cash and Waylon Jennings to create the **Highwayman** LP and hit single of the same title.

Me And Bobby McGee, Kris Kristofferson, Courtesy Monument Records.

Jesus Was A Capricorn, Kris Kristofferson. Courtesy Monument.

Albums:
Kristofferson (Monument/Monument)
Me And Bobby McGee (Monument/
Monument)
Jesus Was A Capricorn (Monument/
Monument)
Full Moon – with Rita Coolidge
(A&M/A&M)

LaCosta

Elder sister of Tanya Tucker, LaCosta (born Seminole, Texas, April 6, 1951) entered her first talent contest, in Snyder, Texas, at the age of four. During her early years, her family switched location frequently, as Beau Tucker (the girls' father) travelled from one construction job to another. During one stay in Arizona, LaCosta and Tanya worked with a band called the Country Westerners but at that time LaCosta saw no future in a musical career and opted to become a medical records technician.

For a while she worked in a local hospital in Toltrec, Arizona, and it was not until after Tanya's 1972 success with **Delta Dawn** that LaCosta decided to return to music once more, initially joining her sister in Las Vegas, then gaining a record contract of her own with Capitol Records. Her first release, **I Wanta Get To You** (1974) went to No. 25. Her next, **Get On My Love Train**, climbed to No. 3.

With All My Love, La Costa. Courtesy Capitol Records.

For a while, it looked as if LaCosta might even get to outshine Tanya. During 1975 she came up with three Top 20 hits (**He Took Me For A Ride**, **This House Runs On Sunshine**, **Western Man**) and during 1976–80 she continued to provide Capitol with a steady flow of worthwhile releases, but since then has only had one really successful record, **Love Take It Easy On Me**, a 1982 Elektra release that saw her charting under her full name of LaCosta Tucker.

Albums:
Get On My Love Train (Capitol/–)
With All My Love (Capitol/–)

Cristy Lane

One of the best sold singers in country music – her albums have been advertised extensively on US TV and through scores of magazines, from the National Enquirer to TV Guide and Good Housekeeping – Cristy's husband, Lee Stoller, a one-time Fuller Brushes salesman, revealed her story to the world through 'One Time At A Time', a 1983 biography penned by himself and writer Peter Chaney.

Born Eleanor Johnston, in Peoria, Illinois, on January 8, 1940, the eighth of 12 children born to a family living in a depressed area, Cristy met and married country music fan Leland Stoller in 1959. He encouraged her to sing and she began working local clubs, in 1968 gaining a date on the National Barn Dance radio show. Later she made the trip to Nashville recording a single, **Janie Took My Place**, which surfaced on K-Ark. By 1969 she was touring Vietnam where her jeep came under attack and its driver killed.

Owners of a nightclub in Peoria, Cristy and her husband, together with their three children, sold up and moved permanently to Nashville in 1972, Lee forming a company, LS Records, and releasing his wife's records. Her first chart single came with **Tryin' To Forget About You** in 1977. Later that same year she went Top 10 with

Let Me Down Easy, following this with another major hit in **Shake Me I Rattle**. During 1978 came three further hits, **I'm Gonna Love You Anyway**, **Penny Arcade** and **I Just Can't Stay Married To You**. The last-named title seemed ironic – Lee Stoller was indicted for extortion and bribery and the authorities seemed set on sending him to jail.

Following another Top 10 record with **Simple Little Words** (1979) Cristy's discs began emerging on the UA label, Stoller being $1,500,000 in debt. But the hits continued, Cristy winning the Top New Female Artist Award of 1979 given by the ACM. In 1980 she achieved her first No. 1 with **One Day At A Time**, her other best-sellers of the time including **Sweet Sexy Eyes** (1980), **I Have A Dream** (1981) and **Lies On Your Lips** (1982).

It was during 1982 that the law finally caught up with Lee Stoller – he was jailed

Below: Cristy Lane. Her One Day At A Time was a UK hit for Lena Martell.

for three years, the sentence later being reduced to one year. Since his release, still protesting his innocence on all charges, Stoller has continued to famepush the soft-voiced Cristy. During 1985 he continued to buy ad-space in scores of magazines and sold Cristy Lane associated products, including a 14-inch Cristy Lane doll, through a mailing list which is said to comprise two million names. A massive seller of TV albums – her One Day At A Time LP is reputed to be the biggest selling gospel album of all time – Cristy Lane looks likely to remain a crowd-puller as long as Lee Stoller wants her to be.

Albums:
Cristy's Greatest Hits (LS/–)
Ask Me To Dance (UA/UA)
Simple Little Words (UA/UA)

Red Lane

A singer-songwriter of some consequence, Lane was born near Bogalusa, Louisiana, on February 9, 1939,

The World Needs A Melody, Red Lane. Courtesy RCA Records.

but spent much of his early life in Michigan.

Initially entering the music scene as a guitarist, he arrived in Nashville during the early '60s, finding some session work, then going on the road with the Justin Tubb Band. In 1967, Lane joined Dottie West's band, The Heartaches, as front man and

MC, he and Dottie combining to write **Country Girl**, a West hit of 1968. By 1971 Lane had become a hitmaker in his own right, two of his recordings that year, namely **The World Needs A Melody** and **Set The World On Fire (With Love)** becoming moderate sellers for RCA, the former sparking off a number of cover versions.

Though he has had no hit records of his own since **It Was Love While It Lasted** in 1972, Lane's songwriting ability has not waned, his songs being recorded by Merle Haggard, Eddy Arnold, Tammy Wynette and many others. The recipient of several NARAS superpicker awards for his work on various discs, Red has often toured as guitarist with Merle Haggard's Strangers.

Album:
The World Needs A Melody (RCA/–)

Brenda Lee

Once known as 'Little Miss Dynamite' – she is only 4 feet 11 inches tall – Brenda Lee was born Brenda Mae Tarpley, in Lithonia, Georgia, on December 11, 1944, and was educated in Nashville. She won a talent contest at the age of six and at a later contest, in 1956, she was heard by Red Foley who asked her to appear on his Ozark Jubilee Show. Her success on that show led to further TV stints and a Decca record contract in May, 1956. After her initial record release – a version of Hank Williams' **Jambalaya** – she began chalking up an impressive tally of chart entries, commencing with **One Step At A Time**, which became both a country and pop hit in 1957. Later came a series of hard-headed rockers like **Dynamite** (1957) and **Sweet Nuthin's** (1959), Brenda proving equally adept at scoring with such ballads as **I'm Sorry** (1960) and **As Usual** (1963). For a while she was undoubtedly one of the world's most popular female singers, five of her singles selling past the million mark. But after a major hit with **Coming On Strong** in 1966, her record sales tapered off considerably.

After a few years in an easy-listening wilderness, Brenda made a return to the

Now, Brenda Lee. A mid '70s album, Courtesy MCA Records.

country Top 10 in 1973 with a version of Kris Kristofferson's **Nobody Wins**, following this with such other major records as **Sunday Sunrise** (1973), **Wrong Ideas**, **Big Four Poster Bed**, **Rock On Baby** (1974), **He's My Rock** (1975), **The Cowgirl And The Dandy**, **Broken Trust** (1980), and, more recently, a joyous version of **Hallelujah I Love You So**, a 1984 duet with George Jones.

Still an energetic on-stage performer,

Above: Brenda Lee. She now spends much of her time working for the CMA.

Brenda has appeared in the movie 'Smokey And The Bandit 2' and has her own syndicated radio show. She has also put in a lot of time on behalf of country music in her capacity as a director of the CMA.

Album:
The Brenda Lee Story (MCA/MCA)

Dickey Lee

A singer-songwriter whose compositions have also found favour with pop audiences, his song **Never Ending Song Of Love** became a standard in this respect, Britain's New Seekers making it into a huge pop hit.

Born in Memphis, on September 21, 1900 (real name Dickey Lipscomb), Dickey was already playing professionally by the time he left high school. While still at school he and his group won a talent contest and thus secured a regular 15 minute spot on a radio station in Santa Barbara, California. He joined Memphis' Sun label in 1957, recording **Good Lovin'**, and played rockabilly in Florida. His other great love is boxing and he became welterweight champion in Memphis, attending Memphis State University partly on a boxing scholarship.

His songs have achieved a remarkable record of success, some of them also proving big hits for other artists, **She Thinks I Still Care** becoming associated with George Jones, who had a No. 1

single with it in 1962. Other artists who have covered Dickey's material include Glen Campbell, Don Williams, Anne Murray and Brenda Lee.

His own early pop hits included **Patches** (written by Barry Mann and Larry Kolber) on Smash Records in 1962, **I Saw Linda Yesterday** (1962), **I Don't Wanna Think About Paula** (1963) and **The Girl From Peyton Place** (1965), after which Lee moved on to RCA and began logging such country winners as **The Mahogany Pulpit** (1971), **Never Ending Song Of Love** (1971), **Rocky** (1975), **Angels, Roses And Rain** (1976), **9,999,999 Tears** (1976), plus others.

By 1979 Lee, now a Nashville resident, had moved on to the Mercury label continuing his hitmaking ways through to 1982, at which point devoted his time to songwriting, and very successfully too.

Albums:
Rocky (RCA/–)
Ashes Of Love (RCA/RCA)

Ashes Of Love, Dickey Lee. Courtesy RCA Records.

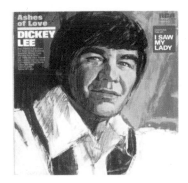

Johnny Lee

East Texan John Lee Ham was born in Texas City, Texas, in 1946. Raised on a farm at Alta Loma, he formed a high school band called Johnny Lee and Roadrunners, winning various talent contests. After high school he joined the navy, becoming a bosun's mate. Upon discharge he worked for a while in California but later returned to Texas, working in honky-tonks and gaining a job as singer and trumpet-player with Mickey Gilley's band.

By 1971 he was heading Mickey's band at Gilley's own Houston club whenever the headliner was out playing tours. He also signed a number of series of short-lived record deals, gaining a fair sprinkling of local hits and even grabbing a place in the country charts with **Sometimes**, a 1975 ABC-Dot release. By 1976 he climbed into the Top 30 with **Red Sails In The Sunset**, on GRT, following this with another major hit in **Country Party** (1977).

National fame really began heading his way in 1979 when the TV movie 'The Girls In The Office', starring Barbara Eden and Susan St James, was shot in Houston, Lee and his band being given a spot in the film. The following year, the John Travolta movie 'Urban Cowboy' used Gilley's band as a focal point. Travolta heard Johnny Lee sing **Looking For Love**, a pop song penned by two Gulfport, Mississippi, schoolteachers, and insisted it went on to the film soundtrack. Released as a single by Full Moon/Asylum Records, it proved a massive crossover hit, reaching No. 1 in the country charts, and Top 5 in the US pop listings. He recorded a best-selling album of the same title and three singles from this, **One In A Million** (No. 1, 1980), **Pickin' Up Strangers** and **Prisoner Of Hope** (1981), all charted high, along with **Bet Your Heart On Me** (No. 1, 1981) the title track of Lee's next album.

He became an in-demand act, playing various TV dates and also playing gigs at venues that ranged from fairgrounds through to Las Vegas nightspots, working

Keep Me Hangin' On, Johnny Lee. Courtesy WEA Records.

with the Urban Cowboy Band, either headlining or co-headlining with former boss Mickey Gilley. He also gained much publicity when he began dating Charlene Tilton ('poison dwarf' Lucy Ewing of TV's 'Dallas' series), the couple getting married on St Valentine's Day, 1982. That same year he logged two further Top 10 singles, **Be There For Me Baby** and **Cherokee Fiddle** – the latter featuring assistance from Michael Murphey and Charlie Daniels – following these with **Sounds Like Love**, **Hey Bartender** (1983), **The Yellow Rose**, with Lane Brody, **You Could Have A Heart Break** (both 1984 No. 1's) and **Rollin' Lonely** (1985). During 1985 he also contributed a track called **Lucy's Eyes** to an album of songs by the stars of 'Dallas'. But by that time, he and Charlene Tilton were already falling apart.

Albums:
Lookin' For Love (Asylum/–)
Bet Your Heart On Me (Full Moon/–)
Hey Bartender (Warner/–)

Zella Lehr

Born into a show-biz family who worked throughout Europe and the East as The Crazy Lehrs from Hollywood, Zella spent 12 years of her life in an almost circus-like environment, dressed up in cowboy gear and singing songs like **I Can't Get Off My Horse 'Cuz Some Dirty Dog Put Glue On My Saddle**. When her parents retired, Zella, her brothers and her sister-in-law continued as The Young Lehrs and decided to return to their US homeland to begin a new career. Their father, who travelled with them, managed to get the troupe a free passage onboard ship on the understanding that they entertained the rest of the passengers. But their father died en route and on arrival in the States the family fell apart, Zella and her mother opting to remain in America while the other Lehrs returned overseas. Zella took singing and dancing lessons and looked around for work, eventually gaining an audition for 'Hee Haw'. This she passed in a literally high position, riding in on a six foot high unicycle to upstage nearly 600 other job applicants.

It was during her second season on 'Hee Haw' – earning a reputation as the girl who rode her unicycle across a field while everyone else threw tomatoes at her – that bookings as a country singer in Las Vegas started coming in. Later she began playing Nashville clubs, attempting to gain a recording deal with a major label. Eventually some RCA executives saw her perform at The Captain's Table and signed her to the label, Zella making an immediate impact with her first single, a version of Dolly Parton's **Two Doors Down**, which went Top 10 in early 1978. She provided RCA with a further half-dozen hits during the next two years but in 1981 moved over to Columbia where she continued her chart ways on a lower level until 1984 when Zella became a Compleat label signing.

Below: Bobby Lewis who turned lute into loot. A frequent Opry guest, he was nominated for two Grammy Awards in 1969. His first Top 10 hit came with How Long Has It Been.

Bobby Lewis

Born in Hodgerville, Kentucky, Bobby Lewis appeared on the Hi-Varieties TV show at the age of 13, later working on the Old Kentucky Barn Dance radio show, CBS's Saturday Night Country Style and the highly rated TV programme Hayloft Hoedown.

Only 5 feet 4 inches tall, Lewis had problems handling his heavy and bulky Gibson J-200 guitar and eventually bought a 'funny shaped small guitar' in a Kentucky music shop, this 'guitar' proving to be a lute, which he fitted with steel strings and adopted as his main instrument.

Signed to UA Records during the mid-'60s, Lewis' first Top 10 hit came in 1964 with **How Long Has It Been**, which he followed with such other sellers as **Love Me And Make It Better** (1967), **From Heaven To Heartache** (1968), **Things For You And I** (1969), and **Hello Mary Lou**

Odd Man In, Jerry Lee Lewis, Courtesy Mercury Records.

(1970). **From Heaven to Heartache**, a crossover hit, earnt him a Grammy nomination as Best Male Performer in 1969. In 1973, after supplying UA with 14 hits of various dimensions, he moved on to Ace Of Hearts and added three more, the biggest of these being **Too Many Memories**. Since then Lewis has had minor hits on GRT Records (1974), Ace Of Hearts (1975) and the ill-fated Capricorn label (1979).

Album:
The Best Of Bobby Lewis (UA/–)

Jerry Lee Lewis

Yet another example of the 1950s interplay between country and rock'n'roll, this pianist-singer with the wild stage manner was originally influenced by the pumping, honky tonk piano style of Moon Mullican. Vocally he incorporated the delivery of black singers into his routine and, finally, after becoming a somewhat notorious rock'n'roll household name, Jerry Lee returned to his country roots, splitting his programmes into half rock, half country affairs, amazingly seeming to satisfy the fans of both factions.

Born in Ferriday, Louisiana, on September 29, 1935, Lewis was exposed to the bayou state's wide range of music and particularly church music – his parents sang and played at the Assembly Of God church. Jerry learned piano and played his first public gig in 1948 at Ferriday's Ford car agency, where to introduce a new model he sang **Drinkin' Wine Spo Dee O Dee**. Like many of his generation, Lewis spent time in the local black clubs and when he cut his first sides for Sam Phillips' Sun label in Memphis, they proved to be some of the wildest rock'n'roll sounds of their time. But amid the frantic rockers such as **Whole Lotta Shakin' Goin' On** and **Great Balls of Fire**, Jerry Lee also snuck in an array of pure country cuts, his first Sun release being a cover of the Ray Price hit **Crazy Arms** that

made the country charts.

His career went through a traumatic period after it was found that he had married his 13-year-old second cousin. He was booed off the stage in Britain and the UK press crucified him. However, by the late '60s he was making a comeback, both public tolerance and rock'n'roll being in vogue once more. Jerry Lee was back and running, making more country records this time. He scored big on the US country charts of the period with out and out honky tonkers like **Another Place, Another Time** and **What Made Milwaukee Famous** (both 1968) and other hits for the Smash label, such as **To Make Love Sweeter For You** (No. 1, 1968), **One Has My Name, She Even Woke Me Up To Say Goodbye** (1969) and **Once More With Feeling** (1970). Additionally, in the late '60s, he also appeared in 'Catch My Soul', a rock musical which ran in Los Angeles.

Ever controversial – in 1976, 'The Killer' was picked up by the police for waving a gun around and demanding entry to Elvis Presley's Memphis mansion – he continued accruing both publicity and hits for the Mercury label throughout the '70s, the latter including **Touching Home**, **Would You Take Another Chance On Me** (1971), **Chantilly Lace** (1972), **Sometimes A Memory Ain't Enough** (1973), **He Can't Fill My Shoes** (1974), **Let's Put It Back Together Again** (1976), **Middle Aged Crazy** (1977), **Come On In**, and **I'll Find It Where I Can** (1978).

By 1979 Jerry Lee had moved over to Elektra, his first Top 10 record for his new label being a bluesy version of the Yip Harburg standard **Over The Rainbow** (1980). During 1981 he played London's Wembley Festival and tore the place apart when he jammed with another son of Sun Carl Perkins, the duo becoming a Sun rock trio when they were joined onstage by Johnny Cash in Germany later that same tour. Also in 1981 Jerry Lee went Top 10 yet again with **Thirty Nine And Holding**. Then he quit Elektra and joined the MCA roster, since which time very little has gone right for him. His health has been poor – a couple of times he has reportedly been on the point of death; he fought the law (or rather the income tax authorities) and happily managed to win through; but

Country Class, Jerry Lee Lewis. Courtesy Mercury Records.

he also lost his fifth wife, Shawn, who died from an overdose of methadone in 1983. Sometimes Jerry Lee's biography seems no less than a horror story – two of his sons have died in accidents, two of his wives have met untimely deaths – but Lewis himself carried on, often making magnificent music, earthy, gutsy, the sort of stuff that is the very roots of both country and rock.

A strange personality, combining arrogance and boastfulness with an apparent respect for religion and traditional southern values, Jerry Lee is the ultimate country music enigma.

Below: Jerry Lee Lewis. A magnificent entertainer, albeit one who is frequently arrogant and boastful.

Albums:
The Sun Years – boxed set (–/Charly)
Odd Man In (Mercury/–)
Country Class (Mercury/–)
The Best Of Jerry Lee Lewis (Mercury/Mercury)
Southern Roots (Mercury/Mercury)
Killer Country (Elektra/Elektra)
I Am What I Am (MCA/–)

Light Crust Doughboys

The Doughboys, basically a western swing outfit, first came to life when Bob Wills and Herman Arnspiger began playing at Fort Worth, Texas, venues as Wills' Fiddle Band. With the addition of vocalist Milton Brown they became the Aladdin Laddies in 1931 and later gained a job – through Burrus Mills' executive announcer and band manager, Wilbert Lee O'Daniel – advertising Light Crust Flour on Fort Worth radio station KFJZ. At which point they became first the Forth Worth Doughboys, then in 1932, the Light Crust Doughboys.

The personnel of the Doughboys changed frequently during the band's career and even by 1933 – the year that the band switched to another Fort Worth station, WBAP – all the original members had departed, O'Daniel restocking the outfit with new members (including his sons).

But despite the changes (the list of musicians who at one time played with the Doughboys is lengthy, very impressive and includes the names of Knocky Parker, Johnnie Lee Wills, Leon Huff and Leon McAuliffe), the band continued their long association with Burrus Mills until 1942, when they became the Coffee Grinders for a while, under the sponsorship of the Duncan Coffee Co. Later, the Doughboys – who in various forms had recorded for Victor and Vocalion – reverted to their former and better-known title, but never again achieved the fame that was theirs during the '30s.

Albums:
The Light Crust Doughboys (Texas Rose/–)
String Band Swing Vol. 2 (Longhorn/–)

Hank Locklin

Elected mayor of his hometown during the 1960s, Locklin is the possessor of a vocal style that somehow endears him to audiences of Irish extraction.

Born in McLellan, Florida, on February 15, 1918, Lawrence Hankins Locklin played guitar in amateur talent shows at the age of ten. During the depression years he did almost any job that came his way – farmwork, roadbuilding, etc – gaining his first radio exposure on station WCOA, Pensacola.

At the age of 20 he made his first

The Era of Hank Locklin, Courtesy Ember Records, a British release.

professional appearance at a community centre in Whistler, Alabama, and then embarked on a series of tours and broadcasts throughout the southern states, becoming a member of Shreveport's Louisiana Hayride during the late '40s. Record contracts with Decca and Four Star were proffered and duly signed, Locklin gaining two hits with Four Star in **The Same Sweet Girl** (1949) and **Let Me Be The One** (1953). The success of the latter helped him obtain Opry bookings, at the same time enabling the singer to become an RCA recording artist.

With RCA he began to accrue a number of best sellers – **Geisha Girl** (1957), **Send Me The Pillow You Dream On** and **It's A Little More Like Heaven** (both 1969), all being Top 10 items. But he surpassed these in sales with the self-penned **Please Help Me I'm Falling**, a 1960 No. 1 that provided Locklin with a gold disc – the composer again recording the song in 1970, with Danny Davis' Nashville Brass, and once more having some chart reaction.

A habitual tourer, Locklin, whose many other hits have included **Happy Birthday To Me** (1961), **Happy Journey** (1962) and **Country Hall Of Fame** (1967), was among the artists who, as part of the 'Concert In Country Music' made the first country music tour of Europe, in 1957. During the '70s, the singer based himself in Houston, appearing on KTR-TV and also on Dallas'

John D. Loudermilk Sings A Bizarre Collection Of The Most Unusual Songs.

20 Of The Best, Hank Locklin. Courtesy RCA Records.

KRID Big D Jamboree and by 1975 had become signed to MGM Records.

Albums:
The First 15 Years (RCA/RCA)
Famous Country Music Makers (–/RCA)
Hank Locklin (MGM/MGM)

Below: Lonzo and Oscar, a top Opry comedy act for many years and a hit duo with I'm My Own Grandpa.

Grandpa, a song penned by the Sullivans. The act went into store while the brothers became part of the armed forces and shortly after their return to civilian life, Ken Marvin retired. John assumed the guise of Oscar, the duo touring with Eddy Arnold until 1947 – in which year the Sullivans became Opry regulars.

Some time after the death of John, Rollin Sullivan again resurrected Lonzo and Oscar using a new partner Dave Hooten. In its various permutations over the years, the act recorded for such labels as RCA, Decca, Starday, Nugget, Columbia and GRC.

Album:
Traces Of Life (GRC/–)

John D. Loudermilk

The writer of such hits as **Talk Back Trembling Lips**, **Tobacco Road**, **Abilene**, **Ebony Eyes**, **Indian Reservation**, **Language Of Love**, **Norman**, **Angela Jones**, **Sad Movies** and **A Rose And Baby Ruth**, also co-writer (with Marijohn Wilkin) of **Waterloo**, the Stonewall Jackson hit, Loudermilk was once a Salvation Army bandsman. Born in Durham, North Carolina, on March 31, 1934, he learned to play trumpet, saxophone, trombone and bass drum at Salvationist meetings, later learning to play a homemade ukelele, which he took to square dances. Although he made his TV debut at the age of 12 – with Tex Ritter, no less – his big break came in the mid-'50s, when he set a poem to music and performed on TV. George Hamilton heard Loudermilk's composition and recorded it, the result – **A Rose And Baby Ruth** – released in 1956, selling more

Lonzo And Oscar

Really the Sullivan Brothers, John (Lonzo) born in Edmonton, Kentucky, on July 7, 1917, and Rollin (Oscar) born in Edmonton, Kentucky, on January 19, 1919, Lonzo and Oscar were the top comedy act on the Opry, their 20-year stint being terminated by the death of Johnny Sullivan on June 5, 1967. Originally there was another Lonzo, a performer named Ken Marvin (real name Lloyd George) teaming with Rollin in pre-World War II days and recording a nationwide comedy hit, **I'm My Own**

than a million copies.

After penning **Sittin' In The Balcony**, a 1958 smash for Eddie Cochran, Loudermilk married Gwen Cooke, a university student and headed for Nashville, there meeting Jim Denny and Chet Aktins, becoming first affiliated with Cedarwood Music, then with Acuff-Rose Publishing, also commencing a recording career with RCA. His own recording of **Language Of Love** became a huge hit on both sides of the Atlantic during the winter of 1961-2, but all his subsequent releases have made but slight chart indentations, possibly due to Loudermilk's reluctance to tour on any major scale. He is, nevertheless, an onstage performer of considerable talent and charm and has always been a great favourite in Britain, where he has compered the Wembley Festival and appeared on several TV shows.

Albums:
A Bizarre Collection Of The Most Unusual Songs (RCA/–)
Country Love Songs (RCA/–)
The Best Of John D Loudermilk (RCA/RCA)
Encores (RCA/RCA)

Louvin Brothers

The Louvin Brothers, Ira and Charlie, once formed one of the finest duos in country music, offering superb close harmony vocals in a manner that often displayed their gospel roots.

Born in Rainesville, Alabama (Ira on April 21, 1924; Charlie on July 7, 1927), the Louvins (real name Loudermilk) were raised on a farm where they first learnt to play guitar, winning their first talent show in the early '40s, some time after the family had moved to Tennessee. Drafted in to the forces during the latter stages of World War II, they returned to music at the cessation of their period of active service, gaining dates on Knoxville's KNOX Mid-Day Merry-Go-Round. However, just when the brothers seemed to be making the grade (they managed to cut one session for Decca) Charlie was recalled for duty during the Korean crisis.

Once more, the Louvins had to re-establish themselves and following some appearances on a radio show in Memphis (where the brothers worked in the Post Office) came in 1951 a recording contract with MGM Records, followed by a signing with Capitol Records. Their fortunes improved further and by 1955 they had become Opry regulars, also having a hit record with their self-penned **When I Stop Dreaming**, a disc which sparked off a run of similarly successful singles by the Louvins during the period 1955–62. Then, after one last duo hit via **Must You Throw Dirt In My Face?**, the Louvins decided to go their separate ways, Charlie proving the more popular of the two, with three 1964 chart records, **I Don't Love You Anymore**, **See The Big Man Cry** and **Less And Less**. Just a few months later, Ira was dead, the victim of a head-on car accident near Jefferson City, Missouri (June 20, 1965), his wife Florence, who sang under the name of Anne Young, also being killed in the crash.

Since that time, Charlie Louvin has continued as a top flight country entertainer, appearing in such films as 'Music City USA', and 'The Golden Guitar'. He also provided Capitol with a number of chart entries – including a number of hit duets with Melba Montgomery – before leaving the label to join United Artists in the fall of 1973 and immediately scoring with **You're My Wife, She's My Woman** (1974). Much on networked country TV shows, he has still notched the odd hit or two in recent times – he and Emmylou Harris charted with **Love Don't Care**, a Little D release, in 1979, while in 1982 he teamed with Jim and Jesse for **North Wind**, a mid-chart entry for the Soundwaves label – and at the beginning of the '80s claimed to be averaging 100,000 miles a year playing concert dates.

Albums:
Louvin Brothers:
Great Gospel Singing Of The Louvin Brothers (Capitol/–)
Tragic Songs Of Life (Rounder/–)
The Louvin Brothers (Rounder/–)
Charlie Louvin:
It Almost Felt Like Love (UA/–)
Best Of Charlie Louvin (Capitol/–)
Somethin' To Brag About – with Melba Montgomery (Capitol/–)
Old Time (Rounder/–)
Songs That Tell A Story (Rounder/–)
Those Louvin Brothers Sing The Songs Of The Delmores (Golden Country/–)

Above: Charlie Louvin. He and his brother Ira formed an unbeatable close-harmony duo.

Lulu Belle And Scotty

Husband-wife teams have long been a staple of country music performance but one of the earliest and most popular was Lulu Belle and Scotty, mainstays of the National Barn Dance from 1933 through to 1958.

Lulu Belle was born Myrtle Eleanor Cooper in Boone, North Carolina, on December 24, 1913. Active musically as a teenager, she auditioned for the National Barn Dance in 1932 and was hired, immediately becoming one of the stars of the show. She often teamed with Red Foley (then bass player with the Cumberland Ridge Runners) in duets, the twosome becoming a popular team.

In 1933 another cast member was added to the National Barn Dance: a guitarist, banjoist, singer and songwriter named Scott Wiseman, known professionally as Skyland Scotty. Born near Spruce Pine, North Carolina, on November 8, 1909, Scotty had appeared on radio over WRVA in Richmond as early as 1927, and on WMMN, Fairport, West Virginia, while attending Fairmont Teachers College. Although he aspired to a career as an educator (a calling he would pursue in later years), he tried his hand at music, becoming an immediate hit upon joining the Barn Dance.

The two hit it off and became a very popular team (although some listeners wrote angry letters to WLS, thinking Scotty had 'stolen' Red Foley's girl), largely on the basis of their smooth duet sound and on Scotty's prolific song writing, which produced such country standards

Above: Husband and wife team, Lulu Belle and Scotty, were regulars on the National Barn Dance for 25 years.

as **Mountain Dew** (co-written with Bascomb Lamar Lunsford), **Remember Me**, the folk favourite **Brown Mountain Light**, and their biggest hit, **Have I Told You Lately That I Love You?**

In their years on the Barn Dance, they recorded for Conqueror, Vocalion, Okeh, Columbia, Vogue, Bluebird and, after the war, on Mercury, London and Starday. They also appeared as stars of several films based around the National Barn Dance cast, including 'Village Barn Dance', 'Hi Neighbor', 'Country Fair', 'Sing, Neighbor, Sing' and 'National Barn Dance'. They spent a brief time away from the Barn Dance at the Boone County

Jamboree in Cincinnati (1938–41) but were and are closely associated with Chicago, where in addition to their network and regular WLS broadcasts, they had a daily TV show over WNBQ from 1949–57.

Scotty began working toward a masters degree in education during the '50s and when the act bowed out of the performing limelight in 1958 he and Lulu Belle retired to their native North Carolina, where Scotty finally fulfilled his early ambition to teach, Lulu Belle spending a couple of terms in state legislature. Scotty died of a heart attack in 1981, Florida.

Albums:
Have I Told You Lately That I Love You?
  (Old Homestead/–)
Lulu Belle And Scotty (Starday/–)
Sweethearts Still (Starday/–)

Bob Luman

Once a teenage rockabilly, Luman became an Opry regular in August, 1969. Born in Nacogdoches, Texas, on April 15, 1937, Robert Glynn Luman spent much of his boyhood listening to various country and R&B shows on the radio. Encouraged to pursue a musical career by his father, an excellent fiddler, guitarist and harmonica player, he learnt guitar but was torn between continuing as a musician or as a baseball player – Luman Jr being a semi-professional ball player of some ability. But after being offered a trial with the Pittsburgh Pirates during the mid '50s, he flunked it and from then on concentrated his energies on becoming a rock star in the Presley mould.

In 1955, Luman recorded tracks for a small Dallas company, then, a short time later, won an amateur talent contest that resulted in a spot on Shreveport's Louisiana Hayride, the Texan becoming a regular on the show after Johnny Cash pulled out of the cast. Record dates with Imperial and Capitol followed, plus Las Vegas bookings and a part in the rock movie 'Carnival' (1957) but it was not until 1960 and the Warner release of a Luman single called **Lets Think About Livin'** that the real breakthrough came, the Boudleaux Bryant song providing the singer with a residency in both the pop and country Top 10. He was, however, unable to capitalize on this position. A reservist, Luman was called up for active duty, Jim Reeves taking over his band during Luman's army stay.

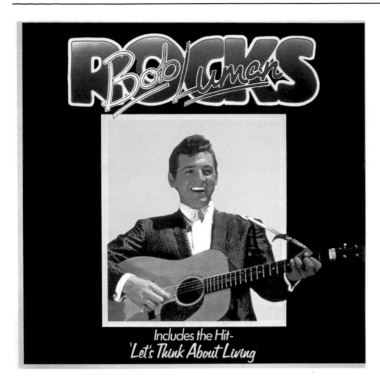

Bob Luman Rocks. A British compilation. Courtesy DJM Records.

With the advent of The Beatles, Luman, like many other former rockers, once more turned to country, signing for Hickory and Epic and logging over three dozen hits, the biggest of these being **The File** (1964), **Ain't Got Time To Be Unhappy** (1968), **When You Say Love**, **Lonely Women Make Good Lovers** (1972), **Neither One Of Us**, **Still Loving You** (1973) and **The Pay Phone** (1977). From 1976 he suffered health problems which affected his career but in 1977 he made an album, produced by Johnny Cash, that proclaimed he was **Alive And Well**. But well he was not. He died in December, 1978.

Albums:
Greatest Hits (Epic/–)
Alive And Well (Epic/–)
The Rocker (–/Bear Family)
Bob Luman Rocks (–/DJM)

Robert Lunn

As 'The Talking Blues Boy' (or 'The Talking Blues Man'), Robert Lunn brought an unusual form of both comedy and blues to the Grand Ole Opry for two decades and was long the country's foremost exponent of the talking blues, a style which was to become a staple of the folk song revival movement.

Lunn was born in Franklin, Tennessee, on November 28, 1912. He apprenticed in Vaudeville before joining the Opry in 1938, and he stayed for the show, except for service in World War II, until 1958. A left-handed guitar player, he rarely sang, relying instead on his droll, dry, talking blues recitations, most of which he wrote himself. His only recording was a long out-of-print Starday album called **The Original Talking Blues Man**. Lunn died of a heart attack on March 8, 1966.

Right: Robert Lunn, whose forte was the talking blues – a mixture of comedy and blues. This style was brought to greater prominence by the late, great Woody Guthrie.

Frank Luther

Often remembered best for his children's records, Frank Luther actually had a long career in country music as well as some success in the pop field. Born Frank Crow in Kansas, on August 5, 1905, he grew up in Bakersfield, California, and his early musical experience was as a singer and pianist with gospel quartets.

He moved to New York in the late '20s, where he teamed up with a fellow Kansan, Carson J. Robinson, as a recording act (frequently called on record Bud and Joe Billings) and as songwriters, collaborating on **Barnacle Bill The Sailor** and **What Good Will It Do?** He and his wife Zora Layman also did extensive recording, some of it with Ray Whitley.

He recorded a wide variety of country material in the '20s and '30s, for such labels as Victor, Conqueror and Decca. He moved into the field of children's recording in the late '30s and '40s, recording stories, ballads and cowboy songs, largely for Decca. In addition, he lectured on American music and even wrote a book on the subject: 'Americans And Their Songs'.

Other achievements include early country music films (c.1933), shot in New York, authorship of some 500 songs and a good bit of popular recording as well as country. In the '50s he moved into an executive role before finally retiring in the New York area.

Few of his country recordings are available, but he can be heard on Carson J. Robinson's **Just A Melody**, an Old Homestead album.

Judy Lynn

Daughter of Joe Voiten, an ex-bandleader, Judy (born Boise, Idaho, April 12, 1936) was once a teenage rodeo rider, a national yodelling champion and a beauty queen, representing Idaho in the 1955 Miss America contest and emerging as runner-up. Signed to the Opry touring show after deputizing for an illness-stricken Jean Shepherd, in 1956 she obtained a recording contract with ABC-Paramount. Her major breakthrough came a year later, when she was selected to co-host (with Ernest Tubb) the first TV screening of the Grand Ole Opry show.

Dressed in flamboyant western attire, Judy began touring with an eight piece band, in 1960 commencing the first of her highly popular TV shows. She signed to UA and in 1961 cut **Footsteps Of A Fool**, a Top 10 single. There were other major hits in 1963 (**My Secret** and **My Father's Voice**) but then her recording career petered out, despite contracts with companies such as Musicor, Columbia, Amaret and Warner Bros, though the by-then Las Vegas based Judy did have a couple of mini-hits during the '70s with **Married To A Memory** (1971) and **Padre** (1975).

Albums:
Live At Caesar's Palace (Columbia/–)
Parts Of Love (Amaret/–)

Coal Miner's Daughter, Loretta Lynn. Courtesy MCA Records.

Loretta Lynn

CMA Female Vocalist Of The Year in 1967, 1972, 1973 and, with Conway Twitty, three times winner of the Association's Vocal Duo Of The Year section, Loretta, the daughter of Melvin Webb, a worker in the Van Lear coal mines, was born in

Below: Loretta Lynn. Her autobiography sold over a million copies and was made into an Oscar winning movie.

I Remember Patsy, Loretta Lynn. Courtesy MCA Records.

Butcher's Hollow, Kentucky, on April 14, 1935.

Part of a musical family, she sang at local functions in her early years, marrying Oliver 'Moonshine' Lynn (known as Mooney) immediately prior to her fourteenth birthday. In the '50s, the Lynns moved to Custer, Washington, where Loretta formed a band that included her brother Jay Lee Webb on guitar. Later, signed to Zero Records, the diminutive (5ft

2in) vocalist hit the charts with **Honky Tonk Girl**, a 1960 best-seller, she and Mooney touring in a 1955 Ford in order to promote the record.

The Wilburn Brothers were impressed enough to ask Loretta to come to Nashville, where Mooney took a job in a garage to support his four daughters, while Loretta and the Wilburns tried to negotiate a record deal – the singer eventually signing for Decca.

With a song appropriately titled **Success**, she broke into the charts in 1962, at the same time winning the first of her numerous awards. And for the rest of the '60s and all of the '70s, Loretta became the most prolific female country hitmaker in Nashville, virtually every one of her releases making the Top 10 during this period, many of them, including **Don't Come Home A-Drinkin'** (1966), **Fist City** (1968), **Woman Of The World** (1969), **Coal Miner's Daughter** (1970), **One's On The Way** (1971), **Rated X** (1972), **Love Is The Function** (1973), **Trouble In Paradise** (1974), **Somebody Somewhere (Don't Know What He's Missin' Tonight)** (1976), **She's Got You** (1977) and **Out Of My Head And Back In My Bed** (1977), reaching the premier position. And her series of duets with Conway Twitty claimed equally impressive sales figures, the duo enjoying joint No. 1s with **After The Fire Is Gone**, **Lead Me On** (1971), **Louisiana Woman, Mississippi Man** (1973), **As Soon As I Hang Up The Phone** (1974), and **Feelin's** (1975).

A grandmother at 32, Loretta now has six children. The owner of various business interests, she also owns the whole town of Hurricane Mills, Tennessee, where she resides. Ever popular – even in the '80s she has notched over a dozen chart records including such

Top 10 singles as **It's True Love** (1980) and **I Lie** (1982) – the singer suddenly found herself with a whole new host of fans in 1980 when her autobiography 'Coal Miner's Daughter' was turned into a much hailed movie, with Sissy Spacek portraying Loretta and Tommy Jones playing Mooney. The first female artist to win the CMA's coveted Entertainer Of The Year award (1972), Loretta has never been above a bit of controversy when acting as a kind of spokesperson on behalf of downtrodden womanhood, her songs (some self-written) including such feminist banner-wavers as **The Pill**, a 1975 hit that endorsed birth control.

Albums:
I Remember Patsy (MCA/MCA)
Greatest Hits Vols 1 & 2 (MCA/–)
The Very Best Of Conway and Loretta (MCA/MCA)
Coal Miner's Daughter (MCA/MCA)
Just A Woman (MCA/MCA)
Don't Come Home A-Drinkin' (MCA/–)
Loretta Lynn Story (–/MFP)

Mac and Bob

Lester McFarland (mandolin and vocals), born on February 2, 1902, at Gray, Kentucky, and Robert Alexander Gardner (guitar and vocals) born on March 16, 1897, in Olive Springs, Tennessee, met each other at the Kentucky School For The Blind in their middle teens and became one of the first – if not the first – of the mandolin-guitar duet teams that became so popular in America in the middle 1930s.

They spent several long stints with the National Barn Dance (1931–4, 1939–50) as well as on KNOX, Knoxville (1925–31) and KDKA, Pittsburgh and KMA, Shenandoah, Iowa. They began recording with Brunswick in 1926 and also recorded for the American Record Company complex of labels, Conqueror, Columbia, Dixie, Irene and others. They were best known for **When The Roses Bloom Again**, but introduced many old time songs and ballads to the repertoires of the duet teams that followed. Although they were long favourites, their sound was rather stiff and they were superseded by later duos like the Delmore Brothers, Monroe Brothers, Karl and Harty, the Blue Sky Boys and others.

Bob retired in 1951, while Mac went on as a solo until 1953. A talented musician, he also played piano, trumpet, cornet and trombone.

Leon McAuliffe

'Take it away, Leon', was Bob Wills' famous cry which made Leon McAuliffe's name a household word in the south west during the heyday of western swing. Although he rose to prominence with the Texas Playboys, he actually had a long career of his own as well.

Born William Leon McAuliffe on January 3, 1917, at Houston, Texas, he joined the Light Crust Doughboys in 1933, at the age of 16, and began his famous association with Wills in 1935. One of the first to electrify his steel, he popularized the sound for many years with Wills, proving ubiquitous on nearly all of his Columbia Records.

Leon joined the armed forces in 1942 and after his return from World War II, set up his own band, the Cimarron Boys, in Tulsa. He recorded for Columbia through to 1955, then Dot, ABC, Starday, Capitol, his own label Cimarron, and also Stoneway, before leading the newly-revived Texas Playboys on Capitol. His biggest hits were **Blacksmith Blues** and **Cozy Inn**, though he wrote and performed many western swing and steel guitar classics while a Texas Playboy. These included the following notables: **Steel Guitar Rag**, **Panhandle Rag**, **Bluebonnet Rag** and many others.

As western swing faded in popularity in the late '50s, Leon developed other business interests including two Arkansas radio stations, while playing and recording only on the side.

But by the late '70s Leon was back in the band business once more, leading a revitalized version of the Original Texas Playboys.

Album:
Bob Wills' Original Texas Playboys Today (Capitol/–)

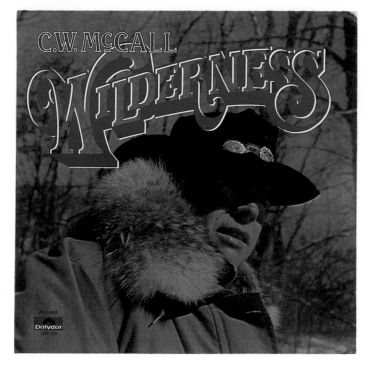

C. W. McCall

McCall (real name William Fries, born Audubon, Iowa, circa 1929) was a fine arts major at the University Of Iowa who, after many years of working his way up the ladder in the advertising industry, won a 1973 Cleo award for a TV campaign he masterminded on behalf of the Mezt Bread Company. Creating a fictional Old Home Bread truckdriver called C. W. McCall as lead character in this series of commercials, he began using his own voice on the soundtracks, later recording a single based on the commercials.

Adopting his McCall guise he cut **The Old Home Filler-Up And Keep On A-Truckin' Cafe** (1974), the result eventually becoming a national hit. With truckers fast becoming the folk heroes of the '70s, Fries aimed further narrative-type singles at this

Let Me Be Your Baby, Charly McClain. Courtesy Epic Records.

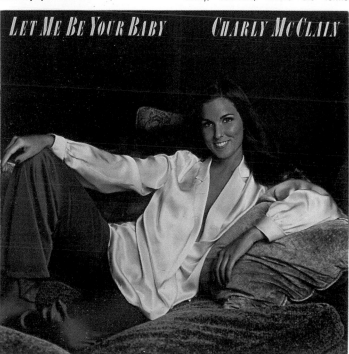

Wilderness, C. W. McCall. Courtesy Polydor Records.

market, scoring with such releases as **Wolf Creek Pass** (a tale about brake failure), **Classified** (which dealt with the perils of buying used vehicles), **Black Bear Road** (about a hectic ride through the mountains of South Colorado) and **Convoy** (which utilized the language of CB radio), the last named becoming a worldwide multi-million seller in early 1976.

That same year, Fries/McCall left MGM Records and signed for Polydor, entering the country music charts with **There Won't Be No Country Music**. During 1977 he went Top 10 once more with **Roses For Mama**, but when his Polydor contract ended a few months later he decided to quit music and return to advertising, gaining some added income when Sam Peckinpah decided to make a 1978 film based on Fries' **Convoy** hit.

In 1982 Fries and his family moved to Ouray, Colorado, where the former performer got into local politics and wound up being elected mayor.

Albums:
Black Bear Road (MGM/MGM)
Wilderness (Polydor/–)

Charly McClain

McClain has had her own TV special 'So You Want To Be A Star', a dramatization of her life on the road. She made her debut as an actress in 'Hart To Hart' and was rewarded by being signed to promote Luck's Country Style Beans and Country Style Soup in TV commercials. Since then she has been onscreen in 'CHiPS' and 'Fantasy Island' and even appeared in a fashion layout for 'Good Housekeeping' magazine. The lives of attractive young country singers have changed a lot since the era when Loretta Lynn and Patsy Cline first blew into Town.

Born Charlotte Denise McClain in Memphis, Tennessee, on March 26, 1956, Charly sang and played bass in her brother's band at the age of nine. At 17 she became a regular on Memphis' 'Mid-South Jamboree', staying two years till the show closed. Urged by Ray Pillow, she went onstage with Shylo at a fair, after which Shylo's producer Larry Rogers cut a demo, which he handed on to Billy Sherrill. By 1976 she had been signed to Epic, her first single being **Lay Down**, which charted. Three more singles also proved low-level hits the following year but in 1978 Charly went Top 20 with **Let Me Be Your Baby**, climbing even higher with **That's What You Do To Me**.

Still Memphis-based, she kept up the flow with four more major singles in 1979 – including **I Hate The Way I Love It**, a duet with Johnny Rodriguez – and an additional quartet during 1980, the year that she gained her first chart-topper with **Who's Cheatin' Who?** Awards were promptly showered on her, Music City News and the ACM both voting her Most Promising Female Vocalist Of 1980, while 'People' magazine had already picked her as 'the country face to watch'. She responded by placing three singles in the Top 10 during 1981 (**Surround Me With Love, Sleepin' With The Radio On, The Very Best Is You**) and also going Top 10 in the album charts. Some predicted a burn out. But this still shows little sign of happening as the girl George Jones dubbed 'the Princess of Country Music' has added to her toll of Top 10 singles with **Dancing Your Memory Away, With You** (1982), **Semtimental Ol' You** (1983), **Paradise Tonight** (a duet with Mickey Gilley that went to No. 1 in 1983), **Candy Man** (another Gilley-McClain duet, 1984), **Radio Heart** (No. 1 in 1985), and **With Just One Look In Your Eyes** (with Wayne Massey, 1985).

Albums:
Paradise (Epic/–)
Women Get Lonely (Epic/Epic)
Surround Me With Love (Epic/–)
Who's Cheatin' Who? (Epic/–)

Obie McClinton

McClinton is a black singer who, during the early '70s, began carving a fairly impressive career in country music.

Born May 28, 1942, Obie Burnett McClinton grew up on his father's farm at

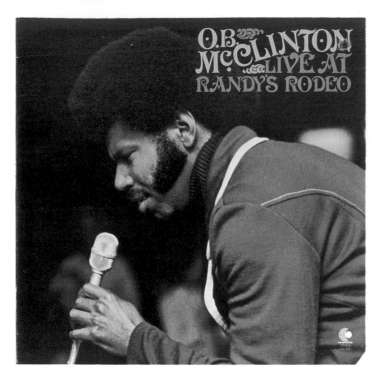

Live At Randy's Rodeo, O. B. McClinton. Courtesy Enterprise Records.

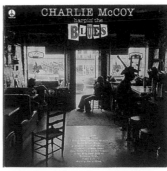

Harpin' The Blues, Charlie McCoy. Courtesy Monument.

Mel McDaniel

A rugged but amiable singer, McDaniel hails from the Creek Indian area of Checotah, Oklahoma. During his high school days he became a trumpet player but, influenced by Elvis Presley, he switched to guitar ("**Frankie and Johnny** was the first song I ever learned to play on my guitar and sing at the same time") and joined a band that played local gigs and cut some singles, one, **Lazy Me**, on the Galway label, being produced by J. J. Cale. After graduation from high school, he married his high school sweetheart and moved to Tulsa, where he pumped gas, and sold car parts. In 1969 he moved to Nashville but still mainly pumped gas. After two years he headed for Alaska where he found he could make a living as an entertainer. Two more years on and he was in Nashville again, this time working at the Holiday Inn. He began selling his songs to a publishing company and also became a demo singer, recording songs for writers who lacked the vocal equipment to do the job themselves.

One of his own songs, **Roll Your Own**, was recorded by Hoyt Axton, Commander Cody and Arlo Guthrie but it was not until 1976 that McDaniel gained a record contract of his own, his debut single for Capitol being a version of a Bob Morrison song, **Have A Dream On Me**, which went Top 50. Throughout the rest of the '70s, his singles charted regularly but modestly. A

Senotobia, Mississippi. Raised on country music he tried to move into R&B as a singer but flunked out. After completing high-school, he headed for Memphis where he worked as a dishwasher. Next came a choir scholarship to Rust College, Holly Springs, Mississipi, where he graduated in 1966, moving back to Memphis once again – this time to work on radio station WDIA. He volunteered for the Air Force in December 1966 (to avoid being drafted into the Army) and began singing on service talent shows, during this period forming a songwriting relationship with the Stax label, contributing songs waxed by Otis Redding, Clarence Carter and others. In 1971 he became a Stax-Enterprise artist himself, cutting several hit singles (including **Don't Let The Green Grass Fool You**, **My Whole World Is Falling Down** (1972), and **Something Better** (1974)) before the label folded. Afterwards he moved on to Mercury, Epic and Sunbird, supplying all three with chart records before surfacing on Moonshine Records during 1984 with a wonderfully titled hit, **Honky Tonk Tan**.

Albums:
Country (Enterprise/–)
Obie From Senatobie (Enterprise/–)

Charlie McCoy

One of the finest harmonica players ever to grace the Nashville scene, McCoy was born at Oak Ridge, West Virginia, on March 28, 1941. Once a member of Stonewall Jackson's touring band, he opted for session work during the '60s, gaining a wide audience through his appearances on various Bob Dylan albums – impressing Dylan by playing bass and trumpet at the same time on one session! He became a member of Area Code 615 in 1969 and was featured on the Code's **Stone Fox Chase**, an instrumental which for a long period was the theme to BBC-TV's 'Whistle Test' rock show.

Signed to Monument since 1963, he

had a minor pop hit with **Cherry Berry Wine** while recording for Cadence in 1961. Since then he has had a fairly active chart

Below: Hip harmonica man Charlie McCoy. His mouth-harp is not quite this big, he just made it sound that way.

career, his biggest solo records being **I Started Loving You Again**, **I'm So Lonesome I Could Cry**, **I Really Don't Want To Know**, **Orange Blossom Special** (all 1972), **Boogie Woogie** (with Barefoot Jerry, 1974), and **Fair And Tender Ladies** (1978), more recently forming a music-making partnership with Laney Hicks and charting with **Until The Nights** (1981) and **The State Of Our Union** (1983). A brilliant all-round musician, McCoy was adjudged CMA Instrumentalist Of The Year in both 1972 and 1973.

Albums:
Goodtime Charlie's Got The Blues
  (Monument/–)
Nashville Hit Man (Monument/Monument)
Harpin' The Blues (Monument/–)
Stone Fox Chase (–/Monument)

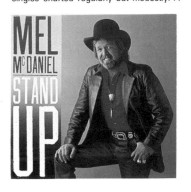

Stand Up, Mel McDaniel, Courtesy Capitol Records.

glance at any chart during this period would always reveal one of Mel's Capitol releases lodged mid-way, among the most successful being: **Gentle To Your Senses** (1977), **God Made Love** (1977) and **Play Her Back To Yesterday** (1979). The buzz was that McDaniel could not make up his mind whether he was a singer or a songwriter. Certainly he was equally proficient in the latter field, providing hits for others like Bobby Goldsboro and Johnny Rodriguez.

As the '80s moved in, Mel McDaniel suddenly became fashionable. In 1981, two of his singles, **Louisiana Saturday Night** and **Right In The Palm Of Your Hand**, went Top 10, while **Preachin' Up A Storm** also sold well. Since then he has gone Top 20 in almost routine fashion, notching hit after hit with such releases as **Take Me To The Country**, **Big Ole Brew**, **I Wish I Was In Nashville** (1982), **I Call It Love** (1983), **Baby's Got Her Blue Jeans On** (a 1984 release that climbed to No. 1 in 1985), **Let It Roll (Let It Rock)** and **Stand Up** (1985). But even these days he does not always win. Some while back he drove his brand new car into a service station where he used to work and planned to yell 'fill her up' to the manager. However, he later ruefully recalled that in the interim they had turned it into a self-service station, so he still had to do the job himself!

Albums:
I'm Countryfied (Capitol/–)
Stand Up (Capitol/–)
Naturally Country (Capitol/–)
Mel McDaniel With Oklahoma
    Wind (Capitol/–)
Take Me To The Country (Capitol)

Skeets MacDonald

A popular singer on the West Coast, McDonald is known best for his 1952 hit **Don't Let The Stars Get In Your Eyes**. Born on October 1, 1915, in Greenaway, Arkansas, he began his career in Michigan, where he played on a number of radio stations in Royal Oak, Flint and Detroit before migrating to the West Coast after his World War II service.

He became a longtime fixture on the Town Hall Party and recorded largely for Capitol (1952–9) and Columbia (1959–67). Other hits included **Call Me Mr Brown** and **You Took Her Off My Hands**. He died of a heart attack on March 31, 1968.

Album:
Going Steady With The Blues (–/Capitol)

Below: Red River Dave McEnery – the king of the saga song – onstage with Bill Fenner and Roy Huxton.

Red River Dave McEnery

Although saga songs have long been a tradition in country music – dating back to broadside sheets – the foremost exponent of the style has been a tall, blue-eyed Texan named Red River Dave McEnery.

Born in San Antonio, on December 15, 1914, he began a professional career in 1935, playing a host of radio stations all across the country but finding success in New York from 1938 through to 1941. Dave returned to Texas in the early '40s, playing the Mexican border stations and then basing himself in San Antonio from then on, though he found time to record for Decca, Savoy, Sanora, MGM, Confidential and a whole host of smaller labels, also appearing in a film for Columbia ('Swing In The Saddle', 1948) and a couple for Universal ('Hidden Valley' and 'Echo Ranch', both 1949).

He really found his niche when he wrote **Amelia Earhart's Last Flight**, however, for though he was long popular as a singer of country songs, it is these modern day event songs which have become his forte. Using the course of current events, he has written **The Ballad Of Francis Gary Powers**, **The Flight Of Apollo Eleven**, and **The Ballad Of Patty Hearst**.

In the early '70s Red River Dave moved to Nashville, where he became a well-known sight, with his gold boots, lariat strapped to his side, big hat and leonine white hair and goatee. At the age of 60 he claimed to be working on a comeback.

Reba McEntire

Adjudged Female Vocalist Of The Year at the CMA Awards in 1986, Reba McEntire was born in Chockie, Oklahoma, on March 28, 1954. Daughter of a world champion steer roper, she became part of a country band while still in her ninth grade, playing at clubs sometimes till the early hours of the morning. A promising rodeo performer, she intended to become a school teacher and enrolled at Southeastern Oklahoma State University as an elementary education major. But in 1974 she was offered the opportunity to sing the national anthem at the National Rodeo Finals, where she met Red Steagall. Impressed by her voice, Steagall arranged for her to cut a demo tape in Nashville, the results gaining her a contract with Mercury records.

Her first chart record, **I Don't Want To Be A One Night Stand**, came in mid-1976. For the first couple of years, her records sold well enough, but only a duet with Jacky Ward (**Three Sheets In The Wind**, 1978) pierced the barrier into the Top 20. By 1979 she had a Top 20 single of her own with **Sweet Dreams**, while 1980 saw her in the Top 10 with **(You Lift Me) Up To Heaven**. This set her on the way to becoming what one publication described as 'Mercury Records' crown jewel of country music', the next few years seeing her chart in major fashion with such singles as **I Don't Think Love Ought To Be That Way**, **Today All Over Again**, **Only You (And You Alone)** (1981), **I'm Not That Lonely Yet** (1982), **Can't Even Get The Blues** (No. 1, 1982), **You're The First Time**

I've Thought About Leaving (No. 1 1983), **Why Do We Want (What We Know We Can't Have)**, and **There Ain't No Future In This** (1983). Then, as Mercury boasted about having the next Nashville superstar, she switched her affiliation to MCA, at the same time, finding a new booking agency, trying new producers, ditching her longtime manager and playing her first dates in Las Vegas. But she did not intend to move into cross-over country. She told 'Billboard', "We're wanting to go traditional country – no, I'll take that back – we want to go new country. We're wanting to go new Loretta Lynn – to get new pickers, young pickers who are like me and want to stay country."

So she stayed real country but threw in little bits of business dreamed up by choreographers, lighting directors and others who could help her act stay imaginative. And the results paid off in record sales. Her first three singles for MCA, **Just A Little Love**, **He Broke Your Mem'ry Last Night** and **How Blue**, all went Top 20 in 1984, the last-named reaching the top of the charts. In October 1984 she received her just reward – the CMA named her Female Vocalist Of The Year.

During 1985 she logged yet another No. 1 with **Somebody Should Leave**, and clambered twice more into the Top 10 via **Have I Got A Deal For You** and **Only In My Mind**. And in October that year, the CMA reported: "A teary-eyed Reba McEntire won the prestigious Female Vocalist Of The Year, for the second year in a row. Reba McEntire is now a member of an elite group of repeat winners that includes Dolly Parton, Loretta Lynn and Barbara Mandrell."

Just A Little Love, Reba McEntire. Courtesy MCA Records.

Albums:
Unlimited (Mercury/–)
Behind The Scene (Mercury/–)
My Kind Of Country (MCA/MCA)
Just A Little Love (MCA/MCA)
Whoever's In New England (MCA/MCA)

Sam and Kirk McGee

Members of Uncle Dave Macon's Fruit Jar Drinkers, the McGee Brothers (both born Franklin, Tennessee, Sam on May 1, 1894, Kirk on November 4, 1899) were musically influenced by their father, an old-time street fiddle player and the black street musicians of Perry, Tennessee, where the McGees spent part of their boyhood. With Sam on banjo and Kirk on guitar and fiddle, they became part of Uncle Dave Macon's band in 1924, joining him on the Opry two years later. In 1930 they worked with fiddler Arthur Smith, forming a trio known as the Dixieliners (which recorded for Bluebird), Smith leaving in the early '40s, at which time the brothers occasionally joined a popular Opry act, Sara and Sally.

Occasional members of several of the Opry's old-time bands in ensuing years, the duo eventually opted to go their own way again, becoming favourites at many folk festivals in the '60s, when a new generation afforded the McGees the recognition their music deserved.

Sam, who claimed to be the first musician to play electric guitar on the Opry (a claim disputed by others), was killed on his farm on August 21, 1975, his tractor falling on him. But Kirk soldiered on and was still appearing on the Opry up to the time of death on October 24, 1983.

Albums:
Sam McGee – Grand Dad Of Country
   Guitar Pickers (Arhoolie/–)
The McGee Brothers With Arthur Smith
   (Folkways/–)

Warner Mack

Nashville-born, on April 2, 1938, singer-songwriter Warner McPherson was raised in Vicksberg, Mississippi. While at

Love Hungry, Warner Mack. Courtesy MCA Records.

Vickburg's Jett High School he played guitar at various events, from there moving on to perform in local clubs. During the '50s, McPherson became a regular on KWKH's Louisiana Hayride and was also featured on Red Foley's Ozark Jubilee, his record career making progress in 1957 when his recording of **Is It Wrong?** charted in fairly spectacular manner. In the wake of this initial success, McPherson – who had become Warner Mack after his nickname had inadvertently been placed on a record label – decided to return to Music City. But there was a lull in his record-selling fortunes until 1964 when, following a moderate hit with **Surely**, Mack suddenly hit top gear, providing Decca with 14 successive Top 20 entries between 1964 and 1970, one of which, **The Bridge Washed Out**, was the best selling country disc for a lengthy period during 1965.

An ever-busy songwriter, Mack has written over 250 songs including **The Bridge Washed Out**, **Is It Wrong** and several of his other chart climbers including **Talkin' To The Wall** (1966) and **How Long Will It Take?** (1967).

During the early '70s, Mack continued on his chart-filling way with such lower order singles as **Draggin The River**, **You're Burnin' My House Down** (1972), **Some Roads Have No Ending**, **Goodbyes** and **Don't Come Easy** (1973) all for Decca/MCA. Mack's last chart appearance came on Pageboy in late 1977 with **These Crazy Thoughts**, but still he continues playing successful tours. In recent times, Mack has completed two, well-received jaunts around Europe.

Uncle Dave Macon

Known variously as The Dixie Dewdrop, the King Of the Hillbillies and The King Of Banjo Players, David Harrison Macon was the first real star of the Grand Ole Opry.

Born in Smart Station, Tennessee, on October 7, 1870, he grew up in a threatrical environment, his parents running a Nashville boarding house catering for travelling showbiz folk.

Following his marriage to Mathilda Richardson, Macon moved to a farm near Readyville, Tennessee, there establishing a mule and wagon transport company which operated for around 20 years. A natural entertainer and a fine five-string banjoist, David Macon played at local functions for many years but remained unpaid until 1918 when, wishing to decline an offer to play at a pompous farmer's party, he asked what he thought was the exorbitant fee of 15 dollars, expecting to be turned down. But the fee was paid and Uncle Dave played, being spotted there by a Loew's talent scout who offered him a spot at a Birmingham, Alabama, theatre.

In 1923, while playing in a Nashville barber's shop, he met fiddler and guitarist Sid Harkreader, the two of them teaming to perform at the local Loew's Theatre, then moving on to tour the south as part of a vaudeville show. A year later, while playing at a furniture convention, the duo were approached by C. C. Rutherford of the Sterchi Brothers Furniture Company,

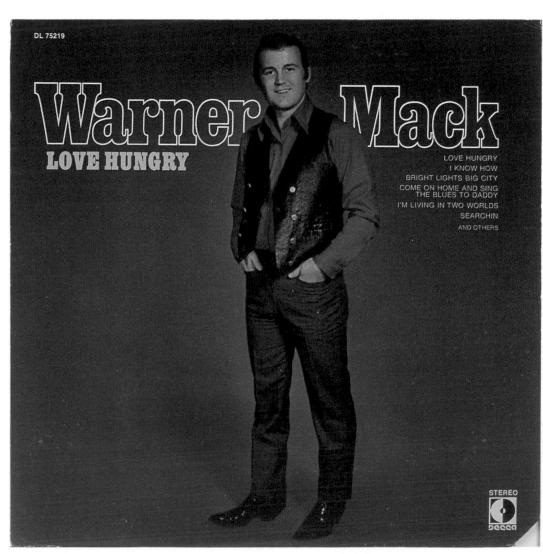

The Gayest Old Dude In Town, Uncle Dave Macon. Courtesy Bear Family.

who offered to finance a New York recording date with Vocalion. Macon and Harkreader accepted, cutting 14 sides at the initial sessions, returning in 1925 to produce another 28 titles. Macon's next New York sessions (1926) found him playing alongside guitarist Sam McGee, cutting such sides as **The Death Of John Henry** and **Whoop 'Em Up Cindy** – and that same year he first appeared on the Opry, where the jovial, exuberant Macon, clad in his waistcoat, winged collar and plug hat, soon became a firm favourite.

An Opry performer – usually accompanied by his son Dorris – almost up to the time of his death, the fun-loving banjoist cut many records during his lifetime, sometimes recording solo, sometimes as part of the Fruit Jar Drinkers Band (not the same as the Opry band of the same name) or, on more religious sessions, as a member of the Dixie Sacred Singers, usually employing fiddler Mazy Todd and the McGee Brothers as supporting musicians. He appeared – and virtually stole the show – in the 1940 film 'Grand Ole Opry' with Roy Acuff and others.

He died aged 82 on March 22, 1952, in Readyville, just three weeks after his final appearance on the Opry, his burial taking place in Coleman County, Murfreesboro, Tennessee. In October, 1966, he was elected to the Country Music Hall Of Fame, his plaque recalling that the man known as The Dixie Dewdrop was 'A proficient banjoist and singer of old time ballads who was, during his time, the most popular country music artist in America.'

Albums:
Gayest Old Dude in Town (–/Bear Family)
Uncle Dave Macon 1926–1939 (Historical/–)
Early Recordings (County/–)
Laugh Your Blues Away (Rounder/–)

Rose Maddox

Born in Boaz, Alabama, on December 15, 1926, Rose Maddox began her show business as part of a family band, an outfit justifiably known as 'the most colourful hillbilly band in the land'. With Cal on guitar and harmonica, Henry on mandolin, Fred on bass, Don providing the comedy and Rose handling the lead vocals in her

On The Air, Maddox Brothers And Rose. Courtesy Arhoolie Records.

full-throated, emotional style, the Maddox Brothers and Rose established a reputation first in California (where the family had taken up residence during the Depression) then on to the Louisiana Hayride in Shreveport.

During the '50s, the Maddoxes produced several fine records, also putting in appearances on the Grand Ole Opry and other leading country music shows, moving their band of operations back to California as the decade came to a close. Shortly after, the group disbanded and Rose became a solo act, recording for Capitol and supplying the label with such successful records as **Gambler's Love** (1959), **Kissing My Pillow** (1961), **Sing A Little Song Of Heartache** (1962), **Lonely Teardrops** (1963), **Somebody Told Somebody** (1963) and **Bluebird, Let Me Tag Along** (1964).

During this period she also recorded a number of duets with Buck Owens – one of which, **Loose Talk/Mental Cruelty** proved a double-sided hit in 1961 – and cut an album called **Bluegrass**, a disc made at the suggestion of Bill Monroe, who played mandolin on the sessions, Don Reno and Red Smiley also taking part.

After being in semi-retirement for a while, she began working again, often in partnership with Vern Williams and his band, this unit playing many benefits for Rose in order to pay her hospital bills when she became gravely ill in the late '70s. During 1983 Rose and Vern Williams again joined forces to record **A Beautiful Bouquet**, an album of gospel music, recorded in honour of Rose's son Donnie, who died in August, 1982.

Albums:
The Maddox Brothers And Rose – On The Air (Arhoolie/–)
Rockin' Rollin' Maddox Brothers And Rose (–/Bear Family)
Maddox Brothers And Rose 1946–1951 Vols 1 & 2 (Arhoolie/–)
This Is Rose Maddox (Arhoolie/–)
A Beautiful Bouquet (Arhoolie/–)

J. E. Mainer

The leader of the Mountaineers, one of the first string bands on record, banjoist and fiddler J. E. Mainer was born in Weaversville, North Carolina, on July 20, 1898.

A banjo player at the age of nine, by his early teens he had become a cotton mill hand, working alongside his father at a Glendale, South Carolina mill. In 1913, he moved to Knoxville, Tennessee, there witnessing an accident in which a fiddler was killed by a railroad train. He then claimed the musician's broken instrument as his own, had it repaired and learnt to play it, soon becoming one of the finest fiddlers in his area.

By 1922, Mainer had hoboed his way to Concord, North Carolina, there marrying Sarah Gertrude McDaniel and, later, forming a band with his brother Wade (banjo), Papa John Love (guitar) and Zeke Morris (mandolin/guitar). The band gained a fair degree of fame locally, though J.E. was still employed in the textile industry. But in the early '30s came a change of fortune, when Mainer's unit, adopting the

Left: Mainer's Mountaineers, c.1936. J. E. is top left, Wade is bottom right.

title of the Crazy Mountaineers, began a series of broadcasts from Charlottesville, sponsored by the Crazy Water Crystal Company. Record dates for RCA Bluebird followed, the Mountaineers cutting such tracks as **John Henry**, **Lights In The Valley**, **Ol' Number 9** and **Maple On The Hill**.

The band's popularity continued throughout the '30s and '40s, Mainer and the Mountaineers recording over 200 sides for RCA and broadcasting over WPTF, Raleigh, North Carolina. And by the late '60s J.E. was still performing and recording — one of his releases being a single featuring unaccompanied Jew's harp — but the grim reaper eventually caught up with him in 1971.

Albums:
J. E. Mainer's Mountaineers (Arhoolie/–)
J. E. Mainer's Mountaineers Vols 1 and 2
　(Old Timey/–)
Good Old Mountain Music (King/–)

Wade Mainer

The banjo-playing younger brother of J. E. Mainer, Wade had a long and influential career of his own. Born on April 21, 1907, near Weaverville, North Carolina, Wade developed an advanced two-finger banjo picking style which led to a distinctive sound on his records as well as those he made with his brother.

After splitting from Mainer's Mountaineers (who had a big hit in 1936 with **Maple On The Hill**), Wade formed hs own group, which at times included Clyde Moody and Wade Morris of the Morris Brothers, called Wade Mainer and The Sons Of The Mountaineers.

Possessed of a strong clear voice, his **Sparkling Blue Eyes** was a major hit in 1939, one of the last commercial releases by a string band. Wade recorded for Bluebird until 1941, and after the war spent several years with King but without much commercial success. After a brief retirement in North Carolina, he moved to Flint, Michigan, where he worked for Chevrolet until his retirement. In later years he recorded for Old Homestead and proved that his strong, pure country voice and unique banjo style had not been affected by his advanced years.

Albums:
Sacred Songs Of Mother And Home (Old
　Homestead/–)
Wade Mainer And The Mainer's
　Mountaineers (Old Homestead/–)

Barbara Mandrell

Barbara is the singer who, probably more than anyone else, has managed to weld Las Vegas pzazz to the relatively more down-homey sounds of Nashville. She picks but she is slick, she sings songs like **I Was Country When Country Wasn't Cool** yet still manages to make them sound as though they had originally been penned for some Hollywood disco-flick. She is beautiful and glossy enough to have just walked off the Dallas set. She has also got brains, business-sense and enough talent to win the CMA Entertainer Of The Year award in 1980 and 1981, along with several

with such other major hits as **Married But Not To Each Other**, **Woman To Woman** (both 1977), **Tonight** (1978), **Sleeping Single In A Double Bed** (No. 1, 1978), and **(If Loving You Is Wrong) I Don't Want To Be Right** (No. 1, 1979), before ABC/Dot sold out to MCA.

With her new label, Barbara went on hitmaking, **Fooled By A Feeling** (1979) being succeeded by **Years** (No. 1, 1979), **Crackers**, **The Best Of Strangers** (1980), **Love Is Fair** (1981), **I Was Country When Country Wasn't Cool** (No. 1 1981), **Wish You Were Here** (1981), **Till You're Gone** (No. 1, 1982), **Operator, Long Distance Please** (1982), **In Times Like These** (1983), **One Of A Kind Pair Of Fools** (No. 1, 1983), **Happy Birthday** (1984), **Only A Lonely Heart Knows** (1984) and **To Me**, a duet with Lee Greenwood (1984).

During the early '80s, her popularity soared as a result of a TV series on which she and her sisters Irlene and Louise played myriad instruments, sang gospel, country and pop, danced and even jammed with puppets in an effort to display their versatility.

In 1984 the Mandrell luck momentarily changed and Barbara narrowly escaped death when she and her children were driving home from a shopping trip, her Jaguar becoming involved in a head-on collision with a car that had jumped lanes. Hospitalized for 19 days, she suffered a broken leg and ankle, a crushed kneecap and severe concussion. But by January, 1985, while still on crutches, she gave a press conference to announce the making of a second made-for-TV movie (the first was 'Burning Rage' in 1984), and a networked TV special with guests Lee Greenwood and Roy Acuff. Her more recent hits have included **There's No Love In Tennessee**, **Angel In Your Arms** (both 1985) and **Fast Lanes And Country Roads** (1986).

Albums:
The Best Of Barbara Mandrell (Columbia/–)
The Very Best of Barbara Mandrell (–/ Ronco)
Live (MCA/MCA)

Louise Mandrell

Born in Corpus Christi, Texas, on July 13, 1954, Louise is the fiddle and bass playing member of the Mandrell girls. A member of Barbara's Do-Rites at 15, mainly playing bass, she toured with the group for several years, but during the '70s became part of the troupe headed by Opry star Stu Phillips, playing an increasing role in the programme. Next came a musical liaison with Merle Haggard, Louise singing both lead and back-ups on Haggard live dates and recordings, after which she decided to go it alone, signing a deal as a solo act with Epic, the label also signing R. C. Bannon, whom Louise married in 1979.

The first hit, a minor one, was **Put It On Me**, in 1978. But the following year things took off, Louise garnering no less than five successful singles including a Top 20 shot with **Reunited**, a duet with Bannon. By 1981, the couple had signed to RCA, immediately making some impression with **Where There's Smoke There's Fire**, the following year charting with **Christmas Is Just A Song For Us This Year**, the reverse of Alabama's Xmas single. Given considerable exposure by her weekly appearances on her sister's TV show, during 1983 Louise experienced a

Above: Barbara Mandrell has her own museum on Nashville's Division Street. It contains a reproduction of the trophy room in her own home.

Clean Cut, Barbara Mandrell. Courtesy MCA Records.

other major plaudits. Next to Dolly Parton, Barbara Mandrell is Nashville's hottest female property.

Born in Houston, Texas, in 1948, but raised in L.A., she became part of the family band, headed by her father. At the age of 11 she could play pedal-steel, demonstrating her prowess at Las Vegas' Showboat Hotel that same year. Also before hitting her teens she could find her way around a piano, bass, guitar, banjo and saxophone. At 13 she toured with Johnny Cash and in 1966–7 played at military bases in Korea and Vietnam.

During the late '60s, she began recording for the minor Mosrite label cutting titles that included **Queen For A Day**. But following a family move to Tennessee, she set her sights on a Nashville contract, eventually signing for Columbia in March, 1969, and gaining her first hit that year with her version of Otis Redding's **I've Been Loving You Too Long**, establishing a successful country-meets-soul format that saw her achieving further chart status with such R&B material as **Do Right Woman – Do Right Man** (1971), **Treat Him Right** (1971) and Joe Tex's **Show Me** (1972). During 1971 she had her first Top 10 record with **Tonight My Baby's Coming Home**, following this with **Midnight Oil** (1973). In 1975 she signed to ABC/Dot and immediately went Top 5 with **Standing Room Only**, providing the label

Louise Mandrell remained in the shadow of Barbara for many years but gained her own TV special in 1983.

considerable increase in her solo fortunes, two singles, **Save Me** and **Too Hot To Sleep**, both going Top 10, while a third, **Runaway Heart**, went Top 20. During 1984 she again had a Top 10 record with **I'm Not Through Loving You Yet**.

Albums:
Inseparable – with R. C. Bannon (Epic/–)
Too Hot To Sleep (RCA/–)
I'm Not Through Loving You Yet (RCA/–)

Zeke Manners

An accordion player, singer and songwriter, Zeke Manners is best known as a co-founder of the Beverly Hillbillies and for his long association with Elton Britt.

Manners befriended Britt when he joined the Hillbillies in 1932 and in 1935 the two of them broke away from the group and headed for New York, where they proved popular – sometimes playing together, sometimes as solo acts – for many years.

Aside from his Brunswick recordings with the Beverly Hillbillies, Manners recorded on his own for Variety, Bluebird and RCA, collaborating with Elton Britt in the late '50s for the **Wandering Cowboy** album on ABC-Paramount.

Joe and Rose Maphis

A husband and wife team whose popularity peaked during the '50s and '60s, Otis W. 'Joe' Maphis (born Suffolk, Virginia, May 12, 1921) and Rose Lee (born Baltimore, Maryland, December 29, 1922) met on Richmond, Virginia's WRVA Old Dominion Barn Dance in 1948. Shortly after meeting, they married and moved out to the West Coast, there playing on Cliffie Stone's Hometown Jamboree and Crompton's Town Hall Party for several years, also performing vocally and instrumentally (Joe played fiddle, guitar, banjo, mandolin and bass, while Rose Lee played guitar) on various recording sessions. Joe, who is Barbara Mandrell's uncle, is possibly best known for the time he spent on the road and in the studio with Rick Nelson. He died in June 1986.

Album:
Honky Tonk Cowboy (CMH/–)

Linda Martell

From South Carolina, Linda was initially an R&B singer who regularly entertained at the USAF base in Charleston. Discovering that she received more response whenever she employed country material,

she turned increasingly to this type of music and was eventually recommended to Nashville music businessman Duke Rayner, who auditioned her and then organized some Music City demo

Fly Me To Frisco, Jimmy Martin And The Sunny Mountain Boys. Courtesy MCA.

sessions. The results impressed Shelby Singleton and he signed Linda for his Plantation label, her first release, **Color Him Father**, reaching No. 22 on the country charts in 1969. Subsequent recordings failed to make any great impact (**A Bad Case Of The Blues** being the biggest of them) but Linda nevertheless made country music history by becoming the first black female singer to guest on the Grand Ole Opry.

Album:
Color Me Country (Plantation/–)

Jimmy Martin

Born in Sneedville, Tennessee, in 1927 James Henry Martin rose to prominence as a member of Bill Monroe's Bluegrass Boys, with which outfit he was lead vocalist, guitarist and front man for much of 1949–53, his last session with the band taking place in January 1954. Next came some fine sides for Victor, which found Martin in the company of the Osborne Brothers, fiddler Red Taylor (who had played alongside Martin on Monroe's classic **Uncle Pen**) and bassist Howard Watts, a luminary of both Monroe's band and Hank Williams' Drifting Cowboys.

Some time later, Martin formed his own regular outfit, the Sunny Mountain Boys, and began recording for Decca, sometimes employing material of a novelty nature but always using musicians of quality, J. D. Crowe, Vic Jordan (later with Lester Flatt), Bill Emerson (with Country Gentlemen) and Allan Munde (of Country Gazette) being amongst those who worked with the band.

Maligned for his use of drums – thus horrifying some purists – Martin is perhaps one of the more unsung heroes on the bluegrass scene, though his contribution, both vocally and instrumentally, has been of inestimable value.

Albums:
Big Instrumentals (MCA/–)
Jimmy Martin (MCA/–)
Jimmy Martin And The Sunny Mountain Boys (MCA/–)
Good'n'Country (MCA/–)

Above: Jimmy Martin and his Sunny Mountain Boys. The girl is Lois Johnson.

Frankie Marvin

Following in the footsteps of his elder brother Johnny, Frankie Marvin (born Butler, Oklahoma, 1905) journeyed to New York and joined him at the peak of his popularity, doing comedy as well as playing steel guitar and ukelele. He also worked with the Duke Of Paducah in a comedy team known as Ralph and Elmer, and cut numerous records for a host of companies, being among the earliest country sides recorded in New York.

He joined Gene Autry – whom he had befriended in New York in 1929 – in Chicago in the early '30s, as Autry's popularity began to grow. He then went west with him to Hollywood in the mid-'30s. Frank toured, broadcast and recorded with Autry for the next two decades, adding the distinctive steel guitar styling that was so much of the Autry sound. He left the Autry show in 1955 and later retired in the mountains near Frazier Park, California.

Johnny Marvin

Born in Butler, Oklahoma, in 1898, young Johnny ran away from home at the age of 12 to pursue a career as a musician, singer and entertainer. His quest eventually took him to New York City where he became popular on Broadway, also logging a couple of hit records on Victor: **Just Another Day Wasted Away** and **Wait For Me At the Close Of A Long, Long Day**, which was his theme song.

He also became popular in the country field as 'The Lonesome Singer Of The Air' and used his steel guitar playing alongside brother Frankie both as a comedian and as a musician. The two befriended Gene Autry in 1929, and after the Depression took the wind out of Johnny's sails, he went to work for Gene as songwriter and

producer on the Melody Ranch radio show. He contracted an illness while entertaining GIs in the South Seas during World War II and died in 1945 at the age of 47.

Louise Massey (And The Westerners)

Milt Mable, vocals and various instruments; Allen Massey, vocals and various instruments; Curt Massey, fiddle, trumpet, piano, vocals; Dad Massey, vocals and various instruments; Louise Massey, vocals; Larry Wellington, vocals and various instruments.

One of the earliest, most popular and most professional Western bands in country music was known as the Musical Massey Family, then as The Westerners and, finally, as Louise Massey And The Westerners. Natives of Texas, they were the first to dress in flashy cowboy outfits and exploit a Western image. They appeared for several years on WLS, beginning in 1928, and also on Plantation Party and other popular radio shows.

The main vocals were by Louis Massey, whose growth in popularity is reflected in the changing band name, with many other solos by her brother Curt, who had an active and successful career in popular music both before and after his association with The Westerners, ultimately being musical director and writer of the theme songs for the 'Beverly Hillbillies' and 'Petticoat Junction' TV shows, actually singing the latter. Supporting vocals were done by all the band members, most notably the third sibling Allen, and Louise's husband Milt Mable. They recorded for the ARC complex of labels, Vocalion, Okeh and Conqueror. Their biggest hit was probably **The Honey Song**, although they are best known for Louise's composition **My Adobe Hacienda**.

Ken Maynard

Ken Maynard (born July 21, 1895, Vevay, Indiana) was a major cowboy film star in both the silent and sound era, making and losing several screen fortunes in his many years on the screen. His place in country music was assured firstly by his being the first cowboy to sing on film, in 'the Wagon Master' in 1930; secondly by being the first to use a Western song as a film title (**The Strawberry Roan**, 1933); thirdly by introducing Gene Autrey to films, as a singer in 'In Old Sante Fe' in 1934; and lastly by his 1930 recording session for Columbia at which he cut eight traditional cowboy songs.

A fiddler, banjoist, guitarist, and rough but appealing singer as well as a stunt man, rodeo star and film hero of over two decades (1922–45), Ken Maynard died in California on March 23, 1973.

Below: Ken Maynard fiddles his way through the movie 'Strawberry Roan'.

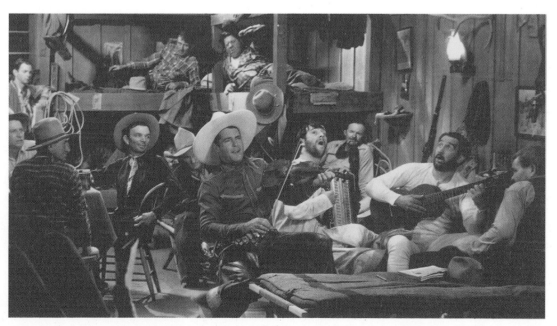

ROLL ME ON THE WATER
TRY ME AGAIN
YOU CAN BE REPLACED
WON'T YOU STAY (JUST A LITTLE BIT LONGER)
MAYBE I SHOULD'VE BEEN LISTENIN'
MONTANA COWBOY
SPREAD A LITTLE LOVE AROUND
WHEN THE NEW WEARS OFF OUR LOVE
THIS IS US
I DON'T BELIEVE YOU'VE MET MY BABY

Jody Miller

The complete cross-over singer, Jody Miller is equally at home in pop, country or folk setting, a trait that leads to most articles on her talents commencing with the words: 'Jody Miller is difficult to classify.'

Born in Phoenix, Arizona, on November 29, 1941, the daughter of a country fiddle player, Jody grew up in Oklahoma, where she and school friends formed a trio known as The Melodies. Upon graduation, she decided on a solo singing career, but after heading for California she broke her neck and was forced to return home to Oklahoma once more. Recuperation completed, she began establishing herself locally, joining the Tom Paxton TV Show, and gained a reputation as a folk singer. Through actor Dale Robertson she became signed to Capitol Records in 1963, making a fairly commercial folk album in **Wednesday's Child**, later cutting a hit single, **He Walks Like A Man** (1964), and obtaining a place in the Italian San Remo Song Festival. A year later, Jody's version of **Queen Of The House** – Mary Taylor's sequel to Roger Miller's **King Of The Road** – became a monster country and pop hit. But, despite some enjoyable pop-country albums that included **Jody Miller Sings The Hits Of Buck Owens** and **The Nashville Sound Of Jody Miller**, there were no further hit singles for Capitol except **Long Black Limousine**, a minor success in 1968.

Following a short retirement during

which Jody spent her time on her Oklahoma ranch raising her daughter Robin, she returned to performing once more, cutting sides for Epic, an association with producer Billy Sherrill providing her with a 1970 chart entry called **Look At Mine**, a Tony Hatch song. Her other Top 10 hits have included **He's So Fine**, **Baby I'm Yours** (1971), **There's A Party**, **Good News**, **Darling You Always Come Back** (1972), while another 1972 single, **Let's All Go Down The River**, a duet with Johnny Paycheck, also sold well. During the remainder of the '70s, the hits kept coming – albeit on a lower level, the biggest of these being **Reflections** (1974), **When The New Wears Off Our Love** (1976), and **Kiss Away** (1978).

A popular act at such diverse venues as the Wembley Country Festival and Las Vegas' Riviera and Frontier, Jody spends most of her spare time on the family farm in Oklahoma, where she breeds and raises quarter horses.

Here's Jody Miller. Courtesy Epic Records.

Albums:
There's A Party Going On (Epic/Epic)
He's So Fine (Epic/Epic)
Here's Jody Miller (Epic/Epic)

Roger Miller

The voice and songs of Roger Miller have been heard in films ranging from 'Waterhole 3', a zany Western, through to

the Disney version of 'Robin Hood'. He has also paid some dues as a TV actor while his records made him one of the most successful pop stars during the '60s. He was also one of the most original.

Born in Fort Worth, Texas, on January 2, 1936, Roger Dean Miller was raised by

Supersongs, Roger Miller. Courtesy CBS Records.

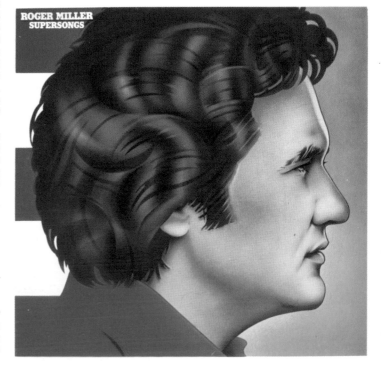

his uncle in Erick, Oklahoma, and performed his first song at the age of five, his audience being the 36 other children who attended Erick's one-room schoolhouse. Influenced by the singing of Hank Williams, Miller saved enough money to buy a guitar, later also acquiring a fiddle.

Following a period spent as a ranch hand, Miller spent three years in the US Army in Korea, spending most of his time as a jeep driver. Upon discharge, he made his way to Nashville, booking in at the Andrew Jackson hotel for one evening, the next morning obtaining a job as a pageboy at the same establishment. In the sleeve notes to his **Trip In The Country** album, Miller describes himself at this period as being 'a young ambitous songwriter, walking the streets of Nashville, trying to get anybody and everybody to record my songs. All in all, I wrote about 150 songs for George Jones, Ray Price, Ernest Tubb and others. Some were hits and some were not. In the beginning I created heavenly, earthy songs.'

Ray Price was one of the first to benefit from the Miller songwriting skill, having a 1958 hit with **Invitation To The Blues**. And signed to RCA in 1960, Miller began accruing his own country winners with **You Don't Want My Love** (1960) and **When Two Worlds Collide** (1961). In 1962 he joined Faron Young's band as drummer, also that same year, guesting on the Tennessee Ernie TV Show. After one last hit for RCA in **Lock, Stock And Teardrops**, Miller moved to Smash, having an immediate million seller with **Dang Me**, following this with other gold disc winners in the infectious **Chug-A-Lug** (1964) and the lightly swinging **King Of The Road** (1965). His endearing mixture of humour, musicianship and pure corn continued to pay dividends throughout the '60s, **Do Wacka Do** (1964), **Engine, Engine No. 9**, **One Dyin' And Buryin'**, **Kansas City Star**, **England Swings** (all 1965), **Husbands and Wives**, **You Can't Roller Skate In A Buffalo Herd** (1966), **Walkin' In The Sunshine** (1967) and **Little Green Apples** (1968) all becoming Top 40 US pop hits.

The '70s, which saw Miller switch labels first to Mercury then to Columbia, brought less success to the then California-based singer-songwriter and hotel chain owner, though he kept up a steady flow of moderately sized hits. Contracts with Mercury Records (1979) and Elektra (1981) did not change the situation and it was not until 1982 and a liaison with Willie Nelson and Ray Price on **Old Friends**, a Columbia release, that Miller climbed back into the Top 10 for the first time since 1973.

But by 1985 he had moved on to a new stage in his career as 'Big River', a Miller musical based on the writings of Mark Twain, opened on Broadway. At the same time, MCA recorded an original cast album, the first album of its type to use a Nashville-based producer (Jimmy Bowen) and to be partly cut in Nashville. Additionally MCA announced that the singer-composer would also be making a solo album for the label, Miller's first since **Making A Name For Myself**, which he cut for Windsong in 1977. Not that Miller has ever worried too much about records in recent years. At nights he probably gets to sleep by merely counting his haul of gold records and numerous industry awards, the latter including an astonishing feat of 11 Grammies in two years, an achievement which has so far not been repeated by anyone.

Albums:
Spotlight On Roger Miller (–/Philips)
Supersongs (Columbia/CBS)
The Best Of Roger Miller (Mercury/ Philips)

Ronnie Milsap

The winner of the CMA Male Vocalist Of The Year award in 1974 and Entertainer Of The Year 1977, Milsap is equally at home with the blues as with country ballads.

Born blind in Robbinsville, North Carolina (1944), he learnt the violin at the age of seven and could play piano just a year later. By 12 he had also mastered the guitar. Attending the State School for the Blind in Raleigh, he became interested in classical music but formed a rock group, The Apparitions, 'because it was the thing to do'. Upon completing high school, Milsap attended Young Harris Junior College, Atlanta, studying pre-law and planning to go on to law school at Emory College, where he had been granted a scholarship.

However, he quit studies to play with J. J. Cale and in 1965 formed his own band, playing blues, country and jazz, also signing with Scepter Records and cutting **Never Had It So Good/Let's Go Get Stoned**, two R&B tracks for his first single release. Attaining an essentially black sound, Milsap soon found himself playing dates alongside such artists as Bobby Bland and The Miracles.

By 1969, he and his band had moved to Memphis, becoming resident group at a club called TJ's, Milsap recording for the Chips label and coming up with a hit disc in **Loving You Is A Natural Thing** (1970). After a stint with Warner Brothers Records, Milsap, who had always featured some country material in his act, decided to devote his career to becoming a fully-fledged country entertainer. At that point he moved to Nashville, there gaining a residency at Roger Miller's King Of The Road motel and signing a management deal with Jack D. Johnson, the Svengali behind the rise of Charley Pride. In April 1973 he became an RCA recording artist, his first release on the label being **I Hate**

Ronnie Milsap, Courtesy RCA Records. He edges further towards pop sounds.

You, a Top 10 single.

His hits since then are too numerous to list in full but his chart-toppers alone include **Pure Love, Please Don't Tell Me How The Story Ends, (I'd Be) A Legend In My Time** (1974), **Daydreams About Night Things** (1975), **What Goes On When The**

There's No Getting Over Me, Ronnie Milsap. Courtesy RCA Records.

Sun Goes Down, (I'm A) Stand By My Woman Man, Let My Love Be Your Pillow (1976), **It Was Almost Like A Song, What A Difference You've Made In My Life** (1977), **Only One Love In My Life, Let's Take The Long Way Around The World** (1978), **Nobody Likes Sad Songs** (1979), **Why Don't You Spend The Night, My Heart, Cowboys And Clowns, Smokey Mountain Rain** (1980), **Am I Losing You, (There's) No Getting Over Me, I Wouldn't Have Missed It For The World** (1981), **Any Day Now, He Got You, Inside** (1982), **Don't**

You Know How Much I Love You, Show Her (1983) and **Still Losing You** (1984).

These days Milsap edges further towards pop sounds than he did previously. Nevertheless, though some rue his ditching of his previous honky-tonk approach, he remains one of the most potent performers on the country scene.

Albums:
Greatest Hits (RCA/RCA)
A Legend In My Time (RCA/RCA)
Images (RCA/RCA)
Pure Love (RCA/RCA)
Live (RCA/RCA)
Night Things (RCA/RCA)
Vocalist Of The Year (Crazy Cajun/–)

Monroe Brothers

The virtual base on which the whole of bluegrass music rests, William Smith (Bill) Monroe was born at Rosine, Kentucky, on September 13, 1911, the youngest of eight children. Brother Charlie was next youngest having been born eight years previously on July 4, 1903. This gap, coupled with Bill's poor eyesight, inhibited the youngest son from many of the usual play activities and gave him an introverted nature which carried through into later life, many people mistaking his shyness for stand-offishness. However, this sense of isolation did allow him to develop his musical talents with great alacrity. The family farmed 655 acres and Bill, working way out in the fields where no one could hear him, developed his lung power without hindrance. Church was also a major formative influence, as with so many Southern musicians. In Bill's case he could not see to read the shape note

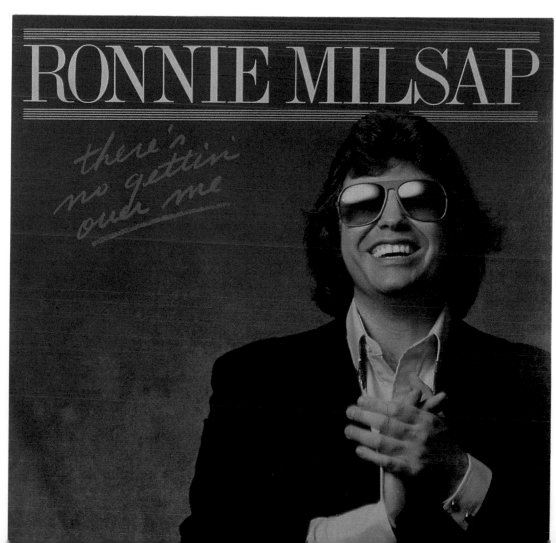

hymnals too well and so learnt the music by ear. The shaped notes were to appear later in Bill's bluegrass music and the ear training was also important since it has obviously contributed to the man's fine sense of harmony in high vocal ranges.

The Monroe family was musical on both sides. Brother Charlie could play guitar by 11 and Birch could play fiddle. Bill's mother's side, the Vandivers, were the more musical and Uncle Pendleton Vandiver (later immortailized in Bill's most famous composition, **Uncle Pen**) would often stay overnight at the household, occasions of great musical festivity. Uncle Pen was a rated fiddler locally and Bill was playing publicly with him by 13, travelling to local square dance and backing Pen's fiddle with guitar.

Also influential on Bill at this time was a black musician from Rosine, Arnold Shultz. Bill would gig with him too and rated him a fine musician with an unrivalled feel for the blues. At this time he also started to hear the gramophone records that were being produced featuring such performers as Charlie Poole and the North Carolina Ramblers.

Birch and Charlie left to seek work in Indiana and Bill joined them in 1929, when he was 18. Until 1934, in East Chicago, Indiana, they worked manual jobs by day (Bill washed and loaded barrels in an oil refinery) and played dances and parties at night. For a while they went on tour with the Chicago WLS station Barn Dance, doing exhibition dancing. In 1934, Radio WLS, for whom the three brothers (Birch on fiddle, Charlie on guitar and Bill on mandolin) had been working on a semi-professional basis, offered them full time employment. Birch decided to give up music but Charlie and Bill reformed as a duet, the Monroe Brothers, and then followed much other radio work until in 1935 they were sponsored on Carolina radio by Texas Crystals. In that same year Bill married Caroline Brown – their children, Melissa (born 1936) and James (1941) have both performed with Bill, James eventually forming his own band, the Midnight Ramblers.

The Monroe Brothers, engaged on radio work in Greenville, South Carolina, and Charlotte, North Carolina, were persuaded forcefully (by Eli Oberstein of Victor Records) to cut some records in 1936. That year, in the Radio Building at Charlotte, they cut 10 sides during February, including an early best-seller **What Would You Give (In Exchange For Your Soul)**. At first they did not feel interested in the idea of recording since they were already doing well via radio and live broadcasts, but sales of the early sides were impressive enough to warrant five more such sessions during the next 12 months. Besides featuring popular traditional material from such sources as the Skillet Lickers, Carter Family, Bradley Kincaid and Jimmie Rodgers (the Monroes did not write their own songs at the time), they had pioneered a distinctive style in which then-advanced mandolin and guitar techniques were coupled with a high, clear, recognizable vocal sound.

In 1938 they went their separate ways, partly due to differing artistic ideas, partly due to personal tensions resulting from many years of touring together. Bill formed the Kentuckians in Little Rock, Arkansas and then moved on to Radio KARK, Atlanta, Georgia, where the first of the Blue Grass Boys line-ups was evolved. At this time, Bill began to sing lead and to take mandolin solos rather than just

Above: Bill Monroe, the man who invented bluegrass music.

remaining part of the general sound. In 1939 he auditioned for the Opry and George D. Hay was impressed enough to sign him, promising that if Bill ever left it would be because he had sacked himself. The following Saturday Bill played his first Opry number, the famous **Mule Skinner Blues**.

Bill Monroe's music then started to undergo subtle changes. He added accordion and banjo (played by Sally Ann Forester and Stringbean respectively) in 1945 when he joined Columbia Records and this period saw the evolution of a

The High Lonesome Sound Of Bill Monroe, Courtesy MCA Records.

fuller sound with the musicians taking more solos. But in 1945 the accordion was dispensed with, never to return, and in that year the addition of Earl Scruggs, with a banjo style that was more driving and syncopated than anything heard previously, put the final, distinctive seal on Monroe's bluegrass sound. Flatt and Scruggs remained with Bill until 1948.

Songs from this period include **Blue Moon Of Kentucky, I Hear A Sweet Voice Calling, I'm Going Back To Old Kentucky** and **Will You Be Loving Another Man?** Other musicians with Bill at this time were Chubby Wise (fiddle) and Howard Watts – also known as Cedric Rainwater – (bass).

Bill left Columbia in 1949 because he objected to them signing the Stanley Brothers, a rival bluegrass group. With his next label, Decca, his main man was

Jimmy Martin, a musician with a strong, thin, highish voice, whose talents enabled Monroe to fill in more subtle vocal harmonies alongside. This was Monroe's golden age for compositions. He wrote **Uncle Pen, Roanoke, Scotland** (a nod towards the source whence so much in the way of string band jigs and reels had evolved), **My Little Georgia Rose, Walking In Jerusalem** and **I'm Working On A Building**, the last two being religious 'message' songs, always part of the Monroe tradition from the earliest days.

By the end of the decade, bluegrass, though it had added a new dimension to country, was in decline due to the onset of rock'n'roll (it is interesting to remember that when Elvis Presley released his **Blue Moon Of Kentucky** in 1954, Bill's record company rushed out a re-release of Monroe's (very different) original). But the '60s saw a folk revival and, apart from the regional audience which had remained loyal to some extent, Bill now found hordes of students eager to embrace indigenous rural white folk music. In 1963 Bill made his first college appearance at the University of Chicago; later that same year he played to 15,000 people at the Newport Folk Festival.

Bill Monroe was elected to the Country Music Hall Of Fame in 1970. He has always trodden his own musical path, never bowing to commercial pressure, and his contribution to country music is inestimable.

As for Charlie, he had a long and successful career – though not nearly as spectacular as Bill's – with his own band, The Kentucky Pardners, well into the '50s. He returned from retirement in the early '70s to appear on the bluegrass circuit – displaying great grace and charm – before dying of cancer in 1975.

Bill Monroe Albums:
The Original Bluegrass Band (Rounder/–)
16 All Time Greatest Hits (Columbia/–)
Best Of Bill Monroe And The Bluegrass Boys (–/MCA)

16 All-Time Greatest Hits, Bill Monroe, Courtesy CBS Records.

Bluegrass Instrumentals (MCA/–)
Bluegrass Ramble (MCA–)

Charlie Monroe Albums:
Who's Calling You Sweetheart Tonight (Camden/–)
Charlie Monroe On The Noonday Jamboree (County/County)

Monroe Brothers:
Early Blue Grass Music (Camden/–)

Patsy Montana

Patsy Montana, born Rubye Blevins, on October 30, 1914, in Hot Springs, Arkansas, became the first woman in country music to have a million-selling record when **I Want To Be A Cowboy's Sweetheart** was released in 1935. She began her early career with silent film cowboy star Monte Montana (no relation), but was long associated with the Prairie Ramblers on the National Barn Dance radio show (1934–52), the Ramblers backing her on **Cowboy's Sweetheart** and most of her other hits. She recorded with them on the ARC complex of labels (1935–42) and then Decca (1942–9) and RCA (1949–51) before leaving them and Chicago for the West Coast in 1952.

She has been in and out of retirement ever since, occasionally appearing with her daughter Judy Rose, and recording in later years on Surf and Starday.

Album:
Early Country Favourites (Old Homestead/–)

Melba Montgomery

Born in Iron City, Tennessee, on October 14, 1938, Melba was raised in Florence, Alabama. She began her singing at the local Methodist church where her fiddle- and guitar-playing father taught singing,

she and her brothers later becoming part of an act that got to the finals of a talent contest organized by Pet Milk.

Melba moved to Nashville, there catching the attention of Roy Acuff, with whose show she stayed for four years. In 1962 she went solo and released her first singles, her initial Top 10 entry coming with **We Must Have Been Out Of Our Minds**, a duet with George Jones, released by UA in 1963. That same year she made her solo chart debut with **Hall Of Shame** and charted with another three releases – two of them being duets with Jones. Her voice had both strength and purity and it soon became obvious that she was a find of some importance. She continued recording for UA and Musicor in moderately successful fashion through to 1967, when her musical partnership with George Jones ended, Melba moving on to Capitol Records and a series of hit

Melba Montgomery. Courtesy Elektra Records.

Above: Melba Montgomery, great cheek-bones, great voice. Once a member of Roy Acuff's band, she has made records with George Jones and Charlie Louvin.

duets with Charlie Louvin which spanned 1970–3. In fact duets were a speciality of

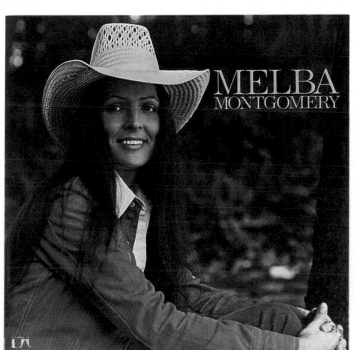

Melba's – she had already made an album with Gene Pitney in 1966.

Her time at Capitol saw the start of a liaison with Pete Drake that carried over fruitfully into her stint with the Elektra label. Elektra was, at that time, the West Coast's hippest record label, having made its reputation first with folk acts, then with such rock acts as The Doors and MC5. Melba was to represent the label's initial move into modern country and the result was a series of albums that were slap bang in Melba's country style but sparklingly well produced too. She was also served well by the label for her singles. By 1974 she had a No. 1 record with **No Charge**, a sentimental 'talkover' song penned by Harlan Howard that in 1976 provided J. J. Barrie with a British pop hit. She also went Top 20 with **Don't Let The Good Times Fool You** (1975) but, by 1977, was back on UA once more, doing pretty well with a version of **Angel Of The Morning**. But after this her name became absent from the annual list of chart contenders, her only hit of any size coming with **The Star**, a Kari release in 1980.

Albums:
Baby, You've Got What It Takes – with Charlie Louvin (Capitol/–)
Don't Let The Good Times Fool You (Elektra/–)
No Charge (Electra/–)
We Must Have Been Out Of Our Minds – with George Jones (RCA/RCA)

Clyde Moody

Born in Cherokee, North Carolina, in 1915, Clyde Moody rose to prominence in the '40s as the Hillbilly Waltz King, largely on the strength of his gold record for **Shenandoah Waltz** for King Records, which sold some three million copies.

Moody apprenticed with Mainer's Mountaineers, spent several successful years with Bill Monroe, with whom he recorded the classic **Six White Horses**, and spent a bit of time with Roy Acuff before joining the Opry on his own in the mid-'40s. He left the Opry in the late '40s to pioneer television in the Washington DC area, then returned to his native North Carolina, where he had a long-running TV show and several business interests. But later he could be found in Nashville, resuming his musical career, appearing at numerous bluegrass festivals yearly (those fans did not forget his years as a Blue Grass Boy) and touring over 300 days a year with Ramblin' Tommy Scott's Show.

Album:
Moody's Blue (Old Homestead/–)

George Morgan

The writer and singer of **Candy Kisses**, the biggest country song of 1949, Morgan, for a brief period, looked capable of usurping Eddy Arnold's position as the undisputed king of country pop.

Born in Waverly, Tennessee, on June 28, 1925, he spent his teen years in Barberton, Ohio. On completing high school, Morgan worked as a part-time performer, but mainly earned his keep by stints as a truck driver, salesman, etc. Obtaining a regular singing spot on WWVA Jamboree, Wheeling, West Virginia, he established something of a reputation there and became signed to Columbia Records. His first release was **Candy Kisses**, which reached No. 1 in the

Above: Clyde Moody – North Carolina's Hillbilly Waltz King.

country charts (subsequently selling a million) while Elton Britt's cover version reached No. 3. Invited to join WSM in 1948 in the dual role of DJ and vocalist, he soon became an Opry regular, scoring with further 1949 hits in **Rainbow In My Heart**, **Room Full Of Roses** and **Cry-Baby Heart**.

Establishing a smooth, easy style that came replete with fiddle and steel guitar, Morgan became a popular radio and concert artist but, despite major successes with **Almost** (1952), **I'm In Love Again** (1959) and **You're The Only Good Thing** (1960), his record sales remained little more than steady throughout the rest of his association with Columbia.

In 1966 he joined Starday, who provided him with elaborate orchestral trappings, a ploy which gained Morgan a quintet of mini-hits during 1967–8. But soon he was on the move again, recording with Stop, Decca and Four Star, but only twice attaining Top 20 status, with **Lilacs And Rain**, a 1970 Stop release, and **Red Rose From The Blue Side Of Town**, a 1973 MCA item. By 1975 he was signed to 4-Star.

Morgan's death occurred in July, 1975, following a heart attack sustained while on the roof of his house, where he had been fixing a TV aerial.

Sounds Of Goodbye, George Morgan. Courtesy Starday.

Above: George Morgan. His Candy Kisses was the biggest country song of 1949.

Albums:
Remembering (Greatest Hits) (Columbia/–)
The Best Of George Morgan (Starday/–)

The Morris Brothers

Wiley Morris, mandolin and tenor vocals; Zeke Morris, guitar and lead vocals.

Yet another of the fine duet acts which flooded country music in the mid-'30s, the Morris Brothers became well known for their smooth harmony singing and songs like **Salty Dog** and **You Give Me Your Love And I'll Give You Mine**, although they are probably best known for their version of **Tragic Romance**.

Wiley actually had a long career playing mandolin and guitar for a number of bands, including Wade and J. E. Mainer both together and with their separate bands, and with Charlie Monroe and his Kentucky Pardners.

The Morris Brothers' career lasted well into the '40s, although they retired to their native western North Carolina and remained relatively inactive in latter years, making a brief appearance on **Country Music And Bluegrass At Newport** (Vanguard) and on Earl Scruggs' 90-minute TV special, 'Earl Scruggs, His Family And Friends', plus the Columbia album of the same name. One further

remaining fame to claim – in 1940 they were the first to give Earl Scruggs a job as a professional banjo player.

Gary Morris

Like country pioneer Vernon Dalhart in that he is able to sing both country and opera, Gary Morris was born and raised in Fort Worth, Texas. A junior high school guitarist who sang in the church choir, he formed a trio that, during the late '60s, was booked into a Denver nightclub after playing a Hank Williams medley at a live audition in front of an audience.

After several years at the club, Morris went solo and headed back to Texas, there meeting Lawton Williams, writer of **Fraulein**, a massive hit for Bobby Helms. Williams introduced Morris to various music-biz people and in 1978 he was invited to play at a White House party hosted by President Carter, after which he was asked to record a number of sides for MCA Nashville – though nothing happened as a result of these sessions. For a while Morris went back to Colorado forming a band called Breakaway. But in 1980 he flew to Nashville once more, meeting producer Norro Wilson, who had seen him at the White House gig, and cutting **Sweet Red Wine** and **Fire In Your Eyes**, both going Top 40 on Warner.

Late in 1981 he had his first Top 10 single in **Headed For A Heartache**. The following year he had three major singles, the biggest of these being **Velvet Chains** and by 1983 he had become a fully fledged

Born on his family's farm near Corrigan, Polk County, Texas, on March 29, 1909, as a boy he learnt guitar from a black farmworker. His family came from religious stock and his father once bought an old pump organ in order that Mullican's sisters could practise church music – but Aubrey used the instrument to fashion his blues style, much to his father's dismay.

At 21 he hoboed his way to Houston aboard a freight train, upon arrival finding work in various houses of ill-repute, sleeping by day and working by night, thus earning the nickname 'Moon'. During the '30s he formed a band and began playing on radio and at clubs in the Louisiana-Texas area. He joined Leon Selph's Blue Ridge Playboys for a while in 1940 after appearing on a 1939 recording session with the band. He also played with Cliff Bruner and the Texas Wanderers during this same period.

By the mid-'40s, Mullican had become a major solo attraction, his 1947 reworking of the Cajun tune **Jole Blon** (released by King as **New Jole Blon**) selling a million copies within three years of release. This he followed with **Sweeter Than The Flowers**, a 1948 high flyer, and **I'll Sail My Ship Alone**, a 1950 release that provided yet another million-seller for King. In 1949 Mullican joined the Grand Ole Opry for a period of six years, during which time he achieved further hits with **Mona Lisa**, **Goodnight Irene** (1950), and **Cherokee Boogie** (1951).

During the late '50s and '60s he toured throughout the States and overseas, becoming part of Governor Jimmy Davis' staff and band for four years (1960–3). During this period he gained one further hit record, **Ragged But Right**, on the Starday label, but he often found himself dogged by a combination of bad luck and ill health. The king of pumpin' piano, he died from a heart attack in Beaumont, Texas, on January 1, 1967.

Albums:
Seven Nights To Rock (Western/–)
Sweet Rockin' Music (–/Charly)

Danny's Song, Anne Murray. Courtesy Capitol Records. Like Hank Snow and Wilf Carter, Anne Murray hails from Nova Scotia.

Anne Murray

A deceptively light-voiced Canadian singer, Anne Murray packed enough punch on her **Snowbird** hit in the '60s to score a major international pop hit.

Born in Spring Hill, Nova Scotia, on June 20, 1946, Anne was the only girl in a family of five brothers. She obtained a bachelor's degree at the University of New Brunswick and taught physical education. Eventually, finding that singing was taking more and more of her time, she quit and moved entirely into show-biz when offered a contract by Capitol Records.

Snowbird was one of her first releases and its light airy melody was soon on everyone's lips. It scored in both the pop and country charts in 1970 and provided Anne with two potential markets which she proceeded to tightrope-walk for many years.

She made some high-selling singles during 1972, including **Cotton Jenny**, **Danny's Song** and **Love Song** but had to wait until 1974 and **He Thinks I Still Care** before gaining her second No. 1. After this she had Top 10 singles with **Son Of A Rotten Gambler** (1974), **Walk Right Back**, **You Needed Me** (1978), hitting a winning streak in 1979 when **I Just Fall In Love Again**, **Shadows In The Moonlight** and **Broken Hearted Me** all went to No. 1. Then came **Daydream Believer**, **Lucky Me**, **Could I Have This Dance?** (1980), **Blessed Are The Believers**, **It's All I Can Do** (1981), **Another Sleepless Night**, **Hey! Baby!**, **Somebody's Always Saying Goodbye** (1982) and **A Little Good News** (No. 1, 1983). The last named is lyrically at least, the finest song that Murray has ever recorded and one that won her a Grammy Award as Best Country Female Singer, helping her accrue a tally of major awards that includes four Grammys, three CMA awards and no less than 22 Canadian Juno plaudits, a feat which caused the 'Toronto Sun' to suggest that these awards be renamed the 'Annies'.

During 1984 she logged two further country No. 1s with **Just Another Woman In Love** and **Nobody Loves Me Like You Do** and the following year had a further hit

---

Above: Gary Morris. When you're a friend of the Colbys, anything is possible – even a part in La Boheme!

Top 10 act, logging three solo hit records – **The Love She Found In Me**, **The Wind Beneath My Wings**, **Why, Lady, Why?** – and **You're Welcome Tonight**, a high-selling duet with Lynn Anderson, recorded for the Permian label. The next year saw things going pretty much the same way, Gary netting three further Top 10 records, **Between Two Fires**, **Second Hand Heart** and **Baby Bye Bye** (the latter becoming his first No. 1) and being acclaimed as country's premier male sex symbol.

After that, everything headed his way. He was chosen to star opposite Linda Rondstadt in the New York Shakespeare Festival production of the opera 'La Boheme', this leading to regular guest appearances in the TV soap 'Dynasty II – The Colbys'. And still the hitmaking has continued, the most recent being **Lasoo The Moon**, **Making Up For Lost Time** (a duet with Crystal Gayle), **I'll Never Stop Loving You** (all 1985) and **100% Chance Of Rain** (1986).

Albums:
Faded Blue (Warner Bros/–)
Second Hand Love (Warner Bros/Warner Bros)

Tex Morton

One of Australia's greatest country artists, Morton was actually born in Nelson, New Zealand, in 1916. In 1932, together with some fellow entertainers, he decided to try his luck in Australia, existing there by taking jobs that varied from fairground boxing to riding the Wall Of Death on a motorcycle. A fine singer and yodeller, Morton made his first records for Regal Zonophone in 1936, gaining instant popularity, his stage debut at Brisbane attracting a crowd of over 50,000.

When scout Ralph Peer visited Australia in 1948, he saw Morton and felt that he had found an heir to the crown once worn by Jimmie Rodgers. A move to the USA followed but he was soon forced to leave by the immigration authorities, after which he resided in Canada for some time, there becoming The Great Morton – The World's Greatest Hypnotist, also continuing with an acting and singing career.

In 1959 he returned to Australia once more, spending his remaining years until his death, on July 23, 1983, there or in his native New Zealand, and always, but always, maintaining his reputation as a top-line entertainer.

Album:
You And My Old Guitar (Festival/–)

Moon Mullican

The originator of a highly personal, two-finger piano style, Aubrey 'Moon' Mullican influenced many later country keyboard players including Mickey Gilley and Jerry Lee Lewis.

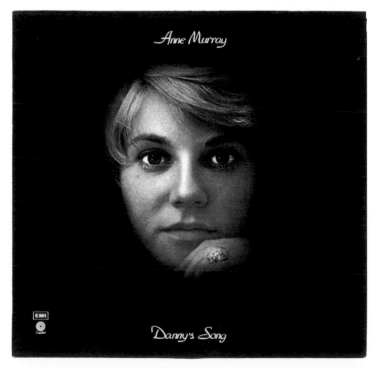

with **Time Don't Run Out On Me**. But the 'country' categorization was beginning to hurt. 'Awards are one thing,' she claimed at the start of 1986, 'Platinum records are another.' Accordingly she came up with an album which she claimed was her first real pop album in six years. From it Capitol culled a single called **Now And Forever (You And Me)**. And it immediately went to No 1 in the country charts. Meanwhile, in the pop listings it did next to zilch.

Albums:
Anne Murray's Greatest Hits (Capitol/ Capitol)
A Little Good News (Capitol/Capitol)

Buck And Tex Ann Nation

To Buck (born Muskogee, Oklahoma, 1910) and Tex Ann (born Chanute, Kansas, 1916) goes the credit for starting the now popular country music parks, where Sunday afternoon crowds can picnic, relax and listen to country music. Active in the north-east, Buck and Tex Ann opened their first park in 1934 and found their greatest success in Maine, of all the unlikely places.

After the duo split up, Tex Ann moved to the west coast, where she found wartime employment with the bands of Merle Travis, Ray Whitley, and others as both a vocalist and a fine bassist.

Jerry Naylor

Once front man with The Crickets, Naylor won 'Billboard' awards in 1973 and 1974 for providing the best syndicated country radio show.

Born in Stephenville, Texas, on March 6, 1939, he formed his own group at the age of 14 and soon proved able enough to perform on the Lousiana Hayride show, touring alongside such acts as Johnny Cash, Elvis Presley and Johnny Horton. A DJ during his high school days, he later enrolled at the Elkins Electronic Institute, employing his radio know-how for AFRS in Germany during 1957.

Following discharge from the army after a spinal injury, he returned home and recorded for Sklya Records, also befriending Glen Campbell. The duo moved to L.A. where Naylor worked for KRLA and KDAY, and in 1961 he became a member of The Crickets, replacing bassist Joe B. Maudlin (although both musicians are depicted on the sleeve of the **Bobby Vee Meets The Crickets** album!). But he suffered a heart attack in 1964 and left the group, taking up a solo career in country music, recording first for Tower, then for Columbia and MGM before signing for Melodyland – for which label he provided a hit in **Is That All There Is To A Honky Tonk?** in 1975.

Along the way, Naylor, who once recorded for Raystar under the name of Jackie Garrard, has notched hits for Hitsville (1976), MC (1978), Oak (1980), also working for Hoyt Axton's Jeremiah Records (1980–2) without much success. He now concentrates mainly on DJ work and lives in Angoura, California with his wife Pamela and three children.

Album:
Love Away Her Memory (MC/–)

Rick Nelson

The child of a showbusiness family (his parents Ozzie And Harriet had a radio and later a TV show), Nelson made the transition from teenage idol to modern country artist.

Born on May 8, 1940, in Teaneck, New Jersey, he signed as Ricky Nelson first for Verve and then Imperial; his lonesome, teenthrob voice was allied to light, country-influenced backings on songs such as **Poor Little Fool, It's Late** and **Lonesome Town**, sagas of jilted love and dating frustrations, and perfectly in tune with the softening tone of rock 'n' roll.

This was the major record companies' answer to the more raw, sharper music of Memphis. Since Nelson was also blessed with archetypal boy-next-door looks, his appeal was further propagated via concerts and TV, and riots ensued when he played.

The coming of the British Invasion swept away many of these clean-cut American teen rockers, although Nelson was by then signed to MCA and had shortened his name to Rick. Although he had James Burton in his band, he failed to make a real impression; however, two country albums, **Country Fever** and **Bright Lights And Country Music**, found favour

Above: The late great Rick Nelson. The plane in which he crashed once belonged to Jerry Lee Lewis.

with some people.

The formation of the Stone Canyon Band in the '70s saw Nelson being accepted as a viable country rocker. This band included, at one point, Randy Meisner, also known from Poco and The Eagles, and Tom Brumley, Buck Owens' rated steel player for five years (Brumley, it should be noted also manufactures the famous ZB pedal steel guitars).

Garden Party, a poignant autobiographical piece of country-rock, made the American pop Top 10 in 1972 and won Nelson yet another gold record. Although he recorded some outstanding country-rock albums during the '70s for MCA, Epic and Capitol, he failed to make any further inroads into the charts.

During the early '80s, Rick and his excellent Stone Canyon Band were mainly working rock 'n' roll revival shows, but his musical integrity was always maintained by his insistence on not just going through the old songs, but giving many of them fresh, new arrangements. He successfully toured Britain during November 1985 with fellow rock 'n' roll stars Bo Diddley, Bobby Vee and Frankie Ford. Two months later, on December 31, 1985, Rick, along with his

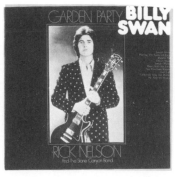

Garden Party, Rick Nelson, Courtesy MCA Records.

fiancee, Helen Blair, and members of his band were in a fatal air crash while en route to a show in Dallas, Texas.

Albums:
Country (MCA/–)
Garden Party (MCA/MCA)
In Concert (MCA/–)
Rudy The 5th (MCA/MCA)
Sings Rick Nelson (MCA/MCA)
Singles Album (–/UA)
String Along With Rick (–/Charly)
Playing To Win (Capitol/Capitol)

Tracy Nelson

The bluesy-voiced Tracy (born Madison, Wisconsin, December 27, 1947) began her career in Madison as a folk singer, later joining the Fabulous Imitations, an R&B outfit. After a stint with the White Trash Band, she headed for San Francisco in 1967, there becoming part of Mother Earth, a unit which began life as a pure blues and soul aggregation but gradually became heavily country oriented. The band split after five years, Tracy going solo and cutting **Tracy Nelson**, an Atlantic album that employed the talents of Willie Nelson, Linda Ronstadt, Mac Gayden, Reggie Young and others, her **After The Fire Is Gone** duet with Willie being released as a Grammy nominated single.

After a brace of albums for MCA, Tracy signed for Flying Fish (1979–1980) and Adelphi (1980). An in-demand session vocalist, she has appeared on records by Guy Clark, Dianne Davidson, Happy and Artie Traum, Townes Van Zandt, Amazing Rhythm Aces, etc. A strong songwriter, Tracy's **Down So Low** has been covered by many singers including Linda Ronstadt.

Albums:
Mother Earth Presents Tracy Nelson Country (Mercury/Mercury)
Tracy Nelson (Atlantic/–)
Homemade Songs (Flying Fish/–)

Help Me Make It Through The Night, Willie Nelson, Courtesy RCA Records.

Above: Tracy Nelson – with non-playing Nashville cat.

Willie Nelson

Willie Nelson has run a long, hard race in country music but has won through as a premier stylist. Born in Abbott, Texas, on April 30, 1933, Nelson was raised by his grandparents after his own parents separated.

His grandparents taught him some chords and by his teens he was becoming proficient on guitar. In 1950, he left Abbott to join the Air Force and on his subsequent discharge he married a Cherokee Indian girl by whom he had a daughter, Lana. Living in Waco, Texas, Nelson took various salesman jobs, but anxious to gain a proper intro into music he talked his way into an announcing job on a local station.

Soon after, he was hosting country shows on a Fort Worth station, doubling at night as a musician in some rough local honky tonks and, whenever he could, he was jotting down songs. It was during this period that he wrote **Family Bible** and **Night Life**, songs which have become standards.

When he finally made his way to Nashville and found a job in Ray Price's band as a bass player, he found that he was placing his songs at last. Price, a huge name of that era, made **Night Life** his theme tune. Faron Young cut **Hello Walls**, Patsy Cline **Crazy** and Willie himself recorded **The Party's Over**. They were

Right: Willie in Honeysuckle Rose, a road movie that also featured Hank Cochran, Johnny Gimble and Emmylous Harris.

sombre but haunting melodies, true 'white man's blues', and Willie has since incorporated them tellingly into his sparse, bluesy act. More than 70 artists have recorded **Night Life** (Willie's songs are often potential cross-overs but the artist himself presents them usually in a very different tone).

After poaching most of Ray Price's band from him, Nelson went on the road. At this time his first marriage broke up and he went off with the wife of a DJ Association president and married again, settling variously in Fort Worth, Los Angeles and Nashville.

Besides recording 18 albums in these years, he also helped the career of Charley Pride, featuring him on his show in the deepest South during the racially sensitive years of civil rights.

During the '60s the smooth Nashville Sound was in its ascendant and Willie found himself becoming increasingly disillusioned with big business methods, hankering as he was to make his mark as a singer rather than as a songwriter and preferably on his own terms. A spell living in Texas, while his Nashville home was being rebuilt after a fire, did nothing to salve Willie's restlessness. By the early '70s he was determined to get out of his RCA contract, and with the help of one Neil Reshen (afterwards Nelson's manager) he landed a new contract from Atlantic, which company was just opening a Nashville office. However country music was new to Atlantic, who had built their reputation on black music. But with Atlantic's Jerry Wexler producing in New York, Willie came up with **Shotgun Willie** and **Phases And Stages**, the second particularly a new, intense country sound displaying a deep sense of lonesome identity and making no concessions whatsoever to modern Nashville.

Nelson had by now settled in Austin with his third wife, Connie. He became a godfather there – a whiff of hardnose country authenticity amid some dedicated but basically folk-influenced young artists. Texas had always been the centre for barroom music, and now the tradition was back home again in a slightly different, but nonetheless intense, way. The glossy magazines began to home in on the phenomenon.

By this time Atlantic's Nashville operation had folded and Willie signed with Columbia, for whom he made **Red Headed Stranger** and **The Sound In Your Mind**. Like **Phases And Stages**, **Red Headed Stranger** was a concept album, but even more personal. It threw up the national cross-over hit single **Blue Eyes Cryin' In The Rain** and established Willie Nelson as a nationally known figure.

Willie, recognized as the unofficial Mayor of Austin, reconciled hip and redneck musical interests and helped lead a new explosion of interest in country

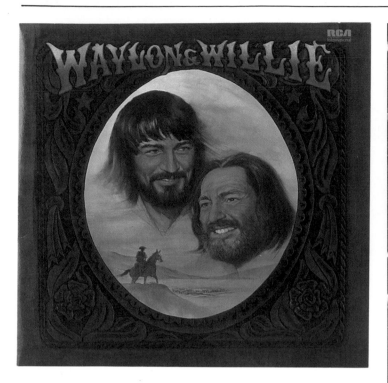

Waylon and Willie. The Hit City outlaws ride again. Courtesy RCA.

music. Teaming up with fellow Texan, Waylon Jennings, they topped the country charts in 1976 with **Good Hearted Woman** and were both featured on the compilation album, **Wanted: The Outlaws**, the first certified platinum album in country music, and so started the Outlaw Movement.

Although Nashville was cagey about The Outlaws' intentions and the way they went outside the system to get what they wanted, it recognized the pair's contribution towards restoring massive new interest in country music generally and voted them into top positions in the annual Country Music Association awards, a sure sign of industry acceptance.

Refusing to be tied down to commercial considerations, Nelson has recorded such diverse album projects as **Stardust** (a set of popular standards), **The Troublemaker** (a gospel set featuring Larry Gatlin, Sammi Smith and Doug Sahm), **To Lefty From Willie** (a tribute to Lefty Frizzell) and **Angel Eyes** (featuring the jazz guitar artistry of Jackie King).

Willie also instigated the now legendary Fourth Of July Picnics, massive outdoor festivals in Texas which have featured stars such as Leon Russell, Kris Kristofferson, Roy Acuff, Waylon Jennings, Tex Ritter, Charlie Rich and Asleep At The Wheel, in conditions which have at times been far from perfect due to the difficulties of trying to organize such a large event.

During the early '80s, Willie became acknowledged as the 'king' of the country duets. Alongside his highly successful duets with Waylon Jennings, which resulted in the chart-topping **Mammas Don't Let Your Babies Grow Up To Be Cowboys** winning a Grammy in 1978, he has recorded duet albums with Roger Miller, Ray Price, Faron Young, Webb Pierce and Merle Haggard, as well as guesting on albums and singles by Emmylou Harris, Pam Rose, Rattlesnake Annie and many others.

Poncho And Lefty, a duet album recorded with Merle Haggard, was named CMA Album Of The Year (1983) with the title song topping the country

charts. Nelson achieved even more success the following year when he teamed up with Julio Iglesias for the international pop and country hit, **To All The Girls I've Loved Before**, which also won CMA and Grammy awards.

Willie has also made his mark in films, appearing in 'Electric Horseman' with Robert Redford, 'Barbarossa' with Gary Busey, 'Honeysuckle Rose' and 'Coming Out Of The Ice'. There is little doubt that Nelson has been one of the most successful country artists of the '70s and '80s and he has continued to chalk up the hits with such songs as **My Heroes Have Always Been Cowboys** (1980), **Angel Flying Too Close To The Ground** (1981), **Always On My Mind** (1982), **Why Do I Have To Choose** (1983), **Without A Song** (1984), **Me And Paul** (1985), **If Loving You Was Easy** (1985) and **Highwayman** (with Cash, Kristofferson and Jennings 1986).

Albums:
Phases And Stages (Atlantic/–)
Shotgun Willie (Atlantic/–)
Live (RCA/RCA)
Red Headed Stranger (Columbia/CBS)
Famous Country Music Makers (–/RCA)
The Sound In Your Mind (Columbia/CBS)
Somewhere Over The Rainbow (Columbia/–)
20 Of The Best (–/RCA)
Tougher Than Leather (Columbia/CBS)
Take It To The Limits – with Waylon Jennings (Columbia/CBS)
Me And Paul (Columbia/–)
Always On My Mind (Columbia/CBS)

The Troublemaker, Willie Nelson. Courtesy CBS Records.

Above: Willie Nelson. After hearing Bob Dylan protest on behalf of American farmers on Live Aid, he set Farm Aid concerts in 1985 and 1986.

Michael Nesmith

One of the fabulously successful Monkees, a teenybopper quartet whose main claim to artistic fame was that they were usually given good commercial song material, Nesmith left in 1969 to carve a modestly notable career as a sort of freewheeling cosmic cowboy.

Although he claimed to be only nominally into country, his songs have provided good country fodder, and Nesmith's records with the First and Second National Bands have their own cult audience.

Born in Houston, Texas, on December 30, 1942, Nesmith only learned to play guitar after his air force discharge in 1962. However, he was writing songs and his **Different Drum** was covered by Linda Ronstadt.

Becoming increasingly disenchanted by the big business aura surrounding the Monkees, he had, by 1968, produced an album of self-composed instrumentals, **The Wichita Train Whistle Sings**.

Nesmith was the creator of the First National Band, which included pedal steel player Red Rhodes, and was signed to RCA. In 1970 they put out the album **Magnetic South**, a Nesmith composition from this album, **Joanne**, being covered by Andy Williams among others. Another

album that year was **Loose Salute**.

The First National Band split in 1971 and James Burton and Glen D. Hardin were brought in to help complete the album then being recorded, **Nevada Fighter**. Another line-up (again including Red Rhodes) recorded **Tantamount To Treason, Vol. 1**, and in 1972 only Nesmith and Rhodes made **And The Hits Just Keep On Comin'**.

Nesmith founded his own label, Countryside, a subsidiary of Elektra, with the intention of milking some of the country music talent that was going to waste in Los Angeles. But a change of leadership at Elektra, where David Geffen replaced Jac Holzman, saw Countryside closed down.

However, Nesmith had formed another band during this time, the Countryside Band (again including Rhodes) and 1973 saw them releasing **Pretty Much Your Standard Ranch Stash**. He then moved from RCA and formed Pacific Arts, which has seen him involved in mixed media projects, notably 'The Prison', a book with a soundtrack.

One of the first to recognize the importance of video in music promotion, Nesmith became an innovative director/performer in the video field. His 1977 album, **From A Radio Engine To The Photon Wing**, was possibly the first record to utilize video images for effect and resulted in a British hit single for the self-penned **Rio**.

It is generally agreed that Nesmith has written some very good country, or country-influenced songs, one of the most famous being **Some Of Shelley's Blues**.

Nevada Fighter, Mike Nesmith. Courtesy RCA Records.

Albums:
And The Hits Just Keep On Comin'(–/Island)
Pretty Much Your Standard Ranch Stash (–/Island)
The Prison (Pacific Arts/Island)
The Best Of Mike Nesmith (–/RCA)
From A Radio Engine To The Photon Wing (Pacific Arts/Island)

New Grass Revival

A young, electric, bluegrass band, New Grass Revival evolved a distinctive hard-

Too Late To Turn Back, New Grass Revival. Courtesy Flying Fish/Sonet.

edged picking sound during the early '70s and helped spread the appeal of bluegrass to a youth audience.

Based around the jazz-tinged fiddle talents of Sam Bush (who also plays guitar and mandolin and sings) the four-piece group had some success with the single, **Prince Of Peace**, an evocative reworking of a Leon Russell song, this number subsequently appearing on **New Grass Revival** (Starday), the band's debut album. Later, the Revival moved on to Flying Fish cutting several albums before touring with Leon Russell, playing a wide range of dates across the States and in Australasia (1980). One of those gigs, at Pasadena's Perkins' Palace, was recorded, the results appearing on the Paradise Records album titled, **Leon Russell And The New Grass Revival**.

As the '80s moved on, the Revival signed to the Sugar Hill label, in 1984 cutting **On The Boulevard**, an album that featured the foursome playing material that ranged from Bob Marley's **One Love**

and Curtis Mayfield's **People Get Ready**, through to **County Clare**, an original on which bluegrass renewed acquaintance with Irish folk music. The line-up at that point comprised Bush and long-time member John Cowan (bass, vocals) plus Pat Flynn (guitars, vocals) and Bela Fleck, a banjoist with a penchant for the occasional jazz lick.

Albums:
New Grass Revival (Starday/–)
Fly Through The Country (Flying Fish/–)
Barren Country (Flying Fish/–)
Live Album – with Leon Russell (Paradise/Paradise)
Too Late To Turn Back (Flying Fish/Sonet)
On The Boulevard (Sugar Hill/–)

New Riders Of The Purple Sage

Originally formed as a splinter group from San Francisco's leading acid rock band the Grateful Dead, the New Riders eventually became a name in their own right.

The album **Workingman's Dead** saw the Grateful Dead moving from rock towards a more earthy, sometimes country sound, and the New Riders were the natural off-shoot of this movement.

The New Riders at first played gigs with the Dead and were able to utilize Dead guitarist Jerry Garcia's latent talents on pedal steel guitar. Garcia was eventually replaced by Buddy Cage. Famed West Coast rock artists who have been in NRPS include Mickey Hart and Phil Lesh (Grateful Dead), Spencer Dryden (Jefferson Airplane) and Skip Battin (Byrds).

The band originally recorded for Columbia, but in the mid-'70s they changed labels and recorded for MCA. However, they subsequently appeared to lose direction and their music reflected a tired, worn-out approach. To their credit, though, in their hey-day the NRPS were a fine trucking, country rock band.

New Riders Of The Purple Sage, Courtesy CBS Records.

Albums:
New Riders Of The Purple Sage (Columbia/CBS)
Powerglide (Columbia/–)
Gypsy Cowboy (Columbia/CBS)
The Adventures Of Panama Red (Columbia/CBS)
Home, Home On The Road (Columbia/CBS)
The Best Of New Riders Of The Purple Sage (Columbia/CBS)
New Riders (MCA/MCA)

Mickey Newbury

Called 'a poet' by Johnny Cash, Newbury's often ultra sad songs have been recorded by Elvis Presley, Jerry Lee Lewis, Ray Charles, Lynn Anderson, Andy Williams, Kenny Rogers and countless others.

Born in Houston, Texas, on May 19, 1940, Newbury travelled around in earlier years, eventually joining the Air Force for four years, during which time he was based in England.

"After that", he says, "I worked on the shrimp boats in the Gulf, diddled around, did a little writing and lots of other things. I started playing guitar when I was a kid, just enough to be able to go through three or four chords and sing something with it. But when I went into the Air Force, I ditched it all. One day I wound up at a place where they served snacks and had a piano. I began playing it because I just had to get my hands on something that made music. Later I borrowed a guitar from a guy because I didn't have enough money to buy one of my own – but I didn't really start working at things and trying to write until I was 24."

Moving to Nashville in the mid-'60s, Newbury began writing songs for artists of many different styles, at one time having four songs simultaneously in the R&B, Country, Easy Listening and Pop charts.

As a recording artist he began cutting albums for RCA and Mercury, without making much impact, though his Mercury release **It Looks Like Rain** became a collectors' item hauling in high bids before it became repackaged as part of a double album set following Newbury's signing by

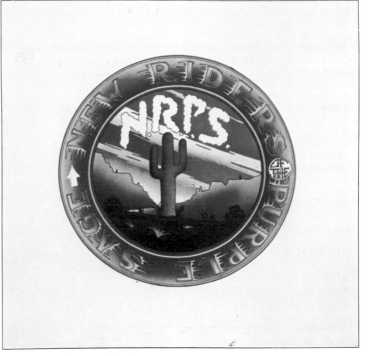

Above: Mickey Newbury formed his American Trilology from Civil War songs.

Elektra in 1971.

His biggest hit to date has been via **American Trilogy** (1972), a composition formed from three Civil War era songs, which also became an international hit for Elvis Presley and was well recorded in country music circles.

Throughout the '70s Newbury recorded a series of albums, carefully crafted works that won him high critical praise, but no large sales. He has continued to provide country acts with hit songs, including Tompall & The Glaser Brothers (**I Still**

characteristics. During the early '50s, he became a regular on Shreveport's Louisiana Hayride and signed with the major Dot label, obtaining a Top 10 disc with **Cry, Cry, Darling** in 1954. An Opry regular by 1956, he celebrated by cutting **A Fallen Star**, his most successful record, during the following year.

Next came an MGM contract and such winners as **You're Making A Fool Out Of Me** (1958), **Grin And Bear It** (1959), and **Lovely Work Of Art** (1960), before Newman became a long-term Decca

Alligator Man, Jimmy 'C' Newman. Courtesy Charly Records.

artist, his run of hits continuing with the chat-filled **Bayou Talk** (1962), **DJ For A Day** (1963), **Artificial Rose** (1965), **Back Pocket Money** (1966), **Blue Lonely Winter** (1967), **Born To Love You** (1968) and others.

Proficient on virtually any type of country material, it was with the formation of his band, Cajun Country, in the mid '70s and a return to his Cajun roots that Jimmy made a big impact. With a musical style that mixed traditional Cajun with contemporary country, he built up a sizeable following in Europe, especially Britain, and recorded some fine modern Cajun albums.

Albums:
Cajun Country (–/RCA)
Alligator Man (–/Charly)
Progressive C.C. (–/Charly)
The Happy Cajun (–/Charly)

Juice Newton

Country-rock singer Juice was born in Virginia Beach, Virginia, the daughter of a Navy man and the only musical person in a family of five. She started to play acoustic guitar and sing folk songs in her early teens, influenced at the time by people like Bob Dylan, Joan Baez and Tom Paxton. At college in North Carolina she began to consider a career in music. She started working in local bars, some nights waiting on tables and others taking to the stage with her guitar and entertaining.

In the late '60s, Juice moved to northern California where she attended Foothill College and first met her longtime boyfriend and partner Otha Young. At first she performed in local folk clubs then, combining her folk interest with rock 'n' roll, formed an electric band with Young called Dixie Peach.

A move to Los Angeles in 1975 led to Juice and Otha forming a new band called Juice Newton & Silver Spur. They signed a recording deal with RCA and released their debut self-titled album, a mixture of country, rock and pop which spawned a minor country hit in **Love Is A Word** in 1976.

One more album followed on RCA, **After The Dust Settles**, then Juice and the band moved on to a new deal with Capitol Records. After **Come To Me**, the first album for the new label, was completed, Juice disbanded Silver Spur, opting to work closely as a solo artist with Otha.

Her first solo album, **Well Kept Secret**, paved the way for the new Juice Newton and by the beginning of 1980 she was making inroads into the country charts with **Sunshine** and **Let's Keep It That Way**. A year later her major breakthrough came with the album simply titled **Juice**, which was released in February 1981 and produced two country number ones in **Angel Of The Morning** and **Queen Of Hearts**. Both singles also made it into the pop Top 10 and Juice started picking up awards including a Grammy for **Angel Of The Morning**, an Academy of Country Music award for the album and several gold discs. Her next single, **The Sweetest Thing**, written by Otha Young back in the

Mickey Newbury Sings His Own. Courtesy RCA Records.

Love You, After All These Years), Marie Osmond (**Blue Sky Shinin'**), Johnny Rodriguez (**Makes Me Wonder If I Ever Said Goodbye**) and Don Gibson (**When Do We Stop Starting Over**).

Albums:
Frisco Mabel Joy (Elektra/Elektra)
Heaven Help The Child (Elektra/Elektra)
Live At Montezuma/It Looks Like Rain
  (Elektra/Elektra)
I Came To Hear The Music (Elektra/Elektra)
Rusty Tracks (ABC/ABC)
After All These Years (Mercury/–)
His Eye Is On The Sparrow (ABC/–)

Jimmy C. Newman

Born of part-French ancestry, in Big Mamou, Louisiana, on August 27, 1927, Jimmy began singing in the Lake Charles area, his style employing many Cajun

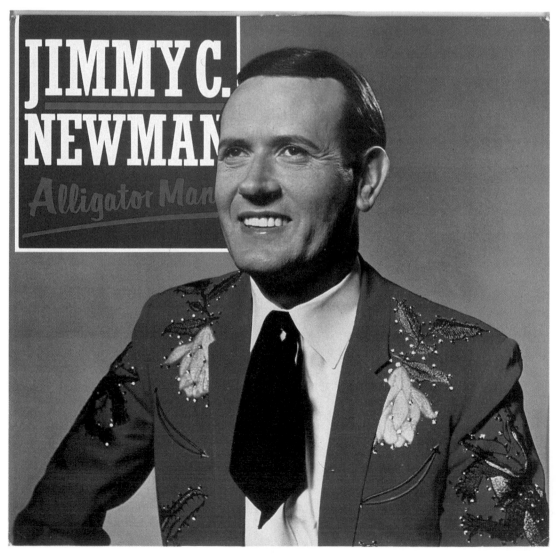

Above: Juice had 1985 No. 1s with Hurt and You Make Me To Make You Mine.

mid '70s, also shot to No. 1 on both country and pop charts.

Gradually Juice moved away from that successful country-rock sound to a more pronounced rock styling that saw her consolidate her success on the pop charts, but lose much of her country following.

Her last album for Capitol, **Dirty Looks**, in 1983, received bad reviews in the country press and with a move back to RCA and the album **Can't Wait All Night**, she had almost completely forsaken her country audience.

Albums:
Juice (Capitol/Capitol)
Quiet Lies (Capitol/Capitol)

Olivia Newton-John

An extremely competent British pop vocalist, Olivia Newton-John won the CMA Female Vocalist Of The Year award in 1974, but soon after turned her back on country and embarked upon a more lucrative film and pop-dance career.

Born in Cambridge, England, on September 26, 1948, she grew up in Australia, where her father headed a college. During the late '60s, she performed as part of an all-girl group, eventually going solo and winning a contest that provided her with a trip to England.

Following a short-lived stint with Tommorrow, a highly hyped pop group,

Olivia embarked upon a solo act once more, achieving a British and US hit with **If Not For You** (1971). British chart successes continued with **Banks Of The Ohio** (1971), **What Is Life?** (1972) and **Take Me Home Country Roads** (1973).

Then came **Let Me Be There**, a countryish hit immaculately produced by John Farrar, which scored in both US pop and country charts, thus earning Olivia no less than three Grammies and the CMA

Come On Over, Olivia Newton-John, Courtesy EMI Records.

award. After her failure in the 1974 Eurovision Song Contest, she spent most of her time in the States, initially logging country-pop chart entries with **I Honestly Love You** and **If You Love Me** (both 1974), **Have You Ever Been Mellow?** and **Please, Mr. Please** (both 1975) and **Let It Shine** (1976).

Hollywood beckoned and she starred in such films as 'Grease' and changed her musical stylings to accommodate rock and dance audiences.

Olivia now has little connection with country music.

Albums:
If You Love Me, Let Me Know (MCA/–)
Let Me Be There (MCA/–)
Come On Over (MCA/EMI)
Don't Stop Believing (MCA/EMI)
Greatest Hits (–/EMI)

Nitty Gritty Dirt Band

A Californian country-rock band, The Nitty Gritty Dirt Band finally gained country acceptance in the early '80s with country chart toppers **Sharecroppers' Dream (A Long Hard Road)**, **I Love Only You** and **High Horse**, following 17 years of releasing critically acclaimed albums covering a sort of all-American eclecticism with strands of a whole musical range: blues, hillbilly, cajun, folk, boogie, traditional and modern country.

Formed in Long Beach in 1966 by Bruce Kunkel and Jeff Hanna as the Illegitimate Jug Band (Jackson Browne was a one time member), they engaged other like-minded local students: Jimmie Fadden, Leslie Thompson, Ralph Barr and John McEuen. Then, changing their name to The Nitty Gritty Dirt Band, John's elder brother, Bill, became their manager and producer.

They signed with Liberty Records in 1967 and made the American pop charts with **Buy For Me The Rain** (1967), **Mr Bojangles**, **House At Pooh Corner** and **Some Of Shelly's Blues** (all 1971). Good musicians and fine songwriters, they made an impression with their albums which covered all kinds of musical styles, but it was the historic recording sessions they undertook at Woodland Sound

Above: Nitty Gritty Dirt Band. In 1986 they proved show-stoppers at London's Wembley Festival.

Studio, Nashville in 1971 which really put The NGDB on the musical map.

A three-record set entitled **Will The Circle Be Unbroken**, conceived by The NGDB but in no way dominated by them, was an ambitious project. It was the first of its kind and required total co-operation between contemporary and old country artists as The NGDB shared the studio with Doc Watson, Mother Maybelle Carter, Roy Acuff, Merle Travis, Jimmy Martin and The Scruggs Family. Even more astounding is the fact that the whole thing was mixed live on a two-track tape machine.

Despite the presence of all these greats of traditional country music, The Nitty Gritties kept their cool splendidly, with John McEuen's banjo and Jimmie Fadden's mouth harp proving particularly outstanding. It is probably the highest-energy acoustic music ever recorded (not a single electric instrument on the whole thing) and a testimonial to both the musicians involved and the music they play. When finally released in 1973 in a lavish booklet sleeve, it became one of the most discussed albums of the time and gave old-time country music a big boost, bringing country to many rock fans not yet acquainted with it.

Throughout the mid '70s The NGDB continued to release albums which showed they were not to be tied down by musical labels, as they mixed old rock 'n' roll songs, country tunes, folk numbers, self-penned songs and material by contemporary writers like Michael Murphey, J. D. Souther and Jackson Browne. Sadly they failed to achieve any kind of commercial success on record,

though they were in continuous demand as an exciting stage act.

In 1976 they shortened their name to The Dirt Band and began to formulate a more straightforward country-rock sound, making a brief return to the American pop charts in 1978 with **In For The Night**. After reverting to the name The Nitty Gritty Dirt Band at the end of 1982, the group had their first taste of success on the country charts with **Shot Full Of Love** and **Dance Little Jean**, which rose to Nos. 19 and 9

Pure Dirt, the Nitty Gritty Dirt Band's first album. Courtesy UA Records.

respectively in 1983. The following year the band changed labels for the first time in 17 years, joining Warner Brothers Records and so beginning a series of country number ones.

Their initial album, **Plain Dirt Fashion**, established a fine modern country sound utilizing self-penned songs along with those of Rodney Crowell, Steve Goodman, Dave Loggins, Don Schlitz and Bruce Springsteen. Amazingly, apart from drummer Bobby Carpenter, all members of The NGDB have been with the group from the beginning, almost 20 years earlier.

They paid tribute to their illustrious,

sometimes disappointing but always fun career in the title tune of their next album, **Partners, Brothers And Friends**. It gave them another country chart topper in the summer of 1986, shortly after they had played a show-stopping set at the annual Wembley Country Music Festival.

Albums:
Will The Circle Be Unbroken (UA/UA)
Plain Dirt Fashion (Warner/–)
Partners, Brothers And Friends (Warner/–)
Let's Go (UA/UA)
Dirt, Silver And Gold (UA/–)

Eddie Noack

Born in Houston, Texas, on April 29, 1930, Armond A. 'Eddie' Noack Jr graduated from the University of Houston in Journalism and English. Opting for a singing career, he won an amateur talent contest at the Texas Theatre, Houston, later making his first radio appearance at Bayton, Texas, in 1947.

In 1949 he signed for Gold Star Records, his first release being **Gentlemen Prefer Blondes**, but by 1951 he was to be found on Four Star, a year later appearing on the TNT label, recording **Too Hot To Handle**. The success of the song led to a contract with Starday, with whom he stayed for nearly five years.

While performing on the Hank Williams Show, he met Hank Snow, who expressed interest in a Noack composition titled **These Hands**, Snow eventually recording the song and taking it into the 1955 charts. More artists, including Lefty Frizzell, Hawkshaw Hawkins, Ernest Tubb and George Jones, all covered Noack's songs but the Texan had little recording success of his own until 1958 when he joined

Pappy Dailey's D Records, cutting rock discs using the name Tommy Wood but scoring with a country disc **Have Blues Will Travel**.

When the D label was purchased by Mercury, Noack sides continued to be released but few raised much in the way of sales, and in 1960 he ceased recording for a while and moved into the publishing and songwriting scene, supplying George Jones with such songs as **Barbara Joy, Flowers For Mama, The Poor Chinee, No Blues Is Good News** and **For Better Or For Worse**. However, Noack later returned to the recording studios once more, cutting sides for K-Ark, Ram and Wide World, making a fine album, **Remembering Jimmie Rodgers**, for the last named.

In the mid '70s, Eddie moved to Nashville where he represented Pappy Dailey's publishing interests and also became an executive on the board of the Nashville Songwriters' Association. He recorded his second album, **Eddie Noack**, in Nashville in 1976 and it was released on Look Records, a small label based in Huddersfield, England.

Eddie died on February 5, 1978, but since his death several compilations of his early recordings have been made available as country fans have re-discovered one of the great unknowns of '50s country music.

Albums:
Eddie Noack (–/Look)
Gentlemen Prefer Blondes (–/Del Rio)
Eddie Noack (–/Ace)

Norma Jean

A highly regarded performer during the '60s, Norma Jean was brought up in Oklahoma City, where she learnt guitar and performed at square dances during her teen years. By 1958 she had become a regular on Red Foley's Ozark Jubilee TV show – and two years later she had not only joined the Opry but also earned a feature spot on Porter Wagoner's Chattanooga Medicine sponsored TV programme. Provided with such exposure Norma Jean could hardly fail – and so it was that her pure country voice soon began giving birth to such Top 20 hits as **Let's Go All The Way, Go, Cat, Go** (1964), **I Wouldn't Buy A Used Car From Him** (1965) and **Heaven Help The Poor Working Girl** (1967). Replaced on the Wagoner show by Dolly Parton in 1967, Norma Jean's record sales dipped accordingly though her name was still in the charts well into the '70s.

And yes, she really was Norma Jean, her family name being Beasler, while her place of birth was Wellston, Oklahoma, where she made her first, no doubt melodic, yell, on January 30, 1938.

Albums:
Let's Go All The Way (RCA/–)
Norma Jean (RCA/–)
Hank Cochran Songs (RCA/–)

Kenny O'Dell

One of Nashville's most successful songwriters, Kenny, who was born in Oklahoma and raised in California, began writing songs in his early teens. After graduating from Santa Maria High School in California, he formed his own record label, Mar-Kay Records and recorded his

Above: Bill, Joe, Richard and Duane – The Oak Ridge Boys.

own song **Old-Time Love**, which received only minimal attention from the public.

Unperturbed by this failure he worked for a while with Duane Eddy, gaining experience along the way before forming a group called Guys and Dolls, which played clubs and hotel lounges throughout the States, including seasons in Hawaii and Alaska.

Success finally came his way with the self-penned **Beautiful People**, a release on the small Vegas Records which made the American pop 40 in 1967, only to be overtaken by a cover version by Bobby Vee which made the Top 10. Another of Kenny's songs, **Next Plane To London** as recorded by Rose Garden, made the Top 20 at the end of that year.

Kenny made a move to Nashville in 1971 to write songs and take over the running of House of Gold, Bobby Goldsboro's publishing firm. Soon his songs were appearing on the country charts beginning with **Why Don't We Go Somewhere And Love** by Sandy Posey and **I Take It On Home** by Charlie Rich.

In 1973 Kenny came up with **Behind Closed Doors**, a song that made Charlie Rich a major country-pop crossover star and was named Song of the Year by the CMA and ACM. This success led to Kenny signing a recording contract with Capricorn Records and scoring minor hits with **You Bet Your Sweet Love** (1974) and **Soulful Woman** (1975), before scoring Top 10 hits with **Let's Shake Hands And Come Out Lovin'**, and **As Long As I Can Wake Up In Your Arms** (both 1978).

Kenny, who has served on the Board of Directors of the CMA and the Board of the Nashville Songwriters Association, has continued to pen hits for such artists as

Billie Jo Spears (**Never Did Like Whiskey**), Tanya Tucker (**Lizzie And The Rainman**), Kenny Dale (**When It's Just You And Me**) and The Judds (**Mama He's Crazy**), though his own recording career seems to have come to a halt with no further releases since 1979.

Albums:
Kenny O'Dell (Capricorn/Capricorn)
Let's Shake Hands And Come Out Lovin' (Capricorn/–)

Seasons, Oak Ridge Boys. Courtesy MCA Records.

Oak Ridge Boys

Duane Allen, lead; Joe Bonsall, tenor; William Lee Golden, baritone; Richard Sterban, bass.

For many years, The Oaks (as they now prefer to be called) were one of the top groups in Gospel music, winning 14 Dove Awards from the Gospel Music Association and four Grammys. Then in 1975 they decided to make a move towards country music and within three years they won the first of many Country Music Association awards as Best Vocal

Above: The Oaks have gained a reputation for exciting, live performances.

Group of 1978.

The Oaks' beginnings go back a long way to shortly after the second world war when they were originally known as The Country Cut-Ups and performed at the atomic energy plant in Oak Ridge, Tennessee. The group was reformed in 1957 by Smitty Gatlin as the Oak Ridge Quartet and began working on a part-time basis, but became fully professional in April 1961, commencing a recording career that has encompassed work on

Y'All Come Back Saloon, Oak Ridge Boys. Courtesy MCA Records.

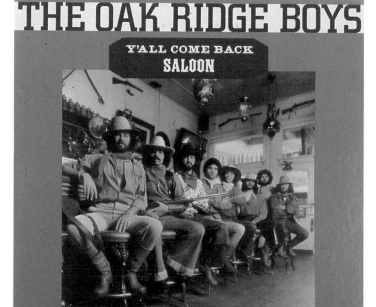

such labels as Cadence, Checker, Warner Brothers, Starday, Skylite, Heart Warming and Columbia.

Their initial appeal lay in the fact that they performed high quality sacred material in an infectious, foot-stomping fashion. In 1971 they received a Grammy Award for their recording of **Talk About The Good Times** and in 1976 did the same thing for **Where The Soul Never Dies**.

William Lee Golden (born January 12, 1939, Brewton, Alabama) is the longest serving member of the group, having joined in 1964. Lead singer Duane Allen (born April 29, 1944, Taylortown, Texas), formerly a member of The Southernaires Quartet, joined in 1966 and is generally regarded as The Oaks' spokesman.

Newer members are Richard Sterban (born April 24, 1944, Camden, New Jersey), who worked with The Stamps Quartet backing Elvis Presley before joining in 1972, and Joe Bonsall (born May 18, 1944, Philadelphia, Pennsylvania), who had worked in pop groups on Dick Clark's American Bandstand and was a member of the Keystone Quartet before joining a year later in 1973.

The foursome made a move towards country acceptance in 1975, scoring a minor hit on the country charts with their secular recording of **Family Reunion** for Columbia the following year. Soon after, they provided the back-up on Paul Simon's **Slip Sliding Away**, which became a million-seller upon release.

Encouraged by Johnny Cash, who asked them to open for him in Las Vegas, and signed by booking agent Jim Halsey, The Oaks began recording for ABC-Dot, and shortly had their first Top 5 country hit with **Y'all Come Back Saloon**.

Since then The Oaks have been red-hot with their gospel flavoured country-pop songs, scoring hits with **I'll Be True To You** (1978), **Come On In** (1978), **Sail Away** (1979), **Leaving Louisiana In The Broad Daylight** (1979), **Trying To Love Two Women** (1980) and **Beautiful You** (1980).

The inevitable pop chart breakthrough came with the multi-million selling **Elvira** (1981) and **Bobbie Sue** (1982), the quartet commanding a huge following in America and each album achieving platinum status within weeks of release. They have continued to dominate the country charts with **American Made** (1983), **Love Song** (1983), **I Guess It Never Hurts To Hurt Sometimes** (1984), **Make My Life With You** (1985) and **Come On In (You Did the Best You Could)** (1986).

With their own six-piece Oak Ridge Boys Band, The Oaks have gained a reputation for their exciting live performances, a fast-paced showcase with dynamic, almost choreographed

presentations from each of the four members.

Albums:
Room Service (ABC/ABC)
Deliver (MCA/MCA)
American Made (MCA/MCA)
Step On Out (MCA/MCA)

W. Lee O'Daniel

Wilbert Lee O'Daniel, born on March 11, 1890 in Malta, Ohio, became the first of many politicians to use the grass roots appeal of country music to propel him to high political office.

O'Daniel grew up in Kansas, but moved to Texas as a flour salesman, eventually rising high in the Burrus Mills company, maker of Light Crust Flour. In 1930 he formed a band around a group of struggling musicians to form the Light Crust Doughboys to advertise the product over radio – early members included Bob Wills, Johnnie Lee Wills, Herman Arnspiger and Milton Brown, and later Leon McAuliffe.

O'Daniel himself did not play an instrument or sing, but personally ran the band (with a heavy hand, if the rapid turnover of fine musicians is an indication), as well as serving as its announcer. In addition, he added considerably to the Doughboys' popularity by reading news, amusing stories, and his own poetry, and wrote several important songs as well, **Beautiful Texas** and **Put Me In Your Pocket** among them.

By 1935 he severed his ties with Burrus Mills and with the Doughboys, setting up his own company and brand, Hillbilly Flour, and a new band as well – the Hillbilly Boys, led by Leon Huff and including O'Daniel's sons Pat and Mike (banjo and fiddle) and Kitty Williamson, Bundy Bratcher, Wallace Griffin and Kermit Whalen.

However, his aspirations had begun to run higher than that of flour company executive; in 1938 he waged a grass roots campaign (taking with him the Hillbilly Boys) for Governor of Texas, winning easily, and went on to serve a term in the US Senate representing the Lone Star State as well.

Molly O'Day

There are more than a few people – her ex-producer Art Satherley among them – who feel that Molly O'Day is the greatest female country singer ever. Her earnest exhortative style – not unlike that of Roy Acuff and Wilma Lee Cooper – is the epitome of a style and brand of old time music not found today.

She was born LaVerne Williamson in Pike County Kentucky, on July 9, 1923, and embarked on a professional career in the summer of 1939, when she joined her fiddling brother Skeets in a band which also included Johnny Bailes. Here she went by the first of her many stage names, Mountain Fern, which she changed to Dixie Lee in the autumn of 1940. She married her longtime husband – and, at the time, fellow bandmember – Lynn Davis on April 5, 1941.

Molly and Lynn made the rounds of a number of south eastern radio stations for the next few years – Beckley, West Virginia; Birmingham, Alabama; Louisville (where she finally chose the name Molly O'Day), Beckley again and then Dallas and finally Knoxville, where they were heard by Fred Rose who interested Satherley in recording them.

Their first Columbia session (December 16, 1946) produced many of her classics: **Tramp On The Street** (written by Hank Williams), **Six More Miles**, **Black Sheep Returned To The Fold** and others. The session also marked the recording debut of Mac Wiseman, who played bass on the recordings.

The records were minor hits, and they resumed the circuit of radio stations, also doing more Columbia recordings: **Poor Ellen Smith** (with Molly on the banjo), **The First Fall Of Snow**, **Matthew Twenty-Four** and others.

In 1950 they began recording only sacred material for Columbia (the content had already been high), and when Molly contracted tuberculosis in 1952, she and Lynn both left musical careers to become ministers in the Church of God, careers which they both follow to this day, Molly occasionally broadcasting over a Christian station based in Huntingdon, West Virginia.

There is no question that Molly O'Day quit performing and recording well before her prime; she certainly had all the talent and appeal to become country music's first really great and really popular woman singer, a role that fell to Kitty Wells just a few years later.

Albums:
Molly O'Day And The Cumberland Mountain Folks (Old Homestead/–)
The Heart And Soul Of Molly O'Day (Queen City/–)
Living Legend Of Country Music (Starday/–)

Below: Carl Perkins, Jerry Lee Lewis, Roy Orbison and Johnny Cash reunite in Memphis' Sun Studios to cut the Class Of '55 album during 1985.

James O'Gwynn

Known as the Smiling Irishman, O'Gwynn won a modicum of fame with **My Name Is Mud**, a Mercury release of 1962.

Born in Winchester, Mississippi, but spending much of his early life in Hattisburg, O'Gwynn was part of a large musical family, his mother teaching him to play guitar. Resident in Texas during the early '50s, he played on the Houston Jamboree but later moved on to become part of Shreveport's Louisiana Hayride (1956), joining the Opry in December, 1960.

On record he has cut sides for Starday, D, Mercury, Pep, UA, Hickory, Stop, Plantation, MGM, etc, his most potent period occurring during 1958–62 when he accrued six hits, O'Gwynn's popularity amazingly diminishing after the release of **My Name Is Mud**, his biggest hit.

Nevertheless, he has remained extremely active in the southern States, touring on a wide basis, and in 1976 he made a long overdue visit to Britain to play dates on the local country club circuit.

Album:
The Best Of James O'Gwynn (Mercury/–)

Roy Orbison

Born in Vernon, Texas, on April 23, 1936, Orbison's roots were deep country, his first band, the Wink Westerners, being named after the town of Wink, where he was raised. He was one of the many youngsters who fell under the spell of rockabilly, and under the guidance of Sam Phillips, had his first hit on Sun Records, **Ooby Dooby**, in 1956.

However, his high, piercing, totally unique voice owes nothing to any particular genre and he moved into

The Classic Roy Orbison. Courtesy London Records.

popular music, where after some seven million-selling singles he remains a major international star, though in the US itself he has dropped out of the limelight.

A victim of tragedy since leaving Monument Records in 1965 – his career immediately plummeted, his wife Claudette was killed in a motorcycle accident and two of his children died in a fire during 1968 – Orbison resumed his relationship with Monument in 1977, a subsequent album, **Regeneration**, proving to be his strongest since the early '60s.

In 1980 he made his debut on the country charts with **That Lovin' You Feeling' Again**, a stylish duet with Emmylou Harris that was featured in the film 'Urban Cowboy' and won a Grammy award. And during 1985, Orbison took part in the Sun reunion – with Johnny Cash, Jerry Lee Lewis and Carl Perkins – that produced the **Class Of '55** album.

Albums:
All Time Greatest Hits (Monument/Monument)
Regeneration (Monument/Monument)
The Sun Years (–/Charly)
Dig O Country (–/Decca)

Osborne Brothers

Among the first of the so-called progressive bluegrass outfits, the Osborne Brothers (both born at Hyden, Kentucky, Bob on December 7, 1931, Sonny on October 29, 1937) made their radio debut on station WROL, Knoxville, in the early '50s.

After teaming for a time with Jimmy Martin, recording for RCA, in 1956 they signed for MGM Records and became regulars on WWVA's Wheeling Jamboree show, where they specialized in precise, sky-high three-part harmony with guitarist Benny Birchfield.

Their gig at Antioch College in 1959 was a milestone, sparking off a series of campus dates, while also in '59 they found themselves accepted on the Opry, later electrification enabling the group to obtain bookings at swank night clubs and even play the White House.

Constantly dismaying purists with their electric sounds and their use of steel guitar, drums and piano, the Osbornes became Decca artists in 1963, terminating their seven year relationship with MGM. As electric bluegrass began to prosper, the group (later featuring Ronnie Reno or Dale Sledd as the third vocalist) began accumulating a number of low chart singles: **The Kind Of Woman I Got** (1966), **Rocky Top** (1968), **Tennessee Hound Dog** (1969) and **Georgie Pinewoods** (1971).

In 1976 they cut their first album for the new CMH label, featuring accompaniment more sparse than in past years, focusing as always on Bob's awesome tenor voice

with Tina Records (1979), Elektra (1979–81), AMI (1982) and Gervasi (1983–4).

Albums:
Heaven Is My Woman's Love (Dot/–)
This Is Tommy Overstreet (Dot/–)
Greatest Hits Vol. 1 (Dot/–)
Welcome To My World Of Love (–/Ember)
I'll Never Let You Down (Elektra/–)

Bonnie Owens

The ex-wife of Merle Haggard and mother of Buddy Allan from a previous marriage to Buck Owens, Bonnie Campbell Owens was born in Blanchard, Oklahoma, on October 1, 1932.

In her early years she sang at clubs throughout Arizona, working with Buck Owens as part of the 'Buck And Britt Show' on a Mesa radio station, later joining him in a band known as Mac's Skillet Lickers. During the '60s, Bonnie – by this time sans Buck – moved to Bakersfield, California, there recording with the Tally and Marvel labels and meeting Merle Haggard, whom she married in 1965.

Some Things I Want To Sing About, Osborne Brothers.

and impressive harmony singing. They have since recorded several more albums for CMH, including new versions of their old hits, an album devoted to Boudleaux and Felice Bryant songs, and one in partnership with long-time friend Mac Wiseman.

Albums:
Voices In Bluegrass (MCA/–)
Ru-bee (MCA/–)
Pickin' Grass And Singin' Country (MCA/–)
Number One (CMH/–)
From Rocky Top To Muddy Bottom (CMH/–)

Tommy Overstreet

Born in Oklahoma, on September 10, 1937, Overstreet began his career in Houston, Texas, working on a Saturday morning TV show in the guise of Tommy Dean from Abilene, a name suggested by one of his relations, the late Gene Austin, a pop singer who had recorded million-selling versions of **Ramona** and **My Blue Heaven** in the late '20s.

In 1956–7 he studied radio and TV production at the University of Texas, then, following a short stint as a touring performer, came a spell of army duty. He claims to have 'just coasted' for the next few years – at one stage recording for Dunhill but gaining little recognition – his fortunes changing in 1967 when, following a move to Nashville, he became manager

of Dot Records' Nashville office, at the same time becoming a Dot recording artist.

His initial singles failed to make much impression, but following the Top 5 success of **Gwen (Congratulations)** (1971), virtually every release made the Top 20. These hits include **Ann (Don't Go Running)**, **Heaven Is My Woman's Love** (1972), **Send Me No Roses** (1973), **Jeannie Marie (You Were A Lady)** (1974), **Here Comes That Girl Again** (1976) and **Don't Go City Girl On Me** (1977).

A regular guest on such shows as TV's Hee Haw, Tonight and Midnight Express, Overstreet built up a reputation as a top class entertainer. In recent years he has failed to make a major impression on the charts, though he has had recording stints

Below: Tommy Overstreet. He began working as Tommy Dean from Abilene.

Just Between The Two Of Us, Bonnie Owens with Merle Haggard (Capitol).

The twosome became signed to Capitol Records, cutting an album of duets entitled **Just Between The Two Of Us**, which led to them being voted Best Vocal Group of 1966 by the Academy Of C&W Music, Bonnie also winning the top female vocalist award. Prior to this, the duo had cut a single of the same name for Tally, which had become a 1964 hit, Bonnie also achieving two solo successes with Tally via **Daddy Don't Live Here Anymore** (1963) and **Don't Take Advantage Of Me** (1964).

Following a small clutch of other minor chart entries – including **Number One Heel** (1965) and **Lead Me On** (1969), Bonnie officially retired from performing in 1975, and though she and Merle were divorced the following year, she has continued to work for Merle, mainly organizing his various business activities, but sometimes taking part in his on-stage performances.

Albums:
That Makes Two Of Us – with Merle Haggard (Hilltop/–)
Lead Me On (Capitol/–)

Buck Owens

Mainman behind the California Sound and the establishment of Bakersfield as a country music capital, Alvis Edgar 'Buck' Owens, the son of a share-cropper, was born in Sherman, Texas, on August 12, 1929.

Buck Owens – Vol. 3. A compilation of hits. Courtesy Capitol Records.

While Buck was still young, the Owens family moved to Arizona in search of a better standard of living, but they failed to find prosperity, Buck having to leave school while in his ninth grade and involve himself in farm labouring. A fine guitarist and mandolin player, he began playing with a band over radio station KTYL, Mesa, Arizona when he was barely 17. At the same age he got married – by 18 he was a father.

In 1951 he moved to Bakersfield, forming a band, the Schoolhouse Playboys, with whom he played sax and trumpet. He also established himself as a first-class sessionman on guitar, backing such Capitol recording stars as Wanda Jackson, Sonny James and Faron Young. Following a stint as a lead guitarist with Tommy Collins' band, he became signed as a Capitol recording artist on March 1, 1957.

His first chart entry was with **Second Fiddle** (1959), then followed a long sojourn in the Top 5 via such releases as **Under Your Spell Again** (1959), **Above And Beyond**, **Excuse Me, I Think I've Got A Heartache** (1960), **Fooling Around** and **Under The Influence Of Love** (1961) – by which time Owens had become one of the biggest stars in country music.

With his band the Buckaroos – an outfit that has featured such fine musicians as Don Rich, Doyle Holly and Tom Brumley – Owens began playing to sellout crowds at such prestigious venues as New York's Madison Square Gardens and Los Angeles' Olympic Auditorium, his record sales becoming increasingly phenomenal, Owens registering no less than 17 No.1 hits between 1963-9, these recordings including such titles as **Act Naturally** (1963), **My Heart Skips A Beat** (1964), **I've Got A Tiger By The Tail** (1965), **Buckaroo** (1965), **Waitin' In The Welfare Line** (1966), **Sam's Place** (1967), **How Long Will My Baby Be Gone?** (1968) and **Tall Dark Stranger** (1969), many of these being written or part-written by Owens himself.

During the early '60s, the bandleader had recorded a series of extremely successful duets with Rose Maddox and at the onset of the '70s Owens revived this practice, employing Susan Raye as a partner and logging up hits with **We're Gonna Get Together**, **Togetherness** and **The Great White Horse**. Although some had begun to suggest that Owens had become **Too Old To Cut The Mustard** – the title of a 1971 chart single featuring Owens and his son Buddy Allan – the Baron of Bakersfield continued to supply Capitol with such major discs as **The Kansas City Song**, **I Wouldn't Live In New York City** (1970), **Bridge Over Troubled Water**, **Ruby (Are You Mad?)**, **Rollin' In My Sweet Baby's Arms** (1971), **I'll Still Be Waiting For You**, **Made In Japan** (1972) and **It's A Monster's Holiday** (1974).

However, in 1976 he terminated his long association with Capitol, signing instead with Warner Brothers and releasing an album entitled, characteristically, **Buck 'Em!** This marked the end of his days as a Top 10 regular, though he did make a brief return to the Top 10 with **Play Together Again, Again**, a duet with Emmylou Harris in 1979.

Whilst his old hits are kept alive with updated versions by today's country stars, Owens continues to be a familiar figure on the TV show 'Hee Haw'.

Albums:
The Best Of (Capitol/–)
Best Of Vol. 4 (Capitol/–)
Buck 'Em (Warner Bros/–)
No. 1 Country Hits (–/Music For Pleasure)
Our Old Mansion (Warner/–)

Tex Owens

Born in the Lone Star State in 1892, Tex Owens was a popular star and co-host of the KMBC Brush Creek Follies as well as the WLW Boone County Jamboree and several other radio shows. But he is best known and remembered for writing and singing his 1935 hit, **Cattle Call**, on Decca.

Owens died at his home in Baden, Texas, in 1962. From a musical family, his daughter, Laura Lee had a long career as Bob Wills' first girl singer and later with husband Dickie McBride; in addition, his sister was Texas Ruby, longtime Opry star.

Vernon Oxford

Highly regarded in Europe, Oxford was born June 8, 1941, in Benton County, Arkansas, one of seven children of one of the area's leading fiddle players. In his early childhood, Oxford would join the whole family in evening singing, later – after a move from the Ozarks to Wichita, Kansas – becoming a member of the local church choir. Like his father, he became a fiddler, entering the well-known Cowtown contest and also the Kansas State championship.

After forming his own band and touring throughout the mid west, Oxford then moved on to Nashville, where he was turned down by several record companies as being 'too country'. Eventually, in 1965, he became signed to RCA, who released seven singles and an album before dropping him. He also signed for Stop, with continued lack of real recognition.

In 1971, fans in Britain and Sweden organized a petition urging RCA to release Oxford's discs once more and, two years later, British RCA duly obliged with a double album in their **Famous Country Music Makers** series, a release which accrued impressive sales figures.

This encouraged RCA Nashville to re-sign Oxford in 1974, the singer immediately responding by providing, first, a minor hit in **Shadows Of My Mind** (1975), then a major one with **Redneck** (1976).

Below: Vernon Oxford. He keeps it country in best '50s tradition.

Albums:
Famous Country Music Makers (–/RCA)
I Just Want To Be A Country Singer (RCA/RCA)
Keepin' It Country (Rounder/Sundown)
Tribute To Hank Williams (–/Meteor)

Ozark Mountain Daredevils

A country-rock band from Springfield, Missouri, the Daredevils sprang from an outfit known as Cosmic Corncob And His Amazing Mountain Daredevils.

Their first album for A&M Records came out in 1973 and was well received. By 1974 they had a pop hit single with **If You Want To Get To Heaven**, their next album **It'll Shine When It Shines** – generally considered to be their best – spawning yet another hit in **Jackie Blue**, penned by band members Steve Cash (vocals, harmonica) and Larry Lee (drums). Mixing pure rock'n'roll with slick country picking, the Daredevils pushed ahead for a while, heading for Nashville to cut their third LP, **The Car Over The Lake Album**.

But interest began to wane and by 1977 members Randle Chowning (guitar, vocals) and Buddy Brayfield (piano) had quit. Original members Steve Cash and John Dillon (vocals, guitar, keyboard, fiddle) appeared on Paul Kennerley's all-star **White Mansions** album in 1978 but they were not destined to stay with A&M much longer. In the wake of a live double,

THE CAR OVER THE LAKE ALBUM

The Car Over The Lake Album, Ozark Mountain Daredevils. Courtesy A&M.

they moved on, signing with Columbia, for whom they cut an eponymously titled album in 1980. But by that time only Dillon, Cash and Mike Granda (bass) remained from the line-up that cut their first sides at a ranch in Missouri.

Albums:
Ozark Mountain Daredevils (A&M/A&M)
It'll Shine When It Shines (A&M/A&M)
The Car Over The Lake Album (A&M/A&M)

Andy Parker (And The Plainsmen)

Born near Mangum, Oklahoma, on March 17, 1913, Andy Parker began his radio career at the age of 16 over KGMP, Elk City, Oklahoma – a career which eventually took him to San Francisco, where he assumed the role of the singing cowboy on NBC's 'Death Valley Days' from 1937–41. After working in defence plants, he moved to L.A. in 1944 and by 1946 had formed a western harmony group known as Andy Parker And The Plainsmen, with KNX, Hollywood, as their home base.

Andy and The Plainsmen appeared in some eight PRC films with Eddie Dean, and signed with Capitol Records in December, 1947. However, they were never able to establish a firm identity apart from the host of rival groups abounding at the time, despite Parker's fine lead voice, excellent harmony and the strong line-up of Charlie Morgan (of the Morgan Family) on lead guitar, Clem Smith on bass, George Bamby (who had worked with Spade Cooley before and would work with the Songs Of The Pioneers afterwards) as arranger and accordionist, and legendary jazz steel guitarist Joaquin Murphy.

The band had no particularly big selling records on either Capitol or Coast Records, although they did cut a fine series of Capitol Transcriptions, before Parker was forced to retire, suffering from a heart condition.

Gram Parsons

A seminal figure in the country-rock movement of the late '60s. Born Cecil Connor in Winterhaven, Florida, on November 5, 1946, his father 'Coon Dog' Connor owned a packing plant in Waycross, Georgia. Coon Dog shot himself when Gram was 13 and Gram's mother married again, to Robert Parsons, a rich New Orleans businessman. Parsons formally adopted Cecil and changed the boy's name to Gram Parsons.

With much drinking in both real and adopted families and a hitherto uprooted life, Gram ran away at 14 and two years later was in New York's Greenwich Village singing folk songs. At one point he formed a folk band with Jim Stafford, and with a later band, Shiloh, Gram specialized in a commercial and regionally successful

Grievous Angel, Gram Parsons. Courtesy WEA Records.

Gram Parsons   Grievous Angel

brand of folk.

Studying theology at Harvard in 1965, Gram formed the International Submarine Band. After he dropped out of university, the band reformed in New York and an album, on Lee Hazelwood's label, showed them to be following a fairly purist country path.

By the time that album came out, Gram had joined The Byrds. Meeting Chris Hillman of that band in LA in 1968, he convinced Hillman that the hitherto rock-oriented Byrds should experiment with country. The result was **Sweetheart Of The Rodeo**, the first real country-rock album. Although much of Gram's contribution was mixed out, the album set a new style among rock groups and reminded many a Southern-bred rocker just where his roots lay. The Byrds appeared on the Grand Ole Opry and sang Gram's own composition **Hickory Wind**.

Gram's fantasy about marrying country with rock charisma was nurtured by his association with the Rolling Stones. He quit The Byrds on the eve of a South African tour, causing a welter of ill feeling. However, he reunited with Chris Hillman in 1969 when his country aspirations were more fully realized in the Flying Burrito Brothers, that band's **Gilded Palace Of Sin** album being hailed as a country rock-classic, showcasing compositions that have since become standards via the talents of Emmylou Harris.

But Parsons was getting into the West Coast drug lifestyle and by the recording of the band's second album, **Burrito Deluxe**, he seemed more interested in hanging out with Jagger and Richard in Europe. With his trust fund providing him extensive monies to indulge his lifestyle and a fantasy about getting to rock superstar level, Gram's preoccupations were tending more towards drugs and drink than productive musical output. However, Warner Reprise came up with a contract and, better still, was the possibility of Merle Haggard producing his next album. Parsons went to visit Haggard but Merle appeared to have a change of heart at the last moment. Even so, the session went ahead using Haggard's engineer Hugh Davis. Also booked were Glen D. Hardin, James Burton and a new girl singer from Baltimore, Emmylou Harris.

Gram was evidently drunk to the point of falling down for the first sessions. Nevertheless, the album showed that his writing ability was still there. **GP** was not a big commercial success on its release in 1972, and it was followed by **Grievous Angel**, which featured a similar line-up and more classic Parsons songs. A tour around that time, with Emmylou Harris and The Fallen Angels Band gave hints of what might have been for Gram had he lived. It has been left to Emmylou to perpetuate the songs and the legend.

Parsons probably did not expect to live long and on September 19, 1973, he died

Sleepless Nights, Gram Parsons. Courtesy A&M.

of a heart attack at Joshua Tree, in the California desert. The causes were apparently a heavy mix of drink and drugs, followed by (according to Byrd Roger McGuinn) a lovemaking bout with his wife. Later, at L.A.'s International Airport, his body was snatched and instead of ending up in New Orleans for a family funeral, was driven to the desert at Joshua Tree and unofficially cremated, the result of a pact between Gram and manager Phil Kaufman that whoever died first would be taken to the desert and cremated.

Because of this bizarre incident no autopsy was possible and no official cause of death established. Parsons has since become a cult figure, following one of his country idols, Hank Williams, to an early and mysterious death. But, unlike Williams, Parsons had to wait until after his demise for recognition.

Albums:
Sleepless Nights – with The Flying Burrito Brothers (A&M/A&M)
GP (Reprise/Reprise)
Grievous Angel (Reprise/Reprise)
Live 1973 – with The Fallen Angels (Sierra/Sundown)
The Early Years (Sierra/Sundown)
The International Submarine Band (HLI or Shiloh/Edsel)

Dolly Parton

Born on a farm in Locust Ridge, Sevier County, Tennessee, on January 19, 1946, Dolly Rebecca Parton was the fourth of 12 children born to a mountain family. At the age of ten, she was already an accomplished performer, her first regular radio and TV dates being on the shows of Cas Walker, in Knoxville. At 13 she was cutting sides for a small Louisiana record company, the same year making an appearance on Grand Ole Opry.

Graduating from Sevier County High School in June 1964, she immediately left for Nashville, where she at first scraped by as part of a songwriting team (with her

Jolene, Dolly Parton. Courtesy RCA Records.

Above: Dolly – she claims she once lost a Dolly Parton lookalike contest!

uncle, Bill Owens), her first success coming in 1967, with two hit records on Monument (**Dumb Blonde** and **Something Fishy**) and a contract to join the Porter Wagoner TV and road show. Also that year, Dolly began recording for RCA, her duet with Wagoner on Tom Paxton's **Last Thing On My Mind** entering the charts in December 1967 and rapidly climbing into the Top 10.

For the next six years, the Parton-Wagoner partnership continued to flourish, over a dozen of their duets becoming RCA best sellers. However, it seemed that Dolly was gradually becoming the major attraction on disc, obtaining a No. 1 with her recording of

All I Can Do, Dolly Parton. Courtesy RCA Records.

Joshua in 1970. By 1974, she had branched out as a true solo act, though continuing to record duets with Wagoner and utilize his talents on some of her sessions. The result was a move away from mainstream country in an attempt to gain a wider audience. And the bid proved profitable, Dolly's recording of **Jolene** (1974) becoming a world-wide hit, this being followed by such other '70s winners as **The Bargain Store**, **The Seeker**, **We Used To** (1975), **Hey Lucky Lady**, **All I Can Do** (1976), **Light Of A Clear Blue Morning** (1977) and then five No. 1s in a row with **Here You Come Again** (1977), **It's All Wrong But It's All Right**, **Heartbreaker**, **I Really Got The Feeling**, **Baby I'm Burnin'** (1978) and **You're The Only One** (1979).

During this period Dolly began exploring every pop avenue, from bluegrass through to disco, her albums ranging from **Great Balls Of Fire**, on which she provided her own versions of earlier pop and rock hits,

to **New Harvest, First Gathering**, a release which featured half of Nashville (Roy Acuff, Kitty Wells, Minnie Pearl, Grandpa Jones, Bashful Brother Oswald, Ernest Tubb and many others) providing back-up assistance on **Applejack**, one of Dolly's own songs.

By this time, Dolly had become a pop personality and the best known country performer in the world. Unfortunately much of this was down to her cheesecake poses rather than her unquestioned singing ability and her outstanding talent as a songwriter. For, despite all the cover shots on magazines, the TV shows, the country hits and a major film career which was sparked by a starring role in the comedy '9 to 5' (1980), the public, other than the ever-faithful country fans, neglected to buy Dolly's records, the

Just Because I'm A Woman, Dolly Parton. Courtesy RCA Records.

singer only achieving four Top 20 pop records from the time she went solo up to 1986.

Still, she has had further country No. 1s with **Starting Over Again**, **Old Flames Can't Hold A Candle To You**, **9 To 5** – also one of her pop hits (1980), **But You Know I Love You** (1981), **I Will Always Love You** (1982), **Island In The Stream** (a duet with Kenny Rogers that went to No. 1 in many countries, 1983), **Tennessee Homesick Blues** (1984), **Real Love** (another Parton-Rogers duet, 1985), and **Think About Love** (1986). There have been other film roles in 'The Best Little Whorehouse In Texas' (1982) and 'Rhinestone' (1984) – the latter garnering Dolly a reported three million dollars – and she has continued to accrue an imposing array of awards, these currently including CMA Female Vocalist of the Year (1975 and 1976) and the coveted CMA Entertainer of The Year (1978). Nevertheless, there is still much for Dolly Parton to achieve. And nobody knows that better than she.

Albums:

Best Of Dolly Parton – 1973 (RCA/RCA)
The Best Of Porter Wagoner and Dolly Parton (RCA/RCA)
Coat Of Many Colours (RCA/RCA)
My Tennessee Mountain Home (RCA/RCA)
Jolene (RCA/RCA)
New Harvest First Gathering (RCA/RCA)
Burlap And Satin (RCA/RCA)
Greatest Hits – 1984 (RCA/RCA)

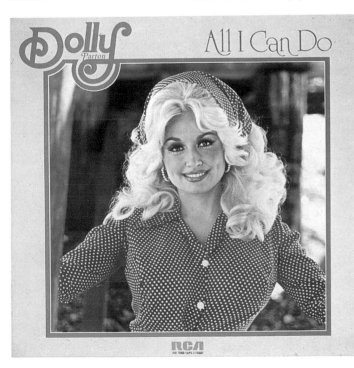

Stella Parton

The sister of Dolly Parton and the sixth of Lee and Avie Lee Parton's twelve children, Stella (born Sevier County, Tennessee, May 4, 1949) married while still at high school and was pregnant by the time she graduated. A TV performer in Knoxville at the age of 9, she recorded early on for some minor Nashville labels and formed a gospel group The Stella Parton Singers, working as performer, manager and booking agent. She formed her own label Soul, Country and Blues Records in the early '70s and in 1975 released **Ode To Olivia**, supporting Olivia Newton-John's right to be acclaimed Top Female Vocalist by the CMA. Also that same year she recorded a song of her own called **I Want To Hold You In My Dreams**, which provided her with her first Top 10 single.

By 1976 she was with Elektra-Asylum, her records being produced by Jim Malloy. The partnership proved successful and resulted in two major records in 1977, **The Danger Of A Stranger** and **Standard Lie Number One**, the former becoming a pop hit in Britain, where she made a promotional tour, explaining to one journalist that someone had airbrushed the cover-shot on her Stella Parton album in order to make her breasts bear a family resemblance to Dolly's!

1978 was another good year for Stella, bringing three sizable hits including **Four Little Letters**, a Top 20 entry. Two more chart entries followed in 1979 but since then it has been all quiet on the vinyl front for a lady who has valiantly fought a battle to be accepted for her own ability, generally steering clear of any situation that might make it seem that she owed anything to Dolly's influence.

Albums:
Stella Parton (Elektra/Elektra)
Country Sweet (Elektra/Elektra)

Les Paul

One of the most influential guitarists in popular music history, Les Paul (born

Stella Parton, Courtesy WEA Records. Check the airbrush art!

Lester William Polfus, Waukseha, Wisconsin, June 9, 1915) began his career as a country musician-comedian named Hot Rod Red, later becoming Rhubarb Red. He toured for some time with a popular Chicago group, Rube Tronson And His Texas Cowboys, but his growing interest in jazz led him to play with big bands and small combos for a time. At one point, from 1934 to 1935, he had a country show as Rhubarb Red over WJJD, Chicago, in the morning and an afternoon jazz show as Les Paul on WIND.

In 1936, he, plus vocalist and rhythm guitarist Jim Atkins (Chet's half-brother) and bassist Ernie Newton (a longtime Opry and Nashville session bassist in the '40s and '50s) auditioned in New York as the Les Paul Trio and spent the next five years

Everybody's Got A Family, Johnny Paycheck. Courtesy Epic Records.

with Fred Waring.

Les moved to L.A. late in 1941, where he spent much of his time in the studios as well as a stint in the services. In 1947 he teamed with a girl singer, an ex-Gene Autry bandmember named Colleen Summers, who was such a fine guitarist she played lead guitar in Jimmy Wakely's band, singing harmony with him on **One Has My Name, The Other Has My Heart**.

Colleen, whom Paul later married, became Mary Ford, and the combination of her singing, his extraordinary playing and his then unique use of multiple track recording for guitar and voice made the team immensely popular in the '40s and early '50s, producing eleven No. 1 pop hits for Capitol, including **Nola**, **Lover**, **How High The Moon** and **The World Is Waiting For The Sunrise**.

Les had experimented with electric guitars as early as the late '30s – in fact he had never stopped being fascinated by electronics since his first crystal set in 1927 – and in 1952 Gibson began putting out their fabulously successful series of Les Paul guitars, designed by Les himself. These solid body electrics are now increasingly commonplace in country.

After he and Mary Ford divorced in 1962, Les retired from performing, turning to inventing in his New Jersey home. The boom in interest in the Les Paul guitar, however, made his name a household word among musicians, and in 1973 he began performing again on a limited scale. Using a guitar called a Les Pulveriser which was light years ahead of the standard Gibson production model, he recorded a number of albums with Chet Atkins, one – **Chester And Lester** – winning a Grammy for the Best Country Instrumental Performance of 1976.

Albums:
Chester And Lester – with Chet Atkins (RCA/RCA)
Guitar Monsters – with Chet Atkins (RCA/RCA)

Johnny Paycheck

A one-time Nashville renegade who, during the mid-'70s temporarily adopted

the name John 'Austin' Paycheck in honour of the Music City's greatest rivals, this singer-songwriter (born Don Lytle, Greenfield, Ohio, May 31, 1941) began his career as a Nashville sideman, enjoying a brief stay as bass-guitarist with Porter Wagoner's Wagonmasters. Later he became a member of Faron Young's Deputies before moving on to play with both George Jones and Ray Price. During this period he switched to steel guitar, rejoining Jones' band as a guitarist during 1959–60.

As a rockabilly he cut some sides for Decca using the pseudonym Donny Young – then came sessions for Mercury and Hilltop, Paycheck having two fair-sized hits on the latter label with **A-11** (1965) and **Heartbreak, Tennessee** (1966). He then helped to form Little Darlin' Records, providing the label with several good sellers during the '60s, the biggest of these being **The Lovin' Machine**, a Top 10 entry during 1966. It was around this time that Paycheck also made the grade as a writer, his **Apartment No. 9** affording Tammy Wynette her first hit. **Touch My Heart**, another of his compositions, went Top 10 via a version cut by Ray Price.

Little Darlin' folded at the end of the '60s, a period during which Paycheck virtually hit rock bottom, becoming a self-confessed alcoholic. However, he proved not to be a quitter. He took the cure and fought back with considerable determination, teaming up with producer Billy Sherrill to cut some sides for Epic, his first release on the label being **She's All I Got**, which reached the top of the country charts in 1971.

For the next couple of years, he was rarely out of the Top 20, thanks to singles such as **Someone To Give My Love To**, **Love Is A Good Thing** (1972), **Something About You I Love**, **Mr Lovemaker** and **Song And Dance Man** (1973). And though the hits continued, for a while they came at lower-order level. Even so, it was surprising when in 1976 Paycheck was reported to be bankrupt. Once again he bounced back and in 1977 took the Top 10 by the scruff of the neck by notching three major hits, **Slide Off Your Satin Sheets**, **I'm The Only Hell (Mama Ever Raised)** and **Take This Job And Shove It**, the latter, one of David Allan Coe's anti-establishment anthems, becoming one of the year's biggest records. He teamed with George Jones for a session that produced hits in **Maybellene** (1978), **You Can Have Her** (1979), and **You Better Move On** (1980), the duo adopting a gruesome twosome guise for the sleeve of **Double Trouble**, a rock'n'fun album that came out in 1980.

By 1981 he was working with Merle Haggard, Hag turning up on Paycheck's Columbia album **Mr Hag Told My Story**, which provided a spin-off single in **I Can't**

Heartbreak, Tenn. An early Paycheck release on Hilltop Records.

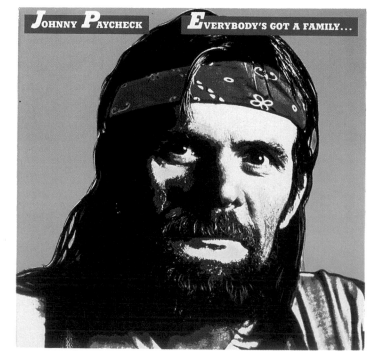

Minnie Pearl

With her flower-bedecked straw hat and old-time summer dress, Minnie Pearl is the most instantly recognizable lady in country entertainment today.

Born Sarah Ophelia Colley in Centreville, Tennessee, on October 25, 1912, she majored in stage technique at Nashville's Ward-Belmont College during the '20s, then taught dancing for a while before joining an Atlanta production company as a drama coach in 1934. By 1940, Sarah had become Minnie Pearl from Grinder's Switch (Grinder's Switch is a railroad switching station just outside Centreville) and made her debut on the Grand Ole Opry in this guise. She became an instant Opry favourite and has since appeared on numerous tours, radio and TV shows, also appearing on the first country music show ever to play New York's Carnegie Hall (1947).

Much honoured by the music industry, Minnie – Nashville's Woman Of The Year in 1965 – was elected to the Country Music Hall Of Fame in 1975. She has recorded for such labels as Everest, Starday and RCA and though not many of her records are currently to be seen in the racks, she continues with her stage and TV career, but was cruelly treated by presenter Jonathan King on the BBC series Entertainment USA in 1985, King letting the cameras dwell on Minnie as she slipped out of character.

Album:
Stars Of The Grand Ole Opry – one track only (RCA/RCA)

Hank Penny

One of the few easterners who tried to bring a western swing sound to country music in the '40s was Hank Penny, born in Birmingham, Alabama, on August 18, 1918.

He began his career as early as 1933 but rose to prominence over WWL in New

Stars Of The Grand Ole Opry (RCA) – Minnie performs Jealous Hearted Me.

Above: Minnie Pearl. "Howdy, I'm jest so proud to be here!"

Hold Myself In Line. But, despite fine records, Paycheck's popularity seemed to be waning again. By 1983 he had slipped his Epic/Columbia connection and was on AMI, charting with **I Never Got Over You**. Maybe he will be back again and climbing even higher. As Epic once claimed in a press handout: "With a life story that fits impeccably into the 'rags to riches to rags to riches' stereotype, the only truly amazing thing about Johnny Paycheck is that no-one has yet seen fit to put his biography on the silver screen. Change a couple of names to protect the guilty and avoid lawsuits and you'd have an instant smash."

Albums:
Double Trouble – with George Jones (Epic/Epic)
Greatest Hits (Little Darlin'/–)
Take This Job And Shove It (Epic/Epic)
Armed And Crazy (Epic/Epic)
Everybody's Got A Family (Epic/Epic)

Jimmy Payne

A fine songwriter, Payne was born in Arkansas in 1939, moving to Gideon, Missouri in the mid-'40s. While in the army, during the late '50s, he met Chuck Glaser of the Glaser Brothers and played guitar with the Glasers' band.

However, it was as a songwriter that he first moved to Nashville in 1962, where,

encouraged by the Glasers, he cut a single, **Ladder In The Sky**, for the K-Ark label, gaining no reaction. He then left Nashville, taking up a job as a paint sprayer in St Louis but later returned to Music City where in 1963 he recorded a version of John Hartford's **Every Pretty Little Girl** for Vee-Jay.

Signed to the Glasers' publishing company, Payne co-wrote **Woman, Woman**, which Union Gap turned into a 1967 pop million seller and since that time he has continued to provide hits for others. However, as a solo record artist, he has made little impact, having achieved only a few minor chart entries with **L.A. Angels** (on Epic, 1969), **Rambling Man** (Cinnamon, 1973), and **Turning My Love On** (Kik, 1981).

Leon Payne

A smooth-voiced singer and multi-instrumentalist, Payne was blind from childhood. Born in Alba, Texas, on June 15, 1917, he attended the Texas School For The Blind between 1924–35 learning to play guitar, piano, organ, drums, trombone and other instruments.

During the mid-'30s he began playing with various Texas bands, occasionally joining Bob Wills and his Texas Playboys. In the late '40s, he became a member of Jack Rhodes' Rhythm Boys, in 1949 forming his own outfit, The Lone Star Buddies, and playing on Grand Ole Opry. A prolific songwriter, Payne penned a great number of much covered songs including

Lost Highway, **Blue Side Of Lonesome**, **They'll Never Take Her Love From Me** and **I Love You Because**, the latter providing him with his own hit in late 1949.

Payne, who recorded with such labels as MGM, Bullet, Decca, Capitol and Starday, suffered a heart attack in 1965 and during his last few years had to curtail many of his performing activities. He died on September 11, 1969.

Orleans and spent a good bit of time on the Midwestern Hayride over WLW in Cincinnati, before departing for the West Coast in the mid-'40s. In later years he turned his talents from vocals to that of comedy and is still active in the Southern California area as a comedian. In his heyday he recorded for Columbia, RCA, King and Decca, his biggest hit being **Bloodshot Eyes**, for King.

Album:
Rompin', Stompin', Singin', Swingin' (–/ Bear Family)

Carl Perkins

Although Perkins is known as one of the seminal figures of Memphis rock'n'roll, he came from a solid country background and his albums have always been dotted with pure country songs.

Born in Lake City, Tennessee, on April 9, 1932, in a poor farming community, he started his career performing at local country dances and honky tonks, along with brothers Jay and Clayton. Independently of Elvis Presley, Carl realized that country was moving in new directions, but when he first approached Sam Phillips at Sun studios in Memphis, Phillips insisted that he cut country music only since Elvis had the other scene tied up. The result was three country singles, **Turn Around**, **Let The Jukebox Keep On**

Carl Perkins. The Blue Suede Shoes man's 1985 album for MCA.

Playing and **Gone, Gone, Gone**. But Perkins persuaded Phillips to let him do some faster material, this plea resulting in **Blue Suede Shoes**, a Perkins original which in 1956 topped the pop, country and R&B charts simultaneously. Perkins looked set to be the next superstar from the Sun stable but later that year he was on his way to do the Perry Como and Ed Sullivan shows in New York when, in his own words: "The Chesapeake Bay Ferry was the last thing I remembered for three days". A car crash had left Perkins with multiple injuries and a broken career. His brother Jay later died as a result of that same crash. However, Elvis had recorded **Blue Suede Shoes** and Perkins at least was assured of a place in the rock'n'roll honours list.

Nevertheless, Carl's solo career seemed to be at a standstill, Elvis had overtaken him as a rock star (Perkins claims that there were times in the early days of package tours when Elvis would completely run out of steam trying to follow him onstage) and Perkins began drinking heavily. But a tour of Britain in 1964, and another as a headliner in 1965, convinced him that he was at least a star in some countries. Also the Beatles had recorded his **Honey Don't**, **Matchbox** and **Everybody's Trying To Be My Baby**.

After this, Perkins was approached by Johnny Cash to become part of his road show and for many years remained a mainstay of the Cash package. He began cutting country records and also recorded an album with the eclectic NRBQ in 1970. In 1978 he released a UK album titled **Ol' Blue Suede's Back**, which saw him

Carl Perkins (CBS). A country singer who is also one of rock's seminal figures.

rockin' once more. He also began touring with hs sons on drums and bass.

A frequent visitor to Britain, where he has appeared on several Wembley Festival bills, he turned up on Paul McCartney's **Tug Of War** album in 1981, was recorded live in Germany with Johnny Cash and Jerry Lee Lewis (forming three-quarters of Sun's legendary million-dollar quartet) and was the subject of a magnificent Charly Records boxed set, **The Sun Years**. Still a crowd-pleaser – he and Jerry Lee raised enough heat to virtually set Wembley on fire in 1982 – Carl signed to MCA in 1985, cutting a strong debut album for the label, also taking part in the Sun Records reunion with Cash, Orbison and Jerry Lee Lewis.

Albums:
Long Tall Sally (–/CBS Embassy)
The Sun Years – boxed set (–/Charly)

Bill Phillips

Long a part of the Kitty Wells–Johnny Wright Roadshow, William Clarence Phillips was born in Canton, North Carolina, on January 28, 1936. A guitarist during his high school days, Phillips originally became an upholsterer by trade, his musical career blossoming in 1955, when he joined the cast of the Old Southern Jamboree on WMIL, Miami, Florida – in which city he gained a residency at the Granada club.

In 1957 he moved to Nashville, there signing as a songwriter with Cedarwood Publishing, and supplying Webb Pierce with **Falling Back To You**, a 1958 Top 10 hit. This resulted in its composer obtaining a record contract with Columbia. With the label, Phillips began cutting such titles as **Sawmill**, **Georgiatown Blues** and **You Are The Reason**, promoting few sales but creating enough interest to obtain dates on the Opry during the late '50s.

After becoming a Decca act in 1963, he began accruing a desirable number of chart entries, the first being **I Can Stand It (As Long As She Can)**, the most successful proving to be **Put It All Off Until Tomorrow**, **The Company You Keep** (both 1966) and **Little Boy Sad** (1969), all Top 10 discs.

A Phillips composition, **We'll Stick Together**, was the first song that Kitty Wells and Johnny Wright recorded as a duet.

Albums:
Bill Phillips (Decca/–)
Action (Decca/–)

Webb Pierce

Born in West Monroe, Louisiana, on August 8, 1926, Webb Pierce became a distinctive stylist in the heavily electric country of the '50s. Early in his youth he learned to play good guitar and was soon gaining notice playing at local events. After regular stints on Radio KMLB, Monroe, Pierce moved to Shreveport, home of the Louisiana Hayride, to try and gain attention. He was noticed by no less than Horace Logan, programme director of KWKH, the sponsoring station of the Hayride, and was quickly to become a popular radio performer.

He joined the Hayride. During this period, the early '50s, his band included many who were themselves to find fame: Faron Young, Jimmy Day, Floyd Cramer.

Early '50s hits with Decca included **Wondering**, **That Heart Belongs To Me** and **Back Street Affair**, while Pierce also

Webb's Choice, Webb Pierce. Courtesy MCA Records.

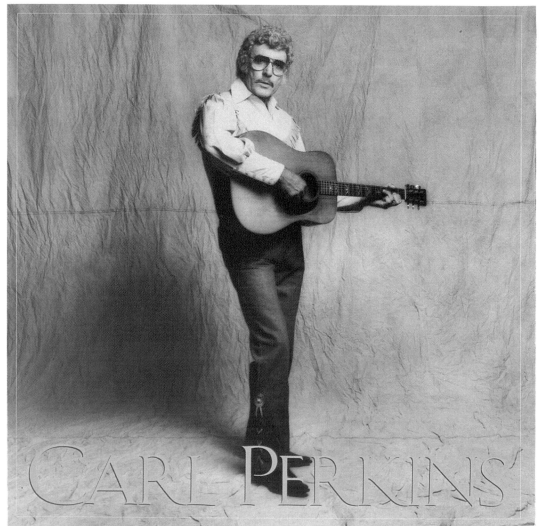

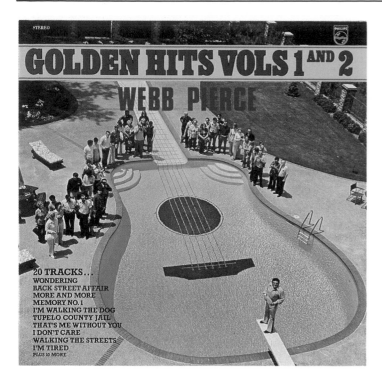

Golden Hits Vols 1 & 2, Webb Pierce. Courtesy Phonogram Records.

co-wrote his **The Last Waltz** success. By 1953 he had become popular enough to win the No. 1 Singer award given by the American Juke Box Operators. Soon after he moved to Nashville and joined the Grand Ole Opry. In 1954 he recorded **Slowly**, a No. 1 single that featured a ground-breaking pedal steel solo (by Bud Isaacs), while during 1955 he had three No. 1 hits: **In The Jailhouse Now**, **Love, Love, Love**, and **I Don't Care**. 1956 saw him scoring duet hits with Red Sovine – **Why, Baby, Why?** and **Little Rosa**. Getting in also with the burgeoning spirit of the times, he recorded **Teenage Boogie**, an item now much sought after by rockabilly collectors. He followed up with more Top 10 hits including **Bye Bye Love**, **Honky Tonk Song** and **Tupelo County Jail**.

Below: Ray Pillow. He became an Opry member back in 1966.

His voice had the authentic, nasal, modern country ring and his songs had a bar room edge, uncluttered by the excessive orchestration later to dominate Nashville recording. But this very authenticity seems dated and Pierce has become something of a museum piece.

He became extensively involved in the business side of things – a record company, radio stations and a publishing company or two. He was also the first star to actually own that Nashville cliché, the guitar-shaped swimming pool. However, though Webb had the occasional mini-hit during the '70s and even charted as recently as 1982, when he teamed with Willie Nelson on a revival of **In The Jailhouse Now**, he is no longer the trendsetting force he once was. His movie credits include 'Buffalo Guns', 'Music City USA' and 'Road To Nashville'.

Albums:
Greatest Hits (MCA/MCA)
I Ain't Never (–/Charly)

Ray Pillow

Voted Most Promising Male Country Artist Of The Year by Billboard and Cashbox in 1966, singer-guitarist Pillow was born in Lynchburg, Virginia, on July 4, 1937. Following four years in the forces during the late '50s, he completed a stay at college, earning his degree, then opted for a singing career, working on the local club circuit.

Later signed to Capitol Records, he gained his first sizeable hit with **Take Your Hands Off My Heart** in 1965 and obtained a Top 20 entry that same year with **Thank You Ma'am**. During 1966 came four more chart fillers, including **I'll Take The Dog**, a duet with Jean Shepherd that was destined to become Pillow's most successful record. And on April 30, 1966, he became a member of the Grand Ole Opry, thus fulfilling one of his greatest ambitions.

Still an Opry regular, Pillow has not had the best of luck with his records since the '60s. Nearly every year he has managed to log an entry or two in the lower regions of the charts, working for such labels as Mega (1972–4), Dot (1974–5), Hilltop (1978), MCA (1979), and First Generation (1981), but the big one still has not come his way.

Albums:
Slippin' Around (Mega/–)
Countryfied (Dot/–)

Poco

A country-slanted rock band, Poco formed in 1969 when ex-Buffalo Springfield cohorts Richie Furay (guitar and vocals) and Jim Messina (guitar and vocals), linked with Rusty Young (pedal steel, banjo, guitar, vocals), George Grantham (drums) and Randy Heisner (bass).

Three desertions took place during the band's nine album stay with the Epic label – Messina moving out to join Kenny Loggins as half of a hit-making duo;

Poco (CBS). The band was originally named Pogo after a comic strip.

Seven, Poco (CBS). It included Rusty Young's Rocky Mountain Breakdown.

Meisner becoming part of Rick Nelson's Stone Canyon Band before joining the Eagles; and Furay eventually helping to form the Souther-Hillman-Furay Band. In the wake of some commercially unsuccessful but musically interesting attempts to create an 'orchestral country' style – as exemplified by the title track of their **Crazy Eyes** album (1973) where Bob Ezrin's full-blooded string orchestrations are permeated by some pure mountain banjo picking – Poco completed their obligations to Epic and signed a deal with ABC Records. The immediate result was **Head Over Heals** (1975), one of their best received albums. But though Poco were moving into a period when their albums would sell more than ever before, they remained much in the shadow of the far more successful Eagles, who mined a similar vein of music. Though it had been rumoured that the band would fold in 1973, a version of Poco still existed in 1982, cutting an album called **Ghost Town** for Atlantic, after cutting three albums for MCA, two of which did not even rate a UK release.

The band at that time was headed by Paul Cotton (guitar, vocals), who had joined Poco in 1971, the only survivor of the original line-up being Rusty Young.

Albums:
Poco (Epic/CBS)
Deliverin' (Epic/Epic)
Crazy Eyes (Epic/Epic)
Cantamos (Epic/Epic)
Rose Of Cimarron (ABC/ABC)

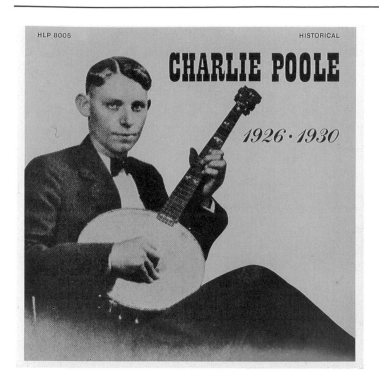

Charlie Poole 1926–1930. Courtesy Historical Records.

Charlie Poole

Leader of the North Carolina Ramblers, one of the most popular bands to emerge from that area in the '20s, five-string banjo player, singer and hard drinker, Charlie Poole was born in Alamance County, North Carolina, on March 22, 1892.

A textile worker for most of his life, in 1917 he met Posey Rorer, a cripped miner who played fiddle. They teamed up and played together in the West Virginia–North Carolina area, eventually adding guitarist Norman Woodlieff and recording for Columbia on July 27, 1925. Among their first sides was **Don't Let Your Deal Go Down**, one of the band's most requested numbers.

Personnel changes followed throughout the ensuing years, Roy Harvey replacing Woodlieff on the band's Columbia sessions of September 1926 and Posey Rorer leaving in 1928 to be succeeded first by Lonnie Austin, and later by Odell Smith.

Invited to provide background music for a Hollywood movie in 1931, Poole readied himself for a move to California. But later that same year, on May 21, he suffered a heart attack and died having reached the grand old age of 39.

Albums:
Charlie Poole And The North Carolina
 Ramblers Vols 1–3 (County/–)
Charlie Poole (Historical/–)

The Prairie Ramblers

The Prairie Ramblers, long associated with WLS and the National Barn Dance, were one of the most influential of the early string bands, although their style progressed through the years from south east string band to western swing in their National Barn Dance tenure 1932-1956.

Holmes (guitar, harmonica, jug), in western Kentucky.

Originally called the Kentucky Ramblers, they began on radio on WOC, Davenport, Iowa, but within a few months were members of the National Barn Dance, where they teamed for many years with Patsy Montana, backing her on her records and in person. Their early style was excellent string band and they introduced many important songs like **Feast Here Tonight**, **Shady Grove**, and **Rolling On**.

As time went on, however, their style became increasingly swingy. An interesting aside – they also recorded a number of risqué songs under the name Sweet Violet Boys.

Atchison left the band in 1937, heading for California, where he appeared in many films and with the bands of Jimmy Wakely, Ray Whitley, Merle Travis and others. Holmes left and returned, then went on to a career that took him to the Opry for a time with his wife Maddie (Martha Carson's sister) as Salty and Maddie. Atchison was replaced by Alan Crockett, who shot himself in 1947, and he was replaced in turn by Wade Ray, later to lead his own swing band and record for RCA. Wally Moore was his replacement, and when the band finally ground to a halt in 1956, Hurt and Taylor (the original members) were playing with a polka band, Stan Wallowick And His Polka Chips, which they continued to do for nearly another decade.

They recorded for the ARC complex of labels, Conqueror, Vocalion, Okeh, Mercury, Victor and Bluebird.

There were numerous personnel changes in the band throughout its life but the nucleus of the Ramblers was formed by Chick Hurt (mandolin, tenor banjo) and three of his neighbours, Jack Taylor (string bass), Tex Atchison (fiddle) and Salty

Roustabout, Elvis Presley. Courtesy RCA Records.

Elvis Presley

When Elvis Presley took country music into undreamed-of realms in 1955, many thought that he had killed it for all time. For there was no doubt that Presley was a country singer up till then and that, until the term rock'n'roll was coined, the new music was believed to be just country with an extra hard backbeat and some wild gimmicks.

Elvis Aaron Presley was born in Tupelo, Mississippi, on January 8, 1935, and brought up in a religious family atmosphere. He sang with his parents at revival meetings, at concerts and in church, also learning to play some guitar. The family moved to Memphis when he was 13 and he began to sing at local dances. After graduating from high school he was employed as a truck driver, playing with local groups at night.

That year he cut his first record, a private recording of **My Happiness**, to give his mother as a birthday present. The people at Sam Phillips' Memphis studio became interested in the country boy with the strange inflections in his voice and, later that year, they set up some experiments in the studio with Presley, Scotty Moore and Bill Black, to find a sound that suited Elvis. Country songs were found to be not quite suitable but when Elvis started a wild version of blues singer Arthur Crudup's **That's All Right, Mama**, they knew it was the missing piece of the puzzle, a piece that linked fast, almost breathless country backups

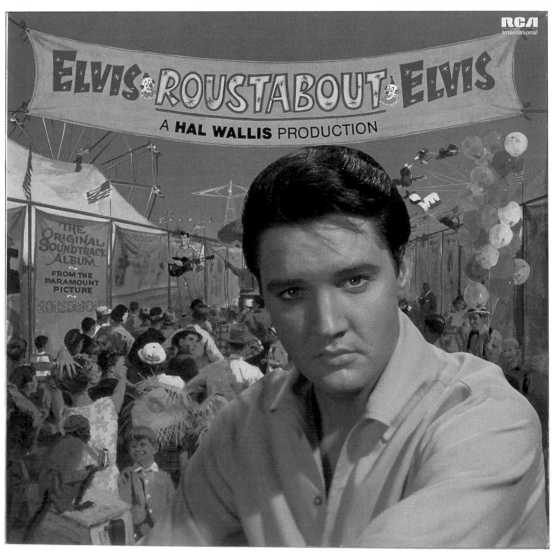

Elvis Country, Elvis Presley. Courtesy RCA Records.

Kenny Price

Known as the Round Mound Of Sound, Price a chunky singer-multi instrumentalist and Hee Haw regular was born in Florence, Kentucky, on May 27, 1931. Reared on a farm in Boone County, Kentucky, he learnt to play a guitar bought from Sears Roebuck and began playing country music at local functions.

Stationed in Korea throughout much of his service career, he successfully auditioned for the Horace Heidt USO Show and upon discharge decided to pursue a serious career in music. After

Below: Kenny Price, a mid-'70s shot of the Round Mound Of Sound.

enrolling at the Cincinnati Conservatory of Music, he joined Cincinnati's WLW in 1954, becoming a regular on the station's Mid-western Hayride for several years – initially as lead singer with the Hometowners, later spending two years as compere – before moving on to Nashville, where he eventually joined the Hee Haw TV show. While with the Hayride he met Bobby Bobo, another cast member, who founded his own company, Boone Records.

Signed to Boone, Price registered an immediate hit with **Walking On New Grass** (1966), that same year obtaining a second Top 10 record with **Happy Tracks**, both songs being Ray Pennington compositions. Further hits for Boone flowed, the biggest of these being **My Goal For Today** (1967). But in 1969 Price

with Presley's frantic, uninhibited vocals. However, he was to keep his country connections, backing each single he released with a country title. Indeed, Charlie Feathers has described Presley's version of **Blue Moon Of Kentucky** as classic rockabilly – bluegrass, speeded up and with a black music feel. Presley was particularly influenced by the blues and by black musicians generally. He tended to dress in the extravagantly-coloured suits of the black street hipsters, this proving an upfront pose that sometimes courted trouble when he began touring in the hardcore redneck South.

That's All Right Mama was doing well locally, where DJ Dewey Phillips had plugged it. A local country agent, Bob Neal, Presley's manager for a while, got him some bookings on local country shows. But it was his next manager, 'Colonel' Tom Parker, a hustling wheeler-dealer who undoubtedly would have been running a medicine show in earlier days, who procured him vital exposure on the prestigious Louisiana Hayride on March 3, 1955. The Hayride was the next most important radio show to the Saturday night Grand Ole Opry from Nashville, which the then 'Hillbilly Cat' was also to play.

He toured on country bills with people like Hank Snow and Johnny Cash and the receptions got wilder, girls trying to get at

Elvis At Madison Square Garden. Courtesy RCA Records.

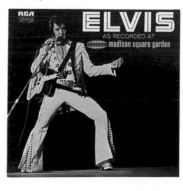

him and tear his clothes. Parker eventually negotiated a deal for him to join the major RCA label and Presley's days as a country-styled rock'n'roller were over as RCA smoothed him gradually into a singer acceptable to both kids and parents.

Although the biggest of superstars, Presley would never again reach those primitive but exciting heights as he settled into a career of Las Vegas concerts and second-rate films. He had taken country music to the limit, making even honky tonk country seem tame by comparison. But in so doing, he badly bruised the country music for many years. However, it is as well conversely to remember country's contribution to rock'n'roll. When archivists came to rediscover the roots of rock years later, they were led to a whole wealth of half-forgotten '50s music and were able to bring it from the shadow of the then prevailing Nashville Sound. Elvis Presley may have utilized black music to launch rock'n'roll but country enthusiasts might argue that he sounded not unlike the fashionable bar room wailers of the day, taken to their wild, bopping conclusion.

Found dead at his Gracelands home in Memphis on August 16, 1977, his death being attributed to 'acute respiratory distress' (though later investigation revealed that drugs may have been a contributory factor) Elvis amassed well over 100 US Top 40 hits during his lifetime, though he was outsold by many on the country chart. Nevertheless, that his contribution to country music history was important is undeniable, as demonstrated by the number of Elvis Presley exhibits (including his solid gold Cadillac) that draw visitors to Nashville's famed Museum of Country Music.

Gracelands, where Elvis laid in state prior to being buried in a mausoleum at Forest Hill Cemetery, in Memphis, was opened to the public in late 1982, the singer's ex-wife claiming that funds were needed to maintain the property.

Albums:
The Sun Sessions (–/RCA)
I'm 10,000 Years Old – Elvis Country (RCA/ RCA)
World Wide 50 Gold Award Hits – four album set (RCA/RCA)

took his happy sound to RCA – two of his 1970 releases, **Biloxi** and **Sheriff of Boone County**, becoming Top 10 entries. During 1972–3 he logged seven further hits but the run began to slow up in 1974 and by 1977 the singer had moved on to MRC Records, where, for a while, it seemed that he might make the climb back into the upper chart brackets. But again his attempt ran out of steam and in 1980 he signed for Dimension, seeing lower chart placings with two singles, **Well Rounded Travellin' Man** and **She's Leavin (And I'm Almost Gone)**.

Albums:
Turn On Your Love Light (RCA/–)
Supersideman (RCA/–)
The Red Foley Songbook (RCA/–)
North East Arkansas Mississippi County Bootlegger (RCA/–)

Ray Price

Born on a farm in Perrybille, East Texas, on January 12, 1926, Ray Noble Price, the 'Cherokee Cowboy', was brought up in the city of Dallas. After high school, he spent several years in the forces, returning to

Below: Ray Price. One of classiest singers, he often works in a dress suit and is backed onstage by a string section.

civilian life in 1946 and attending college with the avowed intention of becoming a veterinary surgeon. However, an able singer-songwriter-guitarist, he began performing at college events and local clubs, eventually making his radio debut as an entertainer in 1948 on station KRBC, Abilene. Later came further exposure on Big D Jamboree, a Dallas show that received some network coverage.

Price began recording for Bullet during the early '50s, his first release being a song called **Jealous Lies**. Then in 1951 came a contract with Columbia, many of his early records reflecting the influence of Hank Williams – Price's band, the Cherokee Cowboys was formed from the remnants of Williams' outfit, the Drifting Cowboys.

By the end of 1952 Price was an Opry regular with two hit singles to his credit – **Talk To Your Heart** and **Don't Let The Stars Get In Your Eyes**, both charting during the year. And though his name was absent from the charts for the next 14 months, in February 1954 he began a run of major hits that continued through to 1973, the most prominent of these being **Crazy Arms** (a 1956 million seller), **I've Got A New Heartache** (1956), **My Shoes Keep Walking Back To You** (1957), **City Lights** (another million seller, 1958), **Heartaches By The Number**, **The Same Old Me** (1959), **One More Time** (1960), **Soft Rain** (1961), **Make The World Go Away** (1963), **Burning**

Hank'n'Me, Ray Price. Courtesy CBS Records.

Memories (1964), **The Other Woman** (1965), **Touch My Heart** (1966), **For The Good Times**, **I Won't Mention It Again** (1970), **I'd Rather Be Sorry** (1971), **Lonesomest Lonesome**, **She's Got To Be A Saint** (1972), and **You're The Best Thing That Ever Happened To Me** (1973), all Columbia releases.

An astute judge of current trends and possessing an ear for up and coming songwriters – he was one of the first to realize Kris Kristofferson's potential – Price realized that country had to appeal to a wider audience in order to forge ahead. Accordingly he began using large back-up units, often employing full string sections, in his plan to take country to a non-country audience. He ditched any pretensions to a cowboy image and began appearing onstage in a dress suit, as though every gig was of Carnegie Hall status. Yet the ballads still sounded as though they came out of Texas and the ploy worked, offending no one but the sort of purists who were still decrying the arrival of the drum-kit.

In 1974 Ray began recording for Myrrh, obtaining a Top 10 single for this mainly gospel label with **Like Old Times Again** and following it with another in **Roses And Love Songs** (1975). He then signed for ABC/Dot and during 1975 had hits on three different labels, Columbia still cashing in on his back-catalogue material. But Price, unwilling to tour as frequently as he once did, had decided to go into semi-retirement. He preferred to spend his time hunting or rearing horses on his Texas ranch. Nevertheless, his records still sold better than most and the ABC/Dot hits continued, albeit at a lower level, through to 1978, when Ray decided to make a comeback, signing to Monument Records and gaining an immediate Top 20 single with **Feet**. During 1979 he provided three more hits, htting the Top 20 again with **That's The Only Way To Say Goodbye**, while in 1980 he teamed with Willie Nelson to cut an excellent duet album that spawned the hit single **Faded Love**. By 1981 Ray had switched to the Dimension label, cutting three hits, including such

Top 10 entrants as **It Don't Hurt Me Half So Bad** and **Diamonds In The Stars**, his 1982 haul containing **Old Friends**, a single made with Roger Miller and Willie Nelson. The following year he had label-jumped yet again, this time to Warner, scoring with two tracks recorded for the soundtrack of the movie 'Honkytonk Man', and next he turned up on Viva, his 1984 trio of chart records being labelled as by 'Ray Price And The Cherokee Cowboys'. But, despite such a long and distinguished career, Ray has only landed one CMA Award: in 1971 being adjudged maker of the Album Of The Year for **I Won't Mention It Again**.

Albums:
Greatest Hits (Columbia/CBS)
Greatest Hits Vol. 2 (Columbia/–)
For The Good Times (Columbia/CBS)
Willie Nelson And Ray Price (Columbia/ CBS)
Like Old Times Again (Myrrh/–)
Hank'n'Me (ABC/–)

Charley Pride

Easily the most successful black entertainer to emerge from the country music scene, Charley Pride was born on a Delta cotton farm in Sledge, Mississippi, March 18, 1938. One of 11 children, Pride picked cotton alongside his parents during his boyhood days, eventually saving enough cash to purchase a $10 Silvertone guitar from Sears Roebuck. Despite being born in blues territory, Pride preferred playing country music – but it was to baseball, not show business, that he turned initially – playing for the Memphis Red Sox as a pitcher and outfield player in 1954. Two years later, he was drafted into the forces, during this period marrying Rozene, a girl he met in Memphis. Returning to civilian life in 1959, he quit baseball following a wage disagreement, becoming a construction worker for a time. Several jobs later he settled down in Helena, Montana, working at a zinc smelting plant, also playing semi-pro ball in the Pioneer League. And though he continued efforts to break into major

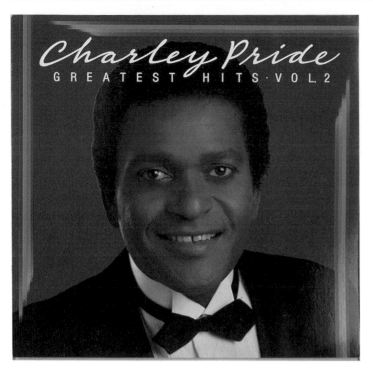

Greatest Hits Vol. 2. Charley Pride
Courtesy RCA.

league ball, he was turned down by the California Angels in 1961 and by the New York Mets, a year later.

However, his secondary career reaped some reward when, in 1963, Pride sang a song on a local show headed by Red Sovine and Red Foley, earning praise from Sovine, who urged him to try his luck in Nashville. Taking this advice, Pride made the move, Chet Atkins eventually hearing some of his demo tapes and signing him to RCA.

Pride's first RCA single, **Snakes Crawl At Night**, was released with little in the way of accompanying publicity in December 1965, few of the DJs who played the disc realizing that the singer was anything but pure Caucasian. But, by the following Spring, the Mississippian

Everybody's Choice, Charley Pride.
Courtesy RCA.

was nationally known after coming up with **Just Between You And Me**, his performance gaining him a Grammy nomination. A couple of hits later, in January 1967, and he was on the Opry, his introduction, by Ernest Tubb, receiving a warm reception.

As the '70s rolled in, Pride reached superstar status. Having logged five No. 1s in a row with **All I Have To Offer Is Me**, **I'm So Afraid Of Losing You** (1969), **Is Anybody Goin' To San Antone?**, **Wonder Could I Live There Anymore** and **I Can't Believe That You've Stopped Loving Me** (1970), he was adjudged Performer Of The Year 1971, by the CMA, also winning the association's Male Vocalist Of The Year award, a title he retained in 1972.

Basically a honky tonk singer who, like many others, moved towards a smoother, more pop-oriented country sound, Pride has proved one of the most consistent record sellers on the RCA roster, his No. 1 records alone being: **I'd Rather Love You**, **I'm Just Me**, **Kiss An Angel Good Mornin'**

(1971); **It's Gonna Take A Little Bit Longer**, **She's Too Good To Be True** (1972); **A Shoulder To Cry On**, **Don't Fight The Feelings Of Love**, **Amazing Love** (1973); **Then Who Am I?** (1974); **Hope You're Feelin' Me** (1975); **My Eyes Can Only See As Far As You** (1976); **She's Just An Old Love Turned Memory**, **I'll Be Leaving Alone**, **More To Me** (1977); **Someone Loves You Honey** (1978), **Where Do I Put Her Memory?**, **You're My Jamaica** (1979); **Honky Tonk Blues**, **You Win Again** (1980); **Never Been So Loved (In All My Life)**, **Mountain Of Love** (1981); **You're So Good When You're Bad**, **Why Baby Why?** (1982); and **Night Games** (1983).

The possessor of a warm baritone voice, Charley Pride sounds as pure country as Hank Williams, a hero whom he honoured in 1980 via **There's A Little Bit Of Hank In Me**, a No. 1 album containing some excellent versions of songs associated with the legendary Williams. Paradoxically, he had become RCA's biggest-selling country act since Elvis Presley – a country boy who tried his hardest to sound black.

Albums:
(Country) Charley Pride (RCA/RCA)
There's A Little Bit Of Hank In Me (RCA/RCA)
Greatest Hits (RCA/RCA)
The Best Of Charlie Pride Vol. 2 (RCA/RCA)

Ronnie Prophet

Described by Chet Atkins as 'the greatest one-man show I've seen', singer-guitarist Prophet was born near Montreal, Canada, on 26 December, 1937, and raised on a farm at Calumet. He began playing at square dances in his early teens and soon moved to Montreal, later playing club dates in Fort Lauderdale, his first Nashville appearance coming in 1969.

He obtained a residency at Nashville's Carousel Club, his drawing power proving such that the venue became renamed Ronnie Prophet's Carousel Club. His first American album was released on RCA in 1976, the LP containing such tracks as **Shine On**, **Sanctuary** and **It's Enough**, all US hit singles. He played the British

Music, also being booked for Mervyn Conn's 15-date Nashville Cavalcade British tour.

Since that time, Prophet, a major figure on the Canadian scene, has enhanced his standing in Europe, been given his own BBC-TV series and also been booked for further British dates.

Albums:
Ronnie Prophet (RCA/RCA)
Ronnie Prophet Country (RCA/RCA)

Jeanne Pruett

Jeanne, a singer-songwriter from Pell City, Alabama, was one of 10 children who spent a fair proportion of their childhood indulging in harmony vocals or joining their mother and father in listening to the Opry on an old battery radio. She first headed for Nashville in 1956, along with her husband Jack, a guitarist who played lead guitar with Marty Robbins for almost 14 years.

It was Robbins who was responsible for her being signed to RCA Records in 1963, at which time she cut six titles. And though there was little reaction, the following year found her making her debut on the Grand Ole Opry.

Despite spending much of her time raising her children, Jeanne continued writing and performing, eventually securing a new record contract with Decca in 1969 and enjoying a minor hit in 1971 with **Hold On To My Unchanging Love**.

But the real breakthrough came in 1973 when the recording of **Satin Sheets** became a phenomenal seller, crossing over to enter the pop charts. Nominated for four CMA Awards that year, on July 21 she became the 63rd member of the Opry, celebrating this with another Top 10 single in **I'm Your Woman**.

Throughout the rest of the '70s, Jeanne graced the country charts with such MCA singles as **You Don't Need To Move A Mountain** (1974), **A Poor Man's Woman** (1975), and **I'm Living A Lie** (1977),

Below: Jeanne Pruett. She worked with Marty Robbins for several years.

Ronnie Prophet. The all-rounder's debut RCA album.

Wembley Festival of 1978 and broke the place up, looning around with compère George Hamilton IV ('your flies are open, George'), playing **Yankee Doodle** and **Dixie** simultaneously while singing **Silent Night**, also regaling the audience with his **Harold The Horny Toad**, a hilarious tale that came complete with electronic gimmickry. The following year he was asked back to compère all three days at the 11th International Festival of Country

Pure Prairie League

Formed in Cincinnati in 1971, this country-rock band took their name from a Women's Temperance Society that appeared in an Errol Flynn movie. Their trademark, which decorated all of their album covers, was 'Luke', an oldtimer originally created by 'Saturday Evening Post' artist Norman Rockwell.

League signed for RCA, the line-up then

Pure Prairie League (RCA). Norman Rockwell provided the sleeve.

Welcome To The Sunshine, Jeanne Pruett. Courtesy MCA.

switching to Mercury for a while then making something of a comeback with **Back To Back** (1979), **Temporarily Yours** and **It's Too Late** (both 1980), three IBC releases that all went Top 10. But a shift to the Paid label in 1981 resulted in lower chart placings, since which time Jeanne's name has appendaged no hits of any description. She still tours, however, and spends much of her spare time either cooking – an art in which she is reputedly up to gourmet standard – or winning prizes for her garden plants and vegetables.

Albums:
Encore (IBC/RCA)
Introducing Jeanne Pruett (–/MCA)

Riley Puckett

One of the pioneers of recorded old-time music, George Riley Puckett was born in Alpharetta, Georgia, on May 7, 1884. When only three months old he suffered an eye infection and following incorrect treatment of the ailment lost his sight. Educated at a school for the blind in Macon, Georgia, he learnt to play five-string banjo, later moving on to guitar. During the early '20s, Puckett worked with a band led by fiddle player Clayton McMichen, then joined Gid Tanner's Skillet Lickers in 1924, remaining featured vocalist with the outfit until its disbandment some 10 years later. Puckett's many solo recordings include **Rock All Our Babies To Sleep**, reputed to be one of the first discs to feature a country yodeller, cut three years prior to Jimmie Rodgers' initial sessions.

From 1934 to 1941, Puckett recorded for RCA Victor – also cutting a few sides for Decca in 1937 – and worked on radio stations in Georgia, West Virginia, Kentucky and Tennessee up to his death in East Point Georgia, on July 13, 1946. At the time of his death, caused by blood poisoning from an infected boil on his neck, Puckett was working with a band called the Stone Mountain Cowboys, on

radio station WACA, Atlanta.

His exuberant – sometimes even wild – bass-run guitar style was very influential on country guitarists of his day, the forerunner of the pulsing style which characterizes bluegrass.

Albums:
The Skillet Lickers Vols 1 & 2 (Country/–)
Riley Puckett (Old Homestead/–)

Below: Pure Prairie League – the John David Call, Mike Reilly, William Frank Hinds, Larry Goshorn, George Ed Powell and Michael O'Connor line-up of the early 1970s.

Pure Prairie League Collection. Courtesy RCA Records.

being Craig Fuller (guitars, vocals), George Ed Powell (guitars, vocals), Jim Lanham (bass, vocals), Jim Caughlan (drums) and John David Call (steel guitar). By the time their second album, **Bustin' Out**, appeared, only Fuller and Powell remained from the original band.

In 1973, after further personnel problems, PPL ceased recording and their record company thought they had broken up. But the group continued playing live dates and caused such a response by these appearances that RCA was forced

to reissue **Bustin' Out**, plus **Amie**, a single taken from the album, the latter going into the US pop charts during 1975.

That year, the group, then comprising original members Fuller and Call plus Larry Goshorn (lead guitar), Michael Connor (keyboards), Mike Reilly (bass) and William Frank Hinds (drums), cut **Two Lane Highway**, an album that featured such guests as Chet Atkins, Emmylou Harris, Johnny Gimble and Don Felder. But, despite further albums and the odd hit like **That'll Be The Way** (1976), the line-up continued to fluctuate, Powell quitting in 1977 along with Larry Goshorn and his brother Timmy Goshorn, who had earlier replaced Call. The band, by then West Coast based, regrouped yet again, one of the new members being singer-songwriter and multi-instrumentalist Vince Gill (born Oklahoma City, Oklahoma, April 1957), who had earlier worked with Boone Creek and Byron Berline's band.

By 1980, still unable to make the breakthrough that would take them up a notch on the concert circuits, PPL moved on to the Casablanca label. The switch brought the band immediate benefits. By the middle of the year they had gone Top

10 in the pop charts with **Let Me Love You Tonight**, following this with other major pop hits in **I'm Almost Ready** (1980) and **Still Right Here In My Heart** (1981). But Gill left first to work with Rodney Crowell and Rosanne Cash and then to pursue a solo career with RCA, and soon PPL were having problems once more and searching for a label deal.

Albums:
Pure Prairie League (RCA/RCA)
Bustin' Out (RCA/RCA)
Two Lane Highway (RCA/RCA)
Dance (RCA/RCA)
Just Fly (RCA/RCA)

Eddie Rabbitt

Considered by many pundits to be pure MOR, singer Eddie Rabbitt (real name Edward Thomas, born in Brooklyn, New York on November 27, 1944) has, nevertheless, won many friends among country music buyers.

A onetime truck driver, soda jerk, boat helper and fruit picker, Rabbitt recorded for 20th Century Fox and Columbia during the 1960s. He achieved little until, as a staff writer with music publishers Hill and Range, he wrote **Kentucky Rain**, which Elvis Presley recorded and turned into a hit (1970). In 1973, Ronnie Milsap waxed Rabbitt's **Pure Love** and grabbed a No. 1, this leading to the New Yorker gaining an Elektra recording contract of his own and getting his chart career underway with **You Get To Me**, a middle-order hit.

By 1975, his records were hitting the Top 20, the first No. 1 being with **Drinkin' My Baby (Off My Mind)** in 1976, a year in which Rabbitt also went Top 10 with

Below: Eddie Rabbitt. He once wrote hits for Elvis Presley and Ronnie Milsap.

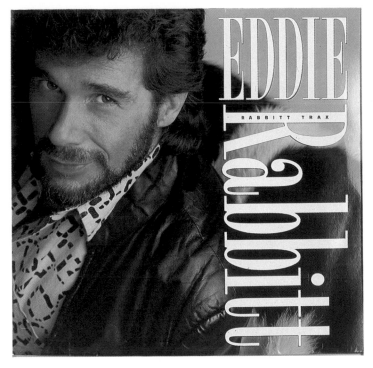

Rabbitt Trax, Eddie Rabbitt. Courtesy RCA Records.

Rocky Mountain Music and **Two Dollars In The Jukebox**. But the best was yet to come for, in the wake of three more Top 10 singles, he provided Elektra with three chart-toppers in a row during 1978 – **You Don't Love Me Anymore**, **I Just Want to Love You** and **Every Which Way But Loose**, the latter being the title track of a Clint Eastwood movie. There was another No 1 in 1979, **Suspicions**, three in 1980: **Gone too Far**, **Drivin' My Life Away** and **I Love A Rainy Day** (the latter topping the US pop charts and also becoming a

British hit); and two more in 1981: **Step By Step** and **Someone Could Lose A Heart Tonight**, Rabbitt's **Step By Step** album becoming the best-selling album in the country market.

He became guest host on the late IV show 'The Midnight Special' and even had a TV special of his own. But CMA Award nominations never came his way. Rabbitt was still a pop kid whom Nashville was allowing to play with its toys – albeit in a fashion that paid off pretty well.

Not that the lack of acclaim in Music City meant much to Rabbitt. He just kept on doing the thing he was good at – notching hits. And in 1982 he notched a couple more; one, a duet with Crystal Gayle (**You And I**), providing the singer with yet another chart-topper that crossed over into the pop listings.

So far he has hardly faltered. He supplied another No. 1 in 1983, **You Can't Run From Love**, and yet another in 1984, **I Got Mexico**, while during 1985 Rabbitt notched two Top 10 records with **Warning Sign** and **She's Comin' Back To Say Goodbye**. But still (gold records apart) his awards cupboard stays somewhat bare.

Albums:
Rabbitt (Elektra/Elektra)
Loveline (Elektra/Elektra)
Radio Romance (Elektra/Mercury)
Step By Step (Elektra/Mercury)
Horizon (Elektra/Elektra)

Marvin Rainwater

Of Indian ancestry, Rainwater – a singer and prolific songwriter who also plays guitar and piano – became a star during the 1950s, when several of his records sold well over a million each. Born in Wichita, Kansas on July 2, 1925, his real name was Marvin Percy, Rainwater being his mother's maiden name which he later adopted for his stage work. Although he was always interested in music as a child and began composing songs at the age of eight, he actually began his career by training as a veterinary surgeon, becoming a pharmacist's mate in the Navy during World War II. Upon dis-

Gonna Find Me A Bluebird, Marvin Rainwater. Courtesy MGM Records.

charge, he opted for a career in the music business, his first major breakthrough coming in 1946 when he debuted on Red Foley's Ozark Jubilee Radio Show, that station receiving so many enquiries about 'that singer with the Indian name' that Rainwater was signed to a regular spot on the programme.

During the early 1950s, he began touring and cutting records for Four Star and Coral, another high point in his career occurring when he entered the Arthur Godfrey CBS Talent Scout TV Show in 1955 and was brought back for four consecutive weeks, this gaining him a position on Godfrey's morning radio show.

In January, 1956, he signed with MGM Records and with his second release, the self-penned **Gonna Find Me A Bluebird**, won his first gold disc. Promoted by MGM as a full-blooded Cherokee brave, Rainwater then usually appeared bedecked in Indian head-dress and similar paraphernalia. And the idea seemed to work for him because in 1958 his rocking **Whole Lotta Woman** became a world-wide hit, reaching the top of the British charts and ensuring Rainwater a season headlining at the London Palladium. However, in the USA reaction to the disc was mixed and some radio shows banned the song as being 'too suggestive'.

Soon after – following another million seller with his version of John D. Loudermilk's **Half-Breed** (1959) – Rainwater and MGM parted company, the singer moving on to record for such labels as Warner Brothers, UA, Warwick and his own Brave Records, with little success. Then in the mid-1960s came a serious throat ailment that resulted in an operation, after which Rainwater was not to record for nearly four years.

In 1971 he again visited Britain, recording an album with UK band, Country Fever. Since that time he has been a constant visitor to Britain, like George Hamilton and Vernon Oxford, enjoying a higher reputation in Europe than in his homeland.

Especially For You, Marvin Rainwater. Courtesy Westwood Records.

Albums:
Rockin' Rolling Rainwater (–/Bear Family)
With A Heart With A Beat (–/Bear Family)

Boots Randolph

A premier Nashville session man, Homer Louis 'Boots' Randolph III, born in Paducah, Kentucky, originally learnt to play trombone but later switched to saxophone, playing first in a high school unit then in bands throughout the middle west.

Eventually he was spotted by Homer and Jethro, who saw him at a Decatur, Illinois club and promptly relayed their enthusiasm to Chet Atkins. Later, Atkins was to hear a tape of Randolph playing **Chicken Reel** in his good-timey, slap-tongued style, and was similarly impressed. He invited Randolph to Nashville and enthused about the sax-man's talents to his friends. Within a few days, Owen Bradley hired him for a Brenda Lee session and from then on he became a much-sought-after sessioner and an established part of the Nashville Sound, recording as a solo act for both RCA and Monument.

In 1963 he obtained a major hit with **Yakety Sax,** following this with such other pop successes as **Mr Sax Man** (1964), **The Shadow Of Your Smile** (1966) and **Temptation** (1967). But perhaps the most interesting Randolph disc, at least to country fans, is **Country Boots,** a 1974 album made in the company of Maybelle Carter, Chet Atkins, Uncle Josh Graves and a host of other stellar pickers. The majority of his other album releases fall outside the scope of this book.

Below: Eddy Raven. During the 1960s, he played in blues bands headed by Edgar and Johnny Winter.

Country Livin', Rattlesnake Annie. Courtesy Rattlesnake Records.

Rattlesnake Annie

A singer whose stage name comes from her habit of wearing a rattlesnake's rattler on her ear, her real name is Annie McGowan and she was born in Tennessee of Cherokee Indian heritage. From a poor family who worked in the tobacco and cotton fields near Puryear, she grew up in a home music-making environment, Annie singing and playing piano at the local church. At the age of 12 she and two cousins formed The Gallimore Sisters and had their own radio show on a Paris, Tennessee, station.

Later, Annie headed for Memphis where she sang the blues on Beale Street, travelling through the South and ending up in Austin, where she befriended Willie Nelson, Billy Joe Shaver and David Allan Coe, the latter co-writing **Texas Lullaby** with Annie and recording it on his 1976 **Long Haired Redneck** album.

The first woman from the West to record a country album in Czechoslovakia – she has a cult following in Europe and has made a brace of highly-acclaimed appearances at the UK's Wembley Festival, in 1986 blues-duetting with Bill Munroe – she released a brilliantly conceived album, **Rattlesnakes And Rusty Water,** on her own Rattlesnake label during 1980. Featuring such guests as John Hartford, Josh Graves, Vassar Clements and Charlie McCoy, and merging blues and traditional country in a fashion Jimmie Rodgers would have approved of, it was voted one of the year's 10 best releases by British country buffs – even though it was on import only!

Nowadays a resident of Nashville, albeit one without a major record deal, Rattlesnake Annie is, in terms of reaching into the past and repackaging it country music's Tom Waits.

Albums:
Rattlesnakes And Rusty Water
    (Rattlesnake/–)
Country Livin' (Rattlesnake/–)

Eddy Raven

Eddy was born and raised in the bayou country of southern Louisiana, one of nine children whose father travelled all over the South as a musician and trucker. At seven Eddy had his first guitar and at 13 his first band. Although his father advised him towards country music, Eddy followed the prevailing rock'n'roll path, even though he was concerned about lyrics.

He lived in Georgia and had his own radio slot on WHAB, even gaining a local hit on the Cosmo label. Then his father moved the family back to Layfayette, Louisiana, where Eddy met Lake Charles record entrepreneur, Bobby Charles, and

This Is Eddy Raven. Courtesy MCA/Dot Records.

wrote a country-blues hit for him which sold 60,000 on Charles' label.

After an experimental period in the 1960s when Eddy performed all around the Gulf Coast (at one time playing with albino brothers Edgar and Johnny Winter), he tired of travelling and, in 1970, went to Nashville where fellow cajun, Jimmy 'C' Newman, put him on to Acuff-Rose.

Eddy's first writing success was **Country Green,** which provided a hit for Don Gibson. He did likewise for Jeannie C. Riley (**Good Morning Country Rain**) and Don Gibson again (**Touch The Morning**). A one-time lounge performer at Nashville's King Of The Road Inn, he became a headliner and grabbed the attention of ABC Records, a label for whom he began providing hits in 1974 (starting with **The Last Of The Sunshine Cowboys),** continuing in a moderately successful way with two or three middle of the chart hits each year, through to 1976. Meanwhile, his songwriting activity continued to pay off through the records of others like Roy Clark, Roy Orbison, Moe Bandy, Connie Smith and Roy Acuff.

In an effort to get his own recording career into higher gear, Eddy signed for Monument in 1978, gaining just one mini-hit with **You're A Dancer.** He switched again, this time to Dimension, and at last began really chart-climbing, one 1980 single, **Dealin' With The Devil,** gaining him access to the Top 25 for the first time. A year later he was on Elektra and reaching even higher through releases such as **I Should Have Called** and **Who Do You Know In California?**

By 1982, 12 years after making the trip to Nashville, he made his Top 10 debut with **She's Playing Hard To Forget.** But the long hard climb to the very top was not achieved until 1984, when Raven, now with yet another record company, RCA, got to No.1 with **I Got To Mexico,** following this with such other Top 10 entries as **I Could Use Another You, She's Gonna Win Your Heart** (1984), **You Should Have Been Gone By Now** and **I Wanna Hear It From You** (1985).

Eddy Raven is perhaps one of the most celebrated examples of the Robert The Bruce theory winning through in recent country music history. And when Billboard reported, in mid-1984, that the singer "because of his artistic longevity, was able to turn his 55-minute showcase into a triumphant 'best of' display with no filler and no slow spots", nobody doubted that this was the truth and nothing but.

Albums:
I Could Use Another You (RCA/–)
That Cajun Country Sound (La Louisianne/–)
This Is Eddie Raven (Dot/–)
Eyes (Dimension/–)
Desperate Dreams (Elektra/–)

Ko-Ko Joe, Jerry Reed. Courtesy RCA Records.

Susan Raye

Above: Susan Raye, a long-time regular on the Buck Owens Show, had a number of hit singles 60s–70s.

A long time regular on 'Hee Haw' and the Buck Owens Show, singer Susan Raye had a number of hit singles during the late 1960s and early 1970s. Once a member of a rock group, Raye (born in Eugene, Oregon in 1944) switched to country after auditioning and winning a regular spot

Love Sure Feels Good, Susan Raye. Courtesy Capitol Records.

with a radio station that was looking for a country singer. Later, after stints as a DJ and nightclub singer, she was invited to Bakersfield to meet Buck Owens, whose show she joined. She also gained a contract with Capitol, her first release, **Maybe If I Closed My Eyes** (1969), being an Owens original.

Her other hits have included a series of duets with Ownes plus such Top 20 solo efforts as **L.A. International Airport, Pitty, Pitty, Patter, (I've Got A Happy Heart)** (1971), **My Heart Has A Mind Of Its Own, Wheel Of Fortune, Love Sure Feels Good In My Heart** (1972), **Cheating Game** (1973), **Stop The World (And Let Me Off),** and **Whatcha Gonna Do With A Dog Like That** (1974), all on Capitol. Later she signed with UA without too much in the way of results. But by 1984, her name still appeared in the charts, aboard **Put Another Notch In Your Belt,** a Westexas release.

Albums:
Best Of Susan Raye (Capitol/–)
Whatcha Gonna Do With A Dog Like That (Capitol/–)

Jerry Reed

One of Nashville's most remarkable guitarmen, Reed was born Jerry Hubbard in Atlanta, Georgia on March 20, 1937. A cotton mill worker in his early days, he began playing at local Atlanta clubs, obtaining a record contract with Capitol in 1955 and cutting some rockabilly tracks. However, these made little impact, Reed's first claim to fame arising through his songwriting ability, predominantly with **Crazy Legs** which Gene Vincent waxed in 1956. Following a two-year stint in the forces, Reed then settled in Nashville, there providing Columbia with two minor 1962 hits in **Goodnight Irene** and **Hully Gully Guitars.**

The Uptown Polka Club, Jerry Reed. Courtesy RCA Records.

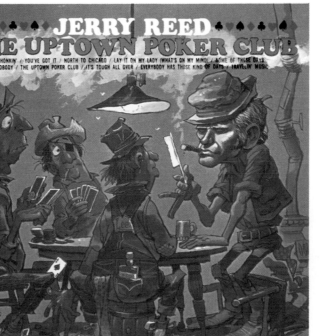

Establishing himself as a superior sessionman, Reed was signed to RCA as a solo act in 1965, his first hit for the label being the rocking **Guitar Man** (1967), which Elvis Presley covered in 1968 thus providing the song with pop chart status. That same year, Presley also scored with **US Male,** another Reed composition. The Georgian's own records all sold increasingly well, **Tupelo Mississippi Flash** (1967), **Remembering** (1968), **Are You From Dixie?** (1969), **Talk About The Good Times** (1970) and **Georgia Sunshine** (1970) all reaching high chart positions. Then, late in 1970, came **Amos Moses,** one of Reed's swamp-rock specials. The song proved to be a Top 10 pop hit and resulted in Reed being nominated CMA Instrumentalist Of The Year. He also won a Grammy for Best Country Male Vocal Performance of 1970.

A maker of somewhat erratic albums – Reed tends to mix hard-headed rockers with sunshiny singalongs – his guitar duet LPs with Chet Atkins, cut during the mid-1970s, resulted in some fine music. Additionally, he has become much acclaimed as an actor, an appearance in 'WW And The Dixie Dance Kings' (1974) resulting in an association with Burt Reynolds that his since seen the duo pairing in 'Gator' (1976), 'Smokey And The Bandit' (1977) and 'Smokey And The Bandit II' (1980). A performer with a larger-than-life personality, Reed has also starred alongside Claude Akins in a TV series 'Nashville 99' and has continued his hit single way with such Top 10 records as

When You're Hot, You're Hot (No.1, 1971), **Lord Mr Ford** (No.1, 1973), **East Bound And Down** (1977), **(I Love You) What Can I Say?** (1978), **She Got The Goldmine (I Got The Shaft)** (No.1, 1982) and **The Birds** (1982), 1984 proving to be the first year since 1967 that failed to provide Reed with chart action of any kind.

Albums:
Me And Chet – with Chet Atkins (RCA/ RCA)
20 Of The Best (–/RCA)

Del Reeves

Singer-Songwriter, multi instrumentalist, Franklin Delano Reeves was born in Sparta, North Carolina on July 14, 1934. At the age of 12 he had his own radio show in North Carolina. Then, after attending Appalachian State College and spending four years in the Air Force, he became a regular on the Chester Smith TV show in California.

By the late 1950s, Reeves had his own TV show which he fronted for four years before moving to Nashville, signing for Frank Sinatra's Reprise label (the first country artist to do so) and writing songs with his wife Ellen Schiell Reeves – these being recorded by Carl Smith, Sheb Woolley, Roy Drusky and others. Reeves own initial hit single came with **Be Quiet Mind,** a 1961 Decca release. But, despite label changes and a couple of minor chart entries on Reprise and Columbia, it was not until 1965 and a contract with UA that he obtained his first No.1 with **Girl On The Billboard.**

In October, 1966, just four hits later, Reeves became a member of the Grand Ole Opry, his reputation as a hit artist being maintained by a stream of chart singles that included such Top 10 records as **Looking At The World Through A Windshield, Good Time Charlies** (1968), **Be Glad** (1969) and **The Philadelphia Fillies** (1971). Del continued supplying such hits for UA – albeit of an increasingly low chart order – right through to 1978, cutting duets with Penny DeHaven and Billie Jo Spears.

By 1980 he was on the Koala label and

The Del Reeves Album, Courtesy UA Records.

back in the charts once more, logging minor hits – the biggest of these being **Slow Hand** (1981) – through to 1982.

Del Reeves has often been tagged 'The Dean Martin of Country Music' because of his laid-back stage manner. The multi-talented Reeves has, along the way, appeared in such movies as 'Second Fiddle To A Steel Guitar', 'Sam Whiskey', 'Cottonpickin' Chickenpickers' and 'Forty Acre Feud'.

Del Reeves

Live At The Palamino, Del Reeves. Courtesy UA Records.

Albums:
Live At The Palamino (UA/–)
10th Anniversary (UA/–)
By Request – with Billie Jo Spears (UA/–)

Goebel Reeves

An early century Woody Guthrie figure, Reeves, known as the Texas Drifter, specialized in songs of hobos and hard times, writing from his own experience on the road.

Born in Sherman, Texas, on October 9, 1899, he came from a solid middle-class background but chose to live a rough travelling life. After a stint in the army, during which time he saw front-line action in World War I, he wandered around the USA, noting the things he saw and eventually turning his thoughts into songs, some of which he recorded for the Okeh and Brunswick labels. He played in vaudeville, the main outlet for music at that time, and also did some radio work. He claimed to have taught Jimmie Rodgers his yodelling style. His songs include **Hobo's Lullaby, Hobo And The Cop, Railroad Boomer, Bright Sherman Valley** and **Cowboy's Prayer.** A one-time member of the Workers Of The World Organisation, he died in California in 1959.

Jim Reeves

Originally a stone country singer, smooth-toned Jim Reeves from Texas reached amazing heights as a pop ballad singer and since his death in an air crash his fame has burgeoned into cult proportions.

James Travis Reeves was born on August 20, 1923, in Galloway, Panola County, Texas. His father died when he was young and his mother supported a large family by working in the fields. Early in his life he heard the sound of Jimmie Rodgers on the phonograph and thus was born his interest in music. He acquired a

guitar at the age of five; it had strings missing but an oil construction worker fitted it up for him and taught him some basic chords. At nine he made his first radio broadcast, a 15-minute programme on a Shreveport, Louisiana, station.

At high school in Cathage, Texas, he was just as interested in sport as in music and became star of the school baseball team, although he still performed at local dances and other events. He entered the University of Texas in Austin, and his baseball prowess as a pitcher soon attracted the attention of the St Louis Cardinals scouts who signed him up. But an unlucky slip on a wet pitch gave him an ankle injury that was to halt his career.

In 1947 he met and married school-teacher Mary White, who encouraged his musical interest. Jim had majored from university in phonetics and pronunciation and now sought a job in radio, becoming a DJ and newsreader at station KGRI in Henderson, Texas. He aspired to the position of Assistant Manager (and later bought the station).

Jim then made a momentous journey. He and Mary, having decided to make a determined effort to further Jim's career, drove out in their car and, at the crossroads of Highway 80 in Texas, they tossed a coin to determine whether to proceed to Dallas or Shreveport. Shreveport won and Jim moved there,

The Abbott Recordings, Jim Reeves. Courtesy RCA Records.

ending up with a job as announcer on KWKH, the station that owned the Louisiana Hayride.

It was one of Reeves' jobs to announce the Saturday night Hayride show and he was even allowed to sing occassionally. One night in 1952, Hank Williams failed to arrive and Jim was asked to fill in. In the audience was Fabor Robinson, owner of Abbott Records, who immediately signed Reeves to a contract. Jim had already made four obscure sides for the Macy label (belonging to a Houston chain store) – these records only coming to light in 1966. However, his Abbott deal soon began bearing fruit, via **Mexican Joe,** his

Below: Jim Reeves. His hit duet with Patsy Cline was recorded many years after the twosome had died in plane crashes.

period including **I'm Getting Better** (1960), **Losing Your Love** (1961), **Adios Amigo** (1962), **I'm Gonna Change Everything** (1962), **Is This Me?** (1963), **Guilty** (1963) and **Welcome To My World** (1964). But on a flight back to Nashville from Arkansas on July 31, 1964, following the negotiation of a property deal, Jim and his manager Dean Manuel reported that their single engine plane had run into heavy rain while crossing remote hills just a few miles from Nashville's Beery Field airport. The plane was making its approach to land at five pm when it disappeared from the airport radar screen. A search was instigated involving 12 planes, two helicopters and a ground party of 400. But it was not until two days later that the wreckage and the bodies were discovered amid thick foliage.

On August 2, 1964, services were held for Reeves and Manuel, most of the country music fraternity being present. Jim's body was flown back to Cathage where hundreds filed past the coffin. Honorary pall bearers included Chet Atkins and Steve Sholes, the man who had signed him to RCA.

But the legend lived on and Reeves' records continued to hit the charts, his after-death No.1s outnumbering those made while he was alive and including **I Guess I'm Crazy** (1964), **This Is It, Is It Really Over?** (both 1965), **Distant Drums, Blue Side of Lonesome** (both 1966) and **I Won't Come In While He's There** (1967). Voted into the Country Music Hall of Fame in 1967, Reeves continued to log hits as the 1970s moved in, going Top 10 with **Angels Don't Lie** (1970), **Missing You** (1972), **Don't Let Me Cross Over** and **Oh How I Miss You Tonight** (both 1979). And even in the 1980s, Reeves' name has cropped up in the Top 10 via electronically created duets with Deborah Allen **(Take Me In Your Arms And Hold Me** – 1980) and Patsy Cline **(Have You Ever Been Lonely?** – 1981).

Albums:
The Abbott Recordings Vol.1 (–/RCA)
The Abbott Recordings Vol.2 (–/RCA)
50 All-Time Worldwide Favourites – four album set (RCA/RCA)

Bobby G. Rice

Rice started in rock'n'roll and although he later switched to country, his records have often retained a strong commercial feel. Born in Boscobel, Wisconsin on July 11, 1944, he grew up on a farm with four sisters and a brother, all musically minded. They ran a popular dance hall called the Circle D and by the mid-1950s had their own radio show on WRCO, Richmond, a gig that lasted for seven years.

The family broke up in 1964 when two sisters married and Rice then formed a duo with his sister Lorraine, adapting to a more country style and doing local TV. When his sister quit, he formed the Bobby Rice Band and was signed by Royal American Records, 1970 seeing such country chart hits as **Sugar Shack,** a version of Bruce Chanel's **Hey Baby, A Hundred Pounds of Clay** and **Lover Please**. Royal American was purchased by Metromedia, for which label Rice scored with **You Lay So Easy On My Mind** (1972) and **You Give Me You** (1973). The vocalist-guitarist-banjoman moved on to GRT in 1975 and kept up his tally of major hit singles with **Write Me A Letter** and

Distant Drums, Jim Reeves. Courtesy RCA Records.

second release, which went to No.1 in the country charts during 1953. That same year he also released **Bimbo**, one of the 36 tracks he recorded for Abbott. This too sold well and attracted the attention of RCA who signed him in 1955 amid considerable competition. That same year, he joined the Grand Ole Opry at the recommendation of Ernest Tubb and Hank Snow.

A string of country hits followed and from the release of **Yonder Comes A Sucker** in 1955 through to 1969, Reeves' name was never absent from the country chart, virtually every hit going Top 20 and most Top 10. The February, 1957 release of **Four Walls** proved the real turning point. That year, Reeves had undertaken a European tour in the company of The Browns, Del Wood and Hank Locklin and was unaware the song had hit both pop and country fields, earning him his third gold disc. He returned to find radio and TV offers in abundance, including a spot on NBC-TV's prestigious Bandstand Show. He also gained his own daily show on ABC-TV.

In the wake of **Billy Bayou**, a 1958 No.1, Reeves recorded his all-time greatest hit, **He'll Have To Go**, a 1959 chartbuster. The theme was familiar enough. Some years earlier it might have been called a honky-tonk song. But the treatment, with Reeves' dark, intimate, velvet tones gliding over a muted backing, was something different again. The result brought him international stardom.

Over the next few years, Jim travelled to every state in American and to most parts of the world. His 1962 tour of South Africa with Chet Atkins and Floyd Cramer reportedly broke every known attendance record in the entertainment field.

During 1963 he returned to South Africa

20 Of The Best, Jim Reeves, Courtesy RCA Records.

to star in his only film, 'Kimberley Jim', the story of a con man in South Africa's diamond strike era. He had not toured British venues in these years because of Musicians' Union restrictions, but in 1964 he arrived in Britain for some TV dates and to promote his current single, **I Love You Because**. During the early 1960s, he also continued to dominate the US country charts, some of his many hits during this

Freda Comes, Freda Goes (1975), plus such lower chart entries as **Pick Me Up On Your Way Down** (1976), and **Just One Kiss Magdelena** (1977). Since then he has signed for Republic (1978), Sunbird (1979) and Charta (1981), providing each with moderately successful singles

Albums:
She Sure Laid the Lonelies On Me (GRT/–)
Instant Rice (GRT/–)

Charlie Rich

Originally a cult favourite in the field of rockabilly, in the mid-1970s Rich, for a while, became the darling of the 'countrypolitan' crossover set.

Born in Forrest City, Arkansas on December 14, 1932, the 'Silver Fox' (his hair turned prematurely white at 23) was the son of a hard-drinking father and a Bible-thumping mother. Legend has it that at the age of seven he hid out in the hills for three days after seeing his brother killed by a tractor. Rich's high school and University of Arkansas era saw him heavily influenced by jazz and blues. He studied music formally at college and when the USAF posted him to Oklahoma in the early 1950s, one of his first groups, The Velvetones (a jazz-blues outfit that featured Charlie's wife Margaret as vocalist), secured a spot on local TV. Upon his discharge, Rich moved to West

Greatest Hits, Charlie Rich, Courtesy Epic Records.

Classic Rich, Charlie Rich. Courtesy UA Records.

Memphis, Arkansas, to work on his father's cotton farm. After sitting in one night with Bill Justis' band, Rich was invited to Sam Phillips' Memphis studio to lay down some trial tracks. He was told he was too jazzy, handed a pile of Jerry Lee

Lewis records and told to come back when he could get that bad!

After playing sessions with Warren Smith, Ray Smith and Billy Lee Riley, Rich landed his own rockabilly hit in 1959 – **Lonely Weekends**. The demise of Sun saw Rich without a record label and Bill Justis, then an employee of RCA, persuaded him to sign for Groove, an RCA

subsidiary, in 1963. From this period came a foot-stomping hit single, **Big Boss Man**.

In 1965 Rich moved to Smash, where Shelby Singleton encouraged Rich to utilize both rock and country influences. That year he scored another hit single in the national charts with **Mohair Sam**.

After an unproductive stint with Hi, the Memphis label, Epic signed him in 1968 and made him part of their modern country push under producer Billy Sherrill. However, even Sherrill had trouble stimulating more than average sales with Rich, though local critical acclaim was voiced for such titles as **Raggedy Ann** and **I Almost Lost My Mind**.

But in 1972, the smoothly soulful country **I Take It On Home,** backed with **Peace On You,** proved a country and pop hit and was nominated for a Grammy award. The album **The Best Of Charlie Rich** swept up many of the earlier Epic titles, re-presented them to the public and suddenly Rich was a big country name. But success really came with the next album, **Behind Closed Doors.** By this time, Sherrill and Rich had become a winning combination and the new urbane country sound known as 'countrypolitan' became the talk of the 1973 CMA Awards. For, not only was Rich topping the country charts with such singles as **Behind Closed Doors** and **The Most Beautiful Girl** (both 1973 No.1s), he was also selling records to those who formally had spent their all on the likes of Frank Sinatra. Rich was big, massively big. So much so that when RCA released his old **There Won't Be Anymore** single, that also went to No.1 (1973).

In 1974, Charlie had four chart-toppers in a row, two (**A Very Special Love Song, I Love My Friend**) stemming from Epic, and two (**I Don't See Me In Your Eyes Anymore, She Called Me Baby**) from RCA. Even Mercury re-released such earlier sides by Rich and were rewarded with chart hits.

There were further Top 10 records in 1975 but gradually interest waned. It looked as though he might be running out of time but in 1977, following a Top 20 record in **Easy Look**, he returned to the top of the charts once more with **Rollin' With The Flow.** By 1978 he was as massive a seller as ever, with four hits on two different labels (Epic and UA) – his No.1 that year, **On My Knees**, being achieved with the vocal aid of Janie Fricke. By 1979 Charlie had signed for Elektra and had a Top 10 record in **I'll Wake You Up When I Get Home.** But it was getting difficult to ascertain exactly who he was working for. He had five other hits that same year, four for UA and one for Epic. Perhaps there were just too many Rich records around. But whatever the reason, the punters tired of buying his singles. By the mid-1980s, the man who hogged the middle of the road market had been pushed (record sales-wise, at least) on to the sidewalk. But then, considering that Charlie never really slotted into any set category, it is something of a wonder that he ever made his name as a country singer in the first place. A soulful performer, whose gospel album **Silver Linings** is highly regarded, Charlie Rich won the CMA's premier award in 1974 when he was named Entertainer Of The Year.

Albums:
Behind Closed Doors (Epic/Epic)
Boss Man (Epic/Epic)
Classic Rich (Epic/–)
Nobody But You (UA/UA)
Silver Linings (Epic/–)

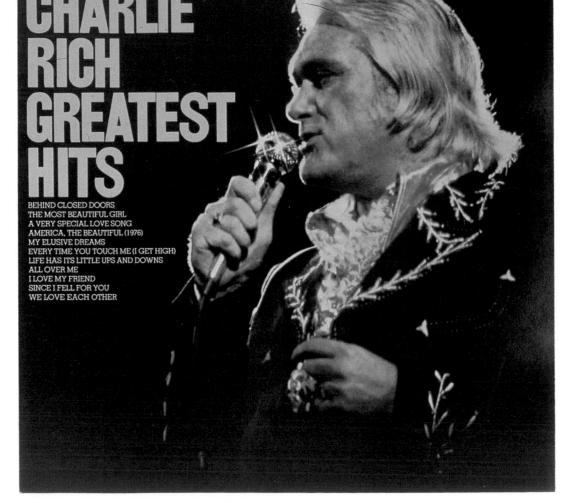

Jeannie C. Riley

An international star on the strength of just one record – a multi-million selling version of Tom T. Hall's **Harper Valley PTA** (1968) – the booted, mini-skirted Jeannie (born in Anson, Texas, on October 19, 1945) had only minimal experience in the entertainment industry prior to her arrival in Nashville.

In Music City she worked as a secretary for some time, cutting a few demo discs but generally having little success, until Shelby Singlton signed her to launch his new Plantation label with **Harper Valley PTA**, an ably constructed song dealing with small town hypocrisy. An immediate hit which sold four million copies in the US alone, the single sparked off an album which qualified for a gold disc, while Jeannie C. was awarded a Grammy as Best Female Country Vocalist of 1968.

The Girl Most Likely (1968), **There Never Was A Time** (1969), **Country Girl** (1970), **Oh Singer** (1971) and **Good Enough To Be Your Wife** (1971), were other Plantation releases that achieved Top 10 status for Jeannie C., but following a switch to MGM in 1971, sales of her discs began to taper off and it's now been a long time since she had a major record, although her name appeared on the charts in 1974 with **Plain Vanilla**, on Mercury, and in 1976 with **The Best I've Ever Had**, a Warner Bros release. A born again Christian, these days she exclusively records gospel songs and only plays dates where the sale of alcohol is banned.

Albums:
Harper Valley PTA (Plantation/Polydor)
Jeannie (Plantation/Polydor)

Tex Ritter

Born near Murval, in Panola County, Texas on January 12, 1905, Woodward Maurice Ritter aspired to a career in law at the University of Texas and at Northwestern before abandoning it for a career on the Broadway stage, where he appeared in five plays in the early 1930s, including 'Green Grow The Lilacs' in 1930. During his New York years, he also appeared as a dramatic actor on radio's popular 'Cowboy Tom's Round-Up' and co-hosted the WHN Barn Dance with Ray Whitley, making his first records for ARC in 1934. One of the first to follow Gene Autry into films as a singing cowboy, Tex moved to Hollywood in 1936, where he was to star in some 60 films for Grand National, Monogram, Columbia, Universal and PRC up to 1945. And, after several unsuccessful years as a Decca recording artist, he was the first singer to sign with the new Capitol label in 1942, responding by providing a long string of hits for them, thus becoming one of country music's biggest sellers of the 1940s.

When his film career declined, he turned to touring and had few rivals in the number of miles travelled year in and year out. In addition, he and Johnny Bond co-hosted 'Town Hall Party' from 1953 to 1960, during which time his rendition of the theme song for the film 'High Noon' won an Academy Award (1953).

Ritter moved to Nashville in 1965, where he joined the Grand Ole Opry and took over a late night radio programme on

Fall Away, Tex Ritter. Courtesy Capitol Records.

WSM. He acted on a long-standing desire to run for political office, when he stood (unsuccessfully) for the US Senate in 1970,

Border Town Affair, Marty Robbins. Courtesy CBS Embassy.

incurring debts that were to haunt him for the rest of his life.

A lifelong student of western history, he was instrumental in setting up the Country Music Foundation and the Country Music Hall of Fame, to which he was elected in 1964. Rated purely as a singer, he did not have a great voice but his unusual accent, odd slurs and phrasing, allied to a strong

feeling of genuine honesty, made his voice one of the most appealing in country music history. His long string of hits included **Jingle Jangle Jingle** (1942), **Jealous Heart** (1944), **There's A New Moon Over My Shoulder** (1944), **I'm Wasting My Tears On You** (1945), **You Two Timed Me Once Too Often** (1945), **Rye Whiskey** (1945), **Green Grow The Lilacs** (1945), **High Noon** (1952), **The Wayward Wind** (1956), and **I Dreamed Of A Hillbilly Heaven** (1961). Tex died on January 2, 1973, after a heart attack at the Metro Jail, Nashville (where he was arranging bail for one of his band) and was pronounced dead on arrival at Baptist Hospital.

Albums:
An American Legend (Capitol/–)
Blood On The Saddle (Capitol/Capitol)
Songs Of The Golden West (Capitol/MFP)
High Noon (–/Bear Family)

Marty Robbins

In a music where 'western' has often been considered a misnomer, Marty Robbins emphasised the western of country and western through a series of memorable cowboy/Mexican style ballads, many of them crossing over to the pop fields.

Born in Glendale, Arizona on September 26, 1925, he grew up in a desert area, his earliest musical recollections involving his harmonica-playing father and the songs and stories of

Above: Marty Robbins – originally known as 'Mr Teardrop' because of his penchant for cry-in-your-beer balladry.

his grandfather, Texas Bob Heckle, a travelling medicine man. Many of Robbins' own songs, such as **Big Iron**, owed much to his grandfather's tales.

Influenced by the films of Gene Autry, Robbins developed an ambition to become a singing cowboy and, following a three year term of service in the Navy, he began playing clubs in the Phoenix area, also appearing on radio station KPHO. Soon he gained his own TV show, 'Western Caravan', at one time having Little Jimmy Dickens as guest, Dickens being so impressed by Robbins' performance that he contacted Columbia records who immediately signed him, releasing his first disc entitled **Love Me Or Leave Me Alone**, back in 1952.

With his third Columbia release, **I'll Go On Alone**, Robbins hit the country music Top 10, also that year (1953) making a return visit with **I Couldn't Keep From Crying**. He had already guested on the Grand Ole Opry and in 1953 became a regular on the show, celebrating his signing with two 1954 hits in **Pretty Words** and **That's All Right**, the latter being the

same Arthur Crudup up-tempo blues with which Elvis Presley made his name. Robbins thus established a rock'n'roll connection that haunted him for many years, following up by recording the hummable **Singing The Blues**, **Knee Deep In The Blues**, **The Story Of My Life**, **White Sport Coat** and **Teenage Dream**, some of these becoming huge international hits and spawning equally successful cover versions in Britain. Robbins was a convincing rock'n'roller, a fact not lost on the British Teddy Boy fraternity, who tended to shout "You gotta rock, Marty" at Wembley Festivals when it became apparent that the singer was bent on providing an exclusively country set.

The crossover hits continued, at least in America, where Robbins had success in 1958 with **She Was Only Seventeen** and **Stairway Of Love**. And in 1959 came his biggest ever, **El Paso**, the lyrics of which would have made a convincing western film and the rhythm of which slipped insistently along, tinged with Mexican nuances. This was the archetypal Robbins, purveying a mixture of macho Western feel and melodic sentiment in a dramatically powerful but held-back voice.

Following **Don't Worry**, a 1961 country No.1, **Devil Woman** brought the same

response as **El Paso** among pop fans and again they brought Robbins into the pop charts on both sides of the Atlantic. That same year (1962) he again climbed high on the pop charts with **Ruby Ann**, but it was to be his final sally into such areas. From then on, his wares were to be found in the country charts only, where he logged hits every time from 1956 through to his death, topping these charts with **Begging To You** (1963), **Ribbon Of Darkness** (1965), **Tonight Carmen** (1967), **I Walk Alone** (1968), **My Woman, My Woman, My Wife** (1970) during his first stay with Columbia.

He signed with Decca/MCA in 1972 and stayed with the label for three years, still having hits but not of the dimension he was used to. So, in 1976 he returned to Columbia and moved back into the area of former glories with **El Paso City**, re-establishing himself at pole position in the chart, a neatly crooned version of the old standard **Among My Souvenirs** providing him with his second No.1 of the year.

With the irony that so often besets singers (Hank Williams releasing **You'll Never Get Out Of This World Alive** just prior to his death), Marty went Top 10 in 1982 with **Some Memories Just Won't Die**. But on December 8, 1982, just after the song had drifted out of the chart and two months before his induction to the Country Music Hall of Fame, Marty himself died, the victim of a heart attack.

An actor of some substance – Robbins appeared in such films as 'The Gun and The Gavel', 'The Badge Of Marshal Brennan' and 'Buffalo Gun' – he was also a successful album artist and maintained a fairly prolific presence in this areas, showing an ability in later years to appeal to the MOR market with his releases. He also appeared on most major American TV shows and toured heavily, displaying a varied, entertaining style in which his own mickey-taking chit-chat featured predominantly. An Opry favourite, the one-time desert rat held the distinction of being the last person to perform at the Ryman Auditorium. A top racing-car driver, he lived dangerously, even though he suffered from a bad heart. He survived major heart surgery in 1970 and made a

return to the Opry where he was forced to remain on stage for 45 minutes by his appreciative fans. But in 1982 his luck finally ran out. Even so, the name Robbins still crops up in the charts these days, Marty's son Ronnie taking over where his father left off and logging hits for such labels as Artic, Columbia and Epic, though his singles are often outsold by Marty's re-releases.

Albums:
Gunfighter Ballads And Trail Songs (Columbia/CBS)
More Gunfighter Ballads (Columbia/CBS)
Rock'n'Rolling Robbins (–/Bear Family)
A Lifetime Of Song 1951–1982 (Columbia/CBS)
El Paso City (Columbia/CBS)
The Marty Robbins Files Vol. 4 – 1957–1958 (–/Bear Family)

Kenny Roberts

A super-yodeller known best in the north and north-east, although he was actually born in Lenoir City, Tennessee, on October 14, 1927. He has recorded for Decca, Coral, Dot, King and Starday, his biggest hits being the yodelling extravaganzas, **Chime Bells** and **She Taught Me How to Yodel.**

Album:
Yodelin' Country Songs (Vocalion/–)

Eck Robertson

Born in Delaney, Madison County, Arkansas on November 20, 1887, old-time fiddler Alexander 'Eck' Robertson grew up in Texas and was probably the first country musician to make records.

Following a Confederate reunion held in Virginia in 1922, he and fiddler Henry Gilliland dressed as Western plainsmen and travelled to New York where they persuaded Victor to let them record. On June 30 and July 1, 1922, they cut six titles, the first of these – including Robertson's version of **Sally Goodin** – being released in April, 1923. A month earlier, Robertson

Devil Woman, Marty Robbins. Courtesy CBS Records.

had played **Sally Goodin** and **Arkansas Traveller** – the latter also being among the recorded tracks – over radio station WBAP, thus becoming the first country performer to promote his own discs over the air. The duo's **Arkansas Traveller** can be heard on the RCA release, **60 Years Of Country Music.**

Carson J. Robinson

Composer of such songs as **Barnacle Bill The Sailor, Open Up Them Pearly Gates, Carry Me Back To The Lone Prairie, Little Green Valley, Blue Ridge Mountain Home, Left My Gal In the Mountains** and the hit monologue, **Life Gets Teejus Don't It?,** Robinson's formula of vaudeville, new songs and pure hillbilly made him one of the most popular country songwriters of his era.

Born in Oswego, Kansas on August 4, 1890, he first sang at local functions in the Oswego area, moving to Kansas City in 1920, where he became one of the first country singers to ever appear on a radio show. In New York during 1924 he recorded as a whistler for Victor, teaming (as guitarist and co-vocalist) with ex-opera singer Vernon Dalhart to form a formidable hitmaking partnership that lasted for four years.

After the termination of this association, Robinson formed another duo – with Frank Luther (Francis Luther Crowe) whose

Famous Country Music Makers, Jimmie Rodgers. Courtesy RCA Records.

voice resembled Dalhart's, also moving on to lead such bands as the Pioneers, the Buckaroos, the Carson Robinson Trio and the Pleasant Valley Boys throughout the years.

Based in Pleasant Valley, New York, during the 1940s and 1950s, Robinson remained an active performer and writer right up to his death on March 24, 1957, one of his final MGM recordings being a rockabilly track, **Rockin' And Rollin' With Grandmaw!** Known as the Kansas Jayhawk, he recorded many hundreds of songs during his career, working for RCA, Conqueror, Supertone and a host of others.

Album:
Just A Melody (Homestead/–)

Jimmie Rodgers

Known as The Father Of Country Music, James Charles Rodgers was born in Meridan, Mississippi on September 8, 1897, the son of a section foreman on the Mobile and Ohio Railroad. Always in ill health as a child (his mother died of TB when Rodgers was four), he left school in 1911, becoming a water carrier on the M&O.

He later moved on to perform other tasks on the railroad, holding down a job as a brakeman until ill health caught up with him once more and he was forced to seek a less strenuous occupation. An amateur entertainer for many years, he became a serious performer in 1925,

initially becoming a black-face artist with a travelling medicine show but in 1926 appeared in Johnson City, Tennessee, as a yodeller, assisted by guitarist Ernest Helton. Also in 1926, Rodgers and his wife Carrie – whom he married in 1920 – moved to Ashville, North Carolina, there organising the Jimmie Rodgers Entertainers, a hillbilly band comprising Jack Pierce (guitar), Jack Grant (mandolin/banjo), Claude Grant (banjo) and Rodgers himself on banjo.

Together they broadcast on station WWNC, Ashville in 1927 for a period of six weeks, then set out to play a series of dates throughout the south east. Upon hearing that Ralph Peer of Victor Records was setting up a portable recording studio in Bristol, on the Virginia-Tennessee border, the entertainers headed in that direction. But due to a dispute within their ranks, Rodgers eventually recorded as a solo artist, selecting a sentimental ballad, **The Soldier's Sweetheart,** and a lullaby, **Sleep, Baby, Sleep,** as his first offerings, these tracks being released in October, 1927, alongside the first release by the Carter Family. The record met with instant acclaim, achieving encouraging sales, thus causing Victor to record further Rodgers sides thoughout 1927, these including **Ben Dewberry's Run, Mother Was A Lady** and **T For Texas,** the latter originally issued as **Blue Yodel** and becoming a million-seller.

By the middle of 1928, two more **Blue Yodels** (the series was eventually to include 13 such titles) were in the catalogue and Rodgers had become America's 'Blue Yodeller', his amalgam of

My Time Ain't Long, Jimmie Rodgers. Courtesy RCA.

blues, country, folk music and down-to-earth songs, having worldwide appeal, thus making him the first true country superstar. Victor began to provide the ex-brakeman with various backing groups, jazzmen accompanying him on some tracks, Hawaiian musicians being drafted in to assist on others, even a whistler named Bob McGimsey being signed to accompany Rodgers on **Tuck Away My Lonesome Blues.**

Rodgers' popularity grew daily, **Brakeman's Blues** becoming his third million-selling disc. And even though the Depression had hit America, his fans still bought his records by the tens of thousands. But Rodgers was gradually wasting away, the illness that he sang about in songs such as **TB Blues,** often forcing him to cancel performances. In 1931, he joined humourist Will Rodgers in a series of concerts in aid of the drought sufferers in the south eastern regions, while in 1932 he began a twice-weekly radio show from station KMAC, San Antonio, Texas, but quit when he became hospitalised in early 1933. However, later that year, though critically ill, he returned to Victor's New York recording studios on 24th Street, there cutting 12 sides over a period of eight days, a special cot being erected in which Rodgers rested between takes. The final song, **Fifteen Years Ago Today,** was completed on May 24, but during the following day Rodgers began to haemorrhage and then lapsed into a coma from which he never regained consciousness. He died on May 26, 1933.

Rodgers never appeared on any major radio show or even played the Grand Ole Opry during his lifetime. But he, Fred Rose and Hank Williams were the first persons to be elected to the Country Music Hall Of Fame in 1961, which is indicative of his importance in the history of country music.

Albums:
Famous Country Music Makers Vol.1 (–/ RCA)
Famous Country Music Makers Vol.2 (–/ RCA)
My Rough And Rowdy Ways (RCA/–)
This Is Jimmie Rodgers (RCA/–)
Train Whistle Blues (RCA/–)

Johnny Rodriguez

Chicano country star Juan Raul Davis Rodriguez was born in Sabinal, Texas, on December 10, 1952, the second youngest of nine children born to Andre and Isabel Rodriguez. Given a guitar by his brother Andres at the age of seven, during his high school days he became vocalist and lead guitarist with a rock outfit. At 17 he recorded a demo disc in San Antonio but

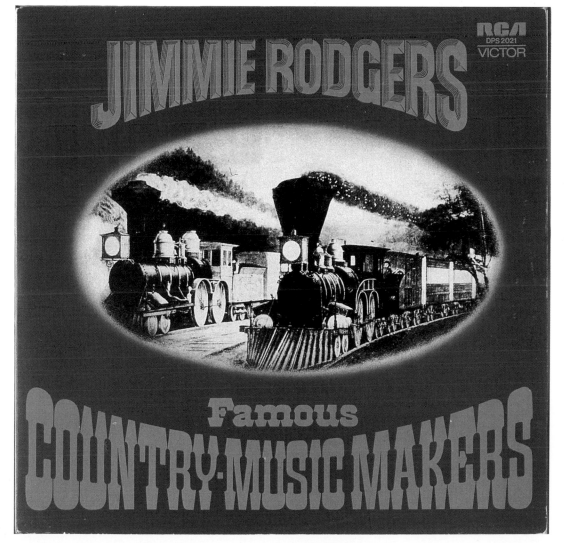

Above Johnny Rodriguez, the man who put 'chic' in Chicano.

a possible record deal fell through. Then, following a couple of minor offences (including the barbecuing of a goat he and some friends had stolen), Rodriguez was taken by a friendly Texas Ranger to see Happy Shahan, the owner of the Alamo Village resort in Bracketville – the belief being that if he obtained a regular job in music he would be more likely to stay out of trouble. Employed by Shahan (who became Rodriguez's co-manager) he spent the summers of 1970 and 1971 at the village, driving a stagecoach, riding horses and singing for the tourists. It was during 1971 that Tom T. Hall and Bobby Bare heard Rodriguez in Bracketville and urged him to come to Nashville.

This he did a few months later when, following the deaths of both his father and his brother Andres, he headed for Music City to become a guitarist with Tom T. Hall's band the Storytellers. Hall, signed to Mercury Records, obtained the Chicano an audition with the label, Rodriguez proving impressive on the session and gaining an immediate contract.

His first release, **Pass Me By**, became a Top 10 hit before the end of 1972, his next three singles, **You Always Come Back (To Hurting Me)**, **Riding My Thumb To Mexico** and **That's The Way Love Goes**, all hitting the No.1 spot. In 1975 he logged three more No.1s with **I Just Can't Get Her Out Of My Mind**, **Just Get Up And Close The Door** and **Love Put A Song In My Heart**,

his flood of winners (mostly Top 20) for Mercury continuing through to 1979, when he signed to Epic Records. That year he had four further Top 20 records, the biggest of which was **Down On The Rio Grande**, one, **I Hate the Way I Love It**, being a duet with Charly McClain.

One of the most good-looking of the younger singers on the country scene, Rodriguez, still only in his late 20s, possessed both teen-appeal plus the ability to make those who had been around longer go out and buy his every release. At one point, it seemed that even if he had recorded a nursery rhyme it would have charted. But during 1981 his appeal started to ebb and his releases began charting in lowly positions only. Later he admitted that a long stint with drugs had led to a careless attitude, this in

Reflecting, Johnny Rodriguez. Courtesy Mercury Records.

turn being translated into poor record sales. At an all-time low in late 1983, he sacked his band and, at some time later, phoned producer-drummer Richie Albright to ask if he would form a new band to work with him. Albright agreed on the understanding that Rodriguez quit drugs, became totally professional and took a more serious attitude to his work. The singer agreed and his record sales showed an almost immediate response, Johnny climbing back into the Top 10 with **Foolin'** and **How Could I Love Her So Much?** during 1984, also notching four hits, including a Top 20 entry in **Too Late To Go Home** the following year.

Albums:
Rodriguez (Epic/Epic)
For Every Rose (Epic/–)
Introducing Johnny Rodriguez (Mercury/ Mercury)
All I Ever Meant To Do Was Sing (Mercury/Mercury)
My Third Album (Mercury/Mercury)
Country Classics (–/Philips)

David Rogers

Rogers grew up in a country music environment, listening to the Grand Ole Opry every Saturday night of his boyhood. Born in Atlanta, Georgia on March 27, 1936, the singer set his sights on becoming an entertainer at an early stage. But although in 1956 he was auditioned by

Roger Miller, then part of the Third Army Special Services Division, he failed to become a forces entertainer, merely being drafted in the normal manner. On his return to civilian life in 1958, he began working at various venues in the Atlanta area, in 1962 singing for the city's Egyptian Ballroom, where he continued to work for nearly six years.

In October, 1967, he became a full member of Wheeling WWVA's Jamboree show, his first strong disc coming in 1968 via **I'd Be Your Fool Again**, a Columbia release.

After further success that year with **I'm In Love With My Wife**, Rogers decided on a move to Nashville. It was here that he began appearing on various package shows, also receiving bookings for top flight clubs and a number of syndicated TV programmes.

Following a run of money-spinning discs including **A World Called You** (1969), **I Wake Up In Heaven** (1970), **She Don't Make Me Cry**, **Ruby You're Warm** (both 1971) and **Need You** (1972), Rogers signed for Atlantic, becoming the label's first country act. Immediately he provided a Top 20 hit in **Just Thank Me** (1973), following this with **Loving You Has Changed My Life**, a Top 10 hit during 1974. After a hit album with **Farewell To The**

Farewell To The Ryman, David Rogers. Courtesy WEA Records.

Ryman, Rogers then switched to the Republic label and continued with his flow of chart contenders through to 1979, the biggest of these being **Darlin'** (1979). Since that time his name has appeared on releases from Kari (1981), Music Master (1982), Mr Music (1983) and Hal Kat (1984), providing some modicum of success for each of these labels.

Album:
Farewell To The Ryman (Atlantic)

Riders in the Sky

The group is a current-day cowboy trio, who offer loving (if frequently tongue-in-cheek) renditions of Sons Of The Pioneers songs plus material of a similar bent. Nashville-based, the group comprises Ranger Doug (guitar, vocals), Woody Paul Chrisman (fiddle, vocals) and Fred 'Too Slim' LaBour (bass, vocals), Ranger Doug in reality being Doug E. Green, the noted country music historian who contributed so much to this very book.

Extremely popular and filling a gap that other bands have not dared to reach, Riders In The Sky are regulars on the Grand Ole Opry and also host 'Tumbleweed Theatre', a western movie programme screened by the Nashville Network.

Albums:
Cowboy Jubilee (Rounder/–)
Live (Rounder/–)
Three On The Trail (Rounder/–)

Kenny Rogers

One of the real superstars of country music, Kenneth Donald Rogers was born in Houston, Texas on August 21, 1938, the son of a dock worker who played fiddle. A member of a high school band, The Scholars, who had a pop hit with **Crazy Feeling** in 1958, Rogers later attended the University of Houston where he studied music and commercial art. After working with the Bobby Doyle Trio, a harmony quartet called The Lively Ones, plus the New Christy Minstrels, he and other ex-Minstrels formed The First Edition in 1967, the group signing for Reprise Records and having a Top 10 pop hit in 1968 with a version of Mickey Newbury's **Just Dropped In (To See What Condition My Condition Was In)**. Other monster discs followed including **But You Know I Love You** (1969), **Ruby, Don't Take Your Love To Town**, an outstanding Mel Tillis song about a disabled war veteran (1969), **Reuben James** (1969), **Something's Burning, Tell It All, Brother** and **Heed The Call** (1970), the group's popularity gradually tapering off following the success of **Someone Who Cares**, in 1971.

Later becoming a solo artist – it had always been his grainy voice that had helped sell the Edition's mixture of folk, country and pop – Rogers gained a recording contract with UA, making some headway on the country scene with **Love Lifted Me**, a chart single in early 1976. By 1977 he was really on his way. UA

Below: Kenny Rogers. Lucille, one of his biggest hits, was also his mother's name.

The Gambler, Kenny Rogers (UA). The title song inspired a movie.

released his version of **Lucille**, a pure country saga regarding an unfaithful wife, reaching No. 1 in the country charts. It also crossed over to become the first of many of his pop Top 10 singles, and gained the bearded six-footer a Grammy award for Best Country Vocal Performance. Additionally, **Lucille** provided Rogers with both Single Of The Year and Song Of The Year at the CMA Awards ceremony.

From there on, it became difficult deciding just what CMA award he was not going to win. In 1978 and 1979, he and Dottie West claimed the Vocal Duo title. During 1979, too, Kenny was declared Male Vocalist Of The Year, while **The Gambler**, another Rogers million-seller, was Song Of The Year. In the interim Rogers notched further No. 1s with **Daytime Friends** (1977) **Love Or Something Like It** (1978), and **Every Time Two Fools Collide** (with Dottie West – 1978), 1979 providing four further chart-toppers in **All I Ever Need Is You** (with Dottie West), **She Believes In Me**, **You Decorated My Life** and **Coward Of The County**.

The 1980s have seen little let-up in the Rogers plan for country world domination. Though purists may knock him for being too pop, and rock fans may consider him pure MOR, the man with the silver hair and a cupboardful of gold and platinum records continues to add to his collection. He has also made further inroads into TV, in 1980 starring in 'The Gambler', a TV movie based on Don Schlitz's outstanding song, since when he has also appeared in 'Coward Of The County' (1981) and 'The Gambler II' (1983).

But it is his records that continue to provide Rogers with an entry into most homes. His 1980 album **Kenny** is reputed to have sold five million copies worldwide, while **Lady**, a song penned for him by Lionel Richie, not only topped the country charts as expected but also provided Rogers with his first US pop No. 1, hanging onto that position for six straight weeks in 1981. In the wake of further No. 1s with **I Don't Need You** (1981), **Love Will Turn You Around** (1982) and **We've Got Tonight** (with Sheena Easton, 1983), after five years with UA/Liberty – during which time he sold some 35 million albums – Kenny signed to RCA for a reported 20 million dollars. He immediately recouped part of that fee for his new label by providing them with one of his biggest ever hits **Islands In The Stream**, a duet with Dolly Parton that again went to No. 1 in both the US country and pop charts.

Since then there have been further chart-toppers with **Crazy** (1984), **Real Love** (another duet with Dolly Parton – 1985) and **Morning Desire** (1986). Kenny and Dolly also lit up the end of 1984 with a TV Christmas Special, while 'Gambler III', starring Kenny plus Linda Evans and Tom Sellick, was also on the boards for CBS-TV's 1985–86 season. Much married – Marianne Gordon, once of 'Hee Haw', is his fourth wife – Kenny Rogers is now one of the richest men in country music and lives in a multi-million Italian palace in Bel Air that has 13 bathrooms, an Olympic-size swimming pool and a servants wing. He also has other equally ritzy homes in Malibu and Beverly Hills. But he has his problems. "I've got a custom-built Stultz, a

Rolls, a Mercedes, a Ferrari, a Corvette and a station wagon," he once announced, "but I've only got a three-car garage!"

Albums:
Kenny Rogers (UA/UA)
Daytime Friends (UA/UA)
The Gambler (UA/UA)
Gideon (UA/UA)
The Kenny Rogers Story (–/Liberty)
Eyes That See In The Dark (RCA/RCA)

Linda Ronstadt

These days, Linda is a rocker who, amazingly enough, has notched some of her biggest albums with Sinatra-styled standards and made an on-stage impact by singing Gilbert and Sullivan on Broadway. But once she sang plenty of country and employed some of the best country-rockers in the business.

Born on July 16, 1946, in Tuscon, Arizona, she arrived in LA in 1964 and formed the folksy Stoney Poneys. After kicking around for a year they signed to Capitol, 1967 seeing the release of two albums, **Stoney Poneys** and **Evergreen**, **Stoney Poneys** yielding a hit single in Linda's version of Mike Nesmith's **Different Drum**.

Linda next went out as a solo act and made two more albums, **Hand Sown, Home Grown** (1969) and **Silk Purse** (1970), the first featuring the talents of such musicians as Clarence White, Red Rhodes, and Doug Dillard, while the latter was made with the aid of Nashville pickers. By 1971, however, she made the first move in a new direction, forming a backing band consisting of future Eagles, Glenn Frey, Don Henley and Randy Meisner and releasing an album called **Linda Ronstadt**, which contained a version of Hank Cochran and Harlan Howard's **I Fall To Pieces**, recorded live in LA with the help of steelie Sneaky Pete Kleinow, fiddler Gib Guilbeau and others.

Since that time she has moved further and further away from her original

Hasten Down The Wind, Linda Ronstadt. Courtesy WEA Records.

Above: Roy Rogers swops licks with Bob Hope in the 1952 movie, 'Son Of Paleface'.

country-oriented sound, though every now and then she has cut a track that serves to remind country music fans of days gone by, her hit singles including **Silver Threads And Golden Needles, I Can't Help It (If I'm Still In Love With You)** (both 1974), **When Will I Be Loved** (No. 1, 1975), **Crazy** (1976) and **Blue Bayou** (1977). An Asylum artist from 1974, during late 1978 and 1979 she worked on a trio album with Emmylou Harris and Dolly Parton, the project being shelved before completion, though all three singers have since intimated their desire to try again.

Album:
Linda Ronstadt – A Retrospective (Capitol/Capitol)

Roy Rogers

A major Western movie star between 1938 and 1953 and known as the King Of The Cowboys, Rogers started out as Leonard Slye, born in Cincinnati, Ohio on November 5, 1911, his biggest early musical influence being his father, who played mandolin and guitar. He grew up on a farm in the Portsmouth, Ohio, area and, following High School, became employed in a Cincinnati shoe factory for a while. During the 1920s he began playing and singing at local functions and in 1930 hitched a ride to California initially becoming a peach picker then a truck driver.

After stints with such groups as the Rocky Mountaineers and the Hollywood Hillbillies, he formed his own band The International Cowboys, later – with the aid of Tim Spencer and Bob Nolan – forming the Sons Of The Pioneers.

Though this outfit established a considerable reputation, Slye set his sights higher and began playing bit parts in films, first under the name of Dick Weston and then assuming his guise as Roy Rogers, eventually winning a starring role in 'Under Western Skies', a 1938 production. With his horse Trigger and frequent female partner, Dale Evans (whom he married in 1947) and occasional help from such people as the Sons Of The Pioneers and Spade Cooley, Rogers became Gene Autry's only real rival, starring in over 100 movies and heading his own TV show in the mid-1950s. His films include 'Carson City Kid' (1940), 'Robin Hood Of The Pecos' (1942), 'The Man From Music Mountain' (1944), 'Along The Navajo Trail' (1946), 'Son Of Paleface' (1952), 'Pals Of The Golden West' (1953), and 'Mackintosh and TJ' (1975).

Still seen on TV guesting on series such as 'The Fall Guy', Rogers was a recording artist with RCA-Victor for many years, later recording for Capitol, Word and 20th Century, gaining a Top 20 single **Hoppy, Gene And Me** (1974) while with the latter label. Even in 1980, then signed to MCA, Rogers was still charting, he and the Sons Of The Pioneers linking once more for **Ride Concrete Cowboy, Ride**, a song stemming from the movie, 'Smokey And The Bandit II'. The owner of a chain of restaurants, Rogers is estimated to be worth something over 100 million dollars.

Albums:
Best Of Roy Rogers (Camden/–)
Happy Trails To You (20th Century/–)

Johnny Russell

A show-stopper at the Wembley Festival, 1985, John Bright Russell was born in Sunflower City, Mississippi on January 23 during the early 1930s, his family moving to California when he was 12. A singer-songwriter and guitarist, he became a regular talent contest winner, gradually building up a highly-polished act and getting booked for classier venues. He got a job plugging for the Wilburn Brothers' music publishing company and also pushed his own songs – one, **Act Naturally**, becoming a chart-topper for Buck Owens in 1963, the song providing a favourite for The Beatles, who also recorded it.

A Burl Ives type character himself, big and bluff, warm and weighty, he wrote songs for Burl plus Loretta Lynn, Del Reeves, Patti Page, Dolly Parton and Porter Wagoner. Eventually, after being turned down by almost everybody, he got his own recording career underway with RCA in 1971 and by 1972 had Top 20 hits with **Catfish John, Rednecks, White Socks And Blue Ribbon Beer** and **Baptism Of Jesse Tylor**. But despite such singles as **She's In Love With A Rodeo Man** and **Obscene Phone Call**, Russell's only other major hit for the label came with **Hello I Love** (1975) and in 1978 he turned up on Mercury. The hits again had thought-provoking titles – **While The Choir Sang The Hymn, I Thought Of Her**, being a 1980 Russell special – but few climbed really high.

Not that Russell really worries. For his onstage act simply gets better and better – Entertainer Of The Year would look well on him – while his songs continue to bring in an abundant supply of royalties, Russell's **You'll Be Back (Every Night In My Dreams)** going Top 5 for the Statlers in 1982, while **Let's Fall To Pieces Together** made it to No. 1 in the charts for George Strait in 1984.

Albums:
Rednecks, White Socks And Blue Ribbon Beer (RCA/RCA)
She's In Love With A Rodeo Man (RCA/RCA)

Mr and Mrs Untrue, Johnny Russell. Courtesy RCA Records.

Buffy Sainte-Marie

Hardly a pure country singer – she began as a folk singer and has since headed

Below: Buffy Sainte-Marie. She did a memorable theme song to 'Soldier Blue'.

every which way – Buffy has nevertheless made several recordings of interest to C&W enthusiasts, her musical pleas on behalf of the Indian nation also being worthy of investigation by those professing an interest in western culture.

Her birthplace is clouded in mystery though Sebago Lake, Maine (February 20, 1941) is the location most generally accepted. Born to Cree Indian parents, she was adopted at an early age and raised mainly in Massachusetts, never knowing her real family.

She broke into the folk scene via appearances at New York's Gaslight Cafe in Greenwich Village during the early '60s, learning to play Indian mouth-bow from singer-songwriter and fellow Cree, Patrick Sky. A codeine addict at one point in her career, she wrote a classic song, **Cod'ine**, about her experiences, though it proved to be Donovan's version of her **Universal Soldier** that brought her songwriting into perspective.

Achieving considerable kudos through her appearances at the Newport Folk Festivals during the '60s, Buffy signed to Vanguard Records, cutting her first album, **It's My Way** (containing both **Cod'ine** and **Universal Soldier**) for the label in 1964.

By 1968, Buffy's intense vibrato was to be heard in a Nashville studio where she cut a pure country album **I'm Gonna Be A Country Girl Again**, achieving a mild pop hit with the title track, but having even more success with **Soldier Blue** (1971), the theme song from a somewhat horrific film dealing with the massacre of the Indians during the last century.

Leaving Vanguard in 1973, she signed for MCA but after only two albums moved on to ABC, making a strong album, **Sweet America**, in 1976.

One Sainte-Marie composition, **Until**

It's Time For You To Go, recorded by Buffy in 1965, later became a 1972 million seller for Elvis Presley and she was also co-writer of the 1982 Grammy Award winning **Up Where We Belong**, the theme song for the acclaimed film 'An Officer And A Gentleman'. Much of Buffy's recorded work lies outside the scope of this book but **I'm Gonna Be A Country Girl Again** and **A Native North-American Child** (both Vanguard), the latter album being a plea on behalf of the North-American Indians, should be heard.

Albums:
I'm Gonna Be A Country Girl Again (Vanguard/Vanguard)
Sweet America (ABC/ABC)

Doug Sahm

Although Doug Sahm became known originally through his teeny-bop hits, **She's About A Mover** (1965), and moved on to utilize blues, Mexican music, rock and country in his recordings, it is his involvement in the so-called Outlaw community of Austin, Texas that has won him his large and loyal cult following.

Born on November 6, 1941 and raised in San Antonio, he was subject to the varied root musical influences of that area, but nevertheless found himself part of the mid '60s garage band movement in which many young American groups emulated the English bands of the day, with long hair and trendy clothes playing at least as important a part as the music.

She's About A Mover featured a pumping 4/4 beat, Sahm's strange whining vocal and the amateurish sounding organ dabs of Augie Meyer. It is a sound that

has since become Sahm's trademark, with various refinements. The Sir Douglas Quintet, as his band was known, then moved to the burgeoning San Francisco and scored another, similar hit with the catchy **Mendocino**.

But Sahm was still a native Texan (a sentiment he has expressed in the song **I'm Just A Country Boy In This Great Big Freaky City**) and the '70s found him in more ethnic mood, pursuing his love of blues, Mexican conjunto and good-time country. His country orientated albums, **Doug Sahm And Band** and **Texas Rock For Country Rollers**, have shown his natural flair for the music and utilized the talents of Bob Dylan, Willie Nelson and David Bromberg.

Albums:
Mendocino (Smash/Oval)
Texas Rock For The Country Rollers (ABC/ABC)
Hell Of A Spell (Takoma/–)
Wanted – Very Much Alive (Texas Records/Sonet)

Junior Samples

From Cumming, Georgia, Alvin Junior Samples (born in 1927), weighed nearly 300 lbs, and was proud of being dubbed 'the world's biggest liar'. A sawmill worker for most of his life, during the early 1960s Samples could be usually found with his wife and six children or merely fishing, drinking and relating his hilarious tales.

One such story told to a game warden eventually came to the ears of a Macon, Georgia, DJ, who interviewed Samples for his radio programme. When the tape was

Below: Sawyer Brown, who took their name from a Nashville Street.

played on the air, it caused such a reaction that Chart Records purchased the recording and released a single, **The World's Biggest Whopper**, which became a mild hit in mid 1967.

This was followed by an album, **The World Of Junior Samples**, and a second ad lib LP, **Bull Session At Bull's Gap**, with Archie Campbell. A a result of this success on record, Samples became one of the mainstays on the Hee-Haw CBS-TV Show. Samples died of a heart attack on November 13, 1983 at his home in Cumming, Georgia.

Sawyer Brown

Gregg (Hobie) Hubbard, keyboards; Mark Miller, lead guitar; Bobby Randall, lead guitar; Jim Scholten, bass; Joe Smyth, drums.

Country-rock band Sawyer Brown made their breakthrough in 1984 when they won Star Search, an American syndicated television talent contest. This led to a recording contract with Capitol and tours with such stars as Kenny Rogers, Dolly Parton, Crystal Gayle, The Oak Ridge Boys and Eddie Rabbitt.

Prior to their long run on Star Search, Sawyer Brown had been together for two years, working the American club circuit and building a reputation as one of the most musically proficient acts to have emerged in country music.

Their first single release, **Leona**, made the country Top 20 at the end of 1984, and the self-contained five-piece outfit has had further hits with **Step That Step**, **Used To Blue** (both 1985), **Heart Don't Fall Now** and **Betty's Bein' Bad** (1986).

Album:
Shakin' (Capitol/Capitol)

John Schneider

Actor turned singer, John was born on April 8, 1954 in New York, and came to prominence as Bo Duke in the TV series 'The Dukes Of Hazzard'. He then found success in country music, scoring his first hit in 1981 with **It's Now Or Never**.

John first demonstrated an inclination towards a career in showbusiness during his early schooldays, landing a part in 'L'il Abner', which was being staged by a community theatre group called the Jay Players in Westchester, New York. Following his parents' divorce in 1968, John moved to Atlanta Georgia with his mother.

While in high school he became active in the drama club and played the lead roles in such musicals and dramas as 'Fiddler On The Roof', 'Annie Get Your Gun', 'The Pyjama Game' and 'The Odd Couple'. Following graduation he appeared in several community theatre productions, sang in Atlanta's clubs and co-wrote the musical score for a play called 'Under Odin's Eye'.

His big break came in 1978 when he auditioned for, and won, the coveted role of Bo Duke, the youngest Duke of Hazzard. When he is not on the Dukes' set, John turns his attention to music. He signed a recording contract with Scotti Brothers Records in 1981 and scored a Top 5 country hit with his update of the Elvis Presley classic **It's Now Or Never**.

Further country hits followed with **Still** (1981), **Them Good Ole Boys Are Bad** (1982), **Livin' For Saturday Night** (1983), **It's A Short Walk From Heaven To Hell** (1985) and his first No. 1, **Country Girls** (1985).

Now signed to MCA Records, John has been busy starring in films like 'Eddie Macon's Run', and making guest

appearances on such TV shows as 'Dinah' and 'Merv Griffin'.

Albums:
Tryin' To Outrun The Wind (MCA/–)
Now Or Never (Scotti Bros./–)

Dan Seals

A Texan singer-songwriter, Dan Seals' background is steeped in country music. His family were originally settlers in mid Tennessee, who moved to Texas in the 1920s. Here, Dan's father gained a reputation as an accomplished guitar player, and later with his son Jimmy (Dan's older brother, who later became part of Seals and Crofts) on fiddle, played backup for many of the country music stars who toured the Midland-Odessa area of Texas.

Later Jimmy joined The Champs (along with Glen Campbell) and played on such pop hits as **Tequila**, **El Rancho Rock** and **Limbo Rock**, in the late '50s and early '60s. Dan started playing in bands whilst at high school and teamed up with John Ford Coley to form Southwest F.O.B. (Freight On Board), scoring a minor pop hit in 1968 with **Smell Of Incense**.

Moving to Los Angeles, the pair eventually landed a recording contract with Atlantic, by this time working as a duo called England Dan and John Ford Coley. During the '70s they released a string of pop hits including **I'd Really Love To See You Tonight**, **We'll Never Have To Say Goodbye Again** and **Nights Are Forever Without You**, and toured with such acts as Elton John, Chicago and Olivia Newton-John.

Eventually, Dan found the urge to return to his roots and in 1982 he uprooted his family from Los Angeles and moved to Nashville, determined to make his mark in country music. A contract with Liberty/EMI America Records resulted in minor country hits with **You Really Go For The Heart** and **Everybody's Dream Girl** (both 1983).

A No. 2 country hit at the beginning of 1985, **My Baby's Got Good Timin'**, was followed later in the year by country No. 1s, **Bop** and **Meet Me In Montana**, the latter a duet with Marie Osmond, firmly establishing him in country music.

Albums:
Won't Be Blue Anymore (EMI America/–)
San Antone (EMI America/–)

Troy Seals

Singer-songwriter Seals (born in Big Hill, Kentucky on November 16, 1938) became a guitar player in his pre-teen years, later forming a band that played both rock and country material.

While touring he met and married pop singer Jo Ann Campbell, forming a duo that recorded for Atlantic, but getting little reaction. Disenchanted, they left the music business, Seals working for a construction firm in Indianapolis.

A year later he arrived in Nashville and began writing songs with such partners as Will Jennings, Don Goodman and Donnie Fritts. He also struck up a friendship with sessionman David Briggs, who obtained Seals' many bookings as a guitarist on record dates – the Kentuckian appearing on sessions with Ray Stevens, Waylon

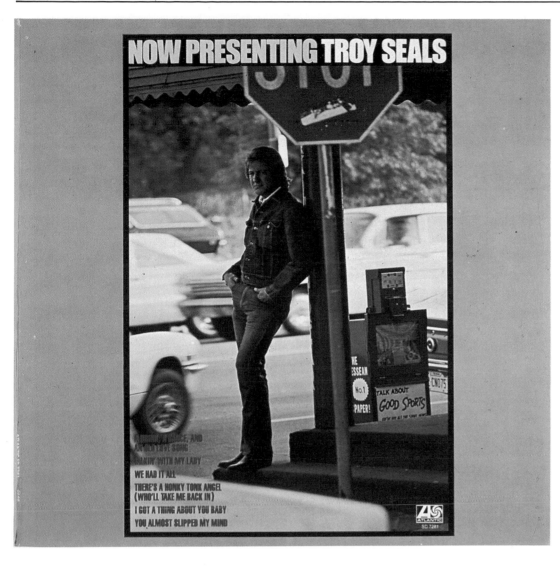

Now Presenting Troy Seals. Courtesy WEA Records.

Jennings, Dobie Gray, Brenda Lee and others.

After cutting demos for Monument under the direction of Ray Pennington, some sides were mooted for Polydor but plans proved abortive and Seals eventually became one of Atlantic's initial country signings. However, within a year the company decided on a change of policy and Seals found himself label-less and forced to move on once more – this time to Columbia.

Despite his lack of success on disc, Seals has fared well as a songwriter, either by himself or in partnership with Max D. Barnes, Eddie Setser, Mike Reid, etc, providing Top 10 hits for Conway Twitty, Waylon Jennings, Gary Stewart, Ronnie Milsap and many other country and pop singers.

Album:
Troy Seals (Columbia/–)

Jeannie Seely

An Opry member since 1966, Jeannie was born in Pennsylvania on July 16, 1940 and grew up in the Titusville area. She began singing on local radio in Meadville, Pennsylvania at the age of 11 and during her high school era appeared on the prestigious Midwest Hayride show.

Although she studied banking and associated subjects at the American Institute of Banking, Jeannie preferred the trappings of showbiz and moved to LA, signing for Four Star Music as a writer and cutting a couple of unsuccessful discs for Challenge Records.

With encouragement from Hank Cochran, who later became her husband, she moved to Nashville in 1965, becoming a writer for Tree International Music. She also signed for Monument Records and had an instant hit with Cochran's **Don't Touch Me** (1966), a release which won her a Grammy award for the Best Female C&W Vocal Performance.

In the wake of eight chart singles for Monument – these including **It's Only Love** (1966), **A Wanderin' Man** (1966) and **I'll Love You More** (1967) – Jeannie became a part of the Jack Greene Show in 1969. Joining Greene on the Decca label, the duo favourably impressed record buyers via **I Wish I Didn't Have To Miss You**, a Top 5 disc in 1969, Jeannie's biggest solo hits arriving with **Can I Sleep In Your Arms?** in 1973, and **Lucky Ladies** (1974).

Album:
Greatest Hits (Monument/–)

The Seldom Scene

A 'newgrass' supergroup, they were formed by the Country Gentlemen's John Duffey in 1971 and played in the Washington D.C. area, the other members of the band being Mike Audridge (dobro),

Ben Eldridge (banjo) John Sterling (guitars and vocals) plus former Country Gentlemen bassist Tom Gray.

Named the Seldom Scene because of their infrequent concert appearances, the group merged both traditional and current chart material, proving popular with the

At The Scene, The Seldom Scene. Courtesy Sugar Hill Records.

THE SELDOM SCENE
...At The Scene...

younger set, their once-a-week residency at Bethesda's Red Fox Inn proving a huge draw in the area. Following a number of appearances at various bluegrass festivals, they gained even more fans and by 1974 they topped the 'Muleskinner News' Awards.

Audridge, often considered the genius of the group – at the very least, he is quite a remarkable dobroist – is the nephew of Ellsworth T Cozzens, the Hawaiian steel guitarist who played on several Jimmie Rodgers records.

Albums:
Act Four (Sugar Hill/–)
At The Scene (Sugar Hill/–)

Ronnie Sessions

A singer who looked set for the big time in the late '70s, Ronnie (born on December 7, 1948, in Henrietta, Oklahoma) had faded from the limelight by the mid '80s, though he continues to work the club and honky tonk circuit, where his driving country music is best appreciated.

Something of a child prodigy Ronnie, who grew up in Bakersfield, California, made his first records for the small Pike Records when he was nine and spent six years as a regular on the Herb Henson Trading Post.TV show.

Throughout the '60s he worked on the West Coast, continuing his television career with an array of popular performers including Billy Mize, Wes Sanders and the Melody Ranch Show. He also embarked upon recording stints with such small labels as Starview and Mosrite, before signing with Gene Autry's Republic Records in 1968, where he notched up regional hits with **Life Of Riley** and **More Than Satisfied**.

Touring in the company of such stars as Buck Owens, Merle Haggard and Glen Campbell presented him with much needed entertainment experience, and by the time he moved to Nashville in 1972 he was already regarded as a very talented entertainer.

Befriended by Hank Cochran and his wife Jeannie Seely, he was signed as a writer to Tree Publishing and started recording for MGM Records, making his first appearance on the country charts with **Never Been To Spain** (1972). A few more minor hits followed, then he joined MCA Records in 1975, achieving success with **Makin' Love** (1975) and his first Top 20 entry **Wiggle Wiggle** (1976).

Sessions soon established himself with his rocking country music, scoring more hits with **Me and Millie**, **Ambush** (both 1977) and **Juliet And Romeo** (1978). Then, with his records only just making it into the country Top 100, he was dropped by MCA in 1980 and has hardly recorded since.

Album:
Ronnie Sessions (MCA/MCA)

Billy Joe Shaver

A new wave singer-songwriter who rose to prominence while in his mid '30s, Shaver was a part-time poet who set his sights on Nashville after hearing Waylon Jennings sing.

Born in Corsicana, Texas, he moved to Waco at the age of 12, spending his early life employed at a sawmill, punching cattle, doing carpentry or performing various menial tasks as a farmhand.

His ambitions as a songwriter later led him to Nashville where he found his wares rejected by every publisher. Shaver, on the brink of starvation, was forced to return to Texas. However, on a later trip to the Music City he sold a song to Bobby Bare that became the B side of a hit and also signed as a writer to Bare's own Return Music Publishing Company, achieving something of a breakthrough when Kristofferson recorded his **Good Christian Soldier** (1971).

Next, Tom T. Hall latched on to Shaver's songs, likewise Dottie West, Jan Howard, Jerry Reed, Tex Ritter and Jim Ed Brown, his reputation as one of the most potent new writers in Nashville being established when Waylon Jennings cut **Honky Tonk Heroes** (1973), an album of songs, nearly all penned by Shaver.

I'm A Believer, Jean Shepard. Courtesy UA Records.

An often controversial writer – one of his songs **Black Rose** deals with the subject of inter-racial marriage – he became a fully fledged recording artist when Kris Kristofferson produced **Old Five And Dimers Like Me**, Shaver's first album, for the Monument label. Further recordings for Capricorn and Columbia received critical acclaim but were commercial failures, though he has continued to score as a writer, providing John Anderson with his first chart topper, **I'm Just An Old Chunk Of Coal** (1981) and hits for Johnny Cash, George Jones and Conway Twitty.

Albums:
Gypsy Boy (Capricorn/–)
I'm Just An Old Chunk Of Coal . . . But I'm Gonna Be A Diamond Someday (Columbia/–)

Dorothy Shay

Known as the Park Avenue Hillbilly, Dorothy's gimmick was to attire herself in exquisite gowns, then perform incongruous, novelty hillbilly numbers such as **Another Notch On Father's Shotgun** and **Makin' Love, Mountain Style**. Very popular during the 1940s, she recorded for Columbia, her biggest hit being **Feudin' And Fightin'** (1947), a song originally from the score of a Broadway show. Born 1923, she appeared in an Abbott and Costello movie, 'Comin' Round The Mountain' in 1951.

In later life she played a recurring role in the TV series 'The Waltons' but died in Santa Monica, California on October 22, 1978.

Jean Shepard

Born in Pauls Valley, Oklahoma on November 21, 1933, Jean originally sang and played bass with an all-girl western swing outfit known as the Melody Ranch Girls.

After impressing Hank Thompson via a Melody Ranch Girls – Brazos Valley Boys

Above: T. G. Sheppard. Known as 'The Good Sheppard', he is one of the most sucessful country-pop artists of the '80s.

joint gig, Jean became signed to Capitol Records in 1953, that same year gaining her first No.1 with **Dear John Letter**, a duet recorded with Ferlin Husky. Next came a sequel, **Forgive Me, John** (1953), then a brace of 1955 solo winners with **Satisfied Mind** and **Beautiful Lies**.

Jean became a regular on the Red Foley Show over KWTO, two years later moving to Nashville and attaining Opry status. But her hits remained infrequent until 1964 (shortly after the death of husband Hawkshaw Hawkins) when her recording of **Second Fiddle (To An Old Guitar)** sparked off a long flow of

Solitary Man, T. G. Sheppard. Courtesy Hitsville Records.

successes that have included **Happy Hangovers To You** (1966), **If Teardrops Were Silver** (1966), **Your Forevers (Don't Last Very Long)** (1967), **Then He Touched Me** (1970), **Another Lonely Night** (1970), **Slippin' Away** (1973) and **At The Time** (1974).

During the mid '70s, Jean made a big impact with British country audiences through her outspoken insistence on keeping country free from pop contamination. Her repertoire of pure '50s type country, full of hard-sob ballads and full throttle honky tonk won her standing ovations at the Wembley Festivals in 1977 and 1978 and subsequent concert tours.

Albums:
I'm A Believer (UA/Music For Pleasure)
Mercy Ain't Love Good (UA/UA)
The Very Best Of (–/UA)
I'll Do Anything It Takes (–/Sunset)

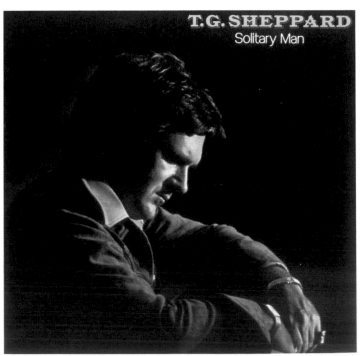

T. G. Sheppard

One of the most successful country-pop artists of the '80s, T. G. (real name Bill Browder) was born July 20, 1944 in Humboldt, Tennessee and moved to Memphis in 1960 where he became a guitarist and backup singer in Travis Wammack's band.

Securing a contract with Atlantic Records and using the name Brian Stacy, he had a number of pop-styled singles released in the early '60s, including **High School Days**, which was a small pop hit. In 1965 he got married and took a hard look at his modest singing career, but as he still wanted to stay in records he became a promotion man.

After a stint as RCA's Memphis promotion man, he formed his own independent production and promotion company, Umbrella Productions. He picked up **Devil In The Bottle** from writer Bobby David and in desperation, after several companies turned it down, demoed it himself, eventually finding an unlikely outlet in Tamla Motown who were just getting into country.

Since the name Bill Browder would coincide with his promotional activities, he called himself T. G. Sheppard, after spotting a bunch of German shepherd dogs through an office window. The record was released on Motown's Melodyland label in 1974 and rapidly climbed to the top of the country charts, crossing over to the pop charts the following spring.

Further hits followed with **Tryin' To Beat The Morning Home**, **Motel And Memories** (both 1975), **Solitary Man** and **Show Me A Man** (both 1976), by which time the record label Melodyland had become Hitsville, because there was a Los Angeles church also named Melodyland, which claimed the name exclusively as their own.

Finally, Motown closed down its country division and T. G. signed with Warner Brothers, making a return to the Top 20 with **Mr DJ** in 1977. This new association turned out to be T. G.'s most successful. Following Top 10 hits with **When Can We Do This Again** and **Daylight** (both 1978), he changed producers and under the guidance of Buddy Killen scored No. 1s with **Last Cheater's Waltz**, **I'll Be Coming Back For More** (both 1979), **Smooth Sailin'** and **Do You Wanna Go To Heaven** (both 1980), and crossed over to the pop charts in 1981 with the million-selling **I Loved 'Em Every One**.

With his good looks, slightly sexy song lyrics and dynamic stage act, T. G. has appealed mainly to woman, creating mob scenes that are usually associated with pop stars rather than mature country singers. His success on record has been maintained with such songs as **Finally** (1982), **Faking Love** (a duet with Karen Brooks, also 1982), **Slow Burn** (1983), **Make My Day** (with Clint Eastwood – 1984) and **Home Again** (this time with Judy Collins – 1985).

He changed labels in 1985, moving over to Columbia, his run of hits continuing with **Doncha?** (1985), **Fooled Around And Fell In Love** and **In Over My Heart** (1986).

Albums:
The Nashville Hitmaker (–/Hitsville)
¾ Lonely (Warners/–)
I Love 'Em All (Warners/–)
Livin' On The Edge (Columbia/–)

Billy Sherrill

An ex-R&B producer who developed a smooth line in modern country production during the 1960s, Sherrill sparked off success for Tammy Wynette and later for Tanya Tucker. In the early '70s he helped revitalise the career of ex-rock 'n' roller Charlie Rich, the seductive, soporific, late-night sound being dubbed 'Countrypolitan' by the critics.

Working for Columbia and Epic, Sherrill evolved a masterly way of balancing steel guitars and orthodox country instruments against orchestras. Such was the success of this fine balance, with all the rough edges knocked off, that records made by Sherrill sold in spectacular quantities and helped identify the 'Nashville Sound' as mainstream country to most people when in fact it was just part of a larger whole.

He has also worked in the studio with such differing singers as Johnny Paycheck, Elvis Costello, George Jones, Marty Robbins, Lacy J. Dalton and David Allan Coe, illustrating the scope of his musical styles. Over the years he has co-written dozens of country hits including **Too Far Gone**, **Stand By Your Man** and **Almost Persuaded**.

Shel Silverstein

Cartoonist with Playboy magazine for over 20 years, Silverstein is the most eccentric figure in popular music – 'a zany character on the Nashville scene'. A bald hipster from Chicago, who writes poetry and children's books, he has made a number of bizarre solo albums, and is a highly professional country songwriter.

Silverstein's musical past does not suggest much affinity with country music. He grew up with Chicago jazz, blues and folk music. On his own records his humour comes from hipster tradition – he uses black language like Leiber and Stoller did with the Coasters. A highly sophisticated

Above: A mid-'70s shot of Billy Sherrill, the one-time R&B piano and saxman who became Nashville's leading producer.

lyricist, it is hard to believe that he could approach country without cynicism, derision or calculation, but he does! His best songs use a conventional form to tell pointed stories, and he has kept faith with the popularity and reality that still underlie country sentiment.

Songs like **One More On The Way** (a hit for Loretta Lynn), make their humorous point through self-commentary. He also wrote **A Boy Named Sue**, a Grammy award winner for Johnny Cash in 1969, and is best known in the wider pop world for his work with Dr. Hook, for whom he

The Great Conch Train Robbery, Shel Silverstein. Courtesy Flying Fish.

wrote **Sylvia's Mother** and such comic songs as **The Cover Of Rolling Stone** and **Freaker's Ball**.

In country circles, he is best known for his work with Bobby Bare, who enjoyed hits with **Daddy What If**, **Marie Laveau** and **Alimony**, and a series of concept albums including **Hard Time Hungrys**, **Lullabys, Legends And Lies** and **Drinkin' From The Bottle, Singin' From The Heart**, which were all penned by Silverstein.

Although as a songwriter he specialises in the catchy and clever, occasionally he proves himself capable of the sincerity and sensitivity inherent in country songwriting, as with his **Here I Am Again** (recorded by Loretta Lynn).

Album:
The Great Conch Train Robbery (Flying Fish/–)

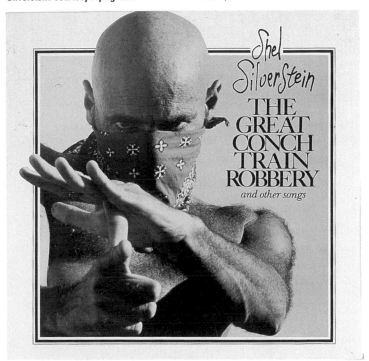

Asher And Little Jimmy Sizemore

One of the early professional bands on the Grand Ole Opry consisted of Asher Sizemore (born on June 6, 1906, in Manchester, Kentucky) and his young son Jimmy (born on January 29, 1928), who specialised in sentimental hearth and home type ballads and songs, and were one of the first Opry acts to put out a very successful songbook.

Asher had little Jimmy on the radio as early as the age of three, and the Opry's Harry Stone, having heard them on WHAS in Louisville, brought them to the Opry where they stayed for some ten years (1932–1942), recording for Bluebird Records as well, although no big hits emerged.

After the war they appeared on KXEL, Waterloo, Iowa, SMOX, St. Louis, WHO in Des Moines, and WSB in Atlanta, often with Asher's younger son Buddy Boy, who was killed in Korea late in 1950. Jimmy Sizemore is currently a radio executive in Arkansas, while Asher died some years ago.

Below: Ricky Skaggs. His vocals still come mountain-flavoured.

Ricky Skaggs

The success story of Ricky Skaggs is perhaps the most amazing in contemporary country music. His roots and sound are pure bluegrass, western swing and traditional country and his vocals mountain-flavoured, yet he dominated the country charts in the early 1980s with No. 1 singles and gold albums, and won CMA awards as Male Vocalist of the Year (1982) and Entertainer of the Year (1985).

Born on July 18, 1954 near Cordell, Kentucky, Ricky had an old-fashioned, mountain upbringing, traditional music and religion being a vital part of family life. A child prodigy, in bluegrass terms, he appeared on TV with Flatt & Scruggs when he was seven and joined Ralph Stanley's band when he was just 15.

His reputation as a tenor vocalist adept at high harmonies, and his skill on mandolin, fiddle, acoustic guitar and banjo, landed him a job with the bluegrass group, Country Gentlemen, in Washington. D.C. Ricky later formed his own band, Boone Creek, and recorded two very good albums.

When Rodney Crowell left Emmylou Harris' Hot Band in 1977, Ricky filled the vacancy as acoustic guitarist, fiddle

Favourite Country Songs, Ricky Skaggs. Courtesy Epic Records. He signed with the label in 1981.

player, mandolinist and, above all, second voice to Emmylou. In his three years with the band, he played a big part in influencing her musical direction and had a key role in her **Roses In The Snow**, an LP widely acclaimed as a bluegrass masterpiece.

In 1980, Ricky decided to branch out on a solo career and recorded for the small North Carolina label, Sugar Hill. With the help of Emmylou, Albert Lee, Jerry Douglas and Bobby Hicks, he came up with the acclaimed **Sweet Temptation** album. This led to a move to a major label and, signing with Epic in Nashville in 1981, he made his debut on the country charts with a fine update of Flatt & Scruggs' **Don't Get Above Your Raising**.

The album that followed, **Waitin' For The Sun To Shine**, resulted in the chart-topping singles **Crying My Heart Out Over You** and **I Don't Care** and his CMA award as Male Vocalist of the Year (1982). Ricky's pure country styling and the sharp instrumentation of his band brought a breath of fresh air to the country charts and also won him a following by pop and rock audiences, as shown by a sell-out appearance at London's Dominion Theatre in 1985, which was captured on a live album and TV and video showcases.

Ricky has also cut an enviable number of country chart-toppers including **Heartbroke** (1982), **Don't Cheat In Our Hometown** (1983), **Honey (Open That Door)** (1984), **Country Boy** (1985) and **Cajun Moon** (1986). Now married to Sharon

Live In London, Ricky Skaggs. Courtesy Epic Records.

White of The Whites family group, Ricky has shown that traditional country music can be commercially successful, having achieved his own world-wide success simply by being himself and playing and singing the music he loves best.

Albums:
Sweet Temptation (Sugar Hill/Ritz)
Country Boy (Epic/Epic)
Highways And Heartaches (Epic/Epic)
Favourite Country Songs (Epic/Epic)

The Skillet Lickers

Ted Hawkins, mandolin, fiddle; Bert Layne, fiddle; Clayton McMichen, fiddle; Fate Norris, banjo, harmonica; Riley Puckett, guitar; Hoke Rice, guitar; Lowe Stokes, fiddle; Arthur Tanner, banjo, guitar; Gid Tanner, fiddle; Gordon Tanner, fiddle; Mike Whitten, guitar.

An extremely popular and influential Atlanta-based string band of the 1920s and 1930s, The Skillet Lickers was led by Gid Tanner. The band included two other country music figures of great importance in their own right: Clayton McMichen and Riley Puckett.

Tanner (1885–1960), a Georgian like all the band-members through the years, first recorded with Puckett (1894–1945), the blind guitarist, for Columbia in 1924 and continued to record with various permutations of the Skillet Lickers for Columbia and Victor for the next decade, although the band name did not actually

Below: Arthur 'Guitar Boogie' Smith and his Crackerjacks. His original Guitar Boogie sold over three million copies.

exist until McMichen (1900–1970) joined Tanner, Puckett and Norris in 1926.

Their material, for the most part, was composed of fiddle breakdowns, minstrel songs and a bizarre and hilarious series of eighteen spoken comedy records called **A Corn Likker Still In Georgia**, although the fiddle breakdown **Down Yonder** is most closely associated with them.

Their sound together was rough and wild, typically featuring the fine twin fiddling of McMichen and Layne, falsetto shouts and snatches of verses by Tanner, and often Puckett's bluesy singing. All three mainstays went their separate ways after 1934, Tanner dying on May 13, 1960, but the legacy of The Skillet Lickers is one of humorous, extremely good-natured, old-time music played in the most spirited of styles. They were unique, but their sound was in many ways the sound of an old-time substyle of country music already on the way out as they were recording it.

Albums:
The Skillet Lickers (County/–)
The Skillet Lickers, Vol. 2 (County/–)
Gid Tanner And His Skillet Lickers (Rounder/–)

Jimmie Skinner

A songwriter of some skill, Skinner never really climbed past the half-way stage on the ladder of success as a performer. At one time he was probably better known as the owner of a mail order record store, the Jimmie Skinner Music Center, in Cincinnati, though he later gave up this business and moved to the Nashville area.

Born near Berea, Kentucky, Skinner's first success came as a songwriter, one of his compositions, **Doin' My Time**, proving a minor hit in 1941. A DJ during the 1940s,

he had his own show on WNOX, Knoxville, Tennessee, and appeared on other stations.

He signed as a performer with Mercury Records during the mid '50s and had Top 10 hits with **I Found My Girl In The USA** (1957) and **Dark Hollow** (1957), also gaining further chart entries and cutting a much sought after album of Jimmie Rodgers' songs.

Since that time, he has recorded for such labels as Decca, Starday, King and Vetco. Many of his songs have become standards in bluegrass repertoire, including (in addition to the above) **You Don't Know My Mind** and **Will You Be Satisfied That Way**. Jimmie died of a heart attack on October 28, 1979 in Hendersonville, Tennessee.

Albums:
Sings Bluegrass (Vetco/–)
Original Greatest Hits (Power Pak/–)

Arthur 'Guitar Boogie' Smith

Leader of an outfit known as the Crackerjacks, guitarist-banjoist-mandolin player Arthur Smith was born on April 1, 1921, in Clinton, South Carolina. One of the State's most popular performers, he played on radio station WBT, Charlotte for over 20 years, achieving national fame when his recording of **Guitar Boogie**, originally issued by the Superdisc label, was subsequently released on MGM, providing Smith with a 1947 million-seller.

After several years of hits for MGM, many of which were of the eight-to-a-bar genre, Smith moved on to other labels. He signed to Starday and Dot during the '60s

and has since recorded for Monument and CMH. His **Feuding Banjos** (frequently called **Duelling Banjos**) became internationally well known as a result of its prominent part in the film 'Deliverance'.

Albums:
Battling Banjos (Monument/–)
Feudin' Again – with Don Reno (CMH/–)

Fiddlin' Arthur Smith

Born in Dixon County, Tennessee, Smith was a railroad worker who, during the early 30s, joined Sam and Kirk McGee in a trio known as the Dixieliners. Becoming an Opry favourite, Smith toured under the auspices of WSM for several years, sometimes playing with the McGees, at other times working with his own trio; the latter group acquiring a national reputation with their recording of **There's More Pretty Girls Than One** in 1936.

Later, Smith moved on to play with the Delmore Brothers and throughout the '40s and '50s worked variously as a sideman or with units of his own, much of it on the West Coast, where he appeared in western films with Jimmy Wakely etc.

The 1960s brought him a new lease of life, thanks to the advent of the folk festivals and the rediscovery of many folk heroes by a new and youthful audience. This period was marked by **Fiddlin' Arthur Smith**, an album for Starday in 1963, and a Mike Seeger-masterminded Smith-McGee Brothers set for Folkways.

Album:
The McGee Brothers With Arthur Smith (Folkways/–)

157

Cal's Country, Cal Smith. Courtesy MCA Records.

Cal Smith

Born Calvin Grant Shofner on April 7, 1932, Gans, Oklahoma, Smith was raised in Oakland, California. After the usual round of talent contests and local engagements, he became a regular on the California Hayride TV show, gaining his first regular club job in San Jose, California, during the early 1950s.

Later, after engagements that included a spell as a DJ, Smith became MC and vocalist with Ernest Tubb's Texas Troubadours, remaining with the band for a period of five and a half years. Through Tubb, Smith became signed to Kapp Records, initially charting with **The Only Thing I Want**, in 1967, then continuing to keep the label supplied with a number of lower-level hits (**Drinking Champagne**, **It Takes All Night Long**, **Heaven Is Just A Touch Away**, etc.) through to 1971. From this tiome, his discs began appearing on Decca.

Around the same time, his chart placings began to rise; **I've Found Someone Of My Own** became a Top 5 hit in 1972, a year during which Smith spent 202 days on the road, playing in such places as Alaska and Hawaii. In 1973, he earned yet another top placing with **The Lord Knows I'm Drinking**, capping even this success with that of **Country Bumpkin**, a massive seller during mid 1974 and a release that won him his first CMA award – for Single Of The Year.

Further hits followed with **Jason's Farm** (1975), **MacArthur's Hand** (1976) and **I Just Came Home To Count The Memories** (1977).

Then, mysteriously, Cal faded from the country charts, though he continued to record for MCA until early 1980 and has since had recordings released on the small Soundwaves label.

Albums:
Cal's Country (MCA/MCA)
Introducing (MCA/MCA)
I Just Came Home To Count The
  Memories (MCA/–)

Carl Smith

Born in Maynardsville, Tennessee on March 15, 1927, Carl Smith sold flower seeds to pay for his first guitar, then cut grass to pay for lessons.

His first break in show business came a few years later, with radio station WROL, Knoxville, Tennessee. Then in 1950, Jack Stapp, at that time programme director of WSM, asked Smith to come to Nashville and work on the WSM morning show.

Soon after, he won a place on the Opry, signed a contract with Columbia Records and, with his second release, **Let's Live A Little**, had a smash hit. That same year (1951), he was voted No. 1 country singer by several polls and accrued three further chartbusters via **If Teardrops Were Pennies**, **Mr. Moon** and **Let Old Mother Nature Have Her Way**.

A Way With Words, Carl Smith. Courtesy DJM Records.

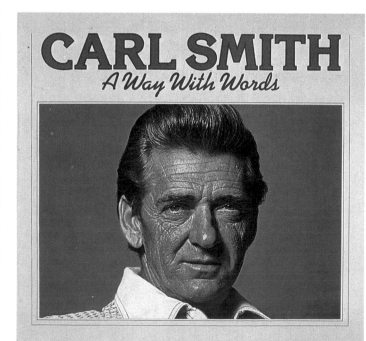

Famous Country Music Makers, Connie Smith. Courtesy RCA Records.

During the '50s and '60s he was rarely out of the charts, averaging around three hits per year, the biggest of these being **Don't Just Stand There**, **Are You Teasing Me?** (1952); **Trademark**, **Hey, Joe** (1953); **Loose Talk**, **Go, Boy, Go** (1954), **Kisses Don't Lie**, **There She Goes** (1955) and **Ten Thousand Drums** (1959), all Top 5 items.

Following his success on radio, Smith moved on to TV, working for such shows as Four Star Jubilee (ABC/TV) and Carl Smith's Country Music Hall, a weekly networked show in Canada, syndicated to several US stations. He has also guested on many other shows and been featured in two films – 'The Badge Of Marshall Brennan' and 'Buffalo Guns'.

In 1957, Smith married country singer Goldie Hill (his second wife; the first having been June Carter) and moved to a ranch near Franklin, Tennessee, to bring up his four children, Carlene, Lorri Lynn, Carl Jnr. and Larry Dean.

Today, he owns a 500 acre ranch with a ranch-styled home, a two storey colonial house converted into an office, another house used for storage, plus some 50 horses and 200 head of cattle.

Early in 1974, the singer left Columbia Records after a 24-year stay with the label (during which time he sold around 15 million discs) and moved on to Hickory Records, for whom he had some minor successes. In recent years, however, Carl has preferred to spend most of his time on his ranch, though he has re-recorded his older hits for a successful TV advertised album.

Albums:
Sings Bluegrass (Columbia/–)
Legendary (Gusto-Lakeshore/–)
This Lady Loving Me (Hickory/DJM)
Greatest Hits (Columbia/–)

Connie Smith

In 1963, Connie Smith was just another pretty Ohio housewife, but in winning an amateur talent contest she was heard by Bill Anderson. The result was an offer to sing with Anderson and an opportunity to embark on a recording career which has, at the present time, allowed her to accrue a tally of nearly 30 Top 10 hits.

Born in Elkhart, Indiana on August 14, 1941, one of a family of 16, Connie learned to play guitar while hospitalised with a serious leg injury. A performer at local events, she later married and settled down to a normal life of household chores. But following her discovery by Anderson, she became signed to RCA Records, creating a tremendous impact with her initial release **Once A Day**, an Anderson-penned song that became a country No. 1 in 1964.

An overnight success, Connie was signed to make her TV debut on the Jimmy Dean Show, won the plaudit Most Promising Singer of 1964 from Billboard and – in the wake of three early '65 hits with **Then And Only Then**, **Tiny Blue Transistor Radio** and **I Can't Remember** – she became an Opry star on June 13, 1965.

Since that time, Connie has appeared on scores of TV and radio shows and has featured in such country-oriented films as 'Las Vegas Hillbillies', 'Road To Nashville' and 'Second Fiddle To A Steel Guitar'. Also, recording mainly Bill Anderson and Dallas Frazier numbers, she has had hits with **Ain't Had No Lovin'**, **The Hurtin's All Over** (both 1966), **Cincinnati, Ohio**, **Burning A Hole In My Mind** (both 1967), **I Never Once Stopped Loving You** (1970), **Just One Time** (1971), **If It Ain't Love, Just For What I Am** (both 1972), **Love Is What You're Looking For** (1973), **Till (I Kissed You)** and **I Don't Wanna Talk About It Anymore** (1976).

One of the many country artists with deep religious convictions, the diminutive Connie, who spends a great deal of her time doing social work, toured Australia, New Zealand and Japan during 1972, raising funds for the children of Bangladesh.

Albums:
Famous Country Music Makers (–/RCA)
Songs We Fell In Love To (Columbia/CBS)
God Is Abundant (Columbia/–)
If It Ain't Love (RCA/RCA)

Below: Connie Smith. Dolly Parton rates her as the finest female country singer.

Margo Smith

A petite, ex-school teacher from Dayton, Ohio, Margo at one time used her talents singing country and folk songs as a teaching aid for the children in her kindergarten classes.

Margo had always nurtured ambitions to be a singer, but chose teaching first because of the financial security it could give. Nevertheless, she started writing songs in her spare time and cut a demo tape which she took to Nashville and promptly signed a recording contract with Chart Records.

A few singles were released, but they made little impression. However, in 1975 she signed a new contract with 20th Century Records and made her debut on the country charts with the self-penned **There I Said It**, which slowly headed towards the Top 10. At this point, Margo gave up teaching in favour of a singing career.

Shortly after this, 20th Century closed their Nashville offices and Margo was without a label. Eventually she signed with Warner Brothers and was soon back in the Top 10 with **Save Your Kisses For Me**, **Take My Breath Away** (both 1976) and

Love's Explosion (1977), before making the coveted top spot with **Don't Break The Heart That Loves You** (1978).

For the next couple of years Margo was rarely out of the charts, scoring another No. 1 with **It Only Hurts A Little While** (1978), a Top 5 hit with her update of **Little Things Mean A Lot** (1978) and Top 10 entries with **Still A Woman** and **If I Give My Heart To You**. She also recorded duets with Rex Allen Jr. of **Cup O' Tea** and **While The Feeling's Good** (1980 and 1981), with plans for an album to follow.

Changes at Warner Brothers during 1981 meant that Margo was dropped by the label, but she has since recorded for smaller labels like AMI, Moonshine and Bermuda Dunes, achieving minor hits but failing to make a return to the Top 10. A tremendously talented young lady and exciting stage performer, Margo is one of the few country ladies who yodel on stage.

In 1986 she began her climb back to the top once more by signing with Dot/MCA and cutting an album, simply titled **Margo Smith**.

Albums:
Diamonds And Chills (Warners/–)
Just Margo (Warners/–)
Song Bird (Warners/–)

As Long As There's A Sunday, Sammi Smith. Courtesy WEA Records.

Sammi Smith

Considered as a country rebel, to be mentioned alongside Jennings, Nelson and Co., Sammi originally made her mark as a crossover artist of some potential, her version of Kristofferson's **Help Me Make It Through** (CMA Single Of The Year, 1971) selling over two million copies.

Born in Orange, California on August 5, 1943, she grew up in Oklahoma, playing clubs in that area at the age of 12. Encouraged in her career by Oklahoma City songwriter/recording studio owner Gene Sullivan, she was heard by Tennessee Three bassist Marshall Grant, who persuaded her to make the inevitable trip to Nashville where she became a Columbia recording act.

Some moderate hits followed including **So Long, Charlie Brown** (1968) and **Brownsville Lumberyard** (1969), after which Sammi moved on to the Mega label in 1970, recording Mega's first album, **He's Everywhere**, the title track becoming a chart single. A second track from the same album was then selected as a follow-up, the amazingly successful **Help Me Make It Through The Night**, the sales of which prompted Mega to title the parent album in line with the single and to embark on a re-promotion campaign.

However, since that initial monster single, Sammi has found it hard to hit the charts consistently, though she has enjoyed Top 20 hits with **I've Got To Have You** (1972), **Today I Started Loving You Again** (1975), **Sunday School To Broadway** (1976), **Loving Arms** (1977) and **What A Lie** (1979) as she has moved through such labels as Elektra, Zodiac, Cyclone and Sound Factory.

One of the most soulful singers in country music, Sammi has the ability to transform even the most banal lyrics into a charged, emotional experience. Frankly, she is too good for country music, and not saleable enough by far.

Albums:
Girl Hero (Cyclone/–)
New Winds, All Quadrants (Elektra/–)
Mixed Emotions (Elektra/–)

Hank Snow

The most revered of all Canadian country performers, Clarence Eugene Snow was born in Liverpool, Nova Scotia on May 9, 1914. Leaving home at 12, he became a cabin boy on a freighter for four years but in his teens began singing in Nova Scotia clubs, obtaining his first radio show in 1934, on CHNS, Halifax, Nova Scotia.

Known initially as the 'Yodelling Ranger'

Country Music Hall Of Fame, Hank Snow. Courtesy RCA Records.

and later as the 'Singing Ranger', he became signed to RCA-Victor in 1934, his first sides being **Lonesome Blue Yodel** and **Prisoned Cowboy**.

Despite a move to the US during the mid '40s and appearances on such shows as the WWVA Jamboree, Snow remained virtually unknown south of the Canadian border until 1949 when, following a disappointing Opry performance on January 7, his recording of **Marriage Vows** became a Top 10 hit.

In 1950 he became an Opry regular, that same year seeing the release of **I'm Moving On**, a self-penned hit that became a US No. 1, remaining in the country charts for well over 40 weeks. Throughout the '50s and early '60s, Snow continued to provide RCA with a huge number of Top 10 singles – several of them being train songs, revealing his debt to Jimmie Rodgers, a singer he had idolised as a boy. His immaculately enunciated ballads also attracted the attention of myriad record buyers.

Too numerous to list, Snow's hits include **Golden Rocket** (1950), **Rhumba Boogie** (1951), **I Don't Hurt Anymore** (1954) and the tongue-twisting **I've Been Everywhere** (1962), all country No. 1s, **I'm Moving On** and **I Don't Hurt Anymore** both becoming million sellers.

Snow, who has consistently fought against what he believes to be over-

Still Movin' On. Hank Snow's 104th album. Courtesy RCA Records.

commercialisation of country music, has proved to be one of C&W's most travelled ambassadors, appearing in his somewhat stagey cowboy attire at venues all over the world, including some that were close to the Vietnamese war front.

His eldest son, Jimmie Rodgers Snow, is both a country performer and a travelling evangelist. Hank still appears on the Opry, though he rarely tours nowadays, and he has had no inclination to record since being dropped by RCA after a record breaking 45 years with the same company. He was elected to the Country Music Hall Of Fame in 1979.

Albums:
Famous Country Music Makers (–/RCA)
Award Winners (RCA/RCA)
Grand Old Opry Favourites (RCA/RCA)
Hits Covered by Snow (RCA/–)
Best Of Hank Snow (RCA/RCA)

20 Of The Best, Sons Of The Pioneers. Courtesy RCA Records.

Sons Of The Pioneers

Originally a guitarist/vocals trio when formed by Roy Rogers, Bob Nolan and Tim Spencer in 1934 as the Pioneer Trio, the name changed to the Sons Of The Pioneers in deference to the American Indian heritage of new members Karl and Hugh Farr.

They did much radio work during the '30s and recorded variously for Decca, Columbia and RCA. Films also figured large for them and they appeared in many of those featuring Rogers after he had left the band to pursue his film career. A few of the films in which the Sons were involved included 'Rhythm On The Range' (1936), 'Hollywood Canteen' (1944), 'Gay Rancheros' (1944) and 'Melody Time' (1948).

Other members of the group have included Lloyd Perryman, Ken Carson, Ken Curtis, Pat Brady, Doye O'Dell, Dale Warren, Deuce Spriggins, Tommy Doss, Shug Fisher and Rusty Richards.

Bob Nolan composed the group's biggest hits **Tumbling Tumbleweeds** and **Cool Water**, and Spencer, who left in 1950 but managed the Sons until 1955, composed **Cigarettes, Whiskey And Wild Wild Women**, **Careless Kisses** and **Roomful Of Roses**. Spencer died on April 26, 1974 aged 65, in California. However, the Sons were still performing at that time, led by Perryman who had originally joined the group back in 1936 and passed away on May 3, 1977, aged 60.

A word should be said about Bob Nolan, whose songwriting may be the finest ever to appear in country music. A brilliant poet with an inventive ear for melody and harmony, he virtually invented the sound and style of western harmony singing single-handedly, and he supplied the once thriving field with the great majority of its classic songs, which, in addition to the above, include **Trail Herding Cowboy**, **A Cowboy Has To Sing**, **One More Ride**, **Way Out There** and **Song Of The Bandit**.

Nolan himself recorded an acclaimed solo album, **Sound Of A Pioneer**, for

Elektra in 1979. The following year he died at his home in California on June 15, aged 72, and The Sons Of The Pioneers were elected to the Country Music Hall Of Fame the following October.

Albums:
20 Of The Best (–/RCA)
Cowboy Country (–/Bear Family)
Riders In The Sky (Camden/–)
Sons Of The Pioneers (Columbia/CBS)

Red Sovine

King of the truck driving songs and narrations, Woodrow Wilson Sovine was born in Charleston, West Virginia on July 17, 1918.

Like many other country entertainers, he learnt guitar at an early age and tuned in to C&W radio stations, obtaining his own first radio job with Jim Pike's Carolina Tar Heels on WCHS, Charleston, West Virginia, in 1935. Later the unit moved on to play the WWVA Jamboree, Wheeling, West Virginia.

During the late 1940s, Sovine formed his own band, The Echo Valley Boys, he and the group gaining their own show on WCHS. Then on June 3, 1949, Hank Williams left the Louisisana Hayride to become an Opry regular and Sovine's band was drafted in as a replacement, the Echo Valley Boys also taking over Williams' daily 15 minute Johnny Fair Syrup Show stint.

From 1949 until 1954, Sovine remained a star attraction on the Hayride, during that period striking up a friendship with Webb Pierce. The twosome performed duets on the show, combining to write songs and, in turn, both becoming Opry regulars. On disc they joined up for **Why, Baby Why?**, a country No. 1 in 1956, following this with **Little Rosa**, a Top 10 hit that same year.

Though Sovine remained a top rated performer throughout the late '50s and early '60s, his name disappeared from the charts until 1964, when a Starday release, **Dream House For Sale**, climbed into the listings. This was followed a few months later by **Giddyup Go**, which provided the singer with yet another No. 1.

From that time on, Sovine continued adding to his list of chart honours, making a major impression in 1967 with **Phantom 309**, his classic tale of a truck-driving ghost. Then in the mid '70s, following a flood of recordings based on tales of CB radio, Sovine came into his own, achieving one of his biggest-ever successes with **Teddy Bear**, a highly sentimental tale regarding a crippled boy, his CB radio and a number of friendly truckers. He had, at the age of 58, finally earned a million-selling record.

Teddy Bear, Red Sovine. Courtesy RCA Records.

Red was killed in a motor accident in Nashville on April 4, 1980, but had a posthumous British pop hit with **Teddy Bear** when it was re-released due to popular demand and reached No. 2 in the charts in 1987[1], selling more than half-a-million copies.

Albums:
Little Rosa (–/Release)
Teddy Bear (Starday/RCA)
Woodrow Wilson Sovine (Starday/–)

Billie Jo Spears

Though she has got a voice that is hardly in Opry tradition – take away the country backings and you are left with a bluesy sound befitting an uppercrust torch singer – Billie Jo was country raised (born on January 14, 1937, Beaumont, Texas) and appeared on the Louisiana Hayride in her early teens. She performed **Too Old For Toys, Too Young For Boys**, a ditty which she recorded on the reverse of a Mel Blanc Bugs Bunny type disc at the age of 13.

Graduating from high school, she worked in a variety of jobs, becoming a car-hop at a Beaumont drive-in for a period of four years. In 1964, country songwriter Jack Rhodes heard her sing and talked her into a trip to Nashville where she became signed to UA Records. However, her first country hit came with **He's Got More Love In His Little Finger**, a Capitol release of 1968, Billie Jo reaching the Top 5 during the following year with **Mr. Walker It's All Over**. Apart from an elongated chart stay with **Marty Gray** (1970), her other Capitol sides, though fair sellers (five other titles reaching the charts) failed to emulate the success of **Mr. Walker**.

A change of fortune occurred following a switch to UA Records in 1974, **Blanket On The Ground** (1975), a Roger Bowling song dealing with the delights of alfresco lovemaking, establishing Billie Jo with an international reputation.

Since then she has scored with **What**

The Best Of Billie Jo Spears. An early hits collection from Capitol.

I've Got In Mind, **Misty Blue** (both 1976), **If You Want Me** (1977), **Lonely Hearts Club**, **'57 Chevrolet** (both 1978) and **I Will Survive** (1979). She has maintained her success in Britain due to regular tours and pop successes with **What I've Got In Mind** and **Sing Me An Old-Fashioned Song**, though in America she has failed to gain a contract with a major label for a number of years.

Albums:
We Just Came Apart At The Dreams (–/Premier)
For The Good Times (–/Music for Pleasure)
Special Songs (–/Liberty)
Singles Album (–/United Artists)

Carl T. Sprague

Known as the Original Singing Cowboy, Sprague was born near Houston, Texas, in 1895. A cowboy music enthusiast in his college days, he led a band while at Texas A&M, playing on the campus radio station.

In August, 1925, inspired by Vernon Dalhart's hit record, **The Prisoner's Song**, he recorded ten songs for Victor, his initial release – **When The Work's All Done This Fall** – selling nine hundred thousand copies. Further sessions (in 1926, '27 and '29) ensued, at which Sprague recorded mainly traditional cowboy material from the late nineteenth century.

A man of many occupations – including insurance salesman, army officer, coach, garage operator, etc – Sprague, who settled in Bryan, Texas, performed at various folk festivals during the 1960s and recorded for the German Folk Variety label in 1972.

Album:
Carl T. Sprague (–/Bear Family)

Joe Stampley

Born on June 6, 1943 in Springhill, Louisiana, Stampley was influenced by both country entertainers and rock 'n' rollers like the Everly Brothers and Jerry

I Don't Lie, Joe Stampley. Courtesy Epic Records.

Lee Lewis. His first forays into recordings were made in 1959 when he cut some rock 'n' roll records for Imperial and Chess.

Becoming a member of the Uniques, a pop outfit that had pop hits in the late '60s with **Not Too Long Ago** and **All These Things** on the Paula label, Stampley started making a name for himself as a songwriter, signing with Gallico Music in Nashville. This led to him making a move towards country music and signing a contract with Dot Records in 1969.

He achieved a minor country hit via **Take Time To Know Her** (1971), finally making the Top 10 with **If You Touch Me (You've Got To Love Me)** in 1972 and achieving his first number one with **Soul Song** the following year. Since then he has achieved an impressive tally of major hits with such releases as **I'm Still Loving You** (1974), **Roll On Big Mama** (1975) – his first release for Epic Records, **All These Things** (1976), **Everyday I Have To Cry Some** (1977), **Do You Ever Fool Around** (1978) and **Put Your Clothes Back On** (1979).

In 1979 Stampley teamed up with Moe Bandy, resulting in the pair having a No. 1 hit with **Just Good Ole Boys** and being voted Top Vocal Duo by the ACM (1979) and CMA (1980). Now regarded as a fully-fledged honky-tonk singer, Stampley has consolidated his position in the '80s

Soul Song, Joe Stampley. Courtesy Ember Records.

with such hits as **There's Another Woman** (1980), **Whiskey Chasin'** (1981), **Back Slidin'** (1982) and **Double Shot Of My Baby's Love** (1983), plus more duets with Moe Bandy, including the 1984 chart-topper **Where's The Dress**.

Albums:
Soul Song (–/Ember)
Saturday Nite Dance (Epic/–)
Ten Songs About Her (Epic/–)
After Hours (Epic/–)
I'm Goin' Hurtin' (Epic/–)

Stanley Brothers

Responsible for some of the most beautiful harmony vocals to ever emerge from the bluegrass scene, guitarist and lead vocalist Carter Glen Stanley (born in McClure, Virginia on August 27, 1925) and his brother, banjoist and vocalist Ralph Edmond Stanley (born in Stratton, Virginia on February 25, 1927), formed an old-time band, the Stanley Brothers and The Clinch Mountain Boys, in 1946, and began broadcasting on radio station WCYB, Bristol, Virginia.

Recording for the small Rich-R-Tone label in 1948, they cut **Molly And Tenbrooks**, the band switching direction and playing in the bluegrass style of Bill Monroe, Ralph Stanley utilising the three-finger method of banjo playing popularised by Monroe sideman, Earl Scruggs.

In March 1949, the Stanleys signed for Columbia records and began cutting a series of classic bluegrass sides (all vocals), retaining mandolin player and vocalist Pee Wee Lambert from their previous band and adding various fiddle and bass players at different sessions, George Shuffler replacing Lambert and becoming part of the Stanley Brothers' sound just prior to the band's last Columbia session in April, 1952.

Throughout the '50s and '60s, the Stanleys recorded for such labels as Mercury, Starday and King, often cutting purely religious material. They also engaged on many tours, playing a prestigious date at London's Albert Hall as part of their European tour in March, 1966.

Above: Bluegrass harmony vocal duo, Carter (left) and Ralph Stanley.

But it was to be the Stanley Brothers' only British appearance; Carter Stanley died in a Bristol, Virginia, hospital on December 1 that same year.

Since the death of his brother, Ralph Stanley has kept the tradition of the Clinch Mountain Boys alive – though his music has become increasingly traditional in character.

Below: A fresh-faced and innocent Kenny Starr.

The music of The Stanleys, however, has been reactivated by younger, contemporary artists like Emmylou Harris, Dan Fogelberg and Chris Hillman, who have used many of their classic songs like **The Darkest Hour Is Just Before Dawn** and **Think Of What You've Done** in their repertoires.

Albums:
Recorded Live Vol. 1 (Rebel/–)
Recorded Live Vol. 2 (Rebel/–)
The Best Of . . . (Starday/–)

Ralph Stanley Albums:
Ralph Stanley, A Man And His Music (Rebel/–)
Old Country Church (Rebel/–)

Kenny Starr

Loretta Lynn protégé Kenny Starr was born in Topeka, Kansas on September 21, 1953, his family later moving to Burlingame, Kansas, where Starr grew up.

At an early age he began visiting the local Veterans Of Foreign Wars hall, where he would unplug the jukebox and sing for nickles and dimes. By the age of nine he was leading his first band, The Rockin' Rebels, this being quickly superseded by another group, Kenny And The Imperials, which toured the area, earning Starr 10 to 15 dollars a night.

At 16 he became a country entertainer, initially leading a band called The Country Showman, later winning a talent contest held in Wichita after singing his version of Ray Price's **I Won't Mention It Again**.

Local promoter Hap Peebles saw Starr's performance on the show and asked if he would appear on a forthcoming Loretta Lynn and Conway Twitty concert, which Starr did, winning a standing ovation. After the concert, Loretta suggested that he should move to Nashville and offered him a job in her own road show. Soon after, she also helped him obtain a recording contract with MCA.

A singer-songwriter-guitarist, Starr had a No. 1 country hit with his own **The Blind Man In The Bleachers** in January, 1976, following this up with minor successes like **Tonight I Face The Man Who Made It Happen** (1976), **Hold Tight** (1977) and **Slow Drivin'** (1978), before mysteriously fading from the limelight.

Album:
The Blind Man In The Bleachers (MCA/–)

Statler Brothers

Vocal Group:
Philip Balsley, born Augusta County, Virginia, August 8, 1939; Jimmy Fortune, replaced Lew De Witt, who retired from the band in July, 1982 due to ill health; Don Reid, born Staunton, Virginia, June 5, 1945; Harold Reid, born Augusta County Virginia, August 21, 1939; Lew DeWitt, born Roanoke County, Virginia, March 8, 1938.

Voted CMA Vocal Group of the Year every year between 1972 and 1977 and again in 1979 and 1980, the Statlers – then Harold (bass), Lew (tenor) and Phil (baritone) – began singing together in 1955 at Lyndhurst Methodist Church in Staunton,

Virginia. In 1960, Harold's younger brother Don joined the group – then known as the Kingsmen – and became front man, the quartet passing an audition to become part of the Johnny Cash Show some three years later. At this point, they changed their name to the Statler Brothers after espying the name Statler on a box of tissues in a hotel room.

In 1965 they went further up the ladder after recording **Flowers On The Wall**, a song penned by DeWitt, this Columbia release becoming a Top 5 pop hit, also gaining a high place on the country charts. The group won two Grammy awards (Best New Country Group and Best Contemporary Performance By A Country Group) as a consequence.

Further hits followed – **Ruthless** and the delightfully titled **You Can't Have Your Kate And Edith Too** (both 1967) proving among the most popular – but it was not until 1970 and a new recording contract with Mercury that the Statlers moved into top gear, immediately gaining a second crossover hit with **Bed Of Roses**.

They became undisputed kings of country vocal groups, winning a Grammy in 1972 for Best Vocal Performance for **Class Of '57** and scoring such No. 1 country hits as **I'll Go To My Grave Loving You** (1975), **Do You Know You Are My Sunshine** (1978), **Don't Wait On Me** (1981), **Elizabeth** (1983) and **My Only Love** (1985).

Though The Statlers are now challenged by such groups as The Oak Ridge Boys, Alabama and The Judds, they are something of a country music institution, the name associated with a certain meticulous attention to detail, an immediately recognisable sound and an

Above: The Statler Brothers, winners of four Music City News Awards in 1986.

almost unflagging compositional quality. Even when Lew De Witt had to leave the group in 1982 and was replaced by young Jimmy Fortune, the group just carried on, Fortune emerging as a songwriter of note,

Oh Happy Day, The Statler Brothers. Courtesy CBS Records.

coming up with several of The Statlers' recent hit songs.

Albums:
Today (Mercury/Mercury)
Sing Country Symphonies In E Major (Mercury/–)
The Originals (Mercury/–)
Pardners In Rhyme (Mercury/Mercury)
10th Anniversary (Mercury/–)
Country Classics (–/Phillips)

Red Steagall

Writer of the brilliant **Texas Red**, an allegory concerning the life of Christ, Russell 'Red' Steagall (born in Gainsville, Texas) learned his music in an atmosphere pervaded by the sounds of Bob Wills.

Polio struck when he was 15, leaving Steagall without the use of his left hand and arm. He used the months of therapy and recuperation to master the guitar and mandolin, and later began playing in coffee houses during his stay at West Texas State University, where he studied animal husbandry – just in case he did not make it in show biz.

However, his first job found him working for an oil company as a soil chemistry expert, with performing remaining a sideline until 1967 when **Here We Go Again**, a Steagall original penned with the aid of co-writer Don Lanier, provided Ray Charles with a chart record.

Other Steagall songs subsequently found their way on to disc and the Texan became involved on the song publishing

If You've Got The Time, I've Got The Song, Red Steagall. Courtesy Capitol.

side of the industry, eventually signing a recording contract with Dot in 1969 without too much success.

He joined Capitol Records in 1972, coming up with such hit singles as **Party Dolls And Wine**, **Somewhere My Love** (both 1972) and **Someone Cares For You** (1974). He then rejoined ABC-Dot, finally making the Top 10 with **Lone Star Beer And Bob Wills Music** (1976). That success was short lived, and though he has recorded some fine albums, mainly with a western swing or cowboy feel, he has remained very much an in-demand performer on the rodeo circuit. Here he often makes a spectacular entrance on a flashy looking horse, delighting the rodeo crowds with his western swing tunes for the rodeo dance-time in the evening.

Albums:
Cowboy Favourites (Delta/–)
Party Dolls And Wine (Capitol/–)
Lone Star Beer And Bob Wills Music (ABC-Dot/–)

Keith Stegall

A talented Nashville-based songwriter, Keith, born in 1955 in Wichita Falls, Texas, the son of Bob Stegall who played steel guitar for Johnny Horton, has seen his songs score on the country, pop, R&B, adult contemporary and jazz charts.

At the age of eight he made his stage debut on a country music show in Tyler,

Texas, and before he reached his teens he had formed his own four-piece combo called The Pacesetters. Soon after this, Keith's family moved to Shreveport, Louisiana and, following a stint in a high school rock band, he joined a folk group called The Cheerful Givers.

By this time he was busy writing songs, his musical diversity surfacing in the early '70s when, at different times, he served as a music director for his church and later held down a job as a night club singer. After receiving a B.A. in Religion from Centenary College, he managed to arrange a meeting with Kris Kristofferson and played him some songs.

He was urged to make a move to Nashville and between 1975 and 1977 Keith made many trips to Music City in search of a publisher for his songs. Eventually finding a job writing songs for CBS Songs (then called April/Blackwood) in Nashville in 1978, he rapidly distinguished himself as a writer for the likes of Al Jarreau (**We're In This Love Together**), Leon Everette (**Hurricane**), Dr. Hook (**Sexy Eyes**), Mickey Gilley (**Lonely Nights**) and The Commodores (**The Woman In My Life**).

After a brilliant start as a songwriter, Keith made a dismal one as a recording artist, signing with Capitol in 1980 and making the lower rungs of the charts with **The Fool Who Fooled Around**. Never able to score higher than the mid-50s with Capitol (and subsequently with its sister label EMI America), Keith signed with Epic in 1984 and made No. 25 with **I Want To Go Somewhere**, followed by **Whatever Turns You On** (No. 19), **California** (No. 13) and finally cracked the Top 10 in September 1985 with the self-penned **Pretty Lady**.

He has continued to concentrate on his writing, usually as a co-writer with such tunesmiths as Stewart Harris, Tom Schuyler and Roger Murrah, coming up with hits for such varied artists as Kenny Rogers, Juice Newton, Charley Pride, Johnny Mathis, Reba McEntire and Glen Campbell.

Album:
Keith Stegall (Epic/–)

Ray Stevens

A talented singer-songwriter, arranger, producer and multi-instrumentalist, Stevens (born Ray Ragsdale in Clarkdale, Georgia, 1939) studied music at Georgia State University. He then moved to Nashville where he began recording such novelty hits as **Jeremiah Peabody's Poly Unsaturated Quick Dissolving Fast Acting Pleasant Tasting Green And Purple Pills**

Nashville, Ray Stevens. A self-produced album for Barnaby Records.

(1961), **Ahab The Arab** (1962), **Harry The Hairy Ape** (1963), **Mr. Businessman** (1968) and **Gitarzan** (1969).

Since the end of the '60s Stevens, who has recorded for such labels as Judd, Mercury, Monument, Barnaby, Janus, Warner, RCA and MCA, has turned increasingly to country music, scoring with such discs as **Turn Your Radio On** (1971), **Nashville** (1973) and a semi-bluegrass version of **Misty** (1975), for which he was awarded a Grammy for Best Arrangement Accompanying A Vocalist.

From time to time he still produces pieces of sheer lunacy like **The Streak** (a pop No.1 in 1974), **Shriner's Convention** (1980), **Mississippi Squirrel Revival** (1984) and **It's Me Again, Margaret** (1985).

Albums:
Misty (Barnaby/Janus)
Greatest Hits (RCA/–)
He Thinks He's Ray Stevens (MCA/MCA)
Greatest Hits (–/Spot)

Gary Stewart

An exciting honky tonk singer-songwriter whose vibrato-filled voice places him in a love or hate category, Stewart was born on May 28, 1945 in Letcher County, Kentucky, moving to Florida with his family when he was 12.

His recording career began in 1964 with **I Loved You Truly**, a single for Cory which did little. Stewart then went on the road, playing bass with the Amps, a rock outfit,

Below: Gary Stewart. Hail honky-tonk and viva vibrato!

Out Of Hand, Gary Stewart. Courtesy RCA Records.

eventually returning home to work for an aircraft firm.

In 1967 he met policeman Bill Eldridge, an ex-rocker who had contacts in Nashville. Together they began writing songs, one becoming a minor hit for Stonewall Jackson, commencing a deluge that included **Sweet Thang And Cisco**, a 1969 hit for Nat Stuckey; **When A Man Loves A Woman** and **She Goes Walking Through My Mind**, both 1970 Top 5 discs for Billy Walker, and other material for such artists as Kenny Price, Jack Greene, Johnny Paycheck, Cal Smith, Hank Snow and Warner Mack.

But, with his own recording contract with Kapp petering out, Stewart returned to Fort Pierce, Florida, leaving behind some demo sessions he had made of Motown material, cut while he was working in various capacities at Bradley's Barn studio.

These demos were later heard by Roy Dea, a Mercury producer who was subsequently signed to RCA by Jerry Bradley. He immediately signed Stewart for his new label, his belief in the singer paying off when Stewart's **Drinkin' Thing**, a second-time-round release, became a Top 10 hit in 1974.

Since that time, Stewart has had other major chart discs with **Out Of Hand** (1975), **She's Actin' Single (I'm Drinkin' Doubles)** (1975), **In Some Room Above The Street** (1976), **Ten Years Of This** (1977) and **Whiskey Trip** (1978). He has rigidly stuck to playing the honky tonk clubs where he feels most comfortable, which has restricted his chances of becoming a major superstar.

In 1982, Gary teamed up with singer-songwriter Dean Dillon, and the two wild honky tonkers came up with some dynamic numbers like **Brotherly Love** (1982) and **Smokin' In The Rockies** (1983), but failed to make their mark with the record-buying public.

Albums:
Little Junior (RCA/–)
Brotherly Love – with Dean Dillon (RCA/–)
20 Of The Best (–/RCA)

John Stewart

With over a dozen albums to his name as a solo performer, singer-songwriter John Stewart (born on September 5, 1939 in San Diego, California) has been a major influence on the American country and rock scene for more than 20 years.

He played rock 'n' roll in his youth, but soon turned to folk music. A prolific writer, he performed a couple of his songs for the Kingston Trio backstage after one of their concerts. The Trio liked the songs, **Green**

Cannons In The Rain, John Stewart. Courtesy RCA Records.

Grasses and **Molly Dee**, which led to John being asked to form a similar folk trio by Roulette Records. The result was The Cumberland Three, who recorded three albums for the New York based label between 1959 and 1961.

When founder member Dave Guard left the Kingston Trio at the end of 1961, John was asked to join them. This was after the days of **Tom Dooley**, but before the beat explosion, and the Trio were big news. However, despite appearing before mass audiences and playing an important part in the Trio (he was the only songwriter and was also responsible for them recording the works of such people as Billy Edd Wheeler, Rod McKuen, etc) John never felt a real part of the Trio, or happy with the 'college fraternity' lifestyle they led. Indeed, for the whole six years he was with them until the break-up in 1967, he was on a salary.

Judging by his subsequent music, the split must have been a welcome relief. He was far more in touch with other artists and once before nearly left the Trio to form a new group with John Phillips (of the Mamas & Papas) and Scott McKenzie. For a while after leaving the Trio he hung out with John Denver and, though they never went out as a duo, they recorded demos of **Leaving On A Jet Plane** and **Daydream Believer**, the latter song becoming a multi-million seller for The Monkees in 1967, Stewart surviving for many years on the revenue from the song.

Stewart next found himself with constant lady friend Buffy Ford, and together they recorded **Signals Through The Glass**, an album based around the paintings of Andrew Wyeth, whose subjects of an older, simpler, rural America were to permeate Stewart's work. In the late '60s he worked on the Bobby Kennedy election campaign and utilised some of his experiences in the song **Omaha Rainbow**.

Throughout the '70s John recorded a series of albums as he moved through such labels as Capitol, Warners and RCA. **California Bloodlines**, recorded for Capitol in 1969 and produced by Nick Venet in Nashville, is counted as something of a milestone. Further albums featured the talents of such musicians and singers as James Taylor, Carole King, Doug Kershaw, Chris Darrow, James Burton, Glen D. Hardin, Buddy Emmons, Fred Carter Jr., Pete Drake and Charlie McCoy. But at the centre were John's songs, crammed full of celebratory lyricism, somehow capturing the vastness of America beneath open skies.

He built up a sizeable cult following, especially in Britain, where a magazine, Omaha Rainbow, is named after one of his songs. Finally he achieved the commercial success he deserved when his second

album for RSO Records, **Bombs Away Dream Babies**, made the Top 10 album charts and his single, **Gold**, an ode to songwriters everywhere, reached the American Top 5 and won John a gold disc in 1979.

This turned out to be a short-lived success, and during the '80s John Stewart was once again relegated to being a cult hero, a singer-songwriter who appeals to the more discerning music lovers. He continues to please those dedicated fans with regular album releases, which are now issued on small independent labels such as Allegiance and Sunstorm.

Albums:
California Bloodlines (Capitol/Capitol)
The Phoenix Concerts (RCA/RCA)
Forgotten Songs Of Some Old Yesterday (RCA/RCA)
Bombs Away Dream Babies (RSO/RSO)
Blondes (Allegiance/–)
Trancas (–/Sunstorm)

Below: Redd Stewart, whose Tennessee Waltz was a hit for Patti Page, Jo Stafford, Guy Lombardo, Spike Jones . . .

Redd Stewart

Henry Redd Stewart, born in Ashland City, Tennessee on May 27, 1921, began his career by writing a song for a car dealer's commercial at the age of 14. He then formed and played in bands around the Louisville, Kentucky area until 1937, when Pee Wee King came to Louisville to play on radio station WHAS and signed Stewart as a musician. Eddy Arnold was the band's vocalist at the time, although Redd was Eddy's replacement as vocalist when Arnold went off on his own. Then came Pearl Harbour, and Stewart was drafted for army service in the South Pacific, during which period he wrote **A Soldier's Last Letter**, a major hit for Ernest Tubb.

After the war he rejoined King and began taking a serious interest in songwriting, teaming with King to write **Tennessee Waltz** (a hit for both King and Cowboy Copas but a 1950 six million seller for pop singer Patti Page), following this with **Slow Poke** (a 1951 gold disc for King),

and **You Belong To Me** (which, in the Jo Stafford version, topped the US charts for five weeks during 1952), and the reworked old fiddle tune, **Bonaparte's Retreat**.

Stewart's own career on disc has been less successful – despite stints with such labels as RCA, Starday, King and Hickory – and it seems that he will generally be remembered for his songwriting and his 30-year association with Pee Wee King.

Album:
The Best Of Pee Wee King And Redd Stewart (Starday/–)

Wynn Stewart

Singer-songwriter, born in Morrisville, Missouri on June 7, 1934, Stewart received early singing experience in church, and at 13 appeared on KWTO, Springfield, Missouri. A year or so later his family moved to California and this was where he made his first recording at the tender age of 15.

During the mid '50s, Stewart became

signed to Capitol Records, later that decade switching to Jackpot Records, a subsidiary of Challenge. His song, **Above And Beyond**, provided a big hit for Buck Owens in 1960, while some of Stewart's own Jackpot sides featured the voice of Jan Howard. For Challenge itself, Stewart provided such hits as **Wishful Thinking** (1959), **Big Big Day** (1961) and **Another Day, Another Dollar** (1962), around that period opening up his own club in Las Vegas and appearing on his own TV show.

Some two and a half years later he sold the club and moved to California, signing once more for Capitol and promoting his discs by tours with a new band, The Tourists. Purveying his California style of honky tonk and beer-stained ballads, Stewart made friends and infuenced record buyers, the result being a flow of country chart entries that has included **It's Such A Pretty World Today** (a No. 1 in 1967), **'Cause I Have You** (1967), **Love's Gonna Happen To Me** (1967), **Something Pretty** (1968), **In Love** (1968), **World-Wide Travellin' Man** (1969) and **It's A Beautiful Day** (1970).

Having spent their royalties on cars and other luxuries, the Depression of 1929 hit the Stonemans hard. Only one recording date, featuring Pop and his son Eddie, emanated from this period, and Pop had to resume his former occupation as a carpenter in a Washington DC naval gun factory. Meanwhile, his wife Hattie struggled to bring up her family – which eventually numbered 13 children.

Several of the children became musicians and Pop formed a family band during the late '40s, playing in the Washington area and recording an album for Folkways in 1957 that helped spark off a whole new career.

Proving popular on the major folk festivals and on college dates, the Stonemans became an in-demand outfit, making their debut on the Grand Ole Opry in 1962 and recording for Starday that same year.

During the mid '60s the family moved to Nashville, appeared on the Jimmy Dean ABC-TV show, and were signed to appear in their own TV show Those Stonemans in 1966. A year later, they won the CMA award for the Best Vocal Group, the band then consisting of Pop (guitar, autoharp), Scotty (fiddle), Jim (bass), Van (guitar), Donna (mandolin) and Roni (banjo), the last named becoming a star on the 'Hee Haw' TV show.

However, a stomach ailment began to affect Pop and he died in Nashville on June 14, 1968, his last recording session having taken place that day.

Although the Stonemans were – and still are – considered one of the finest semi-bluegrass bands, Pop's early record

Ernest V. Stoneman And The Blue Ridge Cornshuckers. Courtesy Rounder.

output with his Dixie Mountaineers featured sentimental ballads of the nineteenth century, British traditional melodies, dance tunes, much religious material and even a number of humorous sketches. He is reputed to be the first musician to record with an autoharp.

Albums:
In The Family (MGM/–)
The Stoneman Family (Folkways/–)
The Stonemans (MGM/–)
Stoneman's Country (MGM/–)
Tribute To Pop Stoneman (MGM/–)

George Strait

George Strait (born in Pearsall, Texas, in 1952) emerged in the early '80s as one of the best exponents of unvarnished, clean-cut country music. When he first started recording in 1981, his authentic country sound with twin fiddle breaks and strong steel guitar seemed to breathe fresh air into the somewhat stale Nashville scene.

Above: Wynn Stewart. At five he was singing in his hometown church. At 13 he was appearing regularly on radio.

Moving through a succession of labels including RCA (1973), Atlantic (1974) and Playboy (1975–77), he made a chart comeback with **After The Storm**, which reached the Top 10 in 1976. Subsequent releases failed to bring him the chart success he deserved, and Wynn continued recording for small labels like Win, 4-Star and Phonorama up until shortly before his death at his home in Hendersonville, Tennessee on July 17, 1985.

Albums:
After The Storm (Playboy/–)
Baby It's Yours (Capitol/–)

Cliffie Stone

Born Clifford Gilpin Snyder in Burbank, California, on March 1, 1917, Cliffie grew up in a rich country music tradition; his father was the well-known area banjo player-comedian professionally known as Herman the Hermit. Despite this background, Cliffie began his musical career as bassist for big bands such as Anson Weeks and Freddie Slack.

He soon got into country radio, however, and served as a disc jockey, MC and performer on several Los Angeles area stations, and was bandleader and featured comedian on the Hollywood Barn Dance.

Cliffie moved into the executive end of the music business in 1946 with the newly formed Capitol Records, with whom he stayed for over two decades, recording a half dozen albums of his own as well as guiding the careers of Tennessee Ernie Ford and many others. He stayed busy as a performer, however, and co-writing such hits as **No Vacancy**, **Divorce Me C.O.D.**, **New Steel Guitar Rag**, **So Round So Firm So Fully Packed** and **Sweet Temptation**.

In the mid 1960s, he turned his attention to several music business enterprises, including his publishing company Central Songs, which he sold to Capitol in 1969. Cliffie entered the record field once again in 1974, heading up the Granite label in California, but later retired from the music business.

Albums:
Square Dance USA (Capitol/–)
Cliffie Stone Sing-Along (Capitol/–)

Stoneman Family

One of the most famous family groups in Country Music, the Stonemans revolved around Ernest V. 'Pop' Stoneman (born in Monorat, Carroll County, Virginia on May 25, 1893), a carpenter who in 1924 wrote to Okeh and Columbia seeking an audition.

A Jew's harp and harmonica player by the age of ten and a banjoist and autoharp player in his teens, Pop was eventually heard by Okeh's Ralph Peer who recorded some test sides in September, 1924, cutting a number of finally accepted sides the following January. These included **The Sinking Of The Titanic**, one of the biggest selling records of the '20s.

Between 1925 and '29 Pop, sometimes with his wife or other members of his family, cut well over 200 titles for Okeh, Gennett, Paramount, Victor and other companies, also playing on dates with such acts as Riley Puckett and Uncle Dave Macon.

Mel Street's Greatest Hits, Courtesy GRT Records.

recording contract with the small Tandem Records, releasing his first single, **House Of Pride**, in 1970.

It was the other side of the record, Mel's self-penned **Borrowed Angel**, that gained most response from the public, eventually being picked up almost two years later by Royal American Records and making the country Top 10 during 1972. During the next few years, Mel recorded for a variety of labels including Metromedia, GRT, Polydor and Mercury, achieving Top 20 hits with **Lovin' On Back Streets** (1972), **Walk Softly On The Bridges** (1973), **Forbidden Angel** (1974), **Smokey Mountain Memories** (1975), **I Met A Friend Of Yours Today** (1976) and **Close Enough For Lonesome** (1977).

An excellent song stylist who specialized in honky tonk sagas and barroom ditties, Mel was the first singer to record the songs of such writers as Eddie Rabbitt, Earl Thomas Conley and John Schweers, and was one of the best interpreters of Bob McDill material, scoring with **Shady Rest, Barbara Don't Let Me Be The Last To Know** and filling his albums with McDill's songs.

Depressed due to a heavy workload and personal problems, Mel shot himself at his Hendersonville home on October 21, 1978 – his 45th birthday.

Albums:
Smokey Mountain Memories (GRT/–)
Country Soul (Polydor/–)
Many Moods Of Mel Street (Sunbird/–)

Stringbean

Born in Annville, Kentucky on June 17, 1915, his real name was David Akeman, the son of a fine banjo player. Stringbean made his own first banjo at the age of 12 and began playing professionally six years later in the Lexington area, eventually working with Cy Rogers' Lonesome Pine Fiddlers on radio station WLAP.

It was during this period that the 6ft 2in performer became dubbed Stringbean and adopted a more comic direction with his act. During the late '30s, he worked with Charlie Monroe (Monroe Brothers), then joined Bill Monroe on the Grand Ole Opry in July, 1942, staying with Monroe for three years.

Also known as 'The Kentucky Wonder', Stringbean an outstanding banjo player in the style of Uncle Dave Macon, was a longtime member of the Opry but perhaps won even more fame through his appearances on the Hee Haw TV series. He died on November 10, 1973, he and his wife Estelle being brutally murdered on returning home from the Opry and discovering burglars in their house.

Above: George Strait. His first MCA single came out in 1981. By 1985 he was CMA Male Vocalist Of The Year.

Born the second son of a junior high school teacher, George was raised on a ranch in Texas. After a short spell at college, George eloped with his high school sweetheart, Norma, and then joined the army.

While stationed in Hawaii, George started singing with a country band, using

Something Special, George Strait. Courtesy MCA Records.

the songs of his favourites like Merle Haggard, Bob Wills, George Jones and Hank Williams.

After his discharge in 1975, George returned to Texas and attended the South West Texas State University to complete his degree in agriculture. By this time he had been bitten by the music bug and, assembling his Ace In The Hole Band, was soon living a double life, attending classes by day and playing the clubs at night.

George and his band had built up a strong following on the south west Texas honky tonk circuit when, through the efforts of Erv Woolsey, a one-time MCA promotions man, he landed an MCA recording contract in early 1981, his first single, **Unwound**, reaching the Top 10 in the country charts.

During the next five years, George achieved ten No.1 country hits including **Fool Hearted Memory** (1982), **Amarillo By Morning** (1983), **You Look So Good In Love** (1984) and **The Chair** (1986), not to mention three gold albums and being named CMA Male Vocalist of the Year in 1985, with his LP, **Does Fort Worth Ever Cross Your Mind**, being voted Album Of The Year in the same poll.

Albums:
Something Special (MCA/MCA)
Greatest Hits (MCA/–)
Strait From The Heart (MCA/MCA)
Does Fort Worth Ever Cross Your Mind (MCA/MCA)

Mel Street

One of the finest country singers to emerge in the '70s, Mel (born on October 21, 1933 in Grundy, West Virginia), never really achieved the success or recognition he so richly deserved.

He started out singing on local radio shows in the early '50s and, following his marriage, moved to Niagara Falls, New York to work in the construction industry. For several years he sang in a local night spot and eventually had enough money saved to return to West Virginia, where he opened his own automobile paint and body workshop.

With his own four-piece band, Mel had his own television show in Bluefield, West Virginia called Country Showcase, at the same time working regularly in local clubs and honky tonks. Eventually he gained a

Above: David 'Stringbean' Akeman (left) and his sometime partner, Bijou.

Albums:
Salute To Uncle Dave Macon (Starday/–)
Me And My Old Crow (Nugget/–)

Nat Stuckey

Perhaps an underrated performer – though he has been a consistent supplier of medium sized hits – Nat Stuckey was born in Cass County, Texas on December 17, 1937. Employed for some considerable time as a radio announcer – he studied at Arlington State College, Dallas, in order to enhance his radio career – Stuckey also worked with a jazz group in 1957–58, becoming leader of a country band, the Corn Huskers, in 1958–59.

In 1966, Buck Owens recorded his fellow Texan's **Waitin' In The Welfare Line** – the most programmed country record of the year – at which stage Stuckey who had been working with the Louisiana Hayriders and recording for the Sims label, switched to Paula Records, scoring his own Top 10 hit with **Sweet Thang**.

Seven chart records later, in 1968, he label-hopped once more, this time signing for RCA and immediately scoring five major disc successes with **Plastic Saddle** (1968), **Joe And Mabel's 12th Street Bar And Grill**, **Cut Across Shorty**, **Sweet Thang And Cisco** and **Young Love** (all 1969), the latter a duet with Connie Smith.

Since that time, Stuckey has never really enjoyed the quota of potent singles

New Country Roads, Nat Stuckey. Courtesy RCA Records.

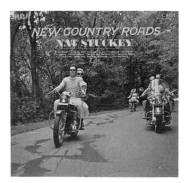

expected of him, only **She Wakes Me Every Morning With A Kiss** (1970) and **Take Time To Love Her** (1973) establishing his name in the upper regions of the charts.

During the mid '70s, he became an MCA artist, scoring Top 20 hits with **Sun Comin' Up** (1976) and **The Days Of Sand And Shovels** (1978) and producing **Independence**, an album acclaimed by the critics, but failing to achieve the kind of lasting commercial success that his talent deserved. Stuckey has since recorded for a variety of small labels but has been unable to make a return to the charts.

Albums:
Independence (MCA/MCA)
She Wakes Me With A Kiss Every
    Morning (RCA/RCA)
The Best Of (RCA/–)

Billy Swan

A comparative unknown when his **I Can Help** single hit the charts in 1974, Swan turned out to have a long pedigree in Southern music generally. Born on May 12, 1942 in Cape Girodeau, Missouri, he had written **Lover Please** at the age of 16. The song was recorded by his band of that time, Mirt Mirley and the Rhythm Steppers, but Clyde McPhatter made it a huge R&B hit.

Swan eventually tried his luck in Nashville and, taking odd jobs, he followed Kris Kristofferson as janitor at Columbia's studios. While working for Columbia Music, Swan became involved with Tony Joe White and produced that artist's first three, and most important, albums. He also backed Kris Kristofferson at the 1970 Isle of Wight Festival. Some time later he was to join Kinky Friedman's band for a while.

The 1974 album release of **I Can Help** revealed an artist with a liking for country, rock 'n' roll and rhythm and blues. Swan

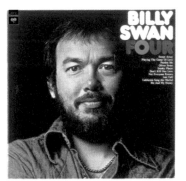

Four. Billy Swan, Courtesy CBS Records.

made an impressive version of Presley's **Don't Be Cruel** and in 1975 he was successful with another pop single hit with **Everything's The Same**.

In the summer of 1978, Swan joined A&M Records, then in 1981 moved on to Epic Records, recording some fine country-rock sides and touring with such highly respected Nashville musicians as Kenny Buttrey and Charlie McCoy as backing musicians.

Billy was back in the musical headlines in the summer of 1986 when he teamed up with former Eagle, Randy Meisner, Jimmy Griffin and Robb Royer of Bread, plus other musicians to form a new band, Black Tie, recording an album, **When The Night Falls**, for Bench Records.

Above: Billy Swan who took over Kris Kristofferson's job as janitor at Columbia Studios.

Albums:
I'm Into Lovin' You (Epic/–)
At His Best (Monument/–)
Rock 'n' Roll Moon (Monument/Monument)
I Can Help (Monument/Monument)

I Can Help, Billy Swan. Courtesy Monument Records.

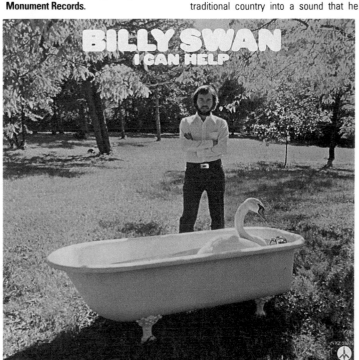

Joe Sun

Joe Sun is one of a talented breed of singer-songwriters who have unselfconsciously absorbed influences across the spectrum from Hank Williams to Waylon Jennings, and drawn from that wide range of styles in their work without going for any predetermined category.

In his music he mixes soul, blues, honky tonk, rock 'n' roll, contemporary and traditional country into a sound that he describes as blues/country. Joe, formerly James Paulson of Rochester, Minnesota, arrived in Nashville in 1972 after having served his time, so to speak, in college, the Air Force and working at various jobs, which included a disc jockey stint at Radio WMAD in Madison, Wisconsin and two years with a computer firm in Chicago.

Whilst in Chicago he sang with a variety of semi-pro bands, working under the name Jack Daniels. Once in Nashville he gave himself five years to make it. For a time he ran a small graphic business called The Sun Shop, then took up independent record promotions, which led to him signing a recording deal with Ovation Records towards the end of 1977.

His first single, **Old Flames (Can't Hold A Candle To You)**, came out in May 1978 and climbed steadily up the country charts reaching the Top 20. Further hits followed with **I Came On Business For The King**, **I'd Rather Go On Hurtin'** (both 1979) and **Shotgun Rider** (1980). Then with his third album, **Livin' On Honky Tonk Time**, just released, Ovation closed down its record division at the end of 1980.

Joe signed with Elektra the following year, and though he has continued to make some fine records, gain rave reviews for his dynamic stage show and command a huge cult following in Britain, he has failed to achieve the commercial success he so richly deserves.

Albums:
The Sun Never Sets (–/Sonet)
Out Of Your Mind (Ovation/Ovation)

Below: Sylvia: "I used to take a deodorant bottle, pretend it was a microphone and practise singing Patsy Cline songs."

Sylvia

One of the most attractive young ladies to have emerged on the Nashville scene, Sylvia (full name Sylvia Kirby Allen) was born in the small town of Kokomo, Indiana in 1957.

Her initial reputation in country music was gained not through performing, but by drawing pencil portraits of top country singers like Barbara Mandrell, Tanya Tucker, Dolly Parton and others when they appeared on the Little Nashville Opry in Indiana. Meeting these stars fuelled Sylvia's ambition to be a singer.

After graduating from high school in 1975, she headed for Nashville, armed with acapella demonstration tapes she had made. Sylvia did not land a job as a singer, but instead took a part-time secretarial position with Tom Collins, at that time producer of Barbara Mandrell and Charley Pride.

She soon persuaded Collins to use her on demo tapes of new songs being written by the songwriters under contract to the producer, and this led to her being used as a back-up vocalist on recording sessions by Ronnie Milsap, Barbara Mandrell and Dave & Sugar. Sylvia was finally offered an RCA contract in the summer of 1979, and her first release, **You Don't Miss A Thing**, made the country charts.

Further hits followed with **It Don't Hurt To Dream** and **Tumbleweed** (both 1980), then Sylvia hit the top of the charts with **Drifter** at the beginning of 1981, consolidating that success with **The Matador** (another No. 1), **Heart On The Mend**, **Sweet Yesterday** and the

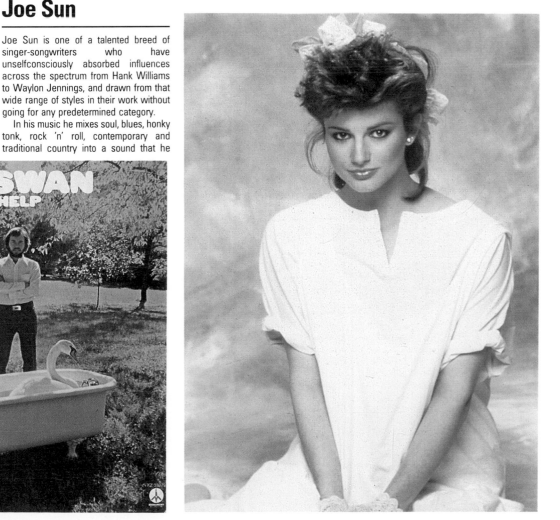

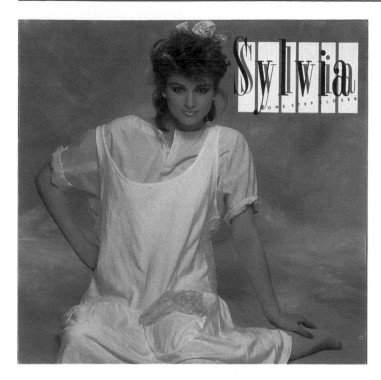

One Step Closer, Sylvia. Courtesy RCA Records.

attractive, pop-styled **Nobody**, a pop-crossover hit in 1982 which went on to win Sylvia a gold disc.

With a wide-ranging voice that has touches of Patsy Cline in the phrasing, Sylvia depicts the young pop-country approach to country, and maintains a close affinity to country – "Young people have been exposed to different influences," she says. "I think I reflect what's country in the 1980s, what's happening now. And ten years from now, I hope I can say I'm country today too."

She has maintained her stature as a pop-country star with such hits as **Snapshot**, **Bobby's In Vicksburg** (both 1983), **I Never Quite Got Back (From Loving You)** (1984), **Cry Just A Little Bit** (1985) and **I Love You By Heart** (a duet with Michael Johnson – 1986).

Albums:
Sweet Yesterday (–/RCA)
One Step Closer (RCA/–)
Drifter (RCA/–)

Jimmie Tarlton

Though his name is now almost forgotten, it was John James Rimbert Tarlton (born in Chesterfield County, South Carolina, 1892) who first recorded and arranged the old folk song **Birmingham Jail**, an oft recorded country favourite.

The son of a sharecropper, Tarlton became proficient on banjo, guitar and harmonica while still a boy, his repertoire being drawn not only from the traditional material learnt from his mother but also from the blues songs of the black workers. During his twenties, he began hoboing his way around the country, his route taking him to New York, Chicago and Texas where he became an oil-field worker. After a spell in the cotton mills of Carolina and a trek through the mid-west with a medicine show, he opted for a full-time career in music, a 1926 partnership with Georgian guitarist Tom Darby proving eminently successful and resulting in a

recording session for Columbia. In November, 1927, Darby and Tarlton recorded **Birmingham Jail** and **Columbus Stockade Blues**, the ensuing disc attaining impressive sales figures.

For the next three years, the duo continued to provide Columbia with discs, their contract finally terminating in 1930. And though no recordings were made in 1931, Tarlton taking up temporary work in a South Carolina cotton mill, dates with Victor (1932) and ARC (1933) followed, the partnership dissolving in 1933 when Darby returned to a farming career.

Tarlton, however, remained an active musician for many years, at one time working with Hank Williams in a medicine show. He was re-discovered by a new generation during the 1960s and began playing club dates and festivals, even cutting an album, **Steel Guitar Rag**, perhaps reminding everyone of his claim to be the first country steel guitar player. But it proved to be his final gesture: he died in 1973.

Albums:
Darby And Tarlton (Old Timey/–)
Darby And Tarlton (–/Bear Family)

The Tenneva Ramblers

Claud Grant, vocals and guitar; Jack Grant, mandolin; Jack Pierce, fiddle; Claude Slagle, banjo.

A relatively popular band of the late 1920s and early 1930s, The Tenneva Ramblers were best known because of their association with Jimmie Rodgers.

Originally known as the Jimmie Rodgers Entertainers, they were set to record for Ralph Peer in that historic week in August, 1927. At the last moment they defected from Rodgers and made up the new band name, which reflected the location of the session: Bristol, a city divided in half by the state line between Tennessee and Virginia. They were moderately successful in their recording efforts but their decision to go it alone harmed Rodgers career not one iota.

Al Terry

Born Alison Joseph Theriot, on January 14, 1922, Al Terry was a cajun who hit it big when rockabilly came along and his **Good Deal Lucille** took off, providing him with a tour with Red Foley and work with various country package shows. However, despite the wide acceptance provided by his monster hit, (covered by Moon Mullican, Jack Scott, Carl Smith, Werley Fairburn and others), Terry has remained pretty much a regional favourite. He recorded for Hickory from 1954–1962 and since for Dot, Index and Rice (having earlier worked with Gold Star and Feature), but another **Good Deal Lucille** has never come his way.

Album:
This Is Al Terry (Index/–)

B. J. Thomas

Born Billy Joe Thomas in Houston, Texas on August 27, 1942, B. J. started out as a rocker, joining a local band, The Triumphs, at the age of 15. His first record with the group was titled **Lazy Man**, but it was with a Hank Williams song, **I'm So Lonesome I Could Cry**, a Scepter label release in 1966, that he obtained his first pop Top 10 hit.

Throughout the 1960s, Thomas continued logging pop Top 40 hits on Hickory and Scepter, the biggest of these being **Raindrops Keep Fallin' On My Head**, from the movie 'Butch Cassidy And The Sundance Kid', a US No. 1 in 1969, and a multi-award winner. From 1970 through to 1972, when he recorded **Rock And Roll Lullaby**, a single that featured the guitar of Duane Eddy, Thomas' name was a constant in the pop charts.

A switch from Scepter to Paramount Records signalled a period of disaster for the Texan. His records failed to sell, and he was into everything from pills to cocaine. One of his lungs was pierced in a stabbing and by the mid-'70s he was

Back In The Swing Of Things, Hank Thompson, Courtesy MCA Records.

bankrupt. Then came a turn about. Billy Joe moved back onto country and recorded Chips Moman and Larry Butler's **(Hey Won't You Play) Another Somebody Done Somebody Wrong Song**, a 1975 ABC Records release that became another pop No. 1. But B. J. was still on drugs when he cut the record and, in his autobiography 'Home Where I Belong', claims that he hardly remembers the session because he was using around 3,000 dollars worth of drugs each week during that period.

However, in January 1976, he became a born-again Christian and opted for a drug-free life. He began cutting gospel material and in 1977 made a gospel album, also called **Home Where I Belong**, that saw him gaining a Grammy award. For a while, his name remained absent from the secular charts, but gradually his MCA releases began edging their way into the country Top 30 once more via such singles as **Everybody Loves A Rain Song** (1978), **Some Love Songs Never Die** and **I Recall A Gypsy Woman** (1981). By 1983 he was back at the top once more. Signed to the Cleveland International label, he headed the country charts with **Whatever Happened to Old-Fashioned Love?** and **New Looks From An Old Lover**, following these with a Top 5 single in **She Meant Forever When She Said Goodbye**. And in 1984 he added to his tally **The Whole World's In Love When You're Lonely** going Top 10, while **Rock And Roll Shoes**, a duet with Ray Charles, also sold well.

Now a multi Grammy and Dove award winner for his gospel releases, B. J. Thomas seems able to slot both sacred and secular songs into his repertoire and is equally happy playing both religious and country venues.

Albums:
New Looks (Cleveland Int./Epic)
Home Where I Belong (Myrrh/Myrrh)

Hank Thompson

For 13 consecutive years (from 1953–1965), Thompson's Brazos Valley Boys won just about every western band poll and even today Thompson's influence pervades the country-rock scene, influencing bands like

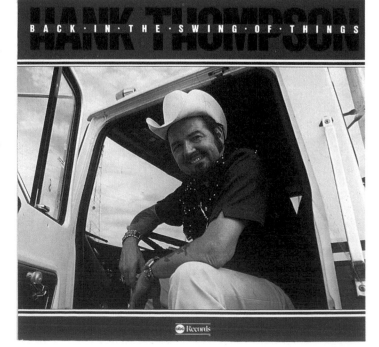

Above: Hank Thompson. His output includes albums of songs made famous by Nat Cole and The Mill Brothers.

Asleep At The Wheel etc.

Born Henry William Thompson in Waco, Texas on September 3, 1925, he initially became a harmonica ace, winning many talent contests by his playing. Later he graduated to guitar, learning to play on a second-hand instrument costing only four dollars. During the early 1940s he began broadcasting on a local radio station and found a sponsor in a flour company, who presented him in a show called 'Hank The Hired Hand'. A few months later, in 1943, Thompson joined the navy for a period of three years, upon discharge returning to country music and winning a spot on Waco station KWTX. He also formed a western swing band, The Brazos Valley Boys, and began recording for Globe Records in August, 1946, the results of the session providing **Whoa Sailor**, a regional hit. This reached the ears of Tex Ritter, who then suggested to Capitol that they sign the Waco singer.

In 1948, Thompson commenced a career with the label that was to last 18 years, scoring immediately with national hits in **Humpty Dumpty Heart** and **Today**, following these with **Green Light** and a remake of **Whoa Sailor** (1949). From then on came a perpetual stream of hits, the biggest being Thompson's version of a Carter-Warren song, **The Wild Side Of Life**, which became a million-seller in 1952. Though his last appearance on the US pop charts was with **She's A Whole Lot Like You**, back in mid-1960, Thompson continued to provide a non-stop flow of country chart winners for several years, these including **Oklahoma Hills, Hangover Tavern** (1961), **On Tap, In The Can Or In The Bottle, Smokey The Bar** (1968) and

I've Come Awful Close (1971), **Cab Driver** (1972), **The Older The Violin The Sweeter The Tune**, and **Who Left The Door To Heaven Open?** (1974). He quit the Capitol label for Warner Brothers in 1966, and then moved on to Dot in 1968.

Although record buyers have, in recent times, veered away from the western swing style that first brought Hank into prominence, he and his Brazos Valley Boys have continued to play an abundance of dates world-wide, also logging the occasional chart entry on such labels as ABC, MCA and Churchill. Reputed to be the first country artist to have recorded in hi-fi and in stereo, Thompson claims that his interest in country music stems from the time, as a boy, when he listened to a neighbour's records. "She was a bootlegger and made good money during prohibition. I'd go over to her place and she'd let me play the records – The Carter Family, Vernon Dalhart, Carson Robinson. I loved those records."

Below: A guitar named Hank Thompson with its clean shaven owner.

Albums:
The Best Of Hank Thompson (Capitol/ Capitol)
The Best Of Hank Thompson Vol. 2 (Capitol/Capitol)
Sings The Gold Standards (Capitol/Capitol)
A Six Pack To Go (Capitol/Capitol)
Back In The Swing Of Things (Dot/ABC)

Uncle Jimmy Thompson

The first featured performer on the Saturday night barn dance show, which was to develop into the Grand Ole Opry, was Uncle Jimmy Thompson, born in Smith County, Tennessee, in 1848. While he primarily farmed for a living for over 50 years in both Tennessee and Texas, he was an avid participant and frequent winner of a nationwide fiddle contest.

Excited by the then new medium of radio, he applied – at the age of 78! – for a spot on WSM, and in 1925 his Saturday night show, the forerunner of the Opry, first came on the air. He stayed with the Opry (then still known as the WSM Barn Dance) until 1928, then toured a bit and recorded for both Columbia (1926) and Vocalion (1930) before passing away, probably of pneumonia, on February 17, 1931, at the ripe old age of 83.

Album:
Nashville, The Early String Bands Vol. 2 – some tracks only (County/–)

Sue Thompson

Known as the lady with the itty-bitty voice, Sue Thompson always sounded like a teeny-bopper. Born in Nevada, Missouri, (real name Eva Sue McKee), she grew up on a farm, listening to country music or viewing Western films. At seven she began playing guitar and, after winning a San José talent contest during her high

The Sue Thompson Story. Courtesy DJM Records.

school days, played a two-week engagment at a local theatre as a reward. Later she became a regular on Dude Martin's Hometown Hayride show, over San Francisco KGO-TV, and after cutting sides with Martin's Round-Up Gang (she was married to Martin for a time and later spent some years as the wife of Hank Penny), she signed to Mercury as a solo act.

Moving to L.A., she appeared in cabaret and in the late 1950s made a number of appearances on Red Foley's portion of the Opry. Following record dates with Columbia and Decca, Sue signed for Hickory Records in 1960 and had an initial hit with **Sad Movies**, a gold disc winner. Others followed including **Norman** (another million-seller), **James (Hold The Ladder Steady), Paper Tiger, Have A Good Time** and **Angel, Angel**, most of her songs being in pure pop vein, though she became increasingly country-oriented during the late 1960s, during which time she made a lengthy tour of the Vietnam war zone. Her last hit of any size was **Never Naughty Rosie** in 1976.

Album:
The Sue Thompson Story (–/DJM)

Mel Tillis

Though Tillis has always had problems with his speech – having a life-long stutter – he has had little trouble putting words (and music) down on paper, his songwriting efforts including **Detroit City, Honky Tonk Song, Ruby, Don't Take Your Love To Town, I'm Tired, One More Time, Crazy Wild Desire, A Thousand Miles Ago** and many other Top 10 entries.

Born in Tampa, Florida on August 8, 1932, Tillis grew up in Pahokee, Florida, there graduating from High School. A drummer in the high school band, he later studied violin but opted out to become a footballer of some distinction. However, next came a spell in the US Air Force followed by a stint on the railroad. During this time Tillis developed his writing and performing ability and in 1957 headed for Nashville with three of his songs – all of which became hits for other singers. Tillis'

he is sometimes announced, is a versatile performer and one who has always been able to turn his speech impediment to good use, becoming, unbelievably, an in-demand guest on all of TV's top chat shows. Also a movie actor, he has appeared in "WW And The Dixie Dance Kings' (1975) and 'Uphill All The Way' (1985).

Albums:
New Patches (MCA/MCA)
The Best Of Mel Tillis (MCA/–)
I Believe In You (MCA/MCA)
The Very Best Of Mel Tillis (MCA/MCA)
The Best Of Mel Tillis And The Statesiders (Polydor/–)

Floyd Tillman

One of country music's most successful songwriters, Floyd Tillman was born in Ryan, Oklahoma on December 8, 1914. A Western Union messenger at the age of 13, he became singer, guitarist, mandolin and banjo player with the Mark Clark Orchestra and the Blue Ridge Playboys during the 1930s, signing for Decca Records in 1939 and cutting the self-written **It Makes No Difference Now**, a country classic.

During the late 1940s, Tillman, who became a Columbia recording artist in 1946, wrote such compositions as **I Love You So Much It Hurts** (1948), **Slipping Around** (1949) and **I'll Never Slip Around Again** (1949), his records of these songs all becoming hits. But they became even bigger hits when recorded by Jimmy

Floyd Tillman Sings His Greatest Hits Of Lovin'. Courtesy Phonogram.

Wakely, big band vocalist Margaret Whiting duetting with Wakely on the two 1949 successes.

Though his name remained absent from the record charts during the 1950s, in 1960 Tillman scored again with **It Just Tore me Up**, a Liberty release.

A honky tonk hero and among the first to utilize electric guitar, Tillman was also responsible for such songs as **Each Night At Nine, I'll Keep On Lovin' You** and **Daisy Mae**.

Album:
Greatest Hits (Crazy Cajun/–)

Tompall And The Glaser Brothers

Born on a ranch in Spalding, Nebraska (Tompall Glaser on September 3, 1933; Charles 'Chuck' Glaser on February 3, 1936 and James Glaser on December 16, 1937),

Above: M-M-M-Mel Tillis. He turned his vocal impediment to good use.

own first hit disc came late in 1958 with **The Violet And The Rose**, a Columbia release. This was followed by **Finally** (1959), **Sawmill** (1959) and **Georgia Town Blues**, a duet with Bill Phillips (1960).

Following a switch to the Ric label and a Top 10 debut with **Wine** (1965), Mel became signed to Kapp (later Decca), his

Heart Over Mind, Mel Tillis. Courtesy CBS Records.

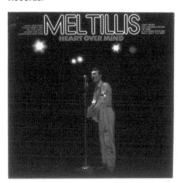

career flourishing from this point. He obtained Top 10 hits with **Who's Julie?** (1968), **These Lonely Hands Of Mine** (1969), **She'll Be Hangin' Round Somewhere, Heart Over Mind** (both 1970), then moved to MGM to continue his personal hit parade with **Commercial Affection, Heaven Everyday** (1970), **The Arms Of A Fool, Brand New Mister Me** (1971), **I Ain't Never** (1972), **Neon Rose, Sawmill** (1973), **Midnight Me And The**

Old Faithful, Mel Tillis, Courtesy MCA Records.

Blues, Stomp Them Grapes, Memory Maker (1974), **Best Way I Know How** and **Woman In The Back Of My Mind** (1975). To this can be added two hit duets with Sherry Bryce and **How Come Your Dog Don't Bite Nobody But Me?**, a diverting duet with Webb Pierce that hit the middle of the charts during 1963.

Adjudged CMA Entertainer Of The Year 1976, Mel moved on to the MCA label and celebrated by logging a No. 1 single with **Good Woman Blues**, following this with other chart-toppers in **Heart Healer** (1977), **I Believe In You** (1978), **Coca Cola Cowboy** (1979) and, on the Elektra label, **Southern Rains** (1980). During 1981 he teamed with Nancy Sinatra for a duet album, **Mel and Nancy**, that spawned a couple of hit singles, but generally his chart entries came on a lower level. Accordingly he switched back to MCA once more and went Top 10 with **In the Middle Of The Night** (1983) and **New Patches** (1984), also recording some sides in the company of Glen Campbell.

One of the most prolific writers in country music – his material has ranged from pure undiluted goo through to raunchy honky tonk – M-M-M-M-Mel, as

The Wonder Of It All, Tompall Glaser. Courtesy MCA Records.

Below: Jim Glaser. Currently the most successful of the Glaser Brothers.

Charlie, Tompall Glaser. Courtesy MGM Records.

studio and an office, the brothers developed differences and split in 1972, Tompall cutting a solo album called **Charlie** (1973) that indicated a change of direction, particularly in terms of lyrics, where Tompall began to delve into more personal, introspective themes. The title song spoke of a man's past and future lives and seemed prophetic. Both single and album were well received critically and salewise.

Later albums saw Tompall in much the same mood, exploring themes that would not have been possible with the more melodic Glaser Brothers. He formed his Outlaw Band and appeared on the million-selling **The Outlaws**, along with Waylon Jennings and Willie Nelson, providing that album's grittiest track with a stomping version of Jimmie Rodgers' **T For Texas**.

Meanwhile, both Jim and Chuck were having some success in more mainstream country, all three Glaser brothers appearing in the country charts during 1974; Chuck with **Gypsy Queen**, Jim with **Fool Passin' Through** and **Forgettin' All About You**, and Tompall with **Texas Law Sez** and **Musical Chairs**, all three brothers still being signed to MGM at that period.

Chuck however became increasingly involved in record production and management but suffered a stroke that put him out of action for some time.

Although Tompall had a critically acclaimed solo career, there remained a bigger demand for the brothers as a threesome. So, in 1978, they got back together again, resuming their joint chart activities with a brace of mid-chart hits for Elektra in 1980. This time, it seemed, they were really going to achieve the breakthrough in record sales they had striven for over the years. Their 1981 version of Kris Kristofferson's **Lovin' Her Was Easier (Than Anything I'll Ever Do Again)** went to No. 2 in the charts, providing the brothers with their biggest-ever single. There were other Top 20 records with **Just One Time** (1981) and **It'll Be Her** (1982). Then the Glasers split once again, Jim – who, with Jimmy Payne, had earlier penned the million-selling hit **Woman, Woman** for Gary Puckett – releasing a single on a new independent label, Noble Vision. Titled **When You're Not A Lady**, it not only went Top 20 in the charts but, after a stay of 22 weeks, became the all-time longest-running debut release by a new record company in the history of those charts.

Tremendously successful since, proffering a soft, romantic line in country that contrasts greatly with Tompall's way of things, Jim has logged a country No. 1 with **You're Getting To Me Again** (1984) along with several other major chart climbers.

their early interest in music was generated by the boys' parents who were both country music devotees. During the early 1950s they formed a band and played local clubs and dance halls. As their reputation spread they gained a 13-week series on KHAS, Hastings, Nebraska. Later, following a win on the Arthur Godfrey Talent Show and consequent national attention, they travelled to Nashville in 1958 and were soon on tour with Marty Robbins. Signed by Decca, they recorded folk music (while performing country on stage) and were not entirely happy with their debut album, **This Land**, which was pure folk.

But in 1962 they became members of the Grand Ole Opry and followed a country direction from then on. Also that year they toured with Johnny Cash, and the dates this package played at Las Vegas and Carnegie Hall provided the Glasers with an even wider audience.

By 1966 they had signed to MGM Records and begun a noteworthy recording career. Their delightful harmony vocals and acoustic guitar work (although they employed full country backing also) were particularly suited to the more melodic country material and they kept abreast of the latest songwriting trends too, utilising material from many sources. Their first hits came with songs like **Gone On The Other Hand** (1966) and **Through The Eyes Of Love** (1967) their first Top 10 being **Rings** (1971). Multi-award winners, they proved a popular live group and stopped the show at the 1970 Wembley Festival. But, after working seven days a week as a band and also trying to run a

Albums:
Tompall Glaser:
Charlie (MGM/MGM)
The Great Tompall And His Outlaw Band
(MGM/MGM)
Tompall Glaser And His Outlaw Band
(ABC/ABC)

Jim Glaser:
The Man In The Mirror (Noble Vision/–)

Tompall And The Glaser Brothers:
Sing Great Hits From Two Decades
(MGM/MGM)
The Award Winners (MGM/MGM)

Diana Trask

An Australian who made it big in Nashville during the late 1960s and early 1970s, Diana Trask was born in Melbourne, Australia on June 23, 1940. Winner of the top talent award at 16, she toured with a group before going to the US in 1959.

Then a pop vocalist, she was on the poverty line for a while but later became signed to Columbia Records, appeared on major TV shows and was even offered a film contact. However, she got married and returned to Australia where she began to raise a family. In the late 1960s, during a trip to the CMA convention, she became bitten by the country bug and stayed on in Nashville, having her first country hit with **Lock, Stock And Barrel**, a Dial release. She then joined Dot and cut an album, **Miss Country Soul**, and had Top 20 entries with **Say When**, **It's A Man's World**, **When I Get My Hands On You** (1973), and **Lean It All On Me** (1974).

She returned to Australia once more in 1975 and had her first hit there in 14 years with **Oh Boy**, a Festival release which went to No. 2. Signed to Australian RCA in 1977 and Polydor in 1980, Diana was back in the US charts in '81 with **This Must Be My Ship** and **Stirrin' Up Feelings**.

Albums:
Diana's Country (Dot/–)
Miss Country Soul (Dot/–)

Miss Country Soul, Diana Trask. Courtesy MCA-Dot.

Above: Merle Travis parades a blues or two in 'From Here To Eternity'.

Merle Travis

Easily one of the most, if not *the* most, multi-talented men ever to enter the music business was Merle Travis, born in Rosewood, Mulenberg County, Kentucky on November 29, 1917.

A singer and songwriter of major proportions and guitar stylist of monumental influence, he also proved adept as an actor, author and even cartoonist.

Merle learned the basics of his celebrated guitar style from Mose Rager (also Ike Everly's teacher) who, in turn, learned it from black railroad hand, fiddler and guitarist, Arnold Shultz. Merle sophisticated the finger style to a degree of complexity unknown in that era (it was to prove extremely influential to Chet Atkins and many others), and his renown won him a job first with a group called the Tennessee Tomcats before joining Clayton McMichen's Georgia Wildcats on WLW's Boone County Jamboree. There he also became part of the Brown's Ferry Four and The Drifting Pioneers and appeared on NBC's 'Plantation Party'.

After a wartime stint in the Marines, Travis relocated on the west coast, perfecting his songwriting, appearing in minor roles in a host of westerns, and playing in bands with Cliffie Stone, Ray Whitley, Jimmy Wakely, Wesley Tuttle and Tex Ritter etc. He also signed with Capitol Records and had several of the biggest hits of the era: **Divorce Me C.O.D.** (1946), **So Round, So Firm, So Fully Packed** (1947) and several others which ranked on the charts, these including **Dark As A Dungeon** (1947) and **Sixteen Tons** (1947), a 1955 hit for Tennessee Ernie Ford.

Writer or co-writer of all his hits, he also co-wrote **No Vacancy** with Cliffie Stone and **Smoke! Smoke! Smoke!** with Tex Williams. He was equally adept at reworking folk tunes, and **John Henry**, **I Am A Pilgrim** and **Nine Pound Hammer** were all adapted by and integrated into the Travis style.

In the 1950s, Merle became a southern California fixture, appearing regularly on the Hometown Jamboree and Town Hall Party, making a striking appearance as a guitar-strumming sailor in the movie 'From Here To Eternity', where he introduced the song **Re-Enlistment Blues**. He moved to Nashville for a short while in the 1960s but later returned to California, using it as a base for frequent tours up to the time of his death in Tahlequah, Oklahoma, on October 20, 1983. Travis, whose last film appearance was in Clint Eastwood's 'Honky Tonk Man', was inducted into the

The Atkins-Travis Traveling Show. Courtesy RCA Records.

Nashville Songwriters Hall Of Fame, 1970.
Both Doc Watson and Chet Atkins named sons after him.

Albums:
The Atkins-Travis Travelling Show – with Chet Atkins (RCA/RCA)
Walkin' The Strings (Capitol/Pathe Marconi)
Travis! (Capitol/Capitol)
Merle Travis And Joe Maphis (Capitol/Capitol)

Ernest Tubb

The sixth member to be elected to the Country Music Hall Of Fame, headliner on the first country music show ever to be presented at Carnegie Hall; a regular member of the Opry from 1943 to the time of his death – these are just a few of the achievements credited to Ernest Dale Tubb, the son of a Texas cotton farm overseer.

Born in Crisp, Texas on February 9, 1914, Tubb's boyhood hero was the great Jimmie Rodgers. Although he had dreams of emulating Rodgers and sang at various local get-togethers during his early teens, Tubb was almost 20 before he owned his first guitar. The year 1934 proved important to him, Tubb then obtaining his initial radio dates on San Antonio KONO. During this period he married Lois Elaine Cook.

But 1935 also brought its incidents – Tubb's eldest son Justin being born that year, and a meeting with Carrie Rodgers (Jimmie's widow). She and Ernest became good friends, Mrs Rodgers loaning him her husband's original guitar and also arranging an RCA recording session at which Tubb cut two sides: **The Passing Of Jimmie Rodgers** and **Jimmie Rodgers' Last Thoughts**. However, Tubb's luck was not always that good. His second son, Rodger Dale, was born on July, 1938, but died after just a few weeks. Things began to look brighter after the birth of a daughter, Violet Elaine, on December 3; Decca offered him a new record contract and he obtained a job on Fort Worth's KGKO, which later led to Tubb being sponsored by Universal Mills, makers of Gold Chain Flour.

It was at this stage that he became the Gold Chain Troubadour, earning 75 dollars a week, promoting Universal's wares. It was a nickname which preceded his famous Texas Troubadour image. By 1941 he had also moved into movies, appearing in 'Fightin' Buckaroos', a Columbia release.

Next came his recording of **Walking The Floor Over You**, a self-penned composition. Released in the Fall of 1942, it became a million-seller, helping Tubb gain his first appearance on the Opry in December, 1942. He was to gain regular membership during 1943.

He continued logging successful discs and film appearances in such productions as 'Ridin' West' (1942), 'Jamboree' (1943) and 'Hollywood Barn Dance' (1947). Also, in 1947, he opened the first of his now famous record shops – near Nashville's Ryman Auditorium – and commenced his Midnight Jamboree programme over WSM, advertising the shop and showcasing the talents of up and coming country artists.

Tubb married again in 1949, his new wife being Olene Adams, mother of Erlene, Olene, Ernest Jr, Larry and Karen Tubb. That year he appeared on hit records with

Above: Ernest Tubb. In 1947 he headed the first country show at Carnegie Hall.

the Andrews Sisters and Red Foley, also managing to achieve Top 10 placings with no less than five of his solo efforts, the biggest of these being **Slippin' Around** and **Blue Christmas**. From then through to 1969 he became the charts' Mr Consistency, thanks to such discs as **Goodnight Irene** (with Red Foley, 1950), **I Love You Because** (1950), **Missing In Action** (1952), **Two Glasses Joe** (1954), **Half A Mind** (1958), **Thanks A Lot** (1963), **Mr And Mrs Used-To-Be** (with Loretta Lynn, 1964) and **Another Story, Another**

Country Hit Time, Ernest Tubb. Courtesy MCA Records.

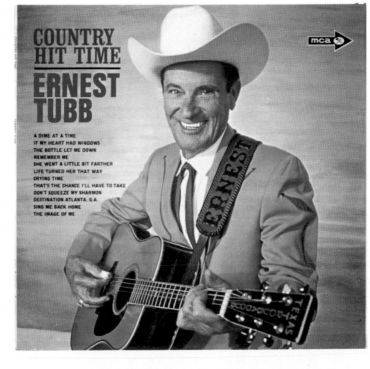

Place (1966). His only real absence from hit listing was between 1952 and 1954 when, following an exhausting Far East tour, Tubb suffered from an illness that kept him off the Opry for some considerable while.

An inveterate tourer, he and his Texas Troubadours (a band which at one point included such stars as Jack Greene and Cal Smith) played around 300 dates a year. An honest singer rather than a great one – emotionally he was a 10-point man, technically he came a lot further down the scale – when ET performed honky tonk you could almost smell the booze. Much loved, when in 1979 he set out to record his **Legend And Legacy** album for First Generation records, virtually everyone who was anyone in Nashville dropped by

to see if they could help out, the album line-up eventually featuring the names of Willie Nelson, Loretta Lynn, Vern Gosdin, Chet Atkins, Merle Haggard, Johnny Cash, Charlie Rich, Johnny Paycheck, Linda Hargrove, Marty Robbins, Conway Twitty, the Wilburn Brothers, Ferlin Husky, Waylon Jennings, Charlie Daniels, George Jones and many, many others. When he died, on September 6, 1984, the whole of Music City mourned the man writer Chet Flippo once accurately described as "honky tonk music personified".

Albums:
The Legend And The Legacy (First Generation/–)
The Ernest Tubb Story (MCA/MCA)
Honky Tonk Classics (Rounder/–)
The Country Hall Of Fame (–/MCA)

Justin Tubb

Eldest son of Ernest Tubb, singer-songwriter-guitarist Justin Tubb was born in San Antonio, Texas on August 20, 1935. One of the many country singers who began entertaining during their high school days, he claims that his career received a real fillup when his father recorded one of his songs in 1952.

That year, he and two of his cousins formed a group and began playing clubs in the Austin area, where Tubb was attending the University of Texas. But after just a year of college came the inevitable move to Nashville and a deejaying job on a radio station in nearby Gallatin, Tennessee, where Tubb not only spun discs but also entertained his listeners with his own songs.

In 1953 he signed with Decca, the following year logging two hits, **Looking Back To See** and **Sure Fire Kisses**, both duets with Goldie Hill. Although Tubb became an Opry regular in 1955, his records sold only moderately well and he began to label hop, leaving Decca in 1959 and cutting sides for Challenge and Starday. Then, after a Top 10 Groove release in **Take A Letter Miss Gray** (1963), came a long association with RCA and some so-so chart visits with **Hurry, Mr Peters** (1965), **We've Gone Too Far Again** (1966) – both duets with Lorene Mann – and **But Wait There's More**, a solo item from 1967.

Once an inveterate tourer, Tubb has played in all but two states and has also appeared in several countries, during 1967 taking a show to the Far East, entertaining servicemen in Vietnam and other areas. Nowadays he tours less regularly but still appears on various country TV shows and is something of a fixture on the Opry. He has also enjoyed considerable success as a writer, his most notable composition being **Lonesome 7-7203**, a No.1 for Hawkshaw Hawkins in 1963.

Albums:
Justin Tubb, Star Of The Grand Ole Opry
(Starday/–)
The Best Of Justin Tubb (RCA/–)

Tanya Tucker

When she was nine years old, people at both MGM and RCA Records wanted to sign her. At 14 she had gained a Top 10 hit and a year later her face bedecked the cover of 'Rolling Stone'. Shortly after, she came up with the biggest country single in

What's Your Mama's Name, Tanya Tucker. Courtesy CBS Records.

the land, also acquiring a reputation as a musical Lolita because of her penchant for employing songs equipped with provocative lyrics.

Born in Seminole, Texas on October 10, 1958, Tanya Denise Tucker, the daughter of a construction worker, spent her early years in Wilcox, Arizona, moving to Phoenix in 1967. There, Tanya and her father began attending as many country concerts as possible, visiting local fairs to hear Mel Tillis, Leroy Van Dyke, Ernest Tubb and others, Tanya often joining the stars onstage for an impromptu song.

Following a cameo role in the movie 'Jeremiah Johnson', Tanya, then 13, cut a demo tape that included her renditions of **For The Good Times**, **Put Your Hand In The Hand** and other songs, the results impressing Columbia's Billy Sherrill, who signed Tanya to the label and promptly produced her recording of Alex Harvey's **Delta Dawn**. The result was a 1972 Top 10 single, after which the Tucker-Sherrill partnership moved into further action to provide such chartbusters as **Love's The Answer**, **What's Your Mama's Name?**, **Blood Red And Going Down** (1973), **Would You Lay With Me (In A Field Of Stone)** and **The Man Who Turned My Mama On** (1974), **Would You Lay With Me**, one of the year's most controversial singles, also proving a hit of international proportions.

In 1976, following a million-dollar deal, Tanya signed for MCA, thus terminating her association with Sherrill and creating some doubts as to her ability to survive without the guiding hand of the Columbia Svengali. But the doubts were quickly dispelled when **Lizzie And The Rainman**, **San Antonio Stroll** (1975), **You've Got Me**

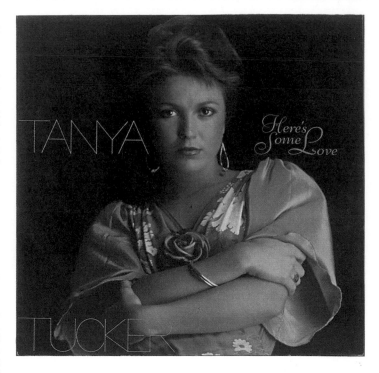

Here's Some Love, Tanya Tucker. Courtesy MCA Records.

To Hold On To (1976), **Here's Some Love** (No. 1, 1976), **It's A Cowboy Lovin' Night** (1977), and **Texas (When I Die)** (1978), all went Top 10.

In the late 1970's, Tanya attempted to move further into the higher stakes of the rock field but, even though she donned

red tights for a highly publicised **TNT** album, things began falling apart a little. Equally publicised was her affair with Glen Campbell, with whom she recorded some duets before the twosome parted in 1981. Nevertheless, she had further solo Top 10 hits in 1980 with **Pecos Promenade** and **Can I See You Tonight** and, after switching to Arista Records in 1982, continued her hit-making way with **I Feel Right**. She is now hitmaking on Capitol.

Albums:
Delta Dawn (Columbia/CBS)
Would You Lay With Me (Columbia/CBS)
Here's Some Love (MCA/MCA)
Greatest Hits (MCA/–)

Wesley Tuttle

Tuttle, born in Lamar, Colorado, became West Coast based after various radio stunts that included a stay on WLW Cincinnati, appearing in films and as a regular on Compton's Town Party along with Tex Williams, Cliffie Stone, Tex Ritter and others.

Tuttle became signed to Capitol Records in 1945, one of his biggest selling records for the label being his version of **Crying In The Chapel** (1953). He also recorded several duets with his wife Marilyn, the duo making some albums for RCA in the late 1950s but later fading from the mainstream country scene when Tuttle began working as an evangelist, recording only religious material.

Conway Twitty

Real name Harold Lloyd Jenkins, born in Friars Point, Mississippi on September 1, 1933, Twitty learnt guitar on board a riverboat piloted by his country music-loving father. Almost signed by the Philadelphia baseball team (he nowadays owns his own team – The Nashville Sounds), Twitty was drafted before the contract could be concluded and spent two years in the army instead.

During the mid-1950s, he became a

Teddy Bear Song
Horseshoe Bend
California Cotton Fields
Rainy Girl
Pass Me By
The Missing Piece Of Puzzle
Song Man
The Chokin' Kind
Teach Me The Words To Your Song
What's Your Mama's Name

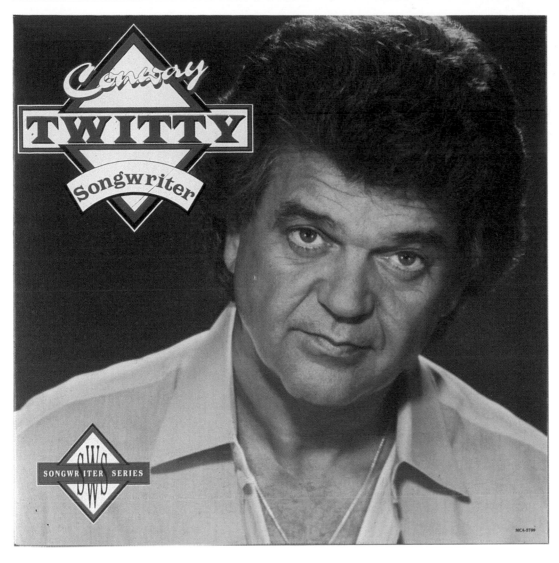

Songwriter. A collection of Conway Twitty originals. Courtesy MCA.

rock'n'roll singer, working on many radio stations and charting with a Mercury single **I Need Your Lovin'** (1957). Shortly after, he joined MGM Records and won a gold disc for **It's Only Make Believe**, one of 1958's biggest sellers. Extremely Presley-influenced at this point in his career, Twitty was hardly out of the pop charts between September 1958 and April 1961, also finding time to appear in three teen-angled movies – 'Sex Kittens Go To College', 'Platinum High School' and 'College Confidential'.

It was at this time that Twitty began writing country songs, his **Walk Me To The Door** being recorded by Ray Price in 1960. By June 1965, he himself was cutting country sides under Decca's Owen Bradley, at the same time settling down in Oklahoma City playing with a band known as the Lonely Blue Boys and (in June, 1966) commencing a syndicated TV programme 'The Conway Twitty Show'. During the late 1960s, Twitty moved to Nashville and began amassing an incredible number of hits – his solo chart-toppers alone including: **Next In Line** (1968), **I Love You More Today, To See My Angel Cry** (1969), **Hello Darlin', 15 Years Ago** (1970), **How Much More Can She Stand** (1971), **(Lost Her Love) On Our Last Date, I Can' Stop Loving You, She Needs Someone To Hold Her** (1972), **You've Never Been This Far Before** (1973), **There's A Honky Tonk Angel, I See The Want To In Your Eyes** (1974), **Linda On My Mind, Touch The Hand, This Time I've**

Hurt Her More Than She Loves Me (1975), **After All The Good Is Gone, The Game That Daddies Play, I Can't Believe She Gives It All To Me** (1976), **Don't Take It Away, I May Never Get To Heaven, Happy Birthday Darlin'** (1979), **I'd Love To Lay You Down** (1980), **Rest Your Love On Me, Tight Fittin' Jeans** and **Red Neckin' Love Makin' Night** (1981) all Decca/MCA releases.

Additionally during this period, Conway, who became a vastly superior singer to the one known only to pop audiences (albeit one who has proved remarkably taciturn between songs) also fashioned an equally impresive number of hits duets with Loretta Lynn, hitting the No. 1 spot with **After The Fire Is Gone, Lead Me On** (1971), **Louisiana Woman, Mississippi Man** (1973), **As Soon As I Hang Up The Phone** (1974) and **Feelin's** (1975). Voted Vocal Duo of The Year by the CMA for four straight years in a row (1972–1975), Conway and Loretta also share several business interests. An astute businessman, Twitty owns a music promotion company, a large slice of real estate and the Twitty City complex (a kind of theme park that includes the homes of Conway, his four children and his mother), one of Nashville's major attractions since it opened in 1982.

Also in 1982, Conway quit MCA and moved on to Elektra Records, immediately claiming three No. 1s (with **The Clown, Slow Hand** and **The Rose**) in his first year with his new label. Switching to Warner Brothers in 1983, Twitty again obliged with three No. 1s in a year during 1984, when **Somebody's Needin' Somebody, Ain't She**

Somethin' Else and **I Don't Know About Love (The Moon Song)** – the last named featuring vocal accompaniment from Conway's daughter, Joni Lee Twitty – all topped the charts.

In 1985, he had three more chart-toppers – **Don't Call Him Cowboy, Ain't She Something Else** and **Between Blue Eyes And Jeans**, confirming Twitty's status as the most consistent hitmaker ever to grace country music.

Originally named after a famous silent film comedian, Twitty took his stage name from the towns of Conway (in Arkansas) and Twitty (in Texas). Made an honorary chief of the Choctaw nation in the early 1970s, he has also been awarded the Indian name Hatako-Chtokchito-A-Yakni-Toloa – which translates into 'Great Man Of Country Music'. Apt for a singer who has despite his pop heritage, never opted for crossover appeal.

To See An Angel Cry, Conway Twitty. Courtesy MCA Records.

Albums:
Greatest Hits Vol. 1 (MCA/MCA)
Classic Conway (MCA/MCA)
Songwriter (MCA/MCA)
Georgia Keeps Pulling On My Ring (MCA/MCA)
Conway (MCA/MCA)
Cross Winds (MCA/MCA)
It's Only Make Believe (–/Warwick)
The Very Best Of Conway And Loretta – with Loretta Lynn (MCA/MCA)
Country Partners – with Loretta Lynn (MCA/MCA)

T. Texas Tyler

Tyler, real name David Luke Myrick, was born on June 20, 1916, near Mena, Arkansas. Educated in Philadelphia, he began his career at the age of 14, heading east and appearing on the Major Bowes Amateur Hour in New York during the 1930s. He became widely known as 'The Man With The Million Friends'.

Later came a further move to West Virginia, while in 1942 Tyler was in Louisiana, becoming a member of Shreveport KWKH's Hayride show. A period in the armed forces followed, Tyler settling down in the Hollywood area upon discharge and forming the T. Texas Western Dance Band, a popular unit. It was during this period that Tyler wrote and recorded **Deck Of Cards**, a hit for Four Stars in 1948. A somewhat sentimental but ingenious monologue regarding a soldier who employed a deck of cards as hs Bible, prayer book and almanac, Tyler's creation became a million seller when recorded by Wink Martindale, also becoming a hit for Tex Ritter and British comedian Max Bygraves. Following this record, which won the 'Cashbox' award for the best country disc of 1948, Tyler came up with several more winners, the most potent of these being **Dad Gave The Dog Away** (1948), **Bumming Around** (1953), **Courting In The Rain** (1954) and his theme song, **Remember Me**.

During 1949, the Arkansas traveller appeared in 'Horseman Of The Sierras', a Columbia movie, and won a fair amount of acclaim for 'Range Round Up', his Los Angeles TV show. During the 1950s and 1960s he continued performing, both live and on TV, but despite some worthwhile Starday releases, Tyler failed to place his name on the record charts during the later stages of his career. He died from natural causes on January 28, 1972, in Springfield, Missouri.

Album:
T. Texas Tyler – His Great Hits (Hilltop/–)

Greatest Hits, T. Texas Tyler. A budget compilation, Courtesy Pickwick.

Uncle Henry's Original Kentucky Mountaineers

A fine and popular old-time string band which, by making certain concessions to modernity, remained active well into the 1940s. 'Uncle Henry' Warren was born in Taylor County, Kentucky in 1903. He possessed a deep love for the music and, although he did not play an instrument, he became the leader of the band as MC and comedian.

The band began as early as 1928, over KFLV, Rockford, Illinois, but rose to prominence in Louisville, where they spent four years over WHAS, hosting the WHAS Morning Jamboree. They also spent time at WNOX, Knoxville, WLAP, Lexington and WHIS, Bluefield, West Virginia, but in 1940 they moved to the WJJD Suppertime Frolic in Chicago, where they spent the war years and well into the 1940s cutting an extensive series of transcriptions for Capitol during this period.

Band members included Paul South, singer and writer of much of their original material; Sally and Coon Hunter, a duet team; Dell Remick, steel guitar; and Jimmy Dale Warren, Uncle Henry's son, who eventually moved to the west coast where he became lead singer with The Songs Of The Pioneers.

The Vagabonds

Herald Goodman, vocals; Curt Poulton, vocals and guitar; Dean Upson, vocals.

A smooth harmony trio who were with the Grand Ole Opry from 1931–1938, The Vagabonds were unique on the Opry at the time – they were all non-Southerners (all were from the midwest), they had acquired and used formal musical training, they were primarily a vocal band using only Poulton's guitar for backup, and they were the first real professional band the Opry ever had, depending on music for their full-time living.

Upson had formed the Vagabonds at WLS in 1925; Poulton joined in 1928 and Goodman completed the trio at KMOX in St Louis in 1930. They were best known for their extremely popular **When It's Lamp Lighting Time In The Valley**, and recorded a host of similar sentimental tunes for Bluebird and other smaller labels.

The Vagabonds broke up in 1938 when Goodman left to head the Saddle Mountain Roundup over KVOO in Tulsa. Poulton turned to MC and occasional guitar work, while Upson eventually became a WSM executive.

Leroy Van Dyke

Co-writer (with Buddy Black) and singer of **The Auctioneer**, a 1956 gold disc winner that incorporated a genuine high-speed auctioneering routine, Van Dyke (born in Spring Fork, Missouri on October 4, 1929) originally decided on a career in agriculture, obtaining a BS degree in that subject at the University of Missouri. After serving with army intelligence during the Korean War, he became a livestock auctioneer and agricultural correspondent, utilizing his writing skills to

Above: Porter Wagoner, the one-time grocery store clerk. In recent times he has worked with an all-girl band.

pen songs. He sang **The Auctioneer** on a talent show and subsequently won a contract with Dot Records, his song providing his first release – ultimately a two and half million seller.

A regular on the Red Foley TV Show, he later signed for Mercury, providing that label with **Walk On By**, yet another million seller, in 1961, following this with **If A Woman Answers** and **Black Cloud**, both hits during the following year. After that his releases rarely charted impressively, only **Louisville** (1968) really making the grade.

Van Dyke, who made his film debut in 'What Am I Bid?' (1967), recorded for Warner Bros, Kapp, Decca and ABC-Dot after leaving Mercury in 1965, his last chart record of any size being **Texas Tea**, an ABC-Dot release in 1977.

Album:
Greatest Hits (MCA/–)

Porter Wagoner

Once a grocery store clerk, Wagoner (born in West Plains, Missouri on August 12, 1930) whiled away slow trading periods by picking guitar and singing, his performances, being so impressive that he was engaged to promote the business over an early morning radio show.

His popularity on radio eventually led to a weekly series on KWTO, Springfield 1951, Wagoner later moving on to TV when KWTO became the home of Red Foley's Ozark Jubilee show. In August, 1952, he signed with RCA Records and, following several flops, had his first Top 5 hit with **A Satisfied Mind** three years later. Following two similarly successful singles in **Eat, Drink And Be Merry** (1955) and **What Would You Do (If Jesus Came To Your House)** (1956), the Missourian joined the Opry (1957), in 1960 moving on to formulate his own TV show with singer Norma Jean (later replaced by Dolly Parton) and his band The Wagonmasters.

Filmed in Nashville and initally syndicated to 18 stations, by the late '60s, the programme was being screened to over 100 outlets throughout the USA and Canada, establishing Wagoner's touring show as one of the most popular on the country circuit.

Predominantly straight country in his own musical approach, although sometimes seemingly a catalyst for more startling innovations (Buck Trent first began playing electric banjo on the Wagoner programme while Porter had also been involved in some of Dolly Parton's more contemporary moves), he managed to gain a consistent foothold in the upper reaches of the charts throughout the years. He had Top 10 solo hits with **Your Old Love Letters** (1961), **Misery Loves Company** (1962), **Cold Dark Waters** (1962), **I've Enjoyed As Much Of This As I Can Stand** (1962), **Sorrow On The**

The Farmer, Porter Wagoner's 1973 tribute. Courtesy RCA Records.

Rocks (1964), **Green, Green Grass Of Home** (1965), **Skid Row Joe** (1965), **The Cold, Hard Facts Of Life** (1967), **Carroll County Accident** (1968) and **Big Wind** (1969), also sharing an impressive number of hit duets with Dolly Parton, including **Burning The Midnight Oil** (1971), **Please Don't Stop Loving Me** (1974) and **Is Forever Longer Than Always?** (1976).

Wagoner's albums have included 'live' recordings made in 1964 and 1966; a bluegrass offering, cut in 1965; some 'downer' sessions, typified by such releases as **The Cold Hard Facts Of Life** and **Confessions Of A Broken Man**, both releases dealing with the seamier side of humanity; and a number of duet LPs with Skeeter Davis and Dolly Parton.

The successful partnership with Dolly Parton came to an end in 1974. Their split was more than a little fraught; Porter didn't want her to leave, but Dolly wanted to be free to develop her own career. This parting marked Porter's rapid fall from the top and, with his records failing to make

Down In The Alley, Porter Wagoner. Courtesy RCA Records.

the Top 10 he finally left RCA in 1981, recording briefly for Warner/Viva during 1982 and 1983. Today, Porter is a very successful Nashville businessman, though he continues to be active in country music, both recording and performing.

Albums:
Best Of . . . (RCA/RCA)
Carroll County Accident (RCA/–)
20 Of The Best (–/RCA)
Today (RCA/–)
Hits Of . . . (–/RCA)
Highway Heading South (RCA/RCA)

With Dolly Parton:
Porter & Dolly (RCA/RCA)
Two Of A Kind (RCA/RCA)
Best Of . . . (RCA/RCA)

Jimmy Wakely

One of country music's major stars during the '40s and early '50s, James Clarence Wakely was born in a log cabin at Mineola, Arkansas on February 16, 1914.

Raised and schooled in Oklahoma, where he took such jobs as a sharecropper, journalist and filling station manager, he became a professional musician during the mid '30s, forming the Jimmy Wakely Trio with Johnny Bond and Scotty Harrell in 1937. The group appeared daily on Oklahoma City's WKY radio station. In 1940, Gene Autry guested on the show, liked the trio and signed them for his Hollywood-based Melody Ranch CBS radio programme.

On Melody Ranch, Wakely quickly established himself as a star in his own right – eventually securing parts in over 50 Hollywood movies (in 1948 he was nominated as the fourth most popular Western film actor – only Roy Rogers, Gene Autry and Charles Starrett being rated higher).

After two years on the Autry show, he left to form his own band, employing such musicians as Cliffie Stone, Spade Cooley, Merle Travis and Wesley Tuttle. By 1949

he had become so popular that he beat both Frank Sinatra and Bing Crosby in the Billboard pop vocalist poll, enjoying a huge hit with his version of Floyd Tillman's **Slippin' Around**. Recorded as a duet with pop vocalist Margaret Whiting, the disc soon became a million-seller for Capitol Records. Other hits with Margaret Whiting followed (including **I'll Never Slip Around Again**), the duo logging no less than seven Top 10 discs within two years.

Meanwhile, Wakely also did well in a solo capacity, such records as **I Love You So Much It Hurts** (1949), **I Wish I Had A Nickel** (1949), **My Heart Cries For You** (1950) and **Beautiful Brown Eyes** (1951) charting impressively. His 1948 hit, **One Has My Name, The Other Has My Heart**, in fact, started a whole cycle of 'Cheatin' songs' which **Slippin' Around** accelerated.

But during the mid '50s, the Wakely career seemed to run out of steam, and

The Hand Of Love, Billy Walker. Courtesy MGM Records.

though he had a CBS networked radio show until 1958 and co-hosted a TV series with Tex Ritter in 1961, his record sales diminished, Wakely forming his own label, Shasta. However, in the mid '70s, Wakely was still in showbiz, mainly playing to clubs in Los Angeles and Las Vegas, using an act that featured his children, Johnny and Linda Lee.

Albums:
Jimmy Wakely Country (Shasta/–)
Slippin' Around (Dot/–)
Big Country Songs (Vocalion/–)

Billy Walker

Once billed as 'The Travelling Texan – The Masked Singer Of Country Songs', William Marvin Walker was born in Ralls, Texas on January 14, 1929.

In 1944, at the age of 15, while Walker was attending Whiteface High School, New Mexico, he won an amateur talent show, the prizes being a chocolate cake and three dollars. But the contest also gained him his own 15-minute Saturday radio show on KICA, Clovis, New Mexico, Walker hitchhiking 80 miles to play on the programme then hitching his way home again.

Joining the Big D Jamboree in Dallas during 1949, he adopted his masked singer guise; the ploy worked, gaining the Texan a considerable following and a subsequent record contract from Columbia.

Other shows followed, Walker appearing on the Louisiana Hayride in the early '50s, the Ozark Jubilee between 1955 and 1960, and joining the Opry in 1960. His first hit disc came in 1954 with **Thank You For Calling**, but it was not until 1962 and the release of **Charlie's Shoes**, a nationwide No. 1, that Walker began to dominate the charts.

The majority of his discs became Top 20 entries during the following decade, providing Columbia with such hits as **Willie The Weeper** (1962), **Circumstances** (1964), **Cross The Brazos At Waco** (1964) and **Matamoros** (1965) before signing with Monument and scoring with **A Million And One** (1966), **Bear With Me A Little**

Longer (1966), **Anything Your Heart Desires** (1967), **Ramona** (1968) and **Thinking About You, Baby** (1969).

By 1970 Walker had joined MGM, gaining high chart placings with **When A Man Loves A Woman** (1970), **I'm Gonna Keep On Loving You** (1971) and **Sing A Love Song To Baby** (1972) but by 1975 he had switched to RCA, obtaining minor chart positions with **Don't Stop The World**, **(Here I Am) Alone Again** and **Love You All To Pieces** in 1976. Billy teamed up with Barbara Fairchild in 1980 to score duet country hits with **The Answer Game** and **Let Me Be The One**.

Though he has failed to score Top 10 hits for many years, he has continued to record regularly for such minor labels as MRC, Scorpion, Caprice, Dimension and his own Tall Texan Records. Due to regular visits to Britain, he has built up a whole new following in the 1980s, the likeable singer scoring with his Mexican-flavoured ballads that have played a major role in his long career. Walker has also made some film appearances, two of which were in 'Second Fiddle To A Steel Guitar' and 'Red River Round-Up'.

Albums:
Alone Again (RCA/–)
Walking Up To Sunshine (Golden Memories/–)
Star Of The Grand Ole Opry (First Generation/–)
The Answer Game – with Barbara Fairchild (–/RCA)
Fine As Wine (MGM/–)

Charlie Walker

Born in Collins County, Texas on November 2 1926, Walker was a precocious singing and writing talent, becoming a good musician in his teens and joining Bill Boyd's Cowboy Ramblers in 1943.

Later he was successful on radio, his announcing style being much sought after and getting him rated in Billboard's Top 10 Country Music Disc Jockey listing.

He signed with Columbia Records in the mid '50s and in 1958 had his first big hit with **Pick Me Up On Your Way Down**.

I Don't Mind Goin' Under, Charlie Walker. Courtesy RCA Records.

During the '60s and early '70s, he recorded for Columbia and Epic, having hits with several songs, among them being **Who'll Buy The Wine?** (1960), **Wild As A Wild Cat** (1965) and **Don't Squeeze My Sharmon** (1967), also cutting a series of honky tonk titles that has included **Close All The Honky Tonks** (1964), **Honky Tonk Season** (1969) and **Honky Tonk Women** (1970).

His announcing capabilities helped him gain many cabaret residencies, most

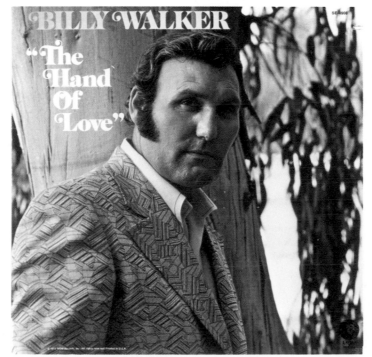

notably at the Las Vegas Golden Nugget. A capable golfer, Walker has won respect as a knowledgeable golfing broadcaster.

In 1972 he became an RCA recording artist, his albums for that label including **Break Out The Bottle** and **I Don't Mind Going Under**. A short spell with Capitol in 1974 proved fruitless, and since recording a couple of albums for Shelby Singleton's Plantation label in the late '70s, Charlie has concentrated on his broadcasting skills.

Jerry Jeff Walker

Originally a folkie operating out of New York, Jerry Jeff (real name Paul Crosby, born in Oneonta, New York on March 16, 1942) became closely associated with the new wave country movement emanating from Austin, Texas during the mid 1970s.

In 1966 he formed a rock group, Circus Maximus, with Austin songwriter Rob Runo, the band recording for Vanguard. However, Walker opted to become a solo act in 1968 and cut the self-penned **Mr. Bojangles**, a memorable song regarding a street dancer he once met in a New Orleans jail, also providing Atco with an album of the same title. But although **Mr. Bojangles** became a much covered song and provided the Dirt Band with a Top 10 hit in 1970, Walker's career seemed to remain fairly stationary for a considerable period.

Signed to MCA in the early '70s, he mixed with fellow Texas singer-

It's A Good Night For Singin', Jerry Jeff Walker. Courtesy MCA.

songwriters, Guy Clark and Townes Van Zandt, and with his own back-up unit, known as The Lost Gonzo Band, recorded a series of good-timey, country-oriented albums that brought him a huge following across Texas.

Jerry Jeff split from The Lost Gonzo Band in 1977, but continued to record for MCA, later joining Elektra and forming The Bandito Band. In more recent years he has preferred to work as a solo performer, though he did team up with Guy Clark for a British tour in the spring of 1986, which included an appearance at the Wembley Festival.

Albums:
Viva Terlingua (MCA/–)
Walker's Collectables (MCA/MCA)
It's A Good Night For Singing (MCA/MCA)
Too Old To Change (Elektra/–)

Jerry Wallace

Billed as 'Mr. Smooth' – though he has been known to rock – Wallace is a one-time pop vocalist who swung into country music during the mid '60s and has since amassed over a score of hits.

Born in Kansas City on December 15, 1933, singer-songwriter-guitarist Wallace was raised and educated in California. Following a brief term of service in the Navy, he made his first chart impact in 1958 when his recording of **How The Time Flies**, on Challenge, reached 11th place in the pop charts. The following year brought even more success when Wallace's version of **Primrose Lane**, a number later

Shutters And Boards, Jerry Wallace. Courtesy Mercury Records.

used as a theme for Henry Fonda's 'Smith Family' TV series, became a million-seller.

After providing Challenge with 11 hit discs, Wallace signed for Mercury and cut more country-oriented material. **Life's Gone And Slipped Away** (1965) gained him his first country chart entry.

Since that time, he has cut sides for such labels as Liberty, Decca, MCA, MGM, 4-Star, Door Knob and BMA, his major country hits including **The Morning After** (1971), **If You Leave Me Tonight, I'll Cry** (a No. 1 in 1972), **Do You Know What It's Like To Be Lonesome?** (1973), **My Wife's House** (1974) and **I Miss You Already** (1977).

A performer on many top TV programmes, Wallace's voice has been heard on myriad commercials, while he has also turned up in such top-rated shows as 'Hec Ramsey' and Rod Serling's 'Night Gallery'.

Albums:
Greatest Hits (MGM/–)
I Miss You Already (BMA/–)
The Golden Hits (4-Star/–)

Steve Wariner

Born in Kentucky on Christmas Day in 1954, Steve Noel Wariner grew up in a musical environment, with his father, a foundry worker, playing in a number of country bands in Indiana where the family moved when Steve was young.

Before reaching his teens, Steve was playing bass in a little country band along with his father and an uncle. Although he was influenced greatly by the music of George Jones and Merle Haggard, Steve's idol was guitar virtuoso Chet Atkins. When he finally signed a recording contract with RCA at the end of 1977, it was Chet who was to act as Steve's producer and to offer him good advice.

Prior to his move to Nashville and joining RCA, Steve had worked the road for three years with Dottie West and spent a little more than two years as front man for Bob Luman's band. An overlooked but very talented songwriter, Steve wrote his first RCA release, **I'm Already Taken**, which was later recorded by Conway Twitty.

Between April, 1978 and the end of 1982, Steve scored a series of minor country hits such as **So Sad (To Watch Good Love Go Bad)**, **Forget Me Not**, **The Easy Part's Over**, **Your Memory** and **By Now**, finally hitting the jackpot with **All**

Midnight Fire, Steve Wariner. Courtesy RCA Records.

Roads Lead To You, a 1982 No. 1. At this time Steve's recordings were patterned very much like the Glen Campbell/Jimmy Webb pop-country classics of the '60s and were produced by Tom Collins.

A change of producer, with Norro Wilson and Tony Brown guiding Steve's recordings, led to a more country-styled approach and such Top 10 hits as **Don't Your Mem'ry Ever Sleep At Night**, **Midnight Fire** (both 1983) and **Lonely Women Make Good Lovers** (1984). When his contract with RCA came up for renewal at the end of 1984, he decided to make a move to MCA where he has rapidly established himself as one of Nashville's most successful country singers.

He also really flourished as a songwriter with such self-penned hits as **You Can't Cut Me Any Deeper**, **Natural History** and **You Can Dream Of Me**. For the first time he was allowed to play lead guitar on his own recordings, being turned loose on guitar solos, which proved to be nothing particularly flashy but certainly

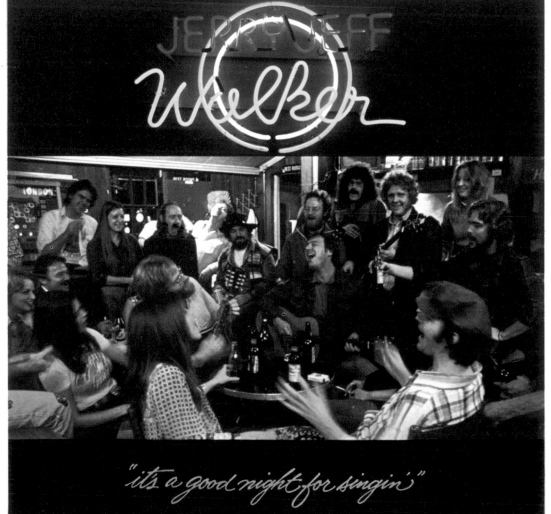

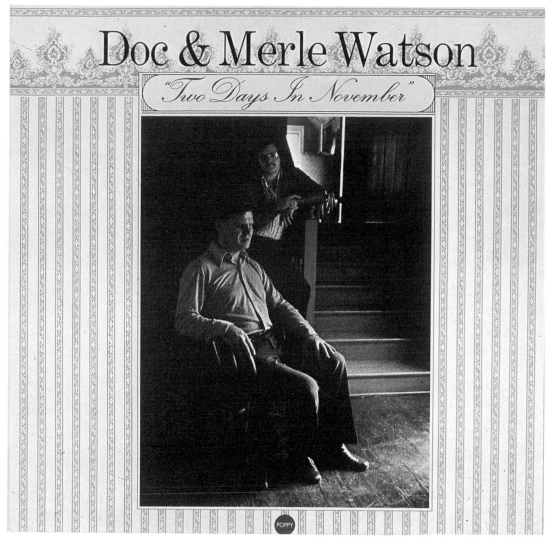

courses in the history of American music, put across by using elements of field hollers, black blues, sacred music, mountain songs, gospel, bluegrass and even traces of jazz.

Albums:
Memories (UA/–)
Two Days In November (UA/UA)
Lonesome Road (UA/–)
The Essential (Vanguard/Vanguard)
The Watson Family Tradition (–/Topic)
In The Pines (–/Sundown)
Guitar Album (Flying Fish/–)
Red Rockin' Chair (Flying Fish/–)

Gene Watson

A singer with an easy-flowing style and a penchant for tearstained ballads, Watson (born on October 11, 1943 in Palestine, Texas) initially worked out of Houston, becoming a resident singer at the Dynasty Club and recording for various independent record labels such as Resco and Wide World during the early '70s.

Obtaining a regional hit with **Love In The Hot Afternoon** (previously recorded by Waylon Jennings, but never released), Gene signed with Capitol Records, who made the record into a Top 5 country chart success in 1975. One of those country singers, well equipped vocally, who found it a long and difficult task to win any real recognition, Gene is not a man to be thrown off balance by the recurrence of his name on the charts, and in a five-year association with Capitol he enjoyed more than a dozen Top 5 hits including **Paper Rosie** (1977), **Farewell Party** (1979), **Nothing Sure Looked Good On You** and **Bedroom Ballad** (both 1980).

Working both on the road and in the studio with his Farewell Party Band, Gene moved over to MCA Records in 1981 and continued to produce first-rate country recordings, choosing his material with meticulous care and singing in a kind of mellow style, but with enough distinctiveness to make it much more than easy-listening. As well as scoring Top 10 country hits with such songs as **Maybe I Should Have Been Listening** (1981), **This Dream's On Me** (1982), **Sometimes I Get**

Two Days In November. Doc And Merle Watson. Courtesy Poppy.

well executed and in keeping with the tone of the pieces.

The result has been such Top 10 country hits as **Heart Trouble** and **What I Didn't Do** (both 1985), **You Can Dream Of Me** and **Life's Highway** (both 1986), plus regular appearances on such TV shows as Austin City Limits, Hee Haw, That Nashville Music and Country Music Comes Home.

Albums:
Midnight Fire (RCA/–)
Life's Highway (MCA/–)
One Good Night Deserves Another (MCA/–)

Doc Watson

Folk legend and heir to an old time country tradition, guitarist, banjoist, singer, Arthel (Doc) Watson was rediscovered in the boom folk years of the '60s and again in the '70s when the Nitty Gritty Dirt Band brought his music to the newly-enthusiastic country-rock public.

Born in Deep Gap, North Carolina on March 2, 1923, Doc was the son of a farmer who was prominent in the singing activities of the local Baptist church. Doc's grandparents lived with his immediate family and they taught the boy many traditional folk songs. He also listened to records of the Carter Family and Gid Tanner's Skillet Lickers.

His first appearance was at the Boone,

North Carolina, Fiddler's Convention. He achieved fame locally but with country music 'smartening up' and with rock 'n' roll finally hitting the scene, the mountain tradition was not foremost in the mind of national America.

In 1960, some east coast recording executives came to cut Clarence Ashley's String Band and Ashley then appeared on a New York 'Friends Of Old Time Music' bill in 1961. Doc was invited along on the bill. As a consequence, he scored a solo gig at Gerde's Folk City in Greenwich Village, being rapturously received. In 1963, he consolidated his reputation considerably with an appearance on the Newport Folk Festival.

Doc relies heavily on traditional material. His voice, his guitar and banjo playing have a simplicity and intense profundity, almost making songs like **Tom Dooley** and **Shady Grove** his own.

During the '60s he recorded for Folkways and Vanguard Records. He has variously been heard on record with his mother, Mrs. G. D. Watson, Jean Ritchie, his brother Arnold, Arnold's father-in-law Gaither Carlton and, most fruitfully, with son Merle, who sadly died when a tractor overturned on him at the Watson farm in Lenoir, North Carolina on October 23, 1985.

Although welded to an acoustic style which has been emulated widely by country-rock guitarists, Doc is no purist. His material runs the gamut of styles from bluegrass through western swing to a more commercial country-pop. During the 1970s he recorded for United Artists in Nashville with such session players as Joe Allen, Chuck Cochran, Johnny Gimble,

Norman Blake and Jim Isbell, and even allowed his producer Jack Clement to surround him with strings on occasion.

A revered figure among old and young alike, drawing wild receptions quite out of keeping with his down-home musical style, Doc's concerts are virtually short

Because You Believed In Me, Gene Watson. Courtesy Capitol Records.

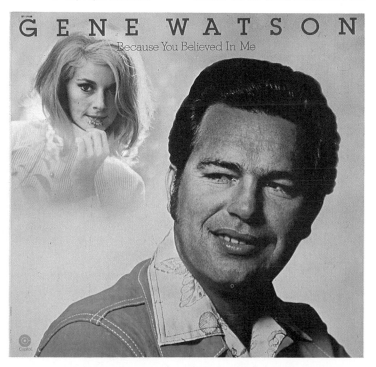

Above: Gene Watson. He cut his first record at 18.

Lucky And Forget (1983), **Forever Again** (1984) and **Got No Reason Now For Going Home** (1985), he has endeared himself to British country fans, though his recent albums have not gained British release.

Towards the end of 1985, Gene changed labels once again, moving to Epic Records and scoring Top 10 hits with **Memories To Burn** (1985) and **Carmen** (1986), this time assisted by Larry Booth, veteran country singer and bass player with the Farewell Party Band, who acted as co-producer with Watson.

Albums:
Beautiful Country (Capitol/–)
Old Loves Never Die (MCA/–)
Little By Little (MCA/–)
Memories To Burn (Epic/–)
Heartaches, Love & Stuff (MCA/–)
Reflections (Capitol/–)

Paper Rosie, Gene Watson. Courtesy Capitol Records.

Dennis Weaver

A character actor best known for his TV role in 'Gunsmoke' (as the limping, slow-drawling Chester – 1958–64), 'Kentucky Jones' (1965) and 'McCloud' (1970 onwards), the easy-going Weaver has acquired both a western image and a reasonable reputation as a country singer. Born in 1924, he hails from Joplin, Missouri. A Western movie addict as a child, he later became a top grade athlete in track events, just failing to qualify for the Olympic Games in 1948.

Following graduation from Oklahoma University, he became part of the New York Artists Studio, making his Broadway debut in 'Come Back Little Sheba' with Shirley Booth (1951). By the following year he had moved into films, appearing in 'The Raiders', later making 'War Arrow' (1954), 'Dragnet' (1954), 'Seven Angry Men' (1955), 'A Touch Of Evil' (1958), 'The Gallant Hours' (1960), 'Duel At Diablo' (1966) and many others.

Recording his first country album, **Dennis Weaver**, for the Impress label in 1972, he subsequently signed for Ovation, for whom he made **One More Road**. By 1976, he had gone the whole hog, spending some time in Nashville with producer Ray Pennington and emerging with a second album titled **Dennis Weaver**. Failing to come up with a hit single, Dennis has now returned to his first love, acting, though he does occasionally make special guest appearances on country shows.

Album:
Dennis Weaver (–/DJM)

Freddy Weller

Born on September 9, 1947 in Atlanta, Georgia, before becoming a country artist and obtaining a contract with Columbia Records, Weller achieved a fair degree of fame in the field of pop, both as a member of hit-parading rock group, Paul Revere And The Raiders, with whom he debuted on the Ed Sullivan Show during April, 1967, and also as co-writer of many songs with Tommy Roe, including the million-sellers **Dizzy** (1968) and **Jam Up, Jelly Tight** (1969).

Once a bassist and guitarist with Joe South, Weller has also worked as a studio musician in Atlanta and toured as part of Billy Joe Royal's backup group.

After achieving a Top 10 country hit with **Games People Play** in 1969, Weller enjoyed a successful patch through to 1971, **These Are Not My People, Promised Land, Indiana Lake** and **Another Night Of Love** all charting impressively during this period. In late 1974, Weller signed for Dot, cutting one album for the label and scoring a couple of minor country hits.

He re-joined Columbia at the beginning of 1976, but has been unable to make it back to the Top 10, only reaching the Top 30 with **Love Got In The Way** (1978) and **Fantasy Island** (1979), leading to him being dropped by the label in 1980.

Albums:
Greatest Hits (Columbia/–)
Go For The Night (Columbia/–)
Roadmaster (Columbia/–)
The Promised Land (Columbia)

Kitty Wells

The acknowledged Queen Of Country Music, Kitty Wells (real name Muriel Deason) was born in Nashville, Tennessee on August 30, 1918. As a child she sang gospel music at the neighbourhood church, at 14 learning to play guitar. Within a year she was playing at local dances, some time later obtaining her first

A Bouquet Of Country Hits, Kitty Wells. Courtesy MCA.

radio dates.

While appearing on station WXIX's 'Dixie Early Birds' show, she met Johnny Wright (Johnny And Jack), whom she married two years later (1938). By this time she had become a featured artist on the Johnny and Jack touring show, adopting the name Kitty Wells from a folk song called 'Sweet Kitty Wells'.

With their backup unit The Tennessee Mountain Boys, Johnny and Jack and Kitty Wells toured widely during the late '30s and the war years of the '40s, their biggest breaks on radio coming in 1940 on WBIG, Greensboro, North Carolina, then later on WNOX Knoxville's 'Mid-Day Merry-Go-Round'.

In 1947 came Johnny, Jack and Kitty's membership on Grand Ole Opry, after which they moved to Shreveport to become the stars of KWKH's new Louisiana Hayride. Five years later came an offer of a regular spot on the Opry, plus a record contract from Decca (she had previously recorded with RCA-Victor), the same year seeing the release of **It Wasn't God Who Made Honky Tonk Angels**, an answer disc to Hank Thompson's **Wild Side Of Life**. This enabled Kitty to become the first female to have a No. 1 country hit – although Patsy Montana's **I Wanna Be A Cowboy's Sweetheart** would have reached No. 1 if charts had existed in 1935.

Since that time, Kitty Wells has amassed an amazing number of chart entries, including duets with Roy Drusky, Red Foley, Roy Acuff, Johnny Wright and Webb Pierce, the biggest of her solo successes being with **Paying For That Back Street Affair** (1953), **Making Believe** (1955), **Searching** (1956), **Jealousy** (1958), **Mommy For A Day** (1959), **Amigo's Guitar** (1959), **Left To Right** (1960), **Heartbreak U.S.A.** (1961), **Unloved, Unwanted** (1962), **Password** (1964) and **You Don't Hear** (1965).

Her awards are equally numerous and include Billboard's No. 1 Country Music Female Artist Of The Year 1954–65, a 1974 Woman of the Year award from the Nashville Association of Business and Professional Women, plus a Most Outstanding Tennessee Citizen citation presented by the late Governor of Tennessee, Frank G. Clement, in 1954.

Kitty, who has three children – Ruby,

Above: Kitty Wells, the first woman to have a No. 1 country hit.

Carol Sue and Bobby – eventually terminated her long association with Decca during the mid '70s, signing for the Macon-based Capricorn label and cutting an album, aptly named **Forever Young**. In 1976 she received the supreme accolade – being elected to the Country Music Hall

Of Fame. Kitty still continues to tour all over America and is busy recording for her own Ruboca Records label, maintaining the style which she is best known for and refusing to be drawn into a modern pop-country sound.

Albums:
Early Classics (Golden Country/–)
Hall Of Fame Vol. 1 (Ruboca/–)
The Kitty Wells Story (MCA/MCA)
The Golden Years (Rounder/–)
Forever Young (Capricorn/–)

Special Delivery, Dottie West. Courtesy UA Records.

Dottie West

Known as the 'Country Sunshine' girl after writing and recording a song of that title for a Coke commercial, Dottie was born in McMinnville, Tennessee on October 11, 1932, one of ten children. Farm raised, Dorothy Marie still had time to gain a college degree while helping to work the cotton and sugar cane fields.

She later incorporated these experiences into her songs, but one of Dottie's strengths has also been her ability to adapt pop stylings, as she has trodden a line between country sentiment and commercial productions with considerable success.

In the early 1950s, she studied music at Tennessee Tech and there met Bill West, her future husband. Bill was studying engineering but he played steel guitar and accompanied Dottie at college concerts. Both eventually majored in their respective subjects and then moved to Ohio where they appeared as a duo on local TV in the Cleveland area.

While visiting relatives in Nashville in 1959, they met some executives from Starday Records and were given a record contract; this resulted in local live appearances but little else, Dottie later switching to the Atlantic label, again with virtually no result.

Success eluded her until 1963 when Dottie, by this time signed to RCA, recorded **Let Me Off At The Corner**, a Top 30 disc. A year later came the big one – **Here Comes My Baby** – a West original that became covered by Perry Como, providing him with a pop hit and also earning Dottie a Grammy award.

From that moment on it was all freewheeling for Dottie – she became an Opry regular (1964), arranged and worked with the Memphis and Kansas City Symphony Orchestra, provided RCA with such major solo hits as **Would You Hold It Against Me?** (1966), **Paper Mansions** (1967), **Country Girl** (1968), **Forever Yours** (1970), **Country Sunshine** (1973) and **Last Time I Saw Him** (1974), and also recorded hit duets with Jim Reeves (**Love Is No Excuse** – 1964) and Don Gibson (**Rings Of Gold** and **There's A Story Goin' Round** – both 1969).

Between collecting numerous awards, making a few films, writing some 400 songs and commercials, and fitting in recording dates and several tours, she has also found time to raise four children and marry again – her second husband being drummer Bryon Metcalf.

In 1978 Dottie teamed up with Kenny Rogers for a successful duet partnership which resulted in the Top 10 hits, **Everytime Two Fools Collide** (1978) and **All I Ever Need Is You** (1979), and the pair being named CMA Vocal Duo in both 1978 and 1979. Dottie had signed with United Artists Records in 1976 and continued to score major country hits with **When It's Just You And Me** (1977), **Come See Me And Come Lonely** (1978), **You Pick Me Up (And Put Me Down)** (1979), **A Lesson In Leavin'** (1980) and **What Are We Doin' In Love** (1981).

The red-haired beauty, who had helped launch the careers of Larry Gatlin and Steve Wariner, found herself something of a country sex queen in her mid '40s with full colour centrespreads in several of the leading American magazines. Her daughter, Shelly West, has also made a name for herself in country music, initially

If It's All Right With You, Dottie West. Courtesy RCA Records.

as a duet partner for David Frizzell and later as a solo performer. Dottie has been recording for the small Permian label since 1985, continuing to chalk up minor country hits.

Albums:
High Times (Liberty/–)
Wild West (Liberty/–)
20 Of The Best (–/RCA)
Special Delivery (UA/UA)
Dottie (UA/UA)
Carolina Cousins (RCA/RCA)
Everytime Two Fools Collide – with Kenny Rogers (UA/UA)
Classics – with Kenny Rogers (UA/UA)

Shelly West

Daughter of Dottie West and her first husband, steel guitarist, Bill West, Shelly (born on May 23, 1958 in Nashville, Tennessee) initially made an impression as the duet partner of David Frizzell on the 1981 chart-topper, **You're The Reason God Made Oklahoma**.

Having grown up in a musical family, it was inevitable that Shelly would end up in the music business. She began performing in Dottie's shows in 1975, soon after her graduation from Nashville's Hillsboro High School. During her year and a half with Dottie, Shelly gradually worked her way up from harmony singing to her own short solo spot.

Towards the end of 1977, she and Allen Frizzell (David and Lefty's younger brother who was employed as Dottie's front man and guitarist) moved to California to pursue their own solo careers. They teamed up with David and worked the honky tonk club circuits across Texas, Oklahoma, New Mexico, Nevada and Southern California.

Eventually David and Shelly began singing together and recorded a duet album featuring **You're The Reason God**

In Session, Shelly West and David Frizzell. Courtesy WEA-Viva Records.

Made Oklahoma, a song that Clint Eastwood insisted on using in his film, 'Any Which Way You Can'. Frizzell and West continued with such duet hits as **Texas State Of Mind** (1981), **Another Honky Tonk Night On Broadway** (1982), **Cajun Invitation** (1983), **Another Dawn Breaking Over Georgia** (1984) and **Do Me Right** (1985).

These duet successes paved the way for Shelly's solo career, and she has made her mark on the charts with **Jose Cuervo** and **Another Motel Memory** (both 1983), **Flight 309 To Nashville** (1984), **Now There's You** and **Don't Make Me Wait On The Moon** (both 1985). For a while Shelly was married to Allen Frizzell, but the couple separated and were divorced in 1985.

Albums:
Don't Make Me Wait On The Moon
  (Warners-Viva/–)
West By West (Warners-Viva/–)
Carryin' On The Family Name – with David
  Frizzell (Warners-Viva/–)

Billy Edd Wheeler

Born in Whitesville, West Virginia on December 9, 1932, Billy Edd is that none too usual animal, the college-educated country artist. He has a BA degree from Berea College, Kentucky, attended Yale Drama School and has been, variously, an editor, a music business executive, a Navy

Nashville Zodiac, Billy Ed Wheeler. Courtesy UA.

pilot and an instructor at Berea College.

The Kingston Trio had a Top 10 pop hit with his **Reverend Mr. Black** in 1963 and Wheeler himself enjoyed a rare hit single with **The Little Brown Shack Out Back**, which nearly (but not quite) topped the country charts in 1964, helping him earn an ASCAP writer's award.

Despite various changes of record company (he has been with such labels as Monitor, Kapp, UA and RCA), his only real influence upon the charts has been through the medium of his songwriting, Johnny Cash and June Carter adding to Wheeler's royalty cheque by recording his **Jackson**, a crossover hit in 1967, and via Kenny Rogers' multi-million selling pop-country smash with **Coward Of The County** in 1979.

A collector of folk material – and author of a folk play – Billy Edd Wheeler was responsible for creating a special music room in the Mountain Hall Of Fame, Richwood, West Virginia.

Albums:
Wild Mountain Flowers (Flying Fish/–)
Nashville Zodiac (UA/UA)
Love (RCA/–)

Clarence White

A rock musician with a bluegrass background, guitarist Clarence White was born in Lewiston, Maine on June 7, 1944. Raised in California, he played with the Country Boys at the age of ten, the group's other members being his brothers, Roland (16) and Eric (12).

The White Brothers, Clarence, Eric and Roland White. Courtesy Rounder.

A bluegrass unit, working at various barn dances and local functions in the Burbank area, the Country Boys materialised into the Kentucky Colonels in 1962, the line-up then being Clarence (guitar), Roland (mandolin), Roger Bush (bass), Billy Ray Latham (banjo) and Leroy

Mack (dobro).

Two albums were recorded, one for World Pacific and the other for Briar, before Clarence left in 1965 to become a sessionman, appearing on disc with Ricky Nelson, the Everlys, the Byrds, Gene Clark, Flying Burritos, Wynn Stewart and many others.

After cutting a never-released solo album for the Bakersfield International label and working sporadically with Cajun Gib and Gene (Gib Guilbeau and Gene Parsons), White formed Nashville West, a short-lived country-rock unit that featured both Guilbeau and Parsons plus bassist Wayne Moore. But in September, 1968, he moved on to become a regular member of the Byrds, remaining with the group until its final demise.

Returning to session work once more, White began fashioning a new solo album, also putting in some gigs with the re-formed Kentucky Colonels. However, the solo album was never completed; White was knocked down and killed by a drunken woman driver while loading equipment on to a van following a gig on July 14, 1973.

Albums:
Clarence White And The Kentucky
  Colonels (Rounder/–)
Nashville West (Sierra Briar/Sundown)
Kentucky Colonels (–/UA)

The Whites

Buck White, piano and mandolin; Cheryl White Warren, acoustic bass; Sharon White Skaggs, acoustic guitar.

Quite the most distinctive and fascinating new group sounds to emerge in the '80s, The Whites, in fact, go back a long way, with father Buck White having roots in western swing music and the distinction of playing piano on the original recording of Slim Willet's **Don't Let The Stars Get In Your Eyes** back in 1952.

Buck, who grew up in Texas, met his wife Pat in the early '50s, and from the very beginning, music played a major role in their family life. At that time he played piano for various swing bands in and

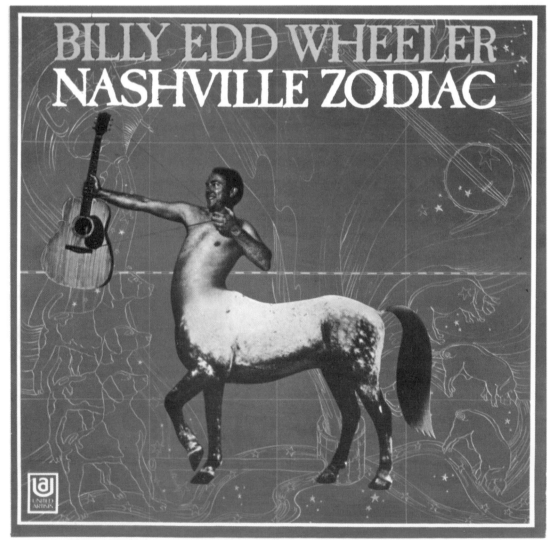

film period, both as a cowboy singer and fronting a western swing dance band for several years during the war. He also continued to record for Decca and later Okeh, Conqueror, Cowboy and Apollo.

An active songwriter, he wrote or co-wrote with Fred Rose many of Gene Autry's big hits, including **Back In The Saddle Again**, **Lonely River**, **I Hang My Head And Cry** and **Ages And Ages Ago**.

In addition, Whitley also managed both the Sons Of The Pioneers and Jimmy Wakely for a time, and helped Gibson design and build their first J-200 guitar, which quickly became popular among country and cowboy singers.

He was still turning up at western film festivals, singing and doing tricks with his bullwhip until shortly before his death in Hollywood, California on February 21, 1979.

Slim Whitman

Born Otis Dewey Whitman Jnr. in Tampa, Florida on January 20, 1924, Whitman's early interest was in sport rather than music. He became a star pitcher with his Tampa high school team and hoped to make a career in the game. However, on leaving school he took a job in a meat-packing plant, where he met his wife-to-be.

Just prior to Pearl Harbour, Whitman bcame a shipyard fitter in Tampa, enlisting in the Navy during 1943 and serving on the USS Chilton until discharged in 1945. While in the Navy he learned guitar and entertained at shipboard events, upon return to civilian life splitting his time between baseball and entertaining when not working in the shipyard.

In 1946 he gained a contract with the Plant City Berries of the Orange Belt

Above: The Whites. Buck (centre) is a fine blues pianist, as well as being an expert mandolinist.

around the Wichita Falls area. In 1962 the family uprooted and moved to Arkansas where Buck became involved in bluegrass music for the first time.

Working as Buck White & The Down Home Folks, the family group, consisting of Buck, Pat and their two daughters Cheryl and Sharon, became popular on the bluegrass festival and other country circuits. In the early '70s, a move to Nashville to further their career was made and they recorded their first album, **Buck White And The Down Home Folks**, for County Records in April, 1972. It was to be another five years before they recorded a second album, **In Person**, by which time Cheryl and Sharon had graduated and were able to work full time with the group.

These were hard times for the family group, though, as bluegrass music was not exactly popular, and the two girls had to find various jobs working in factories, shops and fruit picking to supplement their meagre showbusiness earnings. They were still recording regularly for Ridge Runner and Sugar Hill, slowly building up a sizeable following amongst die-hard bluegrass fans.

A short-lived recording contract with Capitol Records in 1982 came at the same time that they decided to change their name to The Whites. One single was released, **Send Me The Pillow You Dream On**, which made the charts, but Capitol decided not to release any further records.

Emmylou Harris and Ricky Skaggs eventually became involved in the group's career, with Emmylou inviting them to open her tour in support of her **Blue Kentucky Girl** album, and Ricky offering to produce an album for Warner-Curb. This resulted in The Whites being nominated in the CMA 1983 Awards as Vocal Group of

the Year and achieving Top 10 country hits with **You Put The Blue In Me**, **Hangin' Around** (both 1983) and **I Wonder Who's Holding My Baby Tonight** (1984).

Curb Records amalgamated with MCA in 1984 and The Whites continued to score Top 10 hits on that label with **Pins And Needles** (1984), **Hometown Gossip** and **If It Ain't Love (Let's Leave It Alone)** (1985), their style being based upon the distinctive harmonies of Cheryl and Sharon, the expert mandolin playing of Buck and the dobro work of Jerry Douglas, who has been playing with The Whites since the late '70s.

Albums:
Old Familiar Feeling (Warner-Curb/–)
Forever You (MCA-Curb/–)
Whole New World (MCA-Curb/MCA)

Ray Whitley

Despite a late start, Ray Whitley became a quite successful jack of all trades in the era of the singing cowboy. Born on December 5, 1901 near Atlanta, Georgia, Whitley spent some time in the Navy and as an electrician and steelworker in Philadelphia and New York, where he pursued music as a hobby.

He auditioned for radio in New York City, and rapidly rose to co-host (with Tex Ritter) of the WHN Barn Dance in the mid 1930s. Here he also recorded for the American Record Company complex, and also for Decca, his biggest hits being his theme song, **Blue Yodel Blues** and **The Last Flight Of Wiley Post**.

One of the earliest singing cowboys to invade Hollywood, he appeared in films as early as 1936. He spent 1938–1942 at RKO, where he made 18 musical shorts of his own and was the singing sidekick to George O'Brien and Tim Holt before spending some more time in similar roles

at Universal. Film work trailed off in the late 1940s, and his last role was as Watts, James Dean's manager in 'Giant'.

Whitley was active musically during his

Below: Ray Whitley, one of Hollywood's earliest singing cowboys.

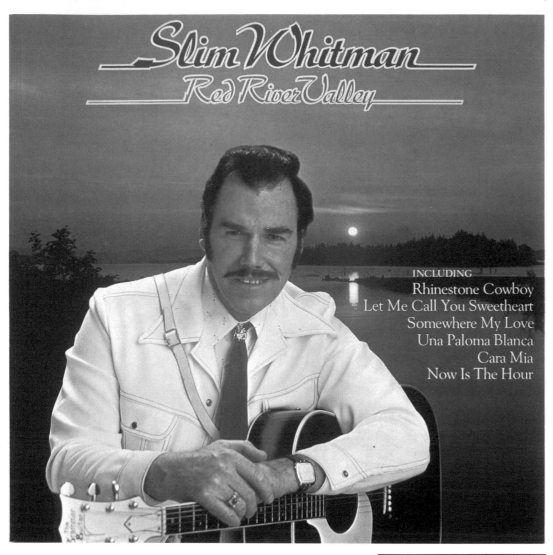

Red River Valley, Slim Whitman. Courtesy UA Records.

League – but his musical career also prospered via radio spots on Tampa WDAE and many local club bookings. It was at this point that Whitman opted for music as a full time occupation and began establishing his reputation beyond the bounds of Tampa, in 1949 winning a record contract with RCA. After gaining some attention with a release titled **Casting My Lasso To The Sky**, he moved to Shreveport, becoming a regular on the Louisiana Hayride.

Later, in 1952, he signed for Imperial Records and staked an immediate claim to stardom with his semi-yodelled version of **Indian Love Call**, a former operetta favourite. This was followed by **Rose Marie**, a massive seller – in Britain it topped the pop charts for eight straight weeks during 1955 – it provided Whitman with a gold disc and an audience ready to snap up such other offerings as **Secret Love** (1954), **Cattle Call** (1955), **More Than Yesterday** (1965), **Guess Who?** (1970) and **Something Beautiful** (1971), all of which have entered the country Top 10.

Whitman's reliance on mainly sweet, romantic ballads, purveyed in a rich voice that switches easily to falsetto, has made him a worldwide favourite. But nowhere is he more popular than in Britain where he became the first country vocalist to perform at the London Palladium. His British tours are usually in the SRO bracket while such albums as **The Very Best Of Slim Whitman** and **Red River Valley** topped the UK charts in 1976 and

1977 respectively.

A special TV advertised set of his most popular numbers became a big seller in America in 1983, introducing Slim to a whole new audience, whilst he has continued to record regularly for United Artists, Cleveland International and Epic with his records making the Radio Two playlists in Britain where he still commands a large and loyal following.

Albums:
15th Anniversary (Imperial/Liberty)
Yodelling (Imperial/Liberty)
Slim Whitman Collection (–/UA)
Songs I Love To Sing (Epic/Epic)
Angeline (Epic/Epic)
25th Anniversary Concert (–/UA)
Country Style (–/Music for Pleasure)
Rose Marie & Other Love Songs (–/Pickwick)
20 Greatest Love Songs (–/Music for Pleasure)

Country Style, Slim Whitman. Courtesy Music For Pleasure.

Henry Whitter

One of the earliest country musicians to be recorded – it is claimed that his earliest recordings were pre-dated only by those of Eck Robertson – William Henry Whitter

was born near Fries, Virginia on April 6, 1892.

Working in a cotton mill to earn a living, he learnt guitar, fiddle, piano, harmonica and organ, and began performing around the Fries area. In March, 1923, he visited New York, gaining an audition with the General Phonograph Company and recording two numbers which were promptly shelved.

However, in the wake of Fiddlin' John Carson's success with his Okeh sides, Whitter was recalled to New York in December, 1923, there waxing nine numbers for Okeh release, the first of these, **The Wreck On The Southern Old '97** backed with **Lonesome Road Blues**, being issued in January, 1924. Later that year, **Old '97** was to be recorded in a slightly different version by Vernon Dalhart, which became a multi-million-selling record.

Whitter continued to record as a soloist, an accompanist (with Roba Stanley – one of the first female country singers to record) and as a bandleader, with Whitter's Virginia Breakdowners. He also formed a successful musical alliance with blind fiddler George Banman Grayson, recording with him several times between 1927 and 1929.

This partnership terminated when Grayson died in a road accident during the mid '30s, and though Whitter continued in a solo role until the commencement of the 1940s, his health gradually deteriorated. He died from diabetes in Morganton, North Carolina on November 10, 1941.

Wilburn Brothers

Once part of a family act that included their father, mother, elder brothers and a sister, Doyle (born in Thayer, Missouri on July 7, 1930) and Teddy Wilburn (born in Thayer on November 30, 1931) began as hometown street corner singers, the Wilburn Family eventually touring the South and establishing a reputation that led ultimately to an Opry signing in 1941.

In the wake of the Korean War, Teddy and Doyle began working as a duo, touring with Webb Pierce and Faron Young. Obtaining a record contract with

A Portrait, The Wilburn Brothers. Courtesy MCA Records.

Decca, they scored a Top 10 disc in 1956 with **Go Away With Me**, this being the first of an impressive tally of hits that extended into the early '70s.

With a repertoire that extended into virtually every area of country music, the Wilburns appealed to a wide audience, a fact reflected in their record sales of 1959 when three of their releases, **Which One Is To Blame?**, **Somebody Back In Town** and **A Woman's Intuition**, major hits.

Founders of the Wil-Helm Talent Agency in conjunction with Smiley Wilson, the Wilburns found themselves representing many of Nashville's leading talents – including Loretta Lynn, whom they featured on their own highly popular TV show and for whom they obtained a recording contract with Decca.

Owners of Surefire Music, a music publishing company, they have published the songs of Loretta Lynn and Johnny Russell, having no fewer than seven songs in the 'Coalminer's Daughter' film. They have enjoyed such Top 10 discs as **Trouble's Back In Town** (1962), **Tell Her No** (1963), **It's Another World** (1965) and **Hurt Her Once For Me** (1966), and though they have not made the Top 10 in more than 20 years, they still work the Opry and record for First Generation Records.

Albums:
A Portrait Of The Wilburn Brothers (MCA/–)
Sing Your Heart Out (Decca/–)
Country Gold (–/Stetson)

Curly Williams

Curly Williams led a popular band on the Grand Ole Opry throughout the 1940s called the Georgia Peach Pickers, and is best known for having written **Half As Much** which, because it was popularised by Hank Williams and because the writer's credit is usually listed as 'Williams', is frequently thought of as Hank's song.

Curly returned to Georgia in the late 1940s and gradually drifted out of performing. He was with Columbia from 1945 to 1951, and his biggest hits were **Southern Belle (From Nashville Tennessee)** and **Georgia Steel Guitar**.

Doc Williams

Although he has never had a hit record, one of the most popular regional acts in country music has been Doc Williams, his wife Chickie and their band the Border Riders. They still play hundreds of dates a year, filling houses in the north east and in the Canadian Maritimes, largely on the strength of their long-time association with WWVA and the Wheeling Jamboree.

Born Andrew J. Smik, of Bohemian descent, on June 26, 1914, he grew up in the musically rich area of eastern Pennsylvania. Except for brief stays at WREC in Memphis (1939) and WFMD in Frederick, Maryland (1945), he has remained in that area: Cleveland from 1934–1936, then Pittsburgh and finally Wheeling, from 1937 until the present day.

In 1948 he married Jessie Wanda Crupe, who became known as Chickie, and they have had many regionally popular records on their own label, Wheeling: **Beyond The Sunset**, **Mary Of The Wild Moor**, **Silver Bells** and Doc's own song **Willie Roy, The Crippled Boy**.

Above: Don Williams, country's Gentle Giant. He may be quiet and laid back, but he is never boring.

A staunch traditionalist and a long-time spokesman for Wheeling, WWVA and the Wheeling Jamboree, Doc Williams never achieved national success or huge record sales, but has been a great influence in the north east and in Canada.

Albums:
From Out Of The Beautiful Hills Of West
  Virginia (Wheeling/–)
Doc 'n' Chickie Together (Wheeling/–)
Wheeling Back To Wheeling (Wheeling/–)

Don Williams

Voted Country Artist Of The Decade by British fans in a 1980 poll, Don (born on May 27, 1939 near Plainview, Texas) has been called 'The Gentle Giant of Country Music' due to his laid-back personality and singing style. He first came to prominence with the pop-folk group, the Pozo Seco singers, in 1965; the group (comprised of Williams, Susan Taylor and Lofton Cline) having a major hit the following year with **Time**.

Between 1966 and 1967, the Pozos also had best sellers with **I'll Be Gone**, **I Can Make It With You**, **Look What You've Done**, **I Believed It All** and **Louisiana Man**, but gradually their popularity waned and in 1971 Williams returned to Texas to join his father-in-law in his furniture business.

A solo recording venture by former

Pozo Susan Taylor had him return to Nashville in a writing capacity, but he soon began singing once more, a solo album **Don Williams Vol. 1** being released on Jack Clements' independent JMI label during 1973.

His debut solo single had been **Don't You Believe** (June, 1972) but it was his second, **The Shelter Of Your Eyes**, that gave him his first major bite at the country charts. Don finally made the country Top 10 with **We Should Be Together**, which reached No. 5 in 1974 and topped the charts a few months later with **I Wouldn't Want To Live If You Didn't Love Me**.

Since then he has rarely missed the Top 5, hitting the top spot with such songs as **You're My Best Friend** and **Love Me Tonight** (both 1975), **'Til The Rivers All Run Dry** and **Say It Again** (both 1976), **Some Broken Hearts Never Mend** and **I'm Just A Country Boy** (both 1977), **Tulsa Time** (1978), **It Must Be Love** (1979), **I Believe In You** (a pop crossover which hit No. 24 on the pop charts in 1980), **Lord I Hope This Day Is Good** (1981), **If Hollywood Don't Need You** (1982), **Love Is On A Roll** (1983), **Stay Young** (1984) and **Walking A Broken Heart** (1985).

Surprisingly he made a British breakthrough with **I Recall A Gypsy Woman**, which made the British Top 10 in 1976, yet was never released as a single in America. Due to regular tours, he has consolidated his following in Britain. He emerged as the number one album seller in 1978 (outselling every rock, country and pop act) and his albums continue to be snapped up by his dedicated fans.

Don tries to keep his public

appearances down to a minimum and spends much of his time writing songs, recording or tending his farm near Ashland City, Tennessee, keeping his private life very much detached from his showbiz career, resulting in him being dubbed 'The Reluctant Superstar'. In 1986 he made a label change, moving over from MCA (formerly ABC-Dot) to Capitol, maintaining familiar Don Williams sound.

Albums:
Visions (ABC/ABC)
Portrait (MCA/MCA)
Listen To The Radio (MCA/MCA)
Cafe Carolina (MCA/MCA)
New Moves (Capitol/Capitol)
Love Stories (–/K-tel)
Very Best Of (–/MCA)
The Best Of The Pozo Seco Singers
  (–/CBS Embassy)
Volume One (JMI/ABC)

Harmony, Don Williams. Courtesy MCA Records.

HANK WILLIAMS JUST ME AND MY GUITAR

This collection conveys the conviction, emotional intensity, and vocal technique which earned Hank his legendary place in country music.

moody and uncommunicative, he was much respected and well loved by the country music fraternity, over 20,000 people attending his funeral in Montgomery, at which Roy Acuff, Carl Smith, Red Foley and Ernest Tubb paid tribute in song.

His songs were well accepted in pop music as well – his compositions providing million-selling discs for Joni James (**Your Cheatin' Heart** – 1953), Tony Bennett (**Cold, Cold Heart** – 1951), Jo Stafford (**Jambalaya** – 1952) etc. Williams' material has been recorded by rock bands, folk singers and black music acts.

Elected to the Country Music Hall of Fame in 1961 his plaque reads: "The simple, beautiful melodies and straightforward plaintive stories in his lyrics of life as he knew it will never die".

His son, Hank Williams Jnr., still carries on the Williams tradition today and in 1964 provided the music to 'Your Cheatin' Heart', a Hollywood scripted film biography, in which George Hamilton portrayed Hank Snr.

Albums:
Rare Takes And Radio Cuts (Polydor/–)
40 Greatest Hits (–/MGM)
The Essential Hank Williams (–/MGM)
The Collectors Hank Williams (–/MGM)
Live At The Grand Ole Opry (MGM/MGM)

Hank Williams Jnr.

Son of the late Hank Williams and his wife Audrey, Hank Jnr. was born in Shreveport, Louisiana on May 26, 1949 – though he was taken to Nashville when only three months old and grew up in the country capital.

During his high school days he excelled in swimming, football, boxing and other sports, becoming a health fanatic. When barely a teenager he toured with his mother's 'Caravan Of Stars' show, at the age of 15 having national hits via MGM releases **Long Gone Lonesome Blues** and **Endless Sleep**.

For many years he was forced to follow in his famous father's footsteps by doing

Hank Williams Snr.

One of the most charismatic figures in country music – his Opry performance of June 11, 1949, when his audience required him to reprise **Lovesick Blues** several times is still considered as the Ryman's greatest moment – he was born Hiram King Williams in Georgia, Alabama on September 17, 1923.

A member of the church choir at six, he was given a $3.50 guitar by his mother a year later, receiving some tuition from Tee-Tot (Rufe Payne) an elderly black street musician. When barely a teenager he won $15 singing WPA Blues at a Montgomery amateur contest, then formed a band, The Drifting Cowboys, which played on station WSFA, Montgomery, for over a decade.

In 1946 Williams signed with Sterling Records, switching to the newly formed MGM label in 1947. Though virtually an alcoholic, he was booked as a regular on KWKH's Louisiana Hayride, and in 1949, having scored with his recording of **Lovesick Blues**, came a contract with the Grand Ole Opry.

An early recording, **Move It On Over**, had already been a minor hit for Williams but after the runaway success of **Lovesick Blues** (a song waxed by yodeller Emmett Miller in 1925), he began cutting Top 10 singles with almost monotonous regularity.

With Fred Rose masterminding every Williams recording session, arranging, playing, producing and often participating

Just Me And My Guitar. Rare sides by Hank Williams. Courtesy CMF Records.

in the songwriting, such hits as **Wedding Belles, Mind Your Own Business, You're Gonna Change** and **My Bucket's Got A Hole In It** all charted during 1949, the following year providing **I Just Don't Like This Kind Of Living', Long Gone Lonesome Blues, Why Don't You Love Me?, Why Should We Try Anymore?** and **Moaning The Blues**.

These were followed by **Cold, Cold Heart, Howlin' At The Moon, Hey Good Lookin', Crazy Love, Baby We're Really In Love** (1951), **Honky Tonk Blues, Half As Much, Jambalaya, Settin' The Woods On Fire** and **I'll Never Get Out Of This World Alive** (1952), the latter ironically released just before his death (from a heart attack brought on by excessive drinking) on New Year's Day, 1953.

He and his Drifting Cowboys had been booked to play a show in Canton, Ohio, and Williams hired a driver to chauffeur him through a snowstorm to the gig. He fell asleep along the way – but when the driver tried to rouse him at Oak Hill, Virginia, he was found to be dead. After his death, his records continued to sell in massive quantities, **Your Cheatin' Heart, Take These Chains From My Heart, I Won't Be Home No More** and **Weary Blue From Waitin'** all charting during the year that followed.

The last months of William's life – though financially rewarding – were ultra-tragic. A drug user in order to combat a spinal ailment caused by being thrown from a horse at the age of 17, he was fired

from the Grand Ole Opry in August, 1952 because of perpetual drunkenness and was also divorced by his wife Audrey Sheperd – though he re-married, to Billie Jean Jones, daughter of a Louisiana police chief, soon after.

A difficult man to work with, being

On Stage, Hank Williams Snr. Courtesy MGM Records.

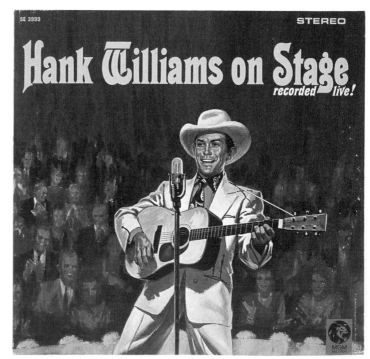

SE 3999 STEREO
Hank Williams on Stage recorded live!

Above: Hank Williams Jnr. who in 1986 became eight years older than his father.

endless versions of Hank Snr.'s songs. He fought against this in songs like **Standing In The Shadows (Of A Very Famous Man)**, which gave him a Top 5 country hit in 1966. Further major hits followed with **It's All Over But The Crying** (1968), **Cajun Baby**, **I'd Rather Be Gone** (both 1969), his first No. 1 – **All For The Love Of Sunshine** (1970), **Ain't That A Shame** and **Eleven Roses** (both 1972) and **The Last Love Song** (1973).

Finally he tired of living in the shadows and being told what to record and sing, and in 1974 he moved from Nashville to Alabama, linked up with an old buddy named James R. Smith and began to forge a new Hank Williams Jnr. sound. He recorded the acclaimed **Hank Williams Jnr. And Friends** album, which featured country-rock musicians including Charlie Daniels and Toy Caldwell.

On August 8, 1975 – about the time the album was being released – Hank Jnr. was involved in a climbing accident on a Montana mountain, suffering appalling head injuries, which he miraculously survived. After two years of recuperation he re-emerged even stronger and made it back to the top with a series of gritty, rough-edged, best-selling country albums.

He changed labels in 1977, moving from MGM to Warner Bros., and although initially his singles failed to make much impression, he finally made it back to the country Top 20 with **I Fought The Law** (1978) and scored Top 5 with **Family Tradition** and **Whiskey Bent And Hell**

Bound (both 1979). Since then he has not looked back, teaming up with Waylon Jennings on **The Conversation** (1979) and topping the charts with such solo hits as **Women I've Never Had** and **Old Habits** (both 1980), **All My Rowdy Friends** (1981) and **A Country Boy Can Survive** (1982), leading to the amazing feat of having 8 albums in Billboard's country charts at the same time.

Albums:
Hank Williams Jnr. And Friends (MGM/MGM)
Greatest Hits (MGM/–)
The New South (Warner/–)
Habits Old And New (Elektra/–)
Man Of Steel (Warners/–)
Are You Sure Hank Done It This Way (–/Warner)
Five-0 (Warner/Warner)
Just Pickin' . . . No Singin' (MGM/—)

Just Pickin' . . . No Singing', Hank Williams Jr. And The Cheatin' Hearts.

Leona Williams

Born Leona Helton in Vienna, Missouri on January 7, 1943, she became part of the Helton family band at an early age – her father, mother, four brothers and seven sisters all being instrumentalists of one kind or another.

Obtaining her own radio show Leona Sings on KWOS, Jefferson City, Missouri, at 15, she married bassist Ron Williams a year later, the duo becoming members of Loretta Lynn's backup unit, Leona playing bass and singing and her husband moving in behind the resident drum kit.

Following a guest appearance on the Grand Ole Opry, a demo recording was arranged by Lonzo and Oscar, the result being a contract with Hickory Records in January, 1968. This association lasted until 1974 when Leona became an MCA acquisition for a spell.

A straight down-the-line country singer, Leona's more successful singles have included **Once More** (1969) and **Country Girl With Hot Pants On** (1971), while her songwriting efforts have been recorded by such as Tammy Wynette and Loretta

A Woman Walked Away, Leona Williams. Courtesy DJM Records.

Lynn.

She joined the Merle Haggard Roadshow as a backing vocalist in 1975 and she not only replaced Bonnie Owens

Those Lazy Hazy Days, Tex Williams. Courtesy PRT Records.

as Merle's duet partner, but on October 7, 1978 became the legendary singer's third wife. It turned out to be a stormy marriage and five years later they were divorced. Leona wrote several songs with Merle and the pair recorded a duet album, **Heart To Heart** in 1983.

As a solo performer she has recorded for MCA, Elektra and Mercury in recent years, but has failed to score any major hits.

Albums:
San Quentin's First Lady (MCA/–)
A Woman Walked Away (–/DJM)
Heart To Heart – with Merle Haggard (Mercury/–)

Tex Williams

Writer (with Merle Travis) and performer of **Smoke, Smoke, Smoke (That Cigarette)** a 1947 hit that sold around two and a half million copies, Williams was, during his heyday, a predominantly West Coast-based bandleader, who appeared in many films during the 1940s.

Born Sol Williams in Ramsey, Fayette County, Illinois on August 23, 1917, he had his own one man band and vocal show on radio WJBL, Decatur, Illinois, at the age of 13, later touring throughout the States, Canada and Mexico with various western and hillbilly aggregations.

During the late 1930s he became Hollywood based, there befriending Tex Ritter and working in films. After a long stay as lead vocalist and bass player with Spade Cooley, he formed his own band, The Western Caravan, in 1946, signing to the up and coming Capitol label.

Following the success of **Smoke, Smoke, Smoke**, the band's third release, Williams became a star of international proportions, working on scores of network TV and radio shows, his band playing to capacity audiences at choice venues. Although his run of record successes seemed to peter out following the release of **Bluebird On Your Windowsill** (1949), he continued recording for such labels as Decca and Liberty.

A record deal with a Kentucky company, Boone, renewed Williams'

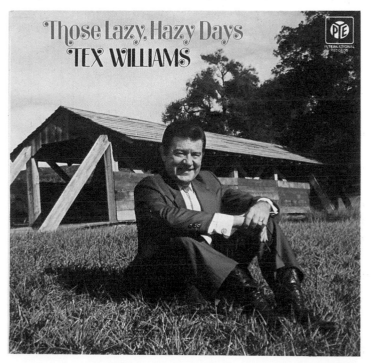

acquaintance with the charts once more – albeit on a lower level – the singer accruing goodly sales with **Too Many Tigers** (1965), **Bottom Of A Mountain** (1966), **Smoke, Smoke, Smoke '68** (1968) and several other titles. 1970 saw him signed to Monument, obtaining a Top 30 disc in 1971 with **The Night Miss Nancy Ann's Hotel For Single Girls Burned Down**, and by the mid '70s Williams had teamed up once more with Cliffie Stone, who had produced his Capitol Recordings, and on Stone's Granite label came up with the album, **These Lazy Hazy Days**.

Albums:
In Las Vegas (–/Sunset)
Oklahoma Stomp – with Spade Cooley (Club Of Spades/–)
Those Lazy, Hazy Days (Granite/Pye)

Foy Willing

Born Foy Willingham in Bosque County, Texas in 1915, Foy aspired to a musical career while still in high school, appearing on radio as a solo singer and with a gospel quartet. He eventually found his way to New York City, where he appeared on radio for Crazy Water Crystals from 1933 to 1935, when he returned to Texas to work in radio as an executive and announcer.

Willing moved to California in 1940 and founded the Riders Of The Purple Sage, originally composed of himself, Al Sloey and Jimmy Dean, although later members included Scotty Harrell, fiddler Johnny Paul, accordionist/arranger Billy Leibert, accordionist Paul Sellers, guitarist Jerry Vaughn, clarinetist Neely Plumb and steel guitarist Freddy Traveres.

The group was formed in 1943 as cast members of the Hollywood Barn Dance, and throughout the rest of the 1940s they appeared on many radio shows including All Star Western Theatre, the Andrews Sisters Show, the Roy Rogers Quaker Oats Show, and appeared in many Republic films as well with Monte Hale and Roy Rogers.

They recorded for Decca, Capitol,

Below: Foy Willing and the Riders Of The Purple Sage.

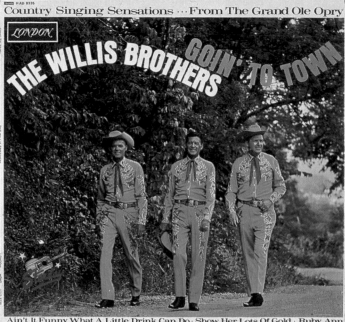

Goin' To Town, The Willis Brothers. Courtesy London.

Columbia and Majestic Records, their biggest hits being **No One To Cry To** and **Cool Water** on Majestic and **Texas Blues** and **Ghost Riders In The Sky** on Capitol.

The Riders Of The Purple Sage disbanded in 1952 when Willing left active performing, although there was an occasional regrouping for special appearances, a couple of quick albums on Roulette and Jubilee and a 1959 tour with Gene Autry.

Foy Willing was still recording, writing songs and appearing at Western film festivals up until shortly before his death on June 24, 1978.

Willis Brothers

The Willis Brothers (Guy, born Alex in Arkansas on July 15, 1915; Skeeter, born in Coalton, Oklahoma on December 20, 1917 and Vic, born in Schulter, Oklahoma on May 31, 1922) were originally known as the Oklahoma Wranglers, their radio career commencing on KGEF, Shawnee, Oklahoma. In 1940, the trio moved on to become featured artists on the Brush Creek Follies Show on KMBC, Kansas City, Missouri.

With Guy as front man and guitarist, Vic on accordion and piano, and Skeeter appearing in his role as the 'smilin' fiddler', the brothers appeared to be on the way to establishing a healthy reputation, but then World War II intervened and the Willis Brothers joined the forces for four years.

They regrouped in 1946 and became Opry members until 1949, striking up an association with Eddy Arnold, on whose show they appeared for some eight years. Also during this period they became the first group to back Hank Williams on Sterling Records, and in a sense were the original Drifting Cowboys, although they did not tour with him.

Rejoining the Opry in 1960, the group enjoyed some hit Starday singles throughout the '60s via such titles as **Give Me Forty Acres** (1964), **A Six Foot Two By Four** (1965), **Bob** (1967) and **Somebody Loves My Dog** (1967).

Often employed as session musicians, the Willis Brothers have recorded for several labels including RCA-Victor, Mercury, Sterling, Coral, Starday and MGM. The first featured act on The Jubilee USA shows in Springfield, Missouri, the brothers, who often impersonated other groups as part of their set, also had the distinction of being the initial country act to play a concert at Washington DC's Constitution Hall, formerly a venue for classical concerts only.

Following Skeeter's death from cancer in 1976 and Guy's retirement, younger brother Vic formed the Vic Willis Trio, using his accordion as lead instrument and performing modern country favourites in a close harmony style, which proved very popular at the Opry. Guy Willis died in Nashville on April 13, 1981.

Album:
Best Of The Willis Brothers (Starday/–)

Bob Wills

Leader of the finest western swing band ever to grace country music, and in fact the originator of the style, the late Bob Wills is acknowledged as having been one of the most influential performers in country music, with Merle Haggard, Asleep At The Wheel, Alvin Crow and Red Steagall all borrowing from his repertoire, and Waylon Jennings paying tribute to the Texas fiddle man with the anthem, **Bob Wills Is Still The King**, a country chart-

Hall Of Fame, Bob Wills and Tommy Duncan. Courtesy UA Records.

topper in 1975.

Born near Kosse, Limestone County, Texas on March 6, 1905, James Robert Wills was the first of ten children of a fiddle-playing father. In 1913 the Wills family moved to Memphis, Texas, where Jim Rob began playing fiddle at square dances, his initial instrument having been mandolin.

Living on a West Texas family farm until 1929, that year he arrived in Fort Worth, becoming 'Bob' Wills after working in a medicine show that possessed one too many Jims. Forming a duo, the Wills Fiddle Band, with guitarist Herman Arnspiger during the summer of 1929, the fiddler began playing for dances in the Fort Worth area.

During 1930 he added vocalist Milton Brown, the unit later metamorphosing into the Light Crust Doughboys, a band whose broadcasts over radio station KFJZ proved extremely popular. The Doughboys recorded for Victor in February, 1932, Brown leaving soon after, to be replaced by Tommy Duncan, a vocalist selected from over 70 other applicants.

Fired from the Doughboys in August 1933 – due to excessive drinking and his inability to get along with Doughboys' leader W. Lee O'Daniel – Wills took Duncan and his banjo-playing brother Johnnie Lee Wills with him, forming his own outfit, Bob Wills And His Playboys

The Greatest Hits Of Bob Wills. Courtesy MCA Records.

Lone Star Rag, Bob Wills. Courtesy CBS Records.

and gaining a regular spot on WACO in Waco. Although beset by legal problems, activated by Wills' ex-sponsors, the Burrus Mill and Elevator Company (the makers of Light Crust flour), the band struggled on, eventually making a base in Tulsa, where they became an institution on station KVOO with Bob and Johnnie Lee heading programmes on the station for the next 24 years.

Now known as Bob Wills And His Texas Playboys, the band began recording for Brunswick, cutting some sides in Dallas during September, 1935. Their record success, KVOO programmes and regular dances at Cain's Academy, as well as the power and inventiveness of the bandmembers, made their Tulsa years their most memorable.

A swing band with country overtones – The Playboys comprised 13 musicians by the mid '30s and grew into an 18-piece during the 1940s – Wills' outfit played a miscellany of country ballads, blues and riffy jazz items with horns and fiddles vying for the front-line positions.

This sound proved tremendously popular and when, in April, 1940, Wills recorded his self-penned **San Antonio Rose** (the band had already cut the number as an instrumental in 1938) as a vehicle for Tommy Duncan's vocal artistry, the resulting disc became a million-seller. Another version of the same song – by Bing Crosby – also sold past the million mark, though it appears that Wills earned little in the way of royalties.

Many more hits followed, but with the advent of Pearl Harbour, the band began to break up as its various members enlisted in the forces, Wills himself joining the army in late 1942. Physically unfit for service life, he was discharged the following July, at which time he headed for California where he appeared on radio shows and made several films.

During the post-war period, with big bands generally fading, Wills was forced to use a smaller band, and began featuring fiddles, electric steel guitar and string instruments more prominently than he had with his earlier Tulsa unit, using Leon McAuliff on steel much in the manner of jazz horn soloists. Again, the public loved the sound but Wills was unsure where he was heading, both musically and home-wise, his wife and children having to move 14 times in 20 years.

His health also began to fail and during 1962 Wills suffered his first heart attack. Still he continued to tour with the Playboys, but in 1964 came another heart attack and he was forced to call a halt to his bandleading days.

Nevertheless, he still made a more limited number of appearances as a solo artist and continued making records – his efforts on behalf of country music receiving due recognition in October, 1968, when Wills' name was added to those already honoured in the Country Music Hall Of Fame.

Also honoured by the State of Texas on May 30, 1969, Wills was paralysed by a stroke the very next day. But although bedridden for many months, with even his power of speech impaired, he fought back and by 1972 began to appear at various functions, albeit in a wheelchair.

In December, 1973, he attended his last record date, many of the original Texas Playboys, plus Merle Haggard, taking part. In two days, 27 titles were cut for UA – but

Tulsa Swing, Johnny Lee Wills. Courtesy Rounder Records.

Wills was only present for a portion of the time, suffering a severe stroke after the first day. He never regained consciousness, although his actual death did not occur until some 17 months later on May 13, 1975.

However, though Wills has gone his music lives on, The Playboys reforming several times since his death and many younger singers and bands recreating the Wills' sound both on record and in live shows.

Albums:
Papa's Jumping (–/Bear Family)
Bob Wills (Columbia/CBS)
San Antonio Rose (Lariat/–)
Anthology (Columbia/CBS)
The Last Time (UA/–)
Greatest String Band Hits (MCA/–)
Leon McAuliff Leads The Texas Playboys (Capitol/–)

Johnnie Lee Wills

Although often cast deep in the shadow of his elder brother Bob, Johnnie Lee Wills actually carved out quite a long and successful career of his own. Born in east Texas in 1912, Johnnie Lee got his start playing tenor banjo with Bob as a member of the Light Crust Doughboys and left the band with him when Bob formed the Playboys, soon to become the Texas Playboys.

Business got so good for Bob around 1940 that he formed a second band around Johnnie Lee, which grew to as many as 14 or 15 pieces. Called Johnnie Lee Wills And His Boys, they became extremely popular in the Tulsa area, and at one time or another contained many of the finest western swing musicians of the era, including Leon Huff, Joe Holley and Jesse Ashlock.

They signed with Bullet Records in mid to late 1940 and had the two biggest country hits that label was to produce: **Rag Mop** and **Peter Cottontail**. They also recorded for Decca, Sims, RCA and a few smaller labels.

When western swing slumped in popularity in the 1950s, Johnnie Lee continued to run his famous Tulsa

Above: Mac Wiseman, an outstanding bluegrass guitarist.

Stampede and opened a thriving western wear shop. He continued to appear at various western swing reunions until ill-health got the better of him in 1982, and he subsequently passed away in 1984.

Mac Wiseman

Malcolm B. Wiseman was born near Waynesboro, Virginia, on May 23, 1925 and raised in an area which he says is "just like The Waltons on TV". Country music in this area of the Shenandoah Valley was very much a folk art and Mac learned his music from the people around him.

He has become known as a bluegrass artist although his music also encompasses old-time, modern and even pop styles as well. Mac has floated in and out of the accepted Monroe-Earl Scruggs bluegrass style in his time and has indeed specialised in more traditional, sentimental material such as **Jimmy Brown The Newsboy** and **Letter Edged In Black**.

He attended the Shenandoah Conservatory of Music in Dayton, Virginia and then joined the announcing staff of radio station WSVA in Harrisburg, Virginia, as newscaster and disc jockey. At this time he also wrote copy for station advertisements and worked nights with local country bands.

Possessing a warm, clear, tenor voice, Mac has been eagerly utilised by some of the top names in bluegrass, notably Bill Monroe and Flatt And Scruggs. Both acts included him live and on record. Mac began his career with another country music legend, Molly O'Day.

On The South Bound, Flatt & Wiseman. Courtesy RCA Records.

He has starred on Shreveport's Louisiana Hayride, Atlanta's WSB Barn Dance and Knoxville Tennessee Barn Dance and has also guested on the Opry. He began recording on the then new Dot Records in 1951 and his hits included **'Tis Sweet To Be Remembered**, **Jimmy Brown, The Newsboy**, **Ballad Of Davy Crockett** and **Love Letters In The Sand**.

In 1957, Mac became Dot's Country A&R director and also ran the company's country music division for a few years. He recorded for Capitol Records during the early '60s, then moved back to Dot where he experimented with a string-filled album. Mac enjoyed a resurgence of popularity when he teamed up with Lester Flatt for some earthy bluegrass albums for RCA during the early '70s and also built a large following in Britain with regular tours and record releases.

Apart from the increasing number of bluegrass festivals he plays, Mac has a very strong student following and has also been active behind the scenes in the industry. In recent years he has recorded for Churchill Records and CMH, maintaining a traditional bluegrass styling.

Albums:
Early Dot Recordings Volume One (Country/–)
Golden Classics (Gusto/–)
Shenandoah Valley Memories (Canaan/ Canaan)
Mac Wiseman Story (CMH/–)
Concert Favourites (RCA/RCA)
Lester 'n' Mac – with Lester Flatt (RCA/RCA)

Del Wood

Probably the second (after Maybelle Carter) female country instrumentalist to achieve any real degree of fame, pianist Del Wood recorded a corny, ragtime version of a fiddle tune called **Down Yonder** (previously a 1934 hit for Gid Tanner of the Skillet Lickers) on the Tennessee label in 1951 and came up with a million-seller.

Born Adelaide Hazelwood on February 22, 1920 in Nashville, Tennessee, Del became an Opry member in 1951 and has remained on the show ever since, even playing on the Japanese version of the Opry during her Far East tour of 1968. Perpetuator of several other best-selling discs in heavy handed ragtime/honky tonk style, Del has recorded for RCA, Mercury, Class, Decca, Lamb & Lion, etc.

Albums:
Ragtime Glory Special (Lamb & Lion/Lamb & Lion)
Tavern In The Town (Vocalion/–)

Sheb Wooley

A highly versatile performer, Wooley was voted CMA Comedian Of The Year in 1968 for his alter ego character Ben Colder, while in 1964 he won a Cashbox magazine award for 'his outstanding contributions to country and popular music as a writer, recording artist and entertainer'.

In the role of Pete Nolan, he co-starred in the TV series 'Rawhide' and as Ben Colder he has scored with such recorded comedy hits as **Don't Go Near The Eskimos** (1962), **Almost Persuaded No. 2** (1966), **Harper Valley PTA (Later That Same Day)** (1968) and **15 Beers Ago** (1971).

Born in Erick, Oklahoma on April 10, 1921, Wooley spent his early years on his father's farm, becoming a competent horseman at the age of four and a rodeo rider during his teens. He formed his own band while still at school, later having his own network radio show for three years. In 1948, he was awarded his first major recording contract by MGM.

It was at this stage that Wooley, who had studied at the Jack Koslyn School of Acting, moved to California and began working on 'Rocky Mountain', a Warner Brothers' film starring Errol Flynn. He has since been featured in more than 30 films, among these being 'Little Big Horn', 'Boy From Oklahoma', 'Giant', 'Distant Drums', 'Man Without A Star' and 'High Noon', in which Wooley received considerable acclaim for his performance as the whiskey-drinking killer, Ben Miller.

Co-star in 105 episodes of 'Rawhide', Wooley has appeared on countless TV shows. As a recording star under his own name (as opposed to releases using his Colder identity), he has enjoyed a six-week stay at the top of the pop charts with his 1959 **Purple People Eater**, three years later topping the country charts with **That's My Pa**.

Albums:
Blue Guitar (–/Bear Family)
Best Of Ben Colder (–/MGM)

Above: Sheb Wooley. He played the killer Ben Miller in High Noon.

Bobby Wright

The son of Johnny Wright and Kitty Wells, Bobby Wright (born in Charleston, West Virginia on March 30, 1942) was brought up in a show business atmosphere, appearing on Shreveport's Louisiana Hayride at the age of eight and becoming a Decca recording artist at 11.

Completing his education at Middle Tennessee State University, he auditioned for and gained the part of Willie in the TV series 'McHale's Navy', remaining with the show for a four-year run. A frequent performer on various syndicated TV shows and a member of his parents' family show, Wright's first hit record came in 1967 with the Decca release **Lay Some Happiness On Me**.

His most successful records have been **Here I Go Again**, a Top 20 entry in 1971 and **Seasons In The Sun**, which climbed to No. 24 in 1974. He has recorded for a number of labels including ABC, MCA and United Artists, but being a part of the Kitty Wells show for most of his career has held him back from making the grade as a singer in his own right.

Album:
Seasons Of Love (ABC/–)

Johnny Wright

Wright (born in Mt. Juliet, Tennessee on May 13, 1914) came from a musical family, his grandfather being a champion old time fiddler and his father a five-string banjo player.

In 1933 he moved to nearby Nashville, then in its infancy as a country music centre, there meeting and marrying Kitty Wells, also working with singer-guitarist Jack Anglin (born in Columbia, Tennessee on May 13, 1916) on radio station WSIX, Nashville and forming a duo, Johnny and Jack, with Anglin in 1938.

During the early '40s, Johnny and Jack toured with their band, The Tennessee Mountain Boys, playing on WBIG, Greensboro, North Carolina, WNOX, Knoxville and many other radio stations. By 1948 they, together with Kitty Wells (still only a featured singer, not yet a star), joined the Grand Ole Opry, then left to become stars of Shreveport's Louisiana Hayride, their popularity on the show leading to an opportunity to rejoin Opry members in 1952, the threesome becoming regulars for a period of 15 years.

Signed initially to Apollo, an R&B label (there cutting such sides as **Jolie Blon** and **Paper Boy**), Johnny and Jack switched to the more country oriented RCA in the late '40s, scoring Top 20 hits with **Poison Love** (1951), **Crying Heart Blues** (1951), **Oh Baby Mine (I Get So Lonely)** (1954), **Beware Of It** (1954), **Goodnight, Sweetheart, Goodnight** (1954), **Stop The World** (1958), **Lonely Island Pearl** (1958) and **Sailor Man** (1959). Other hits included **Ashes Of Love** and **I Can't Tell My Heart That**.

Shortly after one last success with **Slow Poison**, a 1962 Decca release, Jack Anglin was killed (on March 8, 1963) in a car crash en route to a funeral service for Patsy Cline – at which point Wright formed a new roadshow and became a solo recording act, notching a chart No. 1 in 1965 with **Hello Vietnam**.

His son Bobby proving a success chartwise during the late '60s, Wright formed the Kitty Wells-Johnny Wright Family Show in 1969, doing extensive tours and he and Bobby recording an album of Johnny And Jack material for Starday during 1977.

Albums:
Here's Johnny And Jack (Vocalion/–)
All The Best Of Johnny And Jack (RCA/–)

Below: Johnny Wright. With Jack Anglin, he formed the successful duo, Johnny and Jack back in 1938.

Above: Tammy Wynette, subject of a horrific kidnap in October, 1979.

Tammy Wynette

One of the most successful female country singers of all time, Tammy Wynette was adjudged CMA Female Vocalist Of The Year for three consecutive years (1968–70), while her recording of **Stand By Your Man**, a No. 1 in the US during 1968 and a major British hit in 1975, was the biggest selling single by a woman in the entire history of country music.

Tammy began life as Virginia Wynette Pugh, born near Tupelo, Mississippi on May 5, 1942. Her father died when she was but a few months old and her mother moved to Birmingham, Alabama, to engage in war work, leaving her in the care of grandparents until the end of World War II. Brought up on a farm, Tammy learnt to play the collection of instruments owned by her father, taking a lengthy series of music lessons with a view to a career in singing.

But, getting married at 17, she had little time for music during the next three years. Instead she became the mother of three children, her marriage breaking up before the third child was born. The baby, a girl, developed spinal meningitis, and Tammy had to supplement her earnings as a Birmingham beautician in order to pay off various bills incurred as a result of the child's ill health. She turned to music once

more, becoming featured vocalist on station WBRC-TV's Country Boy Eddy Show during the mid '60s, following this with some appearances on Porter Wagoner's syndicated TV programme.

Soon she began making the rounds of the Nashville-based record companies, in the meantime working as a club singer and a song-plugger in order to support her children. Following auditions for UA, Hickory and Kapp, Tammy was signed by Epic's Billy Sherrill and recorded **Apartment No. 9**, a song written by Johnny Paycheck and Bobby Austin. Released in 1966, the disc proved a great success. The next release, **Your Good Girl's Gonna Go Bad** (1967), proved to be even stronger, becoming a Top 5 item. From then on it was plain sailing throughout the '60s as **I Don't Wanna Play House** (1967), **My Elusive Dreams** (with David Houston, 1967), **Take Me To Your World**, **D-I-V-O-R-C-E**, **Stand By Your Man** (all 1968), **Singing My Song** and **The Ways To Love A Man** (both 1969) qualified as chart toppers.

Married five times, Tammy had several well publicised relationships with other partners including film star Burt Reynolds and singer Rudy Gatlin of The Gatlin Brothers, but it was her marriage to singer George Jones that made most of the headlines. The pair announced their marriage on August 22, 1968 in order to silence gossips, but they were not in fact married until February 16, 1969. For several years they toured together and recorded

several big-selling duets, but Jones' regular drinking bouts and Tammy's career aspirations did not mix too well and they were divorced on March 13, 1975.

Womanhood. A highly recommended Wynette release. Courtesy Epic.

However, on disc, Tammy could do little wrong – **Run, Woman Run** (1970), **Good Lovin'** (1971), **'Til I Get It Right** (1973), **Woman To Woman** (1974), **'Til I Can Make It On My Own** (1976), **Womanhood** (1978), **They Call It Making Love** (1979), **Starting Over** (1980), **Crying In The Rain** (1981), I

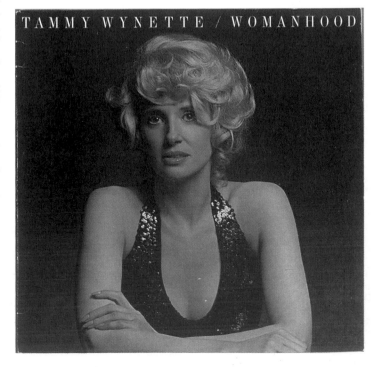

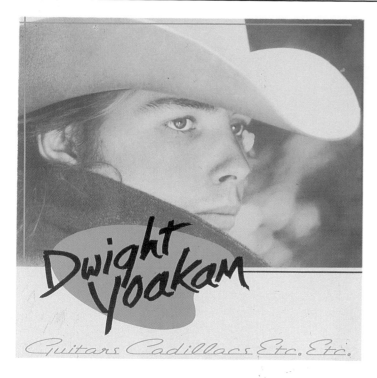

Guitars, Cadillacs Etc. Etc., Dwight Yoakham, Courtesy WEA Records.

Dwight Yoakham

A singer whose debut album for Reprise immediately climbed into the pop charts, Yoakham caught both the attention of traditionalists and even punk rockers.

Born in Pikeville, Kentucky in 1956, Yoakham honed his style of country in bars and roadhouses along Route 23 in southern Ohio, then headed for LA because he felt Nashville music had become too slick, claiming "Those Buck Owens records in the late 1950s and 1960s were some of the hippest hillbilly stuff known to man – and Nashville has all but abandoned it."

He became an opener for roots-oriented rock acts like Los Lobos, The Blasters and Lone Justice and released a six-track EP titled **Guitars, Cadillacs, Etc** on Oak Records during 1985, then moving on to provide Reprise (practically a dead label after Sinatra and Neil Young moved off) with an attention-grabbing album of the same name.

Yoakham, who first sang what he calls 'hillybilly hymns' in a Pikeville church, was, by the mid-1980s, working with a back-up band formed by Pete Anderson (lead guitar), Brantley Kearns (fiddle), J. D. Foster (bass) and Jeff Donovan (drums).

Album:

Guitars, Cadillacs, Etc., Etc. (Reprise/Reprise)

Faron Young

Affectionately known as 'The Sheriff', Faron has been a stalwart of the country music industry for some three decades.

Born in Shreveport, Louisiana on February 25, 1932, he was raised on a farm outside the town and spent his boyhood days picking up guitar chords while minding the family's cows. He formed his first band at school.

After college he found that he had gained something of a reputation in Louisiana and was invited to join KWKH and subsequently the Louisiana Hayride itself. It was then that Webb Pierce employed him as a featured vocalist.

In 1951 he was signed by Capitol Records and had country hits with **Tattle Tale Eyes** and **Have I Waited Too Long?** Joining the Opry in 1952, Young then spent from 1952 to 54 in the US Army, touring widely to entertain the troops. His first major success came with the Ted Daffan song **I've Got Five Dollars And It's Saturday Night**, and with his bid for the

Just Heard A Heart Break (1983), **Sometimes When We Touch** (a duet with Mark Gray, 1985) – being just some of the major hits her crying voice has endowed during the 1970s and 1980s, while her **Greatest Hits** album (which remained in the charts for over 60 weeks) has earned a platinum disc for sales in excess of one million dollars.

Tammy married her longtime friend, and for a time record producer, George Richey, at her Florida home on July 6, 1978. Before their marriage he was musical director for the 'Hee-Haw!' television series, but now spends much of his time guiding Tammy's career, which was captured in her own biography 'Stand By Your Man' and made into a successful 1982 film.

Albums:

The Classic Collection (–/Epic)
Soft Touch (Epic/Epic)
Just Tammy (Epic/Epic)
Greatest Hits (Epic/Epic)
No Charge (–/Embassy)
One Of A Kind (Epic/Epic)
Superb Country Sounds (–/Embassy)

With George Jones:
We're Gonna Hold On (Epic/Epic)
Let's Build A World Together (Epic/Epic)
Greatest Hits (Epic/–)
Together Again (Epic/Epic)

Skeets Yaney

One of country music's great regional stars, who has been unfairly overlooked because of the lack of big record sellers.

A spectacular yodeller, Skeets – born Clyde A. Yaney in Mitchell, Indiana – was a longtime star on KMOX in St Louis, one of the main members of the KMOX Barn Dance in the 1930s and 1940s.

A resident of the St. Louis area towards the end of his career in the late '70s, Yaney died of cancer on January 22 in 1978.

Below: Dwight Yoakham. Top of the charts by mid 1986 with Honky Tonk Man.

Above: Faron Young, a prosperous businessman as well as an entertainer.

teenage market in **Going Steady**.

The '50s saw him gaining many hits and massive popularity, obtaining a No. 1 disc with **Sweet Dreams** and later with **Country Girl** (1959), following this in 1961 with another chart-topper in **Hello Walls**.

Throughout the '60s, the hits continued

The Best Of Faron Young. Courtesy Mercury Records.

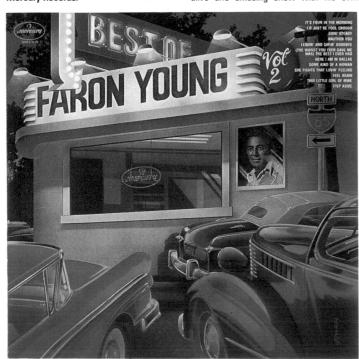

to flow, **Backtrack** (1961), **Three Days, The Comeback, Down By The River** (1962), **The Yellow Bandana, You'll Drive Me Back (Into Her Arms Again)** (1963), **Walk Tall** (1965), **Unmitigated Gall** (1966), **I Just Came To Get My Baby** (1968), **Wine Me Up** (1969) and **Keeping Up With The Joneses**, a 1964 duet with Margie Singleton, figuring among his Top 10 successes for the Mercury label, to which Young became contracted in 1961.

A versatile entertainer who presents an alive and amusing show with his own witty comments much to the fore, Young retained his popularity over an extensive period, as such major '70s hits as **It's Four In The Morning** (a Top 5 pop hit in Britain during 1972), **This Little Girl Of Mine** and **Just What I Had In Mind** clearly demonstrated.

He has appeared in a number of low-budget film productions including 'Daniel Boone', 'Hidden Guns', 'Country Music Holiday' and 'Raiders Of Old California', while his out of showbiz interests include a booking agency, a music publishing firm and magazine publishing – Young having for many years been the owner of the monthly publication Music City News. He has even contributed to Nashville's rising skyline, owning the Faron Young Executive Building near Music Row.

Albums:
The Man And His Music (Mercury/–)
Best Of . . . (Mercury/–)
Free And Easy (MCA/–)

Neil Young

A Canadian singer-songwriter, born on November 12, 1945 in Toronto, Neil worked as a folk singer in Canada in the early '60s before moving to California where he became involved in the West Coast pop movement.

He was a key member of country-rock band Buffalo Springfield, then became part of the soft-rock group Crosby, Stills, Nash and Young. Embarking on a solo career in the early '70s, he formed Crazy Horse, a multi-instrumental unit that mixed strands of country, blues, jazz and rock into a repertoire that proved highly successful in terms of the huge number of albums sold.

The eclectic Young surprised many when he travelled to Nashville at the beginning of 1985 to record a new album, **Old Ways**, which brought him widespread country acclaim. Teaming up with Willie Nelson, Waylon Jennings, Ben Keith, Rufus Thibodeaux, Gail Davies, Leona Williams, Hargus 'Pig' Robbins, Terry McMillan, Ralph Mooney, David Briggs and other notable Music City musicians recorded **The Wayward Wind**, once a hit for Tex Ritter, plus a number of originals all in country mould, the rsult being a best-selling album. "Rock'n'roll has let me down," he claimed later. "It doesn't leave you a way to grow old gracefully."

He subsequently took to the road with a

Old Ways, Neil Young Courtesy Geffen Records.

traditional country band utilizing fiddles, banjo, steel guitar and mandolin.

Album:
Old Ways (Geffen/Geffen)

Appendix

Lack of space prevents us from including a full entry on these following people, organisations and places, etc. Nevertheless, here is a brief run-down on the contribution they have made in the history of country music.

A

WENDELL ADKINS – Born in Kentucky. Raised in Ohio, Wendel was a rock 'n' roll teenage singer. Later he toured the Midwest with a band, moved to Florida, got noticed and ended up in Vegas. Following chunks of aid from Willie Nelson and David Allan Coe, he began an association with Gilley's club that saw him getting fame-pushed.

BUDDY ALAN – Buck Owens' son, born in Tempe, Arizona, 1948, and a singer rarely out of the charts in the late 1960s and early 1970s. But when Dad stopped having hits, so too did 6'4" Buddy.

TERRY ALLEN – Born in Wichita, Kansas in 1953. An art school teacher and singer whose first album (1975) was an incredible concept affair titled **Juarez**. Released by Fate Records of Chicago, it became a cult record among country fans and rock fans alike. Later he cut an essential double album, **Lubbock (On Everything)**, which saw him working with the Joe Ely Band and adding to his reputation as a country songwriter of some piquancy.

AMERICAN RECORD COMPANY – A company that owned five labels of its own and, in addition, recorded material for Conqueror, the Sears-Roebuck label. Once owner of the finest country music catalogue in America, it eventually was taken over by Columbia.

Hylo Brown Meets The Lonesome Pine Fiddlers. Courtesy Starday Records.

JERRY ARHELGER – A Christian country music singer who has worked all over the world, although his base is in Wewahitchka, Florida. His CB/trucking song, **Breaker, Breaker, Sweet Jesus**, is reputed to have once logged over 250 requests in one night on a Mississippi radio station.

ARKIE THE ARKANSAS WOODCHOPPER – Longtime fixture on the National Barn Dance (1928–1970), his real name was Luther Ossenbrink. He was an all-rounder – a singer, guitarist, MC and square dance caller.

AUSTIN – A Texan city that, during the turn of the 1960s, became a centre for a new contemporary 'outlaw' form of country music. The changes evolved around Threadgill's Bar, where, around 1962, students from the university and musicians searching for an identity (such as Janis Joplin) gathered to play folk and country music. Later, performers such as Michael Murphey, Steve Fromholtz and B. W. Stevenson came on like young, homespun idealists, using poetic imagery in their songs, while Kinky Friedman guyed country sounds and Commander Cody presented the whole of the Southern music rainbow. The home of Willie Nelson, Austin – whose place in country music history is the subject of Jan Reid's fine book 'The Improbable Rise of Redneck Rock' – still offers an alternative scene to that promulgated by Nashville. And there are many people who feel that the 'Austin City Limits' show flexes its muscles in a manner that the Opry rarely manages.

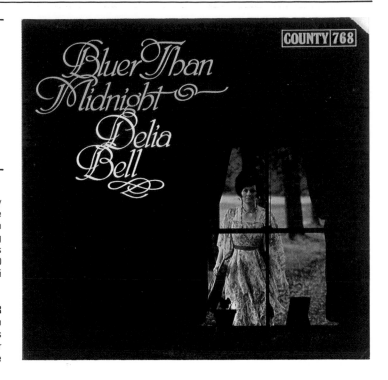

Bluer Than Night, Delia Bell. Courtesy County Records.

B

CARROLL BAKER – Born in Bridgewater, Nova Scotia, she is Canada's Queen Of Country Music. The winner of every award her country can offer, her record sales passed the million mark in 1983.

BAKERSFIELD – A Californian town touted as 'Nashville West' during the mid-1960s, when residents such as Buck Owens, Merle Haggard and Wynn Stewart achieved a fair degree in chart domination.

AVA BARBER – A singer, born in Knoxville, Tennessee, 1954, who made it off 'The Lawrence Welk Show' in the mid-1970s. Signed to Ranwood Records, she had several hits, the biggest being a version of Gail Davies' **Bucket To The South**, in 1978. By 1981 she was with Oak Records.

GLENN BARBER – From Hollis, Oklahoma (born in 1935) but raised in Texas, Barber was a skilled carpenter who built his own recording studio. A multi-instrumentalist and singer-songwriter, he had hits for Sims and Starday in the mid-1960s before moving onto Hickory and continuing his hit-making through to the mid-1970s. In more recent times, he has charted on Groovy, Century 21, MMI and Sunbird.

EARL BALL – Born in Foxworth, Mississippi in 1941. Notable session pianist who tours with the Johnny Cash Show.

J. J. BARRIE – Canadian singer who became a genuine one-hit wonder in 1976 when his version of **No Charge** went to the top of the UK pop charts.

PHILOMENA BEGLEY – A superstar on the Irish country scene. A singer from County Tyrone, her K-Tel album, **The Best Of Philomena Begley**, went platinum in her homeland. She often records duets with Ray Lynam and the two have frequently appeared together onstage at Wembley, though they normally maintain separate careers.

DELIA BELL – A bluegrass lady with a voice that harks back to country's golden era. Loved by those who search the minor label catalogues, she came to the attention of Emmylou Harris in the early 1980s and, unbelievably, got signed by Warner Brothers who released an album in 1983.

BIG TOM – Born Tom McBride in Castleblaney, Ireland. A star in his native Ireland where the song **Big Tom Is Still The King** topped the pop charts in 1980.

BLACKWOOD BROTHERS – The most famous gospel quartet in country music, formed in Mississippi in 1934. Originally comprising Roy, Doyle, James and Roy's son RW, they regrouped after RW died in a 1954 plane crash, J. D. Sumner becoming the group's bass singer. All the original Blackwoods have died but the group continues on its highly successful way, the current line-up including Cecil Blackwood (son of Roy) and Jimmy Blackwood (son of James).

BLUEGRASS – A development of traditional string band music formulated and popularised by Bill Monroe and His Blue Grass Boys. This music form was revitalised during the folk boom of the 1960s when a youthful element added touches of pop, the result being tagged 'New Grass'.

JIMMY BOWEN – Once a hit-making rockabilly, Bowen became president of MCA Nashville in 1984 after a successful period as a Warner Brothers Nashville executive.

CLARENCE 'GATEMOUTH' BROWN – Hugely talented black singer and multi-instrumentalist, born in Orange, Texas in 1924. Though often thought of as a bluesman, he plays great bluegrass and cajun fiddle and has appeared at several international country festivals.

FRANK 'HYLO' BROWN – Guitarist and singer of impressive range who once

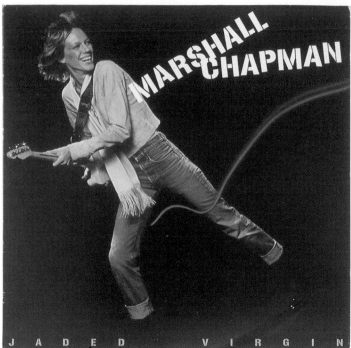

Cross Trackin', Bryan Chalker. Courtesy Emerald Records.

worked with Flatt And Scruggs. His folksy style was well suited to bluegrass and his **Hylo Brown Meets The Lonesome Pine Fiddlers**, a Starday album reissued in 1985 by Guesto, is well worth hanging onto.

ANITA BRYANT – Born in Barnsdall, Oklahoma in 1940. A former Miss Oklahoma (1958), who started out as a country singer, she had a million-seller with **Paper Roses** in 1960, the song that many years later was to prove a country hit for Marie Osmond. These days Anita is best known as a battler against gay rights.

JIMMY BUFFETT – Singer-songwriter from Alabama, born in 1947, who based himself in Key West, Florida and came up with a sunny kind of country variant. His

Havana Daydreamin', Jimmy Buffet. Courtesy ABC Records.

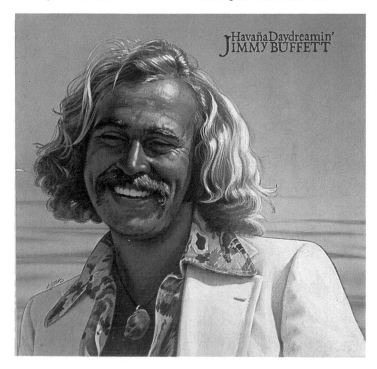

biggest hit to date has been **Margaritaville** (1977) but his best titles are probably **Cheeseburger In Paradise**, and **My Head Hurts, My Feet Stink And I Don't Love Jesus**. He travels with an outfit known as the Coral Reefer Band.

C

CAJUN MUSIC – A product of Louisiana bayou area that merges jazz, blues, country and French folk music. Fiddle and accordion dominate with most vocals still in French.

CONNIE CATO – Born in Carlinville, Illinois in 1955. Signed to Capitol at 17, this singer's big moment came in 1975 when her version of **Hurt** (one of her three hits that year) went Top 20. She was once known as 'Superskirt' and 'Superkitten' following 1974 hits of those titles.

Jaded Virgin, Marshall Chapman. Courtesy Epic Records.

BRYAN CHALKER – Excellent, deep-voiced British singer and guitarist who made several above-average albums, but became disenchanted with the UK club scene and eventually opted to become a country DJ on a Bristol radio station. For a while, Chalker also published one of Britain's leading country music magazines.

MARSHALL CHAPMAN – In the late 1970s, she came on tough and rocky. Different from anything else around, she did **I Walk The Line** and performed in a slow, bluesy, powerhouse way that drove into the brain like a mindworm. But perhaps she was too different. Epic let her go.

LEE CLAYTON – A product of the Nashville 'underground', Clayton also played it tough and rough. Much of the time he was over-produced when all he really needed was his voice and his songs. But he wrote **Ladies Love Outlaws**, so he will be remembered.

PAUL COHEN – A Decca talent scout, Cohen (born in 1908, died in 1970) was the first to recognise the potential of Nashville as a recording centre. He was elected to the Country Music Hall of Fame in 1976.

B. J. COLE – Unquestionably the most successful sessionman in British country music, steelie Bryan Cole has played on hundreds of pop, rock and country records. He also formed his own label, Cow Pie.

COLORADO – A five-piece band from Sutherland, Scotland. One of the most respected British bands, they have toured with many US stars, including Jean Shepard, Boxcar Willie, Melba Montgomery, and Vernon Oxford. To date they have been voted Top British Country Group for five years in a row.

MERVYN CONN – The producer of the prestigious series of Wembley Country Festivals plus numerous European tours featuring just about every worthwhile

name in country music. Often criticized, Conn is, nevertheless, the man who has done most to popularize country sounds in Britain.

COUNTRY MUSIC ASSOCIATION – The CMA is a trade association formed in 1958 by a cadre of businessmen, artists, and DJs to further the cause of country music. The CMA Awards, which take place in Nashville each October, are the most prestigious in country music, the premier accolade being Entertainer of The Year.

COUNTRY MUSIC FOUNDATION – A non-profit organisation which operates Nashville's Country Music Hall Of Fame and Museum, plus the Country Music Foundation Library etc. It sums up its goals as being "dedicated to the study and interpretation of country music's past through the display of artifacts and the collection and dissemination of data found on discs, tape, film and in printed material."

COUNTRY MUSIC HALL OF FAME – Country music's major shrine, based in Nashville, in which the greats of the past and present are honoured for their contributions to their chosen form of music. Two or three members are elected annually, Jimmie Rodgers, Bob Wills, Eddy Arnold, Roy Acuff, Kitty Wells, Minnie Pearl, Hank Williams, Uncle Dave Macon, Tex Ritter and Jimmie Davis being among those who have a commemorative plaque and portrait in the Hall, which is actually part of a larger museum.

COUNTRY ROCK – A trend that grew out of late 1960's west coast rock, particularly around L.A. Gram Parsons can be credited as acting as a catalyst to many of the part-time mandolin players and steel guitarists who were scraping a living in rock-oriented California, while Bob Dylan also helped to encourage the trend with his **Nashville Skyline** album, also leaking the fact that Hank Williams had always been one of his favourite singers.

MAC CURTIS – A hillbilly singer who became a leading rockabilly with the King label, Curtis (from Olney, Texas) still cuts fine country sides from time to time. During the mid-1970s he produced some of Ava Barber's sides for Ranwood.

D

DICK DAMRON – Born in Bentley, Alberta. A Canadian singer-songwriter, highly regarded in Britain. Best known, perhaps, for his song, **Countryfied**, which became a US hit for George Hamilton IV in 1971.

JOHNNY DARRELL – Once a motel manager, Darrell (born in Cleburne County, Alabama, 1940) cut the original version of **Green, Green Grass Of Home** and also had the first hit reditions of **The Son Of Hickory Hollers Tramp** (1967) and **With Pen In Hand** (1968).

LAZY JIM DAY – Born in Creek, Kentucky in 1911; died in 1959. One of the early stars of country radio. A singer, banjoist and guitarist, he originated the singing news routine and by the late 1930s was the leading comedian on the Opry.

JAMES DENNY – a one-time mail clerk, born in Buffalo Valley, Tennessee in 1911; died in Nashville, 1963, who worked his way up the ladder to become talent director at Nashville's WSM radio. He also ran a booking agency business, at one point handling over 3,200 personal appearances throughout the world. He was elected to the Country Music Hall Of Fame in 1966.

KARL DENVER TRIO – British country trio that achieved pop group styled stardom in 1961 when their Decca single, **Marcheta**, went Top 10 in the UK charts, to be followed by **Mexicali Rose** (1961), **Wimoweh** and **Never Goodbye** (both 1962). Two of the original threesome still work with the group.

SYDNEY DEVINE – Scotland's most successful country singer. A would-be Elvis, his **Doubly Devine** double-album on

California Stop-over, Johnny Darrell. Courtesy UA Records.

Philips went Top 20 in the UK during 1976, some 21 years after Devine first began his onstage career.

CAREY DUNCAN – Fresh sounding British vocalist who first made some impact in 1980, touring with George Hamilton IV. Impressed by her ability, Felice and Boudleaux Bryant later decided to write a set of songs especially for her.

DUFFY BROTHERS – British comedy duo who won the Marlboro Country Music competition and then went on tour with Marty Robbins and Tammy Wynette. Since then they have been voted Best British Country Duo for three years in a row, while 1985 saw the act from Peterborough completing their first US album.

E

RAY EDENTON – Frequent winner of the NARAS Superpicker Band Rhythm Guitar award. Born in Mineral, Virginia, he began playing professionally in 1946 and from 1952 to 1962 played on the Grand Ole Opry along with road shows for several stars. Now a sought-after Nashville sideman.

F

J. L. FRANK – One of the great promoters of country music, born in Rossai, Alabama in 1900; died in Detroit, 1952. Known as the 'Flo Ziegfeld of Country Music', he was instrumental in furthering the careers of Gene Autry, Roy Acuff, Ernest Tubb and many others. Elected to the Country Music Hall of Fame in 1967.

RAYMOND FROGGATT – Ever-improving British country singer-songwriter who started out as a pop writer, penning **Red Balloon**, a massive hit for the Dave Clark Five in 1968. A gritty, still slightly rock-oriented performer, these days he brightens up the UK country scene by

mostly performing his own, frequently excellent, material.

G

TERRI GIBBS – Winner of the CMA Horizon Award in 1981. Born blind (in Augusta, Georgia, 1954), she was once a member of a group called Sound Dimension. A bluesy singer and pianist, Terri formed her own group in 1975 and gained a regular gig at Augusta's Steak and Ale House, performing 50 songs a night. Signed to MCA in 1980, she came up with a Top 10 single **Somebody's Knockin'** later that year and for the next three years maintained a steady flow of chart records without ever gaining the monster she undoubtedly deserved.

TONY GOODACRE – British perennial who started out on a Carrol Lewis talent show in 1957. Like many others, he has indulged in 'cover' albums of US hits (**Thanks To The Hanks**, **Roaming Round In Nashville**) but redeemed himself with **Written In Britain**, a release containing all British material by Terry McKenna, Pete Sayers.

THE GRAND OLE OPRY – The greatest show in country music, which has been broadcast on Saturday nights over WSM since 1927 (though it formerly ran as the WSM Barn Dance from 1925). The show has survived many changes of location, first being housed in a WSM studio, then to a larger studio, then to the Hillboro Theatre, before moving onto the Dixie Tabernacle and, for a short spell, to the War Memorial Auditorium, before settling down for over 30 years at the Ryman Auditorium. It is today situated in the modern Grand Ole Opry house in the grounds of a huge amusement complex.

TOM GRIBBEN – Leader of the Saltwater Band, a Florida-based unit that merges a sunny, Jimmy Buffet-like style with tinges of blues, reggae and rock. Once they even covered a Clash song, **The Guns Of Brixton**.

Guest Stars Of The Hee-Haw Show. Courtesy Pickwick Records.

H

THE HAGARS – Identical twins born in Chicago, Jim and John, signed to Capitol in 1969 and notched minor hits through to 1971. Versatile and equipped with ready-to-please comedy routines, they made many appearances on 'Hee Haw', then headed for Hollywood.

BUTCH HANCOCK – Singer-songwriter who has cut his own, often Dylan/Guthrie-like albums for minor labels. He has written some exceptionally fine songs such as **Boxcars** and **West Texas Waltz** – but they only seemed to really come to life when recorded by the Joe Ely Band.

GUS HARDIN – A gutsy singer who spent 11 years singing in Tulsa clubs, one-time mentor Leon Russell describing her voice as "a cross between Otis Redding, Tammy Wynette and a truck driver." Signed to RCA in the early 1980s, she began logging a tally of Top 40 singles, gaining Top 10 records with **After The Last Goodbye** (1983) and **All Tangled Up In Love**, a duet with Earl Thomas Conley (1984).

HEE HAW – A syndicated TV show, established in the summer of 1969. Full of cornporn humour supplied over the years by such funny men as Archie Campbell and Junior Samples plus musicians such as Buck Owens and Roy Clark, the show has continued to be highly popular, despite – or maybe because of – its total lack of anything that seems in the least sophisticated.

KELVIN HENDERSON – British, Bristol-based bandleader who, for many years, has been winning polls in the UK and various European countries.

THE HILLSIDERS – British band that began their long stay at the top in 1965. A Liverpool outfit, they have recorded a Chet Atkins-produced album with Bobby Bare and another with George Hamilton IV. They have had their own BBC-TV show, played a Royal Albert Hall date and even played a two-week engagement at the London Palladium.

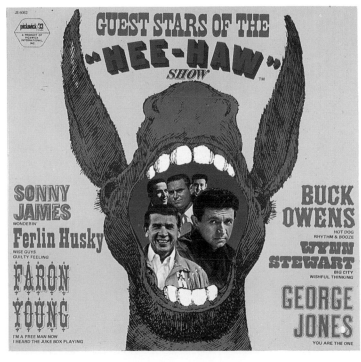

RAY WYLIE HUBBARD – Born in Hugo, Oklahoma in 1946. Singer-songwriter whose **Up Against The Wall Redneck Mother** became the anthem of the Texas outlaw movement during the 1970s. His **Off The Wall** album, made for Willie Nelson's Lone Star label in 1978, is worthy of reasonable outlay – or even unreasonable outlay.

I

JERRY INMAN – Lead singer with the resident band at Hollywood's Palomino for several years. He notched his first hit with the Chelsea label in 1974 and during the late 1970s had a brace of mini-hits on Elektra before fading.

THE IMPERIALS – A country gospel group that, during the mid-1960s, became back-up group for Elvis Presley. Since 1975, they have been recording Christian music exclusively.

J

SHOT JACKSON – Owner of Sho-Bud guitar company, born in Wilmington, North Carolina. Previously a sideman with Johnny and Jack, Kitty Wells and Roy Acuff, Jackson remained with the latter till he and Acuff were injured in a near-fatal auto accident in 1965.

Below: Jana Jae – the beautiful and highly-accomplished fiddler.

JANA JAE – Beautiful and talented fiddler who won the National Lady's Fiddling Championship in 1973 and 1974. A part of the Buck Owens Show for a long period, she had since appeared on many Top TV shows, including 'Hee Haw' and has even played the Montreaux Jazz Festival.

JASON AND THE SCORCHERS – Cowpunk outfit headed by Jason Ringenberg (vocals, guitar, harmonica) from Sheffield, Illinois. Nashville-based, they displayed a wild, breakneck-paced style of rock-oriented country on two EPs for the local Praxis label and in 1984 signed to EMI-America, cutting an album, **Lost And Found**.

FRANK JENNINGS – British singer, heavily influenced by Faron Young, whose band, The Frank Jennings Syndicate, came into existence in 1970 and rose to be the best country unit in the UK, gaining a deal with EMI which did not last as long as it might have done.

K

ANITA KERR – A singer born in Memphis, Tennessee in 1927 who got into the vocal group business early in life and later led the Anita Kerr singers on records by Eddy Arnold, Jim Reeves, Chet Atkins, Skeeter Davis, Floyd Cramer and many other artists. By the 1970s she was based in Europe providing mainly MOR albums.

SID KING – Real name Sidney Erwin, born in Denton, Texas in 1936, leader of the Five Strings, a country outfit that started out as

Heaven Is My Woman's Love, Frank Jennings Syndicate.

the Western Melodymakers. They edged into rockabilly, recorded for Starday, their repertoire including **Who Put The Turtle In Myrtle's Girdle** and, in late 1954, gained a Columbia contract, staying five years. Some of The Five Strings' radio shots can be heard on the Rollercoaster album, **Rockin' On The Radio**.

L

SLEEPY LA BEEF – The man mountain of rockabilly, a 6'6" singer-guitarist who once played the Swamp Monster in the movie 'The Exotic Ones'. The possessor of an amazing baritone voice, La Beef (from

Prairie In The Sky, Mary McCaslin. Courtesy Philo Records.

Smackover, Arkansas) has recorded for Starday, Columbia, Sun, Plantation, Rounder and other labels.

JOHN LAIR – A country music pioneer, born in Livingston, Kentucky in 1894; died in 1985, who produced many country radio shows, formed the Cumberland Ridge Runners and, in 1937, together with the Duke Of Paducah, Red Foley and his brother Cotton Foley, bought and built the Renfro Valley Barn Dance.

RED LANE – Born in Bogalusa, Louisiana in 1939. Singer-songwriter and award-winning guitarist who has worked with Merle Haggard's Strangers. He had a few hits of his own while recording for RCA in 1971–1972.

CHRIS LeDOUX – Highly rated by many, LeDoux is a real singing cowboy. A singer-songwriter since 1972, he has also found time to become the World Championship Bronc Rider in 1976. A fine writer of

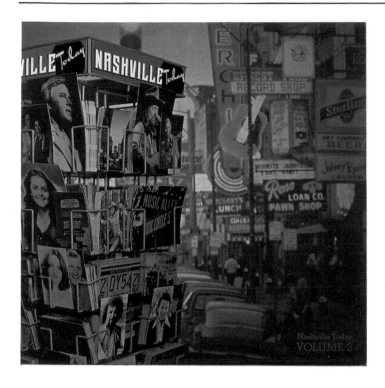

Nashville Today, Volume 2. A Music City compilation.

western-styled songs, he releases material only on his father's Lucky Man label, but nevertheless has scraped a couple of hits, while his albums sell worldwide.

ALBERT LEE – Simply the finest country-rock guitarist ever to come out of Britain. He appeared at London's Royal Albert Hall with Chet Atkins in 1969, played with the group Heads, Hands and Feet in the early '70s, appearing on Jerry Lee Lewis' **London Sessions** album, but later gained true recognition as a member of Emmylou Harris' Hot Band.

THE LILLY BROTHERS – Mitchell 'Bea' B and Everett Lilly (born in Clear Creek, West Virginia in 1921 and 1924 respectively) are

Blue Sky, Night Thunder, Michael Murphey. Courtesy Epic Records.

a bluegrass duo who began as the Lonesome Holler Boys on a Charleston radio show in 1939 but became residents in the Boston area, where they played for around 18 years. During 1973 they visited Japan, cutting several albums.

GEORGE LINDSAY – Comedian-character actor known to the world as 'Goober'. A regular on 'Hee Haw'.

LaWANDA LINDSEY – Once a singer with her father's band, The Dixie Showboys, she signed to Nashville's Chart Records at 14 and had several hits in 1969–1972. Later she moved onto Capitol, Mercury etc., her biggest single to date being **Hello Out There** (1974).

LITTLE GINNY – Full name Ginnette Kirkby. Energetic British singer born in Kingston-Upon-Thames, Surrey. Nominated Top UK Female Country Vocalist 1981.

LONE JUSTICE – Suppliers of a souped-up

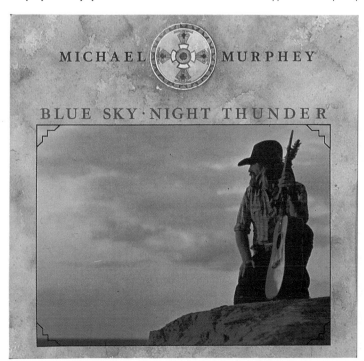

country sound, aimed at the LA rock fraternity, Lone Justice, a band headed by singer Maria McKee and guitarist Ryan Hedgecock, first came to life in mid 1982 and raised such a West Coast storm that they quickly became signed to Geffin Records.

HUBERT LONG – Born in 1923; died in 1972. Elected to the Country Music Hall of Fame in 1979, Long began his career in a Texas dime store record department and later founded Nashville's first talent agency. He was the first person to serve as both president and chairman of the CMA.

LOUISIANA HAYRIDE – An influential show that originated on station KWKH, Shreveport, Louisiana, in 1948, the first programme featuring Johnny and Jack, Kitty Wells, Bailes Brothers, etc. One of the first cast members to attain stardom was Hank Williams.

RAY LYNAM – Arguably Ireland's best known male country singer. A native of Moate, he broke onto the scene in 1970 and, in 1980 recorded an album, **Music Man**, which some hailed as "a milestone in Irish country music."

M

MARY McCASLIN – A singer who grew up in California and became part of Linda Ronstadt's Stone Poneys before going solo and cutting a classic album for Barnaby. Her later albums of western-styled songs for Philo are exceptional.

RONNIE McDOWELL – A singer whose Elvis Presley tribute, **The King Is Dead**, for Scorpion, took him Top 10 in 1977. A Presley-soundalike, he provided the vocals on the soundtrack of the movie 'Elvis' in 1979 and then went on to build a career that was really his own, signing to Epic and gaining a No. 1 single with **Older Woman** in 1981.

Airmail, Wes McGhee. Courtesy Terrapin Records.

WES McGHEE – Leader of the most underrated British country band of recent years. A Texas music nut, he eventually took off for the Lone Star state and toured, his band being augmented by Jerry Jeff Walker drummer Fred Krc and Joe Ely accordionist Ponty Bone. Totally ignored on the UK country club circuit, McGhee has, nevertheless, made some invigorating albums.

TERRY McMILLAN – The man who has replaced Charlie McCoy as the most sought-after harmonica player in

Nashville. A NARAS Super Picker in 1975, his name appears on scores of records.

JAY DEE MANESS – Steel guitar supersessionman, born in Loma Linda, California in 1945, who has worked on hundreds of sides and also toured with Buck Owens and Ray Stevens.

TOKYO MATSU – A real curiosity, a lady trained in the study of voice of classical violin at Japan's Kunitachi School Of Music who now specialises in bluegrass fiddle and portions of pop-country. And yes, she even yodels!

BILLY MIZE – An ACM Vice-President who was once host on Gene Autry's 'Melody Ranch' show, Mize (born in Kansas City, Kansas in 1929) has always had TV connections, eventually heading his own production company. But he still tours with his Tennesseans and from 1966 through to 1974 charted consistently.

TINY MOORE – Another instrumental near-genius, born in Hamilton County, Texas in 1920, who plays both mandolin and fiddle, switching with ease from pure jazz to downhomey country. Once a Bob Wills Playboy, he later worked with Billy Jack Wills but these days plays many dates with Merle Haggard's Strangers.

MICHAEL MURPHEY – A mainstay of the Austin 'progressive country' movement, Murphey (born in Dallas, Texas), a gifted singer-songwriter, went big-time in 1973 with **Wildfire**, a song about a ghostly horse that went to No. 3 in the US pop charts. He has since had several other pop chart successes, while his **Cherokee Fiddle** was featured in the movie 'Urban Cowboy'.

MUSTANG – Yorkshire-based four-piece that won the UK Marlborough Talent Contest in 1979.

N

NASHVILLE – Known as Music City or the Country Capital, this Nashville city started out as the Mecca of country music in 1925 when WSM began its Barn Dance. The first major artist to record in Nashville was Eddy Arnold in 1944, while Capitol was the first major label to commence a Nashville Operation (1950). During the late 1950s and 1960s the famed 'Nashville Sound' took over and the producers, musicians and studios came up with a formula that not only saw such artists as Jim Reeves, Eddy Arnold, Chet Atkins and Floyd Cramer selling huge amounts of records to pop audiences, but also had scores of pop idols heading towards Tennessee in order to add a touch of saleable Nashville magic to their own wares. In 1974 came the opening of Opryland, a modern auditorium amid an extensive amusement park just a few miles outside the city.

NATIONAL BARN DANCE – One of the earliest and the most influential of all radio barn dances for some years. Begun in 1924, it was later overshadowed by the Grand Ole Opry but survived until 1970. Early stars include Bradley Kincaid, Grace Wilson, and Arkie the Woodchoppers, these being followed by John Lair and the Cumberland Ridge Runners, Mac and Bob, Lulu Belle and Scotty and Red Foley.

Above: Orion – masked mystery man and Elvis Presley clone.

O

ORION – Masked mystery man who is the ultimate Elvis Presley clone. Naturally he was recorded by Sun (revived by Shelby Singleton), his albums being pressed as 'Collector's Edition special Gold Vinyl'.

JIM OWEN – Franklin, Tennessee singer-songwriter who is not only a Hank Williams soundalike but also an incredible lookalike. During the early '80s, he has logged a few hits for Sun.

P

PATTI PAGE – Hardly a true country vocalist, Patti (born Clara Ann Fowler in Claremore, Oklahoma, 1927), had one of the biggest all-time country hits with **Tennessee Waltz**, in 1951. Really a pop singer, she switched to country at the start of the 1970s and has since had a fair degree of success in the country charts, particularly during her stay with Shelby Singleton's Plantation label in the early 1980s.

HERB PEDERSON – Born in Berkeley, California, 1944, a singer-banjoist who has played with Flatt And Scruggs, The Dillards, Linda Ronstadt, Emmylou Harris etc., cutting an excellent brace of albums, **Southwest** and **Sandman**, for Epic 1976–1977.

RALPH PEER – The most notable talent scout of the 1920s (born in Kansas City, Missouri in 1892; died in Hollywood, California in 1960. Peer discovered Jimmie Rodgers and the Carter Family, his 1923 sessions with Fiddlin' John Carson proving a landmark in country music history. In 1928 he formed Southern Music, a publishing company heavily involved in the publication of country songs.

MARY KAY PLACE – Born in Tulsa, Oklahoma. An actress who portrayed a country singer called Loretta Haggers in the US TV series 'Mary Hartman, Mary Hartman' (1976), a forerunner of 'Soap'. Accepted as the real thing, she cut an album with Emmylou Harris and The Hot Band, and had a Top 5 hit with **Baby Boy** (1976).

POACHER – British band who won the 'New Faces' TV talent show in 1978. From Warrington, Lancashire, they became sponsored by the local vodka company and threatened an unbelievable breakthrough when, also in 1978, their version of **Darling**, on Republic, entered the US country charts.

MALCOLM PRICE – A perennial on the UK country circuit, where he is warmly regarded. His albums for Decca, made in the early '60s with The Malcolm Price Trio, are ranked highly.

R

RANK AND FILE – An excellent contemporary country-rock band formed from the remnants of West Coast punk band, The Dils. Later they moved to Austin, recording a well-received album, **Sundown**, for Slash Records, thus gaining a UK tour with Elvis Costello.

PAUL RICHEY – Born in Promised Lane, Arkansas, a singer-songwriter, music publisher and Tammy Wynette's brother-in-law. As Wyley McPherson he broke into the charts with **Jedediah Jones** and **The Devil Inside** in 1982.

ROCKABILLY – The first link between country and rock. Carl Perkins has demonstrated the link between the rhythms of certain Hank Williams songs and early rock as part of his act, while chunks of pure rockabilly occur on the Ernie Ford boogies of the late 1940s and early 1950s.

HARGUS 'PIG' ROBBINS – CMA Instrumentalist Of The Year 1976. A blind pianist from Spring City, Tennessee, he gained attention while playing Nashville clubs and became a top sessionman.

JUDY RODMAN – Singer from Riverside, California, who topped the singles charts in mid-'86 with **Until I Met You** on the indie MTM label. Raised mainly in Florida, she studied at Jacksonville University and later moved to Memphis, becoming roommate to Janie Fricke and taking up back-up vocal chores. By 1980 she was in Nashville, doing jingles and back-ups. Later signed to MTM, her first release, **I've Been Had By Love Before**, broke into the Top 40. By 1986 she had been nominated Best New Female Vocalist by the Academy Of Country Music.

FRED ROSE – Founder of the Acuff-Rose Music Publishing Co., Rose (born Evansville, Indiana in 1897, died in Nashville in 1954) was a one-time honky tonk pianist who set up the publishing company in 1942. A fine songwriter – his credits include **Be Honest With Me**, **Blue Eyes Crying In The Rain**, **Take These Chains From My Heart**, **Tears On My Pillow**, **Settin' The Woods On Fire** and others – he often wrote in partnership with such people as Hank Williams, Ray

Rough Tough Trade, Rank And File. Courtesy Slash Records.

Whitley and Hy Heath. In 1961 he became one of the first members of the Country Music Hall Of Fame, sharing the honour with Jimmie Rodgers and Hank Williams.

WESLEY ROSE – The son of Fred Rose, born in Chicago, Illinois in 1918, he has been responsible for expanding the whole horizon of Acuff-Rose's business and making it one of the most successful publishing companies in the world. Initially he moved into the world of record production, at the outset fashioning material for major labels but later forming his own Hickory Records. A music industry leader, Wesley Rose was one of the founder members of the CMA.

PETER ROWAN – Singer-songwriter and brilliant mandolinist, once a member of the Rowan Brothers but, in more recent times, the leader of his own band, switching from folk-rock through to bluegrass, pure country and cajun. He often works with accordionist Flaco Jiminez.

S

ART SATHERLEY – During the 1930s, Satherly (born in Bristol, England in 1889; died in 1986) helped provide ARC with one of the strongest country music catalogues in America, his signings including Gene Autry (1931). In 1938 when ARC became Columbia, Satherley was retained by the company and continued in an A&R role until his retirement in 1952 having added such acts as Lefty Frizzell, Marty Robbins, Little Jimmy Dickens, Bill Monroe and Carl Smith to the Columbia roster. Known as 'Uncle Art' he was elected to the Country Music Hall of Fame in 1971 for his work as a record pioneer.

PETE SAYERS – Versatile British performer (born in Bath, Somerset, 1942) whose finest hour came in 1980 when he compered the Wembley Festival gaining plaudits from even the most acid critics. A multi-instrumentalist of considerable ability and creator of such characters as The Phantom Of The Opry and the Lovely LaWanda, Sayers has often hosted various TV series and has headed his own BBC series 'Pete Sayers Entertains'.

STEVE SHOLES – A&R Manager for RCA's Country Music and R&B Division, Sholes (born in Washington DC in 1911; died in Nashville in 1968) was responsible for the label accumulating one of the most impressive country rosters in the world, signing Jim Reeves, Hank Snow, the Browns, Elvis Presley and Chet Atkins, the latter eventually becoming Sholes' A&R assistant. He was elected to the Country Music Hall of Fame in 1967.

RED SIMPSON – Singer-songwriter-impressionist, multi-instrumentalist and comedian who in the early '70s became associated with the Bakersfield crowd. Winner of Cashbox's New Male Vocalist award in 1972, he came up with an array of hit trucking songs and by 1979 could still be found charting with **The Flying Saucer Man And The Truck Driver**.

SHELBY SINGLETON – One of the shrewdest businessmen in Nashville, Singleton (born in Waskom, Texas in 1931) worked with Mercury Records and became vice-president, signing Jerry Lee

Above: Pete Sayers who compered the Wembley Festival in 1980.

Lewis and Charlie Rich along the way. In 1966 he resigned and formed his own production company, having his biggest success in 1968 when he produced Jeannie C. Riley's **Harper Valley PTA** for his own Plantation label. He has also set up other labels including SSS and Silver Fox and in 1969 acquired Sun Records.

SISSY SPACEK – Award winning movie actress (born in Quitman, Texas in 1950) who in her early days recorded for Roulette as Rainbo. Cast as Loretta Lynn in the film 'Coal Miner's Daughter' (1980), she did all the singing for the soundtrack and promptly got signed by Atlantic, cutting an above-average album **Hangin' Up My Heart**, since when she has had several chart records.

Hangin' Up My Heart, Sissy Spacek. Courtesy Atlantic Records.

BUDDY SPICHER – Session fiddle-player whose career took off as a member of Area Code 615 in 1969. An in-demand picker ever since – he has even worked with Henry Mancini and the Pointer Sisters – he has recorded albums under his own name for two labels: Flying Fish and CMH Records.

STU STEVENS – British singer who, from time to time, has looked likely to cross over and gain recognition from the pop fraternity, predominantly in 1979 when his version of Shel Silverstein and Even Steven's **Man From Outer Space** was picked up by MCA.

J. D. SUMNER AND THE STAMPS – Legendary gospel group that grew out of the Stamps Quartet (formed in 1920). Headed by bass-voiced singer Sumner, they worked with Elvis Prsley from 1971 up to the time of his death. Dave Rowland (of Dave and Sugar) and Richard Sterban (Oak Ridge Boys) both are former members of the Stamps Quartet.

JIMMY SWAGGART – Cousin of Jerry Lee Lewis and Mickey Gilley (born in Ferriday, Louisiana in 1935) who plays the same pumping piano but has aimed his music at the vast country-gospel audience, recording over 50 albums to date.

T

JAMES TALLEY – Singer-songwriter (born in Tulsa, Oklahoma) who performed community work among the Chicanos of New Mexico, then in Nashville's ghetto areas. A superior songwriter who helped build a studio in exchange for studio time, he pressed 1,000 copies of his **Got No Break, No Milk, No Honey But We Sure Got Love** album in 1974 and mailed them to country radio stations, eventually

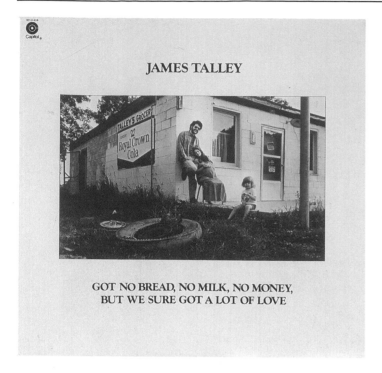

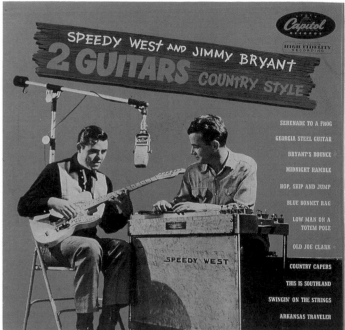

Got No Bread, No Milk, No Money, But We Sure Got A Lot Of Love, James Talley. Courtesy Capitol Records.

2 Guitars Country Style, Speedy West and Jimmy Bryant. Courtesy Capitol Records.

gaining a contract with Capitol, cutting other critically acclaimed albums.

CHIP TAYLOR – Brother of actor Jon Voight (born in New York in 1940). A singer-songwriter who has penned hits for Waylon Jennings, Bobby Bare, Eddy Arnold, Jim Ed Brown and Floyd Cramer. Once a rockabilly singer with King, he did some excellent country-oriented albums with Warner Bros and Columbia.

TUT TAYLOR – A multi-instrumentalist (born in Milledgeville, Georgia in 1923), Robert 'Tut' Taylor is noted for his flat-picking dobro style. Also proficient on mandolin, fiddle, guitar, dulcimer, autoharp and banjo, he has provided back-up on

scores of records and is renowned as a collector, builder and dealer in stringed instruments.

Last Chance, Chip Taylor. Courtesy Warner Brothers.

Friar Tut, Tut Taylor. Courtesy Rounder Records.

KAREN TAYLOR-GOOD – From El Paso, Texas, a singer songwriter who worked her way up through the jingle jungle to work on sessions with George Jones, Dolly Parton, Conway Twitty and others, also working on the soundtracks of 'Best Little Whorehouse In Texas' and 'Smokey And The Bandit II'. In 1982 she and her manager formed Mesa Records, since when she has supplied a regular flow of mid-chart singles.

BUCK TRENT – One of country's most proficient banjoists (born Charles Wilburn Trent in Spartanburg, S. Carolina). He worked with Bill Carlisle in the late '50s and early '60s then moved on to become a member of Porter Wagoner's Wagonmasters. During 1973 Trent teamed up with Roy Clark and put out a number of albums for ABC. Some of these albums were solo and some all-banjo duets with Clark.

GRANT TURNER – Born in Abilene, Texas in 1912. Dean of Opry announcers since 1945. He began his radio career at the age of 16 and joined Nashville's WSM in 1944. Elected to the Country Music Hall of Fame in 1981.

W

HANK WANGFORD – Born Henry Hardman, he is also Dr Sam Hutt, a London, England, gynaecologist. After befriending Gram Parsons, he formed a country band that became increasingly nutty, such monikers as Irma Cetas (the Vera Lynn of Vera Cruz), Brad Breath and Manley Footwear hiding the identities of various well-known sessioneers. A singer who has a love-hate relationship with country and its more 'sincere' aspects, he always seems just on the verge of making the breakthrough into commercial acceptance but, to date, has not quite made it.

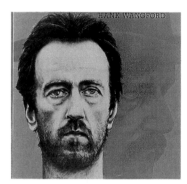

Hank Wangford. Courtesy Cow Pie Records.

GORDIE WEST – Popular Canadian singer – though he was born in Skipton, England. A one-time power engineer, he worked with several country bands but eventually went solo, cutting his first album, **Alberta Bound**, in Wales during 1978.

SPEEDY WEST – One of the most recorded steelies in country music, (born in Missouri in 1924). Once resident on Cliffie Stone's Hometown Jamboree, his 1955 Capitol album with guitarist Jimmy Bryant, **2 Guitars Country Style**, remains an indispensible, instrumental item.

LITTLE DAVID WILKINS – Born in Parsons, Tennessee. Another mail order guitar player who started out with Sun Records in Memphis at 15. A chubby entertainer, perpetually on a diet, he has had hits for such labels as Plantation, MCA, Playboy, and Epic.

X

X STATIONS – Powerful radio stations that operated just inside the Mexican border cutting in on wavelengths used by US and Canadian stations. Many country singers including The Carter Family were helped on their way through border radio.

Index

The performers in this book appear in alphabetical order. Therefore, this index serves mainly as a comprehensive cross-referencing system, listing page number only when performers appear in an entry other than their own. Several performers and personalities who do not have their own entries but who are referred to in the book are also listed.